THE AGENCY

THE
AGENCY

William Morris
and the Hidden History
of Show Business

—

FRANK ROSE

HarperBusiness
A Division of HarperCollins*Publishers*

HarperCollins books may be purchased for educational, business, or sales promotional use. For information please write: Special Markets Department, HarperCollins Publishers, Inc., 10 East 53rd Street, New York, NY 10022.

FIRST EDITION

Designed by Jessica Shatan

Library of Congress Cataloging-in-Publication Data

Rose, Frank.
    The agency : William Morris and the hidden history of show business / by Frank
Rose. -- 1st ed.
        p.   cm.
    Includes bibliographical references and index.
    ISBN 0-88730-749-3
    1. William Morris Agency--History. 2. Theatrical agencies--United States--History.
3. Performing Arts--United States--History--20th century. I. Title.
PN2295.W56R67   1995
792' .06'73--dc20   95-16739

95 96 97 98 99 ❖/RRD 10 9 8 7 6 5 4 3 2 1

Every individual has his price. . . .

—HORTENSE POWDERMAKER,
Hollywood, the Dream Factory

CONTENTS

Photographs follow pages 216 and 376.

PROLOGUE

Los Angeles, June 4, 1983

HILLCREST COUNTRY CLUB WAS AS CLOSE TO INVISIBLE AS 142 ACRES ON the south side of Beverly Hills could be. No sign, just a number on the stone entrance gates: 10000 Pico Boulevard. Black Cadillacs slipped inside one by one, the roar of the traffic falling away as they motored toward the clubhouse, a sprawling pile of wood and glass designed more for comfort than for style. Dense hedges of flowering oleander intensified the hush. Through the darkness lay the fairway, studded with pine and eucalyptus and redolent with memories. Ever since the Depression, this had been the preserve of Hollywood's elite.

All the great moguls had belonged to Hillcrest—Louis B. Mayer and the Warner brothers and Harry Cohn of Columbia and Adolph Zukor of Paramount. Most of the top comics belonged—George Burns, Danny Thomas, George Jessel, Milton Berle, the Marx Brothers. When Groucho said, "I wouldn't want to belong to any club that would accept me as a member," he was referring to Hillcrest—but he joined anyway. Benny Siegel, the mobster who invented Vegas, was admitted, but Joseph P. Kennedy was turned down: Jews only. (Danny Thomas was the exception.) For the men who ran the William Morris Agency, Hillcrest was practically an extension of their offices. And this balmy June evening was their night, the night they'd chosen to celebrate their eighty-fifth anniversary in the talent trade.

Eighty-five years: It was a milestone no other company in show business could boast of. In 1898—before television, before radio, before talkies, before Warner Bros. or Paramount or Metro-Goldwyn-Mayer, almost before cinema itself—a young German-Jewish immigrant named William Morris had set himself up as a booking agent on Fourteenth Street in New York City. Show business at the turn of the century meant vaudeville, and Fourteenth Street, hard by the immigrant quarter of the Lower East Side, was vaudeville's home. From its beginnings in a second-floor walk-up across from Lüchow's Restaurant, the Germanic establishment where the impresarios held court, the Morris office had followed the business uptown to Times Square and across the continent to Hollywood, had followed it into pictures and radio and nightclubs and records and television, until now, in 1983, it represented more talent than any other firm in the world.

Behind the mirrored façade of its sleekly modern headquarters in downtown Beverly Hills, a block removed from the glittering boutiques of Rodeo Drive, some seventy-five Morris agents represented twelve hundred clients, maybe more—actors, directors, writers, singers, athletes, newscasters, politicians. Another fifty or so agents operated out of the upper floors of the MGM Building in midtown Manhattan; two dozen more were stationed in satellite offices in Nashville and Europe. Some estimates put the total number of clients as high as two thousand, but no one outside the agency really knew; the figure was as closely guarded as the amount of commissions they brought in. Morris, being privately held, reported only to the tight circle of senior agents and executives who owned its stock. Yet no one doubted that it was the largest, richest, most powerful agency in the business.

Wattage mattered more than numbers, of course, and Morris handled some of the brightest stars onscreen. Jack Lemmon, named best actor at Cannes for his performance in *Missing*. Barbra Streisand, making her debut as director with *Yentl*. Clint Eastwood, whose Dirty Harry persona—"Go ahead, make my day"—would soon be appropriated by the president. Richard Gere, the star of *An Officer and a Gentleman*, one of the top-grossing films of 1982. Mel Gibson, *The Road Warrior*'s post-apocalyptic hunk, who'd just solidified his star status with *The Year of Living Dangerously*. Barbara Walters, the first TV news personality to win a million-dollar contract. And so on.

As impressive as their current clients, however, were the names the agency had handled in decades past. The story of William Morris, it was frequently said, was the story of show business itself, and to see what that meant, you had only to scan the roster.

In the years before World War I, Will Morris had introduced Harry Lauder to America and Will Rogers to the big time. In the twenties, he brought Maurice Chevalier to America and put the Marx Brothers in the movies. In the thirties, his office built Jimmy Cagney into a star and Mae West into a sex siren. In the forties, it made Rita Hayworth a love goddess and gave Marilyn Monroe her start. In the fifties, it took Frank Sinatra when he'd hit bottom and put Elvis Presley on television. In the sixties, it made a TV husband out of Dick Van Dyke and a TV spy out of Bill Cosby. So proud of all this were the men who ran Morris that a few days earlier, they'd done something so out of character it raised eyebrows all over town: They'd granted interviews to the press.

Morris agents made a point of staying in the background, leaving the spotlight for their clients. But that Saturday morning, their top executives—Sam Weisbord, president, and Morris Stoller, chairman, both seventy-one years old and with one hundred years at the agency between them—had turned up on the front page of the entertainment section of the *Los Angeles Times*. For *Daily Variety*, Weisbord and Stoller had served up the ultimate plum—lunch at Hillcrest with their chairman emeritus, Abe Lastfogel, a cherubic little man wearing an impish grin and his trademark bow tie.

Lastfogel had just turned eighty-five himself, having been born the year the agency was founded. He'd been there longer than any of them—since 1912, when, at age fourteen, he'd gone to work for William Morris himself. He'd seen the company through two world wars, through Prohibition and Depression, through blacklist and Vietnam, and now, in retirement, he'd seen it seed the industry with its progeny. Barry Diller, chairman of Paramount, had gotten his start in its fabled mail room. So had the president of Twentieth Century–Fox, the head of Warner Bros., the vice chairman of Warner Communications in New York. "We have become generic," Stoller confided to the *Variety* reporter, luxuriating for the moment in understandable self-satisfaction. "The world, in a sense, is our oyster."

So the air was full of glory that evening as the two hundred–odd agents and executives gathered in the clubhouse, which felt as familiar and comfortable as an old suit. No stars were present; glitter wasn't the

Morris way. The only outsider invited was Colonel Tom Parker, Elvis's manager, whose ties to the Morris office were so close that even after his client's death, he was considered family. And this was very much a family affair, closed, quiet, a chance to cement their bonds as they gazed out across the deep dark of the fairways, drinks in hand.

Sam Weisbord puffed with pride, a taut, wiry figure in fighting trim, silver hair aglint in the evening light, teeth glowing against the deep bronze of his perpetual tan. Only seventeen when he joined the Morris office in 1929, he'd gone from his parents' corner store in Brooklyn to a penthouse high above Sunset Boulevard, from which he could look out across Beverly Hills to the Pacific. Agenting had made them all rich beyond their dreams, but it had rewarded them in other ways as well. Weisbord, chosen to be Abe Lastfogel's office boy, had become his surrogate son, much as Lastfogel had been Morris's. They were all Lastfogel's children, of course, the family he never had, but Weisbord was the favorite, the one he lunched with every day and had dinner with every night. And while to many of his star clients he was "Uncle Abe," to Weisbord he was still "Mr. Lastfogel," just as Morris had always been "Mr. Morris." The tradition continued.

Unlike Weisbord, who maintained the posture of a bantam cock, Morris Stoller was a genial, avuncular figure with a reassuring smile. Trained as an accountant, he'd joined the agency in 1937 while studying law at Brooklyn College night school. In the late forties, he'd come out to run the West Coast office, and later, with television money pouring into the agency's coffers, he'd put it into real estate—the headquarters complex behind the Beverly Wilshire Hotel, as well as shopping malls, warehouses, and apartment buildings across the country. He made a wrong move once—in 1973, when he launched a sports agency subsidiary that lost some half a million dollars before it was dropped a year later—and that hit him so hard, he suffered a nervous breakdown. But he bounced back a few months afterward, so quickly that few outside the agency knew he'd been gone. Even fewer knew how much had gone awry in his absence.

Of the other men in the gathering, one in particular stood out. Stan Kamen was reserved, even shy, yet aggressive in a low-key way. Raised in the exclusive Brooklyn enclave of Manhattan Beach, educated at Washington and Lee in Virginia, he had a polish few in the agency business could match. As head of the motion picture department—the flagship of any agency—he was a senior member of the Hollywood power structure, that intimate fraternity of studio chiefs and agency heads ("buyers" and "sellers" in the idiom of the trade) who run the business. He spoke for some of the top actors in town—Warren Beatty, Jane Fonda, Goldie Hawn, Al Pacino, Chevy Chase, Barbra Streisand. At fifty-seven, he represented the next generation of Morris men, the one that would take command when Weisbord and Stoller retired. And like Lastfogel, he was the consummate deal maker—unusual for the upper levels at Morris, which had come to be run by lawyers and accountants like Stoller.

The younger agents in the firm had heard innumerable stories about the legendary Abe Lastfogel—the clients he'd built, the deals he'd made—but the man they saw in the office bore little resemblance to the one they heard about. At eighty-five, Lastfogel could be counted on for little more than lunch at Hillcrest, followed by a movie in the screening room. He'd ceded control of the agency after suffering a stroke years before, and at this point he functioned primarily as the embodiment of a glorious past. Everyone regarded him with affection and respect, but younger agents tended to find his presence disconcerting, since the past he represented bore less and less resemblance to the reality they experienced, either in the agency or in the industry.

But it was the past they were celebrating tonight, a past in which—thanks largely to Lastfogel's integrity—the talent agent had been transformed from lowly flesh-peddler, from chiseling ten-percenter growing fat and sleek on the blood of his clients, to an honest broker whose efforts were indispensable to the business. The older men in the room, more than a few of whom had joined the agency just out of high school, felt a vast debt to this man, as if they owed him everything they had. So there was a wave of heartfelt applause as he rose from his seat for the obligatory after-dinner speech, followed by rapt attention as he retold in precise detail a story they'd heard dozens, some of them hundreds, of times before:

It was a rainy afternoon in 1912 when, having turned fourteen and having decided it was time to quit school and get a job, he set out from the tenement where he lived at Third Avenue and Forty-ninth Street with a slip of paper in his pocket. On it were the addresses of two places that had an opening for an office boy—the William Morris Agency on Times Square, and a tailor shop on Thirty-sixth Street. The tailor shop seemed more reliable, but the Morris office was closer, so he went there first. If he'd gone to the tailor . . .

*   *   *

From the house on Angelo Drive, you could take in the entire sweep of the Los Angeles Basin, from the San Gabriel Mountains on the east to the Palos Verdes Peninsula on the south to the Pacific Ocean on the west. Hillcrest was just a dark patch in the shimmering network of lights spread out below. Falcon's Lair, the walled villa Rudolph Valentino bought in 1925 to escape his fans, crowned another hilltop not far away; a few hundred yards down the helter-skelter walls of Benedict Canyon lay the house on Cielo Drive where Sharon Tate and her guests were butchered that August night in 1969. It was a savage landscape, violent and carnivorous. The carefully manicured estates of Beverly Hills lay just below, but there was nothing tamed or polite about these vertiginous slopes; they were as wild as the coyotes that roamed them.

Misty Mountain: That was how the house on Angelo was known. For decades, this mountain hacienda, with its neo-Spanish mansion and its cypress-flanked pool and its rose garden and its orchid house and the movie stars its master could assemble with a snap of the fingers—for decades this place had been home to one Jules Caesar Stein, founder of the Music Corporation of America. Now his widow lived there alone, with only the servants for company.

Jules Stein, talent king: That was how he was identified in a 1946 magazine series. Born two years before Lastfogel, Stein had arrived in Hollywood after opening a band-booking office in Chicago and building it into the biggest agency in the music business. Within a few years, it was preeminent in pictures as well. From 1945 until it was forced out of the agency business by Justice Department trust-busters in 1962, MCA was the dominant force in the talent trade. Unlike Lastfogel, Stein had no desire to be a father figure to his clients or to his employees or even, by their account, to his children. MCA exuded power, not warmth. Its nickname—"the Octopus"—came from its habit of gaining fiduciary involvement in every aspect of its clients' activities, from the automobiles they rented to the television shows they starred in. And then, almost overnight, it dismissed all its agents and clients, shuttered the Beverly Hills mansion that had been its home, and moved to Universal City to begin life anew as MCA/Universal.

The conceit at the Morris office was that William Morris was the one constant in show business—that stars rose and fell, that studios changed hands or went under, that the medium itself might shift from vaudeville to silents to talkies to television, but through it all, the Morris office endured. Jules Stein believed that there is nothing so permanent as change. This realization, he maintained, was the true source of his power.

It may have been fostered by his perspective, for from Misty Mountain you could certainly sense the tenuous interconnectedness of things. Scanning the city at night, you could see every node in the flickering web that was Los Angeles, feel its limitless horizontality and the warp of its existence. The metropolis that sprang up in this vast desert by the sea was invented by visionary real-estate hucksters who saw the climate—three hundred days of sunshine per year—as a marketable commodity. They had only to add water and, presto! buyers would appear. The dream factories that sprang up soon afterward churned out intangible product, but like other factories, they needed a constant supply of raw material—talent, which they bought from agents whose leverage depended on the combined imagined drawing power of the names they had to sell. Agenting is a business based not on power but on the perception of power, a business in which illusion builds on illusion until nothing seems real. A business, as they say, of relationships.

From a spot like Misty Mountain, Los Angeles by night suggests a spectral road map of relationships, a luminous grid in which the pathways connecting agency to studio to box office to public glimmer and glow as if on a video screen. This earthbound web of streets, freeways, and telephone lines is a visual echo of the invisible, skyborne web above, the electronic grid of television, radio, and microwave transmissions. Blips of information appear from nowhere and vanish into geometric infinity. There are no constants. Only change is permanent.

. . . And then there was television.

At that point in his after-dinner speech, Abe Lastfogel's memory seemed to falter. He fumbled for a moment, looked around with pain and befuddlement in his eyes, then slowly took his seat. An embarrassed silence fell across the Hillcrest dining room, followed by a murmur of discomfort.

After a moment or two of confusion, Sam Weisbord jumped up and launched into his General Patton speech, as it was known around the agency. Although Weisbord's own campaigns during World War II had not taken him much beyond Forty-second Street (where he was stationed as a sergeant in the army's USO liaison office), he was inordinately fond of the military metaphor, especially as it applied to William Morris. But as he exhorted them to victory, many of the agents—particularly the younger ones—shifted uncomfortably in their seats.

First, of course, was the sense of loss, the realization that Lastfogel, the one person in the firm who'd truly lived the history of their business, could no longer pass it on. Beyond that was the disturbing fact that the people currently running the Morris office seemed to have little idea where they should go from here. The old guard clung to the notion that William Morris was a family, but Morris didn't feel like a family anymore. It felt cold and corporate. And yet it didn't always act corporate; in the marketplace, where a little ruthlessness would have been appropriate, it too often seemed disorganized and slow. It combined family efficiency with corporate warmth.

Certainly among the younger agents and trainees the attitude was more competitive than familial: How much can we get out of this? These people hadn't come in fresh from high school, as most of their elders had; they were MBAs and law-school graduates who'd turned down astronomical salaries on Wall Street to work for $200 a week in the William Morris mail room so they could take a crack at show business. The training program was almost a hazing ritual—a year spent sorting mail and delivering scripts before they were even qualified to answer the phone for an actual agent. Ambition, impatience, frustration, humiliation—sometimes it got to be too much. Fistfights broke out in the mail room regularly. On one occasion, a pair of trainees were summoned to a senior agent's office by dispatch and handed a white paper bag for delivery to his doctor's office—a stool sample, they discovered when they opened the cup inside. Sitting in traffic in Beverly Hills, staring at the warm cup of shit they'd been handed, they experienced a sudden blinding insight into their status in the business.

The older generation knew exactly what they would get out of William Morris: security. Amid the revolving doors of the entertainment business, the Morris office was rock-solid. If you stayed put and worked hard, you'd get your reward at the end. It was comforting knowledge. Maybe too comforting.

Talent agencies, like any other form of brokerage, are essentially in the information business. They provide information to their clients— what scripts are available, what pictures are in development, what trends are on the horizon—and they use that information to make a sale. By 1983, anyone tuned in to the buzz would have noted the emergence of a new force in the talent trade, created out of William Morris, yet reminiscent of MCA. Creative Artists Agency had been formed in 1975 by Michael Ovitz and four other defectors from the Morris office. It was disciplined and focused and highly aggressive, and already it had made impressive inroads into Morris's client list: Robert Redford, Sylvester Stallone. . . . But Mike Ovitz was after more than Morris's clients. He was changing the rules in show business as radically as his high school classmate Michael Milken, the junk-bond king, had changed the rules in finance.

In the next few years, Ovitz would transform agenting from a sporting enterprise to a cutthroat competition. He would deploy a well-paid, highly motivated, extremely disciplined cadre of agents so effectively as to reverse the traditional relationship between Hollywood's sellers and buyers—between "the people who kiss ass," in the words of one key player, "and the people who have their asses kissed." CAA agents wore dark Armani suits—the equivalent of the black sack suits, white Sulka shirts, and skinny black ties that were the hallmark of the MCA agent in the fifties. They maintained absolute secrecy before the outside world— a stance for which MCA had been famous. Like Jules Stein, Ovitz had created a machine, predatory by nature and despising of weakness.

Once again, William Morris would face an adversary that wanted to corner the market in stars. CAA would be like a hand from the past, a hand of its own creation, a hand of something it had thought buried decades ago. But no one could see this on June 4, 1983. As they climbed into their Caddies at the end of the evening and merged with the infinite stream of traffic on Pico Boulevard, the men who ran the Morris office thought of the future as a linear extension of the past. Why should they fear the traitorous Ovitz and his upstart organization? They were rich in tradition, rich in real estate, rich in manpower. How could they know that before another decade had passed, nearly every-one of consequence that night would be gone from the agency or dead?

PART 1

FAMILY

1898-1969

William Morris, Jr. . . . . asserts firmly that the agency is not primarily concerned with the tawdry aspects of commerce. "We practice in the humanities," he likes to say. ". . . Abe is the epitome of the agent. He looks to the humanities of the situation. He is concerned with the good and welfare of an individual rather than with the individual's mere success. Always and above all, the humanities!"

—E. J. KAHN, JR.,
"THE QUIET GUY IN LINDY'S"

1

THE SHOWMAN

New York, 1898–1932

THOUGH THE MORRIS OFFICE TRIED FOR DECADES TO REVIVE IT, vaudeville died the night William Morris played his final hand of pinochle. Cause of death was talkies, with radio a contributing factor. Demise was not officially announced until some two weeks later, on November 16, 1932, when the Palace Theatre added pictures to its bill. But when Will Morris went, vaudeville went with him.

The Palace was the acme of vaudeville houses, the pinnacle, the top. Situated just across from the Morris office in the heart of Times Square, it was the epitome of the big time—singers, dancers, comedians, magicians, jugglers, acrobats, animal acts, one after another, eight acts a show, two shows a day. Acts that hadn't hit the big time had to scrabble through the small time, playing four shows a day or more in theaters and lodge halls and amusement parks, dodging peach pits and tobacco juice from disgruntled fans, leaving town the next day, or the same night if they didn't get paid. Offstage, vaudevillians lived out of their trunks and enjoyed the social status of vagrants. Onstage, they offered respectable entertainment for the masses—none of the intellectual pretense of legit, but plenty of flash. Even Woodrow Wilson had been a fan.

The Palace had a special significance for Will Morris. It was the flagship of the Keith-Albee theater circuit, which Benjamin Franklin Keith and his successor, Edward F. Albee, had built from a single Boston freak show into the dominant amusement enterprise in the country. Keith and Albee were the robber barons of vaudeville, creators of a monopoly as powerful and rapacious as J. P. Morgan's steel trust or John D. Rockefeller's oil trust. Morris had started fighting them at the turn of the century, when the Keith organization tried to seize control by setting up a central office to book acts into theaters, eliminating independent agents. For almost two decades, he stood at the center of the vaudeville wars, a frenzied melodrama in which Keith and Albee played the mustachioed villains while Morris fought for truth and justice and usually ended up dangling by his fingernails from a cliff. "It's a good thing to give him room when he falls," a critic for the *Cleveland Plain-Dealer* observed in 1912, "because he strikes hard."

Keith died in 1914, but Albee, his chief lieutenant, continued to blacklist Morris's performers while snapping up more and more theaters. Not until 1918, when Albee had all of vaudeville in his grasp and Morris was no longer a threat, did the two make their peace. But over the next ten years, a strange reversal took place. For it turned out that after winning the vaudeville wars, all Albee controlled was . . . vaudeville. Morris represented the talent. During the twenties, when audiences turned to other forms of entertainment—movies, radio— Morris was there ahead of them, encouraging his performers to experiment. Albee fought progress and watched his empire fall apart.

As with vaudeville, so it would later be with movies, radio, television. In the entire history of show business, it would turn out, talent was the commodity that mattered. Control the talent and you control the business.

Albee learned this lesson in 1928, when his theater circuit was wrested away from him by Joseph P. Kennedy, the Boston financier, who was working on a deal with the giant Radio Corporation of America to merge Keith-Albee-Orpheum with a film production company he owned and turn it into the motion picture arm of RCA—the Radio-Keith-Orpheum Corporation, or RKO. Two years later, Albee dropped dead in his Palm Beach hotel room, a rich but embittered old man. *Variety*, the scrappy trade weekly founded by Morris's friend Sime Silverman, coined his epitaph in its obit: "Nothing could stop him, and he stopped at nothing."

Morris survived, but the fighting had taken its toll. He was only fifty-nine in 1932, but he'd been ill with heart disease for some time. Two years earlier, after a mild stroke, he'd retired to his Adirondack retreat and turned the business over to his son, William Morris, Jr., and his personal secretary, Abe Lastfogel. They handled a stable of talent that included Jimmy Cagney and George Raft, Al Jolson and Eddie Cantor, Louis Armstrong and Duke Ellington, S. J. Perelman and E. E. Cummings, Will Rogers and Tom Mix, Sophie Tucker and Mae West, Cab Calloway and George Jessel, Conrad's Pigeons and Singer's Midgets. As the ad in *Variety* read:

NO ACT TOO BIG . . . NO ACT TOO SMALL
(OUR SMALL ACT OF TODAY IS OUR BIG ACT OF TOMORROW)

Morris himself, once a stalwart-looking man with coal-black hair, alabaster skin, and piercing, deep-set eyes, now seemed frail and vulnerable. But it didn't matter what his doctor told him, he couldn't resist the lure of show business. "Don't worry about me," he told his family when they tried to get him to slow down. "When I go, I'll be playing pinochle and smoking a big black cigar."

Morris played his final hand around midnight on the evening of Tuesday, November 1. That morning, he'd braved torrential rains and seventy-mile-an-hour winds to reach his office atop the Mayfair Theatre Building, the former burlesque house at Forty-seventh Street and Seventh Avenue. The gale whipped trees and roofs through Rockaway Beach, sent summer cottages tumbling into Jamaica Bay, smashed an excursion boat to shore in New York Harbor, nearly toppled the ninety-foot flagpole outside the New York Public Library, flung a plate-glass window from the Woolworth Building onto a pedestrian below. Morris went in anyway.

He was there to do battle with Edward Schiller, a vice president of the Loew's theater chain, on behalf of an independent theater manager who was being bullied by the Combine. The quarrel was over movies now—Loew's owned M-G-M, the biggest studio in Hollywood, and was threatening to deny its pictures to the independent. But the principle was the same. If Loew's won, Morris would have to fight the vaudeville wars all over again.

Morris beckoned Lastfogel to a window overlooking Times Square. On the streets below, dwarfed by enormous signs for Pepsodent and Coca-Cola and Chevrolet, jobless men were hawking apples. "To think that we have to go over the same old ground with Ed Schiller," Morris sighed, "when that is what we should be concerned about."

The dispute involved a variety unit the Morris Agency had put together to play movie theaters between picture presentations—a stage show with Eddie Cantor, George Jessel, and the comedy team of George Burns and Gracie Allen. Morris had offered the package to Loew's and gotten the turndown because the price was too high. Now it appeared that when Schiller couldn't afford something, he didn't want anyone else to have it either. A Baltimore theater manager named Izzy Rappaport had taken the show, only to have Schiller threaten to cut off M-G-M's films to his theater.

Morris and Lastfogel marched down Seventh to the Loew's State Theatre Building, headquarters of the Loew's empire. Lastfogel, an almost Pygmy-sized young man with kinky blond hair and bright blue eyes, was much more than a secretary to Morris. He was his chief lieutenant, most trusted aide, almost a son. Morris's real son, now running the Hollywood office, was an aesthetic sort, better at wearing clothes than at making a sale. Lastfogel was a hustler, but a hustler who knew right from wrong. Not unlike Will Morris.

Schiller greeted them pleasantly. He was tall, a prim-looking man with austere features and silver hair. Morris remarked that Schiller's white gloves, which hid a nervous rash, reminded him of the white gloves Eddie Cantor wore for his blackface routines. Lastfogel tried to summarize the situation, but Schiller became more and more upset as he spoke. Loew's played Morris attractions regularly, Schiller told them. It was unfair to book a show like that with a competitor.

Loew's was offered the show first, Morris said.

Schiller jumped up and started pacing the room. Lastfogel glanced at Morris and suggested under his breath that they come back later. Will shook his head. "Ed, please sit down," he said. "You're making me nervous. Listen to me."

Morris knew how to make people listen. Five minutes, it was said, and he could convince a person to do just about anything. He told Schiller about the past—how vaudeville had flourished during the free-for-all of the early years, how Albee had gotten it in his grasp and squeezed the life out of it. Yes, Loew's was facing a weak box office, but it wasn't going to get better if they squeezed out the small fellow.

Schiller knew all about vaudeville, and it didn't interest him. Weak box office? What did Morris know about weak box office? Three years earlier, eighty million people had gone to the movies every week. Now it was sixty million and dropping, and ticket prices had already been slashed. It was . . . it was . . .

As Schiller went incoherent with rage, Morris's voice turned steely. "I came here to reason with you," he said, planting himself in front of Schiller's desk. "If you won't hear reason, hear this. If Loew's puts a ban on Izzy Rappaport, I'll take you to court myself. You'll see not only Cantor and Jessel and George and Gracie on the stand but the entire company. It doesn't matter to me if I only get costs and a dollar damages. Everyone in that courtroom, everyone with the price of a newspaper, will know what one large corporation is trying to do to one small businessman."

Something in Morris's tone had a bracing effect. Schiller folded his white-gloved hands on his desk. "I wouldn't do that, Will," he said quietly. "Let me speak to my booking managers. I think we'll be able to work something out."

Morris had dinner that evening with Lastfogel and Lastfogel's wife, Frances, a vaudeville comedienne whose salty language and blatant delivery reminded people of Sophie Tucker. Then he went around the corner to the Friars Club, an imposing Gothic structure that loomed above the brownstones of Forty-eighth Street like a medieval guildhall. If Walter Kelly were around, he could get in a few hands of pinochle before going home.

Kelly was one of his clients, a Philadelphia comic who was famous as the "Virginia Judge," as famous as his infant niece, Grace, would become a couple of decades later. An inveterate cardplayer whose middle finger had been bitten off in a brawl in Reno years before, he'd carried on his own well-publicized feud with Albee. He and Morris were fixtures at the showmen's fraternity, which counted such fellow clients as George Burns, George Jessel, and Will Rogers among its members, as well as New York Mayor Jimmy Walker.

Morris found him in the Monastery's well-appointed card room. The two men played rummy until midnight. Then Lou Reil, another vaudeville player, and Munro Goldstein, a lawyer who represented many of Morris's clients, came in and joined them for pinochle. Fifteen minutes later, Morris shifted the cigar in his mouth and played the winning trick from a seemingly impossible hand. Then, suddenly, he slumped forward.

IT HAD BEEN AN ADVENTURESOME LIFE, IF NOT A LONG ONE. HE'D BEEN born Zelman Moses in 1873, the son of a prosperous dry-goods merchant in Schwarzenau, a village of five hundred people set amid the green hills and tranquil lakes of Silesia, in the eastern lands of the German Empire. His earliest memories were pastoral, almost idyllic. Watching the local gentry clip-clop down country lanes in their carriages, each one pulled by a matched pair of bays. Receiving his Hebrew instruction at the village school, where the priest taught the Christian children for an hour and the rabbi followed. Then, misfortune.

Zelman's father was a respectable merchant, but his father's brother was a smuggler. Zelman was still a little boy when his uncle was caught bringing in vodka from Poland. Zelman's father, who'd posted bond for him, had to forfeit the store and the house they lived in. The uncle fled to America, and Zelman's father followed, leaving Zelman, his younger brother, his two older sisters, and their mother to make their living peddling thimbles and thread and collecting rags to sell to papermakers. When Zelman was nine, his mother sold everything they had for enough money to book them all in steerage on the S.S. *Ems*, sailing from Bremen to New York.

It was winter, and the crossing was rough. The passengers were packed in like cattle, stacked on bunks in a dank, noisy compartment that vibrated from the turn of the propellers below and reeked of disinfectant, tobacco smoke, and vomit. Numb from the passage, Zelman and his family disembarked at Castle Garden, the massive stone fortress on the Battery where new arrivals were processed. The city was like nothing they'd ever seen, a raucous metropolis of 1.2 million people from every quarter of the globe, all of them jammed into the lower two-thirds of Manhattan Island. They found Zelman's father living with his brother on Broome Street in the Lower East Side, deep in a wretched quarter of rat-infested tenements jammed helter-skelter with Germans, Jews, and Irishmen. There was no grass and little sun, just filthy, shrieking children and grown-ups who were constantly in a hurry, all crushed together in a gray expanse of squalor that stretched for eight square miles.

Zelman enrolled in the public school next door. When the other kids started calling him "Sheeny Moses," he gave in to his parents and changed his name to Morris, as they had. He chose William as his first name. He'd never heard of the other William Morris, the famous one in London, poet, designer, social reformer. His family moved around the corner to 7 Sheriff Street, and Will went to work for Michael Merriman, the coal-and-ice man next door, making deliveries in a horse-drawn cart at five in the morning and studying English at night after school. Then his father abandoned them again, this time for good.

Will quit school and worked as a clerk at the grocery store Merriman bought at Madison and Gouverneur Streets, a few blocks away in the Irish quarter. At night, he ventured a mile and a half west to the Bowery, which in the 1860s had been the center of the theatrical district but now was lined with arcades offering live sex circuses and freak-show attractions—Jo-Jo the Dog-Faced Boy, the Skeleton Dude, Houdini. Or he made his way uptown to Union Square, where in 1881 a showman named Tony Pastor had first taken variety shows out of the drunken squalor of the beer halls and staged them in the somewhat more refined atmosphere of his New Fourteenth Street Theatre in Tammany Hall. Young Will was hooked.

Will's mother wanted him to be a barber. He wanted to go into the show world. But he couldn't find a job, so at sixteen he left Merriman and went to work for the firm of Gallison & Hobrun, publisher of such journals as *Hatter and Furrier* and *Cloak and Suit Review*. He rose rapidly from office boy to subscription clerk to assistant bookkeeper. But he didn't like sitting behind a desk, so when he was offered the position of head bookkeeper, he asked if he could sell advertising instead. By the time he was twenty, he was earning $10,000 a year on commission. Then, as he was about to be made a partner, the Silver Panic of '93 hit.

For three years, the nation's gold reserves had been melting away at a startling rate, ever since the Treasury had abandoned the gold standard and started issuing silver certificates. Wall Street was distracted by furious charges of anti-Semitism: Protestant and Jewish financiers weren't speaking to one another because Theodore Seligman, scion of the powerful Seligman banking house, had just been blackballed by the Union League Club. As credit grew scarce, banks and insurance companies began to fail, railroads went bankrupt, the stock market went into a tailspin. Gallison & Hobrun was not spared. In quick succession, the bookkeeper absconded with all the funds, a junior partner committed suicide, the firm collapsed, and Morris, who'd allowed his commissions to run up, was left penniless. His whole career would be a roller-coaster ride, and this was the start of it.

Morris had been about to get married, to a lovely blonde named Emma Berlinghoff, a German Protestant whose widowed mother ran a candy store on Sheriff Street. Instead, he picked himself up and looked around. He was twenty years old, living with his mother and his brother Hugo at Thirteenth Street and Avenue A. The country was in chaos—hundreds of thousands thrown out of work, mills and factories shuttered, strikes and rioting everywhere. But show business still looked to him as it had when he was a boy, a dream world inhabited by dream people.

He went to the impresario Mike Leavitt, a distant relative who'd started out in 1859 with a troupe that toured New England by wagon. Leavitt had no work for him, but Morris noticed that his office was a mess, so he offered to come by every morning to straighten up. Thus he learned that George Liman, a leading theatrical agent on Fourteenth Street, was looking for a clerk. Swiping one of Leavitt's letterheads, he wrote Liman that he was confidentially looking for a new connection and gave his home address. Liman summoned him for an interview and offered him a job at $8 a week. Morris refused; they settled on $9. After a month, he was put in charge of the office. Later, when Liman went to a spa in Germany for his health, he offered Morris a half-share of the profits to manage the business in his absence.

His future secure, Will and Emma decided they could finally get married. Then Liman died. His widow informed Morris she was revoking his half-share and putting another agent in charge. Urged on by friendly theater managers, he opened his own office across the street, on the second floor of an old row house at 103 East Fourteenth Street, just east of Union Square. Posting his cross-hatch trademark above the door—four X's, representing a W superimposed on an M—he went into business as "William Morris, Vaudeville Agent." Actors followed him over with their photographs, which he tacked to the walls to cover the cracks. When he struck a deal with the widow a few weeks later, it was to buy Liman's office furniture for his own place.

The year was 1898. Morris was twenty-five years old, lean and striking-looking, with black, piercing eyes, pitch-black hair, and pale, milk-white skin. The Lower East Side was teeming with refugees from Southern and Eastern Europe—from Italy, from the vast empires of Russia and Austria-Hungary, from the crumbling domains of the Ottoman Turks. Waves of immigrants were spreading out to cities around the country. The middle classes were expanding rapidly. The excitement of the Spanish-American War and the pride over the consolidation of Brooklyn and the surrounding counties into Greater New York fed a burgeoning optimism. Vaudeville was fresh and new, and Fourteenth Street was its hub—a busy thoroughfare chockablock with theaters and restaurants and jammed with pedestrians dodging horses and hansoms and the cable cars that whipped around Union Square on Dead Man's Curve.

Working on commission, independent agents like Morris competed to book acts into the growing network of theater circuits. How many weeks of work they could promise depended on their connections with the impresarios, and Morris's connections were good. Every day, he walked across the street to lunch at Lüchow's with the theater managers—Percy G. Williams, who'd gone from hawking health belts and patent medicines to running theaters in Brooklyn; Sylvester Z. Poli, who'd come from Italy a sculptor and now had his own vaudeville houses in New Haven and Waterbury; Willie Hammerstein, who ran the Victoria on West Forty-second Street under the supervision of his father, opera impresario Oscar Hammerstein. Performers stopped by to pay their respects. They didn't sit down unless invited.

One of the theater managers Morris booked for was Benjamin Franklin Keith, a New England circus grifter who'd moved up in the world. Keith was a formidable-looking man, his stern visage set off by a bald pate and a walrus mustache that accentuated his pugnacious nature. After starting out in a medicine booth at a Boston freak show, in 1883 he'd opened a dime museum on Washington Street with a single attraction: "Little Alice, the smallest baby ever born live." A few months later, he'd added an upstairs "theater room" with a little stage and an organ. In 1886, he'd moved to the elegantly appointed Bijou Theatre, where he presented variety acts and light opera by the likes of Gilbert and Sullivan. Eight years after that, he'd opened Keith's Union Square Theatre in New York, where he dropped the light opera and assembled a wholesome program of variety acts that he dubbed vaudeville. Now he had a circuit that stretched from Boston to Philadelphia, and ambitions that were bigger still.

In the spring of 1900, Keith launched the Vaudeville Managers' Association, which proposed to standardize actors' salaries and regularize their routes by setting up a central booking office. The VMA functioned as a talent agency like Morris's, except that performers would pay a "booking fee" to their employers instead of paying a commission to an independent broker who sold their talents to the highest bidder.

Together with its counterpart, the Western Vaudeville Managers' Association out of Chicago, it came to be known as the Combine.

Keith had two goals: to keep his competitors from outbidding him, and to get performers to accept lower salaries in exchange for the security of longer bookings. But in order to work, the Combine had to corner the market in talent. If independent agents like Morris continued to sell acts to theaters outside the Combine, the scheme would go nowhere. So the VMA threatened performers who played other theaters with a blacklist. The performers fought back by forming a union, the Exalted Order of the White Rats ("star" spelled backwards), and setting up their own booking agency. In 1902, they struck the Combine's theaters in Boston and Philadelphia. When audiences stayed away, the Keith attempt fizzled.

But only briefly. Keith started luring individual stars away from the White Rats with offers of preferred billing and higher salaries. Those who remained loyal were blacklisted and harassed—trunks and props sent astray, threatened with worse if they didn't cooperate. Morris led the opposition, booking acts into independent theaters—Proctor's Fifth Avenue at Twenty-ninth and Broadway, Hammerstein's Victoria on Forty-second Street, the Circle on Columbus Circle, the Colonial at Broadway and Sixty-second, the Brooklyn Music Hall, and so forth. By the time he moved his offices uptown to Twenty-eighth and Broadway, he was able to offer employment for forty-three weeks at a stretch—an entire season. Then Edward F. Albee, the forty-five-year-old associate Keith had put in charge of the VMA booking office, invited Morris to come in for a meeting. Like his boss, Albee was a New Englander who'd joined the circus, a fellow of good Puritan stock who'd run away from home and toured with P. T. Barnum before linking up with Keith in 1883. Morris was working too hard, Albee told him amiably. Why didn't he take a desk on the Keith booking floor, and bring the other independent agents with him?

Morris said he'd think it over. They both knew what his answer would be.

Albee was right, of course: Morris was working too hard. Shortly afterward, at age thirty, he was stricken with tuberculosis: the white death. A struggle between body and soul in which the body slowly withered as the soul gained supremacy—or that was what they said. The reality was a hacking cough that grew louder and more insistent as you wasted away and sank into fever and started to gasp desperately for air. The only hope was the rest cure, pioneered by Dr. Edward F. Trudeau in the remote Adirondack village of Saranac Lake.

Trudeau had gone to the Adirondacks to die in 1873, the year Morris was born. Instead he'd staged a miraculous recovery, and in 1884 he'd opened his Adirondack Cottage Sanatorium on Mount Pisgah, overlooking the Saranac River and the village along its banks. Now hundreds of desperate victims made the ascent from New York and Boston and Philadelphia every year, forsaking the decay of the lowland cities for a magical realm of dark forests, rugged peaks, crystalline lakes, and pure mountain air. In more fashionable parts of the Adirondacks, consumptives were as welcome as Jews. But the woodsmen of Saranac Lake prospered with the cure industry, turning their homes into cure cottages for boarders who couldn't get into Trudeau's sanatorium. And because the densely wooded shorelines outside town had been bought up by real-estate speculators who didn't mind selling to Hebrews, the lakefronts were dotted with elaborate summer camps built for Jewish industrialists and financiers—Adolph Lewisohn, who'd made his fortune in copper; Otto Kahn, of the Wall Street firm of Kuhn, Loeb & Company.

Leaving the agency in the hands of his staff, Morris took up residence in the Algonquin Hotel, a sprawling Victorian resort on the shores of Lower Saranac Lake, just outside town. It wasn't easy to let go. His mind raced constantly. What was the Combine up to? Would his staff be able to counter their next move? Then the reality of his isolation began to take hold. Enterprise, reason—he'd left that world behind. He was in the realm of death and renewal. Vaudeville was all about time— the big time, the small time, how many weeks of time a showman could offer, how many weeks of time an act had lined up. In vaudeville, time was money. Here, time was all you had left. It was precious in a different way.

The letters stopped. Emma came up and rented a cottage for them on Algonquin Avenue. Her mother, Brigetta, arrived with the children, four-year-old Bill, Jr., and baby Ruth, not yet one. Emma's sister Ella gave up her job in the restaurant at Wanamaker's Department Store to come run the house. Morris slept on an open porch beneath flannel sheets. He was forbidden to touch the children.

A year passed. Two years. Almost three.

*   *   *

In 1905, on one of his first trips back to the city, Morris was sitting in his office at 6 West Twenty-eighth Street when an out-of-work rodeo performer rode in on a horse and lassoed him to his chair. The cowboy was Will Rogers, a young Oklahoma half-breed who'd been doing rope tricks with a Wild West show in Sheepshead Bay, Brooklyn, until it flopped, leaving him with no prospects and a horse to feed. That June, Morris put him to work twirling his lariat on Forty-second Street for $140 a week. Audiences liked him. Soon Morris was booking him in weeklong engagements across the Northeast—at Sylvester Z. Poli's theaters in New Haven, Bridgeport, Hartford, Waterbury, Springfield, and Worcester; at Percy Williams's theaters on Broadway, in Coney Island, in Harlem, and in downtown Brooklyn; at F. F. Proctor's theaters in Newark and on Twenty-third Street. As for Morris, he'd been roped back into the business.

His doctors said he had to live in the country to avoid a relapse, so Emma found them a four-story house on a large plot of land in Washington Heights, the highest point of Manhattan, surrounded by farms and estates on an unpaved road called Fort Washington Avenue. Morris moved his office uptown to the Holland Building, Fortieth and Broadway, to ease the commute. He was only supposed to work three days a week, but he already had big plans. He hired a vaudeville producer named Jesse Lasky and sent him to Chicago to open an office. Lasky was scouting talent at the Majestic Theatre a few weeks later when he was wowed by a blackface singer—not that the voice was so great, but he sounded incredibly sincere. The singer's name was Al Jolson. He and his partner—a crippled Yiddish-dialect comedian who performed in whiteface—billed themselves as "the Hebrew and the Coon." They'd been performing for the WVMA, the Western branch of the Combine, but Lasky signed them to the Morris Agency the next day.

Back in New York, Morris was getting to be friends with Sime Silverman, a square-jawed young man who'd just started a show-business weekly called *Variety* on a $1,500 loan from his father-in-law. Silverman had recently been fired from the *New York Morning Telegraph* for panning the wrong act, a comedy team who'd canceled their Christmas ad as a result. Like Will, he'd lost his head to the gaudy glories of the Rialto, and like Will, he believed in the might and the right of the little man. His paper would champion the actors who made the show world great, not serve the interests of the theater owners who grew fat off their labors. In March 1906, Will took out an ad in the three-month-old paper to ballyhoo his new offices in New York and Chicago and to announce that he could promise forty-nine weeks of playing time to the five thousand acts on his roster. It was time to show them he was back.

Keith wasn't slow to take up the challenge. He called a meeting of the Combine's theater managers and began a bare-knuckles campaign to bring the independent theaters under his sway. He quickly found a weak link among the Morris managers: Frederick Freeman Proctor, an acrobat turned impresario whose flagship was the Fifth Avenue Theatre. Proctor had six years to go on his lease, but there was a cancellation clause in case the property was sold. And Proctor's general manager, who was privy to all his business arrangements, had just left him for Keith. So when Proctor came in one day and was told that his former manager was waiting in the owner's box, and Keith with him, he knew there'd be trouble. When Proctor reached the box, Keith informed him that he'd just purchased the building. Proctor would have to vacate within a year—unless he chose to abandon Morris and merge his circuit with Keith's. Morris learned about the formation of the new Keith & Proctor Company when he picked up the May 13 *Morning Telegraph*.

Sylvester Poli folded next. From his Connecticut base, Poli had assembled a string of vaude houses stretching from Worcester, Massachusetts, to Wilkes-Barre, Pennsylvania, but at the moment his cash was tied up in a new theater in New Haven. When he went for a loan to tide him over, he discovered that Keith had already visited his bankers to tell them he intended to build an opposition theater in every one of Poli's towns. No loans would be forthcoming. Poli knew what he had to do.

Between Proctor and Poli, Morris lost sixteen houses in a week. Yet he still had thirty-three weeks of playing time to offer his acts, including such prime New York locations as Hammerstein's Victoria. Of all the Morris managers, Hammerstein was the most loyal. He and Morris had taken the Victoria to the top with a policy of booking nut acts, from trained fleas to Jo-Jo the Dog-Faced Boy, as well as celebrities like Evelyn Nesbit Thaw, the ravishing beauty whose jealous husband had murdered Stanford White at Madison Square Garden. One of their biggest draws was the Cherry Sisters, billed as the world's worst act, who were so bad they had to perform behind netting to protect them from brickbats hurled by the audience—or actually by Willie, who was standing in the pit. Will and Willie were inseparable. They were the same age, had the same build and the same black mustache, wore the same kind of clothes, and spent so much time together they were known on Broadway as the Siamese Twins. Whatever happened elsewhere, Will Morris would be booking the Victoria.

But ten months later, in February 1907, Morris had a disturbing visit from Percy Williams. Williams owed his success to Morris: He'd been able to move into Manhattan from Brooklyn because Morris had tipped him off to the availability of the Circle Theatre on Columbus Circle, which the smart money said would be the next stop in the theater district's continuing uptown march. Now Williams was telling Morris he could arrange for the two of them to join forces with Keith. Williams would partner with Keith and Proctor in a new venture called the United Booking Office, which would replace the Vaudeville Managers' Association. Morris would run the new booking office as general manager under Albee's supervision. Morris looked at Williams and asked if he'd lost his mind.

It was the Thursday before Lincoln's Birthday. Will and Emma had planned to leave the next day for a four-day weekend in the Adirondacks. But Morris was so upset, he wanted to get away at once. He had some thinking to do, and in the mountains he could think. He phoned Emma in Washington Heights and asked her to pack their bags immediately. They'd meet at Grand Central and take the night train to Saranac Lake.

The doctor in Saranac gave him a good report. Will and Emma swaddled themselves in furs and set off in a sleigh along Forest Home Road, past the rustic entrance gates to the great camps on the lake, skimming deeper and deeper into the snow-covered woods. They went back to the Hotel Berkeley and warmed themselves by the fire. But Morris was restless, and on Sunday night, he announced that he had to return to the city at once. The chauffeur met them at Grand Central on Monday morning and dropped him at his office before taking Emma uptown.

That evening, when Will didn't come home for dinner, Emma called Willie Hammerstein's wife to find out where he was. With Willie and Percy Williams at a big meeting of the Keith-and-Albee crowd, Emma was told.

Then she heard the car in the drive. She met Will at the door and asked if Willie was with him. No, he said, Willie had phoned to say he was going home early. And he'd been unable to reach Percy Williams all day.

She told him about the meeting. There was a long silence.

The meeting broke up at five-thirty Tuesday morning. Before it ended, Percy Williams and Willie Hammerstein and most of the other Morris managers had agreed to Keith's terms. Keith's new United Booking Office would issue franchises permitting agents to book their acts into member theaters—franchises it could revoke at will. Theater managers agreed to book all their acts through the United Office in return for a cut on the performers' commissions.

The deal left Morris flat. Overnight, his business dropped from upward of $100,000 a year to virtually nothing. He'd always worked without a contract, figuring any manager who wasn't happy should be free to leave. Now he had no recourse but to watch them go.

Later that morning, two friendly promoters came to Morris to offer their sympathy. One of them even made a profession of loyalty. Morris directed them to the United Office. They'd made a nice gesture, but the handful of theaters they controlled would do him no good. He needed an invincible ally to fight Keith now, and he'd returned to the city with a scheme for getting one. He walked around the corner to the New Amsterdam Theatre on Forty-second Street, where he was received by Abraham Lincoln Erlanger, the most powerful man in the American theater.

Erlanger was a short, pot-bellied individual known in theatrical circles as Little Napoleon, an appellation he liked, and Dishonest Abe, an appellation he didn't. He ran Klaw & Erlanger, the nationwide theater syndicate that for eleven years had dominated the legitimate stage the way Keith and Albee hoped to dominate vaudeville. Greeting Morris in an office decorated with busts and portraits of his hero, the emperor of the French, Erlanger sat behind his desk in a thronelike chair and cradled his right hand in the fold of his double-breasted jacket. Morris knew that Erlanger and Keith had discussed a joint venture earlier, and that the talks had ended badly. He was betting that Erlanger would be receptive to what he had in mind.

Two days later, Morris stunned everyone by announcing that Klaw & Erlanger would go into vaudeville in association with their archrivals, the Shubert Brothers. It was stupendous news—the robber barons of the theater joining forces with their adversaries to leap into the vaudeville fray, at the inducement of a man everyone had thought crushed just forty-eight hours before. The new enterprise, known as the United States Amusement Company, would present shows in twenty-two theaters previously given over to legit productions—eighteen from Klaw & Erlanger and four from the Shuberts—plus eight more to be constructed soon. Headed by William Morris and given a virtually unlimited budget for talent, it would offer "advanced vaudeville"—solid bills of headliners, thrown head-to-head against anything the UBO could offer. The clash would begin in Philadelphia on April 22.

Morris rationalized his involvement with Klaw & Erlanger on the grounds that it would give actors new stages and free them from domination by Keith. None of them reckoned on the financial panic that set in a few months later, when John D. Rockefeller's brother William tried to destroy Frederick Augustus Heinze, a Montana copper smelter who'd frustrated his attempts to create a copper trust. When Rockefeller managed to bring about the failure of Heinze's Knickerbocker Trust Company, the third largest bank in New York, he set off a panic that threatened to bring down the entire financial community. Box-office receipts held up, but the credit freeze that accompanied the run on the banks hobbled Klaw & Erlanger's backers. The new theater construction had to be postponed indefinitely, and even though the existing theaters were drawing standing-room-only crowds, they couldn't hold enough people to cover the cost of Morris's productions.

Then Morris and Erlanger had a bitter fight. The financial squeeze had them both under pressure, but observers suspected that the breach was really caused by Morris's sudden realization that the great vaudeville war he was waging was in fact just a setup—that Klaw & Erlanger was in it to be bought out. On November 9, Keith did buy them out, reportedly at a million-dollar profit. He offered Morris a job running the United Booking Office. Once again, Morris declined.

This time, Morris really should have been flattened. Two things kept him going. A few days earlier, a Scottish minstrel he'd booked into Klaw & Erlanger's New York Theatre on Times Square had opened to tremendous acclaim. A former coal miner who'd gotten his start on amateur night and become a hit in English music halls, Harry Lauder walked onstage in full Highland getup and broke into a routine that mixed Scottish tunes with wry patter about his drinking, his neighbors, and his "wee wifey." It was his first American appearance, and audiences were ecstatic. "A revelation in vaudeville," *Variety* called him. Morris signed him to a lifelong management contract on the spot. Lauder was already booked in Britain for the next two years, but that was okay—by then, maybe Morris would have someplace to present him.

That was the other thing: In June, Morris had lined up $500,000 in backing and announced his own vaudeville circuit, the William Morris Amusement Company, to operate in cities the United States Amusement Company wasn't planning to enter. His talent was for building stage acts and putting together bills, not heading a far-flung business enterprise. But George Leventritt, his attorney on the Klaw & Erlanger deal, thought he could assemble a new circuit that would carry Morris through the next campaign in the vaudeville wars. And unlike the other venture, this one would not be for sale.

On May 4, 1908, six months after the collapse of his partnership with Klaw & Erlanger, Morris opened his flagship, the American Music Hall at Forty-second Street and Eighth Avenue. He'd spent $50,000 refurbishing the twenty-five-hundred-seat theater in scarlet and gold, with bouquets of American beauty roses in the lobby and a summer roof garden done in an Adirondack-lodge motif. Diamond Jim Brady, the flamboyant Wall Street speculator, was in the audience, as he was on most opening nights. Will and Emma quietly slipped away to Europe to book talent for the fall season, since most American vaudevillians were afraid to risk the Keith blacklist. Because Keith and Albee were having him trailed, they traveled under assumed names.

Morris visited all the major capitals—Paris, Brussels, Amsterdam, Berlin, Vienna. He opened a London office on the Strand and put his brother Hugo in charge. But his most important meeting was in Birkenhead, across the River Mersey from Liverpool, where Harry Lauder was playing. He met Lauder at a pub between performances and made him a staggering offer—$3,000 a week for a six-month American tour, plus expenses for himself, his wife, and his dresser, plus a kilted pipe-and-drum band to escort him to the state capitol or city hall in every city he visited, plus the use of President Roosevelt's private railroad car, the *Mayflower*. He wasn't quite sure how he'd swing this last, but he'd manage it. Lauder knocked the ashes from his pipe, lowered his chin, squinted at Morris over gold-rimmed spectacles, and said he'd take it. Morris had one stipulation: From the moment he stepped onto the dock in New York, Lauder must never again wear trousers in public—only a kilt. They sealed the deal with an oath, and Morris went off to buy out Lauder's commitments in Britain before returning to America on the RMS *Lusitania*.

On October 13, Lauder opened in New York to standing ovations. The demand for tickets was so great that Morris set up camp stools on the stage to handle the overflow. When Albee threatened legal action over the Washington engagement at the Belasco Theater because it was booked by Klaw & Erlanger and the Shuberts, whose surrender agreement prevented them from mounting vaudeville shows, Morris proposed a benefit performance on the White House lawn. Instead, Roosevelt had his secretary phone the Belasco with word that the president would be using his box the entire week of Lauder's performance. The significance of this gesture, coming from a president whose administration was suing to break up John D. Rockefeller's Standard Oil trust under the Sherman Antitrust Act, could hardly be missed. Albee lifted the ban.

Harry Lauder's triumphal procession across America made William Morris the hero of the anti-Keith forces. He even tried his hand at public speaking. "I will never be connected with the United people," he declared at a January 1909 meeting of the White Rats in Chicago. "I will be William Morris forever. I would rather be William Morris and have my apartment and three meals a day and leave my name to my son than have all the fortunes of the United." The actors cheered wildly. "I have always been fighting," he continued. "Even in my school days I was always the arguer and wouldn't stand for the thumb being pressed on me. I would like to tell you more, but I think I will quit. I guess it's stage fright."

Morris had just signed a lease on the New Garden Theatre in Chicago. Later that year, he announced plans to launch a Western circuit, with theaters in Kansas City, Omaha, Denver, Salt Lake City, Oakland, San Francisco, and Los Angeles. When Lauder's second annual tour reached San Francisco in January 1910, Morris laid the cornerstone of his American Music Hall at Ellis and Market Streets to the skirl of bagpipes. His stage fright prevented him from speaking at all that day, but his ten-year-old son was hoisted onto the cornerstone by his associates. After a moment of bewilderment, the boy surveyed the crowd choking the intersection and cried, "Hurrah for all the people!" Then he leaped down, buried his face in father's coat, and burst into tears.

At his American Music Hall in New York, Morris booked Fred Karno's London comedy troupe, then completing a transcontinental tour. They were a big hit in *A Night in an English Music Hall*, featuring twenty-one-year-old Charlie Chaplin as a drunken heckler in the audience. Morris also booked Sophie Tucker, twenty-two years old and fresh from her debut in Florenz Ziegfeld's *Follies of 1909*. Overweight and uncertain of her appeal, Tucker hid her face behind burnt cork and billed herself as "the World's Renowned Coon Shouter." Audiences were going for dialect acts of all sorts—Hebe, wop, coon; the experts said it enabled the new immigrants to explain themselves to each other. Blackface was particularly popular with Jewish acts because it made them strange in a way Americans could understand—hadn't blackface minstrel shows been a staple of popular entertainment since the 1830s? But it could also be a crutch to hide behind. Morris told Sophie she should never go out in blackface again.

Morris's operations were expanding rapidly, but he abhorred business details as much as he loved working with entertainers. So while he scouted for performers and honed their acts, his attorney, George Leventritt, handled the financial and contractual side. Theater by theater, city by city, the thirty-eight-year-old Leventritt was piecing together a nationwide circuit. All that spring of 1910, he conducted intricate negotiations on the East Coast, the West Coast, and points between. On June 13, without warning, he died of a heart attack. His assistant had little idea what deals had been struck, since most of the particulars had never been put down in writing. Morris had no choice but to release all participants.

Pressed by creditors, Morris tried to make a deal with Martin Beck, the West Coast impresario whose Orpheum circuit had been in the Keith camp for years. Beck wanted better access to talent than Keith was giving him, and he was secretly planning to invade Keith's territory by building a theater in Gotham. In July, Morris and Beck met with their lawyers at a resort on Lake Hopatcong, thirty miles away in the hills of New Jersey, and agreed to join forces. The next thing Morris heard, Beck and Keith had agreed to go in together on the theater Beck was planning in New York—the Palace, at Seventh Avenue and Forty-seventh Street. They offered him the job of managing it.

Morris had better luck with Marcus Loew, a short, bulbous, comical individual who owned a small-time vaudeville circuit. The two had first met in the 1890s, when Morris was working for Gallison & Hobrun and

Loew was a furrier on Mercer Street. Since then, Loew had briefly part-nered with another young furrier, Adolph Zukor, in a penny arcade on Fourteenth Street that boasted fortune-telling machines, strength testers, and peep shows. He'd gone on to build his own string of penny arcades and then nickelodeons—storefront amusement halls that offered one-reel films and modest variety attractions. From there, he'd moved into small-time vaudeville, presenting flickers in proscenium arch theaters as a novelty on a par with animal impersonators, dancing bears, and mock hangings in which someone from the audience was invited to pull the rope.

Loew and Zukor had just merged their interests to form a large chain of nickelodeons and small-time vaude houses. Now Morris proposed that Loew take over his own circuit as well. Keith and Albee didn't care about the small time and they weren't worried about the flickers, which seemed to have little potential beyond the novelty stage. So this time, Morris was allowed to dispose of his theaters without a hitch.

Loew also took over Morris's agency, creating a joint Marcus Loew–William Morris Booking Office run by Joe Schenck, one of two brothers who'd gone to work for him after he'd invested in their Pal-isades Amusement Park on the Hudson. Loew moved into Morris's American Music Hall, while Morris rented an office in the new Times Building, which stood like an enormous wedge of wedding cake in the middle of Times Square. Zukor, eager to test his idea that audiences would be even more receptive to full-length feature films than they were to one-reelers, took an office in the same building and formed his Famous Players Film Company, the name inspired by a note he'd scrawled to himself after having an epiphany on the subway: "Famous Players in Famous Plays."

The failure of the Morris circuit was devastating. Morris had to cut his staff down to a secretary-receptionist, a road-show router, and a bookkeeper—Henry Berlinghoff, Emma's brother. He closed the Lon-don branch and advised his brother Hugo to come back to New York and open his own agency under the auspices of the United Office. He bought some land in the Adirondacks—110 acres of evergreen forest on Lake Colby, just outside the village of Saranac Lake—and announced that, except for promoting Harry Lauder, he would go into retirement. But that proved difficult.

In the summer of 1911, while Morris was planning Lauder's next tour, a European agent stopped into his office. As Morris leafed through

his portfolio, a photograph of a tall, bearded man in full rabbinical vest-
ments fell to the floor—Sirota, Cantor of Warsaw. Acting on a gambler's
hunch, Morris contracted to present him at theaters in London and
New York and across the Northeast. By October, Morris once again had
America in the grip of Lauder mania—displays of Scottish regalia grac-
ing the windows at Wanamaker's and Marshall Field's, string ensembles
filling the air in hotels and restaurants with his lilting melodies, pipe-
and-drum parades to city halls and state capitols across the land, an
entire week at the Manhattan Opera House sold out. Then, in February
1912, Cantor Sirota made his debut at Carnegie Hall, creating such
excitement that his listeners, according to the *New York Times*, "literally
besieged" the auditorium.

Morris sailed for England in March with Emma and nine-year-old
Ruth to prepare for the cantor's London appearance at the Albert Hall.
He also wanted to arrange financing for his latest project, a touring
vaudeville show starring Annette Kellerman, the pulchritudinous Australian diver who'd been jailed in the Boston suburb of Revere Beach a
few years before for indecent exposure. Miss Kellerman had an astonishing figure, and she wasn't shy about revealing it—no bloomers, no
middy blouse, no stockings, no laced sandals, no billowing bathing
hat, just a single-piece body stocking that stretched from neck to toe.
After checking into the Savoy, Morris arranged to tour her in Britain
and the States. The climax of the show he had planned, following a
ballet of water sprites in a "sunken grotto" formed by layers of rippling
gauze, would come when she dived into a tank from a springboard just
below the proscenium arch. As a promotional gimmick, he made up
paper tape measures inviting women to compare their measurements
to hers and to the Venus de Milo's. The ensuing scandal made it an
instant craze.

By April, Will and Emma were ready to return to New York. But a few
days before they were to sail, Morris got word that the UBO had offered
Kellerman a two-season tour for more money if she would cancel her
English dates with Morris. Her manager had declined, but theater man-
agers had heard she might cancel and were demanding confirmation.
The only way to convince them she'd show was to see them in person.
Wearily, Morris told Emma to unpack their trunks and pack a bag for
him instead. That night, he'd be leaving for Manchester, Liverpool,
Glasgow, and every other stop on the itinerary. They'd have to cancel
their passage home, though it meant missing the maiden voyage of the

RMS *Titanic*, widely ballyhooed as the safest and most luxurious ship afloat.

That summer, with Morris still in England, Henry Berlinghoff hired a fourteen-year-old office boy named Abe Lastfogel to help them out. Lastfogel was the seventh son of a Yiddish-speaking animal skinner who'd fled Russia in 1889 to escape the pogroms and found work in the Gansevoort Street meatpacking district by the docks of the Lower West Side. Born in 1898, the boy had grown up in a cold-water flat on East Forty-ninth Street, hard by the Third Avenue el in a grim tenement district beset by odors and soot from the slaughterhouses and power plants along the East River. He was a scrappy kid, compact and solidly built, but so nearsighted they joked he had to get the local Irish toughs under a streetlight before he could hit them. After his mother died, he'd been raised by his sister, Bessie, who was eight years older and working at F.A.O. Schwarz, the toy emporium. Bessie had put him through the Merchants' & Bankers' Business School after he finished grammar school, and now that he'd completed his secretarial training there, he was ready to look for a job.

He'd set out that day with ten cents in his pocket and headed uptown to the YMCA on East Fifty-seventh Street, a few blocks away from the Merchants' & Bankers' School on Madison Avenue, because a classmate's older brother ran the employment registry there. Abe found two jobs open—one at Clemons the Tailor on West Thirty-sixth, and one at William Morris on West Forty-second. Both called for interviews before eleven o'clock. Clemons was more than a mile from the Y. That meant a five-cent streetcar ride, and if he spent another nickel on a wiener, his capital would be shot. It looked like a hot day. He didn't want to have to walk home, so he went to Morris first. Henry Berlinghoff hired him on the spot, and he spent the rest of the day preparing for the next Lauder tour—placing newspaper ads, having posters printed up, stuffing press releases into envelopes.

Morris returned full of plans for F. F. Proctor, the manager who'd gone over to the Combine after finding Keith in the owner's box of his Fifth Avenue Theatre. Through extensive legal action, Proctor had finally managed to extricate himself from Keith, and Morris was urging him to move into Times Square, which, contrary to predictions, was still the center of the theater district. Abe Erlanger, the Little Napoleon of the legitimate stage, was eager to lease out his New York Theatre, a block-long entertainment complex at Broadway and Forty-fourth Street, and Morris wanted Proctor to take it.

The New York was a festive-looking place, its ornate exterior capped with flag-bedecked cupolas, standing on Times Square like some immense Venetian pleasure palace. Morris had introduced Harry Lauder to American audiences there in 1907, and for the next four years Florenz Ziegfeld, inspired by the *Folies Bergère* in Paris and backed by Klaw & Erlanger, had presented his racy and spectacular *Follies* on its roof. Directly across from it was the Hotel Astor, where Morris and the other big men of the show world lunched every day in the oak-paneled Hunting Room. Inside was a lavishly appointed theater, two floors of offices, a billiard parlor, and the largest roof garden in New York. But Proctor wasn't interested—so Morris, acting on impulse, took it himself.

His first move was to turn it into Wonderland, a Coney Island–style steeplechase. Wonderland boasted a freak show with offerings like the Skeleton Dude and Krao the Bearded Woman, a beauty contest featuring "girls of all nations," moving pictures and vaudeville acts in the theater, even a merry-go-round. But no one went to Times Square for freak shows and merry-go-rounds, and the building was too enormous to make a profit off passersby. Morris quickly ripped everything out and replaced it with a wisteria-draped rooftop cabaret he called the Jardin de Danse.

Spacious and verdant, high enough above Broadway to catch the summer breezes off the Hudson, Morris's Jardin de Danse was an immediate hit. America was in the throes of a sudden dance craze, and matrons who upholstered their bosoms in fur and diamonds no longer set the tone. The new mode was quick and sassy—lavish floor shows, liquor and gigolos, couples doing the turkey trot, the bunny hug, the monkey glide, the Negro drag, the aeroplane waltz. Crowds came to Morris's open-air pleasure dome to eat and drink and sample the world of dance—can-can girls from France, temple dancers from India, cakewalk contests in which lines of Negro dancers pranced wildly across the floor in wicked imitation of the grand balls of the antebellum South. Morris ran a respectable establishment—formal dress required, no smoking by the ladies—but the sultry tangos and syncopated rags of Big Jim Europe and his all-Negro orchestra were a gust of freedom after the decorous string ensembles polite New Yorkers were accustomed to.

Downstairs, in the theater, Morris booked full-length feature films. Adolph Zukor and a handful of other producers were churning them out regularly now, and they were so popular that some promoters were building palatial theaters expressly to show them. Morris had a long run in 1914 with *Tillie's Punctured Romance*, a hugely successful feature starring one of his favorite comedians, Charlie Chaplin, who'd left Karno's troupe to star in pictures for Mack Sennett's Keystone Film Company. Four years earlier, when Sennett was pulling in $5 a day as a film extra, he'd caught Chaplin at Morris's American Music Hall and resolved to make pictures with him someday. After forming Keystone, he offered Chaplin twice the money Karno was paying to come to the booming cow town of Los Angeles. Chaplin didn't think much of Keystone's frenetic comedies, though they'd developed an enormous following. But he was young and savvy, and he figured a year at this racket would allow him to return to vaudeville a big sensation.

As Harry Lauder's manager, Morris had gotten involved in picture-making himself. Earlier that year, he'd even made a cameo appearance in an impromptu short Lauder made with William Selig, one of the most famous filmmakers in America. Colonel Selig (the title was of dubious origin, but he was too imposing for anyone to take issue with it) was a magician and a tinkerer whose inventions had led him to form the Selig Polyscope Company, with studios in Chicago and Los Angeles. He'd enjoyed great success with a one-reeler called *Hunting Big Game in Africa*, in which a moth-eaten lion and a mustachioed actor and some Negroes from Chicago were done up to look like Teddy Roosevelt on safari. Selig never actually claimed he'd captured the president on film, but he could hardly be blamed if audiences made that assumption. Now Morris had him working on his most ambitious project yet—Harry Lauder Singing and Talking Pictures, which used a system of Selig's devising to meld sound with pictures. But in 1915, when Morris saw the film at the Curran Theatre in San Francisco, he found it a mess. The sound was on disk and the picture was on film, and no one could get them synchronized; Lauder's voice was singing while his face told a joke. Selig went back to the lab.

Morris could still count on Lauder to draw audiences in person, and he'd built another tour around the biggest attraction in vaudeville—Eva Tanguay, the Cyclonic One, an unabashedly corpulent singer whose frantic delivery and outrageous personality made her wildly popular with audiences. But his agency business was in trouble. Small-time vaudeville didn't pay enough to make the commissions worthwhile, so he'd dissolved the joint booking office with Loew and taken the agency independent again. And though Keith had died in 1914, that did Morris no good with the United Office, since Albee ran the Keith empire and continued to blacklist his acts.

Albee now had more than ten thousand theaters under his sway. Yet vaudeville was getting stale: Albee cared more about monopoly than about showmanship, and the war that had just engulfed Europe cut off a major source of entertainers. In the spring of 1915, Morris arranged a meeting to discuss a new scheme—to bring in performers from Britain and France who were too old for war duty. Albee received him in his office atop Martin Beck's Palace Theatre, which he'd seized and made his flagship. He listened to Morris go on about the need for fresh blood in vaudeville until he started to turn purple. Then he rose from his chair and roared, "To hell with that nonsense! *I* am vaudeville!"

Morris had been so excited about his idea that he'd already booked passage on the *Lusitania*, but now he had to cancel. A few days later, on May 7, the *Lusitania* was torpedoed by a German U-boat as she steamed toward the Irish coast. Nearly twelve hundred passengers were lost.

First the *Titanic,* now the *Lusitania:* Albee may have saved Morris from the deep, but he had him where he wanted him all the same. Bills mounting, his agency in decline, Morris seemed ruined. He closed the Jardin de Danse and ceded the New York Theatre to Loew. He dismissed his employees—even his brother-in-law, Henry Berlinghoff, who left to play drums in Berlinghoff's Parade and Dance Band and arrange fair dates for the Australian Wood Choppers. Only Abe Lastfogel refused to go. "Mr. Morris," Lastfogel said, "as long as your name is on the door, I'm working for you." Morris made him his personal secretary. Morris's son, who was a year younger than Lastfogel, left high school soon afterward to join in.

Albee's other opponents seemed destined for extinction as well. He'd been putting the squeeze on *Variety*, banning any performer who was even caught reading it, and by 1916, Sime Silverman was in such trouble that he called a truce, pledging to leave it to the White Rats to attack the United Office. Albee had his own plans for the White Rats: a company union called the National Vaudeville Artists. A new clause in his contracts required performers to certify that they belonged to Albee's NVA to get a booking through the United Office. The White Rats called a strike, but they were demoralized and ineffective. In 1917, when they defaulted on the mortgage to their clubhouse on Forty-sixth Street, their leaders were told that a mysterious 229 West Forty-sixth Street Corporation was ready to assume their debts if they'd vacate the premises. They didn't realize who controlled the corporation until their clubhouse was turned over to the NVA.

Morris got a financial reprieve when the owners of the Park Theatre on Columbus Circle asked him to present a Spanish revue bankrolled by producers in Madrid. But if he wanted to get back into big-time vaudeville, he'd have to make some sort of accommodation with Albee. That February, he did so. With the White Rats out of the way and *Variety* effectively neutralized, he was no longer much of a threat. Since he had clients Albee could use, it made more sense for Albee to bring him into the fold than to continue the feud. So he was allowed to form a joint venture with Pat Casey, a barrel-chested Irishman who served as Albee's troubleshooter. The Morris Agency was exempted from having to pay fees to the UBO, and Morris himself was, as the papers put it, "forgiven."

With an armistice declared in the vaudeville wars, Morris was able to get on with other things, like the Harry Lauder Singing and Talking Pictures. Progress was slow, however, and Morris was an impatient man. "Here is Harry Lauder at present in this country getting advertising like no other Human Being is getting today," he wrote Selig from a road appearance with Lauder in Syracuse that November. "Therefore, why should we not take advantage of this? Let's get a hustle on. . . . We are all out for the money, let's get it now as the time is ripe for it."

Building the agency was easier. Without the threat of a blacklist, Morris was able to take on all sorts of attractions over the next few years—Noble Sissle and Eubie Blake, whose *Shuffle Along* was the first all-Negro musical to open on Broadway; Olympic champion Gertrude Ederle, the first woman to swim the English Channel; the Dancing Cansinos, an exotic brother-sister duo from Madrid; the fantastically popular Borah Minnevitch and his Harmonica Orchestra; Violet and Daisy Hilton, the saxophone-playing Siamese twins from San Antonio. He handled Eddie Cantor, a goggle-eyed young comic from the Lower East Side who'd risen from amateur night on the Bowery to become a Broadway musical-comedy star for the Shubert Brothers. He handled

Clayton, Jackson, and Durante, a song-and-dance team whose propensity for throwing things—plates, telephones, their piano—made them the hottest nightclub act in New York.

Al Shean, a vaudevillian Morris had shot pool with as a boy in the basement of Brigetta Berlinghoff's candy store on Sheriff Street, had asked him years before to keep an eye on his nephews, madcap kids who now played the Keith circuit as the Four Marx Brothers; they came under his wing as well. In 1922, he took them to London with Sophie Tucker to make their English debuts, the Marx Brothers at the Coliseum, Soph at the Hippodrome. Then he slipped over to Paris, where he discovered Maurice Chevalier in the *Folies Bergère*. He was wrong about the Marx Brothers having international appeal—"Twaddle!" "Utter rot!" cried the hecklers as Groucho knee-dipped his way across the stage, flicking his cigar and telling rapid-fire jokes in an incomprehensible twang—but no matter. By this time, the Morris Agency was the undisputed leader in vaudeville.

With success, Morris turned his attention to civic affairs. He founded the Jewish Theatrical Guild in 1924 in response to the anti-Semitic rant of Henry Ford, whose *Dearborn Independent* ran a series on show business with headlines like "Jew Supremacy in the Motion Picture World." Ford had called off his attacks after deciding to run for president in 1922, but others picked up the cudgel; there was even talk of a theatrical branch of the Ku Klux Klan to combat "the Jew and Catholic control of show biz." When Dr. Edgar Mayer, the physician who cared for tubercular vaudevillians at Saranac Lake, told Morris his patients would be better off in a sanatorium than in the lonely cottages the NVA maintained in the village, Morris chaired a luncheon at the Forty-sixth Street clubhouse so Mayer could present his plan to Albee publicly. In 1925, the NVA bought thirty-seven acres on a hilltop outside town to be the site of a future lodge.

Albee could afford to be generous, for, like Morris, he'd achieved his goal. His Keith-Albee circuit in the East and the interlocking Orpheum circuit in the West enjoyed a coast-to-coast monopoly on the big time. And vaudeville seemed as popular as ever, twelve thousand performers playing to 1.6 million people every day. But it no longer had a monopoly on the mass audience; some vaudeville theaters were even switching over to films.

Albee still regarded the moving picture as a brash interloper. Yet movies were no longer a curiosity to be presented between the acrobats and the animal acts; it was more the other way around. When the Chicago chain of Balaban & Katz came up with the idea of offering vaudeville acts as a diversion between films, the Morris office arranged to book its performers with them. The man who struck the deal was Abe Lastfogel.

For a decade now, ever since Abe had shown up at the door with ten cents in his pocket, Bill Morris, Jr., and Abe Lastfogel had been the prince and the pauper—Morris tall and fair-haired and very much the playboy, Lastfogel short and squat and always working to get ahead. As a child, young Morris had been given his own pint-sized desk in his father's office, but until he was sixteen, he was too immature to be much help. Now that he was in his twenties, he could go to Europe on an agency expense account. Once he had to wire home for money from the middle of the Atlantic: He'd boarded a liner in New York for a bon voyage party for his friend Bob Tausig (whose father ran the top travel agency in show business), and after some champagne he'd decided the evening would be infinitely more fun if he didn't get off. Lastfogel, who sat behind Coke-bottle glasses in New York and kept in touch with theater-circuit managers in the United States and abroad, didn't venture overseas until he was twenty-two, when Harry Lauder asked him to engage a theater in London. Another agent suggested they go on to Paris for a New Year's Eve spree, but Lastfogel insisted on taking the next ship back to New York.

Lastfogel was living with his older sister Bessie and their young niece Henrietta on West Ninety-second Street, in a third-floor walk-up in a brick row house just off Riverside Drive. As the favored young man, he got the bedroom while Henrietta slept on a cot in the kitchen and Bessie took a foldout sofa in the front room. He and Bessie spent so many evenings at home with Will and Emma Morris and so many holidays at Camp Intermission, the retreat Morris had built on Lake Colby, that they were almost part of the family. Bessie also went along when he scouted acts at speakeasies and vaude theaters. The rest of his family—his two older brothers, butchers like their father; his three older sisters; and his younger sister, Rose—she kept at bay. As for their father, Ben Lastfogel, the day he came to the office looking for Abe was one they talked about for years.

The humble butcher from Brest-Litovsk was a deeply religious man, and he'd prospered during his thirty years in New York—had bought real estate and opened his own butcher shop and even endowed a Hebrew nursery. But he'd never learned English, and he looked lost in the hustle of Times Square, where the Morris office was situated amid movie palaces, vaudeville theaters, legit theaters, burlesque houses, office buildings, hotels, and flashing electric signs. Asking in Yiddish to speak with Abe, the old man was told in Yiddish that Abe was busy and couldn't come out. Busy? How busy could the boy be, Ben Lastfogel cried, that he couldn't see his own father? Hearing the ruckus, Sophie Tucker sauntered out and told him—also in Yiddish—not to worry: Abe was either schtupping or making money.

Odds were good he was making money. But in 1925, while scouring theaters for a single-woman act he could send to England, he met a vaudeville singer who called herself Frances Arms. A delicatessen owner's daughter who lived on East 116th Street in Italian Harlem, Frances Armhaus was a fresh-faced blonde who made $1,000 a week singing dialect songs—Yiddish, Irish, Italian. (Lastfogel was bringing home about $100.) She wasn't interested in England, but she did agree to a dinner-date, which he canceled at the last minute because of business. She was livid. He was charmed. He followed her around the country and proposed to her backstage at one theater after another until she accepted. They were married in 1927 at their new home—the Ansonia Hotel, a sumptuous turn-of-the-century establishment on upper Broadway that was also home to Babe Ruth and Flo Ziegfeld. To Lastfogel's chagrin, the quiet little wedding they'd planned for 20 turned into a five-hour party for 150.

There were a dozen or so others in the office. Uncle Henry Berlinghoff was back, keeping the books. A very short, very baby-faced young man named John Hyde had joined them in 1926, after eight years as assistant to the booking head for the Loew's circuit. Born Ivan Haidabura in the Black Sea town of Novorossiysk in 1895, he came from a family of acrobats who billed themselves as the Nicholas Haidabura Imperial Russian Troupe. When he was a small child, they'd come to America under the aegis of William Morris. Now he was in charge of vaudeville bookings for the man who'd booked them into the States.

But the real action now was in the movies. The struggle for control that had started with the vaudeville wars had spiraled into a frenzy of mergers aimed at linking the theater chains, which were putting up dazzling new air-cooled picture palaces across the country, to the production companies and distribution operations that kept them filled.

Adolph Zukor merged his Famous Players with a production company Jesse Lasky had formed, with a national distribution outfit called Paramount Pictures, and with the Balaban & Katz theater chain to create the Paramount-Famous–Lasky Corporation, better known as Paramount. Marcus Loew bought Metro Pictures and merged it with Goldwyn Pictures and Louis B. Mayer's independent production unit to create Metro-Goldwyn-Mayer. William Fox, a nickelodeon operator turned small-time vaudeville impresario, ventured into film distribution and then production and now seemed determined to buy up every theater in the country.

Production had become centered in Los Angeles, especially its Hollywood district. Laid out forty years earlier by prim midwestern real-estate speculators (no liquor allowed), Hollywood was now overrun by moviemakers. In 1927, Morris opened a West Coast branch in the State Theatre Building, eight miles away in the Broadway theater district downtown.

WILLIAM MORRIS
CALL BOARD
TALKIES TALKIES TALKIES

screamed the ad in *Variety*.

Talking pictures had been pioneered by Warner Bros., an upstart company founded by four brothers from the roughneck steel town of Youngstown, Ohio. They'd started out with a nickelodeon and eventually gone into film production, with Harry and Albert, the older brothers, handling the business end in New York while Sam and Jack supervised the filmmaking in Los Angeles. Their biggest star was a German shepherd named Rin Tin Tin. They had ambitions, but they lacked the capital to see them through until Harry made a deal with the Wall Street house of Goldman, Sachs & Company in 1925. Then, backed by a multimillion-dollar line of credit, they'd bought movie houses and a faltering movie studio named Vitagraph and gone into partnership with the Western Electric Corporation, whose engineers had succeeded in doing what Colonel Selig and countless others had not—synchronizing sound with film. While Sam Warner made short films of vaudeville routines and musical performances at the Vitagraph studio in Brooklyn, Jack Warner went to work in Hollywood on a feature film using the new Vitaphone sound process to create a synchronized score.

The coming of sound was heralded in August 1926 with the release of Jack's Vitaphone feature, *Don Juan*, a costume epic starring John Barrymore as the great lover. Two months later, the studio released a second Vitaphone program—a feature-length comedy coupled with some of Sam's vaudeville shorts. One short featured Al Jolson—whose success in Broadway musicals for the Shuberts had turned him into Will Morris's biggest star—singing three of his most popular songs in blackface. Another showed George Jessel, also a Morris act, doing a comedy sketch. J. J. Murdock, Albee's general manager, responded with the announcement that vaudevillians under contract to the Keith circuit would not be allowed to perform in sound pictures. But it wasn't until October 1927 that Jolson showed talkies could really work. "Wait a minute. Wait a minute," he cried, playing nightclub singer Jack Robin in *The Jazz Singer*. "You ain't heard nothin' yet. . . ."

The Jazz Singer was Jolson's own story—a backstage drama about a young, Americanized Jew caught between the lure of the stage and the old-country ways of a disapproving father. Jack Robin (born Jakie Rabinowitz) was the cantor's son who had to choose between appearing on Broadway and singing Kol Nidre at the synagogue to please his dying father. Al Jolson (born Asa Yoelson) was the rabbi's son who'd put on blackface and formed an act called "the Hebrew and the Coon." But it could have been Abe Lastfogel or Jack Warner or any of them talking when Jack Robin declared, "Tradition is all right, but this is another day—I'll live my life as I see fit." For that matter, it could have been George Jessel, who'd played Jack Robin on Broadway for the entire 1925–1926 season.

That summer, Jessel had made a silent comedy called *Private Izzy Murphy* for Warner Bros., and while he was on the coast, he urged the studio to buy *The Jazz Singer*. He took the play on the road that fall as Warners announced he'd star in a silent-picture version. There were subsequent disagreements about money and about whether Warners would use its Vitaphone process for the songs—Jessel wanted more pay if they did. But in May 1927 he returned to Los Angeles and ended up sharing a suite at the Biltmore Hotel with Jolson, who was in town for a two-week run of *Big Boy*, a musical he was touring for the Shuberts. Jessel woke up early one morning to find his pal getting dressed. "Go back to sleep, Georgie," Jolson said. "I'm going to play golf." Instead Jolson went to Warner Bros. and signed the contract he'd been discussing, the one that would make him the star of Jessel's picture.

*　　*　　*

The success of *The Jazz Singer* set off a stampede for the coast. Talkies might put vaudeville out of business, but they were also opening up incredible opportunities. At least vaudevillians could talk, unlike most silent-screen stars. Hollywood stars who'd been thrilled to stay in movies at all were soon chagrined to discover that actors from New York and London were getting upward of $5,000 a week.

Morris did all he could to help his clients make the jump. He and Bill Perlberg, one of his agents, were at the train station to greet Fanny Brice, the Ziegfeld *Follies* singer who'd become one of Broadway's biggest musical-comedy stars, when she arrived in Los Angeles in 1928 to star in *My Man*, a waif-girl-makes-it-on-Broadway picture she'd contracted to do for Warners. Al Jolson was there, too, but he became enraptured over a girl who got off shortly afterward, an eighteen-year-old hoofer named Ruby Keeler whom the agency had booked on a six-week tour of West Coast picture houses at $1,250 a week. When Ruby dropped by the Morris office in the State Theatre Building the next day to sign her contract, she was startled to find Jolson waiting for her. She was even more startled when she opened at Grauman's Egyptian on Hollywood Boulevard and found a bouquet of long-stemmed roses with a card that read "Guess Who?"

Fanny Brice, it turned out, was not destined to become a screen idol. As a stage performer she'd always played the defenseless woman victimized by love, and as the innocent wife of feckless gambler Nicky Arnstein, who after years of scandal was sent to prison for securities fraud, she lived out the image in real life. But the movie she made for Warner Bros. turned out to be little more than a crude attempt to capitalize on her story. Before long, she was back in New York.

Even Jolson had trouble making the transition to Hollywood. When he met Ruby Keeler he was about to start in his second Warner Bros. musical, *The Singing Fool*, the mawkish tale of a blackface comedian whose career goes into a tailspin after his son dies. The picture was a huge success; Jolson was the biggest draw in show business. But as audiences grew accustomed to sound, his hysterical overacting and maudlin sentimentality started to seem ridiculous. Talkies demanded subtlety, not broader performances as Jolson thought. His next picture, *Say It with Songs*—a shameless rehash of *The Singing Fool*—was a bomb. So was the next one, and the one after that. He fared better with Miss Keeler: Shortly after he finished *The Singing Fool*, the two of them set off on a honeymoon cruise to Europe.

Other Morris clients clicked with screen audiences and were admitted to the pantheon. Morris hadn't been able to interest anyone in Maurice Chevalier, but when sound created a vogue for film musicals, he saw his chance. Even then it was hard: Where Morris saw a handsome boulevardier whose silken style and knowing manner could speak to women in any language, producers saw a guy who was French. But when Jesse Lasky, now Zukor's production chief at Paramount, went to Europe in 1929, Morris cabled him in Paris to make sure he caught Chevalier's act. Lasky wasn't impressed, but his wife was, and she talked him into signing Chevalier to a movie contract. The negotiations dragged on for six weeks, thanks to the skepticism of Lasky's associates. Yet when Chevalier's first picture, *Innocents of Paris*, reached the screen, audiences proved Morris right.

One of Morris's biggest successes was the Marx Brothers, who were playing the Casino Theatre in New York when he offered them and their hit play *The Cocoanuts* to Walter Wanger of Paramount for $75,000. Zukor was eager for people who could star in talkies, and Wanger thought Morris's deal was a good one until he told Zukor the price. "I'll spit in his eye!" Zukor cried, employing one of his favorite expressions. So Bill Morris, Jr., showed up at Zukor's office with Zeppo Marx to set things right.

Morris was a dapper young man, clear-eyed and handsome and stylish enough to invite comparison with Mayor Jimmy Walker and the Prince of Wales. But he wasn't much of a salesman. While he listened, Zeppo romanced the studio chief shamelessly—What a great showman he was! How wonderful it was to meet him! Finally Zukor said to Zeppo, "So what's the problem between Walter and you?" Zeppo explained that the show contained all their gags, everything they'd ever done, their life's work, but they were willing to commit it to film for only $100,000. At which Zukor turned to Wanger and said, "Walter, what's wrong with that?"

The Marx Brothers were the exception: For most vaudevillians, radio proved an easier jump than pictures. The movies made performers seem distant, unknowable, larger than life; vaudeville was a homey, gemütlich sort of entertainment, short on glamour but long on warmth. Vaudevillians had been through a lot—the ordeal of life on the road, the indignities of the small time, the challenge of working the sticks, the hodgepodge format that put singers and comedians on a par with animal impersonators and freaks of nature. The best of them, like Harry Lauder, exerted a magnetic attraction on their audiences, but their pull had less to do with adulation than with a shared sense of humanity. They touched you somehow. They made you feel like inviting them into your living room—which was what listening to the radio was like.

The year of the Marx Brothers' and Chevalier's first pictures, 1929, was also the year radio became established as a commercial entertainment medium. Wireless telephony had at first been used mainly as a communications device by maritime interests, like the navy and the United Fruit Company, though Morris had employed it to keep in touch with his vaudeville-circuit managers shortly after its introduction. It had made its commercial debut in 1920, when the Westinghouse Electric Company put station KDKA on the air in Pittsburgh to encourage people to buy receiving sets. AT&T launched "toll broadcasting" in 1922 when its station WEAF in New York became the first to carry advertising. Four years later, RCA formed a partnership with Westinghouse and General Electric and launched the National Broadcasting Company, which created two radio networks—central broadcasting organizations that used the telephone lines to distribute programming to stations across the country.

Morris was always looking for another showcase for the talent he represented, and with more and more listeners tuning in and vaudeville on the wane, he told his staffers to get acquainted with broadcasting. Station managers were getting bandleaders and comedians to let them broadcast their acts for the publicity value alone, and at first he urged his performers to cooperate. But by 1926, with the wireless emerging as a national entertainment medium, those days were over. The success of the network idea and of advertising transformed radio into a nationwide medium with unprecedented reach, creating astounding opportunities for singers and musicians and comedians. When Morris got Harry Lauder $20,000 for a pair of fifteen-minute, coast-to-coast broadcasts in December 1929, it signaled the start of a wildcat market for talent.

Morris had equally high expectations for television, a form of radio that had been publicly demonstrated in 1925. By the late twenties a number of experimental transmission stations were broadcasting and rudimentary receivers were being sold to the public. But the technology was too primitive to make these receivers workable for home viewing.

Either the screens were so tiny they came with a magnifying lens, or the whole mechanism was so bulky you could barely move it outside the lab. Then a Chicago inventor named Ulysses Sanabria developed a television receiver with a ten-foot screen—too big for most homes, obviously, but not for the theater.

In 1929, Sanabria demonstrated his system at the Radio World's Fair in Madison Square Garden, the sports arena on the back side of the Broadway theater district, wedged in among the tenements at Eighth Avenue and Forty-ninth Street. He had a small platform set up next to a scanning device and a bank of spotlights; next to all this was one of his ten-foot screens. Spectators were urged to step onto the platform two by two so the crowd could see them onscreen. Morris was fascinated. He came back again and again. Other showmen came as well—among them Adolph Zukor, who that June had acquired 50 percent of the Columbia Broadcasting System, an NBC rival owned by a brash young cigar magnate named William S. Paley.

In September, Zukor also acquired a 50 percent interest in the Morris Agency. Morris and Paramount had long enjoyed a close relationship—Jesse Lasky had once worked for Will Morris, after all, and Abe Lastfogel had made himself indispensable to the Balaban & Katz theater circuit even before its 1925 merger into Zukor's film corporation. By 1929 the Paramount chain, known since the merger as Publix Theaters, had become the largest employer of vaudeville talent in the country, and the Morris office was handling most of its bookings. The deal was a stock swap between Morris and Paramount that left the agency half owned by Paramount-Publix, with each side entitled to choose half its directors. The idea was to ensure smoother bookings, or so it was said; instead it drew a lot of negative chatter and threw a monkey wrench into Morris's attempt to get a license from Actors Equity to represent actors on the legit stage.

Morris's role in the vaudeville wars had left him more accustomed to hosannas than brickbats—three years earlier he'd been hailed in a 112-page testimonial issue of *Variety* as "Morris the hero, Morris the genius and Morris the saint"—but he sloughed off the criticism and kept his eyes on the future. To him, Sanabria's invention looked like a good bet. He figured audiences around the country would flock to theaters to view New York stage productions on Sanabria's oversized screens, just as they'd filled nickelodeons to see one-reel films twenty years before. Singers, dancers, musicians, acrobats, comedians—all would appear onstage through the marvel of the new see-hear waves. But after making a deal to represent Sanabria and his invention, Morris discovered that most of the theater chains—Warners, Fox, the Shuberts—weren't interested in popularizing a potential competitor. Neither were radio broadcasters. Venture capitalists weren't willing to finance a Sanabria company unless Morris himself was willing to head it, which he wasn't. But he still thought television would be a great outlet for talent, so he set up a studio in the back of his offices and got scores of clients—George Jessel, Sophie Tucker, the ever-popular Borah Minnevitch—to do their routines before the scanning machine.

Late that summer, Morris hosted a luncheon at Camp Intermission for his onetime nemesis, E. F. Albee, who'd come up to Saranac Lake to view the almost-completed sanatorium Morris had maneuvered him into building in the woods outside town. Morris was spending much of his time in Saranac now. He'd just built a big new house overlooking Lake Colby, a three-story fieldstone and clapboard lodge designed by William Distin, the local architect whose firm had produced the great camps of Otto Kahn and Adolph Lewisohn and was working on one now for William Rockefeller. He and Emma—Mother Morris, as she'd come to be known—kept an open house for show people driving up to Canada and back, with Emma's sister Elizabeth (Aunt Ella) as the camp cook. Their guests ranged from Sophie Tucker to Rabbi Stephen Wise, the spellbinding Zionist leader from New York. They were also among the village's chief benefactors, starting a Rotary Club and a nursery school, directing carnivals and barn dances, arranging benefit shows with performers like Cantor and Jolson and Lauder. But the biggest project he'd undertaken in town was the sanatorium.

It had been nearly thirty years since the vaudeville wars had begun, and fortune had treated the two men very differently. Morris, who liked to think of show business as a mansion with many rooms, had opened every new door that technology made available. Albee had finally succeeded in bringing all of big-time vaudeville under his dominion when he merged his Keith-Albee circuit with the Orpheum circuit in 1927, only to lose it all a year later to a far more powerful combine dedicated to exploiting the new technologies he feared.

When Joe Kennedy won control of the new Keith-Albee-Orpheum chain and amalgamated it into his Film Booking Office to form Radio-

Keith-Orpheum, the motion picture arm of the giant Radio Corporation of America, vaudeville was so weak that people were saying the circuit would go into receivership in six months without a change in direction. Albee was just a pawn, his theater chain the prize Kennedy delivered to David Sarnoff, the grasping, hard-driving RCA executive who'd already created NBC to dominate broadcasting and now wanted RKO to guarantee a market for a movie theater sound process that RCA controlled. "Didn't you know, Ed?" Kennedy snapped to Albee not long after taking control. "You're washed up, you're through."

This pronouncement was reinforced by other developments. Albee had recently been maneuvered out of the National Vaudeville Association, the company union he'd started to break the White Rats; Eddie Cantor had been named president, and William Fox, the movie magnate, had taken over as president of its Benevolent Fund. Albee hadn't even been invited to the dedication of the NVA Sanatorium in September, a month away. So he came up to tour the place before it opened, and afterward he and the NVA's chief physician went to Camp Intermission for lunch. They had a pleasant meal. No mention was made of the past. Albee and his party drove off. But when his limousine reached the gate, Albee ordered it to a halt, clambered out, and walked the quarter-mile through the woods back to the house. With one foot on the doorstep, he held out his hand and said, "I'm sorry, Will. I played ball with the wrong crowd." And then he left.

The stock market crash that came in October, two months later, had little effect on show business. Most of the damage seemed to be confined to Wall Street speculators, a group there'd admittedly been no shortage of. Sound was still such a novelty that audiences continued to crowd into motion picture theaters. In 1930, as unemployment started to go up and wages to go down, radio's escapist entertainment became more and more popular with listeners. Advertisers saw its growing audience as a ready target for the goods they had to sell if they were to have any hope of staying in the black. With banks failing and stocks on the slide again after a brief winter rally, radio began to look Depression-proof—something-for-nothing entertainment, snatched from the ether.

After suffering a mild stroke that year, Morris turned the agency over to Abe Lastfogel and Bill Morris, Jr. Lastfogel stayed in Gotham; Bill Morris went out to the coast to take over the Los Angeles office. He and his wife, Jerry, a striking, vivacious brunette, set up housekeeping with two friends, a New York insurance broker named Albert Ruben and his wife, Ruth, in a rented East Hollywood mansion they dubbed the Villa Voncha—a rambling Spanish-style hacienda on a ridgetop overlooking the Los Angeles River and the rugged San Gabriel Mountains beyond. They lived grandly; Charlie Chaplin came to their parties. But as the Zeppo incident suggested, young Morris had showed less aptitude for agenting than some of his clients. Most of the actual work was done in New York by Lastfogel and his eager new assistant, Sammy Weisbord, a nineteen-year-old Brooklyn boy who went to work for him in 1931. Morris himself was able to relax by a birch-log fire in the great stone fireplace at Camp Intermission and listen to his performers— Amos 'n' Andy, Jack Benny, Eddie Cantor—on the radio.

But even in retirement, Morris did what he could to promote television as a stage attraction. Huge crowds came to watch his acts perform on Sanabria's giant screen at the Radio World's Fair in September 1931. The following month, he was approached by B. S. Moss, who owned a small theater circuit in New York and was looking for some special attractions to offset the weak pictures he was getting from Hollywood. Morris suggested television. He secured a two-week booking at Moss's Broadway Theatre, followed by another week at an independent theater in Baltimore, with Sanabria's television system featured on a stage bill that had Frances Arms, Lastfogel's wife, as the headliner. The lineup got good box office. But Sanabria's machinery was heavy and cumbersome, and after the last show in Baltimore, when it was being carted out of the theater and loaded onto a truck, the heaviest unit crashed partway through a trap door. One of the crew members would have been crushed if Frances hadn't pulled him away.

"Now have the Lauder Singing Pictures working alright, although it has taken some time," William Selig finally wrote to him that fall. Too much time. In the decade and a half since Selig had taken up the challenge, talkies had become ubiquitous, television had appeared on the horizon, and Harry Lauder's star had begun to fade. Audiences were flocking to gangster movies now, not to see some ancient Scottish minstrel stroll onstage in a tam-o'-shanter and kilt to tell tales about his "wee wifey." Radio and movies were knitting the country together in a way that traveling stage shows never could, changing entertainers from vagabonds to celebrities, transforming audiences from hicks to sophisticates. And as for Morris—well, he'd seen show business through the vaudeville wars; he'd broken through the four walls of the theater to beam his headliners into homes across the country. Now it was time for him to make his exit. It would be a show finish, as they said in vaude. But before he went, he had some unfinished business to take care of in the city.

AT FIRST, AS THEY WERE PLAYING PINOCHLE THAT NIGHT AT THE FRIARS, Walter Kelly thought Morris had dropped a card and was leaning forward in his chair to pick it up. Then Morris fell from his chair and toppled to the floor. They tried to revive him, then rushed to the phone. They called Flower Hospital on Fifth Avenue. They called the Hotel Piccadilly just down the street. By the time the hotel doctor arrived, Morris was dead.

Someone had to call his family. Bill Morris, Jr., was in Hollywood, but Emma and their daughter Ruth, who'd made a name for herself as a columnist for Variety's women's page, were at their apartment on West End Avenue at Eighty-third Street when the phone rang. They sped down Broadway to the Friars, but by the time they got there, it was too late to do anything but mourn his passing. At least he'd gone quickly.

Morris's fifty-year progression uptown, from the squalid, airless tenements of the Lower East Side to the grand apartment houses of the West End, matched that of show business itself, which had long since forsaken the carny hustle of Fourteenth Street for the bright lights and jazzy sophistication of the Great White Way. But his time had passed. Marcus Loew in 1927, Ed Albee and Abe Erlanger in 1930, Flo Ziegfeld in July, and now Will Morris—one by one, the men who'd defined showmanship since the turn of the century were exiting the scene. Joe White, the Silver-Voiced Tenor, sang two of Morris's favorite songs over the NBC networks as an aerial tribute, and show business was passed to a new generation.

2
────

THE PRINCE
AND THE PAUPER

Los Angeles/New York, 1932-1939

ABE LASTFOGEL HAD A SITUATION ON THE COAST.

The Hollywood motion picture studios, squeezed by the Depression on one hand and the high cost of switching to sound on the other, were trying to economize by slashing the price of talent. That meant cutting out the ten-percenter.

As far as the moguls were concerned, agents existed to make them spend too much. Any number of shady practices were employed to further this end, but one of the worst was the enticement to steal. It cost money to build a star, and to have one stolen away in the full flush of success was to be denied a proper return on your investment. A "gentlemen's agreement" against star-poaching already existed among the studio heads, but not all moguls were gentlemen. So in January 1932, the members of the Association of Motion Picture Producers—that is, the studios—had formalized their pledge not to raid one another's stables. Under their new agreement, no studio would approach anyone under contract to a competitor until thirty days before said contract was due to expire. If competing bids did come in when the contract was up, the original studio would have six months to match them.

"Fadeout for Agents," *Variety* announced in a banner headline later that month. What were they needed for, anyway? Without that extra 10 percent, studio executives pointed out, actors and writers could absorb a pay cut and not even feel it. So contracts were allowed to lapse, to be replaced with new deals in which the agent didn't figure. In a case the Morris Agency had brought against a screenwriter at Paramount, a Los Angeles court ruled that a client could repudiate his agency contract at will—precisely what the studios were urging all writers to do, and actors and directors as well. Jimmy Cagney had just done it to William Morris, and the agency was suing him, too.

Cagney had been discovered playing a supporting role with Joan Blondell in *Penny Arcade*, a short-lived Broadway play about a carny barker and a penny arcade owner's daughter. After signing with the Morris office, the two of them had headed for the coast in 1930 to star together in a movie version called *Sinner's Holiday*, which Warner Bros. shot in fifteen days flat. Then Cagney was cast as a mobster's sidekick in *Doorway to Hell*, the first of a string of gangster flicks Warners made under the aegis of its boy-wonder production chief, Darryl F. Zanuck. While it was being shot, Warners offered Cagney a seven-year contract guaranteeing him forty weeks of work a year at $400 a week. That was $100 less than he was getting under his short-term contract, but big money compared to what he'd been getting in Gotham. Hollywood looked like a mirage, about as real as the celluloid fantasies it spun out. He never thought it would last. But the Depression was on, and he signed.

Like most contract players, Cagney had no say over the pictures he was cast in and no standing to demand a raise should he suddenly click at the box office. The studio was free to drop him after any forty-week period if it wished. He was given several supporting roles, including one as the good guy in a buddy picture about a pair of Chicago street kids called *Beer and Blood*, with Joan Blondell and Jean Harlow. At the last minute, however, the director convinced Zanuck to recast Cagney as the tough, a thug who pushes his mother around, squashes a grapefruit in his wife's face, and ends up dead on his own doorstep. Retitled *The Public Enemy* to mollify the guardians of decency at the Hays Office (the Motion Picture Producers and Distributors of America, which the studio chiefs had created in the twenties to fight off censorship demands and labor union threats), the picture became a box-office smash when it was released in the spring of 1931. Suddenly, Cagney was a star.

Three months earlier, when Edward G. Robinson—who did not have a long-term contract—won stardom as the Al Capone figure in *Little Caesar*, he'd been able to get a two-year, six-picture deal paying $40,000 per picture. But Jack Warner refused to bargain with Cagney: "You got a contract," he said. "I expect you to honor it." So in September 1931, Cagney did what frustrated clients invariably do: He fired his agent, Murray Feil of the Morris office.

Warner could take the stance it did because the studios owned the store. The merger frenzy of the twenties had ended with five major companies—Fox, Paramount, Loew's/M-G-M, RKO, and Warner Bros.—which owned their own theater chains, and two minor ones, Universal and Columbia, which did not. (An eighth company, United Artists, functioned as a distribution outlet for independent filmmakers like Samuel Goldwyn.) Each of the majors was headquartered on Times Square or in the vicinity, amid blazing electric lights and crowds of theatergoers, and each maintained in Hollywood or nearby a stable of actors, writers, directors, producers, and technicians whose job was to keep the marquees lit and the seats filled. The optical illusion of moving pictures had become the basis for a nationwide real-estate empire—vast theater circuits that were directed from New York and that the Hollywood movie colony labored to support.

Because among them they owned the studios, the distribution channels, and most of the important theaters, the five major studios and the three smaller ones enjoyed absolute control. But merely creating a monopoly wasn't enough to guarantee a profit, especially in the face of the Depression. The novelty of sound kept audiences coming in for a while, but ticket sales had started dropping precipitously when the economy began to falter in 1930, and costs were up. Talkies were more than twice as expensive to make as silent films, and they required an enormous capital investment in studio and theater equipment from companies that had piled themselves with debt to finance the merger frenzy. In 1931, Fox had lost $3 million, RKO $5.6 million, Warner Bros. $8 million; Paramount's profits dropped from $18 million to $6 million. In February 1932, with its Publix theater chain now contracted to buy stage shows from the rival Fanchon & Marco Agency, the stock swap between Paramount and the Morris office was reversed and the agency became independent again. With theaters the studios had borrowed money to acquire going dark for lack of audiences, this was no time for a studio and a talent agency to be married.

The studios' situation seemed desperate, the solution obvious: Cut the cost of talent. "Actors are like children," declared Irving Thalberg, M-G-M's strong-willed young production chief. "No matter how many gifts are under the Christmas tree, they always want the ornament on . top." The agent's job was to get it for them. It was all a function of the star system, which the studios themselves had developed as a marketing strategy to sell their pictures.

The star system wasn't the first scheme moviemakers had thought up, but it was the only one that worked. Early studios like Vitagraph and Biograph had relied on their own trademarks to market their films; the public yawned. Next they tried stories. But in 1911, when *Motion Picture Story* magazine asked readers to pick their favorite stories, it was inundated with questions about actors instead. The conclusion was inescapable: Stars sell pictures. Every star had some unique drawing power, and the more effectively a star was promoted, the more money he or she could generate at the box office. And so the star was born.

Stars had existed in other fields for centuries, of course; but movie stars were different from opera stars or vaudeville stars. Acting was still a vagabond calling when pictures began. Apartment buildings bore signs that read "No Dogs or Actors Allowed." But as the fantasy appeal of celluloid began to take hold, screen actors began to exert a fantastic pull, drawing people not just into theaters but to Hollywood itself. To sense stardom's magnetic power, you had only to drive out to Culver City, a drab and dusty burg on the western fringe of Los Angeles, to the intersection where M-G-M was headquartered in a shabby colonial-style building across from three gasoline stations and a drugstore. There on any given afternoon, you'd find mothers holding their children aloft in their arms in hopes that some studio exec would spot them from his car before turning into the lot.

It wasn't just stage mothers on Washington Boulevard; everywhere you turned there were starstruck hopefuls. Thousands of them came to Hollywood each year—teenage beauty-contest winners, best-looking and best-dressed boys and girls fresh from high schools in the Midwest, hurling themselves into a Klondike of celebrity. Their chances of getting even occasional work were no better than ten to one, so after throwing away their savings on fly-by-night acting schools, most of them ended up as extras, where their chances were even slimmer. By the early thirties, the colony's four hundred or so regularly employed players were overshadowed by some ten thousand would-be actors and seventeen thousand extras—an army of aspirants waiting to be discovered. They fit right in with everything else about Los Angeles, a rootless boomtown with no industry save the dream factories but plenty of marginal characters on the make—canary farmers, pet morticians, avocado peddlers, psychics, swindlers, boosters, bookies, addicts, polygamists, racketeers, con men, storefront evangelists, incipient suicides. The only thing unusual about these folks was their numbers.

The desperation they brought to Hollywood was fed by the almost unimaginable luxury that existed a couple of miles away in Beverly Hills, which the silent-era stars had discovered as an alternative to the scandalous pleasures of Hollywood and the censorious reserve of Hancock Park, home of the downtown Protestant elite. Douglas Fairbanks and Mary Pickford settled there first, in a manor house above Benedict Canyon that was legendary for its waterways and bridle paths, its rolling lawns and vast swimming pool, its fabulous parties studded with genuine European royalty. Gloria Swanson bought a twenty-two-room mansion on Crescent Drive, which she fixed up with a black marble bathroom and a solid gold tub. Will Rogers followed, and Charlie Chaplin, and John Barrymore, and Buster Keaton, and Rudolph Valentino. There was a brief scare in 1923 when a subsidiary of the Rodeo Land and Water Company, which had developed the town out of the old Rancho Rodeo de las Aguas in the early 1900s, announced that it was running out of water and pushed for annexation by the city of Los Angeles; but the stars banded together and fought off the threat. So while Hollywood and most of the other towns were taken into the water-bearing arms of Los Angeles, Beverly Hills remained a private Shangri-la, a refuge from the leapfrogging hydropolis.

As the contrast between Hollywood's hopefuls and the instant gentry of Beverly Hills suggested, the studios had created a monster. But the moguls cared as much about extras as the Southland's landowners cared about the migrant farmworkers who labored in the vast orange groves that surrounded the city. What concerned the moguls was the handful of stars who powered the system. How could the studios tap the bonanza the stars generated without cutting them in on too big a share? Because it didn't take much imagination to realize that if the stars used their leverage effectively, the studios could be held for ransom.

By 1932, it took no imagination at all, because Myron Selznick had just proved it. Selznick was Hollywood's enfant terrible, a wiry-haired, solidly built young man who drank too much, liked using his fists, and didn't mind carrying a grudge. His father, Lewis J. Selznick, had once owned a powerful film distribution company in New York, but he'd feuded bitterly with some of the top men in the business—Zukor, Mayer, Fox—and in 1923, not entirely by coincidence, his firm had suddenly and dramatically collapsed. Hounded by creditors and attorneys, he'd had to dismiss the Japanese butler, give up the seventeen rooms on Park Avenue, hock the rugs and furniture, and move into a cramped little apartment. Myron's younger brother, David O., had learned to make peace with his father's enemies, as his production job at Paramount and his marriage to Louis Mayer's daughter attested. Myron had not.

Most of the Hollywood boys were chiselers, sharpies, two-bit players who promised but didn't deliver. Selznick was different. He'd gotten into agenting more or less by accident, because his roommate, Lewis Milestone, was having problems with Jack Warner, who had him under contract as a writer-director for $400 a week. In 1927, when Howard Hughes, then a fledgling producer, approached Milestone to direct a comedy called *Two Arabian Nights*, Selznick did the talking. Milestone was hoping for at least $750 a week; Selznick asked for $2,000. The Hughes representative protested vehemently and threatened to end the discussion, but as Milestone looked numbly on, Selznick negotiated a salary of $1,500. "It isn't enough," Selznick said as they closed the deal. That phrase became his trademark, a cry that was likened to the call of a bird.

When he learned that three of Paramount's biggest stars were unhappy with their salaries and that their contracts were about to expire, Selznick sold them to Warner Bros., which had no stars to fill its new theater chain. The Warner deal, which put William Powell and Ruth Chatterton on the payroll at $6,000 each and Kay Francis at $4,000, earned them the enmity of Zukor, Mayer, and the rest, but it wasn't enough to assuage Selznick's anger. At night, when he was drunk and there weren't any moguls around, he was liable to take a swing at anyone—John Barrymore, the black sheep of the acting family, who said something that set him off at the Ambassador Hotel one Saturday night in 1928. Or Erich von Stroheim, who traded blows with him at the door to the Mayfair Club on New Year's Eve 1931. Or a fellow reveler at three that same morning at the Cocoanut Grove (somewhat embarrassing to Selznick, since he was sent sprawling across the dance floor while David, David's wife Irene, Jean Harlow, and Myron's own wife all looked on). David might be content to play the game, but Myron wasn't, and he wasn't going to be intimidated. These were guys he played poker with. One way or another, he was going to make them pay.

Socially, of course, he was courting oblivion merely by becoming an agent. Agents were despised within the movie colony. People called them flesh-peddlers, parasites, bloodsuckers, leeches, and worse. It was said that they never drank tomato juice in public because they were sick of hearing people say, "I see you're drinking your client's blood." When visiting the studios, they went in through the back gate if they were let in at all. Some studios barred them from their clients' dressing rooms and assigned guards to shadow them when they were on the lot. Not that they were hard to spot in any case: They were the ones in the aurora borealis suits, the dragon's blood shirts, the flags-of-all-nations ties.

But the colony's distrust of agents ran deeper than that. It was one thing to be rapacious in selling a product, even a product as insubstantial as shadows flickering in a darkened hall; but there was something unseemly about selling another person's talents. It besmirched the purity of the creative process. As one screenwriter candidly explained to the *Saturday Evening Post*, "I'm worth about one-third what I get. I'm honest, and if I talked for myself, I'd admit that I'm two hundred per cent overpaid, and my salary would be cut to pieces. So I get a dishonest fellow to represent me. He has no scruples about claiming that I am worth three times as much as I am, and he gets it for me. An agent is an unprincipled fellow who prevents an honest man from suffering because of his honesty."

Attitudes like that, plus the red ink of the Depression, made it easy for the studio brass to argue that the ten-percenters were destroying the business. But it was no accident that Warner Bros. and Jimmy Cagney were in the midst of the fray. Warner Bros. movies were known for their tough-guy stance, their gritty social realism, their hard-bitten, cynical edge—and for young, unproven actors like Jimmy Cagney and Edward G. Robinson, novices who could be expected to work long hours for low pay and not give a lot of guff. The house style was partly dictated by financial reality: The drive to acquire theaters and pioneer sound had put the studio more than $100 million in debt, and a stockholder revolt in 1930 had nearly cost the brothers control of the company. But it was also a projection of the Warners themselves. Harry Warner fancied himself the Henry Ford of the movie business, so much so that production at Warner Bros. was on an assembly-line basis. Directors worked on four or five pictures a year, shooting one and then another and then another, with no say in story development or editing or any of the other niceties. Actors were driven relentlessly, often from nine in the morning until two or three the next morning. As for Jack Warner, he saw himself as a survivor, scrappy, cynical, and rebellious, a man without pretense or illusion. The actors he employed were his alter egos. Conflict was inevitable.

Especially with Cagney, who was as explosive as the characters he played. The success of his next films—*Smart Money*, a gambling drama in which he was teamed with Robinson, and *Blonde Crazy*, in which he and Joan Blondell costarred as con artists—convinced Warner to throw him a bonus of $1,000 a week. But that was it; Cagney was still making less than half what Robinson was pulling in, and he wasn't happy. In April 1932, on the day he was supposed to start shooting *Blessed Event*, he took the train to New York instead. He was "through with pictures," he announced, and would study medicine at Columbia University.

Warners retaliated by putting him on suspension, a limbo status that cut off his salary and kept him from getting work at any other studio, and by banning his new agents, Frank & Dunlap, from its lots—the old one in Hollywood and the big one it had just acquired over the hills in Burbank. Myron Selznick and his partner, Frank Joyce, were banned as well, along with all the other agents who'd incurred Jack Warner's wrath. Clients of the banned agencies were told to deal directly with the studio casting director. At the same time, company execs approached William Powell, Ruth Chatterton, and Kay Francis about cutting the salaries that Selznick had negotiated for them the year before.

Selznick and Joyce tried to negotiate a truce. They met with a producers' committee headed by M-G-M production chief Irving Thalberg and his newly appointed counterpart at RKO, David Selznick. They even offered to help the studios cut salaries if the studios would admit agents to casting meetings and guarantee they'd be paid their commissions. (Warner Bros. and Paramount had a blanket rule barring agents from casting discussions.) The producers made noises about accepting agents as legitimate members of the community. Then the agents made the mistake of asking for membership in the Academy of Motion Picture Arts and Sciences, the association of actors, directors, writers, cameramen, and musicians that was the closest thing the Hollywood professionals had to a union. Suddenly, the talks came to a halt.

But the face-off between Cagney and Warner Bros. was resolved in September, when a mediator from the academy negotiated a new salary of $3,000 a week, plus (if gossip columnist Louella Parsons was to be believed) a handsome bonus at the end of the year that Cagney would forfeit if he caused any more trouble. On the same day, a superior court judge ruled in Cagney's favor in the suit William Morris had brought against him. The judge rejected the agency's claim that it was entitled to 10 percent of the actor's earnings from the work it had gotten him. Instead, he ruled that in writing his letter of discharge a year earlier, Cagney had canceled his agency contract and ended his liability. Instead of the $4,013 the agency wanted, he only owed $110.

CAGNEY WAS ALMOST THE LEAST OF IT. THE MORRIS OFFICE FACED A LOT of situations as 1933 began. They'd regained their independence from Paramount, but after turning a $53,000 profit in 1930, they'd lost $18,000 in 1931 and $27,000 in 1932. Harry Lauder had just limped back to Scotland after a fourteen-week American tour without bothering to play his planned weeklong finale on Broadway. The Los Angeles office had moved into swanky quarters in the Taft Building at Hollywood and Vine (across the street from Selznick & Joyce and half a block away from the Brown Derby, where everybody in the industry came for lunch), but the studios were putting on the squeeze, and vaudeville commissions on the coast were barely enough to cover the light bills, let alone the rent. There was even trouble in radio, where executives were grousing that the networks, like the studios, could do fine without agents. And the Boss had just dropped dead at the Friars.

As expected, Bill Morris, Jr., was named president of the firm that March. But when it came to hustle, Bill was not his father's son. The incident at Paramount, where he sat mute while Zeppo Marx sold Adolph Zukor on *The Cocoanuts*, was hardly out of character. Morris hated agenting. He was shy. He was lousy at making chitchat. Nothing about him suggested a showman. His sandy hair and fair complexion and courtly manner gave him a patrician look, as if he'd grown up on an English estate. And his love of the high life was coupled with a starry-eyed idealism that found expression in his internationalist worldview and his support for liberal causes. Commerce seemed somehow tawdry to him. He was a dreamer, not a salesman.

His father had been both, which was why actors loved him so. But sentiments his father might have expressed came out sounding callow or forced when Bill gave them voice. "You are sprinkled with stardust!" he cried on venturing into a Brooklyn vaudeville house and discovering a blackface performer named Bob Burns, whom the Gotham office was now building into a radio star. Abe Lastfogel was serious and subdued, but he was also a born agent—like the Boss, a superb judge of talent, and like the Boss, never at a loss for words. At thirty-four, he was as down-to-earth as Bill Morris, Jr., was ethereal. It was as if Will Morris had two sons, each of whom had inherited different sides of his personality—one of them his flair for salesmanship, the other his idealism. So Lastfogel stayed in New York as general manager, a job that seemed to carry with it most of the responsibility for running the agency, while Bill Morris returned to the coast.

He was operating in a different world from the one he and Abe had grown up in in New York. Agenting in vaudeville meant honing acts and booking them into theaters around the country, week after week, year after year. In Hollywood, it was more like an employment service for a factory system. Hollywood agents brought talent to the studios, negotiated the standard seven-year contract, and represented their clients' interests on the lot. If a client became popular with moviegoers, the agent could ask for more money or even shop him to another studio the way Selznick had done, but if he crossed an invisible line with a studio chief, he could find himself instantly banned. That would be catastrophic, since it kept him from standing up for his clients in meetings and often ended in his clients defecting to some other agency. But banning was drastic; more common, especially for smaller agents, was the brush-off—nothing official, just calls not returned, requests for meetings ignored.

Despite its early involvement in talkies, the operation Bill Morris headed in Hollywood wasn't nearly as well established as Selznick & Joyce. It had lost Jimmy Cagney. Al Jolson was already a has-been. But it did have Johnny Weissmuller, the twenty-eight-year-old Olympic swimming champion M-G-M had cast in *Tarzan the Ape Man*, based on the Edgar Rice Burroughs jungle novel. And it had a budding box-office sensation in Mae West.

La West had been a little-known vaudevillian until 1927, when she starred in *Sex*, a torrid stage show that couldn't be advertised in the newspapers because of its title but ran for 375 performances all the same—until Mayor Jimmy Walker, under pressure from the Society for the Suppression of Vice, had it raided and the theater padlocked. She'd made her film debut in 1932, after a Morris agent learned that Paramount was looking for "a Mae West type" for a small part in *Night After Night*, a George Raft picture about a former prizefighter who buys a nightclub. Bill Morris had come to her with an exceptionally good offer—$5,000 a week for ten weeks—and within days, she was on a train for the coast.

Mae West might have been rotund and fortyish, but with her come-hither walk and her knowing smirk, she had no trouble stealing the film. "Goodness, what lovely diamonds!" the hatcheck girl cries, to which she retorts, "Goodness had nothing to do with it, honey." An avalanche of fan mail convinced the studio to give her a second picture, starring as a Gay Nineties saloonkeeper in a screen version of her Broadway hit *Diamond Lil*. Retitled *She Done Him Wrong*, the film drew packed houses for its February 1933 premiere, and when La West appeared in person at the Paramount on Times Square, there were crowds in the streets.

Bill Morris didn't have to handle Hollywood on his own, of course. There was Bill Perlberg, who'd been at the original West Coast office in the State Theatre Building downtown, and Murray Feil, a vaudeville agent newly arrived from New York who represented Mae West. Perlberg was the strong-arm type, muscular and tough, a natty dresser with a mobster's flair. Feil was milder, quieter, a private man who seemed to enjoy being alone. He'd joined the Morris office in 1930, after dissolving the agency he'd formed with Will Morris's younger brother Hugo years earlier, when the Morris vaudeville circuit failed and Hugo threw his lot in with Keith. Feil had clout, as anyone would who handled a star like Miss West. But he didn't have the kind of clout that came from being dealt in on the moguls' poker games. That was what Bill Morris was there to provide.

But the job facing Morris wasn't just to establish the Morris office in Hollywood. The whole idea of agents was on trial now. If the studio chiefs had their way, they'd be cut out entirely.

Early in 1933, it became clear why Selznick's attempt to bring agents into the academy had backfired. The academy—which Louis Mayer had set up six years earlier to stave off organizing efforts by Actors Equity, the Broadway actors' league—was now being used as a mechanism to further the studios' cost-cutting efforts. It set up committees to deal with cost issues, including one to investigate agency practices and come up with an agency code of ethics. To admit agents on an equal basis with the other five branches would be like admitting the wolf to the barnyard. But the academy's committees had barely started their work when the movie industry was overcome by financial disaster.

Box-office receipts were already down to $3 million a day, from a 1929 high of $5.5 million. In March, as banks closed their doors and Franklin Roosevelt declared a nationwide "bank holiday" on being inaugurated as president, they suddenly dropped by a third. RKO had already tumbled into receivership in January, and Paramount and Fox were on the brink; Warner Bros. was barely hanging on. As they struggled to meet their payrolls and fight off their bankers, the industry's corporate chieftains in New York unilaterally decreed a 50 percent pay cut, effective for the next eight weeks, for all salaried employees earning more than $25 a week. The alternative, they declared, was to shut down the business entirely.

Meanwhile, Metro issued an edict barring all agents from the lot unless sent for, along with salesmen, peddlers, and bootleggers.

The movie colony erupted. For four days, Hollywood was rife with meetings—producers' meetings, actors' meetings, writers' meetings, union meetings, meetings of various boards and committees of the academy. "Squawks Galore," *Variety* reported. All production ceased. On March 10, a massive earthquake struck in Long Beach, collapsing schools and bridges and storefronts across the region in a heap, forcing one meeting to abandon the Roosevelt Hotel for a parking lot on Hollywood Boulevard, next to Sid Grauman's Chinese Theatre. So great was the uproar that when Mae West came back to Hollywood in April to start work on *I'm No Angel,* the L.A. dailies didn't even turn out for her arrival—though the box office for *She Done Him Wrong* was continuing to build.

The agents set up a committee with Frank Joyce as its chairman and Myron Selznick and Bill Morris, Jr., among its members. But the studio heads refused to see them, and the academy's emergency committee ignored their suggestions. With the academy fast losing credibility as a talent union, some agents took on the role of labor organizers, trying to line up stars for a guild that would be recognized by the American Federation of Labor. The screenwriters, the most militant of the talent groups, did form a guild in April, but the actors rebuffed the idea. Meanwhile, the New York industry bosses—Harry Warner of Warner Bros., Nick Schenck of Loew's/M-G-M, and the others—descended on Hollywood for a weeklong series of meetings with their studio chiefs to set things straight. Tension was so high that Louis Mayer fainted from exhaustion after playing eighteen holes of golf with Schenck at Hillcrest.

The bosses saw the financial crisis as a way to eliminate the agency threat for all time. They proposed a nonprofit Central Artists Bureau that would negotiate talent contracts without the rigors of competitive bidding—a revival, it was quickly noted, of B. F. Keith's old United Booking Office from vaudeville days. But memories of the Keith-Albee trust were too fresh and too raw for anything like a Central Artists Bureau to fly. The bosses were looking for another answer when President Roosevelt handed it to them in his National Industrial Recovery Act of 1933.

The idea behind this engine of the New Deal was to revive industry by allowing monopolies, while protecting workers by sanctioning collective bargaining and free organization of labor. Business and labor would both get their way, and the whole country would benefit. The act called for fair practice codes to be created for every industry—standards that would be drawn up and administered by a National Recovery Administration in Washington. Since Washington couldn't be expected to know much about the movie industry, the producers volunteered to help out.

The code proposed by the academy and the Hays Office, which functioned as a central liaison for the picture corporations, enshrined every monopolistic procedure the studios had put into practice since they were formed in the twenties, as well as several they'd tried to achieve but hadn't. The academy's agency practices committee contributed some reasonable recommendations, including a maximum agency commission of 10 percent (one silent star had been paying his agent $2,500 of his $4,000-a-week salary), a provision allowing clients to free themselves of agents who didn't get them work, and another to keep studios from barring agents from the lot. But other provisions in the code were designed to defuse the star system by eliminating the temptation to steal. If the studios couldn't restrain their own appetites, maybe they could get the government to do it for them.

Under these rules, agents would be forbidden to "foment dissension, discord or strife" or in any way advise a client to violate his contract. As with the "gentlemen's agreement" the producers had already approved in 1932, agents were barred from shopping a client to another studio until thirty days before the client's contract expired. Any studio that made a competing offer would have to register it with the authorities and send a copy to its rival, which would have months to decide whether to match it. And the punishment for offenders was draconian: Producers could have their pictures banned from the theaters, talent could be barred from the industry, agencies could be declared off-limits to everyone.

When a preliminary draft of the proposed code was released in late August, the movie colony came apart at the seams. Actors and agents were furious over the academy's involvement and livid over a last-minute provision in the agency section that allowed studio execs to bar agents from client meetings involving anything other than money. A group of agents, reportedly headed by Selznick & Joyce, circulated petitions calling for an independent committee to represent actors when the NRA held public hearings the next month in Washington. Eddie Cantor was on the list of committee members, along with Clark Gable, Groucho Marx, and George Raft.

When the NRA hearings were held in September, a quarter-century of Hollywood rancor was laid bare. B. B. Kahane, president of the bankrupt RKO, blamed most of the business's woes on disreputable agents—troublemakers bent on sowing dissatisfaction. The president of the new Screen Writers Guild demanded that the agency control and antiraiding sections of the code be thrown out. Then, after the hearings, the studio bosses threw a new clause into the code creating a salary-fixing board—a government agency with the power to fine any producer who tried to pay too much for talent. That did it.

Two months earlier, eighteen dissident actors—none of them major stars—had announced the formation of a guild. Now others were ready to join. In early October, Groucho Marx and Charles Butterworth arranged a meeting at which twenty-one stars—including Jimmy Cagney, Gary Cooper, Fredric March, and Adolphe Menjou—agreed to resign from the academy and join the new Screen Actors Guild. Four days later, in a Sunday night meeting at the lavishly appointed El Capitan Theatre on Hollywood Boulevard, more than eight hundred actors cheered wildly when Eddie Cantor, the guild's new president, called for an organization "of, by, and for actors alone."

Cantor was a good leader for the guild—a major picture star ever since the 1930 hit *Whoopee!*, a Florenz Ziegfeld musical that was already a smash for him on Broadway when Sam Goldwyn bought it for the movies. He was making his own movie deals (the Morris office handled his radio and stage performances only), but at his suggestion, Goldwyn had hired another Morris client, a young Broadway choreographer who called himself Busby Berkeley, as dance director. Goldwyn had followed *Whoopee!* with two more Eddie Cantor–Busby Berkeley extravaganzas, *Palmy Days* and *The Kid from Spain*, and now Cantor was one of the top money-earners in Hollywood.

A week after the first mass meeting, twelve hundred people showed up at the El Capitan for a joint meeting with the Writers Guild. Amid the tumult, they managed to draft a telegram to President Roosevelt, who had yet to sign the code. The telegram blamed management for the industry's woes, charging "that the motion picture companies have not been bankrupted by salaries to talent, but by the purchase and leasing of theaters at exorbitant prices, caused by the race for power of a few individuals desiring to get a strangle hold on . . . the box office." But though half the actors in Hollywood earned less than $2,000 a year before taxes and expenses (according to a subsequent NRA study), the new guild still had to explain why a handful of actors were entitled to $5,000 a week when twelve million people were out of work.

Eddie Cantor went to New York and held a press luncheon at Sardi's on November 13. He explained that studios could make pictures with any actor they wanted, but they wanted the actors with the biggest drawing power—Mae West, for instance. By September, Paramount had grossed $3 million on *She Done Him Wrong*, letters were pouring in at the staggering rate of fifteen hundred a week, twelve hundred newspapers had signed up for a "life story" series penned by the Paramount publicity department, and every magazine in the country, from *Vanity Fair* to *Cosmopolitan* to *True Confessions*, was scrambling to do a profile. As Cantor pointed out, if La West—a new convert to the Guild—was going to bring the studio $2.5 million as a lion tamer in *I'm No Angel*, her new picture, then she was certainly worth $5,000 a week—or any amount she asked for.

Strike talk mounted as the deadline for signing approached. Roosevelt invited Cantor to his retreat in Warm Springs, Georgia, along with Joe Schenck, the older brother of Loew's chief Nick Schenck and one of the handful of producers who supported the actors. The Monday after Thanksgiving, when Roosevelt signed the code, it contained most of the producers' demands—blind bidding, for example, which forced independent theater owners to rent a studio's output without knowing what it would be, and block booking, which forced them to take a studio's B-pictures if they wanted its A-pictures. But the sections dealing with talent raiding, agency conduct, and star salaries were suspended by executive order. The talent won out.

EDDIE CANTOR AND MAE WEST MAY HAVE STOOD AT THE FOREFRONT OF the Hollywood labor strife, but the Morris office took a backseat to Myron Selznick. Bill Morris, Jr., was temperamentally predisposed to union causes, but he was not the most vociferous of champions. Lastfogel thought actors should get whatever the market would bear, but he was an outsider in the picture business. And in any battle between the moguls and the stars, the agent, being a middleman, was going to get caught in the middle. Which is what happened with Joan Blondell, who announced she was terminating her agency contract that fall. When the Morris office refused to let her go, she sued, claiming her agent had told her the way to get a raise was to threaten to walk out just before shooting began—the tactic Cagney had used. She declared it was against her principles.

By the end of 1933, it was obvious that as soon as the ten-percenters fought off the studios, they'd have to deal with the talent guilds. Either way, somebody was going to try to regulate them, and most agents weren't much happier at having their clients do it than at having the studios perform the task. A year and a half later, in May 1935, the Supreme Court declared Roosevelt's National Recovery Administration unconstitutional and the idea of an industrywide code of conduct went out the window. With the government out of the picture, the struggle was between the studios and the talent guilds. That's when Abe Lastfogel decided he'd better come out to the coast and take matters in hand.

Lastfogel's usual method of dealing with a tough situation was to figure out what the Boss would have done and then do it. But this time, he could see that following the Boss's example wasn't going to be enough. It was fine to be able to spot talent, but to sell talent to the studio chiefs, he realized, he'd have to know their jobs as well as they did. After twenty-three years in the business, he was suddenly going to have to start over.

He decided to bring Johnny Hyde out as well. Hyde, the onetime child acrobat who'd gotten his start in the Loew's vaudeville circuit, had early on caught the eye of Joe Schenck, then Loew's general manager, who was nineteen years older but had likewise come over from Russia. It was Joe Schenck who'd run the joint Marcus Loew–William Morris Booking Office when Morris sold out after the failure of his vaudeville circuit. When Hyde left Loew's for the Morris Agency in 1926, Marcus Loew had already patched together Metro-Goldwyn-Mayer to provide his theaters with a steady supply of pictures, and Joe's younger brother Nick had taken over as manager of the parent company in New York. Joe had come to Hollywood, where his good friend Louis Mayer ran M-G-M, and Joe himself was now chairman of Twentieth Century–Fox, formed in the just-completed merger of his Twentieth Century Pictures with the old Fox Film Corporation.

Connections like these brought Hyde and Lastfogel into the tight little circle of filmmakers Myron Selznick had entered at birth. That gave them a chance to establish trust—to demonstrate that they were guys who, when they came to your door with some actor they claimed was hot, could be counted on not to be throwing paper at you. They still didn't have the stars Myron Selznick could claim, but they did have Mae West, whose enormous drawing power conferred immense prestige, and they were rich in featured players and promising hopefuls. And their strength in New York fed their success in Hollywood: When Paramount was making *The Big Broadcast of 1936*, the second in its series of all-star radio movies, Morris provided half the acts, from Amos 'n' Andy to Burns and Allen to the Vienna Boys Choir.

As this list suggested, Morris was still a vaudeville office in spirit. Vaudeville had too much heart for the silver screen, but it was just right for radio, and radio was just right for the Depression. Now that primitive crystal sets had been replaced by ornately carved cabinets that the family could gather around in the parlor, singers and comedians who'd once trod the boards were welcomed into the home like old friends. But unlike vaudeville, radio was for headliners only. About five hundred acts were broadcast regulars in the mid-thirties, compared to the thousands of performers who'd once worked the vaudeville circuits.

Sometimes the ether didn't even work for stars. Sophie Tucker, "the Last of the Red-Hot Mamas," was too ribald for the airwaves—but then, she was too racy for vaudeville as well; from 1916 on she'd mainly worked nightclubs. Al Jolson, in his 1932 debut "Presenting Al Jolson," turned out to be as corny on radio as he was on film. "Some of the gags he poured into the mike crumbled from old age . . . long before they got to the loudspeaker," *Variety* observed. His follow-up efforts, a pair of variety shows called "The Kraft Music Hall" and "Shell Chateau" (for Shell Oil), were almost as bad. But Jolson drew listeners all the same, and other Morris performers who'd gotten their start in vaudeville— Fanny Brice, Martha Raye, Burns and Allen, Amos 'n' Andy—were among radio's biggest stars. By the 1937–1938 season, the agency had a hand in nine of the twelve top-rated evening shows.

The remarkable thing about radio was its ability to reach into the national consciousness. After Fanny Brice brought her "Baby Snooks" character—a seven-year-old child who was nobody's fool—to the "Ziegfeld Follies Show of the Air" in 1936, her lisping voice and mischievous "Why, Daddy?" became a chorus that could be heard across the land. "Amos 'n' Andy"—the Chicago comedy show about a pair of hopelessly unsophisticated darkies who'd come from down South to start their "Fresh Air Taxicab Company, Incorpulated"—had slipped considerably since 1929, when NBC put it on the air and sales of radio receivers soared. Even so, an estimated 3.2 million sets were tuned in to each broadcast in 1937, and stock phrases like "Holy mackerel!" and "I'se regusted" were part of the national vocabulary. Louisiana Senator Huey Long had even taken one character's nickname—"the Kingfish"—as his own.

This ability to shape people's thinking propelled the nation's big new food and soap corporations and their Madison Avenue ad agencies willy-nilly into showbiz. Times Square was not an area where "radio's effete east side ether merchandisers," as *Variety* dubbed them, felt comfortable, but they had no choice. So far, radio had succeeded in generating only one star in its own right—Rudy Vallee, a Yale lad who'd gotten his start with a group called the Connecticut Yankees in New York's Heigh-Ho Club. This was not a good enough track record to justify disdain for anything that smacked of Broadway. "The commercial sponsor, adrift in the unfamiliar world of show business, demands concrete results," *Fortune* reported in 1938. "Rather than gamble on new ideas and new talent, he usually prefers to pay big money for established stars. The resultant competition for names has sent prices skyrocketing, and the talent agent with a stable of 'name' entertainers has been placed in a very powerful bargaining position."

For singers and comedians, that agent was Bill Murray, head of William Morris's radio department. Murray, who'd joined the office in 1932, sold shows that starred the agency's big-name vaudeville performers—Fanny Brice, Burns and Allen, Eddie Cantor. Just as it had provided theaters with traveling vaudeville units in the teens and twenties, the agency now came to radio sponsors with complete packages—everything from writers to stars, wrapped up and ready to go. Many of the ideas came from George Gruskin, the agency's West Coast radio chief, who'd joined the office in 1935 after getting his start with Ulysses Sanabria, the inventor whose primitive television system Will Morris had briefly employed as a vaudeville act. He was known as a brilliant programmer, a guy who could generate hit shows off the top of his head.

Gruskin could afford to be Jewish in the Protestant world of television because he was a creative type, not a salesman. Bill Murray cut an altogether different picture. It was no accident that a mostly Jewish agency handling mostly Jewish performers in a business that smacked of the underworld should employ a lifelong Episcopalian—a parishioner at Trinity Church, where Alexander Hamilton had been laid to rest after his duel with Aaron Burr—to sell its acts to Madison Avenue. Nor was it coincidental that Wallace Jordan, Murray's Chicago department head, was equally Protestant. The big advertising agencies and their corporate clients were quite choosy about the people they'd do business with. Murray and Jordan were there to reassure them.

Morris's long history and solid, businesslike demeanor were reassuring as well. The agency's headquarters—which since June 1936 had occupied half the twenty-eighth floor of the RKO Building in Radio City, high above Radio City Music Hall on the Sixth Avenue end of Rockefeller Center—was as stylized and modernistic as any Hollywood set. But a portrait of the founder hung in every office, and the legend above the plate-glass door—"EST. 1898"—made the point that Morris had been around as long as most of the companies that came to it for shows.

Lastfogel and Hyde set out to deliver the same kind of reassurance in Hollywood. Like many successful agencies, the Morris office had joined the exodus from Hollywood and Vine to the county strip on Sunset Boulevard—a mile and a half of unincorporated territory running from the Chateau Marmont, its pseudo-Norman tower standing incongruously against the Hollywood Hills, to the green hush of the Beverly Hills city limits. Exempt from Los Angeles city regulations (including a $100 licensing fee for agents) and conveniently located along the main road from Hollywood to Beverly Hills, the Sunset Strip had become a magnet for nightclubs, talent agencies, and stylish boutiques. But in place of the Anglo-Saxon Protestants it had in Radio City, the Morris office on the Strip was fronted by a pair of Russian Jews.

Yet there was a yawning gulf between the glitter of the movie colony and the brassy show world of Broadway, where they'd started. Hollywood was where song-and-dance artists came to reinvent themselves as screen idols, where junk dealers and fur traders took up golf and polo in their drive to become moguls. Hyde, who'd traded an apartment at the Century on Central Park West for a mansion in Bel Air, had the kind of class it took to fit in with the Hollywood crowd. Lastfogel, who lived in hotels and never gave parties and was married to a big-time vaudevillian who was liable to shout "How the fuck are ya?" when she spied a friend, had more of a problem. Socially, he and Frances reminded a lot of people of something they were trying to forget. So while Hyde romanced the picture colony, Lastfogel shuttled back and forth between Gotham and the coast, handling talent in every area of the business.

It was Lastfogel's idea to send Nat Lefkowitz, a young accountant who'd joined the company in 1927, to study law at Brooklyn College night school so he could learn contracts. No longer would the Morris office rely on a handshake, leaving clients and theater managers free to take their business elsewhere. Meanwhile, Lastfogel and Hyde functioned as nursemaid, talent scout, salesman, advocate, adviser, and sometimes personal servant all in one. Their lives were an endless series of situations, predictable only in their unpredictability.

They'd think nothing of patching together a three-way telephone hookup connecting Hollywood, London, and New York to find the proper diet for Mae West's pet chimp. In a single day, Hyde might persuade an outraged actor to go ahead and take costume tests for his next picture instead of leaving on vacation as planned; drive to another studio to talk execs into sweetening a long-term contract on an actor who was hot; have lunch at the Brown Derby on Vine with a young client just out from New York; have a long cup of coffee with a studio exec and sell him a new singer they were bringing out; drop by the office at Sunset and La Cienega to check in with Lastfogel and deal with the day's letters and telegrams and phone calls; have dinner with an ad exec and the director of a radio show; see the rough cut of a new film with two Morris clients in supporting roles; and hang out at the Trocadero Café on Sunset until midnight to catch three other clients onstage. Then, if there weren't any more situations, he'd go home.

Frances had her own career, somewhat to Lastfogel's chagrin. She made radio appearances, and in 1938 she showed up at Paramount for a bit part in a run-of-the-mill programmer called *Never Say Die*, starring

Bob Hope as a millionaire hypochondriac whose doctor has given him a month to live and Martha Raye as the Texas oil princess he meets at a German spa. Once a year or so, Sammy Weisbord, Lastfogel's assistant in New York, would book her on a brief tour of RKO picture houses as well. She'd play the Palace in Chicago or the Steel Pier on the boardwalk in Atlantic City, headlining for lesser acts like Abbott & Costello, Frank Elliott's Minstrels, and Al Gordon's Dogs. Tiny yet robust, blond hair dramatically set off by her black gown, she'd regale movie fans who'd come to see Ginger Rogers and Fred Astaire in *Carefree*, say, with a song-and-comedy act that ended Sophie Tucker–style with a song called "Let Them Ramble, Let Them Roam." "She is sure-fire with her dialect songs in Irish, Italian and Yiddish accents," *Variety* declared admiringly. "Whams home with her red-hot 'advice to women' number for the finale."

Bill Morris, Jr., was back in New York, having spent some of the $250,000 he was pulling in yearly on a four-story town house on East Fifty-second Street, a clifftop cul-de-sac that ended at River House, the grand apartment tower where Vincent Astor kept his yacht tied up at dock. The contrasts were stark in this corner of Manhattan, millionaires' mansions nuzzling cheek-by-jowl with squalid tenements full of families on relief; the cold-water flat Lastfogel had grown up in was a few blocks away. Morris's decorator had done the place up with startling verve—crimson sofas and buff walls in the living room, blond wood and white leather against Tabasco-red walls in the dining room. On the top floor was a game room with a white leather bar and tables for Ping-Pong, backgammon, and cards. *House & Garden* wrote it up twice.

Despite his duties as president, Morris spent much of his time enjoying himself. He signed the occasional client—Aldous Huxley was the source of much excitement, until they discovered he no longer controlled the film rights to *Brave New World*—but for the most part, he functioned as a free spirit. He had a great sense of adventure, and he didn't mind indulging it when the mood struck. One day his chauffeured motorcar pulled up outside the house of Al and Ruth Ruben, the couple he and Jerry had shared Villa Voncha with a few years before. The Rubens lived near the Pacific now, in a crisply modern house by Richard Neutra in the lush recesses of Santa Monica Canyon. Their two boys, ages eight and ten, were playing outside. Morris rolled down the car window: How'd they like to see Boulder Dam? Their mother was flabbergasted, but she packed their bags, and an hour later they were speeding across the San Gabriel Mountains toward the wastes of southern Nevada.

They were hardly the first people to make the trek out to Boulder Dam. Every month, thousands of people were driving across the desolate Mojave Desert to gape at the enormous concrete plug that government engineers had managed to insert in the jagged depths of Black Canyon. They got dizzy peering down into the narrow, rocky, thousand-foot gorge; they tingled at the high-tension lines strung up overhead on towers tilted crazily over the edge. And then they drove thirty miles across the desert to Las Vegas, a glorified whistle-stop on the Salt Lake–to–Los Angeles line that was the closest thing to civilization for hours in any direction.

Las Vegas was a town out of some Hollywood Western—a wide-open, anything-goes town full of painted whores and hard-drinking men. Looking for a place to spend the night, Morris got the last room he could find and let the boys sleep on a pallet under the stairs. The false-front buildings outside were full of gambling dens, rough-and-tumble joints with sawdust on the floor and saloon doors swinging open to the street, though the town did boast one medium-lavish supper club that an L.A. bootlegger named Tony Cornero had opened in 1931—the year the Nevada legislature, looking for a way to raise money, voted to legalize gambling, which was ubiquitous on the frontier anyway. The burg didn't look like much, but it was bursting with strangers, and the power lines snaking out across the desert from Black Canyon fed it plenty of juice—a lot more than it really seemed to need.

BY 1938, ABE LASTFOGEL HAD BUILT THE MORRIS OFFICE INTO ONE OF the leading agencies in show business, with several hundred screen actors on its roster and total client earnings expected to hit $15 million, up from a mere $500,000 in 1930. Pictures accounted for only a third of its revenues; radio brought in another third, while the rest came from nine other departments—vaudeville, literary, nightclubs, and the like. For the most part, the smaller departments existed to feed the radio and motion picture operations, although they were more than capable of generating excitement in their own right. The September 1938 opening of Ole Olsen and Chic Johnson's *Hellzapoppin'*—a madcap Broadway revue that had shots ringing out, cast members running riot through the audience, and film footage of Hitler declaiming in Hebe dialect—so outraged the critics with its vulgarity that for a moment even Germany's dismemberment of Czechoslovakia seemed to pale by comparison.

That November, when the talent guilds won recognition from the studios and took up the issue of agency conduct, the Morris Agency's status in Hollywood became obvious. The Actors Guild wanted to limit agency contracts to one year and set commissions at 5 percent—ideas the agents didn't like at all. Thirteen large agencies had formed an Artists' Managers Guild to fight the actors' plan, but eventually they bowed to the actors and agreed to work out a code. Lastfogel was named to head the negotiating committee.

The appointment made sense. Lastfogel might be an outsider, more attuned to the bustle and excitement of Times Square than the studied nonchalance of Hollywood, but he was a reassuring presence in a strangely off-kilter world. His sober, subdued demeanor stood out amid the overfed egos of the picture business. Sleek and gray, invariably clad in an expensive business suit, he gave the lie to the image of the agent as fast-talking hustler. Here was an agent who looked as stolid as a banker—who didn't say much, who'd sit quietly through the rantings of moguls and production chiefs and then, when they paused for breath, settle everything with a couple of well-chosen words.

In December, just as he was taking over the negotiations with the guilds, the Morris Agency left the jazzy pace of the Strip for the hush of downtown Beverly Hills, where the sidewalks were rolled up every night at nine. It was like moving to a fairy-tale village on the M-G-M lot, a palm-shaded oasis of shops and restaurants nestled between the frothy tower of City Hall and the sheltering arms of the Beverly Wilshire Hotel. Morris took over the former UA Building at 202 North Cañon Drive and doubled its size by adding a second story. The results were stylish and Moderne, translucent glass bricks framing a doorway that opened onto a circular lobby with a sweeping staircase. But at a time when most agencies were trying to make a statement, the Morris Building was characteristically restrained. Extravagance and self-aggrandizement weren't Lastfogel's style. He liked understatement.

This was apparent in the way he went after Mickey Rooney, the 1938 box-office champion of the nation, whose low-budget Hardy Family series captured all that was heartwarming and innocent and right about growing up in small-town America. At seventeen, Rooney was Metro's most valuable star, bigger than Clark Gable or Spencer Tracy or Joan Crawford or Greta Garbo. The studio had him under contract at $900 a week, forty weeks a year—and in 1938, he made ten pictures during those forty weeks.

Four years earlier, after George Jessel discovered them while emcee-ing a vaudeville show in Chicago, the Morris office had signed the Gumm Sisters, a struggling vocal trio whose principal asset was a twelve-year-old with a powerful voice and big, wondering eyes and a tender innocence that made her seem fragile and rare. Back home in Los Angeles, little Frances Gumm had blossomed into Judy Garland, but she was a tough sell at the studios—too old to be Shirley Temple, too young to play the ingénue. She finally landed at M-G-M through contacts her mother had made, and her contract was negotiated by an agent far less exalted than Lastfogel. When her mother subsequently went looking for a new agent, Lastfogel offered to represent her at 7.5 percent. Even so, he got the turndown.

That wasn't going to happen with Rooney. Lastfogel called the boy's mother, an ex-vaudevillian named Nell Carter Pankey, and arranged an appointment. She met with him and was impressed. For months, she heard nothing further. Then, late in 1939, shortly after Rooney and Garland had scored their second triumph together—this time as vaudevillians' kids in *Babes in Arms*—he and his mother were summoned to the building on Cañon Drive.

On arriving, they were ushered into Mr. Hyde's office, which had the hush and solemnity of a funeral parlor. Smiling silently, Mr. Hyde showed Mrs. Pankey the new contract they'd negotiated at Metro: $1,000 a week for the first year, $1,250 for the second, $1,500 for the third, with annual options and salary increases until he'd be making $3,000 in his seventh year; plus a bonus of $25,000 per picture and a minimum of two pictures per year. Mr. Lastfogel, also smiling, proffered a fountain pen. She signed. Mickey thanked them. And they left.

It was the new agency style. From now on, when Mickey met with the imperious Mr. Mayer, he'd be flanked on either side by his new friends, Hyde and Lastfogel, the three of them marching in shoulder-to-shoulder, five-four, five-three, five-three, giants all. The ten-percenters had come into their own.

3

BROADWAY
BOOGIE-WOOGIE

Los Angeles/New York/Las Vegas, 1939-1946

THERE WAS ONE THING MISSING IN ABE LASTFOGEL'S SCHEME OF THINGS: At the height of the big-band era, the Morris office had no serious band department. He was reminded of this by the new headquarters of the Music Corporation of America, which had just gone up three blocks from the Morris Building on Cañon Drive. MCA was the top band-booking agency in the country, a Chicago operation that had already spread to New York. Its founder, Jules Stein, had just decided to break into the picture business. He didn't have any picture clients yet, but they'd come. The first step was to build.

Characteristically, Stein built big. He'd bought a piece of land across from City Hall, and to design something for it, he'd hired Paul Williams, the Negro architect whose colonial-style mansions were the cat's pajamas in money-colored suburbs like Beverly Hills or Palos Verdes. Williams gave him grandeur American-style, colonial Williamsburg crossed with *Gone With the Wind*. Visitors pulling up to his white-columned portico stepped into an entry hall graced by sweeping staircases and a glittering chandelier. Upstairs was Stein's office, a paneled drawing room shipped over from England and furnished in eighteenth-century antiques. A freestanding colonnade in the private park outside his windows lent a contemplative touch. Stein's "White House" was designed to suggest that he was the equal of Jack Warner or Louis Mayer. All he had to do now was get the stars to fill it up. And anyone who knew his past could tell you how he'd go about that.

Jules C. Stein had showed an affinity for money early on. Son of an impoverished shopkeeper in South Bend, Indiana, he'd worked his way through West Virginia University and the University of Chicago med school by leading an orchestra. One night he found himself double-booked, so he got another band to take his place and made a 20 percent commission. He quickly realized that booking gigs could be more lucrative than playing them. For a while, he made this a sideline while working as an ophthalmologist in the office of a leading Chicago eye surgeon. But band booking took up more and more of his attention, and in 1924 he went into it full-time, founding the Music Corporation of America with a college chum named Billy Goodheart, Jr.

Stein and Goodheart started out with just $1,000 in capital and a two-room office in the Loop, but their timing was excellent. The dance craze of the teens had matured into the dance craze of the twenties, and Chicago was full of dance halls and ballrooms where people came to do the fox-trot and watch exhibition dancers perform more adventurous numbers like the shimmy. Up to this point, Stein had mainly booked bands into speakeasies on the South Side—Al Capone's turf. But within months of setting up in the Loop, he had Chicago locked up and was booking across the Midwest.

That took more than timing. When Stein began, most dance bands were anonymous ensembles that played under their booker's name, stayed in the same town for years, and sounded more or less like all the others. But this was the Jazz Age; even the stuffiest orchestras were beginning to experiment with their own arrangements. Stein offered them more—a name, a following, a life on the road. In return, he wanted an exclusive—an understanding that he alone would book their gigs.

He cut a similar deal with the dance halls and hotel ballrooms he booked them into. Rotating bands drew crowds and excitement, but it also meant more work for the people who ran the halls. By giving Stein an exclusive, they could turn it all over to MCA and get a steady stream of bands, some of them better than anything they could normally afford. With exclusives from the halls, Stein could give his bands solid bookings the whole year through. Through subsidiaries, he could offer them insurance, cars, even real estate. And for a flat fee, he could provide dance hall managers not just with bands but with linens, glasses, confetti, cigarettes, swizzle sticks, bootlegged liquor, bandstands, hatcheck girls, the whole package.

Reportedly, there were other advantages to doing business with MCA—payola in the form of cash or cars. Venues that didn't go along ran into difficulties—stink bomb attacks in the middle of performances, that sort of thing. Chicago was that kind of place. Prohibition had turned it into a wide-open town, hog butcher to the world and rubout capital of the nation. Labor bosses fronted for gangsters who gave muscle to their threats; business leaders turned to rival gangsters for protection; politicians and judges averted their eyes. The amusement business was one of the worst, on a par with trucking, paving, and construction.

For all the excitement, Chicago was still the hinterlands. Stein and Goodheart didn't represent a single big-name band until 1929, when they opened an office in New York and booked Guy Lombardo and his Royal Canadians, whose suave, subdued arrangements had made them an overnight sensation in Cleveland three years before, into the Roosevelt Hotel on Madison Avenue. The move to New York also enabled them to break into network radio. In 1930, Goodheart talked American Tobacco into sponsoring the "Lucky Strike Hit Parade," featuring a different MCA orchestra every night. Other shows followed—"The Magic Carpet," "Camel Caravan." As with nightclubs and ballrooms, MCA offered advertisers a package deal—not just bands but singers, comedy writers, guest stars, an entire show.

Here Stein introduced a new wrinkle. The American Federation of Musicians, headed by a boyhood chum named James "Little Caesar" Petrillo, flouted its own bylaws by granting MCA an exclusive blanket waiver permitting it to function as both production company and booking agency. As producer, the agency hired its own clients, sold the shows to sponsors, and pocketed the difference, which could be as much as 30 percent. Big bands flocked to its roster, and hotel ballrooms fought to sign them up. By 1938, MCA represented nearly two-thirds of the name bands in the country, including Xavier Cugat, Tommy Dorsey, Benny Goodman, Harry James, and Guy Lombardo.

That was when Lastfogel moved to challenge its lead. He considered buying a half-interest in Rockwell-O'Keefe, a large band-booking firm with offices in New York, Chicago, San Francisco, Los Angeles, and London, but talks collapsed after Rockwell-O'Keefe opened its books.

While casting about for an alternative, he organized a department to package productions for trade shows and fairs—an offshoot of the entertainment business that MCA had recently discovered as well. Meanwhile, MCA was moving into Hollywood, where Morris was already established. After fifteen years in separate corners of the business, the two agencies were about to go head-to-head.

Lastfogel played his hand in April 1939, when he induced Willard Alexander, one of MCA's leading New York execs, to join the Morris office as head of its new band department. A gaunt man with penetrating eyes, Alexander handled some of the top swing bands in the country—Benny Goodman, Count Basie—but his tastes were considered extreme within MCA, where Eddy Duchin and Xavier Cugat were more the ticket. There was another consideration, too. MCA was a cutthroat organization, its top agents competing ferociously for Stein's approving nod, and Alexander was a leading contender to be his successor. But his chief rival, Sonny Werblin, who a few years before had been Billy Goodheart's office boy, scored a major coup just as Morris made its offer. It looked to Alexander like a good time to jump ship.

He regretted it soon after, when Werblin, not yet thirty, suffered a heart attack that threatened to put him out of commission. Alexander brought Count Basie from MCA and worked with Duke Ellington at the Morris office, but he was an outsider there. Some of Lastfogel's top people weren't as impressed as he was with the band business—controller Nat Lefkowitz, for instance, the sour-faced accountant who'd picked up his law degree at Brooklyn College night school. And Alexander had more in common with the Anglo-Saxon Protestants who ran the radio department than with the Broadway types in the rest of the agency. Other Morris agents dined at Lindy's, the showbiz hangout at Broadway and Fifty-first, where the customers shouted at each other across the room; Alexander preferred the clubbier confines of "21," the former speakeasy tucked away in a mansion off Fifth.

That was typical for an MCA man. MCA treated show business as a social disease. Its New York address—745 Fifth Avenue, a white granite office tower rising grandly above the remaining palazzos of Millionaires' Row—was as far from the lights and crowds of Times Square as possible. Stein himself had mastered the quiet exercise of power. He and his wife, Doris, never appeared in gossip columns, never gave flashy parties.

They were beginning to smell like old money, at a time when old money was viewing the amusement business with new interest. The Rocke-fellers were taking in $7 million a year in cabaret and box-office receipts from such Rockefeller Center properties as the Rainbow Room and Radio City Music Hall. Jock Whitney was chairman of David O. Selznick's new Selznick International Pictures, handling the financial end from New York. But all this was just slumming, like a night on the town at the Stork Club and "21" and El Morocco—a fling that like other flings was apt to end with a hangover. And while café society was fluid in a way Boston or Philadelphia could hardly imagine, New York was still a town in which the Astors and the Vanderbilts ruled. It was Doris's idea to move to Hollywood, where everything was make-believe anyway.

Stein may have been allergic to show business, but he had a flair for show. In Chicago, he'd bought a French Renaissance château overlook-ing Lake Michigan; in Los Angeles it was a Spanish colonial hacienda overlooking Beverly Hills. He lived there like a Yankee grandee, sur-rounded by rare cymbidium orchids and exquisite Queen Anne furni-ture. Reversing the standard Hollywood wisdom that visibility makes you real, he spent so much time behind his gates that a certain mystery attached itself to him. When he did grace a party, it was usually to talk business in a corner. Doris was an accomplished hostess, but she gave small, private dinner parties for a handful of powerful intimates. Stars were admitted on occasion, mainly to entertain the children.

On the other hand, stars became a fixture at MCA's new White House across from City Hall. Stein saw no point in trying to build them from obscurity, so he bought or stole from other agents. To lure Bette Davis, whom Warner Bros. was about to put before the cameras in *Dark Victory*, he approached her husband's best friend, an out-of-work character named Eddie Linsk, and put him on the MCA payroll. Miss Davis switched agencies soon after. Other stars followed—Joan Crawford, Errol Flynn, John Forsythe, John Garfield, Paulette Goddard, Basil Rathbone.

When he couldn't buy stars, Stein bought agents, or whole agencies. He bought out Johnny Beck, Jr., the leading agent at Associated Artists, and put him in charge of the motion picture department. In 1940, he bought out the William Meiklejohn Agency, another little office on the Strip, and came away with William Demarest, Jane Wyman, and Ronald Reagan. He didn't get a warm welcome at the studios, but MCA's lock on the band business gave it leverage: Moguls needed orchestras for their pictures, and the home office in New York needed them to play the theater chains. Studio chiefs quickly found themselves listening to Stein much more attentively than they'd intended to.

The motion picture department was soon taken over by Lew Wasserman, a onetime nightclub publicist Stein had hired in 1936 to run advertising and publicity out of Chicago. Tall and gaunt, Wasserman was an ambitious young man whose unsmiling demeanor did not diminish his charm. Stein was clinical and remote, but Wasserman had rapport with the stars—like Reagan, an Iowa radio announcer whom Meiklejohn had landed a contract at Warner Bros., the standard forty weeks a year for seven years. When Warners made *King's Row*, the 1942 melodrama about a small-town rake who loses his legs after an accident in a rail yard, Reagan got such a good response in previews that Warners offered him a new contract at three times his current salary. Reagan wanted to hold out until the film was released, but Wasserman reminded him there was a war on and he might be in it soon.

It was good advice—Reagan was called to active duty not long after and assigned to Culver City to narrate training films for the Army Air Corps. In the meantime, Wasserman saw a chance to write his first million-dollar deal. He figured the most he could get for Reagan was $3,500 a week; forty weeks a year for seven years at $3,500 a week comes to just under $1 million, so he persuaded Jack Warner to use his client for forty-three weeks a year instead. The weekly salary looked good to Reagan, but what mattered to Wasserman, and to MCA, was the deal itself. A million dollars: It was a totemic sum, testament not just to Reagan's worth but to Wasserman's. Fact that most of it might never be collected was beside the point.

WHILE JULES STEIN AND LEW WASSERMAN WERE ESTABLISHING MCA IN Hollywood, Abe Lastfogel was working gratis to mount the greatest vaudeville production the world had ever seen. From Pearl Harbor to V-J Day, USO–Camp Shows had more than seven thousand performers (Humphrey Bogart, James Cagney, Gary Cooper, Bing Crosby, Clark Gable, Marlene Dietrich, Al Jolson, Carole Lombard, Dinah Shore, and James Stewart among them) playing to two hundred million soldiers, sailors, airmen, and marines at military bases and hospitals around the globe. As supreme commander of the Allied amusement effort, Lastfogel staged the show.

Camp Shows had been launched by the nation's big men of affairs. In the fall of 1940, with draftees reporting for duty in the United States as the Luftwaffe bombed Britain and the Japanese advanced across Indochina, Thomas J. Watson, chairman of International Business Machines, organized a citizens committee that put on shows at training camps from the backs of trucks on loan from General Motors. John D. Rockefeller, Jr., heir to the Standard Oil fortune (and landlord to the Morris Agency in New York), helped set up the United Service Organization to coordinate the efforts of the Young Men's Christian Association and other groups concerned with the draftees' morale, and their morals as well. But these worthies would have had the boys on a steady diet of violin recitals if Lastfogel hadn't been recruited to provide something brisker.

When Lastfogel took command, on November 22, 1941, he was confident he could get things moving in six months or so and get back to work. In two weeks, he had eleven vaudeville troupes on the road. Then the Japanese bombed Pearl Harbor, and he realized he'd better forget the agency for a while. He left Bill Morris, Jr., to run the place and Johnny Hyde to handle the West Coast office and threw himself full-time into the war effort.

Bill Morris had his own morale-building plan, a scheme to print up a million red, white, and blue lapel buttons emblazoned with the slogan "Hey Rube!"—for sixty years or more the cry of distress among carnival folk. He wanted to make it a rallying cry against the Axis as it had been against angry circusgoers—rubes, in carny parlance. Ads were taken out in the trade papers:

THE SPIRIT OF THE NEW YEAR . . .
HEY RUBE!
TAKE YOUR PLACES

The traditional circus call to arms—the rallying cry of Show Business—again thunders through the great American world of entertainment. The Big Show has been attacked! Down through the pages of our country's history—whenever security and decent living were endangered by the wanton acts of international outlaws—our fathers and our fathers' fathers closed their fists about every last weapon at hand to defend their nation's life and liberty. Our country needs us now. There are a thousand ways to help—a thousand ways to roll up

our sleeves and heed the traditional battle-cry of Show Business. Take
your places! Grab the best weapon at hand—and come out fighting!

HEY RUBE!
OUR SEASON'S GREETINGS TO SHOW BUSINESS
WILLIAM MORRIS AGENCY

Most of Morris's attention, however, was directed toward the Soviet
Union. He was fascinated by all things Russian, from the Russian language, which he was studying, to the nature of the Soviet experiment. In
October 1941, with the Red Army reeling before the German blitzkrieg
and Pearl Harbor still two months away, he'd joined a host of public figures, from Museum of Modern Art director Alfred Barr to *Los Angeles
Times* publisher Harry Chandler, in calling for a massive benefit for Russian War Relief at Madison Square Garden. Later he went on the board
of Russian War Relief, along with department store magnate Marshall
Field, former New York Governor Alfred E. Smith, and Thomas J. Watson of IBM. In March 1943, he helped found the National Council of
American-Soviet Friendship, an organization devoted to promoting the
Soviet cause in America.

Morris was essentially a figurehead at the agency. He was divorced
now, his marriage to Jerry over. Sitting on the boards of Russian War
Relief and the National Council of American-Soviet Friendship gave
him plenty to do—meetings to attend, dinners to plan, rallies and benefits to organize. In 1943, he led a $150,000 fund-raising drive for the
National Council. In 1944, he worked with Lillian Hellman on the advisory production committee for a Russian War Relief pageant at Madison
Square Garden. Meanwhile, Lastfogel shuttled between Camp Shows'
drab headquarters across from the New York Public Library and a Beverly Hills office around the corner from the Morris Building on Cañon
Drive, strong-arming producers, studio chiefs, union leaders, and fellow
agents into granting the concessions that would make an all-out entertainment effort possible. Stars agreed to work for no pay. Other people
worked below scale under conditions that made a joke of union rules.
The Morris office announced it would waive all commissions. Other
agencies followed suit.

After a couple of false starts, Lastfogel managed to divide the nation's
military bases into two circuits—a Victory Circuit of large bases
equipped to handle full Broadway productions, and a Blue Circuit of

smaller camps that got vaudeville acts—singers, dancers, magicians, comedians, acrobats, ventriloquists, baton twirlers, mind readers, trick golfers, what-have-you. In December 1942, after a six-week tour of Britain with a Feminine Theatrical Task Force composed of Kay Francis, Carole Landis, Mitzi Mayfair, and Martha Raye, he concluded that while American soldiers liked British entertainment "well enough," it was time to add a Foxhole Circuit for troops in the field.

In the ensuing years, he sent Olivia de Havilland to Alaska, Paulette Goddard to Burma, Bob Hope to Panama, André Kostelanetz to Iraq, Ray Milland to Australia, and Spencer Tracy to Hawaii. Camp Show performers followed General Patton into North Africa and Sicily and hopscotched across the Pacific islands with Admiral Halsey. Six and a half weeks after D-Day, twenty-six of them piled out of landing barges and waded onto the beach at Normandy. Sometimes they played to thousands at air bases and sports arenas. Sometimes they'd do a song and dance on a mess hall table in the jungle, or from the back of a truck for a dozen GIs they'd just come across at some remote country cross-roads. "Abe dear," Dinah Shore wrote from Normandy in August 1944, ". . . I can truthfully say that I have sung in some of the best pastures in France. It's really quite an experience, and the most difficult part of the whole trip, believe it or not, is lassoing an audience long enough to do a show. . . . If you hear of us doing a truck-to-truck production on convoy don't be surprised, it's just four ham actors running after an audience."

As civilian noncombatants, Camp Show performers had to be issued uniforms so they wouldn't be taken for spies. Sometimes that wasn't enough, as the comedy team of Jane and Joe McKenna discovered when they were snared by a German patrol in Normandy and had to mime their act to avoid being shot. On occasion, entertainers actually did per-form a military function. When a North African native suspected of traf-ficking with the Germans insisted that he understood no English, the intelligence officer in charge took him to Jack Benny. The man was released when he failed to laugh at Benny's jokes.

Not every Camp Show comedian was that funny. GI audiences were tough, and as the war ground on, fresh talent became harder to find. Hitler was drafting sixteen-year-olds; Lastfogel found himself in a simi-lar predicament. It didn't help that every performer's material had to be passed on in advance by an Army Special Services office in New York. Some people were offended anyway: One chaplain wrote to a friend, in a letter that attained some notoriety, that he needed a bath "both internally and externally" after witnessing a USO show. Nor was filth the only concern. Lastfogel rejected one Broadway show because one of its main characters was a sick mother, and he thought fighting men abroad shouldn't have to worry about sick mothers at home.

One of the toughest jobs performers had to face was entertaining the wounded, whether in field hospitals abroad or on the Hospital Circuit Lastfogel organized at home. Ventriloquist Edgar Bergen tried to get a laugh out of a shell-shocked soldier who hadn't spoken or eaten in more than a week; he finally won a grin when his sidekick McCarthy turned to him and quipped, "Oh, nuts, boss, say something bright. Our pal here is bored." John Steinbeck, reporting for the *New York Herald Tribune*, wrote that Bob Hope and Frances Langford had a hospital ward in stitches until Langford started to sing "As Time Goes By" and a young man with a head wound began to sob. Langford gamely finished, her voice all but inaudible by the end, then hurried out of the room and broke down. The ward was dead silent until Hope stood up between the beds. "Fellows," he intoned with his usual impeccable timing, "the folks at home are having a terrible time about eggs. They can't get any powdered eggs at all. They've got to use the old-fashioned kind you break open."

None of Lastfogel's entertainers were killed by enemy fire, though two died and five were hurt when a Pan Am Clipper went down in Lisbon harbor, and thirty-five more lost their lives in a variety of other mishaps. Several did have close calls in combat, particularly during the Battle of the Bulge, when the Germans' last-ditch counteroffensive overran the Allied rear in the Ardennes forest. A group of baseball players disappeared for several days and was presumed lost until they made their way back to the Allied lines. Marlene Dietrich, whose sister was imprisoned at Belsen and who was herself on Hitler's death list, was on the verge of being captured when soldiers from the Eighty-second Airborne rescued her unit. But the only USO troupe that actually got taken by the Germans was on Broadway, in a 1945 play called *Common Ground*.

Chief villain of the play was an offstage character named Abe Firstwonger, the civilian general who'd gotten them into this predicament. At one point a comedian in the unit recalled, "I was having a corned beef in Lindy's when he crept out from the cole slaw . . . with a *different* idea. A *better* proposition." But as E. J. Kahn, Jr., reported in *The New Yorker*, this portrayal was rife with inaccuracy. In the first place, Abe Lastfogel never assumed an honorific rank higher than captain; and though he certainly was a habitué of Lindy's, he couldn't possibly have crept out of the cole slaw. Truth was, he never touched the stuff.

JULES STEIN'S CONTRIBUTION TO THE WAR EFFORT WAS A SERIES OF DEALS to benefit the Hollywood Canteen, a rustic, barnlike servicemen's club on Cahuenga Boulevard that Bette Davis and John Garfield threw together with his help. The Hollywood Canteen was where servicemen on leave could go for free entertainment (Rudy Vallee, Kay Kyser, Duke Ellington, Eddie Cantor, George Jessel), free refreshments, and a chance to dance with the stars, from Betty Grable to Olivia de Havilland to Greer Garson to Carole Landis. Stein handled the financial end and did it so well the place ended up with a $500,000 surplus, thanks to the fees he charged the radio chains ($5,000 per broadcast, no commercials allowed) and the $750,000 deal he made with Warner Bros. to do a movie, which of course was called *Hollywood Canteen*. He made a similar deal for the Stage Door Canteen in New York. But, unlike Lastfogel, he garnered little publicity for his work.

All agencies, William Morris included, preferred to keep the spotlight on their clients rather than themselves, but MCA made a fetish of it. Jules Stein had transformed a helter-skelter trade into a relentlessly efficient machine, one that turned talent into a commodity and the commodity into money, and the more opaque its operations, the more effective they would be. A mesh of interlocking corporations ticked away inside the MCA shell—the Music Corporation of America, the Management Corporation of America, MCA Artists Ltd., the California Movie Company, and so forth—but information could be had on none of them, not from Moody's or Poor's or Standard Statistics or Dun & Bradstreet. Stein was not listed in *Who's Who* or even *Who's Who in the Motion Picture Industry*. He was rarely photographed and never interviewed. MCA worked in the shadows, its power felt but seldom seen. Then a small-time dance hall operator threatened to blow the lid.

Larry Finley's troubles had started when he made a bid to run a city-owned amusement park in San Diego called Mission Beach. It was a modest place—a Ferris wheel, a roller coaster, a merry-go-round, some scooter cars, a ballroom with country and western bands—but Finley had big plans. Among other things, he wanted to book big-name orchestras in the ballroom, even though so far San Diego had only been able to support one name-band layout—a downtown establishment known as Pacific Square that was owned by the man Finley was trying to get Mission Beach away from. Undaunted, Finley had gone to Beverly Hills to see Larry Barnett, the vice president in charge of MCA's band department.

Barnett was not encouraging. He even told Finley, he later recalled, that it "might not be wise to open up," but Finley wasn't listening. Barnett did not mention that MCA had a San Diego exclusive with the owner of Pacific Square. Finley took over Mission Beach in January 1945; two months later, when he realized the only bands he'd get from MCA were ones that had already appeared at Pacific Square, he sued under the Sherman Antitrust Act. Justice Department investigators had already scrutinized MCA once and dropped the investigation for lack of evidence. Now they started bringing MCA's competitors in for questioning—among them Charles Wick of the Morris office, a former orchestra leader who dutifully explained how MCA was able to coerce its clients and customers.

Meanwhile, MCA continued to consolidate its grasp. It had already bought the CBS Artists' Bureau, the talent agency owned by CBS, which like NBC had ventured into agenting only to be pressured by the Justice Department to get out. In April 1945, Stein concluded a much bigger deal—the purchase of the Hayward-Deverich Agency, which handled some three hundred of the brightest lights in Hollywood and on Broadway. The catch included Greta Garbo, Myrna Loy, Van Johnson, James Stewart, Gene Kelly, Joseph Cotten, Boris Karloff, Fredric March, and Raymond Massey; directors Billy Wilder and Alfred Hitchcock; writers Dorothy Parker, Ben Hecht, Arthur Koestler, Irwin Shaw, and Dashiell Hammett. It also included Leland Hayward and his partner Nat Deverich, both of whom had started with Myron Selznick and both of whom now became MCA vice presidents, at $100,000 a year minimum.

Selznick had died the year before, after a long and painful slide. He despised agenting; what he really wanted was to produce. But the power and the money were too great to give it up, the revenge too sweet even when it curdled in his stomach. By the end of the thirties, he was starting on the Johnnie Walker at mid-morning. When Carole Lombard, Merle Oberon, and Loretta Young each complained that he was neglecting their careers, he invited them to dinner together and announced he'd like to roll them in the hay. His wife, former silent screen star Marjorie Daw, sued for divorce in 1939, shattering a union that had been billed as one of Hollywood's "perfect marriages." Lombard left in 1940; when he claimed she couldn't fire him, she went to an arbitration board and won. But it was his liver that got him in the end. On a Sunday night in March 1944, he was rushed to Santa Monica Hospital with severe abdominal hemorrhaging. Three days later, at age forty-five, he was dead.

Selznick's demise and the Hayward-Deverich merger left MCA the foremost talent agency in the country. To gauge Stein's power, you had only to look at the 1945 Academy Awards, which were swept by Charles Brackett's production of *The Lost Weekend*, a stark and horrifying depiction of a man in the grip of alcoholism. Besides the Oscar for best picture, *The Lost Weekend* took best actor (MCA client Ray Milland), best director (MCA client Billy Wilder), and best screenplay (MCA clients Brackett and Wilder). Jane Wyman failed to get a nomination for best actress, but another MCA artist, Joan Crawford, won the acting award for her role in *Mildred Pierce*. MCA could hardly lose, no matter who won. Stein had more than a third of Hollywood's top stars under contract, a bigger percentage than any studio chief could claim. And while other agencies had stars on their roster, only one could compete with MCA in every area of the business: William Morris.

A month after the Oscar ceremonies, in April 1946, a jury in Los Angeles found for Larry Finley, awarding him $55,000 plus costs. The judge threw out the damages, ruling that it was impossible to put a dollar figure on Finley's loss. But he found ample evidence to support the verdict against MCA, which he described as "the Octopus," its "tentacles reaching out . . . and grasping everything in show business."

Hollywood was eyeing MCA carefully, and after the verdict, the movie colony was rife with rumors of a shake-up. Press speculation centered on Sonny Werblin, now fully recovered from his heart attack and running the New York office. But when the announcement finally came, it was thirty-three-year-old Lew Wasserman who was named president and chief executive while Stein made himself chairman of the board. And there the repercussions stopped. MCA lost its appeal, but in throwing out the damages, the judge apparently saved the agency from an avalanche of similar suits. The Justice Department investigation was aborted on orders from Washington. And for the second time since the start of the century, the Morris office found itself bucking an entertainment trust.

But the Finley decision did have one effect: It dragged MCA into the spotlight. The *Saturday Evening Post* ran a series entitled "Star-Spangled Octopus" that splashed Stein's face across the magazine for week after week, illustrating tales of ruthlessness and woe. "Cursed, threatened and sometimes sued, he's the backstage Mr. Big of show business," the magazine declared. Louella Parsons reported in her column that King Brothers, a low-budget outfit, had offered Stein $50,000 for the film rights, plus casting control. The offer was "too hot to ignore," Parsons reported, "but—P.S. I bet Stein never accepts it."

CAPTAIN LASTFOGEL'S RETURN TO CIVILIAN LIFE HAD BEEN ACCOMPLISHED some months before, at a December 1945 luncheon at the Waldorf-Astoria Hotel. It was a gala affair, with congratulations all around. George Jessel had once quipped that he was looking forward to the day when Lastfogel would be commissioned a fort, and while he had yet to attain that status, Lastfogel was being awarded the Medal of Freedom, the nation's highest civilian honor. And deservedly so, for as the general who pinned it to his chest declared, "Today the American soldier is the best-entertained soldier of any army in the world." The only discordant note came in the keynote address, when John D. Rockefeller, Jr., faulted the country's eagerness to get away from the "restraint and restriction" of wartime. "We the people of this fair land, alone untouched by the ravages of war, in our mad, yes suicidal rush to get back to a normal life, are not only forgetting the war but also the peace, and in so doing are already sowing the seeds of another war," he warned. ". . . God grant that we may come to our senses before it is too late."

Back to normal for Lastfogel meant Lindy's, the touchstone of New York nightlife, a raucous joint strategically situated amid the Times Square theaters. The seating was simple and to the point: headliners at the center, small-timers and business types by the revolving doors, tourists to the rear. Lastfogel, reported E. J. Kahn, Jr., in his *New Yorker* profile, was "the quiet guy in Lindy's": Others would yell and shout and toot their horn, but he just sat there, head turned up, eyes twinkling, cigar planted firmly in the center of his mouth, feet tucked up under him to keep them from dangling above the floor, easily overlooked except by those in the know. Clients called him Kewpie, because he looked like a Kewpie doll, fat-cheeked and wide-eyed. Sometimes they called him the little square man, because he looked like that, too.

The big bands were on the way out now, and Lastfogel didn't hesitate to cut them loose. The agency's band effort had been star-crossed anyway: They'd signed Glenn Miller in the spring of 1944, shortly before the plane crash that took his life, and their efforts to bring Benny Goodman aboard had been thwarted by MCA, whose determination to hold him to his contract had led him to disband his orchestra that March. Lastfogel granted Artie Shaw a release in November 1945 because Shaw wanted to go into pictures and Lastfogel didn't think he had a future there, and a few weeks later he dissolved the band department entirely. Willard Alexander, traumatized by the experience, announced he was taking Duke Ellington, Count Basie, Vaughn Monroe, and several others and going on his own. But Ellington and Basie elected to stay with the Morris office, even though Morris planned to focus on radio and nightclubs and pictures—at least until vaudeville came back.

Frances Arms had retired from show business by this time, at Abe's insistence, but the two of them still lived more or less out of a trunk. They kept permanent hotel suites on both coasts—in the Essex House on Central Park South, an Art Deco pile much favored by the Hollywood set, and in the Beverly Wilshire on Wilshire Boulevard. It was a gay life set to a rhumba beat: limousines, opening nights, a whirl of hotel lobbies and cocktail glasses and showbiz chatter that kept them up till two or three every morning. In Gotham it might be Danny Thomas at La Martinique, the basement show room on Fifty-seventh Street where the wiseguys hung out. Or Milton Berle or Sophie Tucker or Mae West at the Latin Quarter, the big Broadway tourist joint with the razzmatazz floor show—acrobats, jugglers, big-bosomed chorus girls swinging their tassels. Or Joe E. Lewis, the comedian of the chi-chi set, at the Copacabana on East Sixtieth, where his fans included Winthrop Rockefeller and Franklin Roosevelt, Jr., and the management took orders from Frank Costello, the syndicate boss.

The nightspots were all run by the mob, of course—Prohibition had seen to that. Who'd have provided liquor to the speaks if not rumrunners like Costello? It was a short step from delivering the booze to bankrolling a few dives to taking over their management to transforming them into plush and fashionable cafés where the best entertainers of the day could hold forth. El Morocco, the zebra-striped establishment on East Fifty-fourth Street that Howard Hughes and the Duke and

Duchess of Windsor were known to frequent, had been opened two years before by Repeal, an Italian immigrant who'd run a couple of West Side speaks. Sherman Billingsley, proprietor of the Stork Club, had been sentenced to fifteen months in Leavenworth on a bootlegging rap before coming to town, and he and his brothers had done jail time in Seattle before that.

None of this kept FBI director J. Edgar Hoover from palling around with Billingsley, or from mugging for a photographer with a toy machine gun one New Year's Eve as Billingsley and Walter Winchell beamed their approval (after a moment of panic when Hoover, looking for somebody to "arrest," innocently picked a mob killer on parole for extortion and impersonating an FBI agent; fortunately, the fellow proved camera-shy). Nor did it keep Winchell, a chum of both men and of fellow Stork Club regular Frank Costello, from making the place his headquarters. Every night, the king of the Broadway columnists held court behind the velvet rope in the Cub Room, eating Winchellburgers on the cuff and collecting items for his *Daily Mirror* column and chatting up the celebs who gathered by his table for a plug. Small wonder that Billingsley, a semiliterate Okie with a weasel's charm, became the arbiter of café society ("Booze Who," some called it), the one man with authority to decide which actors and writers and socialites and industrialists could slip inside the rope and which could not—at least, not without a hefty tip.

You needed somebody who knew the score if you were going to operate in this world, and Lastfogel had him in the person of George Wood. A genial chap with a taste for the fast life, Wood had gone into business during Prohibition, booking talent into the speaks. His father, Joe Wood, was a legendary Broadway character who'd managed prizefighters and produced vaude shows for the Keith and Orpheum circuits and gotten Eddie Cantor a booking when he was an unknown. George knew everybody and gambled on everything, and when Prohibition was repealed in 1933, a lot of his contacts were said to be loath to let him go. He was still in hock to the loan sharks when he took his list to the Morris office in 1941. A flashy dresser with an owlish beak, he functioned there as Lastfogel's troubleshooter, a high-level operative who specialized in difficult clients and tricky situations. Being pals with Frank Costello made him a natural for the job.

Costello was a good man to know. Not only did he have juice with studio chiefs like Jack Warner of Warner Bros. and Harry Cohn of Columbia; he was in nightclubs and casinos up and down the East Coast. He'd grown up a few blocks away from Frances Arms in Italian Harlem, but he'd gotten a different start in life—quitting school at eleven to run a penny-ante crap game, arrested at seventeen and twenty-one for robbery, sent to jail three years later on a gun charge. Bigger crap games followed, along with a bootlegging operation and a partnership in a novelty company that operated slot machines and another that dealt in Kewpie dolls.

By the time Mayor LaGuardia took a sledgehammer to his slots in 1934, Costello had fallen in with a couple of Jewish bootleggers, Meyer Lansky and Benjamin "Bugsy" Siegel, and with Charlie Luciano, who'd forcibly reorganized the Mafia with the help of the Bugs and Meyer mob. Later, when Luciano was doing thirty-to-fifty on a white slavery rap, Lansky and Costello made a deal with the navy to have him deported to Italy in exchange for the Mafia's help in securing the New York waterfront against Axis saboteurs. That was when Costello took over for him as boss of New York's top Mafia family.

Now that the war was over and the boys were home, Costello and his friends were ready to help the country forget about ack-ack and ration books and have a good time. Aside from his interest in the Copacabana, Costello was partners with Lansky in the Piping Rock, a Moorish-looking establishment outside Saratoga Springs, where Joe E. Lewis entertained the racing crowd while the Copa shut down for August. The Piping Rock was actually two joints in one—a swank supper club and, in an adjacent building guarded by a pair of ex-cops from New York City, the casino itself. Strangers got no farther than the restaurant, but those who were known to the spotters by the door were admitted to the casino, where they found crap tables, roulette wheels, bird cages, chemin de fer, the whole setup, all supervised by a pal of Costello's called Joe Adonis, a fleshy character who counted Brooklyn among his possessions and spent most of his time playing gin with Lewis.

Costello and Lansky were also partners in the Colonial Inn, a grand, white-columned establishment on Florida's Gold Coast, across the county line from Miami and right next door to the palmy Gulfstream Race Track. In 1945, with Lansky's help, Costello opened the equally luxe Beverly Club in Jefferson Parish, Louisiana, just outside New Orleans. Gambling was technically illegal, but each of these nightspots was strategically situated on the far side of some border or other, in a jurisdiction where technicalities didn't count as long as the fix was in. The clientele was loaded: businessmen who'd scored big in black market deals during the war, old-money swells from Park Avenue and Palm Beach, bag men for assorted Latin American dictators. And the profits were handsome—$685,000 for the 1945–1946 season at the Colonial Inn alone. But it wasn't just roulette, bingo, and dice; carpet joints like these offered dining, dancing, a floor show with a chorus line and big-name entertainers—the same lineup you'd see at the Copa, courtesy of George Wood of the Morris office.

Milton Berle, Maurice Chevalier, Jimmy Durante, Joe E. Lewis, Carmen Miranda, Danny Thomas, Sophie Tucker—William Morris had the biggest nightclub roster in the business. Several of these stars, Joe E. Lewis and Sophie Tucker in particular, had serious gambling habits, and virtually all of them were longtime pals of their employers. During the twenties, the antic comedy routines of Clayton, Jackson, and Durante had become a regular feature in the mob-run speaks of New York; after Durante went solo, bootlegger Waxey Gordon backed his 1933 Broadway show *Strike Me Pink* to the tune of $150,000. In 1927, Joe E. Lewis had gotten his throat slit in Chicago after Machine-gun Jack McGurn, a Capone operative, failed to convince him not to abandon his joint to appear in a speakeasy controlled by archrival Bugs Moran; Lewis never fingered his assailants to the cops, but they promptly turned up dead.

George Wood took care of these acts, and if any of them ran into trouble, he handled that, too. He was tight not only with Costello but with Costello's friends as well—with Lansky and Adonis and Jimmy Blue-Eyes Alo and Lucky Luciano himself, the boss in exile. He kept them in entertainers, and sometimes he helped them out in other ways. He was having dinner with Joe Adonis one night at Lindy's when he spied Harold Conrad, a young sportswriter for the *Mirror*. The next thing Conrad knew, he had a job doing public relations for the Colonial Inn.

Wood's friends took care of him in return. One day, he and Adonis were watching a chorus line rehearsal for the Colonial Inn when he noticed Adonis looking at him funny. Georgie, Adonis said, the nose has got to go. The next thing Wood knew, he was seeing a Park Avenue surgeon, the same one who'd done Berle's nose, on Joe Adonis's dime, just so his beak wouldn't embarrass them all when they got down to Florida. That was the thing about these boys: They treated you like family.

Which the William Morris office did, too—as Wood well knew, being Frances Lastfogel's favorite.

Abe Lastfogel, the little square man, might blend into the background in his conservative business suit and his trademark bow tie, but Frances was a pistol. No taller than he and nearly as wide, she packed a mouth that could make a sailor blush. Entering Lindy's one night with Lastfogel and Wood and a younger man from the agency, she spied Winchell coming toward the door and let him have it. Hearst's scandal-mongering columnist, who seldom hesitated to smear a target no matter how powerless, had printed a gratuitous remark about some chorus girl that day, and though the victim was not a client or even an acquaintance, Frances told him exactly what she thought. "Now Frances . . . now Frances . . . " Winchell pleaded, but it did him no good. It was a shriveled Walter Winchell who hit Broadway that night, his vanity punctured.

Lastfogel was Broadway's favorite agent, quiet, patient, and avuncular, "Uncle Abe" to his clients, "Mr. Lastfogel" to his men. About Frances, however, there were two schools of thought. One school (limited largely to men) regarded her as an object of devotion—salty yet maternal, fearsomely curt yet generous and loyal, a Jewish mother with a heart of gold. Other people never got past the brass jockstrap.

Frances Arms had been a big-time woman in vaudeville, and as Frances Lastfogel she was bigger still—if only because of her Abe. She guarded him the way a bulldog might guard a prized bone. But she was always ready to reminisce about her performing days, and she seemed to envy those whose fame was less fleeting. "Boy, is she a bitch!" she sneered one night after making huggy-kissy with Sophie Tucker at a Gotham restaurant. But it wasn't just professional jealousy; Fanny Brice was one of the most successful comediennes on radio, and she was one of Frances's dearest friends. The problem with Soph was that she took up too much of Abe's time.

Abe Lastfogel was a hard-charging man, so much the dynamo that fellows half his age were hard put to keep up with him. Around Hillcrest he was known as the world's fastest golfer—no slouch of a sobriquet at a club where Louis Mayer could make it around the course in seventy minutes flat. But if Abe was the boss of the Morris office, Frances was the boss of Abe. Before, it had been his older sister Bessie; now it was Frances who carried his money, ordered his meals, picked out his clothes. She referred to him as "Mister," as in "Where's Mister?" They didn't have children and they didn't have pets, because Frances, it was said, wanted Abe to herself. So the men of the Morris office subbed as their children, squiring Frances around, accompanying them to nightclubs and restaurants. All of them, clients and employees alike, were considered family.

Abe and Frances never gave parties and seldom attended anyone else's, but they were constantly taking clients and boys from the office out to Lindy's, or to Chasen's or Romanoff's on the coast. There was always a tense moment while everyone waited to see what Frances would order; half the party then ordered the same thing, and the rest selected something in the same price range. Stars passing by were careful to pay their respects lest they be cut dead by Frances's glare. Saturday nights in New York were invariably spent in Italian Harlem with Frances's brother, Harry Armhaus, and his wife, Toddy, who worked as a receptionist at the Morris office. Doc Armhaus—he was a dentist—was a serious cook, and the dinner parties at his brownstone on East 116th Street were as memorable for the food as for the stars Abe and Frances brought along.

For the boys at the office, invitations from the Lastfogels were generally abrupt. Sometimes a secretary would call at the last minute and say, "Mr. Lastfogel is going to the Latin Quarter tonight—would you like to come with him?" Or it might be Frances herself: "He wants you to join him," *click*. But these were invitations you didn't refuse, since if Frances adopted you, there was no limit to how far you could go. It went without saying that wives and girlfriends stayed home.

Like many father figures, Lastfogel maintained an aloofness that none of his children dared breach. Because William Morris had always been addressed as "Mr. Morris," everyone at the agency referred to Lastfogel as "Mr. Lastfogel." This was widely viewed on the outside as peculiar. Once, when Lastfogel brought a couple of his men to Fanny Brice's dressing room after she'd taped her weekly radio show, she exploded in exasperation. "What the hell is this goddamn crap about 'Mr. Lastfogel' this and 'Mr. Lastfogel' that? Abe, these guys have been with you twenty years! Are they always gonna be little boys?"

Answer was obviously in the affirmative.

Being Lastfogel's boys made them all brothers to each other. Most of them had grown up together, having joined the Morris office in their teens, just as Lastfogel himself had. Some of the older ones—members of the second generation of Morris men, along with Lastfogel and Bill Morris, Jr.—actually were brothers. Nat and Harry Kalcheim were Chicago boys who'd started out during the vaudeville wars with the Western Vaudeville Managers Association, the Chicago arm of the Keith Combine. Now they worked out of the Gotham office in the personal appearance division. Nat, who'd joined the Morris Agency in 1928, headed the department. His younger brother Harry had come aboard in 1941, after booking big bands and comedians to play between films in the Paramount theater circuit during the thirties.

Then there were Nat and Julius Lefkowitz, Brooklyn natives who handled the agency's finances. Nat, the controller and head of the New York office, had joined Morris with a business degree from City College and had gone on to earn his law degree from Brooklyn College night school. Julius was the firm's outside accountant, with offices just upstairs in the RKO Building.

The only one who'd left the fold was Nat and Julius's nephew, Ted Assofsky, who'd changed his name to Ted Ashley a few years back because he thought it sounded dignified. Scrawny and unfortunate-looking, with a head too big for his five-foot-five frame, Ashley had grown up in a one-room cold-water flat in Brooklyn, sleeping on a cot on one side of a worn-out curtain while his tubercular father tried to make a living as a tailor on the other. He'd studied shorthand and typing in high school at his uncles' suggestion, then ventured across the river to Manhattan for the first time in his life to take a $14-a-week job in his Uncle Julius's accounting office. That was in 1937, when he was fifteen. A year later he went into the Morris mail room, and four years after that he became an agent. And now, at age twenty-three, he'd just quit the agency to go into business for himself as a personal manager for several Morris clients, like Henny Youngman, the comedian. You had to wait your turn at the Morris office, and Ashley was eager to get ahead. But even though his job as a manager was to guide his clients' careers rather than to get them bookings, his Uncle Nat was livid.

So there was one bad egg; Ashley was the exception. The rest remained faithful, to the Morris office and to each other. None were as close as two agents in the radio department, Sam Weisbord and Phil Weltman—the Damon and Pythias of the Morris Agency.

They'd known each other since they were teenagers growing up in the Stuyvesant Heights district of Brooklyn—Phil on Greene Avenue,

Sammy in a little flat above his mother's corner store on Van Buren Street. In January 1929, when he was seventeen, Sammy had gone to work at the Morris office as an errand boy. Two years later, he'd landed a plum position as Abe Lastfogel's secretary. He was an eager kid, quick and ferretlike, with big, flashy teeth, and Lastfogel had trained him personally—taking him to meetings, sharing his office with him, letting him listen in on phone calls. Phil had gone on to New York University, but with both parents sick, he'd quit after two years and taken a job on Wall Street, clerking at a small government-bond house. He was made a trader after only a year, but when his father died, the partners told him they had a chance to buy a seat on the New York Stock Exchange, and he could have it—if he could come up with $25,000 of the purchase price. He couldn't.

A trader's day was over by four o'clock, so Weltman usually went to a gym uptown to play handball, or up to the Morris office to lounge in the lobby and chat with Sammy or some of the other fellows when they had a moment free. He was contemplating an entire lifetime as a bond trader, his one chance to become a stockbroker blown, when he ran into a guy from Morris at the gym. Why didn't he . . .

Weltman knew nothing about the agency business, but he went in to see Nat Lefkowitz anyway. He came out a trainee at $25 a week— $70 less than he was earning as a bond trader. He figured he'd see what developed. Nine months later, he was contacted by the heads of the nightclub, literary, and radio departments about joining their operations. Weisbord was in the radio department, so he chose that one. Bill Murray, who ran it, was a bald-pated bon vivant who was married to the actress Ilka Chase and read ancient Greek, among other languages. Weltman walked in one day and found him reading a book in Hebrew. "I know you're not Jewish," he said perplexedly—at which point Murray opened a drawer full of books in German, Spanish, and Italian.

When the war came, Bill Morris called Weisbord, Weltman, and his own secretary, a young fellow named Joe Magee who'd previously worked for Interior Secretary Harold Ickes, into his office and offered to get them direct commissions as ensigns in the navy. Magee accepted happily, but Weltman couldn't because he was the sole support of his invalid mother, and Weisbord wanted to help Mr. Lastfogel in the New York office of USO–Camp Shows. In 1943, when Weisbord was drafted, he got himself posted to the army's USO liaison office on Forty-second

Street with the rank of sergeant. Weltman was drafted, too, after his mother died, and sent to Camp Dix, New Jersey, a buck private.

Weltman did okay in the army—hit the beach on D-Day, won the Croix de Guerre for his role in the Battle of Saint-Lô a few weeks later, was commissioned a second lieutenant at the Battle of the Bulge. In June 1945, two months after V-E Day, he returned to New York with five battle stars, a chestful of campaign ribbons, his Croix de Guerre, and a one-month leave before being mustered out for the invasion of Japan. He was backstage at the Roxy visiting Dick Haymes, the singer, with Abe and Frances Lastfogel and Sammy Weisbord, when Haymes's manager, Billy Burton, pulled him aside. "Keep an eye on this guy," Burton said under his breath. He nodded at Weisbord, who was wearing sergeant's stripes on a uniform that may or may not have been hand-tailored, depending on how much faith you put in the office scuttlebutt. "Whaddaya mean?" Weltman asked. Burton pointed to the medals on Weltman's chest—medals that Weisbord didn't have.

Out loud Burton said, "When are you guys going out to the coast so the old man can take it easy?" Lastfogel was forty-seven.

"As soon as they get out of the army," Lastfogel said with a twinkle. It was the first either of them had heard about it.

Abe Lastfogel and Johnny Hyde could have been brothers as well—Hyde born in Russia, Lastfogel born three years later to parents who'd come from Russia. Lastfogel and Bill Morris, Jr., got along despite their differences in temperament, largely because of their shared admiration for Morris's father. But Lastfogel and Hyde were true partners. Each was known as a shrewd judge of talent, and each was numbered among the handful of honest agents in the picture business. They had similar operating styles—quiet, subdued, restrained, their dignity a silent rebuke to the popular image of the talent agent as a heartless bloodsucker in carny garb. And they complemented each other, Hyde working the picture business while Lastfogel straddled Broadway and Hollywood.

Most of the clients Lastfogel favored with his personal attention were either nightclub comedians like Danny Thomas, whom he'd discovered working the 5100 Club in Chicago, or writers like Garson Kanin, whose *Born Yesterday* was one of the top Broadway hits of 1946. But Lastfogel and Hyde often worked in tandem to get a client established in pictures. A case in point was Danny Kaye, a promising young comic who'd been stealing the spotlight in the 1941 Broadway musical *Lady in the Dark* when Lastfogel talked Sam Goldwyn into seeing him. Other producers seemed interested in Kaye as well, but Lastfogel and Hyde saw Goldwyn as their best bet. "Goldwyn is ripe and eager to make stars with comparative unknowns," Hyde explained in a May 1941 letter to Bill Morris in New York, "and of course we believe with Goldwyn's help Danny must reach the top in movies." Launching a funnyman was serious business, however, and Kaye, with his angular face and his prominent nose, presented a familiar problem: extraordinary talent in a not-so-appealing package. Goldwyn was watching screen tests when he hit on the solution—have his hair dyed blond. The next step was to pair him with Dinah Shore in *Up in Arms*, a rewrite of the twenties musical that had been the basis for *Whoopee!*, Goldwyn's 1930 hit with Eddie Cantor. Follow that with a big publicity buildup, and now Danny Kaye was a movie star.

Despite their teamwork, there was one area where Lastfogel and Hyde didn't agree. Lastfogel may have lived in hotels, but he seemed thoroughly domesticated. Hyde was a ladies' man, his life a sea of tempestuous affairs and vitriolic divorce suits. His first marriage, to a Philadelphia dame named Florence Harper, ended in divorce after the birth of two sons, Donald and Jay. In 1928 he'd married again, this time to a Ziegfeld *Follies* girl, but their union foundered twelve years later amid sensational charges of alcoholism and adultery. Did she in fact consume two bottles of gin a day? Did he send three people to their Bel Air mansion one August morning to put her in a straitjacket and carry her off to the state insane hospital at Camarillo, where she was forced to disrobe and perform "all sorts of inexplicable gyrations" in the nude to satisfy a panel of alleged psychiatrists? These were the questions Los Angeles newspaper readers had to ponder as their case came before Superior Court Judge Parker Wood in the summer of 1941.

Hyde won his divorce, his case buttressed by testimony from the superintendent of the Century Apartments in New York, who testified that Anne Hyde not only got drunk almost every day, she also terrorized the elevator boys, coming home plastered at night and accusing them of snitching on her drinking habits to her husband. The judge ordered him to fix her with a $24,000 trust fund paying $250 a month, which wasn't even enough to keep her in servants. (Hyde himself was reportedly making $250,000 a year.) Two years later, he wed his former secretary, twenty-four-year-old Mozelle Cravens, who sacrificed a $150-a-week salary and a nascent screen career at Columbia to become the bride of an agent twice her age.

Now there was trouble again, the third Mrs. Hyde apparently having difficulty accommodating herself to the fact that her husband, though a good provider, had a nasty temper and an incurably wandering eye. The situation deteriorated dramatically one night in June 1945, when (as she later maintained in court papers) Hyde attacked her in loutish fashion—hitting her across the face, threatening to throw her out of the house, locking her in the bedroom, running downstairs for a butcher knife screaming he was going to slit her throat and cut out her heart. In July, two months shy of their second anniversary and less than a year after the arrival of their little son Jimmy, she filed for divorce. The following spring, she took him back.

Whatever his drawbacks as a husband, Hyde was charming and debonair on the dance floor, with a jockey's build and a handsome face. Where Lastfogel was stolid and built like a fireplug, Hyde was graceful and delicate, like a toy person. It was said around the office that he signed more starlets with his dick than most guys did with their fountain pens. One of those starlets later reported that the dick was as tiny as the rest of him, but no matter. His clout was as big as any man's.

It was champ clout, no question. Nineteen forty-six was a banner year for Hollywood, and Hyde and Lew Wasserman of MCA were the top agents in town. Hyde handled June Allyson, a newcomer whose appearance in a string of goopy M-G-M musicals was a sure sign the studio was grooming her for stardom, and Esther Williams, M-G-M's glamorous aquabelle, the pinup girl with the golden freestyle. He made the deal with Columbia for *The Jolson Story*, starring B-picture actor Larry Parks, which became one of the year's top-grossing films and won Al Jolson a new generation of fans. (Columbia boss Harry Cohn had wanted Danny Thomas to play Jolson, but only if he consented to a nose job; Thomas declined.) But his hottest stars were Lana Turner and Rita Hayworth, two bombshells whose 1946 releases captured perfectly the anxiety the country was starting to feel as the swell of victory subsided.

Lana Turner was the starlet Warner Bros. had promoted as the Sweater Girl, on the rationale that people would find it easier to remember her breasts than her name. She'd been discovered at fifteen, sipping a Coke at a soda fountain across from Hollywood High School, by Billy Wilkerson, a debonair gent who'd started the *Hollywood Reporter* and the Tro-cadero Café on the Sunset Strip. Wilkerson sent her to the Zeppo Marx Agency—Zeppo having quit the act and followed his instincts—which sent her to director Mervyn LeRoy, who put her to work at $50 a week, $40 more than her mother was making in a beauty parlor. She followed LeRoy from Warner Bros. to M-G-M in 1937, and the following year she was teamed with Mickey Rooney and Judy Garland in *Love Finds Andy Hardy*. Hyde bought out her agency contract along the way.

On the day she turned twenty, the Sweater Girl impulsively dashed off to Nevada with bandleader Artie Shaw and got married. There was apparently some fantasy chatter involving a home and some kids and a white picket fence, but it was not a smart move career-wise, a point Louella Parsons did not hesitate to make in her column. "If Lana Turner will behave herself and not go completely berserk she is headed for a top spot in motion pictures," Parsons wrote after the wedding. ". . . Lana, of course, has never been in any scandal, but she has always acted hastily and been guided more by her own ideas than by any advice any studio gave her." This little scolding was doubtless meant to buttress the efforts of Louis B. Mayer, who reportedly paid a visit to the groom and advised him not to get his star property pregnant. It happened any-way, but by the time Lana discovered it she'd already filed for divorce. She turned to Johnny Hyde, who told her that if she didn't want to give up her career, she'd either have to go back to her husband or have an abortion. She was hospitalized soon afterward for "exhaustion." Shaw learned the real reason through the grapevine.

The top spot eluded Turner during the war years, but in May 1945, shooting started on *The Postman Always Rings Twice*, a noir tale of mur-der and romance based on the James M. Cain novel, which the studio had bought eleven years earlier. In the film, Turner's all-white wardrobe is the disguise of a murderous sex kitten with a yen for respectability. As the lonely wife of the middle-aged proprietor of a California roadside café, she takes up with a handsome drifter (John Garfield) who comes to work as a handyman. They could run away, but in the interest of financial security, she talks her new beau into snuffing the husband instead. The man-trap theme is set up by a handy pair of shots—Turner's entrance, when Garfield stoops to retrieve a tube of lipstick as it rolls across the floor to her feet, and her exit, when she expires in a sickening car crash and the lipstick drops from her lifeless hand.

But Lana Turner was nothing to Rita Hayworth. The former Mar-

garita Cansino was a vaudeville kid, daughter of Volga Hayworth and
Eduardo Cansino, a Spanish dancer whose bookings had been handled
by the Morris office in the twenties. As a teenager, Rita had passed as
her father's wife in the Mexican casinos and offshore gambling ships
where they worked as a dance team; later, she confided that he'd used
her as a wife as well. The Dancing Cansinos were a hit at Agua
Caliente, the opulent Tijuana gambling resort part-owned by Twentieth
Century's Joe Schenck and frequented by his Hollywood pals. Rita was
shown off at some of Schenck's private parties, and at fifteen she was
"discovered" by the production chief at Fox. The year was 1934.

At Fox, she met a slick operator named Eddie Judson, a former car
salesman more than double her age, who landed her a contract at
Columbia after Fox dropped her, eloped with her when she was eighteen, and supervised her metamorphosis into star material through an
excruciating regimen of dieting, exercise, voice lessons, and electrolysis
to heighten her forehead. Remade into a ravishing American beauty,
renamed so she wouldn't be restricted to exotic-Latin parts, the
painfully shy Rita was then transformed by *Life* magazine into America's
wartime pinup, the fantasy date of every lonesome GI with a hard-on.
Meanwhile, she later alleged, Judson was hiding her money away and
threatening to throw acid on her face if she left him: He'd created her,
and he could destroy her. She divorced him anyway, and after a fling
with Victor Mature, she took up with Orson Welles, who'd seen *Life*'s
"Dream Girl" photo on location in Brazil and come back to Hollywood
to marry her.

They were wed while she was shooting *Cover Girl*, a Jerome Kern–Ira
Gershwin musical about a nightclub dancer who makes it as fashion
model, only to discover that love is worth more than glamour and success—a lesson Hayworth already knew but was having difficulty putting
to use. Now established as one of Columbia's most alluring stars, she
settled into a ten-room house in the verdant Brentwood section of West
Los Angeles and gave birth to a daughter she named Rebecca. But by
the time she showed up to make *Gilda*, Welles's overwork and infideli-
ties and her own drunken, jealous rages were beginning to mar the
happy picture.

The story of a voluptuous temptress at a Buenos Aires casino who
spurns her husband, only to be brought low by the man she loves, *Gilda*
was Rita Hayworth's life retold as twisted film noir parable. Here was a
dame who could turn wet dreams into nightmares, a vixen who'd destroy

every man who came near her if she wasn't destroyed herself. That was a job for Glenn Ford, a fellow Morris client just back from the marines, playing a down-on-his-luck gambler named Johnny Farrell who's rescued by the casino's proprietor and put to work as his right-hand man. The wantonly amoral Gilda—"If I'd been a ranch, they'd name me the Bar Nothing," she purrs—turns out to be not just the proprietor's wife but Johnny's ex-lover. Passion builds. When the husband is given up for dead after a plane crash, Gilda weds Johnny, only to discover that out of loyalty to his boss, he intends never to touch her. Driven to hysteria by his rejection, she retorts with a devastating striptease and a song that says it all:

Put the blame on Mame, boys,
Put the blame on Mame.

Released in February 1946, *Gilda* was a huge hit at the box office, and it made Rita Hayworth a top star. Johnny Hyde's response was to tell Harry Cohn he wanted to renegotiate her contract. It was a predictable request under the circumstances, except that Hyde was proposing she get a cut of the profits. Cohn was giving Al Jolson 50 percent of the profits to *The Jolson Story*—Jack Warner had offered to buy it outright for $200,000, a sum Cohn wasn't prepared to match—but that was for the rights to his life story; actors hadn't been cut in since the studio consolidation in the late twenties. Cohn went ballistic. He still had a year on this broad, he reminded Hyde, and if he had to, he'd put her in every B-picture he had.

Hyde looked at him coolly. "No, you won't," Hyde said. "You won't put her in anything."

"Whaddaya mean?"

"You won't put her in anything," Hyde explained, "because we'll give her a thousand a week to do nothing until her contract runs out." He didn't bother to mention that they could take her to Europe and put her to work there. Plenty of producers would be thrilled to go to Europe to make a picture with Rita Hayworth.

Hyde heard more bellowing, the gist of which was that he should get his ass off the lot and stay off.

It was a gutsy play. Hyde had other clients at Columbia (Glenn Ford, whose next picture was a melodrama called *Framed*; Ann Miller, the budget Rita Hayworth Cohn used for his B-musicals), and life would be harder for them if Cohn banned their agent from the lot. On the other hand, Hyde's clients and connections made him a formidable opponent, and actors had learned that an agent who got himself banned was an agent who was pushing the limit on their behalf.

Hayworth might have been volatile in her private life, but she was a pro on the set: She'd missed one day when she and Welles separated during the shooting of *Gilda,* and the next morning she'd turned up dry-eyed and ready to work. But shortly after production started on her next picture, an expensive Technicolor musical called *Down to Earth,* she declared herself too ill to go forward. She also turned down a role as the sinister nightclub singer in *Dead Reckoning,* a property Cohn was so jazzed about he'd gotten Humphrey Bogart on a loan-out from Warner Bros. to be her costar.

Cohn was wise to Hayworth's game: Feigning illness a couple of weeks into a shoot, with the sets built and film in the can and cast and crew standing by and costs mounting hourly—this had gotten to be the standard gambit for stars on the make for a sweeter deal. And he had no doubt that Hyde had put her up to it. But what could he do? Rita Hayworth was the first star he'd been able to develop. Columbia had started out on Poverty Row, the celluloid shantytown around Sunset and Beachwood, and while it had outgrown its origins, it had never really escaped them. Cohn could rant and fume, but in the end he had to come around.

Which meant that after completing *Down to Earth* and one more film, Hayworth would receive, on top of her weekly salary, 25 percent of the net of every picture she made. She'd also have script approval—something stars had been fighting to get for years. On the advice of the Morris office, she set up her own company, the Beckworth Corporation (a contraction of Becky and Hayworth), to handle the money. Seven years earlier, she'd been doing bit parts in potboilers at $300 a week, $50 of which went straight to her acting coach; now people were saying she'd soon be one of the richest women in Hollywood.

But the impact of the Beckworth deal went way beyond Rita Hayworth's purse. In getting script approval and a piece of the action, Hyde was shifting the balance in Hollywood. Charles K. Feldman, who handled Claudette Colbert and Irene Dunne, had already been high-spotted in the *Saturday Evening Post* for applying the package deal to pictures—putting a screenwriter client together with a producer client and a director client and several actor clients to create a film that played in movie houses as a Charles K. Feldman Production. "Some Hollywood prophets see this as an omen of the day when the agents will run the studios," the *Post* had concluded in 1942, "but that time is probably remote." Hyde had just ratcheted it one notch closer.

As of yet, however, no one had figured out how to control the fame that gave actors and their agents their power. Fame has a fury all its own, Hayworth discovered in July of 1946, when she learned that the atomic test bomb that had just blasted Bikini Atoll had her name on it. American servicemen, paying tribute to the most explosive force they knew, had dubbed the thing Gilda and adorned it with her pinup before dropping it onto the remote Pacific paradise, which it obliterated along with the seventy-five surplus warships and most of the forty-eight hundred animals that had been assembled for the occasion. Rita went hysterical at the news.

NOT EVERY DEAL COULD BE AS BIG AS BECKWORTH. THE NIGHTCLUB BUSIness provided much of the Morris Agency's bread and butter, and if it wasn't as big on the coast as it was in Gotham, it was still a regular source of commissions. There was Slapsy Maxie's, a celebrity-studded watering hole on Wilshire that boasted headliners on the order of Joe E. Lewis. The Trocadero closed in 1946, but Ciro's and the Mocambo, an intimate spot much favored by the movie set, still lent glamour to the Strip. Over on Hollywood Boulevard, a raucous tourist joint called the Florentine Gardens drew crowds to see performers like Sophie Tucker and Harry Richman and his band. There were bookings in the hinterlands as well, in burgs like Frisco and Seattle and the godforsaken desert hamlet of Las Vegas, Nevada.

Vegas had changed since Bill Morris took the Ruben boys there. Much of the thanks were due to a small-time hotel man named Tom Hull, who was driving out of town one day on Highway 91 when he had a flat, found himself counting cars while waiting for help to arrive, and ended up convinced that this would be a first-rate place for a resort. The result was El Rancho Vegas, a Western-themed establishment with rustic cabins arrayed around a swimming pool, a dining room, and a casino. In 1942 El Rancho was joined by a second ranch-style resort, the Last Frontier, which boasted wagon-wheel chandeliers and authentic pioneer furnishings and offered dinner shows for modern-day cowpokes who wanted a little diversion between crap games. In January

1944, fifteen months after it opened, the Morris office provided the Last Frontier with the first big-time performer Las Vegas had ever seen: Sophie Tucker, who strode onstage in spike-heeled cowboy boots and a ten-gallon hat, a pair of six-guns strapped to her ample hips.

Meanwhile, Benny Siegel, Meyer Lansky's old partner from Prohibition days, had moved out to Hollywood to look after the business interests of his East Coast confederates. Tall and square-jawed, nattily attired in silk shirts and cashmere sport coats, Siegel joined Hillcrest and became a regular at movie colony restaurants like the Brown Derby in Hollywood and Romanoff's in Beverly Hills. He went out with starlets—Lana Turner, Ava Gardner. He played the horses at Santa Anita, the palm-shaded racetrack out past Pasadena, where George Raft and Jimmy Durante were regulars and Louis Mayer stabled his mounts. Meyer Lansky, who'd relocated to Miami, sent a roly-poly gunman named Mickey Cohen to be his henchman and bodyguard, and with Cohen's help, Siegel succeeded in pulling together the West Coast gambling operations for his friends back East.

But Siegel had a problem. The boys had been operating some gambling ships just beyond the three-mile limit, two off Long Beach and two more off Santa Monica. Siegel himself had owned a piece of the most luxurious of them, the *Rex*, run by Tony Cornero, the hood who'd started the Meadows in Vegas in 1931. But California's new attorney general, Earl Warren, was cracking down on vice, and after moving against the dog tracks, he'd figured out a way to scuttle the gambling ships, too. Cornero actually managed to fight off a boarding party, but after a ten-day seige, the *Rex* ran low on supplies and had to surrender. His dream of a Monte Carlo on the ocean dead, Siegel started thinking about Las Vegas.

Vegas was a six-hour drive through the blistering Mojave Desert from Los Angeles—considerably less convenient than the syndicate pleasure palaces outside Miami and New Orleans. But it was blessed with a welcoming array of pliant politicians who'd had the thoughtfulness to legalize gambling statewide. Siegel had already established that people would sail out into the ocean to gamble; why not trek through the desert instead? He could even turn the town's isolation to his advantage. All you needed for sucker bait was some big-name stars and the promise of a good time, and once you had them, there was nothing for them to do but gamble. He knew George Wood of the Morris office through Meyer Lansky and Jimmy Blue-Eyes Alo and the East Coast crowd, so he knew he'd have no trouble finding stars.

Siegel wasn't the only one who smelled opportunity in Vegas; other people were said to be scouting properties, too—Frank Sinatra, Mae West, even Roy Rogers. But Siegel moved fast. In December 1945 he took over the El Cortez Hotel downtown, then flipped it at a 25 percent profit. Then he hit upon the lavish new gambling resort the *Hollywood Reporter*'s Billy Wilkerson had started on the highway to Los Angeles, out past the El Rancho and the Last Frontier. Wilkerson was running low on dough, so Siegel and his partners agreed to put in most of the cash from the sale of the El Cortez in exchange for a two-thirds share in the venture, which became known as the Flamingo Hotel.

That summer, while Billy Wilkerson sounded the trumpet against the Red menace in the *Hollywood Reporter*, printing the names and party numbers of prominent screenwriters with the point-blank question, "Are you a member of the Communist Party?" Siegel rushed to complete his new resort. The Flamingo took shape rapidly—fine Italian marble, exotic woods, sunken tub and porcelain bidet in every bath. Inevitably there were setbacks: The boiler room had to be enlarged, the air-cooling system kept breaking down, the luxurious master suite was bisected by a support beam less than six feet above the floor. The budget mushroomed from $1 million to $2 million to $5 million and more, with Lansky and his associates picking up the tab. But by Thursday, December 26, 1946, everything was set.

George Wood had come through for him, with some help from Fred Elswit, one of the new boys in the Beverly Hills office. Elswit was the thirty-one-year-old son of Abe Lastfogel's older sister Sarah, whose husband owned a pharmacy in Brooklyn. He was a good-looking guy, tall and friendly and warm, with the same kinky blond hair that Lastfogel and everybody else in the family had. He'd joined the agency in the mid-thirties, after graduating from City College in New York with a civil engineering degree and learning that engineering firms didn't hire Jews. Frances didn't like people in the family coming to her Abe for jobs, but this time Abe's sister Bessie had put her foot down. Fred had served in the Army Signal Corps during the war and done a stint afterward with the occupation forces in Japan. He'd gotten his discharge in September and come back to run the agency's West Coast personal appearance department, just in time for the opening of the Flamingo.

Not that the place was exactly ready. The casino, the restaurant, the bar, and the nightclub were finished, and laborers working under blinding floodlights the night before had covered the desert with topsoil and stuck it with date palms and cork trees and shrubbery and smoothed it over with thick green sod. But the lobby was still lousy with carpenters and painters, and the hotel rooms were months away from completion. There were plenty of black-chip gamblers on hand—black chips being the $100 kind—but the dealers were untested, so a lot of high rollers won big and then retired to the El Rancho or the Last Frontier to gamble away their winnings. And a sudden storm in Los Angeles grounded the TWA Constellation Siegel had engaged to fly out a much-ballyhooed contingent of stars—Lucille Ball, Ava Gardner, Veronica Lake, Peter Lawford, George Raft—for the final night of his three-night opening spree. The Flamingo's premiere was shaping up as a disaster.

And yet he seemingly pulled it out. Most of the advertised stars didn't show, but George Raft drove out in his Cadillac, and Vivian Blaine and Sonny Tufts made it, too. The former maître d' at Ciro's and the Troc was on hand to preside over the dining room, where diners could chow down on classy victuals like chateaubriand bon viveur. For the floor show they had two of Abe Lastfogel's favorite clients—Rose Marie, child star of the old NBC radio show "Baby Rose Marie," and Siegel's old friend Jimmy Durante. With George Jessel as master of ceremonies and Xavier Cugat providing the music, the crowd got a prime lineup of big-city entertainment. Rose Marie came out in a pink gown and did her gravel-voiced Durante imitation; Durante ripped up a $1,600 piano and scattered Cugat's sheet music across the stage. It was still mighty lonely out there in the desert, but inside the Flamingo it looked as if Benny Siegel and the Morris office just might succeed in giving the people of this fair land, in their mad, yes, suicidal rush to have a good time, a place to rush to.

4

VAUDEO

Washington/Los Angeles/New York, 1947-1949

IT WAS ON THE MORNING OF JULY 21, 1947, THAT BILL MORRIS, JR., WAS first named. Testimony came from one Walter S. Steele, ace Red hunter and all-around patriot. Steele had been diligent in his capacity as national security chief of the American Coalition of Patriotic, Civic, and Fraternal Societies, a league that included the American War Mothers, the Eugenics Society of Northern California, the Order of Colonial Lords of Manors in America, the Southern Vigilant Intelligence Association, and so forth. For nearly twenty years he'd studied subversives, read their literature, noted their leaders and followers, deposited his findings into ever more voluminous files. Now he was spilling before the House Committee on Un-American Activities, Honorable J. Parnell Thomas presiding.

Steele had appeared before the committee once before, in 1938, the year the House had created it at the behest of Samuel Dickstein, New York City congressman aghast at the proliferation of pro-Hitler youth camps and goose-stepping Nazi symps. The committee had been taken over by east Texas Congressman Martin Dies, a man more worried about Reds in the labor movement than about the Heil Hitler crowd. Steele had given him the rundown on hundreds of tainted organizations, from the American Civil Liberties Union to the Camp Fire Girls.

Nine years had passed, and the committee, invigorated by the Republicans' big win in the 1946 congressional elections, was eager to hear more. What were the Communists after? Was it the secret of the atom bomb, rumored to be the target of various Soviet spy rings? Was it the Congress of Industrial Organizations, said to be riddled with Soviet agents bent on fomenting strikes, chaos, and revolution? Or was it the Hollywood movie colony, recently characterized by committee member John Rankin, Jew-hating Democrat from Mississippi, as "the greatest hotbed of subversive activities in the United States"?

Hollywood had already been softened up by Jack Tenney, the state senator who ran his own little HUAC in Sacramento, and by the anti-Communist goons of the International Alliance of Theatrical Stage Employees, led by a former American Federation of Labor troubleshooter named Roy Brewer. While Brewer's stagehands were clubbing down striking members of a rival left-wing union outside the studio gates, some of Hollywood's better-paid citizens—among them Walt Disney, Ginger Rogers, John Wayne, and Sam Wood, the militantly anti-Communist director of such small-town melodramas as *Our Town* and *Kings Row*—had formed a noisy organization called the Motion Picture Alliance for the Preservation of American Ideals. Now the big boys in Washington seemed ready to move in.

Parnell Thomas had laid the groundwork in May, when he led a handful of HUAC members and investigators on a field expedition to the Biltmore Hotel in downtown Los Angeles. Thomas (real name Feeney), the pug-nosed son of a Jersey City police commissioner, had been invited to town by Sam Wood and his Motion Picture Alliance. Like Wood, he saw Communists everywhere, particularly in the New Deal, and the witnesses he heard in Los Angeles confirmed his worst fears.

Robert Taylor told them that government officials had kept him from going into the navy until he finished *Song of Russia*, an M-G-M picture that Thomas promptly denounced as "Communist propaganda." Lela Rogers revealed how screenwriter Dalton Trumbo had tried to get her Ginger to spout Red propaganda in the movie *Tender Comrade*. ("Share and share alike—that's democracy" was the Commie line.) Meanwhile, a couple of miles away at Gilmore Stadium, 27,000 people turned out at a rally for Henry Wallace, last of the New Dealers to leave the Truman cabinet and a likely candidate for Truman's job in the next election. Wallace, who'd been sacked as Secretary of Commerce after attacking Truman's new "Get Tough with Russia" policy at an ICCASP rally in New York the year before, denounced the committee as "a group of bigots."

Now, in Washington, Steele was feeding them names, hundreds of names—names of petition signers, rally sponsors, rally speakers, front-group officers, front-group members, New Dealers, One-Worlders, Soviet-Firsters, dupes, pigeons, pinkos, Reds. He identified Bill Morris (along with Olivia de Havilland, Lillian Hellman, screenwriter John Howard Lawson, Paul Robeson, and others) as a director of ICCASP, the Independent Citizens Committee of the Arts, Sciences, and Professions, a national organization that had supported progressive Democrats in the 1946 elections. HICCASP, its Hollywood branch, had been particularly active—and spectacularly unsuccessful—in that contest, which ended in a statewide Republican sweep that carried Richard Nixon into the House and onto the committee. As Nixon and the others hung on his words, Steele declared ICCASP a Communist front, founded by Reds and serving their ends.

He also named Morris as cofounder and vice chairman of the National Council of American-Soviet Friendship, which the committee had fingered in 1944 as "the Communist Party's principal front for all things Russian." In 1946, the committee had cited its chairman, Corliss Lamont, and its director, Richard Morford, for contempt after they refused to hand over its financial records. Lamont made a particularly tempting target—author, lecturer, socialist, humanist, a man with impeccable credentials in the Ivy League and the upper crust. His father, Thomas W. Lamont, was one of the most powerful men on Wall Street: chairman of the executive committee of J. P. Morgan & Company, adviser to Presidents Wilson and Hoover, friend to Henry Luce of *Time* and Arthur Sulzberger of the *New York Times*, leader of the failed attempt to rally the market in the 1929 crash. "Mr. Morgan speaks to Mr. Lamont," it was said, "and Mr. Lamont speaks to the people." Now Corliss Lamont could be found lecturing in philosophy at Columbia while spreading the gospel of friendship with the Soviets. Here was no swarthy Semite, but a blue-blooded American traitor—or so it would seem—to class and country alike.

Anyone who knew Bill Morris could tell you he'd fall in with the likes of Corliss Lamont. Civilized, urbane men, they shared a privileged background and an idealistic outlook. Lamont, whose father had been among the handful of Republican business leaders to argue for recognition of the Bolshevik government after the Russian Revolution, had written two books on the place, *Russia Day by Day* and *The Peoples of the Soviet Union*, a laudatory survey that looked to the land of Cossacks and commissars for lessons in ethnic harmony. He'd led earlier pro-Soviet groups, all of which Steele suggested took orders from Moscow, before founding the National Council with Morris and three others—Episcopal clergyman William Howard Melish, Rockefeller Institute biochemist Harry Grundfest, and George Marshall of the National Federation for Constitutional Liberties.

Morris's feelings for Russia weren't merely political. He'd just gotten the agency to book the famed Russian cantor Moshe Kusevitsky on a tour of the States, though the guys in the personal appearance department were no longer used to dealing in cantors and the results were not what they might have been. Things had changed since his father's day. Yet when E. J. Kahn, Jr., had come around for his *New Yorker* profile the year before, Morris showed him the eighteenth-century map of the world that hung in his office and remarked, "Father used to say that when you booked acts into these spots marked *Terra Incognita*, you'd have real peace in the world." As far as he was concerned, the *terra* most *incognita* to Americans was Soviet Russia.

It had been respectable to be pro-Soviet when Stalin was an ally, and the left had taken Roosevelt's victory in 1944 as a sign of triumph, for the New Deal at home and One World abroad. In February 1946, when the National Council held its Washington's Birthday–Red Army Day banquet at the Waldorf-Astoria, President Truman's newly designated envoy to Moscow, General Walter Bedell Smith, pronounced his comradeship with the leaders of the Soviet army. But two weeks later, Winston Churchill stood next to Truman and warned of an "iron curtain" descending across Europe. The National Council's new director was summoned before HUAC the next day and shouted down when he objected to the committee's demands. By June, when the council's board elected Morris vice chairman, public opinion was swinging against them with dizzying speed. It was as if Roosevelt's ideals had been revealed as some kind of wanton woman, the temptress who had to be destroyed. The cold war was on, and Bill Morris had picked the wrong side.

A year had gone by since then. It was the summer of 1947. As Walter Steele named names in Washington, committee investigators were visiting the Hollywood motion picture studios to suggest that suspected Commies be fired. *Newsweek*, in a cover story headlined "Enemy Within the Gates," denounced dozens of Communists and fellow travelers, from Corliss Lamont to Lillian Hellman. HICCASP ripped itself apart trying to compose a unity letter that included a statement of anti-Communism. Ronald Reagan, president of the Screen Actors Guild, turned informer in his zeal to rid the organization of Communists. By the time the committee issued its subpoenas in September, Roy Brewer's union of stagehands had broken their rival, and with it the left's only link to the Hollywood proletariat. But there was still the Screen Writers Guild, which Thomas had announced was "lousy with Communists," and that was where the committee directed its spotlight.

It was another Tuesday evening at NBC Radio City in Hollywood, and Phil Weltman flushed with pride as Carmen Dragon and his orchestra took it away with "Rock-a-bye Baby," theme song of "The Baby Snooks Show." He'd just come out to the coast to manage the show, and every detail of the trip was etched in his memory. First, the Twentieth Century Limited out of Grand Central Station, a chrome-and-steel bullet for the sixteen-hour nonstop to Chicago. There he'd stepped off for a visit to Tallulah Bankhead, one of his favorite clients, laid up with shingles. From Chicago he'd taken the Super Chief overnight to Los Angeles, arriving at nine in the morning at Union Station, which looked like some Hollywood set-designer's idea of a Franciscan mission with trains running into it. The date was October 12, 1947.

Sam Weisbord, his best friend from Brooklyn, was there to meet him, flashing his toothsome grin and sporting the darkest tan Weltman had ever seen. Next to Sammy was Morris Stoller, a slender and bespectacled accountant who'd been sent out by Nat Lefkowitz, the controller, to run the West Coast office. Like Sammy and Phil, Stoller was part of the third generation of Morris men, the group a decade or so behind Abe Lastfogel and Johnny Hyde and Bill Morris, Jr. First Sammy, then Stoller, now Phil—the West Coast office was filling up with guys from New York.

Weisbord and Stoller drove him out Sunset to his new home—past the dusty Mexican tourist-trap plaza where the city had gotten its start, past Aimee Semple McPherson's five-thousand-seat Angelus Temple, past the streamlined NBC studios at Sunset and Vine, straight through Hollywood to the spot where Sunset curves to skirt the hills. There, at the foot of a winding lane, they disembarked in front of the Chateau Marmont and led him through pointed arches and past cloistered gardens to a four-room apartment overlooking the Sunset Strip, with Schwab's Pharmacy and Alla Nazimova's Garden of Allah bungalow complex laid out below. The Lastfogels took him to dinner that evening, and then they dropped by to see Fanny Brice in her house on Comstock Avenue, just off Sunset in Westwood. Fanny was in bed, but she was always glad to see Abe and Frances. They introduced her to Weltman. She eyed him with a quizzical look, then stepped back and said, "Well, what do you think? Did you ever think you'd meet someone like me?"

"Not in my wildest dreams," Weltman replied.

That was what they'd brought him out from New York for, to take care of Fanny Brice. Every week, Fanny transformed herself from a fiftyish show gal who'd been through three husbands to the impish little girl who regaled her radio audience on "The Baby Snooks Show." Weltman's job was to make sure it all went smoothly—the script, the rehearsals, the broadcast itself. After that first night she'd virtually adopted him, having him over for dinner, giving him furniture, trying to teach him about art, decorating his apartment just as she'd decorated the grander quarters of Eddie Cantor and Katharine Hepburn. Weltman worked for her and for his other shows day and night, scheduling his time in fifteen-minute increments until nearly midnight, breaking only for lunch at the Brown Derby on Vine and for dinner at Fanny's, on the nights when her cook called and asked what he felt like eating.

Sammy Weisbord lived in the apartment immediately upstairs, on the fifth floor of the Chateau. Late at night, trying to unwind, they'd walk the Strip together, past Ciro's and the Mocambo, past the talent agencies in their fake-colonial bungalows, past the pricey antique shops and gift shops and salons, past the haberdashery where Mickey Cohen made his headquarters. Benny Siegel had just been shot dead on his mistress's chintz sofa in Beverly Hills, apparently on account of the gambling losses at the Flamingo, and Cohen had declared himself king of the L.A. underworld. It was an exotic scene—headlights and car horns swooping past, raucous crowds milling about outside the nightclubs, the jagged hills rising up on one side, the lights of the city spilling off on the other, cedars and jasmine scenting the air, more like the Riviera than anything two Brooklyn boys had ever seen.

California had turned Sammy into a health nut. On weekends he lay on the beach until his skin turned burnt orange. Every morning he was up at six for an hour-long workout at the gym. At the office he was a dynamo, speedy and efficient and maniacally dedicated, his long, lean face a study in charm. He idolized Abe Lastfogel. Every day he had lunch with Mr. Lastfogel at Hillcrest. Nearly every night he joined Mr. and Mrs. Lastfogel for dinner. Lastfogel was too much a creature of habit to make this any great luxury: He went to the same seven restaurants every week in strict rotation, and the moment he finished eating he leapt from the table and said he'd meet you outside. Yet four or five nights a week, Sammy was there. Weltman was beginning to think this a little odd.

A couple of times, when they were walking the Strip late at night, he told Sammy so. It wasn't natural, Phil said, wasn't what he'd do even with his own father. Sammy wasn't interested. He'd gotten his start as Mr. Lastfogel's secretary, and now he'd become Mr. Lastfogel's surrogate, the guy who kept his eye on everything, the guy you went to if you wanted the Boss's ear. Not just his business surrogate either, more like a surrogate son.

Weltman's boss—the boss of the agency's entire West Coast radio operation—was George Gruskin, an eccentric programming genius whose personality was as far removed from the clubby bonhomie of Bill Murray and his second-in-command in the New York office, Wally Jordan, as it was possible to be. Gruskin dressed conservatively enough to be a General Motors executive, but he was an eccentric character, with Coke-bottle glasses and a high-pitched voice that was always screeching on about some new idea. He had a mercurial personality as well—animated and gregarious one day, down in the dumps another. But he'd been responsible for some tremendous successes, like "Burns and Allen" and the long-running NBC comedy "Duffy's Tavern" ("where the elite meet to eat"), whose star, Florence Halop, had become his wife. And though he was only thirty-seven, he operated with autonomy. When Bill Murray failed to read a long memo he'd prepared detailing ways to keep "Burns and Allen" going, he refused to write another memo to anyone on any subject ever. Sammy Weisbord didn't approve—but Gruskin was valuable to the company, so Mr. Lastfogel let him get away with it.

THE SUBPOENAS, BRIGHT PINK DOCUMENTS BORNE BY DEPUTY U.S. MAR-shals, went out to forty-three people in Hollywood, from fervent anti-

Communists like Adolphe Menjou to known party leaders like John Howard Lawson. When nineteen who considered themselves targets— twelve screenwriters, five directors, one actor, and a producer—met at Lewis Milestone's house and declared their refusal to cooperate, the picture colony rallied to their support. HICCASP organized defense rallies and held a Thought-Control Conference at the Beverly Hills Hotel. John Huston, William Wyler, and screenwriter Philip Dunne launched a Committee for the First Amendment and garnered an impressive roster of stars—Humphrey Bogart, Lauren Bacall, Rita Hayworth, Katharine Hepburn, Groucho Marx, Frank Sinatra. The celebrities who packed Ira Gershwin's house for the committee's first meeting were excited, even giddy in their defiance: Here was a fight they could win.

The Morris Agency had just negotiated a new contract for one of the nineteen, Ring Lardner, Jr., who was now getting $2,000 a week to write screenplays for Otto Preminger at Fox. Lardner had come to Hollywood in 1935 to do publicity for Selznick International Pictures and ended up working with Budd Schulberg on *A Star Is Born*. Schulberg had recruited him into the party, and when Lardner and his friend Michael Kanin sold a script called *Woman of the Year* to M-G-M, Kanin's younger brother Garson had arranged for the Morris office to represent them. The deal was sealed with a state visit by Lastfogel and Hyde, who rode out to Kanin's modest Westwood abode in a chauffeured black limousine, gave them some papers to sign, and rode back. In 1944, when Lardner's brother was killed in Germany, Lastfogel pulled strings and got him on a plane to New York to be with his mother. But until the Fox contract came up, that was about the extent of his contact with the agency.

Lardner had tried to get Morris's legal department to delete the standard morals clause—a vague provision forbidding the signer to do anything to "shock, insult or offend the community or ridicule public morals or decency or prejudice"—from his contract. His friend Dalton Trumbo had gotten it taken out at Metro, and it seemed like a good idea in case the Red-menace stuff got any worse. But Fox wouldn't budge, so Lardner signed anyway.

Nobody seemed to care about the subpoena in any case; Lardner already had a new picture to work on. When he and the others flew to Washington, seven thousand people turned out at the Shrine Auditorium to see them off. But on his Sunday night radio broadcast, Walter Winchell issued a frantic call to arms against the Soviet threat. "They are measuring the American Republic for its coffin," he intoned. ". . . Wake up, Americans. Wake up, or you and your children will die in your sleep. . . . " As the National Council of American-Soviet Friendship prepared a bitter but ineffectual rejoinder, the Hollywood nineteen arrived in Washington to find their hotel rooms bugged, the phones clicking ominously, and the lobby full of hovering strangers. Yet when their lawyers asked Eric Johnston, president of the Motion Picture Association of America (the old Hays Office, now headed by the ex-president of the U.S. Chamber of Commerce) about press reports that the producers had agreed to a blacklist, Johnston was adamant. "Tell the boys not to worry," he said. "There'll never be a blacklist. We're not going to go totalitarian to please this committee."

The show began at ten-twenty on the morning of Monday, October 20, when Representative Thomas strode into the Caucus Room of the Old House Office Building on Independence Avenue and took his seat behind a battery of microphones at the rostrum. The vast room was packed with starstruck spectators and buzzing with the whir of newsreel cameras. The first day's witnesses were Louis B. Mayer, Jack Warner, and Sam Wood, who charged five directors (including one whose name he couldn't recall) with trying to "steer us into the Red river." When Mayer tried to defend *Song of Russia* as a harmless boy-girl romance, the committee produced Ayn Rand, Russian-born novelist and screenwriter, who declared that its portrayal of smiling, well-dressed peasants was strictly propaganda.

Adolphe Menjou came to the stand on Tuesday, followed by *Esquire* film critic John Charles Moffitt, a corpulent individual whose efforts as a screenwriter had met with limited success. Moffitt asserted that most of the studios' story analysts were loyal to the party line (possibly explaining his own failures as a screenwriter) and that the literary agencies were "very, very heavily infiltrated" by Communists as well. Asked if he knew any Hollywood Communists engaged in subversion, he said, "Yes, sir," and named John Weber, head of the Morris Agency's West Coast literary department.

What followed was the fantastical tale of one Slick Goodlin, a young test pilot for Bell Aircraft. Goodlin had recently been chosen to fly the experimental X-1 airplane, which Bell had built under army contract to fly faster than the speed of sound—a feat that had been attempted once before, by a pilot who hadn't come back. "Early in the spring Goodlin came to Hollywood on a visit," Moffitt recalled. "Mr. Weber and a number of people of strong left-wing tendencies got to the boy. They told him that one engaged in his activity should most certainly have a wonderful story to sell to the magazines. I understood that he replied that anything he wrote would have to be passed through military intelligence. The reply was, 'Oh, of course, that will be done, but let us see a sample of what you can write, and we will see whether it is admissible,' whether it is practical to be prepared for magazine publication.

"The boy was foolish enough to do this," Moffitt continued, "and his story, his draft of a magazine article containing, as I understand it, much confidential information on the supersonic plane came into the hands of Mr. Weber, the literary agent who was sent to Hollywood by Communist headquarters in New York. I understand that this has been taken up by the F.B.I. At any rate, Goodlin was assigned to the supersonic plane."

Moffitt was wrong about the assignment: Slick Goodlin, whose movie-star handsome features had adorned the pages of *Life* magazine a few months before, had demanded so much money to perform the death-defying task of breaking the sound barrier that the army air force had given the job instead to a World War II fighter ace named Chuck Yeager. Seven days before Moffitt's testimony, for no bonus at all, Captain Yeager had taken the X-1 into the high desert sky north of Los Angeles and accomplished the feat Slick Goodlin and his manager wanted $150,000 to do. But the military had imposed an immediate publicity blackout on the flight, so nobody outside a few flyboys in the Mojave Desert knew he'd even taken it.

Moffitt was wrong about the secrets, too. The Los Angeles newspaper boys got to Goodlin that afternoon at his house in Rosamond, out by the dry lake beds where the X-1 was being tested. When they told him Moffitt's story, he insisted that his article, set to appear in *Air Trails* magazine in January (with a condensed version coming out in *Reader's Digest*), revealed none of the secrets of the mysterious X-1. As for Weber, Goodlin denied ever meeting him. He'd given the article to one of Weber's associates, waited three months and heard nothing, and finally made the magazine sales himself. "I don't know where this man Moffitt got his information, but he certainly got it all wrong," Goodlin told a reporter. "It's the sheerest kind of nonsense."

The only thing Moffitt was right about was John Weber: The head of the Morris Agency's Hollywood literary department was indeed a Communist. He'd worked as a section organizer and as a party spokesman in New York in the thirties, then moved out to the coast. A good-looking guy, vocal and bright and well-read, he'd landed a job in Hollywood with the Morris office, where the pay was considerably better than the $15 a week a party organizer could expect.

Weber's secretary, a little mouseburger type named Helen Gurley, thought he had the dark, smoldering looks of John Garfield, but she had no idea he was a Communist. Neither, apparently, did anyone else at the Morris office. Yet he and his wife, Ruth, were both active in the party's Hollywood section, which had sixty to eighty members in several branches. They were well known to other party members who were Morris clients, like Lardner and director Joe Losey and screenwriter Leo Townsend. But Weber was neither the section organizer nor the dominant personality in it. That would be John Howard Lawson, HICCASP officer and founder of the Screen Writers Guild.

Lawson's appearance the following Monday signaled the start of the committee's confrontation with the Hollywood left, a raucous mêlée marked by much shouting and speechifying and gavel-banging and hauling off of witnesses who lived up to their unfriendly label. But on Thursday afternoon, after calling up ten of the nineteen—Lardner among them—and citing them for contempt when they refused to say whether they were Communists, Chairman Thomas suddenly declared an indefinite adjournment. He announced his retreat bulldog-style, barking out a pledge to expose yet more Communists and conduct "an exhaustive study" of Communist propaganda in the movies. But his opponents were gleeful. Two weeks of grandstanding had yielded a lot of wild accusations but no serious evidence, and the whole exercise was beginning to look absurd.

Certainly, Jack Moffitt hadn't done a lot for the committee's credibility. On Monday, the day Lawson took the stand, Bill Morris, Jr., sent Thomas sworn statements from John Weber and his New York counterpart, Helen Strauss, categorically denying Moffitt's tale. On Friday, the day after Thomas halted the hearings, Lardner was summoned to the New York office for a meeting on the matter. Morris ran it himself, but he didn't seem overly concerned. It broke up after a half-hour with nothing decided except that someone should check out Weber's affiliations. Nobody in the industry was talking about a blacklist, and Bill Morris was hardly one to be consumed with anxiety about the Red threat.

But if Morris wasn't, others were. The American Legion was threatening a boycott of Hollywood pictures. Demonstrations had broken out in California, Kansas, and North Carolina. Fox announced it would dismiss any acknowledged Communist or any employee—such as Lardner—who refused to testify as to whether he was a Communist. Then, in late November, the Hollywood moguls and their New York overseers held a two-day powwow with Eric Johnston at the Waldorf-Astoria to decide what to do. Despite his brave words at the start of the hearings, Johnston had been privately urging the studio chiefs to fire the Reds on their payroll for months. Now he said it again, with meaning.

When Sam Goldwyn made a crack about the panic in the room, Johnston put it to them straight: Were they mice or were they men? If they wanted the respect of the American people, he declared, the Communists would have to go. Dore Schary, production chief at RKO, reminded them there was no law against being a Communist. Eddie Mannix, general manager of M-G-M, reminded them there was a law in California against firing people for their politics. But after Johnston flung his hotel key onto the table and threatened to resign, they didn't even bother to take a vote.

Parnell Thomas's resolution to cite the unfriendly ten for contempt had just passed the House, after hot debate, by a lopsided margin. Ten days later, in a letter to the newly established Loyalty Review Board, Attorney General Tom Clark added the National Council of American-Soviet Friendship to the government's growing list of subversive organizations. But Bill Morris had other things to think about by this time. The Morris office was on the threshold of an entirely new business, one that promised to revolutionize the amusement world, taking the agency back to its roots while rocketing it into the future. As president of the firm and heir to his father's name, Bill Morris was being groomed to make the pitch.

IN MAY 1948, SIX MONTHS AFTER THE HOLLYWOOD STUDIOS IMPLE-mented the blacklist and fifty years after William Morris first posted his trademark on Fourteenth Street, his son announced the Morris Agency's entry into commercial television. "Now's the Time to Get in Video: William Morris," declared the page-one head in *Advertising Age*, the sober ad industry bible. "Vaude-Tele Mated By Texaco at 5G for June 8 Teeoff," cried *Variety*. Translation was provided in the two-page ad inside:

VAUDEVILLE IS BACK!
THE GOLDEN ERA OF VARIETY BEGINS WITH THE PREMIERE OF
TEXACO STAR THEATRE
ON TELEVISION

Gist of the story was this: The Morris office was putting together a one-hour variety show with a $5,000 weekly budget to begin broadcasting June 8. Deal was a four-way involving Morris's radio department, NBC's WNBT television station in New York, top brass at the Texas Company, and the Kudner advertising agency. (Arthur Kudner was celebrated among ad men for discovering an everyday fungus, dubbing it athlete's foot, and hawking it to the public with Absorbine Jr. as the cure.) Packaged by Stellar Radio Enterprises, a Morris Agency subsidiary that had been set up in 1940 to produce radio and television programs, the show would be broadcast live from Studio 6B in the RCA Building, across the street from the Morris office in the RKO Building and more or less at the epicenter of Radio City.

"Texaco Star Theater" had been a fixture on radio for years, with a variety of formats and a variety of stars from the Morris office—Fred Allen, Eddie Cantor, Ed Wynn. Idea behind the new version was to put a complete vaudeville bill on the air—a dumb act (acrobat or puppeteer) as the opener, a single woman in the deuce, a sketch for the trey, and so on, seven acts a show, with Milton Berle as emcee for the first four weeks and Al Jolson and Groucho Marx to follow. "The Palace of television" was how Bill Morris described it to *Variety*, which promptly dubbed the new hybrid "vaudeo."

Coincidentally, it was announced that the real Palace on Times Square, a movie house for the past fifteen years, would likely shut its doors. The movie business was in a spot, and not just because of Thomas and his committee. After setting an all-time record of $1.7 billion in 1946 and doing almost as well in 1947, the box office was starting to drop. Americans were staying home to raise the babies they'd been making so feverishly, and their money was going for mortgage payments on their new suburban tract houses and for the new cars and refrigerators and dishwashers that Madison Avenue was telling them they needed. A survey conducted for the Foote, Cone & Belding ad agency yielded a "loose estimate" (actually an extrapolation from results in a single Long Island town) that television was already cutting into movie grosses at the rate of $3 million a year. The foreign market was drying up because the British Board of Trade had recently imposed a 75 percent tax on foreign film earnings, inspiring other governments to follow suit. And the Supreme Court had just ruled that the structure of the entire industry was illegal.

Even as Congress was probing Hollywood as a seedbed of Communist subversion, the Justice Department had been prosecuting it as a capitalist conspiracy. But the government's antitrust case, *United States v. Paramount Pictures et al.*, had been moving fitfully through the criminal justice system for a decade, so long that it had begun to look like part of the scenery. The suit was aimed at the vertical integration the big-five motion picture corporations had fought so hard to achieve in the twenties—their control of the studios that produced the films, the companies that distributed them to theaters, and the theaters that showed them in every major city—and at the practice of blind bidding and block booking, which forced independent theater owners to take whatever the studios wanted to send them. These rules made it virtually impossible for a studio release to lose money—a good thing, as far as the moguls were concerned.

On the last day of 1945, after a trial and a temporary settlement and then another trial, a federal court in Foley Square in Manhattan had issued a ruling so convoluted that neither the press nor the stock market could make out if the studios had won or lost. It didn't matter, because all sides appealed to the Supreme Court, which issued its ruling just as the Morris office was announcing its scheme to revive vaudeville on television. This time there was no doubt: The studio system was a conspiracy in restraint of trade. It was left to the lower court to decide how the monopoly should be broken up. But clearly the theater chains that had been strung together in vaudeville days, the very theaters whose seats the studios had been created to fill, would have to go. Divestiture and divorcement were the order of the day.

The picture business was manic-depressive by nature, and the studio bosses reacted to their sudden change of fortune with customary panic. Excess gave way to economy with wrenching speed. Production budgets were cut back. Studio payrolls were slashed. Execs waived scheduled pay increases. Long-term contracts were replaced by one-shot deals. Agents for freelance players got offers of a fraction of their usual asking price. The blacklist helped, too. It eliminated Adrian Scott and Edward Dmytryk, producer and director of *Crossfire*, RKO's dazzling attack on anti-Semitism. (When a Philadelphia organization gave them a humanitarian award a few weeks later, Eric Johnston accepted it for them with a rousing speech against discrimination.) Dalton Trumbo was let go by M-G-M, morals clause or no morals clause. Ring Lardner, Jr., was dismissed by Fox, and by the Morris office as well, since there seemed to be little point in representing a man with no career to represent.

To those who were blacklisted, the Red smear against Hollywood meant an end to the privileged existence they'd won for themselves in the lush confines of the movie colony. But to the men who ran the studios, the Red smear was just part of the enormous avalanche of misfortune now befalling them. Sagging box office, overseas taxation, advent of television, evisceration by the Supreme Court, divorcement from the theater chains, subpoenas from Congress, threat of boycotts—it added up to the end of their world, the world they'd created barely two decades before. RKO, weakest of the big-five studios, had just been sold to Howard Hughes, the maverick producer, after losing nearly $2 million in 1947. Dore Schary, RKO's forty-three-year-old production chief, suddenly turned up at M-G-M, ostensibly at Louis Mayer's invitation but reportedly at the behest of Nick Schenck, Mayer's boss in New York. M-G-M was the biggest and the richest of the studios. A shake-up there meant no one was safe.

But bad news for the studio chiefs, or for individual writers or directors, didn't necessarily mean bad news for the talent agencies. Show business was a fluid and fickle enterprise, no easier to pin down than a blob of mercury, but the one constant in it, the only guarantee, was that people would lay down hard cash to be entertained by other people with talent. The agencies had the talent. All they had to do was figure out what to do with it.

Television was an obvious move, but not necessarily a smart one. It could easily turn out to be a fad, and a poorly paying fad at that. In 1948, only 172,000 sets were in use—158,000 more than the year before, but still far from enough to support the kinds of salaries that stars were used to getting. Radio executives were as nervous as movie moguls, because television was going to require a lot of seed money from the parent it seemed destined to destroy. And the talent agencies had their own reason to worry, since most of their revenues came from movies and radio.

But the Morris office had been pushing television ever since Will Morris had demonstrated the Sanabria system nearly two decades before. In 1938, Bill Morris, Jr., had helped connect Paramount with television pioneer Allen B. DuMont to finance the DuMont Television Network. DuMont was a protégé of Lee De Forest, the turn-of-the-century inventor whose vacuum tube made wireless communication possible; DuMont himself invented the first practical cathode-ray tube, which provided the basis for television, and his DuMont Labs manufactured the first television receiver sets. Now the DuMont network was vying with ABC—created when the Federal Communications Commission forced NBC to sell off the smaller of its two networks in 1941—for third place behind NBC and CBS.

The Morris Agency was handling DuMont's most popular show, Ted Mack's "Amateur Hour," with its every-Sunday-night parade of hopefuls waiting for the spin of the Wheel of Fortune: "Round and around she goes, and where she stops, nobody knows." Another Morris client, crooner Lanny Ross, had just launched a half-hour music-and-quiz show on NBC for Swift. Morris had radio chat stars Tex McCrary and his wife, Jinx Falkenburg, doing their "Tex and Jinx" show for Swift on Sunday nights and "The Swift Home Service Club" on daytime. Plus there were sporting events to be peddled, musical telecasts to put together for Count Basie, Duke Ellington. . . .

Vaudeville was just part of what televiewers could expect. CBS announced a one-hour cabaret revue hosted by Ed Sullivan, Broadway columnist for the *New York Daily News*, to debut two weeks after NBC's "Texaco Star Theater." The Democratic National Committee was considering television as a way of portraying Truman as a warm and human guy and countering the strong support for Henry Wallace, newly declared third-party candidate for president, in California and the Northeast, where televiewers were concentrated. Enthusiasts saw no limits to what television could do. As Bill Morris told *Ad Age*, "Television is to the entertainment field what atomic fission is to science."

But first they had to find the raw material. Talent agencies were shifting vaude specialists into their radio departments on the theory that it was more important to know the visual angle than to know broadcasting. The Morris office tapped Harry Kalcheim for the job. As chief booker for the Paramount circuit in the thirties, Kalcheim had brought in big bands—the Tommy Dorsey Orchestra, the Benny Goodman Orchestra, the Glenn Miller Orchestra—to entertain movie patrons, as well as singers and comedians like Danny Kaye, Dinah Shore, and Red Skelton. He and Myron Kirk of the Kudner Agency had developed the Texaco show, and now he'd be in charge of booking it. Meanwhile, Bill Morris flew to London with his seventy-five-year-old mother to catch Sophie Tucker's debut at the Casino Theatre and to scout for talent. He was hoping to bring back Harry Lauder, now knighted and living in retirement in a country manor outside Glasgow.

"Texaco Star Theater" began its regular season on September 21 with Milton Berle as permanent emcee. Berle was a frenzied comic, a brash and unlovable guy with an unquenchable, almost desperate, urge to entertain. He'd flopped in pictures and flopped on radio but he was a big name in nightclubs, big enough to pull in better than $250,000 a year doing appearances ($750,000 in 1946). Born forty years before in a Harlem tenement, he'd gotten his start at age five when his mother dragged him off to an amateur show after she caught him mimicking Charlie Chaplin on the street. When he was six, she took him to Hollywood, where he made his screen debut as a newsboy in *Tillie's Punctured Romance*, the Chaplin picture Will Morris did so well with at the New York Theatre. Mama Berle steered him straight to the top, and if he had to steal everybody else's jokes to get there, too bad. "A parrot with skin on," Fred Allen called him—a parrot with 850,000 indexed gags in his office, a duplicate on microfilm in a bank vault, and another duplicate in his head, which he could riffle through with the speed of an IBM electronic calculator until he hit the right riposte to anything, flip-sort-*chung*, delivering it as smoothly as an ad-lib. He was made for live TV.

Bill Morris had predicted that vaudevillians would fare better on television than in movies or on radio because they needed a live audience to play off and visuals to put themselves across, and Berle's success bore him out. But Berle wasn't just successful, he was phenomenal. So what if his salary was $1,500 a week, versus the $23,000 he'd gotten at the Roxy on Broadway? "Texaco Star Theater" quickly won a weekly Hooperating of 80, meaning that 80 percent of all TV sets that were tuned in at all were tuned in to it. That added up to 4.5 million people in twenty-four cities watching Berle live or on kinescope two weeks later. The second-rated show was nearly thirty points behind.

With numbers like that, NBC didn't even cancel the show for the November 2 election returns. When the city fathers of Detroit tried to find out why the reservoirs were dropping at nine o'clock every Tuesday night, they discovered it was because nobody used the toilet until Berle went off the air. And it wasn't just bathrooms: Restaurants stood empty and nightclubs shut their doors because people were staying home to watch Berle. Those who didn't yet have a TV set at home—and most people didn't—crowded into bars or gathered outside appliance stores. "Berle is responsible for more television sets being sold than anyone else," quipped Joe E. Lewis. "I sold mine, my father sold his. . . . "

Berle's secret—and it wasn't much of a secret once he hit TV—was that he'd do anything for a laugh. He'd ride out on a dogsled, he'd black out his two front teeth, he'd strap on falsies and wriggle into a dress, he'd wrap a scarf around his head with a fruit compote tumbling out of it à la Carmen Miranda. He had a great gash of a mouth and loving-cup ears and a rubber face that could wrap itself around any character from Li'l Abner to the Easter Bunny. For an hour every Tuesday night, his viewers forgot about the Reds and the A-bomb and the mortgage payments and lost themselves in laughter at the glowing mosaic of hyperkinetic electronic dots bursting willy-nilly out of the screen. It was atomic entertainment all right, and it made Berle the hottest comic in America.

HARRY KALCHEIM HAD HIS HANDS FULL. LIVE WEEKLY TELEVISION WASN'T like the movies, where you could negotiate a seven-year contract, motor out to the lot to make sure everything was copacetic, and let the studio take care of the rest. Every week there were shows to book, acts to audition, scripts to commission, rehearsals to sit in on, stars and writers and network brass and ad agency execs and their clients to keep happy. Vaudeo required a constant turnover of smaller acts to surround the top names, so to guarantee the supply, Kalcheim signed up scores of acts he'd normally have spurned. Abe Lastfogel threw the agency's entire sales staff into television to help him out—vaude and café bookers into vaudeo, agents from the legit department handling dramatic programs, and so forth. Commissions weren't yet close to paying their way, but television figured to be the top money-earner in the office in a few years.

Kalcheim was a nebbishy-looking man, short and thin with rimless eyeglasses and a perpetually furrowed brow, hardly your standard Broadway talent agent. He was absentminded and painfully shy. When his secretary buzzed him with a call, she never knew if he'd pick up his Dictaphone by mistake. One morning he asked her to get his doctor on the phone; when she typed out his Dictaphone belt that afternoon, she found him describing an ingrown toenail. He was always going out to the Latin Quarter or La Martinique or the Copa to scout talent, but first he had to be home by six-thirty for dinner. He and his wife, Bea, were dancing at the Latin Quarter one evening when the manager asked him what he thought of the orchestra. "I dunno," he said, "they don't have much rhythm." Bea looked down and cried, "For Christ's sake, Harry, take your rubbers off!"

Kalcheim may have looked too meek to hold his own among the Lindy's crowd, but he was a hard worker with surprisingly adventuresome tastes. All summer, while launching "Texaco Star Theater," he'd been driving ad agency execs out to the Pocono Mountains, ninety miles west of Gotham in the wilds of Pennsylvania, to catch the Saturday night show at a Socialist Party resort called Camp Tamiment. The Tamiment revues—scaled-down versions of big song-and-dance productions like the Ziegfeld *Follies*, directed by a Vienna-born Broadway maven named Max Liebman—had been showcased on Broadway in 1939, in the production that launched Danny Kaye. When the Morris office got Kaye his picture deal with Sam Goldwyn, Liebman had gone to Hollywood to help work up the material for his first film. Then he'd served as a writer-director for USO–Camp Shows and ended up staging a Coast Guard revue in Palm Beach, where he discovered a talented young recruit named Sid Caesar. After working with Caesar in nightclubs and directing him in the 1948 Broadway revue *Make Mine Manhattan*, he'd returned to Tamiment to develop a showcase for television.

The first visitor Kalcheim brought out to the Poconos was Pat Weaver of Young & Rubicam, which had a client who was thinking of going into television. Weaver liked the show, but on television, he reminded Liebman, he'd have to stage a new one every week. Just what they'd been doing for years, Liebman told him. Later, Kalcheim showed up with Myron Kirk, the Kudner exec who'd done the Texaco deal. Kirk was impressed, too. He had Liebman do a presentation for the president of Admiral, a TV-set manufacturer, who agreed to sponsor the program if Liebman could give him an hour every week for $15,000—big money for television. Pat Weaver, who by this time had left Young & Rubicam to become a vice president at NBC, gave the go-ahead for the network, and the show was on.

Liebman's "Admiral Broadway Revue" premiered in January 1949 on both NBC and DuMont, which carried it in cities NBC didn't reach.

For Imogene Coca, a Tamiment player Liebman wanted to pair with Sid Caesar, the first show was an unwitting audition, since Kudner and Admiral didn't want her and Liebman was afraid to tell her until the end of the performance—which was so good they instantly gave her the nod. Critics were wildly enthusiastic, and not just about Coca. Instead of the slapstick humor and the acrobats and animal acts that prevailed on "Texaco Star Theater" and Ed Sullivan's "Toast of the Town," Liebman gave them knowing satire on highbrow amusements like opera ("No, No, Rigolett") and ballet ("P.M. of a Faun"). "I can't think of anything better in New York's expensive nightclubs," wrote the reviewer for the *New York Herald-Tribune*. "Come to think of it, there isn't anything much better on Broadway, either."

A lot of Morris clients were getting into television by this time, or thinking about it, or having second thoughts because they suddenly realized that in one show they could use up material they'd developed over a lifetime. Al Jolson, a star again after the release of *The Jolson Story*, made a deal with NBC to do a minstrel show. Ed Wynn, who'd hit the big time in the Ziegfeld *Follies* of 1914 and become a millionaire as a radio star during the Depression, was talking with CBS about going on television in his guise as "the perfect fool." Eddie Cantor was thinking about doing television in addition to his weekly radio broadcast for Pabst. But in February, when Abe Lastfogel and Sammy Weisbord went to Chicago for talks with brewery officials, he decided once a week was too often. Cantor wanted to go on every other week instead.

Talent agents were as eager to break into television as performers. But broadcasting wasn't a club you could get into automatically. Television was live from New York, so most of the Hollywood boys were out of the picture. And it was as restricted as radio, which left out most of the fellows in New York. It was okay to run a network if you were Jewish— William Paley owned CBS, and David Sarnoff headed RCA, which owned NBC—but it was tough to do business with the networks if your family tree didn't have *Mayflower* potential. To get in the door at the networks and the ad agencies and the giant food and soap and petroleum corporations that controlled the programming, an agency needed both an established setup and people who knew show business yet felt comfortable in the clubbier East Side precincts. That pretty much whittled the list down to Morris and MCA.

Strategically speaking, Abe Lastfogel and Jules Stein both agreed with Bill Morris about the prospects for a vaudeville revival on television. The Morris office, with a client roster that included Amos 'n' Andy, Burns and Allen, Eddie Cantor, George Jessel, Al Jolson, and Ed Wynn—not to mention Milton Berle—clearly had the edge. MCA had always disdained vaudeville in favor of band bookings, which paid a higher commission because of the complex routing and travel arrangements the big bands required.

There was one way around this, however—the same technique Stein had used in Hollywood: Steal them. Not for television, because that wasn't where the money was. For radio. With Milton Berle selling TV sets as fast as RCA could make them, NBC and its corporate parent— which manufactured television transmitters and antennae as well as receivers—had good reason to be committed to the new medium. Not to mention that two years earlier, David Sarnoff had bested Paley when the Federal Communications Commission chose RCA's technically superior black-and-white television system over the flawed color system CBS was pushing. But despite NBC's success with Berle, a lot of people in broadcasting—advertisers, station managers, network executives— thought television cost too much to make sense. Paley was one of them. And now Paley, with Lew Wasserman's help, was wiping out Sarnoff's talent roster, and with it NBC's dominance in the only side of broadcasting that paid.

The raids had begun in September 1948, just as "Texaco Star Theater" was starting its regular season, when Bill Paley announced that "Amos 'n' Andy," one of NBC's and William Morris's longest-running programs, was coming to CBS in a $2 million deal negotiated by Wasserman. Characteristically, Wasserman had structured the deal to give his new clients maximum tax advantages. The top tax bracket for personal incomes above $70,000 was 77 percent. Wasserman got the show's creators, Freeman Gosden and Charles Correll, to incorporate, then sold the program to CBS for $2 million plus a share of the profits, taxable at the capital gains rate of 25 percent. The Bureau of Internal Revenue uttered its benediction.

Wasserman's next move was to sell Jack Benny to CBS in another capital gains deal, this one worth $2.3 million. "The Jack Benny Program" had been a fixture on NBC since 1932, almost as long as "Amos 'n' Andy." But where "Amos 'n' Andy" was clearly on the slide, Benny— with his lousy violin playing, his unvarying stinginess, his perpetual age of thirty-nine, and his running feud with Fred Allen—had the top Hoop-erating on radio. His sponsor, the American Tobacco Company, and its ad agency, Batten, Barton, Durstine & Osborn, tried to kill the move because CBS had fewer listeners and weaker stations than NBC; the commissioner of internal revenue, feeling the heat from Congress over the tax dodge he'd just okayed for Gosden and Correll, vetoed the capital gains setup. Paley won his prize regardless. "I wonder if they have free parking at CBS?" Benny supposedly quipped when the story broke.

In January and February 1949, MCA got three more stars for Paley—Edgar Bergen and Red Skelton from NBC and Bing Crosby from ABC. "Paley's Comet," *Variety* dubbed his suddenly star-spangled network. By March, CBS had nine of the top fifteen radio programs, yet Sarnoff couldn't believe mere star appeal would outweigh RCA's technological prowess and industrial might. "A business built on a few comedians," he groused to a friend as radio audiences deserted his network, "isn't a business worth being in."

Sarnoff wasn't a programmer. It was up to Harry Kalcheim and Bill Murray and their people at the Morris office, working with the ad agen-cies and their sponsors, to come up with something people actually wanted to see. The radio-television department, so rapidly expanded, was overwhelmed. They had dozens of shows on the air—Milton Berle, Sid Caesar, Ted Mack on television; Fred Allen, Fanny Brice, Burns and Allen, Eddie Cantor on radio. Looking back, you'd think no one would have been surprised at what happened next.

On March 9, after a full day at the office, the fifty-nine-year-old Mur-ray, head as smooth as a bowling ball above a perfectly tailored suit, took his wife to the opera—his third wife, the marriage to Ilka Chase having ended some years before. It was a Wednesday night; they had one-year-old twins at home. Suddenly she felt ill, so they left the opera house and went to their apartment on East Fifty-seventh Street. Murray was stricken by a heart attack while tending to her. He died in the hospital the next morning.

Lastfogel flew in with George Gruskin, Murray's opposite number on the coast. Scores of show folk made their way through the unfamiliar canyons of Wall Street for the Saturday morning funeral at Trinity Church. Lastfogel held a meeting at his Essex House apartment the next day to announce that Murray's deputy, Wally Jordan, would take over the department. Then he rode to the airport for the flight back to Los Angeles.

Jordan was brusque and to the point, an ex–radio producer who'd joined the Morris office in Chicago in 1938 after working with Bob Hope, the Marx Brothers, and Will Rogers. He'd been running the department in tandem with Murray since 1942, but he had a big job ahead of him all the same, and it wasn't just servicing the shows they had. A few weeks after the funeral, just as the Morris office was preparing a $300,000 suit against Gosden and Correll for lost commissions on the "Amos 'n' Andy" deal, Burns and Allen pulled the same stunt they had.

George Burns was Jack Benny's best friend, so once MCA made the deal for Benny, it was obvious he and Gracie might follow, even though they'd been handled by the Morris office since vaudeville and had renewed their agency papers just two years before. But Lastfogel didn't get sore. Of course clients would leave; why hold a grudge? He went about his business, as quiet and composed as ever. His associates marveled at his equanimity. So did his clients. Finally it got to be too much for Burns, who went up to him and said, "Abe, would you do me a favor? Would you please call somebody a son of a bitch?"

5
―――

PYGMALION

Los Angeles/New York, 1949-1950

JOHNNY HYDE WASN'T USED TO THIS KIND OF TROUBLE SELLING A STARLET. Usually, it just took a little adjustment, like the nose job that reputedly helped him land Ann Miller her contract, and look what that had led to—a big career in pictures, from queen of the B's at Columbia to a role in M-G-M's lavish Technicolor musical *Easter Parade*, not to mention an affair with Louis Mayer that culminated in his suicide attempt when she opted to marry elevator heir Reese Milner instead. Ann Miller was easy. But nobody wanted to hear about Marilyn Monroe. Everywhere he took her—Columbia, Fox, M-G-M—they just laughed at him. Men he'd done business with for years were starting to think of him as a bore and a pest. And the funny thing was, he didn't care. After three marriages, three divorces, and conquests too numerous to count, he was finally in love.

He knew something, too: This one would go a lot farther than Ann Miller or any of the other girls he'd signed to their seven years of studio servitude. She had looks, she had spirit, she had drive, and she could act. The kid was a knockout; she was going straight to the top. But in the meantime, she had to eat.

Hyde looked up from his desk. Marilyn was sitting beside him, looking morose. Milt Ebbins, a personal manager who handled Count Basie and Billy Eckstine, wandered into his office. *"Milt!"* Hyde cried. "For God's sake, can *you* get her a job?"

Ebbins sputtered, nonplussed. Him? What could he do? Marilyn just sat there, mute. You could see why people called her a dumb blonde—number one, she was blond, and number two, she never said anything. She was in way over her head with Johnny's crowd, but she figured she could stay out of trouble by keeping her mouth shut. So people took her for a dumb blonde.

Marilyn was a too-familiar sight in Hollywood, a dazed, somewhat slovenly youngster who yearned, ached, *needed* to become a movie star. Most people saw little to distinguish her from the pack. Yet ever since he'd met her, at the beginning of 1949, Hyde had been spellbound. She seemed so willing, so malleable, so perfectable. She was his to create, his Galatea. The work he'd put into creating and preserving those other stars—the nose job for little Ann Miller, the abortion for Lana Turner—was nothing to this.

Hyde's reconciliation with his last starlet, the former Mozelle Cravens, hadn't lasted long. In November 1946, seven months after taking him back, Mozelle had discovered she was going to have a second child. A bad scene ensued. She'd filed for divorce again, claiming he'd threatened to put out her eyes, to mar her face, to wait until she got nice and large and then kick her in the belly so she'd be sorry she'd ever gotten pregnant. At the trial she merely told the judge he'd called her "bowlegged," which was enough in itself to win a divorce and $1,000 a month in alimony. Hyde kept the house, a rambling, white-clapboard mansion on North Palm Drive in Beverly Hills, just below the palatial movie-star estates on Sunset. Then he met Marilyn.

A film cutter's knockabout daughter, Marilyn Monroe—real name Norma Jeane Dougherty—had been saturated in the kind of fantasy Hollywood was in business to create. She had no idea who her father was; her mother had made a living piecing together raw footage for pictures like RKO's *Flying Down to Rio*, which had scenes of scantily clad maidens dancing across the wings of airplanes in flight, before disappearing into a series of mental institutions. Raised at various times in a Pentecostal foster home in the fringe village of Hawthorne, in her mother's starstruck household in Hollywood, in an orphanage hard by the RKO lot, by her aunt's mother in Compton, by her mother's best friend's aunt in West L.A., and by her mother's best friend herself in a San Fernando Valley bungalow, she'd been repeatedly abandoned and sometimes sexually abused. At sixteen she'd quit school to marry a twenty-one-year-old neighbor she called "Daddy." She was childlike, uneducated, and confused. All she knew was what her mother had told her—that someday she'd be just like Jean Harlow, Metro's Depression-era bombshell.

By the time she met Johnny, three years into her assault on stardom and more than two years after her divorce, she'd been around the track. She'd been bedded by a couple of photographers during her brief modeling career, and when things were lean she'd turned tricks on the side streets off Hollywood Boulevard for a meal. One night while serving as decoration for a party she'd met Joe Schenck, Hyde's cigar-chomping friend at Fox, a big bear of a man who sent a limousine the next evening to fetch her to his Mediterranean-style mansion for an intimate dinner à deux, after which he encouraged her to slip off her clothes so he could regale her with tales of old Hollywood. Fox had already signed and dropped her at this point, but Schenck pulled some strings with Harry Cohn and got her a contract at Columbia. There'd been other men, too. She'd been passed around. She'd had men laugh in her face.

Hollywood was some creep town.

Then she met Johnny.

Columbia had just dropped her, after dyeing her chestnut-brown hair a luxuriant blond and taking the fuzz off her face with electrolysis for the B-musical *Ladies of the Chorus*. Fred Karger, the studio's handsome and available young vocal coach, had even taken her to an orthodontist and paid for braces to correct her overbite and for bleaching to whiten her teeth, which was decent of him since he was screwing her at the time and he didn't mind telling her that screwing was the only real talent she had. Now she was trying to get over him. If he wouldn't marry her, she could do worse than to hook up with a top agent like Johnny Hyde. Even if Karger was the one she loved.

Hyde was different. Not the way he treated her—he told her she was a chump, criticized her constantly, just as Karger had—but the way he believed in her. She already knew she was a chump, but to be told she was a chump with possibility—that was something new. So what if he was a lecher like the rest of them, a man who graded women as tramps, near-tramps, and pushovers? In that one way he was unique, and she loved him for it. Tried to love him, anyway, even though he was two inches shorter and more than twice her age and weakened by a bum heart and not quite the lover he thought he was. That was okay, sex wasn't something she sought for satisfaction, it was what she had to barter. And he got such a thrill from it—not just from having her, but from having her to show off.

But for all his top-level relationships, Hyde didn't seem able to do much more for her than Columbia's thirty-two-year-old vocal coach. He'd gotten the Morris office to buy out her contract with Harry Lipton at National Concert & Artists Corporation, the little agency she'd signed with in 1946 when she was nineteen. He got her a bit part in *Love Happy*, a lackluster Marx Brothers picture for United Artists: For $500 she did a brief walk-on that sent Groucho's eyebrows arching toward the ceiling. He tried to get her a $25 spot on "The Pinky Lee Show," a TV variety program on the local NBC station, but Pinky—an ex-vaudevillian handled by the Morris office—wasn't impressed: "What can she do that's worth $25?" he wanted to know. Charles Wick in the radio-television department arranged an audition with Ken Murray, who was taking his famous *Blackouts* from the El Capitan Theatre to television and needed a replacement for his star, Marie Wilson, who'd given 3,126 live performances and wanted a change. That didn't work out either.

Maybe it was the nose. Karger had started the transformation from tousle-haired innocent to blond sexpot, but the job was only half done. The tip of her nose was still a mite long, and her lower jaw could use some rounding out as well. Hyde arranged for a Beverly Hills plastic surgeon to take care of it. He also introduced her to music and literature, and he tried to tutor her in the social graces, which her hardscrabble upbringing hadn't given her much exposure to.

Then again, maybe it wasn't the nose. Maybe it was the signals she sent. Marilyn wasn't the vixen Rita Hayworth had been made out to be; she was a little lost kitten who seemed natural and uninhibited. She made men want to take her into their arms and protect her, until they realized she was coming on helpless and breathy and seductive and ambitious and manipulative and determined all at the same time. Women often liked her, maybe because they sensed the truth at the core of her helpless act, maybe because they realized she wasn't a cobra at heart: She wanted a career, not a husband. Men never got past the realization that beneath the playful, kittenish exterior was a gal on the make, a gal who wouldn't mind using them on her way to the top. They were too smart for her. They were going to use her first.

Marilyn was living in a tiny efficiency apartment in the Beverly Carlton Hotel on Olympic Boulevard, an unassuming establishment on the south side of Beverly Hills. But she was spending most of her nights with Hyde in his big house on Palm Drive. In the evenings he squired her around town—dinner at Chasen's and Romanoff's, dancing at Ciro's and the Mocambo—or showed her off at little dinner parties at his house, in the dining room she called "my own private Romanoff's" because it had little booths and round tables just like the real one. But getting Jack Warner to ogle her on the dance floor was the easy part. The tough part was getting the studio bosses to take her seriously. She was no longer a fresh face by 1949, and the studios were dumping starlets, not signing them. They already had their screen goddesses—M-G-M had Lana Turner, Fox had Betty Grable, Columbia had Rita Hayworth. At least, Harry Cohn thought he had Rita Hayworth.

Rita Hayworth was a problem. She'd sailed to France the summer before, in 1948, and Elsa Maxwell, the society writer, had given a party in Cannes to introduce her to Prince Aly Khan, the thirty-seven-year-old playboy whose father led the Ismaili Muslim sect. The prince, though technically married, had proved an ardent suitor, whisking her off to Spain, following her to Los Angeles, accompanying her on a spur-of-the-moment jaunt to Mexico and Cuba with scandalized reporters in hot pursuit. Meanwhile, Cohn was putting together a Western for her, the second picture under the lucrative Beckworth contract Hyde had negotiated. But though the contract gave her script approval, Cohn didn't send her the script until the cast and crew were ready to go. When she rejected it, he put her on suspension and proclaimed her a shirker, abandoning her duty amid the industry's traumas. Pilloried by the press, she sailed with Aly and little Becky for Europe, where it was announced that he would divorce the current princess and marry her.

Cohn went livid at the idea that "the bum," as he called Aly, was going to marry his most lucrative screen property and turn her into some kind of Muslim princess. Rita didn't care. She detested Cohn, she loathed Hollywood, she hated stardom, she wanted only the love and protection of a husband who would be faithful to her as no man ever had. Still, there was one man in Hollywood she respected, even regarded in a fatherly way, because she knew he believed in her.

Johnny Hyde had served as Cohn's go-between with Hayworth before, particularly during her entanglement with Orson Welles. Cohn's Western was a dead issue. But would Rita star in *Born Yesterday*, Garson Kanin's hit Broadway play, which Lastfogel had sold to Cohn two years earlier for an unprecedented $1 million? For that matter, would she ever work in Hollywood again? As the prince and his staff made feverish preparations for the May 27 wedding at the Château de l'Horizon, his sumptuous villa on the Riviera, Hyde flew to Cannes to find out.

BACK IN HIS OFFICE A FEW WEEKS LATER, HYDE TURNED HIS ATTENTION to another client. He'd met a lot of dames in his life, but never one quite like this: a black orchid, frail and willowy and lovely, raven hair framing a pale and perfect face. Her name was Jane Harvey, and she was fast on her way to becoming the hottest singer in America. She'd sung with some of the top bandleaders in the business—with Benny Goodman at the Blue Angel in New York, with Desi Arnaz at Ciro's, and the day after she opened every studio in town called to talk to her. She was a household word waiting to happen. Everything Marilyn was fighting so hard to get, she could have for the asking. And she wanted to throw it all away to marry Hyde's son.

Not that he was necessarily opposed to the boy's getting married. The younger of the two children he'd had with his first wife, Florence Harper—Polly, as she was called—Jay Hyde clearly needed somebody to take care of him. That's why he was living in Johnny's house. He was a handsome guy, with wavy golden hair and big blue eyes, but there was something soft about him. People saw him as a sweet, lovable puppy, pleasant but dull. Donald, the older son, was a liar and a cheat. Hyde had made Donald head of the West Coast literary department, over Lastfogel's objections, and Donald had disgraced him so thoroughly he didn't even want to think about it. Then he'd given the two boys $20,000 to start their own agency down the street, and Donald was blowing it on custom sofas and extravagant dinners. He wouldn't wish Donald on any girl. Jay should get married to someone. But to a born star?

"So," he said, warming to the subject. "What would you like to do in your career? Would you like to play Chicago? Would you like to work the Copa?"

Jane looked at him strangely. "Oh, no," she cried. "We're going to get married!"

He was patient, testing her. "But wouldn't you like to have a career?"

"No, no! Jay and I are *in love*." Hadn't he seen Janet Gaynor in *The*

Farmer Takes a Wife? That was what she wanted, to live happily ever after in a tar-paper shack.

Hyde regarded her as if she were a Martian. Did she actually believe the stuff she saw in the movies? Life didn't work that way. He ought to know.

If only Marilyn wanted to get married as badly. But Marilyn wanted to be a star, and as hard as it was now, she knew nobody would ever take her seriously if she tried to pass herself off as Mrs. Johnny Hyde. Anyway, she wasn't the kind of girl who'd marry someone just to get ahead. She'd already decided that the next time she got married, it would be for love. She liked Johnny a lot, she loved going out to fancy restaurants and nightclubs with him, she appreciated all he was trying to do for her. But the man she fell in love with was going to be tall and handsome, like Fred Karger. She didn't love Johnny, and she'd told him so.

So he told her he had a bad heart, told her he didn't have long to live, told her she'd be a rich woman when he died. The heart stuff was no joke: Nicholas Hyde, Johnny's father, had died of a heart attack when he was sixty-three, and Johnny's older brother Victor had died in 1943, at fifty-eight, after fighting heart disease for nearly eleven years. Johnny himself had had a heart attack a year before; his face was constantly flushed, and he was popping nitroglycerin tablets under his tongue regularly to fight off the suffocating pain of his angina attacks. Marilyn felt sorry for him, but not sorry enough to marry him. Being a rich young widow had never been part of her plan.

Hyde was persistent, as a suitor and as an agent. He wanted above all else to make her happy, and what made her happy was becoming a movie star. In August, shortly before Jay married Jane Harvey in the backyard on Palm Drive, he took her to an audition at Fox, where she landed a bit part in a Technicolor Western farce called *A Ticket to Tomahawk*. Then he took her to M-G-M, where John Huston was casting *The Asphalt Jungle*, a fast-paced film noir about a bunch of grifters looking to stage a jewel heist. Hyde wanted Marilyn to play Angela, the mastermind's moll, a slinky, voluptuous blonde who goes through life in a fog of self-absorption. She was petrified at the audition, but she managed to get her lines off before fleeing. Huston was not impressed; he wanted another young blonde, Lola Albright, for the role. But Marilyn had the backing of M-G-M's talent director, Lucille Ryman, who in this case had more clout than Hyde.

Ryman and her husband, B-musical star John Carroll, had met Marilyn when she caddied for him at a celebrity golf tournament two years earlier. Moved by her tale of orphanhood and deprivation (this was when she was turning tricks in Hollywood to eat), they'd befriended her, letting her live in their apartment just off the Strip, inviting her out to their ranch in the San Fernando Valley on weekends, even granting her a weekly stipend so she could continue her classes at the Actors Lab, a local offshoot of the Group Theater in New York. They'd stopped her allowance after she met Hyde, but they were still friendly to her. John Huston stabled his horses at their ranch, but his gambling and high living had caused him to fall some $18,000 behind in board. After reminding him of the debt, Carroll told Huston he thought Marilyn should get another screen test. Huston saw his point.

After three days of careful rehearsal with her drama coach, Natasha Lytess, and a test that impressed even Louis Mayer, Marilyn got the part. She was nervous at the shoot, so nervous that Huston had to talk her down. But she did her three scenes quickly and professionally, in just a handful of takes, and when they looked at the footage, they could see she was generating heat. And then, nothing happened. Hyde was sure he could land her a contract at Metro now, or at any other studio in town. Yet when he went to see Dore Schary, M-G-M's newly installed production chief, he came back disappointed. Schary didn't think Marilyn Monroe looked like a movie star.

THESE DAYS, WHAT STUDIO EXEC COULD SAY WHO DID LOOK LIKE A MOVIE star? The business was shifting beneath their feet, but no one could figure out how. The latest figures showed attendance down from eighty million a week in 1946 to sixty-seven million in 1948 and still falling. "Pix Baffled for B.O. Solution," cried *Variety*. Anxiety hung in the air. Anything could happen, none of it good.

One source of tension was the Justice Department. Attorney General Tom Clark was determined to split the theater chains from the film studios, and most of the studio chiefs, eager to cut their losses after ten years of legal bills in a cause that the 1948 Supreme Court decision had clearly rendered hopeless, were ready to negotiate. In November 1948 Howard Hughes had become the first of the studio chiefs to cave in, signing a consent decree in which RKO agreed to spin off its 124 movie houses—last remnant of the once all-powerful Keith-Albee-Orpheum vaudeville circuit—into a separate company called RKO Theatres. In

February 1949 Paramount followed suit, agreeing to dissolve itself and form two new companies, Paramount Pictures and United Paramount Theatres. Negotiations continued with Loew's/M-G-M and Fox; Harry Warner declared his intention to wage a court fight.

Television was a much bigger unknown. Sales of TV sets were still going up, and with the new twelve- and sixteen-inch screens, they were losing the peep-show connotations the old seven-inch screens had given them. Could movies compete? Sam Goldwyn argued in the *New York Times Magazine* that television was taking the industry into its third major era, just as the coming of sound had signaled the start of the second. "It is a certainty that people will be unwilling to pay to see poor pictures," he declared, "when they can stay home and see something which is, at least, no worse."

So the picture business was in the toilet, Hollywood was supposedly a ghost town, and yet the Morris offices on Cañon Drive were busier than ever. Network television was tough, because both CBS and NBC preferred live shows over film and because the nationwide coaxial cable system that was supposed to link television stations coast-to-coast had yet to reach Los Angeles. Even so, in April 1949 they made a deal with CBS to do a weekly variety show with Ed Wynn, to be televised live on the coast and kinescoped for transmission to the rest of the country. They also set up a Hollywood TV deal for "The Life of Riley," the popular radio comedy about the misadventures of a bumbling riveter in a southern California aircraft plant, though they had to replace William Bendix with Jackie Gleason because Bendix thought television was just a fad.

If the moguls were at a loss, if the studio system was breaking down, then it was up to talent agents and independent producers like Goldwyn to put together movies the public wanted to see. Charles Feldman, whose Famous Artists Corporation was one of the top agencies in Beverly Hills, was showing one way agents could take advantage of the confusion—by going into production. *To Have and Have Not, The Big Sleep, Red River*—Feldman had put together some of the more memorable films of the decade. But Lastfogel's negotiations with the Screen Actors Guild on behalf of the Artists' Managers Guild a decade earlier had yielded an agreement that kept agents out of production, except for a few like Feldman who were already in it and were granted a picture-by-picture waiver. Not that independent production was a road to riches anyway: After the theater owner and the distributor got their cuts, an independent producer might see twenty cents of every dollar his films collected at the box office, out of which he'd have to pay for prints and advertising and promotion and financing charges, not to mention the production itself.

On the other hand, as an agent you could assemble a production with your clients, take a commission on their services, and not have to worry about the box office. The trick was having the clients. Johnny Hyde had made the Morris office a major presence in Hollywood, with a stable of stars and directors that included George Cukor, Glenn Ford, Katharine Hepburn, Judy Holliday, Danny Kaye, Elia Kazan, Vivien Leigh, Peter Lorre, Carmen Miranda, Laurence Olivier, and Mickey Rooney. But Morris was still overshadowed by MCA, which Jules Stein and Lew Wasserman had fashioned into a juggernaut. Lastfogel usually relied on internal growth to build the agency, but now he saw a chance to do what MCA had done—buy their way to the top.

With the possible exception of Famous Artists, the Berg-Allenberg Agency in Beverly Hills had the most impressive client list of any independent Hollywood agency. Between them, Phil Berg and his partner, Bert Allenberg, handled Frank Capra, Linda Darnell, Clark Gable, Judy Garland, Peter Lawford, Joe Mankiewicz, Joel McCrea, Robert Mitchum, Edward G. Robinson, and Loretta Young, among others. When Berg decided to retire, Allenberg bought out his share and went shopping for a merger. He talked with MCA, but nothing came of it. In November 1949 he opened discussions with Lastfogel and Hyde, who owned the Morris Agency in partnership with Bill Morris, Jr.

On December 15, after several days of round-the-clock negotiations involving the principals and their attorneys, an agreement was reached. The Morris office would acquire Berg-Allenberg and its clients for a sum said to be well into six figures. Allenberg and his staff would move into the Morris Building at 202 North Cañon in the early weeks of 1950. It was the biggest merger in the history of the agency business.

BILL MORRIS WAS AS EXCITED AS EVER ABOUT THE PROMISE OF THE future—about new developments like Phonevision, which would allow televiewers to ring their telephone operators, ask to see *Gilda*, say, and get the charge on their monthly phone bill. But while Lastfogel and Hyde worked to make the agency a Hollywood powerhouse, life for

Morris at the end of 1949 seemed mainly taken up with dinners. On October 27, there was a dinner at the Hotel Astor for the New York Variety Club, the local branch of the theatrical charity that had just taken over the tuberculosis sanatorium in Saranac Lake his father had launched in 1924. Housed in a rambling mock-Tudor building overlooking the lake, run by the Will Rogers Fund, which supported it by passing the cup at theaters, the facility was scraping by with X-ray machines from the twenties. Variety International would be able to give it a hefty boost, especially with the help of its New York chapter. Bill Morris was on the entertainment committee.

Two weeks later, he had a dinner honoring Andrei Vishinsky, the Soviet foreign minister, sponsored by the National Council of American-Soviet Friendship and presided over by his old friend Corliss Lamont. Though still a vice chairman, Morris had taken a backseat at the National Council as its critics multiplied. In 1948, a few months after Attorney General Clark put it on his list of subversive organizations, the Tenney committee in Sacramento had issued a report on Communist fronts in which Morris and the National Council figured prominently. "William Morris, Jr., is said to be 'very friendly to Communist writers and exceedingly unfriendly to anti-Communist writers,'" the report noted, adding that the council itself "is a direct agent of the Soviet Union, engaged in traitorous activities under the orders of Stalin's consular service in the United States." The Tenney report also cited Morris as an affiliate of three other front groups—Russian War Relief; the Independent Citizens' Committee of the Arts, Sciences, and Professions; and the Citizens Committee to Free Earl Browder, the Communist Party chief who'd gone to prison on a perjury rap.

Now they were throwing a dinner for Vishinsky on the Waldorf-Astoria's Starlight Roof, a Park Avenue wingding for the Red commissar. No ordinary commissar either: Comrade Vishinsky had prosecuted Nikolai Bukharin in the last of the great Moscow show trials, had refused to let British and American warplanes aid the Polish resistance in the doomed Warsaw uprising of 1944, and was now consolidating the Soviet dominion in central Europe. To the cold warriors in Washington, he was one of Stalin's most bloodthirsty henchmen. To the men and women of the National Council, he was a slender ray of hope. Six weeks earlier, a Communist government had been declared in China; one week before that, President Truman had announced that the Soviets had detonated an atomic bomb. Even so, Vishinsky told his audience, "The Soviet

Union now as in the past advocates the immediate prohibition of atomic weapons and the establishment of strict international control, and thereby the guarantee of security for the people of the world."

Trouble was, only the faithful believed it. Henry Wallace's disastrous defeat in the 1948 presidential election—1.1 million votes, zero states—had signaled the eclipse of the left. As the National Council and its cause became increasingly suspect, members and sponsors headed for the exits. The first rush, in 1946, had claimed such figures as Judge Learned Hand, Interior Secretary Harold Ickes, Raymond Massey, and Massachusetts Senator Leverett Saltonstall. More recently, CBS executive Goddard Lieberson and Florida Senator Claude Pepper had withdrawn. Lillian Hellman, Eugene O'Neill, and Edward G. Robinson were still members, but not for long. With activities on the agenda like next month's "Outlaw the Atom Bomb" rally at Madison Square Garden and a birthday symposium on "Joseph V. Stalin—the Man and His Work," the council was increasingly out on the fringe.

Bill Morris was appalled at the turn the country had taken—at the demise of the New Deal, at the defeat of Henry Wallace and the ideal of one world, at the rout of the left and the hysteria on the right. But he couldn't speak up too loudly for fear of embarrassing the agency, especially since Lastfogel was making it clear his activities were already embarrassing. His one consolation was that he'd found somebody who shared his views. She was Ruth Ruben, the fiery redhead he and his ex-wife Jerry had shared Villa Voncha with in Hollywood some twenty years before.

Ruben was the product of a solid German-Jewish family in Cincinnati, but after sixteen years as an insurance executive's wife, she'd discovered her artistic side. This sudden flowering had been accompanied by a political awakening of the sort that seldom sits well with insurance men. Shortly before the war, she'd left her husband and moved into an apartment in Los Angeles. Bill Morris had encouraged her along the way. They'd seen a lot of each other over the years, beginning when she and the two boys came to New York for the 1939 World's Fair and stayed with him at the house on Fifty-second Street. Now they were driving up to Camp Intermission to be married. Her nickname was Red.

NINETEEN FIFTY FOUND THE NEW YORK OFFICE IN PANDEMONIUM. THE Morris Agency swept the second annual Emmy awards in January, Ed Wynn and Milton Berle taking most outstanding personality, "The Ed

Wynn Show" and Berle's "Texaco Star Theater" taking best show, "The Life of Riley" winning best telefilm. But all this success was just about more than they could handle. Their quarters in the RKO Building were so jammed they had desks rowed up in the hall. Agents were working seven days out of seven; trainees went off every night scouting for talent at little supper clubs like Café Society or Bon Soir in the Village or the Blue Angel or Le Ruban Bleu on the East Side. Everybody was on call twenty-four hours a day.

The "Admiral Broadway Revue" had actually been canceled for being too successful: Admiral couldn't manufacture TV sets fast enough to keep up with demand, so after nineteen weeks, the company decided to use its money to expand production. But NBC's Pat Weaver was a fan, and he'd fixed it for Max Liebman and Sid Caesar to come back in February as part of the two-and-a-half-hour "NBC Saturday Night Revue." The first hour was given over to a Morris package out of Chicago called "The Jack Carter Show"; Liebman followed with "Your Show of Shows," an hour and a half of comedy, opera, and dance, broadcast live from New York at nine.

For Pat Weaver, "Your Show of Shows" was an experiment. "Admiral Broadway Revue," like "Texaco Star Theater" and most other shows on television, had been purchased by the ad agency on behalf of a single sponsor; the network merely provided studio facilities and air time. But "Your Show of Shows" was bought by NBC, which then sold air time to a number of different advertisers the way a magazine would sell pages. Weaver's new magazine concept meant that NBC could get more money for the air time it had to sell, and that it could control the programming that went out under its aegis. "Your Show of Shows" also had a radical new format: Where the Admiral program had been a static presentation of a Broadway stage revue, the new one employed close-ups and camera movements to bring viewers face-to-face with the performers onscreen. Every week there was a different guest host—Burgess Meredith, Rex Harrison. There were violin solos, excerpts from *Carmen* and *La Traviata*, even a Show of Shows Ballet Company. "Really out of the top drawer," the *New York Times* declared. "Big-time entertainment and sales potential," crowed *Variety*.

Getting "Your Show of Shows" on the air every week was a nightmare job for the Morris Agency, but "Texaco Star Theater" was worse. Harry Kalcheim worked all day every day and most of the evening, only to be awakened by a call from Berle at two or three in the morning. It began every Wednesday morning at nine, twelve hours after the end of the Tuesday night broadcast, when Kalcheim and Berle got together with the writers in Berle's tiny office at Broadway and Fifty-first Street. Kalcheim would have a list of stars for next week's guest appearances, but Berle wouldn't let him book anyone until he knew what the script would be like. So Kalcheim would sit there while the writers tried to come up with ideas. The room was hot and thick with smoke, but the window had to stay shut because Berle was afraid of drafts.

Eventually they'd come up with some ideas Berle liked, and then Kalcheim would get on the phone. He had an enormous Rolodex with the name and number of every performer in existence, and he'd spend all day Thursday, Friday, and Saturday flipping through it, lining up guests—singers, dancers, acrobats, comedians, ventriloquists, whatever. Some wouldn't be available, so they'd have more meetings to come up with more names. By Sunday morning Kalcheim would have the show booked and the cast would assemble for rehearsals at Nola Studios on Broadway, upstairs from Lindy's. Invariably some of the guest stars would object to the material that had been written for them, Berle would get into the act, a lot of yelling would ensue, the stars would threaten to walk, and Kalcheim would have to cajole them in their dressing rooms well into Monday. On Tuesday they'd move to NBC's Studio 6B for dress rehearsal, which Berle ran with a towel across his neck to keep the drafts away and a whistle to save his voice and destroy everyone else's ears. If they were lucky, they'd get almost through the show before eight o'clock rolled around and it was time to go live.

Managing the Berle show meant trying to satisfy a maniacal perfectionist with an explosive personality. As director and producer, Berle controlled everything—script, bookings, performances, blocking, camera angles, costumes, lights. But he didn't control Myron Kirk of the Kudner Agency, who was a big cheese now thanks to "Texaco Star Theater." Mike Kirk was one of the toughest men in the ad business, arrogant and demanding and hard to please. When he was angry about something, he could slam his office door hard enough to take it nearly off its hinges. And while he liked to talk about television as the "atomic" sales force, he was petrified that some freelance Red hunter monitoring the airwaves would declare a guest star a Commie and spook the sponsor.

The joke was they couldn't book so-and-so because he'd just been seen coming out of the Russian Tea Room; but this was no joke. Red hunting was a growth industry in 1950, and it turned television into the atomic sales medium that could explode in your face. There was Laurence A. Johnson, the supermarket king from Syracuse, New York, an elderly gent of patriotic mien whose campaign to keep Red symps off the air was preordained to success because so much broadcasting revenue came from supermarket products—food, drugs, cleansers, toiletries. There was Vincent Hartnett, a former naval intelligence officer who kept files on suspect individuals and consulted for such firms as Young & Rubicam and the Kudner Agency. There were Kenneth Bierly, John Keenan, and Theodore Kirkpatrick, ex-FBI agents who'd set up shop on Madison Avenue as American Business Consultants and published a monthly newsletter called *Counterattack* that printed names and affiliations of anyone they considered pink.

In June 1950, a few days after Communist troops launched their sneak attack on South Korea, American Business Consultants issued a guide to fellow travelers in show business called *Red Channels*. Every performer who appeared on the Berle show had to be approved in advance by Mike Kirk, and *Red Channels*, with its conveniently alphabetized lists of suspect entertainers and organizations, became Harry Kalcheim's bible. No one who appeared in its pages could even be considered. Names that passed that test would be offered to one of Kirk's minions, who stood in the office and scanned his own list before saying yes or no. "No" often meant an explosion from Berle, who didn't like some guy having veto power over his guests and was liable to stalk out during dress rehearsal if Kirk didn't back down.

Harry Kalcheim was nervous under the best of circumstances. Between Milton Berle and Mike Kirk, he was almost a wreck. And the Morris office had more shows than ever on the 1950–1951 lineup, including the new "wheels"—weekly variety shows with rotating stars like Jack Carson, Jimmy Durante, Danny Thomas, and Ed Wynn on NBC's "Four Star Revue," or Fred Allen, Eddie Cantor, and Martin and Lewis on "The Colgate Comedy Hour." So they started looking for somebody else to run Berle. But not just anyone, because Berle was picky.

Eventually a call went out to Ben Griefer, New Jersey district manager for the Paramount theater chain, whom Kalcheim had worked with before joining the Morris office in 1941. Griefer wasn't dumb; he could see what Berle was doing to the movie theater business on Tuesday nights. He figured this was a good time to get into television. So he came in from

Newark one evening to be interviewed by Bill Morris and Nat Lefkowitz in Morris's swank office in the RKO Building, and a couple of days later he found himself on one side of a partner's desk in the hall outside the men's room. It was September 1950. The third season was due to begin in three weeks, and all they had booked was a couple of acrobats.

ITEM IN THE NOVEMBER 7, 1950, *LOS ANGELES EXAMINER*:

Johnny Hyde is in Cedars of Lebanon Hospital trying to lick the flu. His girl friend, Marilyn Monroe, will have two escorts to the opening of "All About Eve." Johnny doesn't mind because he believes there is safety in numbers.

Hyde was in Cedars of Lebanon all right, but not with the flu. His heart condition had deteriorated drastically since Jay's wedding fourteen months earlier, to the point that keeping him alive had become a very iffy proposition. Nor was he in much shape to orchestrate Marilyn's social engagements: He hadn't seen her in weeks, and it had been months since she'd stayed over at his house. She'd moved in with her drama coach, Natasha Lytess, who had a one-bedroom apartment on Harper Avenue, just below the Chateau Marmont. But he hadn't slacked off trying to make her a star.

He'd gotten her a couple of bit parts at the beginning of the year—as a roller-derby fan in *The Fireball* at Fox; as a model who fields a pass from a has-been boxing champ played by Dick Powell in M-G-M's *Right Cross*; as a receptionist who gets ogled by her boss in Metro's *Home Town Story*. Three walk-ons, three duds, a one-way ticket to oblivion. Then he'd taken her to meet Joseph L. Mankiewicz, the writer-director-producer whose credits included *The Philadelphia Story*, *Woman of the Year*, and *The Ghost and Mrs. Muir*.

Mankiewicz had become a Morris client with the Berg-Allenberg merger in December, and he was set to direct a picture for Fox, from a script he'd written, about an aging Broadway star and a demure young fan who schemes to supplant her. The project was *All About Eve*. Bette Davis and Anne Baxter would have the lead roles, and Darryl Zanuck was producing. Hyde read the script and decided that the role of Claudia Caswell—a breathless if somewhat dim-witted product of the "Copacabana School of Dramatic Art" who makes herself available to nice men who might advance her career—would be perfect for Marilyn. He didn't let up until Mankiewicz said yes.

The picture took an acid view of the theater, skewering it for, among other things, promoting actors at the expense of writers and directors. "I shall never understand the weird process by which a body with a voice suddenly fancies itself as a mind," complains Addison de Witt, Mankiewicz's sharp-tongued theater critic. "Just exactly when does an actress decide they're *her* words she's saying and *her* thoughts she's expressing?" A would-be actress, Miss Caswell voices thoughts that are naïve but not stupid. Asked to make nice to a producer, she blurts out, "Why do they always look like unhappy rabbits?" Marilyn was horribly insecure during the shoot. She only had two scenes—one in a theater lobby, another at a cocktail party—but she required some two dozen takes for the first and showed up an hour late for the second. Whose girl is *that?* wondered Davis's costar, Celeste Holm.

As Hyde became increasingly obsessed with Marilyn and debilitated by heart disease, MCA began to show a vulturelike interest in some of his clients who'd already attained stardom. That spring, while Mankiewicz was shooting *All About Eve* on the Fox lot, Jules and Doris Stein had dropped in on Rita Hayworth and Aly Khan at the Château de l'Horizon. As connoisseurs of fine art and antiques, the Steins were in a better position than most to appreciate the sun-drenched villa, with its Aubusson carpets, its paintings by Degas and Renoir and Utrillo, its terraces overlooking the Mediterranean. A bon vivant accustomed to maintaining houseguests like the Steins in lavish style even though his father controlled his fortune, Prince Aly seemed eager to see his wife go back to Hollywood—and who better to negotiate her return than Stein? So after a four-day visit, Stein arrived in New York to tell eager gossip columnists that, while Rita had no plans at present to make another picture, she would never make one without a deal for more money. And what about reports that the Love Goddess, as *Life* magazine had dubbed her, was miserable as the wife of a philandering spendthrift who loved her more for her fiery screen image than for herself? "You can discount all those rumors," he declared.

Bert Allenberg had a long talk with Hayworth a few months later that ended in her deciding to return to Johnny Hyde. But with Hayworth still playing princess and Hyde in precarious health, it wasn't much of a victory. By fall, Hyde was too frail even to go into the office. Marilyn, meanwhile, was taking a night-school class in world lit at UCLA and getting private acting lessons from Natasha Lytess and growing chummy with Sidney Skolsky, a showbiz reporter for the Hearst chain. In September, thanks to Hyde, *Photoplay* ran a feature on her called "A Star Is Born." Yet the sicker he got, the more she pulled away from him; and the more she pulled away from him, the more desperate he became. He begged her to marry him. He told her she was the only one who could save his life. She thought he was joking. She talked to him on the phone, but she didn't visit him until late November. Even Lytess, who saw herself as Hyde's rival, told her she was being thoughtless.

In early December, however, she did sign the standard client contract with the Morris Agency. Hyde, released from the hospital and working out of his house on Palm Drive, managed to get her a screen test at Fox, with a long-term contract in the offing. The test was for a project called *Cold Shoulder* that ended up on the shelf, but she did land a small part in an office comedy called *As Young as You Feel*, based on a magazine story by a young writer named Paddy Chayefsky that Helen Strauss of the New York literary department had sold to Fox.

While Marilyn was preparing for the role, Hyde started to put his affairs in order. He asked Harry Cohn to take care of his secretary, Dona Holloway, if anything should happen to him. He spoke with Sam Berke, the West Coast partner of Julius Lefkowitz, the agency's outside accountant, about drawing up a new will that would make some provision for Marilyn. Then he made the 110-mile trip out to Palm Springs, with his chauffeur, Ferde Woldemar, behind the wheel of his black limousine.

He was planning a long stay. The dry heat usually did him good, and Palm Springs, with its masseuses and its golf courses, its flowering oleanders and feathery tamarisk trees, its chic nightclubs and expensive New York shops, was the perfect desert playground. He was eager—desperate—for Marilyn to join him. She told him she couldn't. On Sunday, December 17, just a couple of days out of Los Angeles, the chest pains hit him again. That night, a shrieking ambulance rushed him back— through the San Gorgonio Pass, through the fruit orchards of Banning and Beaumont, through the Moreno Valley wheatfields, through the miles of orange groves around Riverside and Pomona, through suburban Monterey Park, through the gauntlet of gas stations and roadside stands leading to downtown Los Angeles, out Sunset to Cedars of Lebanon. It was no good. He was dead the next afternoon, at age fifty-five.

*   *   *

The funeral was set for Forest Lawn, Rabbi Edgar Magnin presiding. On Wednesday afternoon, two days after Hyde's death, the mourners wound their way up the grassy Glendale hillside, past the half-timbered mortuary and the Wee Kirk o' the Heather, up Mausoleum Slope and Sunrise Slope and Inspiration Slope and Ascension to the Church of the Recessional, a newly minted replica of Kipling's ancient Saxon Church of St. Margaret in Sussex, exact in every detail except for the palm-filled greenhouse where the stained-glass windows should have been. Here in this green swath of earthly paradise, atop a narrow ridge overlooking Hollywood on one side and the sawtooth peaks of the San Gabriel Mountains on the other, it had been decreed that death should be robbed of its sting. No misshapen monuments to mar the vista, no grim reminders of man's mortality, just sunshine and songbirds, splashing fountains and sweeping lawns—a paean to life, eternal life, on the threshold of the hereafter.

Abe Lastfogel and Bill Morris had flown in together from New York Monday night. Now they took their positions outside the church with their fellow pallbearers—Bert Allenberg, Glenn Ford, Danny Kaye, Mickey Rooney. . . . The throng of honorary pallbearers was so large, it threatened to overwhelm the proceedings: Eddie Cantor, Harry Cohn, George Cukor, Jimmy Durante, George Jessel, Garson Kanin, Elia Kazan, Louis Mayer, Laurence Olivier, Joe Schenck, Nick Schenck, Red Skelton, Danny Thomas, Spencer Tracy, Jack Warner, Darryl Zanuck, and some fifty more, a cross-section of Hollywood's elite. Edgar Magnin, Hollywood's rabbi to the stars, led the service in his theatrical manner, as if he were doing a screen test for the mourners. Danny Kaye delivered the eulogy. And then they filed out.

Leaning against the rough stone wall of the church was an uninvited guest—Marilyn Monroe, dressed entirely in black. Her face was pale, her body racked with sobs. In a voice thick with tears, she called out his name: "Johnny, Johnny, Johnny." Had she killed him? Would he still be alive if she hadn't been so selfish?

There was guilt enough to go around. He was only fifty-five, at the height of his powers. Lastfogel couldn't help thinking it was his own fault. It was he who'd left Hyde to run the West Coast operation during the war. If only he hadn't put him under all that pressure . . .

As the mourners stood together on the flagstone terrace outside the church, surrounded by huge stone tablets engraved with Kipling's poems, Lastfogel even told Donald and Jay they'd have a home with the agency any time they wanted it. But the sight of Marilyn was too much for Reece Halsey, the nephew Hyde had put to work in the literary department. "There's the bitch who killed my uncle," he muttered as they all turned away.

6

COMMUNISTS AND

MOBSTERS

Los Angeles/Las Vegas/New York/

Washington, 1951-1952

FOR BERT ALLENBERG, THE NEW YEAR WAS SHAPING UP AS A LARGE-SIZED headache. Take Edward G. Robinson, the tough guy. The Berg-Allenberg Agency had long represented him in movies, while the Morris office handled the radio appearances he did on the side—guest spots on Kate Smith's "A&P Bandwagon," DuPont's "Cavalcade of America," that sort of thing. But Robinson's extracurricular activities in behalf of the Hollywood Ten and Henry Wallace's presidential campaign and various other suspect causes had made him a prime target for the Tenney committee in Sacramento, among others. He'd made the front page of the *Los Angeles Times*: "Film Stars Listed in Red Orbit by Reports of FBI and Tenney." He'd turned up in *Red Channels*. He'd been attacked by Hedda Hopper and the *Hollywood Reporter*. He'd been singled out as "a notorious example" in the Catholic Information Society pamphlet *Red Star over Hollywood*. And so on.

Abe Lastfogel had his own problems—Judy Holliday, for instance. She'd been with the Morris Agency since the late thirties, when Ruth Morris signed up the Revuers, the comedy troupe Holliday had formed with Betty Comden and Adolph Green, and booked them into the Rainbow Room. After the war, she'd done thirty-nine months on Broadway as the star of *Born Yesterday*, the Garson Kanin play, which Lastfogel sold to Columbia. Harry Cohn wanted Rita Hayworth to play Billie Dawn, the dumb-blonde chorus girl who's content to be kept by a junk-yard baron until he makes the mistake of hiring a *New Republic* writer to smarten her up. But Columbia's Love Goddess ran off with Prince Aly the bum, and Cohn ended up testing thirty-eight actresses before settling for Holliday—"that fat Jewish broad," he called her. Now the film had just opened to rave reviews, terrific box office, and a smear campaign in the Catholic press, which was targeting it as Marxist propaganda.

Judy Garland was a problem, too. She'd been with Berg-Allenberg when it closed, and after delaying for months she'd signed with the Morris office. M-G-M, having reared her from the age of thirteen, had let her go weeks earlier after a long series of troubles—pills, suicide attempts, insomnia, more pills, nausea, drink, phobias, work habits so erratic she'd been removed from *Annie Get Your Gun*, the Irving Berlin musical, and sent to a hospital in Boston to dry out. It didn't work, and after barely managing to complete *Summer Stock* with Gene Kelly, she'd been fired from the studio. At twenty-eight, she'd hit bottom.

A nose they could fix; this was trickier. The Lastfogels fussed over her, took her into their family, all but adopted her. Uncle Abe booked her in guest spots on the radio, singing on "The Bing Crosby Show" and "The Bob Hope Show" and "The Big Show," a celebrity-studded Sunday evening variety program NBC had put together with Tallulah Bankhead as emcee. But to make a comeback she'd have to hit the stage—preferably in London, where audiences were eager for American stars and an enthusiastic response would allow her to make a triumphal return to the States. Lastfogel contacted the Palladium and was offered $15,000 a week, then $20,000. Garland was nervous; she hadn't performed live since her USO tour during the war. Finally, Abe and Frances took her to dinner at Fanny Brice's house and got Fanny to talk her into it.

Then there was Elia Kazan, the director, who took the Super Chief out from New York in early January. Kazan was staying at Charlie Feldman's house while they tried to mollify the censors on *A Streetcar Named Desire*, which Feldman had produced. Lastfogel had taken Kazan on years earlier, when Hollywood was eager to grab him because he had simultaneous hits on Broadway, directing Tallulah Bankhead in *The Skin of Our Teeth* and Helen Hayes in *Harriet*. A Greek immigrant's son who'd studied at Yale and worked with the Group Theater in New York, he brought a visceral swagger to his work, and a vision of theater that was raw and emotional and carried a punch. But what served as a tonic on Broadway could get him into trouble in Hollywood, especially with material as provocative as *Streetcar*. Were American movie audiences ready to watch a faded Southern belle, widowed by her homosexual pervert suicide husband, be brutally raped by her brother-in-law? The Breen Office—Joseph I. Breen's Production Code Administration, whose job it was to decide these things—thought not.

And then there were Johnny Hyde's Christmas presents, which started showing up in his friends' mail right after the funeral. Merry Christmas from a dead man: That left everyone spooked. From what Bert Allenberg could see, taking over the Morris Agency's film department was not going to be a picnic.

Allenberg was out of character for the Morris office anyway—tall and patrician, with a long, jowly, almost soulful-looking face. He was affable, but not exactly warm. Born in New York around the turn of the century, he'd started out a broker, then come to Los Angeles in the late twenties and gone to work as a business manager, handling investments for people in the movie colony. In 1931 he'd gone into agenting with Phil Berg, who eventually made him his partner. Allenberg lacked Lastfogel's gemütlich quality, but plenty of stars were devoted to him.

Lastfogel came in every morning and read his mail, then spent the rest of the day being chauffeured to meetings at the studios. One day in January he rode out with Kazan to see Darryl Zanuck at the Fox lot to discuss *The Hook*, a screenplay about union violence on the waterfront written by Kazan's friend Arthur Miller. Zanuck told them he didn't go for the subject matter, but he was eager to move ahead on a picture John Steinbeck was writing about the life of Emiliano Zapata, the Mexican revolutionary. As they left Fox's long, barrackslike headquarters, Kazan suggested to Lastfogel that he offer *The Hook* to Warner Bros., which happened to be Lastfogel's next stop. Kazan stayed on the lot to see his former cutter, who was directing *As Young as You Feel*, the Paddy Chayefsky picture in which Marilyn Monroe had sixth billing.

Marilyn was still grief-stricken over Hyde, but she agreed to go out with Kazan for dinner, and before long she was spending her evenings with him at Charlie Feldman's house. This was fortuitous, for though the Morris office had managed to negotiate the standard seven-year contract for her at Fox after Hyde's death, no one at the agency showed any enthusiasm except Norman Brokaw, Hyde's twenty-three-year-old nephew, who worked with George Gruskin and Phil Weltman in the radio department. Normie was adorable and eager to help, a diminutive lad with a sly, easy smile and a shock of dark brown hair that fell almost over his eyes. His mother had performed with Hyde and the rest of the family in the Haidabura Imperial Russian Dance Troupe, but she'd quit to marry a real-estate man and raise a family in Larchmont. When he was fifteen they'd moved to Los Angeles, where he'd tried to find work in defense plants and movie studios and finally ended up in the William Morris mailroom, thanks to his Uncle Johnny. He enjoyed chauffeuring Marilyn around town, but his only experience in the picture business was covering B-factories like Monogram and Republic. When Marilyn's Fox contract sat in the Morris office for three weeks before anyone notified her, Feldman's Famous Artists began to look after her affairs.

Unlike Lastfogel, Allenberg preferred to do business behind his desk, often with his barber in attendance to touch up his haircut or manicure his nails as the deal was being struck. He left it to junior agents to do the legwork at the studios, chatting up producers and casting directors. One covered the Westside studios, M-G-M in Culver City and Fox in West L.A.; another had the Hollywood studios, Columbia and Paramount and RKO; and still another spent his days out in the Valley, where Warner Bros. and Universal kept themselves. At five o'clock they'd all head back to Beverly Hills with a couple of deals in their pockets and start returning the twenty to thirty phone calls they'd gotten during the day. Once a week Allenberg presided over a department meeting at which they brought one another up to date.

Allenberg was a super salesman, the kind of character who could walk into an empty room and have seven deals going in twenty minutes. Business ignited all around him. Lately, however, some of their clients were getting so cold, it would take an atomic blast to warm them up.

Like Robinson. There didn't seem to be anything definite against him—no evidence he'd ever been a party member, for example. But he'd been active in organizations that had since been branded Communist fronts: the American Committee for Yugoslav Relief, the American Russian Institute, ICCASP. It had been twenty years since he'd shot his way to stardom as the Al Capone tough guy in *Little Caesar*. His star was bright enough to attract the Red hunters but not to withstand their attentions. He'd taken second billing to Humphrey Bogart in John Huston's *Key Largo* (1948), he'd starred in Joe Mankiewicz's *House of*

Strangers (1949), he'd done a couple of smaller pictures, and then—
nothing. So he decided to clear himself.

Easier said than done.

Being accused was simple: Anybody could do it to you. Proving your
innocence was tougher. There wasn't any system for it. After helping
launch a group called the Motion Picture Industrial Council to show
that the industry was cleaning house, Roy Brewer of the Stagehands
Union and Ronald Reagan of the Screen Actors Guild had started meeting with studio chiefs to dictate changes that would be needed before a
questionable project could reach the screen. But so far Brewer and Reagan hadn't managed to work out any way for individuals to clear themselves. The most they could do was to steer people who felt they'd been
wronged to one of the right-wing columnists in the Hearst empire,
Westbrook Pegler or Victor Riesel or George Sokolsky, who might or
might not agree with one another.

It stood to reason that the House Un-American Activities Committee
would be the ultimate tribunal on disloyalty matters, so Robinson peti-
tioned for a hearing. But the committee was getting a lot of these
requests, and it didn't seem eager to handle them. Robinson was turned
down: No accusations against him, he was told. Los Angeles Mayor
Sam Yorty pulled some strings and won him a hearing with the committee's investigators, however, and in December 1950 he'd succeeded in
testifying under oath before some actual committee members, including
Francis Walter of Pennsylvania, who'd taken over as chairman after Parnell Thomas was sent to the pen on a payroll padding scheme. Following the hearing, Robinson announced he'd been cleared. The committee's chief investigator had stated he had no record of Robinson ever
being a Communist or a suspected Communist; what else could they
want? Louella Parsons bought it: "It's time the whispering stopped," she
wrote in her column. Walter Winchell agreed. But when Allenberg and
Lastfogel talked him up with studio chiefs and production heads, they
still couldn't get any interest.

That was the way the blacklist worked: no big pronouncements, nothing you could ever point to, just—no interest. So Robinson sent copies
of his testimony to Louis Mayer, to Jack Warner, to Darryl Zanuck and
the others. No response. Then, on January 25, the anti-Communist
newsletter *Alert* announced that the committee "has not cleared actor
Edward G. Robinson, as Robinson would have the public believe."
Robinson was engaged in a "whitewash." If he'd been serious, he'd have

told who'd lured him into those Commie fronts. He'd have named names.

Robinson was like the man who came home and told his wife he'd been accused of being a rabbit. "That's ridiculous," his wife replied. "You're not a rabbit!" "I know," he said. "But how do I *prove* it?"

Holliday looked to be in much better shape. She was still on the way up, and *Born Yesterday* was so good that Harry Cohn had rushed it into release the day after Christmas so it would qualify for the 1950 Academy Awards. But it had been a bumpy ride. *Tidings*, the newspaper of the Catholic diocese of Los Angeles, had printed an article headlined "Clever Film Satire Strictly from Marx" that pointed out Garson Kanin's support of Henry Wallace and the Hollywood Ten and denounced the picture as "the most diabolically clever political satire I have encountered in almost thirty years of steady film reviewing." This was too much even for Louella Parsons: "If there are any pink ideas infiltered into *Born Yesterday*, they are way over my head," she wrote. Still, the article was reprinted in twenty-two other diocesan papers across the country.

The real satire in *Born Yesterday* wasn't political at all. Though the picture was set in Washington, where junkyard king Harry Brock goes to buy himself a congressman, the model for him was Harry Cohn of Columbia. Cohn didn't mind; he liked being thought of as a tough guy. As for the picture, Billie Dawn's visits to the Capitol and the Jefferson Memorial and the National Archives turned much of it into a Washington travelogue, and the rest was stuffed with bromides about how most congressmen are honest Joes who wouldn't give the time of day to a thug like Harry Brock. But the script did contain a few digs at fascism, and by 1951 it was possible to read any portrayal of a venal businessman as a wholesale assault on capitalism. And Holliday, too, had been listed in *Red Channels*. By March the Catholic War Veterans were picketing outside theaters in New York and New Jersey, and they had her name on their placards.

The Morris office had worked out a seven-year contract with Columbia that committed Holliday to only one film a year, at $30,000 for the first picture and $10,000 more for each one after that. That gave her plenty of time for other work, so they set out to take advantage of her stardom by putting her on the air. They booked her as a semiregular guest on "The Big Show," portraying a Billie Dawn type opposite Tallulah in skits that played off such topical subjects as *All About Eve*, whose main character—the acid-tongued Broadway star played by Bette Davis—bore a less-than-coincidental resemblance to La Bankhead. There was talk about putting Holliday in a television series as well. But as quickly as the picketers and newsletters picked her up, network executives dropped her.

Meanwhile, in Washington, the House Un-American Activities Committee was rousing itself for another investigation of Hollywood. People like Robinson were desperate to clear themselves. Members of Congress were accusing it of slacking off: The panel hadn't produced a decent-sized headline since 1948, when *Time* magazine editor Whittaker Chambers, known homosexual and reformed Communist, testified that Alger Hiss—distinguished former State Department official, veteran New Dealer, and now head of the Carnegie Endowment—was a Red. Donald L. Jackson of California, who'd succeeded Richard Nixon on the committee after Nixon rode the Hiss case to the Senate in the 1950 election, announced he was unhappy with the "implied clearance" Robinson had gotten in December. So a new round of hearings was set to begin March 21, with Morris client Larry Parks as the first witness.

TELEVISION MIGHT BE THE ATOMIC MEDIUM, BUT LAS VEGAS WAS SHAPING up as the atomic town. The military disaster in Korea, where the American push toward the Chinese border had triggered a series of Red Chinese human-wave assaults that had the Eighth Army in headlong retreat, spurred the Truman administration to start testing atomic weapons inside the United States. The site selected, with the support of Nevada's silver-haired political boss, Democratic Senator Pat McCarran, was 350 square miles on an isolated desert gunnery range that became known as the Nevada Proving Ground. The first bomb was dropped on a dry lake bed called Frenchman Flat in January 1951. Four more followed over the next ten days. An eight-kiloton device on February 2 shattered windows in Las Vegas, sixty-five miles away. A second round of tests, aimed at helping the army develop "atomic soldiers" who could use the bomb to break through enemy ranks, was set for October.

People in Vegas were excited. The A-bomb was the biggest thing to hit town since Benny Siegel, maybe bigger. For sheer entertainment value it was hard to beat. If you timed your visit right—and the chamber of commerce made it easy to do so—you could stand in your hotel room in Glitter Gulch and watch a mushroom cloud take shape in the desert sky. Out on the Strip, as the two-lane highway to Los Angeles was being called, you might even be able to watch the whole thing poolside.

The nonatomic entertainment in Vegas was pretty hot as well—Lastfogel's nephew Fred Elswit made sure of that, with help from George Wood in the New York office. The casinos on the Strip were giving the little town of twenty-five thousand a year-round entertainment lineup to rival Saratoga in August or Miami in mid-winter. The Flamingo offered Eddie Cantor, the Ritz Brothers, and Pinky Lee. El Rancho Vegas, which had signed an exclusive with the Morris Agency in 1948, had radio comic Abe Burrows, nightclub comedian Joe E. Lewis, Carmen Miranda, and Sophie Tucker. After doing her show in the Round-Up Room, Soph would set up a table in the lobby and peddle autographed copies of her book, *Some of These Days*, which Reece Halsey of the Morris office was trying to sell to Paramount. Joe E. had a tendency to drop his paycheck at the dice tables, which encouraged the crowd around him to follow suit and so endeared him to owner Beldon Katleman that he became the joint's resident comic.

April 1950 had seen the arrival of a fifth resort on the Strip, the pink-and-green Desert Inn, fronted by an ebullient, fun-loving fellow named Wilbur Clark but controlled by Moe Dalitz and the Cleveland mob. The same pattern of investment held at the Strip's fourth attraction, the Thunderbird, which had been started by a partnership involving Nevada Lieutenant Governor Clifford Jones but got a critically timed boost of cash from Meyer Lansky and his brother Jake. With Jones providing the grease, the Thunderbird became a hangout for Senator McCarran and his cronies, who were too busy to worry about the moral fiber of the boys who ran the place. During the war, McCarran had pulled strings to get the town a magnesium plant and an air base. In 1946 he'd helped Benny Siegel cut through government restrictions to get the steel and other materials to build the Flamingo. In 1948 he'd helped the town get its first civilian airport, McCarran Field, conveniently located near the Strip. "A senator from Nevada is like a college president," A. J. Liebling observed when he covered the opening of the Desert Inn for *The New Yorker*; "his job is to get things."

When he wasn't getting things, McCarran was hunting Reds. Along with Wisconsin's Joe McCarthy, he was one of the "primitives," as Secretary of State Dean Acheson called them—a group of right-wing western and midwestern senators who hated New Dealers, Wall Street fat cats, and card-carrying Communists with equal virulence. McCarran had been pursuing Reds when McCarthy was still developing a taste for whiskey. He'd been on the case in 1939, leading the grill team when Franklin Roosevelt appointed Harvard law professor Felix Frankfurter to the Supreme Court. More recently he'd pushed through the McCarran Internal Security Act, which required all Communist and Communist-front groups to register with a government board, barred Communists from government jobs, stripped them of their passports, and allowed for detention camps in case of national emergency. Truman declared the measure "a mockery of the Bill of Rights," but Congress overrode his veto, and McCarran promptly took command of a new Senate Subcommittee on Internal Security.

The Red hunt might mean big trouble in Hollywood and on television, but thanks to Pat McCarran and the mob, the Morris office had a great new concentration of nightclubs to book in the Nevada desert. The Congress giveth, and the Congress taketh away. The best part, from the agency's point of view, was that the casinos weren't bound by the laws of economics that constrained ordinary niteries. At the Copa or the Mocambo, how much a performer could earn was determined by the club's take from cover charges and drinks and the like. In Vegas, that didn't matter. What mattered in Vegas was whether a performer drew gamblers. It was all about traffic—and with the new casinos opening up and down the Strip, a bidding war for top-drawing entertainers was clearly in the offing.

This was good news for the Morris office, whose nightclub business had been suffering from excess law enforcement. The Colonial Inn, the posh gambling den Frank Costello and Meyer Lansky had opened outside Miami, had been shut down in 1948 at the behest of the local citizenry. Two years later a couple of neighboring joints controlled by Lansky had been closed as well. Lansky, Jimmy Blue-Eyes Alo, and eight others paid fines and walked, but the era of the suburban carpet joint was clearly over. It was beginning to look as if Fred Elswit had been on to something when he championed Vegas even before the Bugsy snuff.

Elswit was a raffish young man, just the type to appreciate a wide-open gambling town. He'd grown up in the Bronx, in an apartment house owned by his grandfather, Ben Lastfogel. As a junior agent in the New York personal appearance department before the war, he'd made a habit of dating every chorus girl he could get his hands on. Eventually he married Dorothy Olson, who was in a roller-skating trio called the Hollywood Blondes that the Morris office booked into the Latin Quarter and the Roxy and Radio City Music Hall, downstairs from the office. She was called Midge, and she was as sweet as she was tiny—five-foot-three and ninety-eight pounds. Elswit was out on a date the night their first child was born.

After he got back from occupation duty in Japan, he and Midge bought a little GI starter house in Mar Vista, a section of West L.A. between the sprawling Twentieth Century–Fox lot and the beach town of Santa Monica. Developments like this were springing up all over now that the war was over, amid the ranch lands and orange groves of the San Fernando Valley, in the beanfields and beetfields north of Long Beach, anywhere there was a broad expanse of more-or-less level ground that could be scraped raw and carved up into little lots and covered with two- or three-bedroom houses that were just big enough to shelter the families everybody was so eager to start. A lot of Mar Vista residents settled there because it was close to the Douglas Aircraft plant on Ocean Park Boulevard, or the Northrup plant next to the Municipal Airport. Elswit liked it because it was close to Santa Monica's Clover Field. He'd had a pilot's license for years, and every chance he got he'd rent a little plane and take it out to Vegas for the weekend. He'd land at McCarran Field and show up at some big opening and catch up with the boys who ran the joints, and then he'd fly back home.

Vegas was a twenty-four-hour party in the middle of nowhere, a floating crap game in the desert where all the players were pals. A little dirt road led from McCarran Field to the Strip, which looked from a distance like a few flickers of neon surrounded by a vast and unfathomable blackness. The first flicker was the Flamingo, low-slung and flamboyantly modernistic. After that was more blackness. Then came Wilbur Clark's Desert Inn, with its contemporary Western look and its eighteen-hole golf course out back. Past that was the Last Frontier, a rambling hitching post of a place with huge sandstone fireplaces and pony-hide ceilings and mounted cattle horns on the walls—"The Early West in Modern Splendor," said the neon sign out front. Next door was the Last Frontier Village, a Wild West attraction with covered wagons, a narrow-gauge railroad, round-the-clock wedding services at the Little Church of the West, and burlesque shows at the Silver Slipper Saloon. Up the road a bit more was the Thunderbird, dedicated to the mythical fowl the Navajos considered "The Sacred Bearer of Happiness Unlimited."

Finally, across from a schlocky casino called the Club Bingo, was El Rancho Vegas, the place that started it all, with green lawns and cabins and a Western-style windmill etched in colored neon. From the El Rancho it was still three miles into town.

One of the hottest acts Fred Elswit booked in Vegas was the Will Mastin Trio, a song-and-dance team out of Harlem featuring a kid named Sammy Davis, Jr., who did unbelievable impressions of—this was the astonishing part—*white people*. Most colored performers shuffled across the stage with downcast eyes, going "Yassuh, yassuh" and acting as if they'd just wandered in from the cotton patch. Davis worked the crowd directly, strutting his stuff like white performers did. Audiences loved him. Innkeepers didn't: The only place the group could find to spend the night was a tumbledown rooming house in the Negro shantytown on the far side of the tracks from Glitter Gulch.

The Will Mastin Trio had first played Vegas at the El Rancho in 1945. They'd opened for Frank Sinatra when he played the Capitol Theatre in New York, and then they'd gotten a gig at Ciro's on Oscar night, when every star in Hollywood was there. Sammy had torn the place up that night, doing Sinatra, doing Mel Tormé, Nat "King" Cole, Frankie Laine, Humphrey Bogart, Jimmy Cagney, Edward G. Robinson—"riotous," said *Daily Variety*. "Show-stoppers," cried the *Los Angeles Times*. Abe Lastfogel had come backstage and signed them to the Morris Agency, and then he'd taken Sammy to lunch at Hillcrest and introduced him to the greats who hung out at the round table there—Jack Benny, George Burns, Al Jolson, Groucho Marx. From there the Will Mastin Trio had gone straight to the top: the Copacabana. The Flamingo. The Riviera in Fort Lee, New Jersey, a glamorous pillbox of a place perched atop the Hudson River Palisades near the George Washington Bridge, where on warm summer evenings the roof swung open and you could dance beneath the strawberry moon with the lights of Manhattan twinkling in the distance.

At the end of February 1951, about a month after the first A-bomb hit Frenchman Flat, Fred and Midge Elswit hopped in a little rented plane and flew to McCarran Field. The Will Mastin Trio was playing the Flamingo again, and Elswit wanted to be on hand. The two boys—Richard, age five, and Robert, eight months—were left with a nanny in Mar Vista. Fred and Midge were planning to spend a couple of days in Vegas, then fly back on Sunday, March 2. A winter storm blew in from the Pacific that weekend, bringing thick clouds and torrential rains. All commercial flights out of Vegas were grounded. But Fred decided to fly back anyway. He'd made the trip dozens of times; he knew the area.

Lastfogel got to the office Monday morning to discover that Fred and Midge hadn't been heard from. His first response was anger. He knew what was right and what was wrong, and bad judgment was wrong. It was stupid to fly in weather like that, and he couldn't imagine why anyone as able and hardworking as Fred would do something stupid. But Fred had always had a reckless streak—like that night before the war, when he'd had a few drinks and run off the road and totaled his aunt Bessie's Packard convertible. "If he survives this," Lastfogel said, "I'm going to kill him." But by then their bodies were already scattered across a barren mountainside near the California-Nevada line.

THAT WAS THE SPRING OF THE GREAT CONGRESSIONAL ROAD SHOWS. ON March 13, the Kefauver committee—the Special Senate Committee to Investigate Organized Crime in Interstate Commerce, headed by Estes Kefauver of Tennessee—opened hearings in New York after a ten-month tour of the underworld that included stops in San Francisco, Kansas City, New Orleans, and Detroit. In Washington, eight days later, the House Un-American Activities Committee resumed the probe of Red subversion in Hollywood it had halted so abruptly in 1947. Both committees sought the same thing—headlines, public acclaim, but also to sound an alarm. Somewhere out there was a massive conspiracy, unseen hands pulling the strings, subverting the natural order of things. By the time these committees were through, both politics and show business would be ravaged.

The Kefauver revelations were shocking. There was "a government within a government in this country," he announced in February 1951, "and that second government was the government by the underworld." A homespun Chattanooga lawyer serving his first term in the Senate, Estes Kefauver had originally faced competition on the crime issue from another freshman senator, Joe McCarthy, until McCarthy got distracted by the news potential of Commies in the State Department. Now Kefauver had the hot seat waiting for the man the press was calling the prime minister of the underworld—George Wood's pal, Frank Costello.

Costello was a notorious figure by now—1949 cover boy for *Time* and *Newsweek*, touted as "America's Number One Mystery Man" in *Collier's*, regarded by millions (according to *Time*) as a "master criminal, shadowy as a ghost and cunning as Satan, who ruled a vast, mysterious and malevolent underworld and laughed lazily at the law." Actually, he was more Satan's caretaker than Satan himself: Charlie Luciano was the real boss, but he'd been sent up to Dannemora and then banished to Italy, where his second-in-command, Vito Genovese, had already fled to avoid prosecution on a 1934 murder beef. Genovese had been sent back to the U.S. to face trial after the war, but when the state's key witness turned up dead in protective custody, he walked. Now he was reasserting his control, yet it was Costello—a man who'd once left an envelope stuffed with $27,200 in cash in a taxi and then tried to claim it—who drew the headlines.

Kefauver hadn't intended for his New York hearings to be televised, but they were anyway—in twenty cities, live, from the East Coast to the Midwest. When Costello's attorney protested the cameras, a technician suggested they show the witness's hands instead of his face. So for more than a week Costello's harsh, raspy voice could be heard dissembling on the subject of his aliases, his criminal record, his citizenship application, his assets, his business interests, his income taxes, his associates, and his political connections, while the camera focused relentlessly on his hands—the hands the newspapers were saying had America by the throat.

George Wood had been trying for years to introduce Costello to Helen Strauss, head of the Morris Agency's literary department, but being a proper woman, she'd resisted the idea. Now he was the guest star in the most popular television series in the country. Housewives, businessmen—more than twenty million people dropped what they were doing and watched, mesmerized by the first glimpse of an underworld that J. Edgar Hoover, top G-man in the nation, had been telling them didn't exist. Con Edison had to add an extra generator to keep all the television sets going in New York. It was the biggest thing to hit TV since Milton Berle. Costello became a celebrity. People came up to him in restaurants and asked for his autograph. Cigarette companies offered him big money to play with their brand on the witness table.

Larry Parks got no such offers when he appeared the following week before the House Un-American Activities Committee. It was funny: Organized crime was a threat, and Communism was a threat, but one seemed glamorous and the other just scary. Parks took the stand the day Alger Hiss went to prison, the day the government rested its case against Julius and Ethel Rosenberg, charged with selling atomic secrets to the Soviet Union. Parks admitted that he'd been a party member from 1941 to 1945, but he asked his questioners not to make him name others who'd been in the party, too. "This is not the American way," he said, and some committee members seemed to agree. "Don't present me with the choice of either being in contempt of this committee and going to jail, or forcing me to really crawl through the mud to be an informer," he begged. "For what purpose?" The willingness to name names, explained Jackson of California, was "the ultimate test of the credibility of a witness." The mud was waiting. Parks crawled.

When they asked him about Edward G. Robinson, Parks said he'd never seen Robinson at a party meeting—but what did that prove? On March 14 character actor Ward Bond, treasurer of the fervently anti-Communist Motion Picture Alliance for the Preservation of American Ideals, had declared in a *Daily Variety* interview that if Robinson and José Ferrer—up for an Oscar as star of *Cyrano de Bergerac*—claimed they weren't Red symps, it was "outright perjury." And if the academy insisted on giving Oscars to Ferrer or Judy Holliday or Sam Jaffe (nominated for his supporting role in *The Asphalt Jungle*), Bond warned, it was going to mean trouble.

The 1950 Academy Awards were shaping up as the latest battleground in Hollywood's ideological civil war. Ostensibly, the struggle was between Fox's *All About Eve* and Paramount's *Sunset Boulevard*—navel-gazing examinations of the acting trade that turned into acts of psychic disembowelment. The two films were competing against each other for best editing, best art direction, best cinematography, best direction, best supporting actress, best supporting actor, best actress, and best picture. The Morris office had several clients in contention, including Joe Mankiewicz as writer and director of *All About Eve*, George Cukor as director and Judy Holliday as lead actress in *Born Yesterday*, and Garson Kanin and Ruth Gordon as writers on another Cukor picture, *Adam's Rib*. But for many the question wasn't whose clients won, or even which studios. It was which side the winners were on.

The ceremonies were held on March 29, hosted by Fred Astaire at Hollywood's Pantages Theatre, a grand Art Deco movie palace whose outmoded faddishness seemed to sum up the fate of the business. Cukor, Holliday, Jaffe, and Ferrer were all in New York, where Ferrer was costarring with Gloria Swanson in a Broadway revival of *Twentieth Century*. So Ferrer hosted a second Oscar gathering at La Zambra, a Spanish cabaret on Manhattan's West Side, which had been fitted out for the evening with a live radio hookup. Holliday was given little chance of winning, not just because of her politics but because of the competition—Swanson in *Sunset Boulevard*, Bette Davis in *All About Eve*.

Jaffe lost to George Sanders, the devastatingly acerbic theater critic in *All About Eve*. Mankiewicz, in Hollywood, was named best screenwriter for the same picture. And best director. When Ferrer—who'd just been subpoenaed by HUAC—was named best actor, he stepped quickly to the microphone. "This means more to me than an honor to an actor," he said. "I consider it a vote of confidence and an act of faith, and, believe me, I'll not let you down." A few moments later, Olivia de Havilland stood onstage in Hollywood and unsealed the envelope for best actress. The winner was . . . *Judy Holliday*!

The crowd at La Zambra erupted. Holliday struggled to reach the mike before the connection to Hollywood was switched off. "Judy, darling!" cried Gloria Swanson, regal in a black sheath dress and white mink bolero jacket set off by a veiled pillbox hat and elbow-length gloves. Then in a whisper she snipped, "Why couldn't you have waited till next year?"

WOULD THERE BE A NEXT YEAR? MAYBE NOT FOR SWANSON, BUT MAYBE not for Holliday either, or for anybody who'd stepped out of line. All spring and summer and into the fall, the House Un-American Activities Committee labored to expose the Red conspiracy as Billy Wilkerson cheered them on in the *Hollywood Reporter*. People agonized over their choices, wept on the witness stand, took the Fifth or named names, tried to explain away their youthful idealism, and occasionally committed suicide. Their agents did what they could to help, the Morris office as much as any other.

Morris had no agency policy. At first, many agents had trouble understanding why these people couldn't just get on the stand and testify to what they'd done. Even when they saw the way people like Robinson were being victimized, there seemed to be little they could do except live with reality and do what they could to help the clients who needed it—try to get them work, steer them toward people who might be able to clear them, line up lawyers, advise them on whether and how to testify. This was no repeat of the vaudeville wars Will Morris had fought, when Keith and Albee tried to blacklist anyone who didn't play by their rules. This blacklist was too big to fight. It was being demanded by political leaders, industry leaders, and a big chunk of the public, and it was being applied—selectively applied, according to criteria no one could really understand—in broadcasting, movies, even the theater. Maybe if Will Morris had been around . . . but he wasn't.

Edward G. Robinson's name surfaced again, courtesy of Edward Dmytryk, a member of the Hollywood Ten who'd done jail time for refusing to say whether he was a Communist and now wanted to redeem himself. He couldn't tell the committee if Robinson was a Communist, but he did mention that the nineteen unfriendly witnesses summoned in 1947 had met at Robinson's house in Beverly Hills after getting their subpoenas. Robinson knew now he was washed up in pictures, so he naïvely asked the Morris office to try to get him TV work. With the *Red Channels* listing, their attempts came to nothing. But he was offered the lead in the road company production of *Darkness at Noon*, based on Arthur Koestler's starkly anti-Communist novel about a Soviet commissar caught in the Stalinist purges. Two years earlier he'd turned down the part on Broadway, but his prospects were bleaker now. It was an arduous role for a fifty-eight-year-old—two hours onstage with barely a break. Yet its portrayal of a man broken and betrayed by his own countrymen was hard to beat for public relations value. It also spoke to his own condition. He took it.

Elia Kazan was in a different jam. The Legion of Decency, censorship arm of the Catholic Church, was threatening *A Streetcar Named Desire* with a "C" rating—C for condemned. There was talk that the Catholic War Veterans might picket, that a boycott might materialize, not just of *Streetcar* but of all Warner Bros. films. Kazan learned that *Streetcar's* premiere at Radio City Music Hall had been canceled. Then he discovered that Jack Warner—after promising the film would go to theaters as is—had sent the film's cutter to New York with orders not to let Kazan know. Kazan was furious. He phoned Steve Trilling, Warner's right-hand man. He spoke to Lastfogel, who suggested he put it all on paper. He wrote Trilling an angry letter, and as soon as he'd finished shooting *Zapata*, he rushed to New York to salvage *Streetcar*.

He ended up in the company of one Martin Quigley, publisher of a couple of motion picture trade papers and friend of Francis Cardinal

Spellman of New York. It developed that the film had already been cut, at Quigley's behest, after Jack Warner asked him what he thought should be done to keep the picture from getting a C. Quigley was a calm man, large and pasty-faced, and he tried to reassure Kazan that he'd done the minimum necessary to avoid censure. Kazan was not calm. He seethed. He went home and had nightmares. He wrote an article for the *New York Times*. None of it mattered. Warner Bros. owned the film, and Jack Warner could no more risk offending the Legion of Decency than Harry Cohn could risk arousing the Catholic War Veterans.

WALLY JORDAN OF THE TELEVISION DEPARTMENT SPENT MUCH OF THAT spring of 1951 in negotiations with NBC, which was eager to nail down the services of Milton Berle. Three years into its run, "Texaco Star Theater" was still the number one show on the air, watched according to the new Nielsen ratings in 62 percent of all households with a television. Berle was much in demand as a guest star on other shows, and he'd been pestering the network about filming the Texaco program for reruns instead of just letting it vanish into the ether. So on May 3 he was presented with the biggest contract in the history of television—a "lifetime" deal guaranteeing him $100,000 a year minimum for thirty years (more when he actually performed) in return for going exclusive with NBC. The terms had everyone gasping. They far exceeded the deals Paley had made for Amos 'n' Andy, Jack Benny, and Burns and Allen two and a half years earlier. MCA had upped the ante by starting a bidding war; now both agencies, and their clients, would benefit.

Morris's television department was also talking with NBC about a show for Judy Holliday, but here they were having less luck. It was customary for Oscar winners to get sweeter terms on their movie contracts, guest shots on TV and radio, that sort of thing. But Holliday was in *Red Channels*, and when the ad agency called the FBI and was told she did indeed have a long string of front involvements, though she'd never belonged to the party, the idea was dropped. Instead, after a brief engagement with New York's City Center Drama Company, Holliday found herself doing summer stock while waiting for a movie role. The Morris Agency negotiated a deal that made summer-stock history—a

$5,000 advance plus fifty percent of the gross (minus $4,000 to go toward script rights and tour expenses) for a three-week tour. But still— summer stock, for an actress who'd just won an Oscar?

At least Holliday had Harry Cohn behind her. Cohn was no left-winger, but like Harry Brock in *Born Yesterday*, he didn't intend to be pushed around by a bunch of politicians. Not that he knew what to do with her, exactly. He'd been thinking of a film version of Anita Loos's *Gentlemen Prefer Blondes*, which was playing on Broadway with Carol Channing as Lorelei Lee, the gold-digging blonde who sets sail for Paris with rocks in her eyes. Holliday was interested in another Anita Loos play, *Happy Birthday*, which Reece Halsey of the Morris office had earlier tried to sell as a vehicle for Claudette Colbert. Garson Kanin and Ruth Gordon had been writing a screenplay called *The Marrying Kind* with Holliday and Sid Caesar in mind, a bittersweet comedy about a lower-middle-class couple who go to court for a divorce but, after telling their story to the judge (and the audience, through flashbacks), decide to try again. Cohn liked it; so did Holliday. Sid Caesar was far too busy with "Your Show of Shows" to make a film, so Cohn gave the male lead to Aldo Ray, a young actor he'd signed, and hired George Cukor to direct.

But Cohn also had to protect his investment in Holliday. He steered her to George Sokolsky, the Hearst columnist, but Sokolsky didn't buy her protestations of innocence. So he hired Kenneth Bierly, one of the ex-FBI agents behind *Red Channels*, to investigate her—a clever move, since if Bierly wanted to please his new boss, he'd have to exonerate her. That summer Bierly reported that he could find no evidence Holliday had ever been a party member. She hadn't meant to do anything subversive, he added, but she'd have to be more careful. He also had a tip: She wasn't going to be called before HUAC.

That was good news, given the drift of the hearings. In September, as Holliday was in New York doing location shots for *The Marrying Kind*, the committee moved its hearings to the Federal Building in Los Angeles: more names for the bonfire. Columbia's story editor, Eve Ettinger, testified that she'd been a party member during the late thirties. A staff investigator asked if she'd known John Weber, head of the Morris Agency's West Coast literary department, as a Communist: No. A week later, the committee heard from Leo Townsend, a journeyman screenwriter who'd joined the party in 1943 and enjoyed little success at the studios despite the persistent efforts of his agent, Reece Halsey of the Morris office.

Townsend was an easygoing sort with a moon-shaped face and a jolly disposition—unusual for party members. He and his wife, Pauline, who'd joined the party with him in the excitement of a wartime discussion of current events, lived in the Malibu Colony, in a house on pylons above the surf. She'd been assigned to run the Los Angeles arm of the National Council of American-Soviet Friendship. He, like a lot of party members in Hollywood, had gone into therapy with Philip Cohen, a lay analyst whose patients later showed a remarkable tendency to cooperate with the FBI. In 1950 Townsend had called the bureau and spoken with two agents in his house. Now, summoned before the committee, he reported that as a party member, he'd been asked to contribute to such groups as the Hollywood Democratic Committee and the National Council of American-Soviet Friendship. He also named thirty-seven other party members. One of them was Reece Halsey's boss, John Weber.

Also that day Senator Harry Cain of Washington called on Truman to explain why he hadn't appointed the detention board authorized by the McCarran Internal Security Act to round up subversives in case of war. There was work to be done, Cain declared: Setting up procedures for sending suspect citizens to internment camps would be complicated and time-consuming. On the other hand, J. Edgar Hoover had already promised he could round up twenty-five thousand Communists in short order.

The next day another screenwriter, Martin Berkeley, took the stand. Tall and blond, Berkeley had worked on the *Dr. Gillespie* and *Dr. Kildare* series for M-G-M—programmers about a crusty old doctor and his young protégé. He produced 161 names, probably a record. One of them was Weber—"Mr. John Weber, W-e-b-e-r, who functioned as a teacher, both for party people and to work with nonparty groups, and later became a very successful agent with the William Morris Agency. I doubt if he is there right now."

Good call. John Weber didn't look forward to hiding in the bedroom with the lights off, hoping to dodge the subpoena servers. He'd never been much for foreign climes, but he and his wife, Ruth, had made a sudden decision to broaden their horizons while they still had their passports. They were headed for Paris.

KEN BIERLY, THE *RED CHANNELS* MAN, WAS RIGHT: JUDY HOLLIDAY WAS not summoned before HUAC. She was subpoenaed by Pat McCarran's

Senate Subcommittee on Internal Security. McCarran's usual territory was the army and the State Department; he wanted answers to the big questions, like who'd lost China. But in the spring of 1952 he broadened his interests to include a hearing on "Subversive Infiltration of Radio, Television, and the Entertainment Industry." Since most of his witnesses were Jews of Eastern European origin, it was assumed that his real motive was to dramatize the need for the new McCarran-Walter immigration bill (cosponsored by Francis Walter of Pennsylvania, the HUAC chairman), which would maintain strict quotas for most countries outside Western Europe. Holliday (real name Tuvim) got her subpoena toward the end of 1951, shortly after shooting was completed on *The Marrying Kind.*

Harry Cohn was caught in a quandary. He didn't want to offend the public by employing people rendered odious through some run-in with Congress. But he had product in the pipeline and money tied up in it, money he couldn't throw away. So he went to work. Columbia attorneys assured subcommittee staffers that Holliday would cooperate; in return they asked that she not be called until after the new picture had opened. The subcommittee agreed. Using his Vegas contacts, Cohn approached McCarran with another request—that the hearing be held in closed session. Again assurances were forthcoming. Holliday's appearance was set for March 26, nearly a year to the day after her Oscar win.

Allenberg and Lastfogel were trying to scare up interest in Robinson for a film version of *Darkness at Noon,* or for anything else they could dig up. He'd been touring since September 28, and as the months wore on, his phone calls from the road became less and less coherent. His brief stopover in Los Angeles in mid-February gave everybody reason to worry. "Please, Eddie, get hold of yourself," Allenberg wired him in Seattle on March 3. "I know you are human and entitled to moments of weakness and depression and God knows you have been strong and courageous beyond belief during this terrible period and you do have good friends who are loyal and working for you myriads of them and you will be on top again higher than ever before so have faith and confidence for yourself just as I have for you. Let me hear from you. All my love, Bert."

Holliday was frantic, too. Cohn's stall gave *The Marrying Kind* time to open before the bad press swung in, but it did little for her mental state. It didn't matter that she'd never been a Communist, or that the worst anyone could claim was that she'd performed at a couple of rallies that might have had Communist Party organizers behind them. She was going to have to testify, under oath. She couldn't take the Fifth without ending her career, and she had no grounds to take it anyway. But once she started, she'd have to answer questions about anyone she knew who might have been a Communist—her best friend, a New York City policewoman; her uncle, who was dead; even her mother.

After preparing a conciliatory statement with the lawyer Cohn had hired for her, Holliday and her husband went to Washington for the hearing. Pickets from the Catholic War Veterans were brandishing signs outside theaters where *The Marrying Kind* was playing: "Judy Holliday Is the Darling of the Daily Worker." She couldn't take a chance on being discovered at a hotel—Oscar-winning actresses weren't going to Washington these days to tour the National Archives—so they stayed with an acquaintance, a public relations man who cannily suggested that she wow the subcommittee with her Billie Dawn routine. The next morning she walked into the Senate Office Building on Constitution Avenue in a black dress with white gloves and a veiled hat, a curvaceous morsel marching *click-click-click* down the endless halls of government. Entering the fourth-floor hearing room, she took her seat beneath the rostrum and submitted to questioning.

The questions were sharp and relentless, the tone disbelieving. They asked about her name, her friends, her uncle, her political activities, this group, that group. They asked if she'd ever urged the repeal of the McCarran Internal Security Act. If she believed in God. If she knew about Thomas Mann and Albert Einstein and their long record of involvement in Communist fronts. She was nervous, almost shaking, but she kept her cool. "I am sure none of them are Communists," she declared in her high-pitched, nasal voice, all dippy and innocent. "I mean, if you are a Communist, why go to a Communist front? Why not be a Communist? Whatever you are, be it!"

It was hard to argue with that logic, and Utah Republican Arthur Watkins didn't try. After two hours and forty minutes of questioning, he dismissed her with a fatherly lecture. "We do not like to quiz you," he intoned. ". . . That is a job, unpleasant as it is. Personally I would much rather find that everybody we brought in here was completely innocent and there were not any subversive elements in this country trying to overthrow it." Then he reminded her not to release anything from the proceedings, like the statement she'd prepared attesting to her patriotism.

"Release anything?" she said. "I'd rather die."

As FAR AS ABE LASTFOGEL WAS CONCERNED, THESE INVESTIGATIONS WERE getting uncomfortably close. It was one thing to represent actors or writers or directors who might be dupes or fellow travelers or even outright Reds—how could a talent agent know what his clients were plotting? It was something else to have potential subversives inside the agency, where they could place these people in key positions. If people thought there was a conspiracy to subvert the American way of life through television and radio and the movies, what better way to accomplish it than by burrowing from within, through the agencies that brokered talent? And if people discovered that the president of one of these agencies— the namesake, in fact, of the very agency whose Hollywood literary chief had just fled the country—was himself a Red . . .

It was a bum rap, but there you had it. The name William Morris, Jr., was one of thousands of threads that ran throughout a vast and loosely woven tapestry of accusation and investigation—never very prominent, always in the background, just waiting to be plucked, or maybe not: You never knew. So far, though plenty of little-known screenwriters had been forced to rat on their colleagues or abandon their careers, the anti-Communist press had mainly seized on stars—John Garfield, Lillian Hellman, Judy Holliday, Dorothy Parker, Edward G. Robinson. Bill Morris had led several of the groups they'd been active in—Russian War Relief, the National Council of American-Soviet Friendship, the Committee to Free Earl Browder, ICCASP—and he'd been cited for it repeatedly by both the Tenney committee in Sacramento and the House committee in Washington. The FBI had already paid the West Coast office a Sunday morning visit to photograph John Weber's files. One unfriendly columnist, one carefully placed leak, one subpoena, and Bill Morris and his agency could find themselves in a maelstrom of accusation.

It wasn't as if good things had been happening to the other leaders of the National Council of American-Soviet Friendship. Morris's friend Corliss Lamont had been pilloried in *Newsweek*, summoned before HUAC, and fingered as a Communist before McCarran's subcommittee—a charge Lamont hotly contended. The State Department had denied him a passport. Reverend William Howard Melish, a cofounder of the council with Morris and Lamont, had been splashed across the front page of the *Brooklyn Eagle* for months, provoking a bitter dispute at the Church of the Holy Trinity in Brooklyn Heights that cost his father his position as rector there. Richard Morford, the council's executive director, had gone to jail for contempt after refusing to give the books to HUAC.

Bill Morris had quietly distanced himself from the organization, stepping down as vice chairman, taking a less active role in its affairs. But the damage had been done. More than one of the agency's clients were being blacklisted for less—Edward G. Robinson, for example. The memory of his sainted father cut Morris a lot of slack with some of the more virulent right-wingers in the press, like Jack Lait, the hard-nosed executive editor of Hearst's *Daily Mirror*, who'd gotten his start as Will Morris's press agent when Morris was building his vaudeville circuit. But there was no guarantee, and things were happening fast.

HUAC had resumed its investigation of Hollywood in January. One of the first to be summoned was Elia Kazan, who'd been a party member in the thirties when he was with the Group Theater in New York. Appearing in closed session, he'd testified about himself but refused to name others. Two months later, arriving at the Bel Air Hotel for the Oscar ceremony (*Streetcar*, having survived the Quigley depredations, was up for every major award, including best director), he got a call from Lastfogel in New York: HUAC had leaked his testimony to George Sokolsky, who was about to expose his Communist past in the *New York Journal-American*. The next day, at a lunch meeting in the producer's dining room at Fox, Darryl Zanuck told him that Fox president Spyros Skouras had managed to kill the Sokolsky column. But Zanuck had heard from Billy Wilkerson that Kazan would be called again, this time in open session. "Name the names, for chrissake," Zanuck said. "Who the hell are you going to jail for? You'll be sitting there and someone else will sure as hell name those people. Who are you saving?"

Abe Lastfogel concurred. Lastfogel was a principled man, so stiff and upright that people called him "the Pope" behind his back. He didn't get involved in politics, but like most of Hollywood's other self-made immigrant businessmen, he was conservative by nature and patriotic to the core. He hated the blacklist, he didn't want to see anyone smeared or put out of work, but he hated Communism more. And he was practical by nature.

On April 10, after an agonizing reappraisal in which he concluded that the Communist Party's efforts to censor members who strayed from the party line (as Budd Schulberg had done in his Hollywood novel *What Makes Sammy Run*) were no different from the Catholic Church's efforts to censor *Streetcar*, Kazan went before the committee again. In a prepared statement he named eleven names, eight of them people he'd worked with in the Group Theater. "I have come to the conclusion that I did wrong to withhold these names before, because secrecy serves the Communists and is exactly what they want. The American people need the facts and all the facts. . . ." Two days later he took out an ad in the *New York Times* in which he not only defended his actions but urged others to do likewise. But people he'd worked with for years now crossed the street to avoid meeting him.

Lastfogel was in New York, wrestling with his own dilemma. Bill Morris had never been more than a figurehead in running the agency, and now he'd endangered it with his left-wing associations. They both knew that any attempt he made to defend himself would place the agency in an untenable position. He would have to go.

The decision was reached quietly, with a minimum of fuss. Lastfogel may have been angry with Morris for what he'd done, but he couldn't deny their past. They'd grown up together, the prince and the pauper. The pauper had become pope; the prince was forever the dilettante, a well-meaning amateur in a game other men were playing for keeps. Yet they were still brothers in a way, united in their admiration for Morris's father. Lastfogel had no wish to destroy the son. The son had no wish to destroy the agency, and no illusion he could run it himself. Lastfogel was everything he wasn't—a shrewd businessman, a canny salesman, a hard-driving executive. Morris could never in good conscience challenge him for control of the agency. Yet it was part of him, it bore his name, he'd never be able to cut himself off from it.

The announcement went out Tuesday, April 29—a terse, four-sentence release. On July 1, William Morris, Jr., would retire from the agency; Abe Lastfogel would continue with the company; William Morris, Jr., would remain a director; end of story. Morris sent out telegrams to friends and family and colleagues—to his sister, Ruth, at Camp Intermission; to Frances Lastfogel at the Essex House; to her brother Harry Armhaus in Italian Harlem; to Abe's sister Bessie; to Nat Lefkowitz on vacation at the Hotel de Crillon in Paris; to Danny Kaye in Beverly Hills; to Jimmy Durante and Sophie Tucker in London; to Jack Lait at the *Daily Mirror*; to Allen DuMont at DuMont Laboratories; to Lee Shubert at the Shubert Organization; to Adolph Zukor at Paramount; to Spyros Skouras at Fox. "Everybody happy," a typical cable ended. "Love and kisses."

The New York staff assembled in the new offices at Broadway and Fifty-fifth Street to hear Morris make the announcement personally. It was a bittersweet moment, a gentle, lovely man wishing them all well. He was gracious and dignified. No one mentioned what was really happening.

The papers handled the story deftly—brief notices in the entertainment columns, a longer article in *Variety* that played up the "taking it easy" theme they were highlighting: "In line with a longtime aim to personally lighten his load, William Morris, Jr. . . . " No scandal, no controversy.

On Saturday night, Morris and his wife, Red, had a big fête at the Waldorf-Astoria, a testimonial dinner for Milton Berle to benefit the Jewish Theatrical Guild, which Morris's father had founded in 1924. George Jessel was toastmaster; Morris sat on the dais with Lastfogel and gave a little speech. Borah Minnevitch, who probably went back longer with the Morris office than anyone except Sophie Tucker, came over from France, where his Moulin de Minnevitch outside Paris had become a mecca for vacationing show people and Broadway expatriates. The following Thursday, May 8, there was a 2:00 P.M. board meeting at the agency, at which Lastfogel, Lefkowitz, Bert Allenberg, Bill Morris, and his sister, Ruth, were to elect Lastfogel president. After that, Bill and Red would start motoring to Los Angeles in easy stages, the beginning of a long life of leisure. Next spring they'd go to England for the Grand National at Aintree, followed perhaps by a trip around the world with their old friends, Bob and Thea Tausig, who lived near the Opéra in Paris. . . .

Others had a harsher world to face. On the afternoon of April 30, the day news of Bill Morris's resignation hit the papers, Edward G. Robinson appeared before the committee for the third and final time. After 250 performances of *Darkness at Noon*, Robinson was shattered. He couldn't get a passport to see his wife in Paris. He couldn't get film work or television. He'd never been a party member, he had no names to name. "I wish to God I had," he told the committee. All he could do was crawl. "I was duped and used," he continued. "I was lied to."

"I think you are number one on every sucker list in the country," committee chairman Francis Walter intoned. Witness dismissed.

MILT EBBINS, THE MANAGER WHO HANDLED COUNT BASIE AND BILLY Eckstine, stepped out of the Morris Building on Cañon Drive and found Frank Sinatra on the sidewalk, head in hands. Sinatra hadn't been having a good time of it lately. Eight years earlier he'd caused a riot in Times

Square—thirty thousand fans stampeding across Broadway, crashing through store windows, snarling traffic for blocks in every direction. Now he sang to mostly empty theaters when he sang at all. The bobby-soxers were gone, the fan clubs disbanded, his record contract dropped. M-G-M had released him from his movie contract; MCA had dumped him as a client in a tangle over commissions, then taken out ads in the trades to announce it publicly, in case there was any confusion. Even his voice had deserted him—one night at the Copa, when he opened his mouth and nothing came out and he had to flee the stage amid a deathly hush. And his marriage to Ava Gardner was a disaster, jealous rages leading to screaming, hair-pulling, furniture-sailing-through-the-air fights, all of it fueled by the hard-to-dodge fact that Metro's spitfire screen star was on the rise while her husband was washed up.

"How ya doin', Frank?" Ebbins asked. After the MCA debacle, Lastfogel had taken Sinatra on as a client at the urging of George Wood. Sinatra and Wood had a number of mutual friends—Frank Costello, Meyer Lansky—so Wood was eager to do what he could to help. But so far their efforts to get him work had yielded nothing.

"Not too good," Sinatra replied.

"You'll do better," Ebbins said.

Sinatra fixed him with a look. "You know what, Milt? There isn't a building high enough for me to jump off of."

More than anything except Ava, Sinatra wanted a part in *From Here to Eternity*, which Harry Cohn was developing at Columbia. Based on James Jones's steamy best-seller about army life at Pearl Harbor on the eve of the Japanese attack, it promised to be a big, sprawling melodrama about America's loss of innocence. Sinatra was desperate for the role of Private Maggio, a scrappy little GI with more pride than sense. Cohn didn't buy it.

Bert Allenberg had been fighting tenaciously for Sinatra while trying to get Robinson back to work at the same time. Robinson was a tough sell, even after his groveling appearance before HUAC. Over the summer he'd met with Roy Brewer, who'd finally gotten together with the American Legion to fashion a workable clearance racket. Brewer was a mild-mannered man, roly-poly and balding, his pudgy face awkwardly punctuated by a pointy nose. He told Robinson that if he really wanted to work in pictures, he'd have to purge himself one more time. What Brewer had in mind was an article in *American Legion Magazine* explaining just how Robinson had gone wrong. It came out in

October: "How the Reds Made a Sucker Out of Me." Soon afterward, Allenberg was able to talk some producer clients of his into giving Robinson the lead in a B-picture about a couple of cop killers on the lam. The pay was peanuts—$50,000. Robinson was happy to take it.

Sinatra was a different problem—a has-been singer with no acting career to speak of, despite more than a dozen movie credits. He'd made his debut in 1941 as a nameless crooner for Tommy Dorsey in *Las Vegas Nights*. After rising to the top of the hit parade and breaking out of a long-term contract with Dorsey—a feat he was said to have accomplished with muscle from one of Costello's lieutenants—he'd signed with RKO for a couple of forgettable pictures. In 1945 he'd costarred with Gene Kelly in M-G-M's *Anchors Aweigh*, which was successful enough to land him a five-year contract at $260,000 per. But he tended to give his most dramatic performances offscreen—singing for Charlie Luciano, Meyer Lansky, Frank Costello, Vito Genovese, and rest of the boys at the Hotel Nacional in Havana in February 1947; punching out the *Daily Mirror's* entertainment editor outside Ciro's two months later; shooting up the desert burg of Indio on a drunken spree with Ava.

This last went unreported, thanks to his press agent's generosity with a thick wad of bills, mostly hundreds and thousands. The mob connections and the illicit romance with Ava did not. Newspaper readers were shocked to discover that the puny teen idol had deserted his loving wife and three young children for a Hollywood homewrecker who'd been through two husbands already. He tried to recoup after M-G-M dropped him by making *Meet Danny Wilson* for Universal, about a crooner who rises to the top with mob backing. But moviegoers weren't interested, and critics thought the story too close to real life.

Sinatra had often played himself, and seldom very well. But growing up in Hoboken, New Jersey, a tough waterfront town across the Hudson from Manhattan, he really could have been Maggio. He made a lunch date with Cohn and pleaded for the role, but it was no go. "Look, Frank, that's an actor's part, a stage actor's part," Cohn told him bluntly. "You're nothing but a fucking hoofer." He called Lastfogel and Sammy Weisbord and begged them to get him the job, even if he had to do it for nothing. They promised to talk to Fred Zinnemann, a client who'd been hired to direct, and see what they could do.

Zinnemann wasn't interested, for the same reason as Cohn. If he gave the part to Sinatra, people would think it was a joke: Was he trying to make a musical? But everywhere Cohn turned, people were bugging him to give Sinatra a shot: Ava Gardner, whom he'd have loved to put in one of his films. Joan Cohn, his own wife, whom Ava had gotten to intercede. Bert Allenberg. Jack Entratter, the ex-doorman at the Stork Club who'd become maître d' at the Copacabana, Frank Costello's joint in New York. George Wood, who reminded Cohn that Sinatra had friends who wanted him to get the part. Johnny Roselli, the national syndicate's emissary to Hollywood, who made the same point.

Cohn was friendly with Costello himself, friendly enough that Costello's operatives wouldn't try anything funny on him. Everybody was polite. The boys were asking him to come through for their pal, and Cohn was saying he wasn't right for the part. But the chorus was beginning to wear him down. Finally he called Sinatra and said he could take a screen test if he wanted to. But weeks went by with no further word, and in November 1952, with nothing better to do, Sinatra flew to Kenya with Ava to hang around the set of *Mogambo*, the love-in-the-jungle picture she was making with Clark Gable. Sinatra left instructions with the Morris office to cable him if they heard from Columbia, and after five days in the bush—five days during which the screaming in their tent rivaled the shrieking from the hyenas outside—he was notified to come back. Eli Wallach was being tested too, and comic Harvey Lembeck.

Lembeck was quickly eliminated. After a lot of argument, Cohn agreed to Zinnemann's demand that Montgomery Clift get the lead role as Private Robert E. Lee Prewitt, the boxer who refuses to go back in the ring because he'd blinded a sparring partner in an accident. Cohn also agreed to Bert Allenberg's suggestion that quiet, ladylike Deborah Kerr play the captain's wife. Burt Lancaster was cast as the sergeant, a tough guy who runs the outfit while the captain chases skirts and ends up on the beach, carnally entangled with the captain's wife. That left Maggio.

Wallach's screen test was dazzling, but his agent demanded twice the money Cohn wanted to pay. Cohn was furious. He watched the two screen tests repeatedly. He got his wife to watch. Clearly Wallach was the better actor—but, she pointed out, he was too sturdy to play a scrawny kid who gets creamed by a pair of MPs. Sinatra looked like Maggio was supposed to look, a pitiful schnook who was born to take it on the chin. And he kept sending them these cables from Africa signed "Maggio." Finally, Cohn decided to offer him the part—eight weeks at $1,000 a week. (Clift was getting $150,000.) "I'll show those mothers," Sinatra muttered when he got the cable. "I'll show 'em!"

IT WAS IN THE FALL OF 1952 THAT VEGAS TURNED INTO A BONA FIDE boomtown. In October you had the opening of the Sahara, a two-hundred-room, $5.5 million hotel and casino on the site of the old Club Bingo, directly across the Strip from El Rancho Vegas. The Sahara was "The Jewel in the Desert," with the biggest swimming pool in town and the biggest cabaret theater and camel statues out front to play up the African theme. But it was about to be eclipsed by the Sands, a two-hundred-room, $5.5 million hotel and casino on the site of the old La Rue restaurant, just up the Strip from the Flamingo. The Sands was fronted by Jake Freedman, a big-time gambler–horse breeder–oil man from Houston, but it was really Frank Costello's operation. With Jack Entratter of the Copa running the show room and George Wood of the Morris office providing the talent, it promised to be the swankiest resort on the Strip.

Costello was doing eighteen months on a contempt charge for refusing to discuss his finances with the Kefauver committee, and Meyer Lansky was facing trial for running a gambling operation in Saratoga Springs; but they'd found a haven in Pat McCarran's Nevada. Not that there were no rules. Postwar steel restrictions still applied, which was why hotels were being built as "expansions" of existing businesses. Gaming operators were licensed by the county and the state, which checked all fingerprints with the FBI. But the Nevada Tax Commission, which was charged with policing these characters, was a parochial body made up of ranchers, miners, and real-estate men, people given to such erstwhile queries as "Who is this Frank Costello?" They were hard-put to deal with the casinos' system of hidden points, which had folks like Jack Entratter of the Sands holding percentages for other individuals unlikely to stand up to public scrutiny. And when it came to reporting casino profits, Nevada put its gaming operators on the honor system—which left them free to skim from the top before they figured the state's 2 percent take.

George Wood was the agency's high-level contact—Abe Lastfogel's emissary to the mob, an indispensable operative who functioned in every area of the business where his particular brand of savvy was required. He dealt with the men whose names never turned up on a government application—Lansky, Costello, Jimmy Blue-Eyes Alo. Most of the actual bookings were made by his associates, fellows like Sam Bramson in New York and Hershey Martin in the Beverly Hills office, the guy who'd taken Fred Elswit's job after the plane crash. Sam Bramson was head of the nightclub department, a natty dresser who was on a first-name basis with every gangster in the business. With all the activity on the Strip, these guys had their hands full.

Hersh Martin had been hearing from Stan Irwin, a young comic who'd moved to Vegas and started booking acts at the Club Bingo. Now Irwin was entertainment director at the Sahara, and he wanted Milton Berle to open his new Congo Room. Martin quoted him a price that made him gulp: $40,000 a week. Irwin might have paid it, but he couldn't tell them exactly when the hotel was going to open, and by the time he found out, Berle was booked. He called Danny Thomas, whom he knew from the nightclub circuit, but Thomas couldn't do it because he already worked the Flamingo in Vegas and the Copa in New York; if he played any other place in Vegas, it would be Jack Entratter's.

So Irwin went back to Hersh Martin and asked for Ray Bolger, the song-and-dance man who'd played the scarecrow in *The Wizard of Oz*. Bolger was a big star on Broadway and a frequent guest star on TV; he didn't play nightclubs, Martin reported. Fine. Feeling a little desperate now, Irwin phoned Mrs. Bolger, who told him the same thing. Of course not, Irwin said; he's much too good for nightclubs. We don't have a nightclub. We have a theater-restaurant, with a full proscenium stage and professional lighting and tiered seating for eleven hundred people. Also, we pay $20,000 a week. Bolger continued not to play nightclubs, but he became a regular at the Sahara.

As the Sahara was opening its doors, Jack Entratter and the other shareholders of record at the Sands were up before the Nevada Tax Commission. Entratter got his license promptly after telling the commissioners his doctor had advised him to move to Nevada for his health. A tall, portly man with a crooked smile and a fondness for big-name entertainment, he set out to re-create one of New York's most glamorous nightclubs in the desert. His Copa Room, just off the casino, would be an oasis of booze and revelry, luxuriantly tricked out in Brazilian-carnival motif, with an open stage and seating for 450. Set amid the sixty-five acres outside were a lot of low-slung, Bermuda-modern buildings named after racetracks (Arlington Park, Belmont Park, Santa Anita) and angled around a pool—the Paradise Pool, because it lay in the middle of the Paradise Valley. But it wasn't the facilities that would make the Sands the "in" spot for Texas high rollers and New York and Hollywood sophisticates. It was Jack Entratter and the people he knew.

For opening night, December 15, the Morris office gave him Danny Thomas at $10,000 a week. The evening was a celebrity spotters' paradise—Lucille Ball and Desi Arnaz, Humphrey Bogart and Lauren Bacall, Jimmy Durante, Nick the Greek, Louella Parsons, Dick Powell and June Allyson, wafting through the blur of slot machines and roulette wheels and crap games as if in some whiskey-soaked vision. Seventy miles away in the barren wastes of the Nevada Test Site, Civil Defense officials were getting ready to build an elaborate "doom town" near ground zero, with cars in the carports and food in the fridge, so they could study the effects of a nuclear blast on a typical American town. But here amid the carefully modulated pandemonium of the Vegas casinos, as on the back lots of Hollywood and in the TV studios of New York and the hearing rooms of Washington, the future of show business was taking shape. Socialist utopia or gambler's paradise? Ban-the-bomb or balance of terror? Was there ever any question which would prevail?

7

PACKAGE DEAL

New York/Los Angeles/Las Vegas, 1953-1958

DANNY THOMAS WAS BACK AT THE COPACABANA WHEN ABE LASTFOGEL found him in his dressing room atop the Fourteen Hotel next door—14 East Sixtieth Street, across from the swanky marble palazzo of J. P. Morgan's Metropolitan Club. Lastfogel had just been talking with ABC, which needed to beef up its television schedule and wanted Ray Bolger to do it. He was happy to sell them Bolger, but if they wanted Bolger they'd have to take Danny Thomas, too. "It's like a horse race," he told Thomas as he handed him a contract to do a pilot, with a fifteen-minute radio show thrown in as a consolation prize in case the pilot didn't work. "Ray Bolger is One and you're One-A. Now, you sign here. They haven't signed it yet, but they will."

ABC needed talent, fast. Not just talent, but complete shows, scripted, cast, and packaged. For a dozen years, the network had struggled along under the ownership of Ed Noble, the penny-pinching Life Savers magnate. But in February 1953 the FCC finally okayed its acquisition by United Paramount Theatres, the movie house chain that had emerged from the court-ordered breakup of Paramount Pictures—final remnant of the old Publix chain with which the Morris office had once been associated. ABC's new chief was the president of United

Paramount Theatres, Leonard Goldenson, who'd been relying on the Morris Agency for stage acts to entertain Paramount audiences between movies since 1937. As soon as he got control of ABC, he'd gone to Abe Lastfogel for help.

At a time when 80 percent of network programming was live, Goldenson wanted to challenge NBC and CBS with filmed programs from Hollywood. Radio audiences had always preferred the you-are-there feeling of live broadcasts, so most network executives assumed that televiewers would, too. But the success of "I Love Lucy," the sitcom on CBS that shot to the top of the Nielsen ratings as "Texaco Star Theater" and "The Colgate Comedy Hour" began to slide, demonstrated otherwise. Maintaining a full weekly program of live drama and comedy and variety shows was an expensive and chaotic undertaking, and with the completion of the transcontinental coaxial cable in 1951, it was now possible to link the West Coast to the rest of the country in a nationwide network hookup. What's more, Goldenson's research showed that the talent on NBC and CBS—Jack Benny, Burns and Allen—appealed mainly to older people, not to the young families in the eighteen-to-forty-nine age bracket who were buying cars and appliances and other big-ticket items that advertisers were eager to push. As the new, young network, ABC wanted to go after new, young audiences.

Goldenson had plenty of money: United Paramount Theatres was loaded with cash, and as part of the takeover deal, he'd pledged $37 million to beef up ABC's operations. But that's all he had. CBS and NBC had more than seventy affiliates each; ABC had fourteen. The only hit show it could claim was "The Adventures of Ozzie and Harriet," featuring bandleader Ozzie Nelson with his real-life wife and kids. There were big gaps in its broadcast schedule—on the air until eleven some nights, others till ten, one night off at eight. Lastfogel suggested several possibilities—Ray Bolger, Danny Thomas, George Jessel, Sammy Davis, Jr. Goldenson was interested in them all, but the one he really wanted was Bolger.

Bolger came back to him with "Where's Raymond?"—a half-hour sitcom about a Broadway star who's always late to the theater, throwing his agent and everyone else into a panic until he shows up at the last minute and breaks into a song-and-dance routine. George Jessel, having appointed himself Toastmaster General of the United States, developed a program called "George Jessel's Show Business," which had him presiding over testimonial dinners honoring the greats of showbiz—sanitized versions of the Friars Club roasts. Sammy Davis, Jr., was a tougher sell.

Sammy had been on television before, when Eddie Cantor had the Will Mastin Trio do their song-and-dance on "The Colgate Comedy Hour" and invited Davis to stay onstage for a little patter. Afterward, NBC, Cantor, and Colgate-Palmolive had been deluged with letters: "Where do you get off wiping that little coon's face with the same handkerchief you'd put on a good, clean, white, American face?" "Dear lousy nigger, keep your filthy paws off Eddie Cantor he may be a jew but at least he is white. . . . " And so on. All the same, ABC spent $20,000 on a pilot called "Three's Company," about a Negro show-business family played by Davis and his partners. Then it started looking for a sponsor.

The only one who couldn't seem to come up with a concept was Danny Thomas. He'd already flopped on television once, as one of four rotating hosts on "Four Star Revue." He wasn't a cutup like Ed Wynn or a mad dervish like Milton Berle, he was a storyteller, and by the time he got halfway through an anecdote it was time to introduce the acrobats. Television was "only for idiots," he'd declared. And movies were for people without enormous beaks, as he'd discovered when he was under contract to M-G-M, when Louis Mayer gave him a talk about movies being a fairyland and how if he had an unsightly wart on the side of his face he'd have it removed. Thomas had been so upset he'd gone home and flung himself on the bed and cried, until Uncle Abe called and said, "Frig him. We're not fixing our nose. We don't need him." And maybe they didn't—only now it was beginning to look like he'd be another Joe E. Lewis, working nightclubs forever.

That was fine for Lewis, who was a lush and a loner, but it was no life for a family man. Thomas had come a long way from the 5100 Club in Chicago. He was a successful entertainer with a wife and three kids and a lovely home in Beverly Hills, but he spent so much time on the road that his kids referred to him as "Uncle Daddy," just as they referred to Lastfogel as "Uncle Abe" and Al Ruben, the insurance man whose ex-wife had married Bill Morris, as "Uncle Al." Television was his ticket home. So Lastfogel put him together with another client, Lou Edelman, who'd produced two pictures Thomas had made for Warner Bros., a biography of songwriter Gus Kahn called *I'll See You in My Dreams* and a forgettable remake of *The Jazz Singer*.

Edelman came over to Thomas's house to kick around some ideas. He brought along Mel Shavelson, one of the writers on the Gus Kahn pic.

Every idea they threw out was promptly shot down. Finally, Shavelson got up to leave. Thomas begged him to stick around—he had to come up with something that would keep him home with his kids before they forgot him entirely. As he went on about how hard it was being gone for months at a time, Edelman cried, "That's the premise!"

What's the premise?

Two days later Mel Shavelson came back with a script about a night-club comic who was trying to make a go of it as a dad but couldn't because he always had to be away. Danny Thomas was recast as Danny Williams, a comedian at the Copa Club in New York who lives with his wife, Margaret, and two bratty but lovable kids in an East Fifty-sixth Street apartment. Thomas's wife, Rosie, suggested they call it "Make Room for Daddy," because when he was away, the two girls slept with their mother and moved all their clothes into his dresser, and when he came back, they had to clear everything out to make room.

The network approved the script, and after making a successful pilot, Thomas went to work with his cast and crew on Soundstage 5 at Desilu Studios, the facility Desi Arnaz and Lucille Ball had set up to produce "I Love Lucy." Right next door, on Soundstage 6, Ray Bolger was shooting "Where's Raymond?" The two shows made their debut a week apart, "Make Room for Daddy" on September 29, 1953, "Where's Raymond?" on October 8. The ratings left no room for doubt: Television audiences were a lot more interested in watching a nightclub comic stay home with his family than in seeing a Broadway song-and-dance man try to get to the theater on time.

Danny Thomas wasn't the first entertainer to turn to television to ease the strain on his family, nor was he the first to build a sitcom around the travails of the entertainer's life. It was the same formula that bandleader Desi Arnaz and his radio-comedienne wife had used to create "I Love Lucy" two years earlier. "I Love Lucy" was about a hot-tempered Latin bandleader and his screwball wife; "Make Room for Daddy" was about a hardworking comic who makes a bumbling schnook of a dad. Danny Thomas, Desi Arnaz, Ozzie Nelson—television was starting to fill up with refugees from a life on the road.

It was as if all the glamour and sophistication of Manhattan's East Side supper clubs and their counterparts in Miami Beach and Chicago and on the Sunset Strip were being sucked into the tube and beamed out as domestic comedy. Millions of people who'd never get to go out on the town to see Danny Thomas at the Copa could stay home with the kids, heat up those new frozen TV dinners, and watch Danny Williams of the Copa Club at home with *his* kids. It was nightlife in a box. No need to blow a wad of dough, just relax in your own living room and look in on the stars as they go about their antic yet carefully scripted lives, courtesy of Philip Morris or the American Tobacco Company or whatever.

"Three's Company" with Sammy Davis, Jr., was supposed to air that fall as well, but it ended up on the shelf: no sponsor. The network set a new date and kept looking. The show was postponed again. And again. And again.

GEORGE WOOD HAD HIS HANDS FULL. ON NOVEMBER 18, JIMMY VAN Heusen, a songwriter who was one of Frank Sinatra's closest pals, had come home to his apartment house on Fifty-seventh Street to find Sinatra sprawled out in the elevator with his wrists slashed. Van Heusen had been through a lot with Sinatra, like the tiff Frank and Ava had in the same apartment that ended with the two lovebirds hurling his furniture at each other, but this was special. Slipping $50 to the doorman to keep his mouth shut, Van Heusen called a doctor and hustled Sinatra off to Mount Sinai Hospital. The wounds weren't serious; Sinatra signed himself out two days later. As far as the press was concerned, the whole thing was just an accident with a broken glass. But somebody had to keep an eye on him to make sure he didn't do it again. Wood got the gig.

Anybody who could read knew that Frank was having dame trouble. M-G-M had announced the breakup of his marriage to Ava Gardner on October 29, two weeks shy of their wedding anniversary. He and Ava had reunited for a brief moment of happiness after he finished *From Here to Eternity*, but the quarreling had commenced shortly afterward. She accompanied him on a disastrous European concert tour—half-empty theaters, booing fans, outraged newspapermen. He canceled the remaining dates and they returned to London, where she was shooting *Knights of the Round Table* for M-G-M. Then he insisted on going to New York to rehearse for a date at the Riviera, which so infuriated her that she didn't bother to tell him when she came back. "I saw a picture of Ava at the airport and that's the first inkling I had that she was in town," he told a reporter. "I don't understand it."

His mother engineered a brief reconciliation, but a few weeks later, when Frank left for Vegas, he left alone. It was his premier engagement at the Sands—he'd played the Desert Inn before, in 1951, but not Jack Entratter's new joint. Arriving from McCarran Field, he was met by a flotilla of motorized carts that zipped him through the complex with his luggage to Churchill Downs, where Entratter himself was on hand to usher him into the Presidential Suite. The new digs came with three bedrooms, a well-stocked bar, and a private swimming pool hidden behind a wall. All on the house, of course.

While Frank made like a pasha in Vegas, Ava went to the *Mogambo* premiere in Los Angeles, then left for Palm Springs to take stock. He was too proud to call her, but not to open himself up to Louella Parsons, Hollywood's aging gossip queen, who was on hand to cover his appearance in the Copa Room. "No, Ava doesn't love me any more," he lamented as Louella gripped the microphone, her sagging features frozen in a paroxysm of excitement. "If she did, she'd be here where she belongs—with me. Instead, she's in Palm Springs having a wonderful time."

Their split was announced shortly afterward. It sent Sinatra on a downhill spiral that had his friends holding their breath. Or ducking for cover, in the case of Peter Lawford.

Like Sinatra, Lawford had just joined the Morris office. He'd spent ten years as a contract player at M-G-M, ten years in which he'd slid from minor roles in major films to B-pictures with B-costars. But now, with profits dropping and management in chaos—Louis Mayer had just resigned after a violent row with Dore Schary—the studio was finding more and more of its contract players expendable. Lawford had already been let go when he went to a party at Charlie Feldman's house. Feldman came up to him at the buffet table and suggested, after a few minutes of casual career chitchat, that he join Feldman's agency, Famous Artists—why, they could get him a big picture deal within forty-eight hours! Lawford pointed out that he already *was* with Feldman's agency. That situation was soon rectified.

When he moved to the Morris office, Lawford also acquired a new manager, Milt Ebbins. One day the two of them ran into Ava Gardner at a Beverly Hills restaurant over lunch. Ava invited them to join her and her sister that evening for drinks. It might have seemed innocent enough, except that Ava was more than just another ex-M-G-M property, she was an ex-flame as well. Lawford wasn't sure it was such a great idea to go out with her, but he did anyway. The next day, Louella printed an item about their "date," which suggested the two might have something going again. That night, Peter got a 2:00 A.M. call from Frank, threatening to kill him.

All this craziness was happening just as Sinatra's career was beginning to rise from the dead. *From Here to Eternity* had opened to fantastic box office and tremendous acclaim, and Sinatra's performance as pathetic little Maggio was so touching and defiant that it stopped cold any talk about whether he could act. He was nominated for an Oscar, as was nearly everyone else connected with the film. His recording career was coming alive as well. Columbia Records had dumped him the year before, and no one else showed any interest until Axel Stordahl, whose dreamy string arrangements had been his trademark when he was the bobby-soxers' idol, talked him up to a producer at Capitol, an upstart outfit that recorded Nat "King" Cole, Peggy Lee, and Les Paul and Mary Ford. The producer went to Alan Livingston, Capitol's artists and reper-toire chief, and urged him to call Sam Weisbord at the Morris office and work out a deal. Capitol refused to give Sinatra an advance and insisted that he pay all his studio costs, but it did give him a record outlet. It also assigned him to Nelson Riddle, whose sophisticated, up-tempo jazz was a lot more appropriate to the world-weary nightclub singer Sinatra was becoming than Stordahl's cream-puff strings would have been.

Best of all, though, was what the boys were doing for him at the Sands. To help him feel more at home, he was being allowed to buy into the place—a 2 percent interest worth about $50,000. This share was reportedly being sold to him by Jake Freedman, the Texas gambler who was the majority stockholder of record, but the idea came from Doc Stacher, who'd grown up with Benny Siegel and Meyer Lansky on the Lower East Side and was the real owner of the place, in partnership with Frank Costello and Jimmy Blue-Eyes Alo. Sinatra's well-known mob connections caused concern on the state tax commission, espe-cially since Jack Lait and his entertainment editor at the *Daily Mirror*—the one Sinatra had punched outside Ciro's a few years earlier—were taking time out from their usual campaign against Reds to castigate him as "the darling of the New Jersey gangsters." But the commission's sec-retary promised Sinatra would receive "the same investigation that everyone else goes through in obtaining a gambling license," and that seemed to augur well.

Jack Entratter and his publicist were already making the Sands the most talked-about spot in Vegas. Their "floating crap game" photo—a bunch of people in bathing suits hunched over a crap table in the middle of the swimming pool—got picked up by virtually every newspaper in the country. Rita Hayworth's wedding to singer Dick Haymes was front-page news, along with the murder threat against three-year-old Princess Yasmin, presumably from some Muslim fanatic upset about Rita's divorce from Aly Khan. With Sinatra in residence, baring his soul twice nightly as the Copa Girls swayed to and fro in their rhinestone bodices and electric-blue ostrich-feather gowns, the Sands would be the only casino worth going to.

Assuming that George Wood could keep his wrists intact. But Georgie was Sinatra's kind of guy. He wasn't like other agents; he didn't have to play by the rules. He'd roll into his big corner office at eleven in the morning and ring up Ed Sullivan or Jack Entratter or Harry Cohn and make any deal he felt like making. He didn't go to meetings. He didn't answer to anybody.

Like Sinatra, Wood was a boxing fan. Every Friday night, after his five-o'clock shave and trim at the Essex House barbershop, he'd head for Dinty Moore's, the Forty-sixth Street grill where the celebs and the tough guys and the New York Copa Girls hung out. After dinner he'd stroll over to Madison Square Garden for the fights, picking up a copy of the *Journal-American* along the way to keep the blood from spattering his face. That's what people bought the *Journal-American* for, to catch the blood. Crossing Eighth Avenue, he'd elbow his way into the dingy fight palace and descend into the gloom. His hair had gone silver by this time, and like a lot of guys in showbiz, he always wore television blue— light blue shirt, dark blue tie, gray-blue suit with pointy-toed alligator shoes. He'd all but disappear into the gray-blue fog of cigar smoke as he waddled past the bookies and the grifters and the tough guys toward the ring. Frank Costello would be at his regular seat, center ringside. Sinatra, too, if he was in town.

Georgie was close to all of Sinatra's pals. He often saw Costello at the Waldorf-Astoria barbershop, where Costello held court every morning, his face swathed in towels while a manicurist labored over his fingernails and a shoeshine boy buffed his shoes. When Wood didn't go to the Waldorf himself, he'd usually send his secretary over to deliver an envelope or pick one up. Other mobsters liked to drop by Wood's office in the Mutual Life Building, the agency's new headquarters at 1740 Broadway. Jimmy Alo came by one day and found a new receptionist on duty. When he told her his name was Jimmy Blue-Eyes, she buzzed Wood and said, "Mr. Eyes is here to see you."

Wood and Alo liked to eat at Rumpelmayer's, the ice cream parlor in the St. Moritz Hotel, next door to 40 Central Park South, the white-brick apartment house where Wood lived. They'd order egg-salad sand-wiches and chocolate malteds and talk about "cocksucker" this and "motherfucker" that and wonder why the blue-haired ladies always scur-ried away from them. George loved to surprise a waitress with a $10 tip, but he was never ostentatious about it—he palmed it off on her instead of leaving it on the table for everyone to see. He was class all the way. And if he liked you, there was nothing he wouldn't do for you.

For the next few weeks he and Sinatra went everywhere together. When Frank ate, Georgie ate. When Frank slept, Georgie slept. When Frank got a haircut, Georgie got a haircut. When Frank felt like taking a walk, Georgie walked with him. And when Frank felt like hanging out, he'd sprawl across a chair in Georgie's enormous office, which looked down Broadway to Times Square, and hang out with whoever was around.

It didn't take long to realize he wasn't really going to kill himself. Even so, things tended to spin out of control. Just before Christmas Frank decided to call Ava in Spain, where she was having a torrid affair with the world's greatest bullfighter. He'd decided he couldn't get through the holidays without her. Wood's secretary was trying to get her on the phone, but the international operator kept telling him there was some sort of emergency and only government calls were being put through. Frank was getting more and more agitated. Finally he grabbed the receiver and screamed, *"I AM the government!"* When the operator cut him off, he slammed the receiver down and went hysterical.

NAT LEFKOWITZ FIXED THE YOUNG MAN SEATED BEFORE HIM WITH AN appraising stare. Job applicant. Law degree. Current firm specializing in estates and trusts. Name: Harold Cohen. Solid-looking kid. Recom-mended by a friend who knew him from volunteer work at the Federa-tion of Jewish Philanthropies. Lefkowitz wanted him for the contracts department, handling back-office details on deals the agents had negoti-ated. How much did he want to come to work for the William Morris Agency?

Cohen was making $65 a week as an attorney. His burning ambition was to pull in $5,000 a year—$100 a week, not counting two weeks unpaid vacation. He mentioned this figure.

Lefkowitz was no Sammy Glick. He was short, middle-aged, conservatively dressed. His manner was sober, even awkward. He spoke in a barely audible mumble, forcing Cohen to lean forward in his chair to make out what he was saying. Right now, he was saying they were prepared to offer him $90 a week.

Cohen was adamant. "I don't want you to think that $10 a week is going to make a material difference in my way of life," he said. "But surely for a company as august as this one, it can mean nothing—and to me, it's meaningful."

Negotiations were not Lefkowitz's forte. As the controller and New York office manager, he stayed in the background, strategizing, supervising the agents, often second-guessing them. He was the éminence grise of the Morris office, one of a second generation of Morris men dominated by more colorful figures—Abe Lastfogel, Bill Morris, Jr., George Wood, Bert Allenberg, the late Johnny Hyde. But he did know how to hire people. Did Cohen have money in the bank? How much interest was he getting? Two percent? Well—did he realize that he'd asked for *11.11 percent more* than they were prepared to pay him?

Just as Lefkowitz suspected. Cohen didn't know, nobody knew—but 11.11 percent was a very significant figure for the Morris office. Ten percent was nice; 10 percent was what everybody thought they were getting. But 11.11 percent was better. Especially when it was attached to television packages that were beginning to generate real money.

The math was simple. When it packaged television shows, the agency waived the normal 10 percent commission on its clients' salaries. Instead, it took a commission on the entire budget of the show. But it couldn't subtract 10 percent from the budget the way it did from artists' fees, so it added its commission onto the top. The packaging fee was 10 percent of the total package price, including the fee itself. To calculate the fee, you totaled up everything in the show's budget and then added one-ninth of that—11.11 percent—to the top. If the show's budget came to $27,000 per week, the commission would be $3,000, bringing the total package price to $30,000.

And that was the best part: $30,000 wasn't even a lot of money for a television show anymore. A couple of years earlier, when the West Coast office packaged a bumbling-dad sitcom called "The Trouble with Father" for ABC, the total price including commission was $10,000 a week and an agency attorney in Beverly Hills was wondering privately if television wouldn't bankrupt itself when shows hit $20,000 or $25,000. But so many people were watching television now, and buying so many products they saw advertised on it, that advertisers were happy to pay more.

By 1954 America had enjoyed nearly a decade of postwar prosperity and the end was nowhere in sight. The fear of subversion was beginning to abate, thanks largely to television: Edward R. Murrow calmly dissected Joe McCarthy's wild accusations on CBS in March, and people got to see for themselves in April, when ABC and DuMont aired the Senate hearings into McCarthy's charges that the army was harboring Reds. As the panic slowly dissipated, people began to notice the awesome scale of their own consumerism. Tract homes, vacuum cleaners, dinette sets, charcoal grills, frozen foods, refrigerators, television sets, new and improved television sets, automatic washing machines, automobiles with aerodynamic tail fins—the American populace was on a buying spree of astonishing proportions, fueled not by pent-up demand as in the late forties but by sheer willingness and ability to spend.

The trick was to get them to keep buying, since business couldn't prosper otherwise. That was where advertising came in. In the old America, the prewar America that harkened to its Puritan past, the newly minted elect would have stashed away their financial reward and the great engine of prosperity would have ground slowly to a halt. But in the new, postwar America of great corporations and sprawling suburbs and nuclear families, people could be encouraged to buy, spend, even go into debt, because the future was always going to be bigger and brighter. And where radio had enabled the new package-goods corporations to reach into the living room, television actually allowed them to show the product on the spot. It was the atomic sales medium all right, fusing a nation of atomized family units into a mass market of consumers.

For the Morris office, as for Madison Avenue, television was like hitting the jackpot, Vegas-style. That 11.11 percent packaging fee, tacked on to the ever-expanding production budgets of an ever-increasing number of shows, promised a revenue stream that threatened to dwarf what Hollywood and Vegas had to offer. And the proliferation of filmed programs from Hollywood meant the agency had to do less work for its money, since it was far easier to mount a sitcom with the same cast each week than to create a live drama or variety show from scratch. With live programs like the new "Buick Berle Show," which Ben Griefer in the New York office put together after Texaco dropped Berle in the face of falling ratings, the agency had to handle the hair-raising details of each week's production. With a filmed show like "Make Room for Daddy," its main function was to get it on the air and keep it there.

The agency did do some administrative work for its money. It handled publicity, kept the books, provided legal assistance to the production company—a company like T&L Productions, formed after Norman Brokaw, Johnny Hyde's winsome young nephew, put Danny Thomas together with Sheldon Leonard, a onetime charactor actor who'd shown a flair for directing when he did a pilot for the "Damon Runyon Theatre" series. The production company owned the series and got paid a package price by the sponsor to make it. After paying the actors, the writers, the cameramen, and all the other expenses, the company took what was left as profit. If the show ran over budget, there wouldn't be any profit. Either way, William Morris collected its fee.

MCA had a similar arrangement with its star clients—people like George Burns and Gracie Allen, who'd moved from radio to television in 1950. But MCA also owned its own television company, Revue Productions, which smaller clients frequently found themselves making shows for.

Revue had been set up in 1949 at the instigation of an MCA vice president named Karl Kramer. With the movie business on the skids, Kramer had come up with the idea of putting some of MCA's unemployed talent to work on a television series called "Stars over Hollywood" and forming an MCA subsidiary to produce it. Most people thought he was crazy. But Lew Wasserman told him to go ahead, and before long he had Armour as a sponsor and a Wednesday night time slot on NBC.

"Stars over Hollywood" lasted only a year, but it led to bigger things. After the show went off the air, MCA started selling reruns directly to local TV stations. Then it started producing other anthology series— "Chevron Theatre," which it sold in syndication as well, and "General Electric Theatre," which appeared on CBS. Production companies were popping up all over Hollywood by this time, and the motion picture studios were starting to film programs as well. But as an agency selling clients to itself, MCA was in a special position. The Screen Actors Guild rule against agents producing motion pictures hadn't been extended to television, but it would be soon. So Larry Beilenson, an MCA lawyer who'd earlier represented the guild, approached Ronald Reagan, an MCA client who was president of the guild, to talk about a deal. In July 1952 Reagan signed a blanket waiver permitting MCA to make an unlimited number of television programs.

The rationale was that this would brighten the employment picture in Hollywood, and indeed Reagan's own employment soon picked up considerably. No longer in much demand at the studios—he'd been the "Errol Flynn of the B's," and with television there was no longer much of an audience for B-pictures—Reagan was being dunned for back taxes by the Internal Revenue Service while trying to make payments on 290 acres of ranchland he'd bought out in Malibu Canyon. In 1954 MCA got him a two-week gig emceeing a show at the Last Frontier in Vegas, but he found that assignment distasteful. So Taft Schreiber, the MCA exec who'd taken over Revue, convinced GE and its ad agency to air "General Electric Theatre" weekly instead of every other week and to hire Reagan as its host.

Limited waivers were granted to a number of other agencies, including Charlie Feldman's Famous Artists. But only MCA had a blanket waiver. By 1954, the year the guild ban went into effect for other agencies, MCA was earning more from its television enterprises than from its agency business. Abe Lastfogel complained loudly about the arrangement and announced that the Morris Agency, following the sainted example of William Morris himself, would not try to emulate it—Morris's brief alliances with the Loew's vaudeville circuit in the teens and Paramount-Publix in the early thirties having by this time been largely forgotten. What you made of this development depended on where you sat. The way MCA people saw it, Lew Wasserman was willing to take risks while Lastfogel was cautious and stodgy. But to the agents at William Morris, not owning television shows was a badge of integrity. As Lastfogel liked to say, the business of the Morris office wasn't making money; it was representing people.

Of course, that didn't preclude their owning other things. The Morris Agency's investments were the province of Nat Lefkowitz and his associates—his brother Julius, who headed the agency's outside accounting firm, and his protégé Morris Stoller, who ran the Beverly Hills office. It was a cozy relationship, rendered even cozier by the fact that Stoller had a brother named Nat who was Julius Lefkowitz's partner.

None of them—not Nat or Julius Lefkowitz, not Morris or Nat Stoller—was ever likely to be mistaken for a talent agent. Nat

Lefkowitz, the dominant one in the group, was thorough and meticulous and widely regarded as brilliant. A short, saturnine figure, he showed tremendous drive, particularly when fighting for their clients. He didn't like to hear the word "no," whether from a buyer or from one of his own agents. When booking clients for variety shows, he insisted that agents hang on to syndication rights: Give them one use only. Outside the office he was a good husband, a devoted family man, and a total square. His social awkwardness was mitigated by his showbiz associations, which left him speckled with stardust: Everywhere he went, people were dying to know what Milton Berle was really like. But it was hard to think of him as creative next to the rapid-fire, idea-a-minute inspiration of George Gruskin, the packaging genius on the coast, or the smooth, slap-on-the-back salesmanship of Wally Jordan, the cigar-smoking television chief in New York. They were there to make the sale. Lefkowitz's job was to worry about the fine print.

Like everyone else at the agency, Nat Lefkowitz was in awe of Mr. Lastfogel. He was not intimidated by anyone else. But he was friendly with several of the senior agents, particularly Nat and Harry Kalcheim, straitlaced family men like himself. Nat Kalcheim, the older brother, was as stiff as Harry, and stern and judgmental as well. He ran the personal appearance department with a sense of moral rectitude that seemed almost quaint—especially given some of the characters who worked under him, like Sam Bramson, the gangster buff who ran the nightclub department. When Nat Kalcheim and his wife, Esther, went out to the Latin Quarter and the girls came out in their pasties, they'd turn their heads and pretend not to notice while the junior agents at the table sat there with their eyes bugging out. And he was far too dignified to use a word like "fag"; he'd say "nance" instead.

Nat Lefkowitz, Abe Lastfogel, Wally Jordan, and George Wood all had their offices on the twentieth floor of the agency's new headquarters in the Mutual Life Building, a muscular gray skyscraper at the top end of the theater district, a couple of blocks up Broadway from Lindy's and around the corner from Carnegie Hall. The Kalcheims were upstairs on the twenty-first floor, along with the theater department and the mail room. The accounting department was on the twenty-fifth floor, next to the offices of Julius Lefkowitz & Company.

Julius Lefkowitz was as short as his brother but far more unfortunate-looking—corpulent and flabby, with thick, protuberant lips. It was his idea to invest in real estate. With the incredible growth of television in the early fifties, the agency was suddenly generating cash faster than it could spend it. Cash was also piling up in the pension fund. Some of the profits could be dissipated in the form of end-of-the-year bonuses— $2,500 to junior agents, $10,000 to $20,000 to senior agents, more to key men like Lastfogel and Lefkowitz. But something had to be done with the rest.

Beverly Hills looked like a good place to buy, especially since the agency was outgrowing the building on Cañon Drive. So they bought a tiny portion of the old Rancho Rodeo de las Aguas—four and a half lots on either side of El Camino, a narrow, flat, tree-lined residential street running south from Wilshire Boulevard and the Beverly Wilshire Hotel, where Abe and Frances Lastfogel kept their apartment. In the spring of 1955, a new West Coast headquarters went up on the west side of El Camino, on a double lot on the corner of Charleville Boulevard. It was an anonymous building, three stories, brick, with the charm of a cardboard factory. Lastfogel didn't share Bill Morris's aesthetic sense, and he didn't spend much time in the office anyway. He thought the agent should go to the client, not make the client come to him. A parking lot went in across the street.

These properties were owned not by the agency itself but by a company known as the Arms Building Corporation, whose president was Frances Arms. The arrangement was unusual, but it made sense. Everybody knew that Frances was Lastfogel's boss. She picked out his clothes when they went shopping, she ordered his meals in restaurants, she carried his money when they went out, she gave him his stake when they went to Vegas. Once, on a rainy day, she even had his secretary phone him at Twentieth Century–Fox, where he'd gone for a meeting with Spyros Skouras, the president of the studio. "Abe, you son of a bitch!" she yelled when she got him on the line. "You left without your rubbers and your umbrella!"

Now she controlled the agency's real estate as well. "You'd better not forget," she liked to remind him. "The money's in my name."

GEORGE GRUSKIN NEEDED HELP. HE WAS MAKING UP TELEVISION SHOWS off the top of his head, spouting ideas that ad agency guys and network execs and other Morris agents all thought were brilliant. But he'd refused to write anything down ever since that run-in with Bill Murray over the "Burns and Allen" memo that Murray never read, even though Murray was now dead and he, Gruskin, invariably forgot all his great ideas as soon as the meeting was over. He needed someone to follow him around and record what he said, and on his last trip to New York, he'd figured out who—a young lawyer in the office there named Stan Kamen. He asked Lastfogel, who said sure, bring him out. Lefkowitz went crazy when he tried to find Kamen a week later and discovered him gone, but by then it was too late to do anything but squawk.

Lefkowitz had been ready to fire Kamen two years before, when he'd come down with hepatitis his first week on the job. But the other two guys in the legal department said no, they'd muddled through short-handed this long, they could hang on awhile longer. Once Kamen recovered, they found out he wasn't such a great lawyer anyway. He screwed up contracts. He didn't even want to be a lawyer. He'd worked for his father's law firm and hated it. He didn't know what he wanted to do.

Hyman Kamen was a successful Brooklyn real-estate attorney who'd raised his two children, Stan and Judy, in Manhattan Beach, a tony oceanfront enclave of large private homes set well apart from the roller coasters, Ferris wheels, Dodgem cars, penny arcades, hot dog stands, chop suey parlors, freak shows, fun houses, carny barkers, shooting galleries, honky-tonks, and teeming summer crowds of nearby Coney Island. Stan had gone to public school, then to New York University, founded a century earlier for the education of the lower and middle classes. He took time off for a stint in the Coast Guard during the war, and then it was decided that he should get his degree at someplace a little more prestigious. But the Ivy League colleges had strict quotas for Jews, so he'd ended up in Virginia at a little men's college known as Washington and Lee University.

Going to Washington and Lee in the mid-forties was like renouncing the real world for a relic of the Old South that had somehow stumbled into the twentieth century. Centered around a row of redbrick, white-columned, Greek Revival temples on the brow of a hill on the edge of a small town in the Valley of Virginia, the school struck Kamen as a kind of Eden, an idyllic retreat from the mayhem and prejudice of the real world. George Washington had endowed it, and Robert E. Lee had served as its president after the Civil War, but after that history had stopped, or at least gone into slow motion. The place had barely made it through the Depression, only to face certain death when World War II stripped it of students. It had survived by becoming home to the army's

Special Services School, where officers and enlisted men were instructed in the art of entertaining the troops. Through it all, it retained the sense of exclusivity and faded glory that put it on the short list of approved sites for a Southern gentleman's education.

Exclusivity was nice, but anti-Semitism was a luxury Washington and Lee couldn't afford. Its president, who made all admissions decisions personally, had decided to recruit some prosperous New York Jews to enhance the dwindling ranks of Southern aristocracy and Yankee elite, which when Kamen was there included not only Robert E. Lee IV but also Fred Vinson, Jr., son of the Chief Justice, and Pat Robertson, a full-tilt carouser who'd grown up in a big Victorian house a few blocks away and whose father sat in the Senate. In addition to the usual fraternities for the blond and blue-eyed, W&L boasted two that took Jews only, Zeta Beta Tau and Phi Epsilon Pi. Kamen was admitted to the PEP house, next door to the Episcopal church on the edge of campus, and he became good friends with people like Rob Lee and Roger Mudd, a journalism student who did wicked imitations of Winston Churchill. In 1949 he graduated with a B.A. and a law degree and returned to New York.

Working with his father just led to screaming matches, so Kamen decided he'd better find something else to do. He was staying at his parents' summer house on Candlewood Lake in western Connecticut when he met David Susskind on the golf course. They started talking, and Susskind, an MCA agent who was about to go into television production, asked Kamen what he intended to do with himself. Kamen didn't know. Susskind suggested the agency business. Kamen said okay, so Susskind arranged an interview at MCA. That didn't work out, but then Kamen went to William Morris, and Lefkowitz offered him a job.

There he'd become known as the baby-faced kid in the legal department. Also, to some at least, as the pansy. Not that it was anything he ever talked about, or hinted at, or gave anybody any real cause to suspect—who in his right mind would? Probably no one would have wondered about him except that he didn't go out with girls. He wasn't an obvious fairy. He was a good-looking guy, a little pudgy perhaps, with dark hair and hooded eyes and that smooth, gentle face. He could have gotten a date if he'd wanted one. But this wasn't something you'd ask him about, even if he were someone you'd ask.

Kamen was quiet and private, intensely private. When he came out to the coast to work with George Gruskin, he moved into a studio apartment in the mid-Wilshire district, between downtown Los Angeles and Beverly Hills. Before long, though, he rented a little place on the beach out toward Malibu, so remote that the only people who lived there were beach bums and movie stars. He'd always loved the water, he explained later to a friend. It was the only place where he felt he could be himself.

HARRY KALCHEIM COULD NOT BELIEVE WHAT HE'D JUST SEEN. HE'D BEEN down south with Eddy Arnold's old manager, Colonel Tom Parker, who'd arranged for him to catch this kid named Elvis Presley who was performing with a traveling country and western show. Kalcheim was a modest man, shy and unassuming, a devoted husband and father, but he wasn't the naïf he appeared to be. He'd dealt with Berle. He knew his way around Nashville. He was used to the hillbilly sound, and he'd heard plenty of race music, too. He'd never heard anything like this.

It was some weird kind of jungle-billy, country twang and Negro blues all mixed together, like a hillbilly coon-shouter in whiteface. Some whiteface, too. Here was a twenty-year-old kid who'd been driving trucks for a living and looked it, a baby-faced greaser with sideburns and a sneer who came out onstage in red pants and a pink shirt and a green jacket and stood there. That was the buildup. Then he sprang into action, humping his guitar, breaking strings all over the place, jumping about in an animalistic frenzy. But that wasn't the amazing part. The amazing part, he told them when he got back to the office, was that the girls in the audience were actually throwing their panties at him—perfectly respectable Southern white girls screaming and ripping their panties off and flinging them at the stage. Here in New York it sounded absurd. But sitting in that auditorium watching it happen, Harry Kalcheim had known right away that the colonel had latched on to something big.

Harry Kalcheim and Tom Parker went back a long way. Years earlier, Kalcheim had signed Eddy Arnold, the Tennessee Plowboy, a hillbilly singer Parker had picked up in 1944. Together they'd taken Arnold from "The Grand Ole Opry," the Nashville radio show, and landed him in the big time—hit records, his own radio show, even a Hollywood movie deal.

Parker was a carny barker at heart, a dumpy, balding man whose slack-jawed expression and greasy, aw-shucks manner failed to mask a

cunning streak that served him well in business. He'd gotten his start in
the thirties with the Royal American Shows, a traveling carnival that
rolled out of Tampa each spring and hit every big fair there was to hit—
the Memphis Cotton Carnival, the Shriners Jubilee, the Red River Exhi-
bition in Winnipeg, the Mid-America Fair in Topeka, the Wisconsin
State Fair, the Louisiana State Fair, and so on until November. The
Royal American was no slouch of a carnival. It was run by Carl
Sedlmeyer, King of the Carnies, and it had everything—a freak show, a
midget show, white and Negro vaudeville revues, roller coasters,
Dodgem cars, even a Motordome with motorcycles roaring around at a
ninety-degree angle.

In 1948, while managing Eddy Arnold, Parker had picked up his
colonelship from the governor of Louisiana. Five years later, when
Arnold suddenly dumped him for reasons that were never explained, he
took on Hank Snow, the Singing Ranger, a Canadian who'd landed in
Nashville and become the number one country artist in the nation. He
also started a booking office, All-Star Attractions, to set up gigs for
Snow and other country performers. Early in 1955, tipped off by a crony
who'd been managing Hank Williams until Williams turned up dead in
the backseat of his car, Parker arranged for Elvis to join the next Hank
Snow tour.

Elvis Presley was a poor boy from Memphis with three local hits on
the Sun label, a fledgling outfit that specialized in recordings by Negro
bluesmen. Memphis was capital of the Delta, that vast alluvial plain
where King Cotton reigned, a world removed from the hillbilly scene in
Nashville. Living there, Elvis was exposed not just to white gospel quar-
tets in church, but to rhythm and blues singers on the Negro radio station, on programs like "Tan Town Jamboree" and "Sepia Swing Time."
He picked up the guitar, and in 1953, having just graduated from
Humes High School and gotten a job driving a truck for the Crown
Electric Company, he walked into Sam Phillips's Memphis Recording
Service and plunked down $4 to make an acetate disk so he could hear
what he sounded like. He sounded pretty good.

Months later, in the spring of 1954, Phillips gave the kid a ring and
asked him to come down and try a ballad he'd been sent from Nashville.
The session didn't go well, but Phillips was intrigued all the same. Many
times, he'd said that if he could find a white man with the sound and
feel of a Negro, he could make a million dollars. Elvis had absorbed all
the Delta had to offer, from the nasal twang of white gospel to the loamy

funk of Negro country blues. Phillips put him together with Scotty Moore, a guitar player with a country and western band called the Starlite Wranglers, and the two of them started jamming with the Wranglers' bass player. In early July they came into Phillips's storefront studio for a session. They were sitting around sipping Cokes when Elvis started clowning with a country blues tune by Arthur "Big Boy" Crudup. The others joined in, loose and crazy and fooling around. Phillips got them to start over while he began the tape. "That's All Right Mama" hit the airwaves two nights later. By the end of the month it was number three on the local charts.

By the time Colonel Parker came on the scene, in February 1955, Elvis had quit his truck-driving job, become a regular on the country radio show "Louisiana Hayride," and signed a management contract with a Memphis deejay who did a little promoting on the side. But Parker was big-time, and booking Elvis on the Hank Snow tour that spring gave him a chance to set the bait. He won Elvis over with sweet talk about New York and Hollywood and with unscheduled "bonuses" that he slipped into the boy's pocket after gigs. He bought off the deejay and went to work on Elvis's parents, Vernon and Gladys Presley, a semiliterate ne'er-do well and his highly emotional wife. Hank Snow got in touch with an RCA Victor exec in Nashville who convinced his bosses to pay $25,000 to buy out Elvis's contract with Sun. An additional $15,000 from Hill & Range, the Nashville music publisher, clinched the deal. And the colonel rang up his good buddy in New York, Harry Kalcheim of the William Morris Agency.

Harry Kalcheim brought an acetate Presley had cut at Sun to the weekly meeting of the television department and played it for the agents who sat crowded around the conference table. Their reaction was cautious, to say the least. A couple of guys snickered a little. The one lady agent in the room started to get excited by the beat, then blushed. Most of them just didn't get it.

So Kalcheim arranged for Elvis to perform for the top brass. No one was quite prepared for what walked in—a slim, greasy-haired youngster who smelled up the room and wore long sideburns and eye makeup and a torn T-shirt. Kalcheim couldn't give him a bath and a haircut, but he did get his secretary to go downstairs with the kid and pick out a sweater. Back in the office, better clad, Elvis struck them all as inordinately polite—"Mr. Kalcheim" this, "Mr. Lefkowitz" that. Then he picked up his guitar and walked into the audition room.

Wally Jordan, head of the television department, watched impassively as he gave them the whole performance—the sneer, the twitching, the grinding, the humping, the crazy splits, the voice that gulped and hiccupped and skittered up and down the register like beads of water on a red-hot griddle. Jordan puffed his cigar judiciously and said nothing. His lieutenants, lined up beside him in their dark blue suits and their pale blue shirts and their dark blue ties, were equally enthusiastic.

What was it with Kalcheim and these cornpone novelty acts? A couple of years earlier he'd come to them with Andy Griffith, this kid out of North Carolina who'd cut a comedy record called "What It Was, Was Football." The idea was that here was this wide-eyed country boy who'd never seen a football game and he gives a play-by-play description. It had already become a regional hit for a little label in Chapel Hill when Capitol put it out nationally, in a deal not unlike the one Colonel Parker had just made with RCA. A Capitol exec who'd been in on the Sinatra deal brought him to George Wood, but Griffith found Georgie's big-city ways a little overwhelming, so Harry Kalcheim had taken over. And the guys in the television department were still trying to figure out what to do with him.

It was Abe Lastfogel who'd given the go-ahead to sign Andy Griffith, after he and Frances caught his routine in the audition room. And it was Abe Lastfogel who shared Kalcheim's excitement now about Elvis Presley. For all his absentmindedness and his awkwardness in front of strangers, Kalcheim could spot talent wherever he found it, from a Socialist summer camp in the Poconos to a hillbilly roadhouse in Tennessee. Lastfogel had the same nose for talent, and he saw right away that this kid was special.

Lastfogel and the colonel got along, too. Parker was a familiar character to him, a throwback to the amusement world of his youth. E. F. Albee, the robber baron of vaudeville, had started out a circus con man, luring suckers into the tent show. Will Morris had been the classic sucker, enticed into the business by his fascination with the Bowery freak shows. It wasn't all that great a leap from presenting the Skeleton Dude and Jo-Jo the Dog-Faced Boy to agenting Frank Sinatra and Katharine Hepburn. There was a bit of the carny barker in all of them, no matter how smoothly they tried to camouflage it. Colonel Parker just hadn't made it as far up the evolutionary ladder as some, that was all.

There was something else about Lastfogel and the colonel—their sense of loyalty. Colonel Parker had gone through several clients in his years as a manager, but he'd dealt with one record company, one music publisher, one talent agent. There were no agency papers with Elvis, nothing formal—just an understanding between Lastfogel and the colonel. The colonel knew the Morris office worked closely with managers, where other agencies might try to cut them out. He had total trust in Lastfogel, and vice versa. Rule number one was: No one from the agency would ever communicate with the client directly. The colonel called the shots, Elvis said "Yes, sir," and the agency took 10 percent.

Going with the Morris office put Elvis right where the colonel wanted him, at the threshold of Hollywood and network television and big-money merchandising. Parker figured he knew everything there was to learn about record contracts and touring and hawking souvenir glossies and buttons on the road, but Hollywood was out of his league. It had the sharpest, slickest, fastest-talking guys in the world, and he wanted someone like Lastfogel on his side, someone who knew all the moves. That was the thing about those two—Parker was a sharpie who told everyone who'd listen he was only in it for the money, but hidden in the pall of cigar smoke was a man who was loyal and square and true. And the little square man whom people called "the Pope" was a big-time wheeler-dealer who knew every trick.

Their first booking, on January 28, 1956, was on Tommy and Jimmy Dorsey's "Stage Show," a Saturday night program on CBS that Jackie Gleason produced as a lead-in for "The Honeymooners." "Heartbreak Hotel," Elvis's first RCA single, had just been released, and as he broke into it now, the contrast between him and the Dorseys was there for the whole nation to see. It was the raw against the cooked, postwar prosperity versus prewar propriety, an atomic burst of sexual vitality obliterating the pallid remnants of Depression-era glamour. The next day, CBS was inundated with angry protests. Within weeks, as "Heartbreak Hotel" climbed the C&W chart and the R&B chart and the pop chart simultaneously—an unheard-of feat—Presley became a lightning rod for controversy. The *New York Times* found psychologists who linked the craze for this wild new rock 'n' roll sound to outbreaks of "spontaneous lunacy" dating back to the Middle Ages. Meanwhile, Elvis was touring the South in a fleet of Cadillacs, creating riot conditions wherever he appeared.

Early that spring Colonel Parker flew to Los Angeles to cut a movie deal. Lastfogel took him to Hillcrest, the Jewish country club across from the Fox lot, where the moguls played golf and the comics played cards. Parker may have looked the bumpkin in his string tie and his hillbilly jacket, but that didn't faze Hal Wallis. Wallis was a veteran producer, one of the most successful in Hollywood. As production chief at Warner Bros. he'd made any number of classics—*Jezebel, High Sierra, The Maltese Falcon, King's Row, Casablanca*. Now he had a deal at Paramount, where he'd been shooting movies with Dean Martin and Jerry Lewis. He'd caught Presley on the Dorsey Brothers show and was eager to make a screen test. Critics were pooh-poohing Elvis as a no-talent hillbilly who'd be gone tomorrow, but Wallis agreed with Lastfogel: This kid had star potential.

This was what Elvis had been waiting to hear. Rock 'n' roll was great, but Hollywood was class.

Elvis flew to Los Angeles toward the end of March. The agency put him up at the Beverly Wilshire, where the Lastfogels lived, just up the street from the new office on El Camino. On Tuesday, March 27, he reported to Paramount for his screen test. He read a scene from *The Rainmaker*, the picture Wallis was planning to shoot next—a little too agreeably at first, but he learned to play tough quick. Wallis, who was shooting *Gunfight at the O.K. Corral* with Burt Lancaster and Kirk Douglas, was happy with the results.

By the following Monday, April 2, Lastfogel, Parker, and Wallis had agreed on a seven-year deal that called for Elvis to make one picture a year for Paramount and allowed him to make one picture a year with another producer as well. The pay was modest—$15,000 for eight weeks of work on the first picture, plus two $25,000 bonuses for a total of $65,000. For the second picture he'd get $100,000—$20,000 for eight weeks, plus a $50,000 bonus and $30,000 in expenses. The pay was so modest, in fact, that Wallis's partner in New York, Joe Hazen, was advised by the studio lawyer that they'd have to get a waiver from the Screen Actors Guild, since the guild required one any time an actor was getting less than $25,000 a year salary.

No sooner was the movie deal in place than Elvis went back on television. Ben Griefer, the New York television agent who worked with Milton Berle, had gone to dinner with Lastfogel and the colonel at Hillcrest, too, and while he was in town he'd arranged for Elvis to go on Berle's latest show, which alternated with "The Martha Raye Show" and "The Chevy Show" and was being beamed from California that spring. Elvis made his appearance the night after the deal with Wallis was struck, singing "Heartbreak Hotel" and his latest single, "Blue Suede Shoes," from the deck of the USS *Hancock* in San Diego Bay as flags snapped in the breeze and Uncle Miltie, dressed in an admiral's uniform, looked on admiringly. It was a spectacular performance, Elvis cool and self-assured, all in black except for white bucks, white belt, and white tie, toying with the audience of sailors and their dates as he grooved on his sudden success: on the air with Mr. Television!

On Thursday, two days later, Joe Hazen got a call from Leonard Hirshan, a young agent in the motion picture department. In the past forty-eight hours, Hirshan had been deluged with phone calls about Elvis. Norman Panama and Melvin Frank even wanted to talk about casting him in their screen version of the Broadway musical *Li'l Abner*—why, wasn't he the boy from Dogpatch? Elvis and the colonel were due at the Morris office at noon Friday to sign the Wallis contract, which Paramount had sent over in octuplicate. But when Hirshan handed the papers to Elvis, Parker told his boy not to sign—he wanted to take them with him to read. Elvis was making his final appearance on "Louisiana Hayride" the next day, then going on a two-week tour of Texas and heading for Nashville to record. Hirshan assured Hazen and Wallis he'd send someone to catch them on the road and return with the signatures.

Hazen and Wallis were already looking for a property for their new star—maybe *The Rat Race*, the Garson Kanin play about a yokel who comes to the big city to join a jazz band? Kanin had refused to sell it for Martin and Lewis, but maybe he'd feel differently about Elvis, especially if he got to write and direct. But for the next few weeks, Hazen found himself talking with the Morris office about how to sweeten the contract.

While Lastfogel and his people were smoothing things out between Wallis and the colonel, they'd also been working the nightclub end. The colonel was capable of booking Elvis in arenas he could pack with screaming teenage girls, but the Morris office could get him prestige engagements. They had a $6,000-a-week offer for two weeks at the Last Frontier, which had just been remodeled and dubbed the New Frontier. First Hollywood, now Vegas—and they were working on a deal at the Copa for the same kind of money.

Billed as "the Atomic Powered Singer," Elvis opened in the New Frontier's lavishly appointed Venus Room on April 23, headlining with comedian Shecky Greene. "Heartbreak Hotel" had hit number one on the *Billboard* chart two days before. But high school girls didn't shoot craps, and it had been a long time since anyone had come to Vegas for the country atmosphere. Vegas's idea of a good singer was Liberace, the wavy-haired pianist with the voice like sweet champagne, who was getting $50,000 a week at the Riviera. Liberace was worth that kind of dough because he drew middle-aged dames who simply adored him and dragged their high-rolling husbands along to share the tingle. Elvis played to empty tables, punctuated here and there by customers who'd come to gawk. Within days he was second-billed below Shecky Greene; by the end of the week he'd been dropped altogether.

The colonel was livid. The next time his boy played Vegas, he vowed, they'd pay ten times as much. Elvis was less concerned. He was having a good time playing bumper cars at the Last Frontier Village next door, and in a couple of months he'd be a Hollywood movie star.

While he was in Vegas, Elvis caught a lounge act called Freddy Bell and the Bellboys who gave a slick imitation of country colored-folks jive with "Hound Dog," a novelty song by Jerry Leiber and Mike Stoller that had been a hit for Big Mama Thornton on the R&B charts. When Elvis gave it the swivel-hipped treatment in his return engagement on "The Milton Berle Show," the nation went wild. Released as a single a few weeks later, "Hound Dog" exploded Elvis into the mass consciousness. Ed Sullivan, who'd long since overtaken Berle as the most popular variety show host on television, was outraged: No such act would ever appear on *his* show. So the guys in the television department booked him opposite Sullivan on "The Steve Allen Show," NBC's new Sunday evening program featuring the popular host of "Tonight."

Allen wasn't a Morris client, but he mainly booked Morris acts because Sullivan, who was handled by MCA, had a lock on MCA artists. He'd seen Presley on the Dorsey show and come away with a healthy respect for his star appeal, if not for his vocal instrument. But Allen wasn't exactly a rock 'n' roll fan, and he wasn't hosting a variety show either. He was doing a comedy show, and his guests had to fit into the format. So the Elvis who appeared on "The Steve Allen Show" on July 1 bore little relation to the Elvis who'd had girls going wild across the South.

"We want to do a show the whole family can watch and enjoy, and *we always do*," Allen told his audience. "And tonight we are presenting Elvis

Presley in what you might call his first comeback." Enter Elvis in white tie and tails to sing "Hound Dog" to a basset hound sitting on a stool. Later in the show he did a comedy sketch with Allen, Andy Griffith, and Imogene Coca, playing a dim-witted country boy in a takeoff on the kind of hillbilly radio show that had helped propel him to stardom. Allen was pleased, especially since he beat Sullivan in the ratings that night. But the numbers weren't even in when Sullivan phoned Colonel Parker backstage and offered him $10,000 a show with a three-show minimum. The colonel was so happy with the way Allen treated them that he let him match Sullivan's bid. But Allen, who had a $7,500 top, couldn't compete.

Just as well, it turned out, since Elvis's fans hated what Allen had done to their hero. Picketers appeared outside the RCA Building the next day brandishing signs that read, "We Want the Real Elvis." The folks back home weren't happy either. "You better call home and get straight, boy," said Dewey Phillips, the Memphis deejay who'd been one of his earliest backers. "What're you doing in that monkey suit? Where's your guitar?"

Three days after his appearance on "The Steve Allen Show," Elvis did go back, for a July 4 benefit at Russwood Stadium. "I'm gonna show you what the *real* Elvis is like tonight!" he promised the screaming crowd. He delivered white-hot renditions of "Heartbreak Hotel" and "That's All Right Mama" and Carl Perkins's "Blue Suede Shoes," then grabbed the mike again. "I just wanna tell y'all not to worry," he cried as the band revved into "Hound Dog." "Them people in New York and Hollywood are not gonna change me none!"

Meanwhile, out on the coast, the colonel was working a deal. The Morris office had put him on to a Beverly Hills merchandising outfit known as Special Projects, which had its offices a couple of blocks away on South Beverly Drive. Hank Saperstein, Special Projects' president, was an old hand at turning television personalities into stuff the public would pay good money for. He'd merchandised Lassie, Wyatt Earp, the Lone Ranger. His partner, Howard Bell, had done Walt Disney characters—Peter Pan, Mickey Mouse, Davy Crockett. They had a vision for Elvis.

Cigar clenched between his teeth, ashes dropping on his amply swaddled frame, Colonel Parker could wheel and deal with the best of them—RCA, Hill & Range, Paramount, Ed Sullivan, whoever. But what delighted him above all else, what filled his carny barker's soul with glee, was exploitation—the chance to mingle with the fans, to feel the heat and the lust and the need, to hawk the glossies and the buttons that would assuage it, if only for a spell. And so it was that on July 26, the colonel, the Morris Agency, and Hank Saperstein executed an agreement on behalf of Elvis Presley Enterprises, which was a partnership between Elvis and the colonel.

In exchange for a $35,000 advance, 10 percent of which would go to the Morris office, Special Projects got the right to exploit the likeness of Elvis Presley for the next year in any number of consumer products—perfumes, bracelets, lockets, anklets, earrings, brooches, blue jeans, play suits, pedal pushers, blouses, skirts, dresses, scarves, handkerchiefs, robes, raincoats, swimsuits, bathing caps, stockings, shoes, bobby sox, bobby pins, slippers, pajamas, underwear, greeting cards, purses, luggage, portable typewriters, notebooks, scrapbooks, picture frames, guitars, belts, and other items too numerous to mention. With the stroke of a pen, Elvis was transformed from threat to trinket. Before long, any fan who wanted to possess a piece of him—and plenty did—would be able to do so for next to nothing. Elvis himself thought the little things were cute.

SAMMY DAVIS, JR., WAS MORE EAGER THAN EVER TO BREAK INTO TELEVI-sion. Desperate, actually. He had to do something: Instead of lines of people when he played the clubs, he was starting to see empty tables. In the spring of 1956 he'd tried Broadway, sacrificing a half-million dollars in nightclub earnings to star in a musical fabrication called *Mr. Wonderful*, about a nightclub entertainer who sings and tap-dances his way to fame and fortune. But the out-of-town reviews were so harsh that the producers had gutted the story, dropping the race angle that gave it its edge and turning it into an expensive bauble with nothing to say. Meanwhile, his debts were piling up—more than $100,000 at last count—and the columnists and critics, the people he needed to keep his name before the public, were showing more interest in his peccadilloes than in his talents.

So Davis walked into the Morris Building on El Camino one day and showed up unannounced outside the office of Sy Marsh, an agent in the television department. Marsh had been a song-and-dance man himself when he was starting out in the late forties, before Sammy Weisbord talked him into joining the Morris office as an agent instead of a client. Davis was tired of hearing excuses from the New York office about how the networks weren't ready to put a Negro on TV. He thought Marsh might be different.

Marsh was an eager young man, tall and blond and lean, with an impetuous disposition and a passion for his work. He was almost as excitable as Davis, whose wide-open smile and row of pearly whites flashed a desperate need to be loved. And Sammy Davis, Jr., was his idol. As they disappeared into his office, Davis explained that he was coming to Marsh because he'd heard Marsh had been a performer once himself. He could work fifty-two weeks a year in nightclubs, Davis went on, but what he really wanted to do was television. He knew it wasn't going to be easy, but he thought he could do okay if he just had the opportunity.

Marsh couldn't believe it: His idol had just walked in and asked him to get him a job. He had an idea. He frequently booked clients on "General Electric Theatre," the anthology series from MCA's Revue Productions that Ronald Reagan hosted every Sunday night on CBS. "GE Theatre" was one of the top-rated shows on television, and it often featured top actors. Marsh rang up the producer, Harry Tugend, an ex-vaudevillian who'd just gone into television after twenty years in pictures.

A few weeks later Marsh and Tugend took a table at the Moulin Rouge on Sunset and watched Sammy do his routine. Davis threw everything he had at them—not just his impressions, but dramatic bits as well, excerpts from *The Caine Mutiny* and *Hamlet* and *Cyrano de Bergerac*. Tugend was mesmerized. Over dinner that night he mentioned a script he was getting, a play called "Auf Wiedersehen" about a Negro GI in occupied Germany. "It's the lead," he told Sammy. "I think you can handle it."

A couple of months after that, Sammy showed up at the Universal lot, where the program was shot. The script had him working on a utility pole across from an orphanage in Germany when a bunch of little kids are led out to play. One of the kids is Negro. He looks up and sees Sammy and announces excitedly that this must be his father. As the kid rubs Sammy's hand to see if the color comes off, a woman explains that he's never seen another Negro before. At that point, the shooting had to be stopped because the mothers who'd supplied the orphans were all crying so hard that it was messing up the soundtrack.

Sammy was working the Moulin Rouge again when Tony Curtis came backstage and invited him to drop by later for a party. He knew most of the people there, and Janet Leigh, Curtis's wife, introduced him to the rest. "I'm awfully glad to meet you," Kim Novak said with a smile. "I admire your work tremendously."

Novak was Harry Cohn's replacement for Rita Hayworth, whose latest husband, nightclub crooner Dick Haymes, had turned out to be even more impossible than Prince Aly the bum. Marilyn Novak had been touring the country as "Miss Deepfreeze" on a promotional campaign for Thor appliances when she was plucked from obscurity and thrust into Columbia's star-making machinery, which had given her a new name, a new bustline, a new hair color, a new career, and a new diet to keep her trim. That was in 1954. Six films later, Joshua Logan's *Picnic* established her as a star. But when she realized she was getting $13,000 to star in *Jeanne Engels* while her male costar was getting $200,000, she fired the agents who'd discovered her and signed with the Morris office.

Cohn had just made a $200,000 deal to loan Novak out to Paramount for Alfred Hitchcock's next picture, *From Amongst the Dead*, costarring Jimmy Stewart. In exchange, Cohn was supposed to get Stewart for Columbia's next Novak picture, a flim version of the stage comedy *Bell, Book and Candle*. The day after the deal was done, the Morris Agency put Cohn on notice that she would not report for shooting on the Hitchcock picture until her contract had been radically revised. Cohn put her on immediate suspension, but the agency ignored his threats and paid her salary.

It was one of the biggest contract disputes to hit Hollywood since the Rita Hayworth set-to a decade earlier. Then it was Harry Cohn against Johnny Hyde; now it was Cohn against Norman Brokaw, Hyde's twenty-nine-year-old nephew. Brokaw had grown up in show business, hopping the train to catch vaudeville shows in the Broadway movie palaces when he was growing up in suburban Larchmont, going downtown every night as a teenager in the West Coast mailroom to catch acts like the Marx Brothers and Señor Wences. In 1951, after four years in the mailroom and four more years as a secretary and junior agent, he'd been assigned to launch the West Coast television department. He'd been on hand when Loretta Young (*Ladies Courageous*, *And Now Tomorrow*, *The Farmer's Daughter*) became one of the first big film stars to make the jump to television. With "Make Room for Daddy" and "The Loretta Young Show"—a half-hour of uplifting drama, followed by a spot of poetry or Bible verse—he was a force to contend with at the agency. He was too young to have Hyde's stature in the industry, but he had the Morris office behind him, and neither Cohn nor Columbia were what they had been ten years before.

In September 1957, Novak called a truce and reported for work. Cohn settled, quadrupling her salary and granting her a small piece of the net. But money wasn't everything. Most of all, Novak was fed up with being a Hollywood property, with feeling owned, with the studio dictating her entire existence. Davis didn't much like being told what to do either. So when Dorothy Kilgallen and Walter Winchell inflated their chance meeting at Tony Curtis's party into a budding romance, the two were intrigued. Why not?

Within days he was sneaking through the neighbors' yards to get to her house for dinner, then dashing out the front door as his car pulled up to her curb and sped away. The papers found out anyway. "Guess which sepia entertainer's attentions are being whispered as the Kiss of Death to guess which blond movie star's career?" one columnist teased. "Advice to Sammy Davis, Jr., before it's too late," another cautioned. ". . . Don't damage a promising career, and probably your own, too. Wouldn't it be more fitting for a man of your prominence to be a credit to his people, instead of one whose life is scandal, scandal, scandal?" And so on.

When Harry Cohn found out, at a banquet in New York, he was so angry he boarded a plane for Los Angeles and had a coronary over the Rockies. This was no time for Columbia's biggest star to be taking up with a *schwartze*. The month before, in November 1957, the company had held a stockholders' meeting in New York and painted a bleak picture: The first quarter could well end in a loss, the second would be little better, and the only thing buoying them after that would be box-office revenues from *The Bridge on the River Kwai* and *Pal Joey*. *The Bridge on the River Kwai* had been approved by the New York office over Cohn's objections; his baby was *Pal Joey*, a Rodgers and Hart musical starring Kim Novak and Frank Sinatra, with Rita Hayworth in a supporting role. But Sinatra didn't come cheap anymore—his price for this one was $150,000, plus 30 percent of the profits—and Cohn had put his name on the line. His older brother Jack had died the year before, and he sensed there might be moves against him. If Novak, the fat Polack, threw it in the toilet shacking up with that . . .

Cohn got George Wood on the phone. "George," he bellowed, "it's that nigger! Take care of it."

This was tricky—two top clients in an explosive romance, a studio chief about to go into orbit. The kind of situation George Wood was born to handle.

More than anything except gambling, Wood loved to brag about his connections. A few weeks earlier, on the morning of October 25, 1957, Albert Anastasia of Murder, Inc., fame had been getting lathered up in a barber chair at the Park Sheraton Hotel behind the Mutual Life Building when a car pulled up and two men emerged with kerchiefs over their faces and guns drawn. As the barber turned away, the gunmen pumped bullets into Anastasia's head with such force that his body rose out of the chair and slammed against a counter full of bottles. Wood's secretary happened by a few minutes later, and when he saw the crowds and the excitement and the police lines and found out what had happened, he ran upstairs to tell his boss. At which point Wood glanced coolly at his watch, a sleek Automa PK, and said, "Yeah, that's right"—as if he'd been privy to the hit all along.

The chances that Georgie Wood in the Morris office had advance word on the Anastasia snuff were next to nil. Wood was close to Frank Costello, and the spray of blood and brains and hair tonic downstairs meant that Costello's days as a mob boss were finished. Anastasia had been the muscle behind Costello's authority. Vito Genovese, Lucky Luciano's longtime second-in-command, had been scheming to take control for years, not just of the Luciano family but of the national syndicate. A few months earlier, one of his henchmen had tried to assassinate Costello in the marble lobby of Costello's Central Park West apartment house. Anastasia, who headed New York's Mangano family, objected to the power grab and got himself spattered across the barbershop as a result. Genovese wasn't about to clue George Wood in to his plans—but to an impressionable kid fresh out of the William Morris mail room, the routine with the watch would be enough to plant the idea that he knew all about it.

Shortly after Harry Cohn made his call to Wood, word started getting around that Davis was in trouble with the boys on account of his liaison with Columbia's top female property. "The boss of a certain moom pitcha company has a photo of SD, Jr., on his office walls," one columnist reported. "Flings darts at it." Another wrote, "Sammy Davis, Jr., has been warned by top Chicago gangsters that if he ever sees that blonde movie star again both of his legs will be broken and torn off at the knee." And so on.

Sam Giancana, boss of the Chicago outfit, was a good buddy of Sammy's, so Sammy rang him up and asked if the reports were true. Not a chance, said Giancana, who'd been heard to call Davis a "nigger weasel" behind his back. But the mob was a fluid enterprise, nothing like the rigid, quasi-military organization the law enforcement types were so fond of charting. There were any number of people Wood could have gone to if he wanted a credible threat to straighten out a recalcitrant client. Mickey Cohen, for instance—Benny Siegel's ex-henchman in Los Angeles. Cohen later maintained that Frank Costello sent him to see Harry Cohn, but he said he turned the studio chief down because he was friendly with Davis's father from the racetracks. Or Jimmy Alo, one of Wood's best friends. Alo later reported that Wood wanted him to talk with Cohn about straightening Davis out, but Alo said no thanks, it wasn't his style. The next thing Alo heard, Wood was putting Cohn in touch with the Chicago boys. New York, Chicago, L.A.—maybe they were all after him, maybe none of them. Who could be sure? Certainly not Sammy.

Eventually a well-connected friend showed up at Davis's dressing room in Vegas. "We gotta talk," the friend said. Sammy closed the door. He had a problem with the boys, the friend explained. Davis said he'd already checked in with Sam Giancana in Chicago. The problem wasn't Chicago. The problem was West Coast . . . a contract . . . his kneecaps. If he didn't want to get hurt, he'd go downtown and pick some nice, sweet, Negro chick off the chorus line and marry her. Fast.

Davis was numb. Here he was, Charley fuckin' Wonderful, and some mogul was planning to rearrange his legs because he might besmirch the studio's prime blonde—like it might rub off, right? He headed for the blackjack tables and started losing big-time—$39,000 in a few lousy hands. He did his second show and stumbled out into the lounge.

He was blind drunk by the time he hit the Silver Slipper, the Wild West saloon in the Last Frontier Village. Through the blur he made out a familiar face. It was Loray White, a showgirl he'd dated once, then dropped because she seemed to be getting serious. Serious? Sure, why not? She was married now but otherwise agreeable, so he called a press conference and made the announcement on the spot. She got her existing marriage annulled, and on January 10, 1958, they exchanged vows.

A few months later, George Wood got married, too, at St. Malachy's Roman Catholic Church on West Forty-ninth Street, just around the

corner from the Latin Quarter and half a block from Madison Square
Garden. Bride was a budding starlet with the Morris Agency, an invigo-
rating beauty whose turned-up nose and saucy blond hair made people
think of a younger Grace Kelly. It was a quiet ceremony. Jimmy Blue-
Eyes was best man, and Anthony Strollo, the Hoboken waterfront boss
better known as Tony Bender, served as a witness. Wedding bells were
breaking out all over.

SY MARSH PICKED UP THE PHONE IN HIS OFFICE ON EL CAMINO. IT WAS
Neile Adams, a wispy young thing who was being touted—along with
Natalie Wood, the former child actress whom the agency also handled—as a rising star. The agency had gotten her an extended booking at
the Tropicana in Vegas, but she had a problem—her husband, Steve
McQueen, an unemployed off-Broadway actor. He was driving her nuts,
racing his Corvette down the Strip, gambling away her earnings. She
was begging Sy, please, take the guy off her hands.

McQueen showed up in Beverly Hills looking like some kind of *Life*
magazine juvenile delinquent, with tight jeans and a butch haircut and
stubble on his chin. In New York he'd been pegged as a young James
Dean type. Like Dean, he was a product of the Actors Studio, the hot-
shot New York drama school that had grown out of the Group Theater.
Unfortunately, McQueen's Dean imitation was no more convincing
than Dean's Marlon Brando act had been at first. The talent in the
family seemed to belong to Neile. But Marsh figured he'd see what he
could do.

In 1953, when Dean was starting out, he'd done live drama on television—"Kraft Television Theatre" pieces like Rod Serling's "A Long Time
Till Dawn," a play about alienated youth, the kind of thing Hollywood
wouldn't touch. But television had changed since then; everything was
Westerns now. McQueen looked as if he'd do better with a switchblade
than a six-shooter, but Marsh took him out to Universal Pictures, where
Revue was shooting some of its series. Could he handle a horse?
McQueen opened his mouth to answer, but Marsh cut him off. You know
those New Yorkers, Marsh said briskly. Ride in Central Park all the time.

By the end of the day they had McQueen in front of a camera on a
San Fernando Valley dude ranch, where he said a few lines and went
home. The following week Marsh got a call from Revue. He'd brought

this actor out, they couldn't think of his name—McQueen, that was it. He had an interesting quality. Maybe they could offer him a contract. . . .

This has potential, Marsh thought. He walked over to see Stan Kamen, the attorney George Gruskin had moved out from New York, and mentioned his new find. Maybe they'd like to do a screen test?

Kamen was now the agency's salesman for Four Star Productions, which an independent Hollywood agent named Don Sharpe had set up in 1952 for Dick Powell, Charles Boyer, and David Niven when he sold their anthology series "Four Star Playhouse" to Young & Rubicam. (The fourth star, Ida Lupino, never owned stock in the company.) In 1956, when the series went off the air, Four Star had signed an exclusive with the Morris Agency, and now it was becoming a force in television to rival Desilu (which Sharpe had also set up) and Revue. As for Kamen, he and Norman Brokaw were the new stars of the West Coast office— bright, attractive young men who made the packages happen. They worked in tandem, Kamen for Four Star, Brokaw for Danny Thomas's T&L Productions. Kamen had a lot more polish than Brokaw, who'd gone into the mail room as a teenager, but they were both great favorites of Frances Lastfogel.

McQueen's screen test was terrific, so Kamen signed him to an agency contract and got him a guest spot on "Trackdown," a Four Star Western starring Robert Culp as a Texas Ranger. The episode was to be the basis of a spinoff series about a bounty hunter. The producers were dubious—McQueen was short and wiry, not brawny and handsome the way a Western hero was supposed to be. But in the end, this worked to his advantage, because the bounty hunter was a heavy, and the producers decided it would be smart to put a guy in the role who was tough yet boyish, maybe even with a hint of vulnerability.

The episode clicked, and "Wanted: Dead or Alive" was slotted to debut on CBS six months later, in September 1958. Things weren't going as smoothly for Sammy Davis, Jr. The agency was having the same problem with the "Auf Wiedersehen" episode of "GE Theatre" that it had had five years earlier with "Three's Company," the abortive pilot for ABC. They had a sponsor this time; it was an air date they couldn't get. Sy Marsh called repeatedly. To no avail.

Finally, Marsh went in and demanded an air date. He was told the show was being killed. GE's ad agency had vetoed it on the grounds that 63 percent of the company's products were sold below the Mason-Dixon line and there was no way they could star a colored man without risking

The Showman: Thirty-six-year-old William Morris in his office in the American Music Hall at Eighth Avenue and Forty-second Street, 1909.
(New York Public Library for the Performing Arts/Billy Rose Theatre Collection)

Benjamin Franklin Keith started out with a single Boston freak show and became the robber baron of vaudeville.
(New York Public Library for the Performing Arts/Billy Rose Theatre Collection)

Edward F. Albee, Keith's chief lieutenant, blacklisted Morris acts while building the Keith-Albee-Orpheum circuit into a nationwide monopoly. Eventually, he would be forced out by Boston financier Joseph P. Kennedy, who used his theater chain as the basis for Radio-Keith-Orpheum, or RKO.
(Apeda Studios/New York Public Library for the Performing Arts/Billy Rose Theatre Collection)

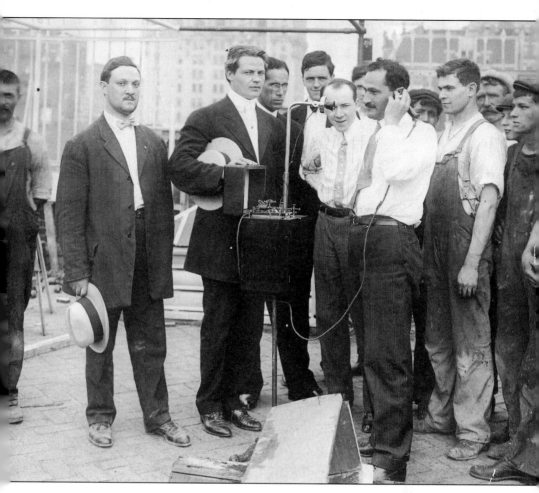

Morris responded to the blacklist by opening his own William Morris Vaudeville Circuit. In 1909, he used a wireless telephone to communicate with theater managers while supervising the construction of his American Music Hall on Forty-second Street. (*Brown Brothers*)

After the collapse of his theater circuit, Morris merged his agency with Marcus Loew's small-time vaudeville operation to form the Marcus Loew–William Morris Booking Office. By 1929, Loew's and its Hollywood subsidiary, Metro-Goldwyn-Mayer, would be the leading motion picture enterprise in the country, and the Morris office would be allied with Paramount. *(New York Public Library for the Performing Arts/Billy Rose Theatre Collection)*

"THE GIBRALTAR OF VAUDEVILLE AGENCIES AND CIRCUITS"

MARCUS LOEW- WILLIAM MORRIS

CONSOLIDATED BOOKING OFFICES AGENCY

JOSEPH M. SCHENCK, General Manager

(AFFILIATED WITH SULLIVAN-CONSIDINE CIRCUIT)

General Offices, American Theatre Building, New York

WILL BOOK ANY VAUDEVILLE THEATRE EAST OF CHICAGO

Giving the same careful attention and consideration received by the

LOEW CIRCUIT OF THEATRES IN NEW YORK, BOSTON AND CHICAGO

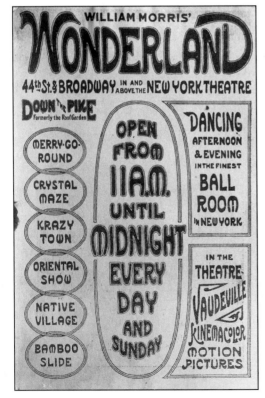

WILLIAM MORRIS'
WONDERLAND
44th St. & BROADWAY IN AND ABOVE THE NEW YORK THEATRE

DOWN the PIKE
Formerly the Roof Garden

MERRY-GO-ROUND

CRYSTAL MAZE

KRAZY TOWN

ORIENTAL SHOW

NATIVE VILLAGE

BAMBOO SLIDE

OPEN FROM 11 A.M. UNTIL MIDNIGHT EVERY DAY AND SUNDAY

DANCING AFTERNOON & EVENING IN THE FINEST BALL ROOM IN NEW YORK

IN THE THEATRE VAUDEVILLE KINEMACOLOR MOTION PICTURES

Instead of retiring, Morris took over the New York Theatre on Times Square and transformed its roof garden, where Florenz Ziegfeld had presented his *Follies*, into Wonderland, a Coney Island–style amusement park that replicated the freak shows of his youth.
(New York Public Library for the Performing Arts/Billy Rose Theatre Collection)

The Great White Way in 1914: William Morris's New York Theatre and Jardin
de Danse stood at the intersection of Seventh Avenue and Broadway, while B. F.
Keith's Palace Theatre reigned supreme. (*Photofest*)

Morris was greeted by Douglas Fairbanks *(left)* and Charlie Chaplin on a 1915 visit to Hollywood. Chaplin had become a picture star after young Mack Sennett saw him at Morris's American Music Hall and vowed to make films with him someday.
(New York Public Library for the Performing Arts/Billy Rose Theatre Collection)

Sir Harry Lauder was the Scottish minstrel whose enormous popularity and deep loyalty enabled Morris to survive the Keith-Albee blacklist.
(*Museum of the City of New York/Theatre Collection*)

During the twenties, along with Al Jolson, Eddie Cantor, and Burns and Allen, Morris booked such popular curiosities as the Hilton Sisters, San Antonio's saxophone-playing Siamese twins.
(Apeda Studios/New York Public Library for the Performing Arts/Billy Rose Theatre Collection)

Frances Arms was a single-woman act belting out Yiddish and Italian dialect songs when Abe Lastfogel married her in 1927. *(New York Public Library for the Performing Arts/Billy Rose Theatre Collection)*

Hired as an office boy at fourteen by Will Morris's brother-in-law, Lastfogel rose steadily to become general manager of the agency. *(Mitchell Studio/New York Public Library for the Performing Arts/Billy Rose Theatre Collection)*

The Marx Brothers were longtime clients when Morris offered their hit play *The Cocoanuts* to Paramount. Bill Morris, Jr., accompanied them to negotiate, but it was Zeppo Marx *(left)* who closed the deal. *(American Museum of the Moving Image)*

As one of the highest-paid movie stars of the thirties, Mae West—shown here with her agent, Murray Feil—helped the Morris office establish itself in Hollywood. *(Rex Hardy, Jr.)*

The Prince: William Morris, Jr., arrives in New York Harbor aboard the S.S. *Normandie,* 1936. (*UPI/Bettmann Archive*)

Camp Intermission, the Morris family retreat in the Adirondacks. After recovering from tuberculosis in the cure village of Saranac Lake, Morris bought 110 acres on nearby Lake Colby and built a rustic lodge that became a magnet for show folk. (*Otto Hagel/Fortune*)

In 1939, Morris moved its West Coast offices to Beverly Hills. Johnny Hyde (*center*) romanced the movie colony, while Abe Lastfogel (*left*) divided his time between Broadway and Hollywood, and Bill Morris, Jr., presided. (*Gene Lester*)

The agency was headquartered in the RKO Building, twenty-eight floors above Radio City Music Hall in Rockefeller Center. The boss's portrait hung above the reception desk and in every office. (*Otto Hagel/Fortune*)

Abe Lastfogel cuts a deal with Louis Mayer of M-G-M. By the end of the thirties, talent agents had become an accepted feature of the movie colony. (*Milton Brown*)

In the forties, while Lastfogel gave his services to the war effort, Jules Stein (*right,* with bandleader Kay Kyser) built his Music Corporation of America from a Swing Era band-booking agency to a Hollywood powerhouse so grasping it became known as "the Octopus." Once again, the Morris office found itself fighting an entertainment trust. (*Gene Lester*)

Sid Caesar (*left*) and Imogene Coca (*right*) star in "Your Show of Shows," a Morris package that originated at a Socialist summer camp in the Poconos. (*American Museum of the Moving Image*)

Radio comedian Milton Berle paints Easter eggs with his daughter, Vickie, in 1948. By fall, he'd be Mr. Television, star of the Morris package "Texaco Star Theater." (*Photofest*)

At poolside in Palm Springs, Johnny Hyde shows off his latest find: Marilyn Monroe, the overeager starlet who declined to become his fourth wife. Marilyn would be his toughest sell, and his last: In December 1950, when he finally had her on the road to stardom, he succumbed to heart disease. (*Photofest*)

In *Born Yesterday* (1950), Judy Holliday played a businessman's moll who's treated to a civics lesson by William Holden. Two years later, she'd be back in Washington for a real-life lesson from Nevada's Pat McCarran and his Senate Subcommittee on Internal Security. (*Culver Pictures*)

boycotts or worse. Marsh said he couldn't allow them to do this—it would break Sammy's heart. He threatened to call a press conference and expose GE. Then he stormed out of the office.

When he got back to El Camino, his secretary told him Abe Lastfogel wanted to see him right away.

Lastfogel was stern. "Sy," he intoned, "we have a very serious situation." Yes, he admitted, the whole Negro thing was unfair. But Revue was a major buyer, and he couldn't allow Marsh to jeopardize their relationship with an entire studio for one client.

Marsh started to argue. Lastfogel eyed him coldly. "Sy," he said, "would you put your job on the line?"

He would.

A smile began to form on Lastfogel's face. "Well," he said, "let's see what we can do." He phoned Revue and said they'd better find a way of putting the show on the air. If they didn't, Marsh would be out of a job and have nothing to lose.

Davis was doing a gig in Lake Tahoe when Marsh showed up at his hotel room door. "I couldn't give it to you over the phone," he said. He laid out the whole scenario, up to the impasse they were at now. Davis was speechless with gratitude. He couldn't believe it. His *agent* was ready to sacrifice his job to get him on television?

He was at the Copa a few nights later when Marsh called on the phone. "You won't believe what I'm going to tell you," Marsh said. General Electric had decided to use the episode to open the 1958 season. But that didn't mean they were showcasing it; it meant they were burying it, because "GE Theatre" ran opposite "The Dinah Shore Chevy Show" on NBC. Dinah had one of the hottest variety programs on the air, and the big guest for her season opener was Rock Hudson. Sammy Davis, Jr., would get to make television history, but no one would notice because Rock and Dinah would be on the other channel.

Except that it didn't work that way, because on October 5, when CBS aired the show, Sammy Davis, Jr., outdrew Dinah in New York, Chicago, Philadelphia, and Los Angeles. The GE execs were ecstatic; as far as they were concerned, Davis could have an episode every season.

"Wanted: Dead or Alive" did equally well in its Saturday night time slot. Within months, Steve McQueen was a star. Never mind that he was dyslexic and unable to memorize extended blocks of dialogue; never mind that he detested horses and hated Westerns. He was television's Method cowboy—scrappy, scrawny, taciturn, and defiant. A Western antihero. The frontier James Dean. Not that he played the sensitive youth; he was tougher, harder, meaner—a bounty hunter. He was quick on the draw, too, but not as quick as Sammy Davis, Jr. They proved that when Sy brought Davis by his house one evening and the two of them got to bragging about how fast they were. After a while there was nothing to do but go out to the backyard for a contest. Sammy beat him, three out of five—*blam, blam, blam.*

SIX YEARS AGO HE COULDN'T GET ARRESTED, BUT NOW FRANK SINATRA was the biggest name in show business—hit movies, million-selling records, even his own TV show. He'd been nominated for an Oscar for his performance as the drug-addicted poker dealer in Otto Preminger's *Man with the Golden Arm.* He'd costarred with Marlon Brando in Sam Goldwyn's *Guys and Dolls* and played Joe E. Lewis getting his throat slashed in *The Joker Is Wild.* Working in tandem with Bert Allenberg, the suave, good-looking agent who'd helped get him that part in *From Here to Eternity,* and operating out of a rented office suite on the second floor of the Morris Building on El Camino, he was able to choose the films he'd make and dictate the terms he'd work under.

It was a total reversal of the old order. When the studios slashed production and freed their contract players to cut costs, they'd inadvertently handed the leverage to the stars—the stars and their agents. Independent producers were going to banks to get financing, and bankers saw a proven box-office draw as good collateral. The asking price for top stars had shot up as a result, and the price for supporting players as well. Both Morris and MCA were assembling actors and writers and directors into packages that could be sold to the studios on a per-picture basis. They weren't packages in the formal sense that prevailed in television, because the agency only took 10 percent of its clients' fees, not 10 percent of the total budget. But they did provide leverage.

As usual, MCA was more aggressive about it than the Morris office. The whole town was talking about the power play MCA had just pulled on *The Young Lions,* a big-budget World War II adventure film from Fox. MCA handled both the picture's stars, Marlon Brando and Montgomery Clift. It didn't handle Tony Randall, a Fox contract player who had the chief supporting role. Four days before the cameras were set to roll, an MCA agent turned up on the lot. He informed the studio's production chief, Buddy Adler, that Brando and Clift didn't want to do the picture with Randall; they wanted to do it with Dean Martin, who happened to be an MCA client. Sputtering, Adler consented to the switch—but he figured the movie industry had come to a sad state when a flesh-peddler could dictate casting to one of the largest studios in Hollywood.

Yet that was exactly what Bert Allenberg of the Morris office, in his smoother, less abrasive way, was doing with Frank Sinatra. For *The Joker Is Wild*, Sinatra had purchased a biography of his pal Joe E. Lewis, invited Charles Vidor to direct, and taken the package to Paramount, which put up the production money and gave him $120,000 plus 20 percent of the profits. For *A Hole in the Head*, about a Miami wheeler-dealer and his solid-citizen older brother, Allenberg hired Edward G. Robinson and screenwriter Arnold Schulman (both clients) and bro-kered a deal between Sinatra and director Frank Capra (also a client) that gave the two a fifty-fifty say in the picture, with Lastfogel to be the tiebreaker in case of problems.

Meanwhile, Lastfogel had negotiated a phenomenal capital gains deal for the TV series Sinatra had hosted the previous season. ABC put up $3 million in cash for "The Frank Sinatra Show," giving Sinatra com-plete artistic control and 60 percent of the residuals. The show turned out to be a disaster, a slapdash effort that drew outraged reviews and dismal ratings. Yet when Lastfogel arranged for ABC chief Leonard Goldenson to fly to Vegas to meet Sinatra in hopes of finding a way to recoup his investment, Sinatra left him to cool his heels at the Sands until he flew away in a rage. So what? Sinatra was pulling in $4 million a year, more than any other star in show business—more than Brigitte Bardot, more than Elizabeth Taylor, more than Marlon Brando, even more than Rock Hudson. Hollywood was running by new rules now, and he and Allenberg were making them.

Allenberg's latest coup was the contract he'd negotiated for Sinatra at Warner Bros. In July 1958, while Sy Marsh and Stan Kamen were sweating the premieres of "GE Theatre" and "Wanted: Dead or Alive," it was announced that Jack Warner had agreed to pay $50,000 for a script about a Las Vegas casino holdup and to finance the picture with Sinatra in the lead. The story involved a group of veterans from a World War II commando team who reunite for a grand heist—robbing six casinos simultaneously in a precision spree on New Year's Eve. Warner's initial reaction was that they shouldn't make the movie, they should pull the heist.

Sinatra had gotten the script from Peter Lawford, who'd gotten it from an acquaintance he'd run into on the beach. Lawford loved the beach, loved it so much he'd bought a piece of it—Louis Mayer's old oceanfront mansion on the Coast Highway in Santa Monica. It was a fitting turn of events, the onetime contract player purchasing the semiderelict estate of the deposed mogul—not that Lawford had exactly prospered since signing with the Morris Agency. His film career was a washout, and the television series George Gruskin had put him into—a sitcom called "Dear Phoebe," in which he played an advice-to-the-lovelorn columnist—was so fraught with tension that he'd pulled out after a single season, even though it had good ratings. But he'd married well, and his wife had gotten him back with Sinatra.

She was Patricia Kennedy, daughter of the financier who'd forced Ed Albee out of vaudeville, sister of the glamorous young senator from Massachusetts. Sinatra and Lawford hadn't spoken since Lawford's "date" with Ava Gardner in 1953. But Pat Kennedy was eager to meet Sinatra, and Sinatra had developed an intense admiration for her brother Jack. Sinatra ignored her at first, but then Gary and Rocky Cooper invited them all to dinner at their house. Peter came late—he was shooting "The Thin Man," a TV series in which he tried to impersonate William Powell—and by the time he arrived, Frank and Pat were deep in conversation. Within weeks the three were great friends.

The reconciliation brought Lawford into Sinatra's extended circle of chums, a boozers' brigade that *Life* magazine dubbed the Clan. They'd started out as the Holmby Hills Rat Pack, after the movie-star district off Sunset where Humphrey Bogart and Lauren Bacall lived. Bogart and Bacall liked to juice it up with their friends, a group that included Sinatra, songwriter Jimmy Van Heusen, Judy Garland, her husband Sid Luft, David Niven, Hollywood literary agent Swifty Lazar, and Prince Michael Romanoff, the phony Russian royal who ran Romanoff's restaurant on South Rodeo Drive, behind the Morris office. Bogey had brought Sammy Davis, Jr., into the clique after seeing him perform at Slapsy Maxie's. Then Bogart died of cancer, and Sinatra brought in a new set of pals—Dean Martin, Joey Bishop, Shirley MacLaine—as most of the old ones dropped away.

Lawford saw the Vegas heist script as the ultimate Rat Pack vehicle. It had already gotten the turndown at every studio in town, but he and Pat decided to buy it for $5,000 apiece. Sinatra flipped, as Lawford knew he would. He could play Danny Ocean, the ringleader, and the rest of them could be his henchmen. With the commitment from Warner Bros., he and Allenberg controlled the film—who'd be in it, what they'd be paid, how the profits would be divvied up. The best roles would go to fellow Clan members, all of them Morris clients except Dean Martin.

Sinatra wanted Lewis Milestone, another client of Allenberg's, to direct. Milestone had returned to Hollywood after waiting out the Red scare in Europe, but for five years he'd had to scrape by directing occasional episodes of "Alfred Hitchcock Presents" and the like—a big comedown for the man who'd made *All Quiet on the Western Front* and *The Front Page*. He'd never worked with Sinatra, though there'd been some talk about his directing *Kings Go Forth*, which Sinatra was making now with Tony Curtis and Natalie Wood. When Milestone asked Allenberg what the new story was about, Allenberg said, "What difference does it make? He'll hand you some kind of script, and if you don't like it, you can rewrite it. There's plenty of money there." Milestone took the job.

Lawford's manager, Milt Ebbins, went in to see Allenberg to negotiate Lawford's participation. Since Lawford had brought in the script, Ebbins wanted a fifty-fifty split on the profits.

"Sinatra can make any picture he wants," Allenberg countered. "Why should he go fifty-fifty with you guys?"

"Because we've got the script."

"Yeah, but we've got the commitment."

"Okay," Ebbins said, "let's make a deal. What kind of deal do you want?"

"Seven and a half percent."

"C'mon."

"What do you say?"

"Forty percent."

Lawford ended up with one-sixth of the gross plus the $10,000 he and Pat had paid for the script plus $50,000 to play in the movie—not bad for someone whose only film role in years was another handout, in the picture Sinatra was about to start now, a war movie for M-G-M called *Never So Few*.

Not long after, in November 1958, Allenberg had a visitor to his house, high above Coldwater Canyon in the Hollywood Hills. It was David Niven, one of the Four Star partners, who'd started as an extra in the thirties and won leading-man status against incredible odds. Success had come with the help of his longtime agent, a hardworking indepen-

dent named Phil Gersh. But at Allenberg's that night, with the city twinkling at his feet on one side and the lights of the valley spilling off in the
other direction, Niven succumbed to vertigo. Allenberg was a giant of
the industry, a man who could walk into moguls' offices unannounced,
and when he told Niven that he'd like to take him on personally and
then laid out some of the things he might be able to do for him, Niven
was undone.

On Monday morning Niven met with Phil Gersh and announced that
he wouldn't be renewing his agency contract, which was due to expire
shortly. Gersh took the news bitterly, but later that day, as Niven sat in
Allenberg's office and his new agent uncorked a bottle of champagne,
Allenberg pooh-poohed the damage. "Gersh'll get over it," he said.
Glowing expansively, he added that he had big meetings lined up at Fox
and M-G-M and told Niven to call him Thursday morning for the news.

Allenberg was at Danny Kaye's house in Beverly Hills that evening
when he tumbled unconscious to the floor. An ambulance rushed him
to Cedars of Lebanon Hospital. Cerebral hemorrhage; coma. For two
and a half days the stars kept vigil by his bedside—Sinatra, Lawford,
Danny Kaye, Sammy Davis, Jr. On Thursday, without regaining consciousness, he died.

The news stunned Hollywood. Allenberg had seemed in the peak of
health. And he was so young—fifty-nine, just four years older than
Johnny Hyde had been. But no one was as shocked as David Niven,
who called that morning as instructed, brimming with expectation, only
to find the secretary in tears: Mr. Allenberg had just passed away.

8

JUSTICE

Palm Springs/New York/Las Vegas/ Los Angeles/Washington, 1959-1962

GEORGE GRUSKIN WAS ON A ROLL. HE WAS IN PALM SPRINGS WITH THE head of J. Walter Thompson's television department, and after dinner they'd dropped by to see Irving Brecher, the Morris client who'd created "The Life of Riley." At forty-nine, Gruskin was one of the most successful agents in television. Thanks largely to his efforts, the Morris Agency was headed for its sixth consecutive record-breaking season, with a network lineup that included nearly a dozen series from Four Star alone, not to mention hits like "The Danny Thomas Show," "The Ann Sothern Show," and "The Real McCoys" and specials by everyone from Milton Berle to Frank Sinatra to Jimmy Durante. This was scant comfort to Brecher, whose latest sitcom—"The People's Choice," featuring a talking bassett hound named Cleo—had been canceled the previous fall. But it had Gruskin in a very ebullient mood.

Maybe too ebullient. Wild mood swings were inevitable in agenting, they all knew that. It was a manic-depressive business—an endless sales pitch in which every phone call could bring success or failure, acceptance or rejection, elation or despair. Gruskin, who combined creative genius with a flair for the spiel, had always been a particularly volatile personality. But lately he'd been more so. Maybe it was the drinking, maybe the pressure, it was hard to tell for sure. In any case, something had snapped.

As they sat in Brecher's living room, the desert night looming just outside, Gruskin started spinning out ideas for more series—twenty of them, thirty, one after another, all with big names attached. Few of them made much sense, but Gruskin didn't notice. He was euphoric, eyes shining, tongue tripping over itself in the gush of fancy. Brecher and Dan Seymour, the J. Walter Thompson exec, eyed each other uncomfortably. Was he drunk or simply hallucinating? They nodded, smiled, and prayed for the evening to end soon.

Brecher was worried. Back in Los Angeles the next day, he phoned the agency to tell Morris Stoller, who ran the West Coast office. They were concerned about Gruskin, too, Stoller told him; he'd been acting strangely on a number of occasions. One night in New York he'd bounced into El Morocco and ordered drinks for everyone in the house, signing the tab for hundreds of well-heeled strangers. Another evening in Beverly Hills he'd run into Peter Lawford and Milt Ebbins coming out of Romanoff's and announced that since Lawford had been such a loyal client, the agency would waive his commissions from now on. On yet another occasion he'd been so transported by a Sammy Davis, Jr., performance at the Mocambo that he'd picked up the tab for the entire audience—a $2,500 expense.

Not long afterward, a couple of men in white coats found Gruskin in San Diego, where he'd just paid the tab for another nightclub full of people, and carried him off in an ambulance. Stoller had him institutionalized at Gateways Hospital in Los Angeles, paid his bills, did all he could to help. But Lastfogel, whose concept of worldly sophistication began and ended with show business, could not accept that anyone who worked for his agency could become mentally ill. George Gruskin was let go, and Sammy Weisbord took charge of the West Coast television department.

By 1959, when Weisbord stepped into Gruskin's job, the case against television seemed conclusive. The past decade had seen a gold rush, and as with other gold rushes, moral and aesthetic considerations had not been uppermost in anyone's mind. The live drama anthologies and variety shows of the early fifties, patterned on live radio but so much tougher to pull off, had given way to canned sitcoms and formula dramas. The same disenchantment with suburban conformity that made best-sellers of *The Organization Man* and *The Man in the Gray Flannel Suit* fueled the fantasy appeal of Westerns, which dominated the Nielsen top ten. Advertisers practiced the hard sell between programs and the covert sell on them, slipping payoffs to writers, directors, actors, anyone who could get a brand-name product into the action. Television, once hailed as the atomic sales medium, was beginning to look like a con game.

The public figured the networks must be to blame. But the networks were merely conduits. To those in the know, the current state of television was due to the agencies—the talent agencies and advertising agencies that between them dictated the content of network TV. A small circle of men, working for companies most people had never heard of, performing a function most people were only dimly aware of, somehow controlled the airwaves. In November 1959, *TV Guide* published an editorial called "NOW Is the Time for Action" which tackled the issue of agency influence head-on:

> Talent agencies control—directly or indirectly—more than 40 percent of nighttime network TV. With the networks so dependent upon MCA and William Morris and a few smaller talent agencies, it is possible for the agencies to sell them routine shows on the basis of special deals, talent tie-ins, or just a good "in." . . . At the heart of the matter is the question of exactly who is to control the medium.

The magazine's immediate concern was the television quiz show scandal, which had reached its climax two weeks earlier when Charles Van Doren, the appealing young man who'd taught viewers the value of learning while winning big on MCA's "Twenty-one," stood before a House committee and admitted he was a fraud. But the issue went well beyond rigged quiz shows. The charge was that through their stranglehold on talent, MCA and William Morris monopolized the medium to the detriment of their clients, the industry, and the public at large. Which was why the Justice Department had launched a secret investigation of both agencies more than two years before.

The Morris Agency had started the quiz show vogue in 1955, when it packaged "The $64,000 Question" for Revlon and sold it to CBS. While the show won praise for its "educational" nature, the real source of its appeal was its crapshoot format—the idea that once contestants' winnings hit the $32,000 mark, they had to decide whether to go double or nothing on the final, $64,000 question, or play it safe and go home. The response was tremendous. Within weeks, the show knocked "I Love Lucy" out of the number-one slot in the ratings. Casinos in Vegas emptied out when it went on the air. Bookies took odds on whether the first contestant to go for the big one—a marine captain whose specialty was cooking—would get the answer right. (He did.) Revlon sold so much Living Lipstick that its factory was unable to meet the demand.

"The $64,000 Question" quickly inspired imitators, among them an MCA package called "Twenty-one." Based on the card game, more or less, "Twenty-one" was a dismal failure at first. "Do whatever you have to do," the sponsor ordered angrily, so the producers put the fix in. In December 1956, when Charles Van Doren, a boyishly attractive English instructor at Columbia University, beat Herb Stempel, a short, squat, nerdy grad student at City College, Van Doren became the first intellectual hero of the television age. Honors and acclaim poured in—the cover of *Time*, letters by the hundreds, offers of movie roles and tenured professorships and a regular guest spot on the "Today" show. But Herb Stempel didn't like being told to lose, especially to some Ivy League snot. He went to the press. The DA's office started to investigate. The walls began to close in.

Meanwhile, the show's producers agreed to sell the rights to NBC for $2 million. One of them started to feel queasy about selling the show without letting the network know the score, so he went to Sonny Werblin, MCA's top man in New York, and asked his advice. Werblin, the man behind such hits as "The Ed Sullivan Show" and "The Jackie Gleason Show," ran the television department as if it were a football team coached by Attila the Hun. "Dan," he asked the producer, "have I ever asked you whether the show was rigged?" No, he hadn't. "And has NBC ever asked you whether the show was rigged?" No, they hadn't either. "Well," Werblin concluded, "the reason that none of us has asked is because we don't want to know."

And with good reason. Not only was "Twenty-one" an MCA package and Van Doren himself an MCA client; Werblin had a special relationship with NBC's president, Robert Kintner. Kintner had been president of ABC until Leonard Goldenson, ABC's chairman, forced him out in his determination to move the network out of third place. MCA used its influence to place him at NBC, where he proved an extremely pliant customer. In the spring of 1957, when the networks were putting together their schedules for the next season, Werblin went to a meeting of NBC programming executives led by Kintner and his boss, RCA chairman Robert Sarnoff. "Sonny, look at the schedule for next season," Kintner said when he walked in. "Here are the empty slots, you fill them."

Abe Lastfogel and Wally Jordan, Werblin's opposite number at the Morris office, were nearly as tight with CBS. They didn't operate as blatantly as Werblin, but that didn't exempt them from criticism. *TV Guide* shone an unaccustomed spotlight on the packaging business when it ran an exposé on the problems of Hugh O'Brian, who played the legendary lawman on "The Life and Legend of Wyatt Earp," a Morris package which was one of ABC's top-rated shows. Like Wyatt Earp Enterprises and producer Lou Edelman, O'Brian was a Morris client. He was getting $1,100 an episode in his third year on the series, plus 4.7 percent of the profits, but the show had made him a star, and he felt he deserved an ownership interest as well. The Morris Agency, which was collecting some $4,000 an episode in packaging fees, plus another $8,000 or so on two other programs Edelman produced, seemed unable to deliver. Yet when *TV Guide* asked Leonard Kramer of the television department if the agency could fairly represent both actor and producer, he took it amiss. "You are showing an enormous ignorance of the television industry by asking such a question," he barked. "I don't have the time to educate you."

Nosy reporters were one thing, wet-behind-the-ears network execs another. Dan Melnick, the new program development manager at ABC, got his education directly from Abe Lastfogel. Melnick's foul-up was to tell Mort Sahl he didn't think Sahl was being well represented by the Morris office. Melnick was at the Beverly Hills Hotel on a business trip to Los Angeles two weeks later when he heard a rap on his door. It was 8:00 A.M. Lastfogel stormed into the room, five feet, three inches of towering rage, and blistered his hide. How dare he interfere with a client? Didn't he know the rules of this game? The Mort Sahls of this world would come and go, but Melnick was a young man with a long future, and he was going to need the Morris office if he expected to stay in this business. Melnick, who'd been under the impression that he was in the power position here, suddenly saw differently.

And yet, however arrogantly the Morris office behaved, MCA could be counted on to do something worse. In February 1958, an MCA subsidiary struck a $50 million deal with Paramount to buy TV syndication rights to all Paramount films made before 1948. MCA was already the biggest talent agency in the business, with revenues of nearly $9 million a year, more than double those of the Morris office. Its production business had just grossed $50 million, up from $9 million only three years before. Now it was going into television distribution as well—the octopus, growing a new tentacle.

Weeks later, newspapers reported that Justice was investigating both MCA and William Morris on antitrust grounds. "It's complete news to me," the Morris Agency's attorney told the *New York Herald-Tribune.* "This is the first I've heard of it," said MCA's chief legal officer. "Thanks a lot!" Not that MCA showed any sign of pulling back. In December it agreed to pay $11.25 million for the Universal Pictures lot—367 acres at the far end of the pass linking Hollywood with the sprawling San Fernando Valley. The deal gave MCA and Revue Productions a veritable fiefdom—a wedge of unincorporated territory unbound by municipal regulations—plus $1 million a year for the next ten years from Universal, which was leasing back part of the lot. It also took MCA another step farther from its roots, another step out on the limb.

Three weeks afterward, in January 1959, J. Edgar Hoover announced an investigation of his own. That summer, as FBI agents wearing ill-fitting suits marched into MCA's gracious Beverly Hills headquarters to comb the files, the Justice Department quietly dropped William Morris from its antitrust investigation. A key consideration was that, unlike MCA, the Morris Agency never took more than 10 percent. "Wm. Morris Agency Parlays Its 'Straight 10%' Philosophy Into Whopping TV Year," *Variety* declared in October, reporting on the agency's biggest television season to date. Hoover's G-men were still sorting papers at MCA when Van Doren took the stand in the quiz show hearings a month later. Despite *TV Guide's* broadside against agency control of television, the Morris office's low-key tactics were protecting it from further scrutiny. Lastfogel meant to keep it that way.

JOHN BONOMI SAT IN HIS OFFICE ACROSS FROM THE TOMBS, THE FORBID-ding gray stone ziggurat that housed the Men's House of Detention, and tried to digest the evidence. A thirty-six-year-old assistant district attorney in the office of Manhattan DA Frank Hogan, Bonomi was not naïve. Two years spent looking into the influence of organized crime in boxing had led him by the fall of 1959 to the conclusion that George Wood was a front man for the mob in the entertainment business. He would even be willing to say that you could identify any entertainer as mob-connected by virtue of the fact that Wood was his agent. And he wouldn't have been shocked to discover that someone like Wood was cozy with a couple of local cops—but with FBI agents? Yet here it was, right off the tap he'd put on the phone at George Wood's apartment—evidence of constant personal contact between Wood and a pair of agents from the FBI's New York office. Bonomi was stupefied.

George Wood was a peripheral figure in the boxing probe. His name had come up when Bonomi got a phone call from Bill Rosensohn, the promoter who was being hailed as the white knight of boxing. Bonomi had tried to put Rosensohn off at first; he was neck-deep in the trial of Frankie Carbo, a gunman in the Lucchese family who functioned as the underworld's commissioner of boxing. When Bonomi finally took a break and met Rosensohn, he found him nervous and upset. A wiseguy from East Harlem was moving in on him.

"Fat Tony Salerno?" Bonomi was taking a flier.

"That's right," he said.

"Tell me about it."

Rosensohn was promoting the first fight between Floyd Patterson, heavyweight champion of the world, and Ingemar Johansson, the Swede. Unfortunately, Rosensohn was short of cash. He'd gone to Gil Beckley, one of the biggest layoff men in the country—a layoff man being a financier who assumes the risk from individual bookies if too many people take one side of the bet. Beckley had put him in touch with Fat Tony Salerno, a high-ranking member of the Genovese family. Now Salerno wanted a third of the proceeds from the Patterson-Johansson match. Rosensohn was in fear for his life.

Fat Tony was living in Florida, so Bonomi couldn't get a tap on him. But George Wood looked to be mixed up with these characters, so Bonomi got a court order to tap Wood's phone. That made for interesting listening, but it didn't yield much on Salerno or the boxing mess. It did reveal Wood's palsy relationship with the two FBI agents. Frank Hogan was apprised of news.

Hogan was "Mr. District Attorney," a racket-busting DA in the Ivy League crusader mold. He'd gone to Columbia Law, he sat on the Columbia Board of Trustees, he was well known to the city's elite. He wasn't very impressed with J. Edgar Hoover or his Federal Bureau of Investigation.

And Hoover was not very impressed with a New York establishment do-gooder who wanted to butt into his affairs. So what if two of his men were friendly with a top agent at William Morris? He had information of his own. It appeared that a detective on the District Attorney's Office Squad had acted as Gil Beckley's courier, carrying bundles from Vegas to Tahoe and making the drop with Jimmy Durante.

Hogan and Hoover were in a standoff. The agents stayed in place. The Rosensohn investigation fizzled. John Bonomi went to work for Estes Kefauver, whose was chairing a Senate subcommittee that was about to hold hearings on the underworld's hold on professional boxing. And George Wood went about his business at the Morris office, unaware that the DA's office had been listening in on the line.

LAS VEGAS, NEVADA: THE APOTHEOSIS OF COOL. PLAYTOWN IN THE DESERT, neon-lit gangster paradise, nights so bright they passed for day. City of booze, city of broads, city of tumbling dice. City that Pat McCarran and Bugsy Siegel had built, and the Morris Agency had sprinkled with stars.

Shooting began on *Ocean's Eleven* in January 1960. *Never So Few* had just opened, with Sinatra and Gina Lollobrigida as the stars and Lawford in a supporting role. Sammy Davis, Jr., was supposed to have had a part, but early in 1959 he'd made the mistake of criticizing Sinatra on a Chicago radio show. "I don't care if you are the most talented person in the world," Davis told his interviewer. "It does not give you the right to step on people and treat them rotten. This is what he does occasionally." Sinatra lost all control, called Davis "a dirty nigger bastard," had him written out of the script. He gave the part to Steve McQueen after Stan Kamen talked McQueen up to John Sturges, a Morris client who'd been hired to direct. Davis was destroyed. Sinatra avoided him for months, ignored his pleas for forgiveness. Then, for no apparent reason, he changed his mind and let him make a public apology—just in time for *Ocean's Eleven*.

The others were there too—Dean Martin, the hitmaster whose big break had come when he was called to fill in for Sinatra at New York's Club Riobamba back in 1944. Joey Bishop, the nightclub comic the Morris Agency had made a regular on "Keep Talking," the audience-participation show hosted by Merv Griffin. Peter Lawford, whose brother-in-law Sinatra was eager to help make president. Angie Dickinson, beauty queen turned Hollywood actress/Rat Pack broad. Richard Conte, Cesar Romero, Henry Silva, longtime Sinatra cronies.

Lewis Milestone was a distinguished director brought low by the blacklist. On this job, he was just a hired hand. *Ocean's Eleven* was Sinatra's picture. If Frank didn't like a scene, he'd have them rewrite the script on the spot. If Frank didn't want to do another take, they didn't do another take. If Frank didn't want to rehearse—well, Frank never wanted to rehearse. Rehearsing was uncool. What if he put himself on the line and it didn't come off? Better to keep it casual, snap the fingers, play it for laughs. He was a performer, not an actor. Repeating the same lines over and over again, standing around day after day with the same bunch of cameramen and sound men and script girls—how could he work his magic? He needed to move fast, in and out, shoot his scenes and head for the action.

The action all happened at night, and it wasn't out there on location but in the Copa Room at the Sands. For nearly a month, from January 20 to February 16, Sands boss Jack Entratter had Sinatra and his Clan booked in a freewheeling, anything-goes show they called the Summit Meeting, after the real one that was about to take place in Paris. "Star-Lite—Star-Bright—Which Star Will Shine Tonight?" the ads teased. Entratter had five—Frank Sinatra, Dean Martin, Peter Lawford, Joey Bishop, and Sammy Davis, Jr.—two or more of whom were guaranteed to show up every evening. Sinatra or Martin alone was a sure draw for the high rollers. Together they were unbeatable. Every hotel room in town was sold out. People stood in line for hours to get in. Only the biggest gamblers were guaranteed a table. The rest had to content themselves with craps, hoping that the action would spill out onto the casino floor—as it often did, Dino dealing blackjack, Sinatra winning big, the chips still changing hands as the sun crept up over the barren peaks outside town.

Inside the Copa Room, it was a party every night. Who knew what would happen? *Reader's Digest* had just run an exposé telling how all the big hotels on the Strip—the Flamingo, the Sahara, the Desert Inn, the Riviera, the Sands, the New Frontier—were funded by the mob. So Joey Bishop would interrupt Sinatra in mid-song: "Don't sing any more, Frank. Tell the people about the *good* work the Mafia is doing." Or Dino would sing as Sammy and Peter and Joey walked out in tuxedo jackets and boxer shorts, trousers draped over their arms. Or Dino and Frank would wheel out their breakfast bar, ready to get juiced, and Joey would announce, "Well, here they are, folks—Haig and Vague."

Cats who weren't hip might dismiss such banter as besotted and infantile. But that kind of talk was strictly from Squaresville. Cats who dug it knew just how cool these guys were. It was like Sammy used to say to the audience: "You can get swacked just *watching* this show!"

But the high point for everybody, the summit of the Summit, came on February 7, the night Jack Kennedy flew in from a campaign appearance in Albuquerque for a little diversion. A month earlier, he'd formally declared his candidacy for the White House; the New Hampshire primary was coming up soon. As Sinatra introduced his new friend, Dino staggered out and quipped, "What did you say his name was?" A few minutes later, Dino picked up Sammy and handed him to Sinatra. "Here," he said. "This award just came to you from the National Association for the Advancement of Colored People."

After the show, Kennedy joined the rest of them upstairs for booze and broads. Sinatra had a girl for him, a twenty-five-year-old beauty named Judy Campbell. He'd been seeing her himself until she decided his tastes were a little kinky and broke it off. Now she could cement the bond between him and the candidate. "How's your bird?"—that's how the fellows liked to greet each other, referring to the male member. It wasn't just an idle question. These guys cared.

A few weeks later, at the end of March, it was abruptly announced that Frank Sinatra would be leaving the Morris Agency in favor of a newly formed personal management outfit. This was a big blow, as Sinatra was Morris's biggest money-earner in the personal appearance field and a major earner in TV and pictures as well. The new company was headed by Hank Sanicola, Sinatra's longtime manager, and it had the services of Milton A. "Mickey" Rudin, the young lawyer at the Hollywood firm of Gang, Kopp & Tyre who'd been handling Sinatra's business for William Morris.

Early reports had it that one of Sanicola's partners would be Milt Ebbins, Peter Lawford's manager, and that their clients were liable to include the rest of the Clan—Lawford, Joey Bishop, Dean Martin, Sammy Davis, Jr. That deal quickly fell apart, and Ebbins ended up taking Sinatra's empty office space on the second floor of El Camino. But the feeling at the agency was one of betrayal.

It wasn't just the commissions he brought in; Sinatra was a mainstay of the Morris family of stars. Some of the guys were livid. George Wood wasn't exactly happy—he'd gone through the bad times with Frank, and his status as a heavyweight had a lot to do with the Frank connection. Sammy Weisbord flew into a rage. But Lastfogel was as unruffled as ever. "Don't worry about it," he said confidently, eyes aglint, leonine head tilted up, feet dangling above the floor. "They'll be back."

SAM WEISBORD WAS ON THE STAND, GIVING THE COMMISSIONERS A GUIDED tour of the package deal. It was October 1960, in the last months of the Eisenhower administration. The elections were three weeks away. The Federal Communications Commission had come to Los Angeles to hold hearings on network programming.

Nearly a year had passed since Van Doren's stunner in the quiz-show hearings. The quiz shows had been abruptly canceled, William Morris's among them. The FCC had lost its chairman, a McCarthy protégé, after a House subcommittee showed that he'd double- and triple-billed the government for travel expenses and spent a week in Bimini on the tab of a station owner who had a case before the Commission. Another commissioner had stepped down after it came out that he'd taken a bribe. But Sammy Weisbord was all smiles as he took the stand, his teeth a dazzling white against the deep, rich copper of his perpetual tan. How could he be of assistance?

First, an explanation of how William Morris works.

Weisbord had come with charts and tables. He walked them briskly through the organization: the motion picture department, the television department, the legit department, the literary department, the concert department, the personal appearance department with its subdivisions for vaudeville, nightclubs, fairs, and the like. The New York television department, with about thirty men under Wallace Jordan, was in touch with every conceivable outlet for talent and for TV packages. Jordan himself handled talent and acted as national sales agent. The twenty men of the West Coast office were in daily contact with their counterparts in New York and with the West Coast branches of the ad agencies and the television networks.

Next, an explanation of the package deal.

Weisbord smiled helpfully. The package deal, he explained, had been around since vaudeville days, when star performers who wanted to establish creative control put together a program of acts to back them on their tours. The practice was extended to radio, where stars like Eddie Cantor and Fred Allen owned their shows and controlled the content. When television came along and the film studios failed to go into program production, the Morris Agency urged its clients to fill the void. The agency starts with a star or an idea, develops a format, puts together writers and actors and a director, and makes the sale to an ad agency or network. It advises the producer on things like picking a production facility, drawing up a budget, getting insurance for the cast, setting up an accounting office. In return, it gets 10 percent of the package fee. It does not take a commission from any of its clients in the package.

Weisbord pulled out some charts that listed television packages by season. For the 1958–1959 season, the agency had seventeen prime-time packages; for 1959–1960, twenty-three packages; for the current 1960–1961 season, twenty-six. They included many of the most popular programs on the air: "The Danny Thomas Show," which Abe Lastfogel had sold to Benton & Bowles and General Foods after "Make Room for Daddy" ran out of steam on ABC and which they'd then placed in the "I Love Lucy" time slot on CBS; "The Real McCoys," first of the shit-kicker sitcoms, which Sheldon Leonard produced for T&L Productions, his phenomenally successful partnership with Danny Thomas; "The Andy Griffith Show," which Leonard had just spun off from "Danny Thomas" after Danny landed in Andy's jail while passing through the mythical town of Mayberry; "The Loretta Young Show," now going into its eighth season on NBC; "The Many Loves of Dobie Gillis," about a typical American teenager and his beatnik buddy, Maynard G. Krebs; "Dick Powell's Zane Grey Theater," a Western anthology series from Four Star; "Wanted: Dead or Alive," the Four Star Western starring Steve McQueen and the sawed-off Winchester rifle that kept him company on his bounty-hunting forays; "The Rifleman," another Western from Four Star, about a New Mexico homesteader and the trick rifle he used to defend himself against frontier violence.

Weisbord was asked about testimony they'd heard the week before from the agent who represented Irving and Norman Pincus, the writers who'd created "The Real McCoys." The agent said the Pincus brothers had gone to the Morris Agency to get Walter Brennan to star in their show, only to be told that if they wanted Brennan, the program would have to be sold as a package, with Morris taking 10 percent off the top.

In fact, Abe Lastfogel had not only sold "The Real McCoys" as a package, he'd given to his pal Danny Thomas a chance to invest in it as a co-owner. Weisbord didn't go into that. Yes, he admitted, the Pincuses had written a pilot script for "The Real McCoys." They wanted Brennan to star in it, and Brennan and Weisbord thought he should do it. Naturally, Brennan was eager to have the Morris Agency's talents and services at his disposal. So Weisbord told the Pincuses that if Brennan were to be in the show, Morris would have to package it because that would give Brennan reassurance.

There was one thing Weisbord wanted to make sure the FCC understood about the Morris Agency. "We own no part of any package," he stressed. "We own no package."

While they were in Los Angeles, the commissioners also wanted to hear from Taft Schreiber, the MCA vice president who ran Revue Productions. *Fortune* had just published a lengthy exposé of MCA that, among other things, detailed the economics of the MCA-Revue setup. On a show it sold for $40,000, MCA would get $4,000 as its package commission, the same fee Morris took on its own shows. But of the remaining $36,000, Revue would take 20 percent—$7,200—for overhead and another $20,000 or so to cover expenses like film and camera crew and studio rental. Of the $40,000 sales price, then, MCA would take $31,000 and pay out $9,000 to the artists involved.

This left the commissioners with a number of interesting queries. But while Taft Schreiber responded to the FCC's subpoena, he refused to answer questions on the witness stand. When pushed to reply, he rose abruptly and exited the hearing room.

The new administration was not slow to signal that its regulatory approach would differ from that of its predecessor. The man John Kennedy picked to chair the FCC was Newton Minow, an idealistic young lawyer who'd clerked for Chief Justice Fred Vinson and gone on to become Adlai Stevenson's law partner. On May 9, 1961, a day that came to be known within the industry as Black Tuesday, Minow gave a forty-minute luncheon address at the National Association of Broadcasters convention in Washington. He was an unassuming-looking man, pudgy and clerkish. Most of the two thousand or so broadcasting executives at the convention had little idea what to expect from him. They got quite a start:

> I invite you to sit down in front of your television set when your station goes on the air and stay there without a book, magazine, newspaper, profit-and-loss sheet, or rating book to distract you—and keep your eyes glued to that set until the station goes off. I can assure you that you will find a vast wasteland. You will see a procession of game shows, violence, audience participation shows, formula comedies about totally unbelievable families, blood and thunder, mayhem, violence, sadism, murder, western bad men, western good men, private eyes, gangsters, more violence, and cartoons. And, endlessly, commercials. . . .

The conventioneers reacted with stunned indignation. In the world outside, Minow quickly became almost as big a hero as Charles Van Doren had been. Thousands of letters poured into FCC headquarters in Washington, nearly all of them favorable. There were even people in broadcasting who secretly applauded his message—people like Hank Brennan, a vice president of McCann-Erickson, the second largest ad agency on Madison Avenue, the one responsible for Chesterfield and Mennen and Coke. Brennan sent a handwritten note to Pierre Salinger, the president's press secretary:

> Dear Pierre:
>
> This is one of those "burn-before-reading" notes but somebody *please* tell Newton Minow that the guy he should be after is "Sonny" Werblin of MCA. His incredible power over talent and booking is the basic source of much of the mediocrity on America's TV screens. . . .
>
> > Regards
> > Hank

Salinger passed the note to the new attorney general, Robert F. Kennedy. But Kennedy was already on the case. Even before Minow's "vast wasteland" speech, Lee Loevinger, the new head of the Justice Department's antitrust division, had advised Kennedy that the MCA investigation he'd inherited from the Eisenhower administration was likely to result in civil or criminal indictments or both. Leonard Posner, the antitrust lawyer heading the investigation, wanted Loevinger to convene a federal grand jury because witnesses were frightened and they couldn't expect to get any cooperation without the cloak of grand jury proceedings. Meanwhile, Posner was fighting off the Senate Interstate and Foreign Commerce Committee, which was eager to hold hearings on the MCA mess. The FBI investigation was continuing, while over at the FCC, a block away, Taft Schreiber had again been subpoenaed and had again refused to testify, even as to what television programs MCA packaged. Newton Minow wanted to know if Schreiber could be prosecuted for contempt.

In the midst of all this, when Jacqueline Bouvier Kennedy announced that she wanted to refurbish the White House to reflect the history of the American presidency, Jules and Doris Stein thought of the perfect gift: some of their furniture. On June 27, the White House announced that Mrs. Kennedy had accepted an offer by the Steins, noted collectors of priceless eighteenth-century antiques, to furnish a sixty-three-foot-long reception hall in the family quarters on the second floor.

Two months later, on August 25, Bobby Kennedy authorized a federal grand jury investigation of MCA—a step that implied suspicion not just of conspiracy but of criminal intent, though the government sometimes used grand juries to gather evidence that ended up yielding only civil charges. The crux of the government's complaint was that, having signed up most of the top names in show business—Marlon Brando, Montgomery Clift, Fred Astaire, Doris Day, Charlton Heston, Janet Leigh, Tony Perkins, Gene Kelly, Shirley MacLaine, Paul Newman, Joanne Woodward, Jack Paar, Ronald Reagan, and Ed Sullivan, for starters—MCA was using its talent roster as a club to make producers do its bidding. When the trades reported shortly afterward that MCA was planning to split off its talent agency from its production operations voluntarily, government lawyers suddenly realized that their case was going to be harder to prove than they'd thought, regardless of whether the divestiture turned out to be genuine. The only solution, they decided, was to step up the pressure.

In early September, as rumors about MCA's future swept Hollywood, the Screen Actors Guild announced that as of December 31 it was canceling all waivers allowing talent agencies to produce. A few weeks later the Guild announced that it was giving MCA eleven months to decide whether to sell off its agency business or its production company. By this time, the FBI had interviewed some 300 witnesses, and Leonard Posner in antitrust had seen 150 more. A secret grand jury was being empaneled in Los Angeles. Lee Loevinger, the assistant attorney general, advised Tish Baldridge, the first lady's social secretary, that it would be unwise to accept any gifts from the Steins. It was not a happy phone call for either of them.

Loevinger also sent a memo to Bobby Kennedy reporting that the grand jury would begin hearing evidence on November 20. Part of the difficulty, he added, was that Justice had only one lawyer on the case. Kennedy returned the memo with a scrawled note: "Within 60 days I want to have made major progress no matter how many lawyers it takes."

DETECTIVE NICHOLSON WAS USED TO THE DRILL. EVERY SIX OR SEVEN days, sometime around midnight, Nicholson—Detective Robert Nicholson, NYPD, assigned to the DA's Office Squad—led a team of police department surveillance experts in a break-in of the Morris Agency headquarters at Broadway and Fifty-fifth Street. Their job: to change the battery pack on the bug that was taped to the bottom of a comfortably upholstered chair in George Wood's office.

For some months now, beginning in April 1961, Wood had been the focus of a new investigation by the Manhattan DA's office. This one was headed by an assistant prosecutor named Jeremiah McKenna, a young lawyer who'd joined the rackets bureau just as John Bonomi was leaving. McKenna was studious and soft-spoken, with wire-rim glasses that gave him a schoolteacherish look. The legwork was being done by Nicholson, a junior gumshoe who'd joined the DA's Office Squad fresh out of detective school after several years as a beat patrolman on the Upper West Side. The squad, a handpicked group of some eighty detectives, had been created by Frank Hogan's predecessor as DA, Tom Dewey, who thought a prosecutor had a duty to serve as the eyes and ears of the public instead of waiting passively for the police to bring in evidence of malfeasance. Nicholson was the kind of guy Hogan was looking for, the kind who liked to dig. Right now, he was digging into Wood's efforts to promote a device called Scopitone, a fancy French jukebox that was supposed to play three-and-a-half-minute music films on a video screen.

Scopitone was going to change the way people listened to music in bars. Instead of just hearing a song, with Scopitone you could drop in a quarter and see it as well. The Scopitone itself was kind of funny-looking, a jukebox with a TV set on top. To finance this innovation, Wood was assembling a Who's Who of shady characters—his good friend Jimmy Blue-Eyes Alo; Danny Brown, New York loan shark and Alo associate; Joe Cataldo, AKA Joe the Wop, owner of the Camelot Supper Club, wiseguy hangout at Forty-ninth and Third; Aaron Weisberg, part owner of the Sands; Francis Breheny, AKA the Irishman, Alo associate with pull in the jukebox racket; Abe Green, head of a New Jersey jukebox manufacturing company with close ties to the Genovese family. Wood had secured U.S. and Latin American distribution rights to Scopitone from Cameca, a subsidiary of the giant French electronics concern Compagnie Générale de Télégraphie sans Fil. He was planning to invest personally, and the Morris Agency would take 10 percent off the production costs of every Scopitone film—a packaging fee, if you will.

The case had landed in Detective Nicholson's lap when Hal Roach, Jr., son of the producer who'd made the Harold Lloyd and Laurel and Hardy films, walked into the DA's office to report that a number of organized crime types seemed to be mixed up in the deal. Roach, a sometime television producer, had been brought in to make the films. Wood had invited him to an upcoming meeting at the Plaza Hotel at which the proposition would be discussed. Several Vegas types would be there, plus the Irishman and representatives of the Stagehands Union and the Teamsters, which were needed to guarantee labor peace and put in some dough. Roach was wired for sound and sent into the meeting. Meanwhile, Nicholson started a background check on George Wood.

A visit to St. Malachy's netted the info that Jimmy Alo had been best man at Wood's wedding. A subpoena on Wood's phone bills yielded a virtual Rolodex of organized crime figures. With that and Hal Roach, Jr.'s indication of criminal conspiracy, Jerry McKenna had no trouble getting court approval to tap the phones in Wood's office. That brought in enough to justify a bug in Wood's office as well, and then a tap on his home phone. Then Wood's mother-in-law came to live with them and he rented a bachelor pad two blocks down the street at 240 Central Park South, so McKenna pulled the tap on his apartment and put in one there.

Taps were easy to install: You just went to the basement and tapped into the phone wire leading up to the apartment. Bugs were another matter. The bug itself was the size of a pack of king-sized cigarettes, and the battery pack that kept it going was four times the size of that. Fresh batteries had to be installed once a week. To pick up the transmissions, you had to establish a receiving station with an unobstructed view of the office where the bug was located.

Diagonally across Broadway from Morris was a building where Horn & Hardart, the Automat chain, had some offices. Detective Nicholson's brother had gone to King's Point—the U.S. Merchant Marine Academy at King's Point, Long Island—with a son of the Horns, so Nicholson was able to get a corner room on the second floor with a clear line of sight to the polished granite lobby of the Mutual Life Building and the offices upstairs. Getting into Wood's office was a little trickier.

A slick bunch of safecrackers had been working Manhattan lately, breaking into offices and lifting cash and securities so deftly that the crimes often went unnoticed for months. Nicholson went to the top executives of Mutual Life and told them he had word that their building was going to be next. We have guards, they told him. Guards can be bribed, he reminded them. He walked out with a letter of introduction to the building superintendent identifying him as the representative of a company that examined buildings for structural weaknesses. The letter gave him and his engineers entrance to the building any time, day or night.

Wood worked in a large, plushly furnished corner office on the twentieth floor. Once a week, Nicholson and his men took the elevator to a floor nearby and walked up the stairs. They picked the locks on the outer door and the door to Wood's office. They turned over the armchair, carefully removed the upholstery tacks holding the underlining in place, taped in a new battery pack, tacked the lining back, tidied up, and left. Once they nearly got caught—on a Saturday night when their lookout radioed them that Wood had just pulled up in a limousine and was on his way up with some cronies who wanted a demo of this Scopitone. Nicholson and his men worked frantically to clean up, then hid in the stairwell while Wood sat around with his pals for an hour and a half. Then they came out and finished the job.

Wood never got to the office before 11:00 A.M., so Nicholson would begin his day at the Tombs, writing up his report for the day before. Then he'd head up to Central Park South to check on the wiretap they had at Wood's bachelor pad. By noon he'd be at the plant across from the Mutual Life Building with his partner, Joe Sanpietro, an older detective who'd taken him under his wing. They'd listen in until six or seven, when Wood walked to a barbershop on Seventh Avenue for a trim and a shave. He'd come out in a fresh blue shirt ready for a night on the town, which could mean stops at swank spots like El Morocco or the Stork Club or the Copa or a visit to Joe the Wop's Camelot Lounge.

Nicholson would go along for the ride, shadowing him, not too close, but close enough to hear. He might take a plainclothes policewoman along if they were going to hit the big clubs; otherwise he'd go it alone. At two or three in the morning he'd get back to his little apartment in Flatbush and catch a few hours of sleep before heading for the Tombs. He was an eager-beaver cop. He didn't have much else to do, being thirty-two and unmarried. And he was a champ at eavesdropping.

Some interesting stuff came into the plant. A day didn't go by that a major wiseguy or somebody connected didn't drop by Wood's office—Jimmy Blue-Eyes or Frank Costello or Tony Bender or Joe the Wop or Roy Cohn, the lawyer, or Manny Kimmel, the ex-bootlegger who'd started the Kinney parking lot chain, biggest in the city. Dames came through by the handful—major stars, minor stars, eager unknowns sent by some club owner in Jersey or Cleveland or Chicago, new to the big town and eager to see what the Morris Agency could do for them. After a while, Nicholson knew the drill by heart: "In this business, baby, it's not how good you are, it's who you know. Now, the guys who control the industry are all friends of mine. I can help you, but you've got to help yourself too. Say somebody's coming in from Chicago for the night—I don't expect you to leave him standing at the front door. 'Cause he'll call me the next day and say, 'Yeah, there's a spot for her in Chicago'—or he won't." Often Wood took her back to his bachelor pad to try her out himself. Sometimes he locked his office door and sampled the goods right there on the sofa, flicking on the intercom so his secretary would listen in.

Nicholson was pretty green, but it didn't take him long to conclude that Wood was some sort of mob pimp. He also caught on that Wood was using certain clients as couriers to move money around the country—the same point John Bonomi had gotten on the previous investigation, when J. Edgar Hoover told them a cop was making drops with Jimmy Durante. Gradually, it dawned on him that this was how the mob controlled the nightclub business—by owning a top agent in the booking agency that dominated the field. They didn't need to run the agency directly, any more than they needed to run the joints they owned in

New York and Miami and Vegas and Chicago. All they needed was a man in place to watch their backs and keep them flush with talent.

It was an efficient system, but it did have one flaw, a point of exposure that Detective Nicholson and Assistant DA McKenna were eager to exploit: George Wood himself. Wood was vulnerable. He made only about $25,000 a year at the Morris office, plus meals and drinks on the cuff and whatever he could claim in expenses, and he had a wife and two little girls to support, not to mention two apartments on Central Park South and a big-time gambling habit. He was forever in trouble with loan sharks and the IRS. And for all that he liked to hang out with hoodlums and boast about his underworld connections, he was actually a pretty gentle guy. He wouldn't want to end up at Dannemora, the Siberia of the New York State penal system, up in the frozen north by the Canadian border. He'd probably do almost anything to avoid it.

Frank Hogan had been looking to get a mole inside the mob for a long time. That was the point of this investigation from the start—not to send George Wood to jail but to turn him. To show him a handful of aces and catch him when he folded. And once they'd turned him, he could never go back. They could ask him to do anything—invite Meyer Lansky up to his office, for instance, and have him talk about things into the armchair—and he'd have to do it. If it ever got out, of course, he'd be dead meat. But as long as it was just their little secret, he could live a normal life. And he'd be theirs forever.

They saw their chance in the fall of 1961, when Jimmy Blue-Eyes called with a job for him to do: Go to Naples to meet Lucky Luciano.

The Genovese family didn't have its affairs in order. No sooner had Don Vitone seized control from Frank Costello than he'd been sent to the federal pen on a drug trafficking beef. A triumvirate consisting of Gerry Catena, Tommy Eboli, and Mike Miranda was supposed to be in charge, but Charlie Lucky, still in Italy after fifteen years of unhappy exile, remained the ultimate authority. Now a money dispute had arisen over an old job. Only Luciano had the records to prove who was right. Meyer Lansky, who generally had the last word on financial matters, wanted Wood to go to Italy to talk with the Boss. Arrangements were made. He'd fly to Paris, take a train to Rome, meet a contact who'd take him to Naples.

When his FBI pals dropped by the Morris office, Wood explained that he had to go to France on Scopitone business. A few days later, he took off for Paris as scheduled. Shortly before he was due to return, his secretary phoned Jimmy Alo to say he'd be bringing back the records. Alo should meet him at Rumpelmayer's that evening to pick up the goods.

As Wood's plane was coming in for a landing at Idlewild, Nicholson was striding into the terminal with a squad of detectives and a search warrant. He alerted customs and told them to send the subject through with only a cursory inspection. Then he stood back and waited for his pigeon to waddle through the gate. It was the chance he'd been waiting for. They'd get him to phone Blue-Eyes and say he'd been held up, postpone the meeting for a couple of hours. Then they'd put him a room and pressure him until he cracked. Meanwhile, they could look over the records he'd brought back from Italy, maybe even doctor them up a little. Then they'd send him out to meet Blue-Eyes wearing a wire, and after that they'd have him solid.

Passengers started to make their way through customs. Wood wasn't among them. Nicholson grew frantic. He checked with the airline to make sure Wood was on the passenger manifest. He sent his men out to search the terminal. Finally he ran out to his car and sped back to Manhattan. As he pulled up in front of the St. Moritz, he caught sight of his pigeon leaving Rumpelmayer's, headed up the street to his apartment. Jimmy Blue-Eyes was nowhere in sight.

Nicholson found out what had gone wrong as soon as he got to the plant the next day. It was all right there on tape—Wood's secretary phoning his FBI buddies, asking if they'd meet George at Idlewild and help him through customs. Later that afternoon, he heard Wood on the phone, expansive as always, bragging about his connections. Guess what just happened? Wood was saying. He had these friends in the FBI and he'd asked them to come out to Idlewild to meet him because he had to rush back to town for this big appointment at Rumpelmayer's. So what do they do? They roll out onto the tarmac in their official car, have him paged on the plane as it's pulling up to the terminal, whisk him out of the airport, and drop him off on Central Park South. How do you like that?

Nicholson didn't.

Until now, the two FBI agents hadn't actually done anything illegal. Nicholson had even heard them telling Wood that their assignment was to follow Jimmy Alo when he came to New York from his home base in Miami. He could make their job a little easier, they'd added, by telling them when he's coming to town. Nothing criminal there. But the caper at Idlewild—that was different.

Frank Hogan was livid. He went directly to Washington to confront Hoover with Nicholson's wiretap. As soon as he left, Hoover phoned the special agent in charge of the bureau's New York office and told him what had just happened. The SAC called in the two agents and passed it along. The renegade agents went straight to Wood's office and told him his phone was being tapped by an inexperienced, overly aggressive, gung-ho young assistant DA named McKenna. They didn't know Nicholson would be listening in on the bug.

Informing a suspect about the existence of a wiretap: This time they'd committed a serious crime. Hogan went back to Hoover. The next day, the two agents were gone from the FBI.

The investigation continued, sans wiretaps. Wood was making progress on the Scopitone deal. He was also putting together a deal to buy the Pioneer Club, a gambling den in Glitter Gulch, AKA downtown Las Vegas. He brought Joe the Wop in on the Pioneer deal. He brought in an associate of Socks Lanza, the Fulton Fish Market boss, who promised to bring in George Raft and Frank Sinatra and Lanza himself. He got Danny Brown, the loan shark, to wire $10,000 to a San Francisco company they were using as a front for the transfer. He made arrangements with Abe Green, the Jersey jukebox king, to have his Runyon Sales Company handle distribution for Scopitone. In return, Green and Gerry Catena of the Genovese family would have approval on all the other partners in the deal.

Detective Sanpietro was at the plant in January 1962 when Wood learned that Luciano had dropped dead. Heart attack, Capodichino airport in Naples, just like that. Jimmy Blue-Eyes and Joe the Wop were in Wood's office across the street, the three of them staring glumly down Broadway from the twentieth floor. They went back a long way, these three, past Vegas and Havana to the Depression, to Prohibition, to the days of Clayton, Jackson, and Durante and the Bugs and Meyer mob and the Keith-Albee circuit. "Whaddaya think of that?" Wood sighed as he turned to his old friend Jimmy, with Sanpietro listening in. "Charlie Lucky just died of a heart attack while waiting for a plane."

THE ANTITRUST INQUIRY WAS HEATING UP FAST. ALTHOUGH JUSTICE Department investigators had found more than one witness who told them the Morris Agency was as bad as MCA or worse, the spotlight now was on MCA. The press was running with the story, painting MCA as a secretive cartel that, as one magazine put it, "decides what you see, like it or not." *Time* held it responsible for "the vampirous attacks of stars" like Marlon Brando, whose $1-million-plus salary for *Mutiny on the Bounty* was driving production costs past the $20-million mark. When word of the federal grand jury investigation leaked out, Bob Hope quipped, "The government better be careful. MCA might declare war and then they won't get any more movies or television in Washington."

Peter Lawford and his manager, Milt Ebbins, were having dinner at the White House when Lawford's brother-in-law brought up the question. It was just the three of them, Lawford and Ebbins and Jack Kennedy, and Kennedy said it didn't look good for MCA. Bobby had this whole thing, and Jules Stein and Taft Schreiber and Lew Wasserman could all go to prison. Lawford and Ebbins were aghast: Prison terms were rare in antitrust cases, unthinkable in Hollywood. "Not Lew Wasserman!" they cried. Kennedy changed the subject.

In April 1962, with the grand jury still hearing witnesses in Los Angeles, an MCA attorney contacted the antitrust division with startling news: MCA was about to buy Decca Records, one of the largest recording companies in the country, and its subsidiary, Universal Pictures. At a time when some studios were cutting back, MCA was planning a relentless expansion—leaping into film production, building three new office towers on its Universal City lot, gambling millions as it strove to reinvent itself. As for the talent agency, MCA intended to sell that to its employees. At Justice, there was no doubt that the divestiture would be cosmetic—that the notoriously taciturn Wasserman, who planned to stay on as president of MCA and its Decca/Universal/Revue subsidiaries, would control the agency through a sweetheart relationship with his longtime associates. The question was what to do about it.

On Friday, July 13, five days before MCA was set to split off its agency business, Justice Department lawyers walked into the federal courthouse in downtown Los Angeles, an Art Moderne slab on a hilltop overlooking the Hollywood Freeway, and filed suit against MCA, the Screen Actors Guild, and the Writers Guild of America West (which had likewise granted MCA a production waiver). They also obtained a temporary restraining order barring MCA from disposing of the agency. MCA's lawyers learned of the action as it was being filed, when they went into a meeting with their counterparts from Justice.

MCA immediately filed suit to block the restraining order, but on Tuesday, the judge upheld it. MCA would not be permitted to sell its talent agency on Wednesday as scheduled. Its franchise from the Screen Actors Guild—its license to represent guild members—was set to expire on Wednesday at midnight. Bobby Kennedy had Wasserman in a corner.

That evening, agents were told the firm was out of business. As they exited the lovely white-brick mansion on Santa Monica Boulevard, they were searched by armed guards, apparently on government orders. Secretaries who came in Thursday morning were told to advise actor clients who called to contact the Screen Actors Guild for information. The White House on Santa Monica took on a hushed, almost funereal air, while all around it, Hollywood was in chaos. Technically, the agency was still entitled to represent writers, directors—anyone other than screen actors. But nobody was representing anybody. Every agent in the firm was trying frantically to make a deal for himself. New agencies were coalescing over the phone and applying for franchises. Agents were fielding employment offers from every other agency in the business. MCA's top executives were closeted with their lawyers, negotiating for a settlement. Producers who wanted to talk terms had no one to call.

Kennedy's price for a settlement was a pledge from Lew Wasserman to abandon the agency business at once. On Monday, ten days after Justice filed suit, an agreement to that effect was entered at the courthouse. Meanwhile, other agencies were competing furiously for the spoils. Ted Ashley, Nat Lefkowitz's nephew, who'd left management a short time after leaving Morris and returned to agenting with another ex-Morris man named Ira Steiner, ended up with a treasure trove—Truman Capote, Ian Fleming, Tennessee Williams, Ingrid Bergman, Danny Kaye, Gene Kelly, Gina Lollobrigida. . . . Only William Morris, suddenly thrust to the top after years as number two, declined to join the free-for-all.

"Don't even contemplate making the calls," Lastfogel told his boys. "Don't do anything to disrupt anybody's business. We don't need it. We have enough." His associates were mystified. Some saw it as arrogance; others thought he didn't want to disturb the family he'd gathered around him. Industry execs suspected the real reason was his desire not to make the Morris Agency the next target.

There was one MCA man the Morris office did hire, a television agent named Jerry Zeitman. Zeitman had joined MCA in 1948, when he was eighteen, and worked for the head of the band department. Then he'd transferred to the television department, where he handled such sitcoms as "Mr. Ed," "The People's Choice," and "The George Burns and Gracie Allen Show," which had gone off the air when Gracie retired in 1958. He still represented Burns—had dinner with him every Thursday night, in fact—as well as Carol Channing, Bob Newhart, and film producers Bud Yorkin and Norman Lear.

Sammy Weisbord had started talking with Zeitman a year before MCA broke up, chatting him up on brisk walks around Beverly Hills, but Zeitman kept telling him he was an MCA man for life. Now Zeitman was out on the street. So he made a deal to join the Morris office, then met with Lastfogel to go over his client list to see who might come with him. "Don't pursue anybody," Lastfogel cautioned him. "We're not ambulance chasers." They went down the list: yes, yes, fine. When they got to Burns's name, Lastfogel's face clouded over.

Burns and Allen had been with the Morris office since they were in vaudeville—until they let MCA take them to CBS fourteen years before. Lastfogel didn't believe in holding a grudge, but loyalty was a quality he very much believed in. "I'd like to sleep on it," he said.

Early the next morning, he stuck his head into Zeitman's new office. "It's fine," he said. "If he wants to be here, I'll have him."

9

MAD, MAD, MAD, MAD WORLD

Palm Springs/Los Angeles/New York, 1962–1969

NINETY MILES AWAY, IN THE BLISTERING DESERT OUTSIDE PALM SPRINGS, Stanley Kramer had assembled the greatest cast of comedians ever put before a movie camera. Jimmy Durante, Milton Berle, Sid Caesar, Buddy Hackett, Jonathan Winters, Ethel Merman, Mickey Rooney— the cast read like a Morris Agency roll call. Abe Lastfogel had even gotten Katharine Hepburn to talk Spencer Tracy, sixty-two and only recently recovered from a tough bout with emphysema, into taking a role. The desert heat would be good for him, Lastfogel assured her, and Tracy would get top billing for a few weeks' work, even though everybody else would be out there for months. Plus, everything about this picture said it would be the biggest, the best, the most—a classic comedy that would harken back to the golden days of Charlie Chaplin and do them one better.

Stanley Kramer was not one to approach comedy lightly. He'd made his name as an independent producer in the early fifties, bucking the Hollywood system just as it was falling apart. Now he was one of Hollywood's reigning rebels, out to free moviemaking from hidebound studio conventions and the straitjacket of McCarthyism. He liked serious issues and big themes. He'd taken on the emptiness of American life in

Death of a Salesman, nuclear doom in *On the Beach*, Nazi war crimes in *Judgment at Nuremberg*, the lunacy of fundamentalism in *Inherit the Wind*, with Tracy playing Clarence Darrow in the Scopes monkey trial. When Kramer made a comedy, it would be comedy with a message. *It's a Mad, Mad, Mad, Mad World* would be nothing less than an inquiry into the human condition, masquerading as a $6 million Cinerama farce. Major stuff, any way you looked at it.

Kramer's subject this time was the Big G: greed. Jimmy Durante is the gangster who sets the whole thing in motion when he runs off a mountain road and spills the secret of his buried loot just before kicking the bucket—literally. Kramer wasn't much for subtlety, but Durante was a nice piece of casting, given his role as a courier for the mob. Five men hear his tale—Milton Berle, a pill-popping neurotic with a ditzy wife and a screaming mother-in-law; Jonathan Winters, a witless truck driver; Sid Caesar, a dentist on a second honeymoon with his wife; and Mickey Rooney and Buddy Hackett, two gag writers on their way to Vegas. For the next three hours they race each other for the booty, speeding across the desert by truck, taxi, bike, and biplane as Spencer Tracy, the police chief, waits and schemes.

Kramer was making an epic comedy in which everyone, from truck driver to chief of police, goes nuts when faced with the prospect of free dough. There was no good versus evil here, no moral center, just an overwhelming sense of American society as corrupt and corruptible, as if Benny Siegel's vision of a casino in the desert had mushroomed to encompass an entire civilization. The sixties had arrived.

THINGS HAD CHANGED ALONG THE SUNSET STRIP SINCE 1947, WHEN PHIL Weltman stepped off the Super Chief and Sammy Weisbord whisked him to his new home at the Chateau Marmont. Ciro's and the Mocambo, the most glamorous nightclubs in movieland, had both shut their doors. The tile-roofed bungalows of the Garden of Allah, long gone to seed, had been bulldozed for a shopping mall. The Strip itself was looking down at the heels, like a dowager star whose drinking was finally catching up with her.

But for fifteen years, Phil and Sammy had lived in the same adjacent suites at the Chateau Marmont, Phil in 4H, Sammy upstairs in 5H. For fifteen years they'd hung out together, confirmed bachelors who spent their spare time catching rays and ogling girls—weekends in Palm Springs or on the beach in Santa Monica, holidays in Europe or Hawaii. And for fifteen years they'd walked the Strip at night, past honking cars and raucous nightspots and crowds of revelers, finding in the tumult a calm that allowed them to hash out the day's events.

As West Coast head of television, Weisbord was more than just Weltman's boss. With the demise of live broadcasting, Hollywood had become a television town. Most of the deals were still made in New York, but as far as production was concerned, New York was where they found the talent and put it on a plane. Hollywood was humming, the studios scaled back and humbled but most of them making money. For every feature film the majors made, they now churned out two television series. And while the FCC was backing the networks in their attempt to wrest programming decisions from sponsors and their ad agencies, the talent agencies found packaging to be as lucrative as ever. So Weisbord had one of the biggest jobs in town, and with television bringing in 60 percent of Morris's commissions, he had one of the biggest jobs at the agency too. Even Wally Jordan, his nominal boss in New York, knew better than to cross him. "Fuckin' Weisbord," he'd say, and roll his eyes.

The job was Weisbord's reward for his devotion to Mr. Lastfogel, which transcended the merely filial. Weisbord was obsessive about everything—tenacious in pursuit of a deal, single-minded in his commitment to exercise and health food, absolutely maniacal in his cultivation of the perfect suntan. Once at a health club on Pico, he took on five junior agents, one after another, doing medicine-ball sit-ups—the kind where two guys lock ankles and toss a medicine ball back and forth. He outlasted them all, though his back was raw and bleeding by the end. His lectures on the benefits of cottage cheese and wheat germ and cranberry juice, which was supposed to be good for the urinary tract, were legendary for their fanaticism. "I don't really care about his urinary tract," Dinah Shore groused one day when she came out of a meeting with him. "I came here to talk about my career."

But nothing brought out Weisbord's obsessiveness more than Abe Lastfogel and the William Morris Agency, twin entities that he regarded with a reverence that veered toward worship. He sported William Morris cufflinks and a William Morris tie clip. He drove a black Cadillac convertible with custom plates that read "WM SW." The reverence with which young Abe Lastfogel had regarded Mr. Morris was negligible compared to the devotion Weisbord showed Mr. Lastfogel. Every day, he accompanied the Boss to Hillcrest for lunch. At the end of every afternoon, he went to the Boss's office to tell him what he'd done that day. Every evening, he went out to dinner with the Boss and Mrs. Lastfogel.

Weisbord had an active, even predatory, social life. Once, when he was planning a trip to Sweden, he'd actually called a trainee in the New York mail room because he'd heard the kid knew a lot of girls. "Sweden?" the guy said. "Mr. Weisbord, I've never *been* to Sweden." Yet Weisbord never took a girl out to dinner; when he had a date, they'd go for a walk after he'd eaten with the Lastfogels. Many people thought this was nuts. Milt Ebbins, Peter Lawford's manager, finally asked him why he never ate with network executives or clients or anybody else in the industry. "I can't do it," Weisbord replied. "I can't. I owe everything to this man."

Phil Weltman was the kind of guy who spoke his mind. He thought this kind of behavior was highly stupid, and as they walked up and down the Strip, he told Sammy so.

"*You* never come into Mr. Lastfogel's office at the end of the day," Sammy would complain.

"Sammy," Phil would reply sarcastically, "I can't sit there and wait for petals of approval to fall on me."

Then Phil would ask Sammy why he didn't take some guy from the mail room and show him the ropes, the way Phil always did. Right now, Phil's secretary was a twenty-year-old UCLA dropout named Barry Diller—son of a wealthy real-estate developer, classmate of Danny Thomas's daughter Marlo at Beverly Hills High. When Diller decided he wanted to go into show business, he'd bugged her dad until he landed an interview at William Morris. But Phil already knew why Sammy wouldn't hire a kid like that—because Sammy preferred babes. Sammy wanted a pretty girl who'd pick up his laundry and keep his refrigerator stocked with cranberry juice. He only used the mail room guys to run to Hillcrest for matzoh ball soup. "Why don't you do for somebody else what Abe Lastfogel did for you?" Phil would say. And they'd have a big fight about it.

But tonight it was something new. A couple of years earlier, Phil and Sammy had decided to leave Palm Springs halfway through a three-day weekend because it was raining. But the sun came out as soon as they got to the edge of town, so they checked into the nearest motel, changed into their shorts, headed for the pool, and immediately laid eyes on a gorgeous pair of gals. Phil ended up with a former Miss New Jersey who lived in Los Angeles. They'd been seeing each other ever since, and even though Phil never thought he'd find a woman who'd put up with the kind of life an agent has to lead, they were actually thinking about getting married. So he told Sammy.

Sammy stopped cold and fixed him with an angry stare. "Have you told Mrs. Lastfogel?" he demanded.

Not the reaction Phil had anticipated. "What are you saying? Are you saying I need to get her *permission?*"

A violent argument ensued.

Sammy acted as best man at the wedding. Afterward, as Phil and his new bride set up housekeeping in a secluded section of Bel Air, Sammy moved into a penthouse in the Sierra Tower, a clean white slab rising against the wooded hills on the far end of the Strip from the Chateau Marmont. Looking west, on a day when the winds whipped across the basin and swept away the smog, he could see the blue Pacific on the horizon; looking east, he could see a handful of towers downtown; looking down, he could see the flats of Beverly Hills—Wilshire Boulevard, the Beverly Wilshire Hotel where Mr. and Mrs. Lastfogel lived, the recently deserted MCA mansion across from city hall, the whole fairy-tale village. His town, at his feet. Thanks to Mr. Lastfogel.

While Sam Weisbord ran West Coast television, Phil Weltman was spending most of his time developing manpower, taking green but ambitious kids like Barry Diller and turning them into sellers. For years, ever since Norman Brokaw's apprenticeship in the forties, Morris trainees had been expected to learn through osmosis as they rose out of the mail room and through the secretarial ranks. Working in the mail room, they got to learn who was who, to deliver scripts and contracts and checks to people around town, to read the confirmation memos that went out setting forth the terms for deals that had just been struck. They were expected to learn typing and shorthand on their own dime. The wages were peanuts—$40 a week—and anyone who screwed up a delivery or had an auto accident quickly found himself back on the street. The others were happy to see him go, since it increased their own chances of advancement.

Those who made it out of the mail room went to work as secretaries for whoever happened to have an opening. They typed up memos, fielded incoming phone calls, listened in to take notes and feed figures to the agent when he needed them. In the process, they learned how to talk to the buyer, how to make a deal, what to go for, and what to leave behind. By the time they graduated to junior agent status, they were expected to have picked up a thorough understanding of the business.

Like any apprenticeship, the William Morris training program worked only as well as the senior agents who administered it. In New York, it had been run for years by Nat Kalcheim, boss of the personal appearance department. Kalcheim was stern and austere, but he encouraged the younger agents and gave them a pat on the back whenever they deserved it. Nat Lefkowitz, the New York office chief, was good at spotting potential manpower but much more stinting in his praise. The one the kids all looked up to was George Wood—worldly and sophisticated, incredibly connected, Mr. Showbiz himself. At five in the afternoon, when Nat Lefkowitz went home to his apartment on Central Park West, Wood's day was just getting started. Being Wood's secretary meant placing a lot of phone calls you weren't allowed to listen in on, but he made up for it by switching on the intercom whenever he humped some dame on the sofa. Nobody knew the NYPD was listening in as well.

Weltman was too strict for any such nonsense. His idea of training was a rigorous exercise in the military mold. He rode herd on the new guys until he was sure they knew the score. When deals came his way, he handed them off to junior agents and coached them on how to handle them. The core of his message was follow-through and integrity. "Be prepared for wild rantings from the buyer," he'd instruct them. "You can always come down." When the deal was struck, he made sure a confirmation letter went out the same day, even if it meant staying in the office until 10:00 P.M. That way, you'd have the terms in writing if the buyer tried to renege.

The agent he wanted them to become was Abe Lastfogel. To Weltman, to all of them, Mr. Lastfogel was the ideal. Quiet. Self-effacing. A man who believed the client came first. A man motivated by incredible passion. Weltman wanted to instill that passion in his boys. He also wanted to give them a sense of teamwork—a feeling that they were in it for their clients and for the agency, not for their own advantage. That's what it meant to be a family, and being a family was what made them special. It was why men who'd grown up at the Morris office, as most of them had, so rarely left it. "They run a good business," he'd say when one of his boys told him a competing agency had made him a generous offer, "but they don't care about people."

Not the way Weltman cared. Sure he was tough—the toughest most of these boys had ever met. When he chewed you out, it was brutal. George Shapiro told him he made his army drill sergeant look like Mary Poppins. Shapiro was typical of Weltman's charges, a young guy from the Bronx who had a connection through his cousin—Carl Reiner, Harry Kalcheim client and former "Your Show of Shows" star—and who'd gone into the New York mail room with his best friend from third grade. After working in the mail room with other promising kids, like Jerry Weintraub and Irwin Winkler, Shapiro had been assigned to the Coast to help Weltman with "The New Steve Allen Show," which ABC had just bought. One day Shapiro got so mad at Weltman that he yelled "I quit!", slammed the door, and stormed out of the office. Young Diller went white-faced. But thirty seconds later Shapiro was back in Weltman's office, crying "What am I doing?" Weltman gave a gruff laugh and took him back. That was the thing about Weltman: He was tough, but you had to love him. He was the heart and soul of the agency.

STAN KAMEN HAD LEARNED TO EXPECT THE OFF-THE-WALL DEMANDS, THE blowups with directors, the anguished 4:00 A.M. phone calls. He knew that when he walked into his office in the morning, he'd find his phone ringing and Steve McQueen on the other end. Even if McQueen was on the other side of the globe, as he was now, shooting *The Great Escape*. Especially if he was on the other side of the globe.

All actors were needy and demanding and insecure, but McQueen was special. Bastard product of a one-night stand, boarded out by an alcoholic mother with anyone who'd take him, he'd grown up a stray cub, rolling drunks and picking up pointers in reform school. Now, at thirty-two, a runty little man with a prematurely crinkled face, he played the tough guy every waking moment—driving fast, picking fights, drinking, gambling, nailing every broad he could find. But inside, he was fragile and vulnerable. Inside, he was Marilyn Monroe. Kamen was old enough to be his big brother. He felt more like his father.

McQueen didn't spend a lot of time mucking around inside. Inside was messy, confusing, a big hole with jagged edges, *vagina dentata*. Instead he'd taken up auto racing, the sport James Dean had broken his neck pursuing four days before the premiere of *Rebel Without a Cause*. Like Dean, he was obsessed with speed. It meant freedom, escape, bliss. But Dean was androgynous and ambivalent; McQueen was out to prove his manhood. Fast cars and motorbikes represented his balls, he liked to say. Women were his way of keeping score. He'd pick them up, screw them, dump them. Sometimes he wouldn't even bother to screw them, just pick them up and dump them. Or he'd share them with his buddies, three or four guys to a chick. But he didn't like queers, didn't like them at all. The idea that someone might take him for one made him crazy with rage.

Stan Kamen may have winced inwardly when McQueen lashed out against queers, but he never said anything. Why should he? He was a man's man himself, at least on the face of it. Nobody knew his secret—nobody at the agency, none of his friends, not even the woman tennis pro he'd been dating in a friendly way. He never talked about himself anyway. As far as his clients were concerned, he was a man with no needs. He was only there for them. He was the perfect agent.

McQueen knew one thing: He couldn't stay in television. He'd gotten a taste of the big screen when Kamen got him Sammy Davis, Jr.'s part in *Never So Few*. He liked it. He'd been offered a role in *Ocean's Eleven* that he couldn't take because it conflicted with the TV series. But when John Sturges wanted him to costar with Yul Brynner in *The Magnificent Seven*, his Western remake of *The Seven Samurai*, Kamen had gone to Dick Powell at Four Star and explained that he might prefer to be working with a happy actor. Powell got the message. Then CBS moved the series to Wednesday night, and early in 1961 it was canceled because the ratings dropped.

But what television star had ever made it in the movies? Clint Eastwood, another Morris client who'd gotten big on TV (playing Rowdy Yates on "Rawhide," Friday nights on CBS), had the same itch, and it was getting him nowhere. Ditto Robert Culp of "Trackdown." Phil Kellogg, Bert Allenberg's longtime deputy, had taken over the motion picture department after Allenberg's death, and he had his hands full with stars—Anne Bancroft, Carol Channing, Katharine Hepburn, Deborah Kerr, Jack Lemmon, Sophia Loren, Marcello Mastroianni, Walter Matthau, Kim Novak, Gregory Peck, Elvis Presley, Ann Sothern, Barbara Stanwyck, Spencer Tracy, Natalie Wood. Abe Lastfogel had begun to show some interest in McQueen, which was certainly a good sign. But if he wanted to be a film star, Kamen would have to make it happen.

Steve and Stan had a system for dealing with scripts. Kamen would screen them first. Anything he approved would go to Steve's wife, Neile. Scripts she thought were right for him would go to Steve. Since Steve only read car and motorcycle mags, this arrangement suited him well. Since Neile had bit by bit given up her own career to become a Hollywood wife and mother (she'd lost a shot at *West Side Story* when she discovered she was pregnant with their second child), it suited her too. But though Steve had gotten work after his series was canceled, he'd seen nothing that would make him a screen idol. Then John Sturges had talked him into doing a World War II prisoner-of-war story called *The Great Escape*—an ensemble piece based on the true story of the largest Allied prison break of the war. So in the summer of 1962, while Stanley Kramer was shooting comedians in the desert and Weisbord and Weltman were yelling at each other as they paced the Strip, Steve McQueen was on location in Bavaria, with Stan Kamen nursing him to stardom long-distance.

McQueen had complaints about everything, but the biggest was that his character was vague and undefined. He liked to come up with little mannerisms to make his character memorable: On *The Magnificent Seven*, he'd spent so much time fiddling with his hat in the background that Brynner hired a full-time hat watcher to let him know when McQueen was stealing a scene. Now he was spending hours with Sturges and the screenwriter, trying to make sure the audience got a vivid impression of Captain Virgil Hilts.

Hilts was a loner. He spent a lot of time in solitary because he kept trying to escape, so McQueen thought of giving him a baseball to bounce against the walls to keep sane, and a catcher's mitt to go with it. Very good: rhythmic, masculine, all-American. Then there was the escape itself. The script called for most of the inmates, having burrowed underground to the edge of the forest, to make their way into town and head for the train station with forged identity papers. Long-legged James Coburn was supposed to peddle off on a bicycle, bony knees pumping away like a praying mantis on the Tour de France. That was fine for Coburn. For himself, McQueen wanted a motorcycle chase. The screenwriter went to work, and McQueen got a class-A escape sequence, ambushing a Nazi trooper, stealing his motorbike and uniform, and streaking off across the Bavarian countryside with the Krauts in hot pursuit. Suddenly, Virgil Hilts no longer seemed undefined.

But what about James Garner? Garner idolized McQueen and seemed bent on copying him, most recently by taking up racing. He'd done some early scenes in a white turtleneck—very flashy. As other parts of the script were rewritten, McQueen began to wonder. Was Sturges expanding Garner's role at his expense? Was Sturges betraying him?

McQueen was unstable at best during a shoot—tense, coiled, as if some feral child were lodged within, ready to spring free. When the pressure built, he blew it off behind the wheel, speeding down narrow roads, driving through flocks of chickens, charging across fields if anyone got in his way. He got more and more irrational as the shoot progressed. Sturges tried to talk him down, but it was no good. Sturges was trying to take his picture away. Desperate, McQueen played the only card he had: He refused to show up for work.

Years of experience had given Sturges great confidence in the Morris office. It was a calming influence, a stabilizing force, a godfather. A call went out to Beverly Hills. The next day, Stan Kamen appeared in Bavaria, talking to McQueen, talking to Sturges, smoothing things out, calming people down. That was what Kamen did best. He was quiet, solid, a rock, and he wasn't afraid to tell McQueen he was out of line. Sturges was a brilliant action director, Kamen reminded him. Sturges had been responsible for *The Magnificent Seven*, McQueen's best picture to date, and now he was giving McQueen the biggest shot of his career. Trust him. He's not going to hurt you.

McQueen looked like a little boy who'd just learned a lesson from his pa. Yeah, he'd go back.

Kamen flew from Munich to Los Angeles on Friday. On Sunday morning, he got another call: McQueen had seen the latest script changes and blown sky-high. Sturges told Kamen not to bother coming out—this time he was taking McQueen off the picture. He knew that would have Kamen on the next plane.

When he got to the set, Kamen found the cast and crew having a beer party outside the prison stockade. He located McQueen and pulled him aside. If McQueen didn't show up for makeup the next morning, Kamen told him, he was off the picture.

Steve wanted to know what Kamen was going to do about those script changes.

Nothing. He'd have to trust Sturges. Kamen left.

It took willpower, but for the rest of the shoot, McQueen managed to project his fears into the camera instead of onto the people around him. The motorbike scenes were brilliant. He rode the way he was—edgy, erratic, out of control. He skittered across the screen, fishtailing around corners, clouds of dust in his wake. Finally, trapped between an advancing Nazi patrol and a barbed-wire barricade on the Swiss border, he gunned his motor and took the leap.

It wasn't really McQueen, of course. The jump was made by Bud Ekins, a motorcycle mechanic McQueen had met in a San Fernando Valley repair shop. Ekins had taught him most of what he knew about riding, and McQueen had brought him to Germany as his stunt double. And now, through Ekins, McQueen made a breathtaking escape—from prison, from authority, from television, from the mundane existence of ordinary folk. The barbed wire was beneath him, stardom shone in his face. Then a higher barricade, more barbed wire, hopelessly caught up. No matter. Virgil Hilts might go back into captivity, but Bud Ekins's daredevil leap for freedom would make McQueen a movie star.

BROADWAY THEATER HAD BEEN FADING FOR YEARS, A VICTIM OF TELEVISION, the movies, rising real-estate values in midtown Manhattan, you name it. Yet in October 1963 the Morris Agency's playwrights and directors were generating enough excitement to make the Great White Way look dazzling again. *Who's Afraid of Virginia Woolf*, Edward Albee's astringent look at modern marriage, had been playing for a year at the Billy Rose Theatre. Abe Burrows was going into his third year with *How to Succeed in Business Without Really Trying*, his wickedly funny musical about an office boy on the make. Meredith Willson, who'd caused a sensation six years earlier with *The Music Man*, had a new musical based on the screen hit *Miracle on 34th Street* about to open at the Shubert. Neil Simon was in previews at the Biltmore with his third play, a lighthearted comedy about newlywed bliss called *Barefoot in the Park*. Jerry Herman was in rehearsals with *Hello, Dolly!*, his musical interpretation of Thornton Wilder's *The Matchmaker*. Harold Prince was directing *She Loves Me*. Richard Nash had written the stage version of his novel *110 in the Shade*. Bob Merrill had written the lyrics and Jule Styne the music for the Fanny Brice musical *Funny Girl*, which Fanny's son-in-law, producer Ray Stark, had announced would star a kooky new singer named Barbra Streisand.

Morris would have been handling Streisand, too, if Harry Kalcheim had had his way. The year before, a twenty-year-old unknown with a

voice so big people forgot her frightful appearance, she'd caused a sensation in a minor role in the Broadway musical *I Can Get It for You
Wholesale*. She was already represented by Associated Booking, but they
were a little outfit and this girl was clearly going places. Big-time agents
were elbowing each other out of the way at her club dates—at the Bon
Soir in Greenwich Village, a basement hole-in-the-wall that had a gay
bar at one end; at the Blue Angel, a tony uptown nightspot upholstered
in pink and gray; at the hungry i in San Francisco and the legendary
Cocoanut Grove in Los Angeles. But though Kalcheim had been eager
to sign her, the initial response in the office was even worse than it had
been for Elvis. Now Morris was being pushed aside by Freddie Fields
and David Begelman, ex-M.C.A. agents who had a new office called
Creative Management Associates, just as Stark was revving up his
Fanny Brice production. They could only hope *Funny Girl* fared better
than *Sophie*, Steve Allen's ill-fated musical about the life of Sophie
Tucker, which had opened the previous spring to devastating reviews
and a short run.

But with or without Streisand, the fellows in the Morris office were
riding high. Show business had transformed their lives—had lifted
them from a drab existence in Brooklyn or the Bronx or wherever to an
exalted realm of action, excitement, success. It was the same with
their clients—like Doc and Danny Simon, brothers whom Ben Griefer
in the television department had gotten work as staff writers at CBS
after the brief, dazzling adventure of "Your Show of Shows." A few
years earlier, walking down Park Avenue, Doc Simon had looked up at
the Ritz Tower, where Goodman Ace lived—Goody Ace, the hottest
writer in broadcasting, a man who'd gotten $5,000 just to take a meet-
ing with Pepsi-Cola's ad agency—and declared that one day he was
going to live there, too. If *Barefoot in the Park* lived up to expectations,
Simon might get his wish. And while the agents might not have
Simon's talent, their jobs gave them entrée to the same rarefied worlds
of Broadway pizzazz and East Side sophistication. For that they were
grateful.

So everyone was in a good mood for the luncheon celebrating Abe
Burrows's twenty-fifth anniversary with the Morris office. Dinty Moore's
was as classy-looking as ever, its brass still polished, its white paint and
evergreen shrubs still brightening the crowded stretch of Forty-sixth
Street west of Broadway. Burrows strolled across the street from the
Variety Arts Theatre, where he was rehearsing the second road company

for *How to Succeed*. Twenty-five years ago, he'd been a gag writer trying to get in the door of the Morris office in the RKO Building; it had taken him a year to get past the receptionist. Since then he'd created "Duffy's Tavern" on radio and appeared as "the bald-headed baritone from Brooklyn" on half a dozen TV quiz shows and variety hours. The corporate ethos he so coolly eviscerated today had been sacrosanct in those earlier years, when he'd found himself listed in *Red Channels* for his involvement in HICCASP; yet now audiences were lining up for his portrayal of a young go-getter who sings "I Believe in You" while staring into a mirror in the executive washroom. But his greatest success had come when he and Jo Swerling strung together some Damon Runyon stories and turned them into *Guys and Dolls*, the musical that captured better than anything else the grit and bustle and excitement of the old Times Square.

That was the spirit of show business, and it was written across the faces of the Morris people who'd gathered in this old hangout to wish their client well—forty-three of them in all, including the dashing and elegant Charlie Baker, head of the legit department, and Wally Jordan of the television department, and the prim and proper Kalcheim brothers and mumbling Nat Lefkowitz and George Wood, who typified the Broadway Damon Runyon had immortalized in his stories, who loved gambling and broads and having a good time. And of course the Lastfogels, who were hosting this affair. They really were a family, these people, which is just the way Burrows thought of them. "I don't think of my commission as a commission," he said as he looked around the table. "It's like sending money home to mother."

"You bet your ass," Frances cried out. "And you'd better keep sending it, too!"

But the Lastfogels weren't in it for the money. That's what made it a family. Lastfogel never even bothered to carry the stuff; anything he wanted he could sign for, and when they went to Vegas Frances would give him a couple of hundred to gamble. Carol Channing, who was set to star in *Hello, Dolly!*, got a lesson in Lastfogel's priorities when she walked into his office one day with a bag slung over her shoulder. He asked her what was in it, so she told him—sandwiches, diamonds, and negotiable securities. His face lit up immediately. "Sandwiches?" he cried. "What kind of sandwiches?"

ALL YEAR, GEORGE WOOD HAD BEEN WORKING THE SCOPITONE DEAL WITH Nat Lefkowitz's deputy, a young man named Lee Stevens who'd started in the mail room ten years before and was as much on the rise as the hero of *How to Succeed in Business*. In May, Stevens had put together an agreement between Cameca, the French corporation behind Scopitone, and a pair of Miami Beach attorneys Wood had recruited to head the investor group he'd assembled. Besides Wood and the two attorneys, the investor group included Aaron Weisberg, part-owner of record of the Sands; Alfred Miniaci, who headed a group of jukebox and vending machine companies in the Bronx; and Jersey jukebox magnate Abe Green, whose Runyon Sales Company had once been headed by the notorious Doc Stacher. The agreement gave the attorneys, who were forming a company called Scopitone Inc., a licensing option for a four-month trial period.

The trial was successful, and in October Stevens put his signature to a contract giving Scopitone Inc. U.S. rights to the invention, with the Morris office acting as agent for both Cameca and Scopitone. The deal was worth more than $1 million in hardware alone, with Scopitone agreeing to buy two hundred machines and manufacture at least fifty-two hundred more over the next ten years. The Morris office stood to get a commission of $12 per machine, plus 10 percent of the $15 sales price of the color films the machines were designed to play.

All of which was very nice, but it wasn't doing much for George Wood personally. Georgie liked the ponies, but the ponies didn't like him. Ditto with football and boxing. He was in hock to his eyebrows to loan sharks, friendly fellows but not the sort you wanted to blow off. By November, he was desperate. Finally he went to Bernie Brillstein, a junior agent whose uncle he knew from radio. As Baron Munchhausen, Jack Pearl had been one of the biggest radio comics of the thirties; now Wood needed a favor from his nephew.

"Bernie, I'm in real trouble," he said. "Do you have any money I can borrow?"

Bernie was making $65 a week. All he had was $2,000 he'd saved from his bar mitzvah.

"Could you lend it to me for a week?"

The two grand bought him some time. There were more games to be played, more wagers to make. His luck would turn, he knew it. By Friday evening he was feeling confident. He went down the street for his customary shave and trim, then headed over to Third Avenue to check

in with the boys at the Camelot Lounge. Detective Nicholson was waiting for him.

Nicholson was still working the Scopitone case for the DA's Office
Squad. The scheme to catch Wood red-handed at Idlewild had failed,
but Nicholson was hoping to turn him some other way. He had nothing
better to do that night, so he figured he'd catch Wood at the Camelot
and see what developed. He was across the street when Wood went in,
around 7:00 P.M.

Nicholson waited about fifteen minutes, then ambled in to scope the
place out. On his way in, he had to step aside for the bouncers, who
were carrying out a man with a bloody towel across his face. Must have
been some rough stuff, Nicholson thought.

He went in and looked around. George Wood was nowhere to be
found.

Wood didn't feel so good when he woke up Saturday morning. He saw
his doctor, who gave him a cardiogram and told him he was okay, but
he'd taken a nasty tumble at the Camelot the night before and the chest
pains weren't going away. Finally he decided to check himself into
Mount Sinai. The doc was an old friend, he took care of all the boys—
Jimmy Blue-Eyes, everybody. Wood went through admissions and settled in. It was comfortable there—he could get away from broads and
work, relax, get one of the guys from the office to bring him a pastrami
and corned beef sandwich. He started to tell the doc a joke. He was
about to deliver the punch line when he fell over dead.

In his pocket was a list of the college ball teams he'd bet on. That
afternoon, most of them lost.

Detective Nicholson spent the weekend trying to figure out what happened. He'd sat in the Camelot Lounge for an hour before going home
to Flatbush. No sign of Wood. Monday morning, he went to his office in
the Tombs and filed his observation report. Then he headed uptown to
the plant to play the tapes back. The first conversation he heard cleared
it up for him. "Is it true what I hear about Georgie?" "Yeah, massive
coronary."

Nicholson was stupefied. There was no way he'd turn George Wood
now.

Funeral was Tuesday at Campbell's, the tony East Side mortuary. Everybody who was anybody showed up—Frank Costello, Tallulah Bankhead,

Jimmy Blue-Eyes, Ed Sullivan, Joe "Socks" Lanza. . . . George Jessel delivered the eulogy, while detectives from the Central Investigation Bureau stood outside on Madison Avenue, taking down license plate numbers.

Something had to be done for his family—not just the wife, but the two little girls as well. Wood was destitute. Worse than destitute—he was into loan sharks for more than $100,000. He had some insurance money coming, but not enough. Nat Lefkowitz made sure the bookies got the money so they wouldn't go after the widow. Jimmy Alo stepped in and covered the rest. What else could he do? Georgie was like family to him, and that's what you did with family—you took care of them.

SHELDON LEONARD WAS WATCHING TELEVISION WHEN HE SAW THE GUY he wanted. It was a Friday night, fall of 1963. Bill Cosby was on "The Jack Paar Program" doing his karate spoof, jumping around ferociously, a black belt defending himself against a mugger—until suddenly he wheels around to find himself up against a midget with a gun. Perfect, Leonard thought.

Cosby was a newcomer, a young comedian the Morris Agency was booking on the nightclub circuit. Sheldon Leonard was the hottest producer in television. His T&L Productions, which Norman Brokaw handled for the agency, was one of the reasons the Morris office could claim twenty-seven hours of television every week—more than three times as much as its closest competitor, Ashley-Steiner Famous, formed when Ted Ashley bought Charles Feldman's Famous Artists the year before. Ashley, forty-one now and operating out of a strikingly furnished corner office on Madison Avenue, had some popular shows—"Candid Camera," "Dr. Kildare," "The Twilight Zone." But Leonard alone had five long-running comedy hits—"The Danny Thomas Show," now in its eleventh season, plus "The Real McCoys," "The Andy Griffith Show," "The Dick Van Dyke Show," and "The Joey Bishop Show." He was about to spin off a new sitcom, "Gomer Pyle, U.S.M.C.," starring Jim Nabors, the doofus filling-station attendant on "Andy Griffith." And for a couple of seasons he'd even gone back to acting, playing Danny's agent on "The Danny Thomas Show"—a character they called Phil Brokaw.

Most of Leonard's business was with CBS, but he'd just gotten a commitment from NBC for an adventure series called "I Spy." The spy fad was as big now as Westerns had been a couple of years before, thanks to *Dr. No* and *From Russia with Love,* the low-budget James Bond pictures Cubby Broccoli had produced in London. Leonard wanted to build his show around a pair of attractive young men who'd go on escapades around the world while working as U.S. intelligence operatives. He'd cast Robert Culp, the Texas Ranger in Four Star's "Trackdown," as one of his stars. He wanted somebody who'd provide contrast for the other role, and Cosby was about as contrasting as you could get.

Like the Smothers Brothers, whom the Morris Agency was booking on college campuses to sell-out crowds, Bill Cosby belonged to a new generation of comics. They weren't like the old guys, the ones George Wood used to book—Henny Youngman or Milton Berle, "the thief of bad gags." Their material was candid and personal; they wrote it themselves. Nor did they have the angry edge of the beat-era comics—Lenny Bruce, Dick Gregory. They were irreverent, but they were also clean-cut, with an earnestness the younger generation found appealing.

The tone was set by the folk music revival, which had been kicked off in the late fifties by the Kingston Trio, three Stanford University students who strummed guitars and thought of their music as intellectually stimulating and had an enormous hit with a ballad called "Tom Dooley." College audiences were ready for serious-minded entertainers who'd give voice to their concerns—nuclear disarmament, the crusade for civil rights, the rise of the "military-industrial complex" that Eisenhower warned about in his farewell address. Folk music struck them as pure and uncommercial, the antithesis of the schmaltzy teen pop that followed the brief rock 'n' roll fad that Elvis ushered in.

While "Tom Dooley" was climbing the charts, the Smothers Brothers—Tom and Dick—were going to San Jose State, in a farm town separated from Stanford by twenty miles of prune orchards and a couple of brand-new semiconductor factories. In the evenings, they sang in an off-campus beer joint with a folk troupe called the Casual Quintet. The Casuals had a limited repertoire, so to pad out their act, they added some stage patter in which Tom, who was blond and intense and totally inarticulate, bounced off his younger brother Dick, who played the straight man. The group broke up after a thirty-six-week run at the Purple Onion in San Francisco, but then Tom persuaded Dick to join him in a duo doing folk songs and topical satire. They got their big break in April 1961, when they went to New York to appear at the Blue Angel, the chic little cabaret on East Fifty-fifth Street where Harry Belafonte and Eartha Kitt had gotten their start.

Bill Cosby was starting out in his hometown of Philadelphia at the time, telling jokes in a hangout called the Cellar while going to Temple University on a track and football scholarship. In the spring of 1962, he headed for New York to try his luck at the Gaslight Café, a folkie hangout in the Village. By this time, the Village had a half-dozen coffeehouses featuring promising young performers, the most widely heralded of whom was Bob Dylan, who'd shown up fifteen months earlier, not yet twenty and fresh out of Hibbing, Minnesota. Roy Silver, a twenty-six-year-old ex–advertising man who'd managed Dylan briefly before selling his contract to Albert Grossman, heard about this Negro comedian who was supposed to be good, so he dropped by the Gaslight one day and found him sweeping the floor. They went to a diner on Sixth Avenue, where Silver announced he was going to make him a star. Cosby signed a hastily scribbled management contract on the spot.

Silver talked up his new find to a pair of junior agents in the Morris Agency's television department, two guys named Marty Litke and Murray Schwartz. Their job was to hit the New York clubs—not Elmo's and the Copa but the little spots, intimate East Side supper clubs like the Blue Angel and Le Ruban Bleu and downtown Boho haunts like Bon Soir on Eighth Street and the Bitter End and the Café au Go-Go on Bleecker. They were scouting for talent to book on the network variety shows that were broadcast from midtown—"The Jack Paar Program," "The Ed Sullivan Show," "The Jackie Gleason Show," "The Garry Moore Show." They dropped in at the Gaslight one night and caught Cosby's act, which consisted mainly of a joke about the first Negro president moving into the White House: "Everything is okay—just a lot of 'for sale' signs on the street." They signed him anyway.

Cosby dropped the Negro stuff at his manager's suggestion and replaced it with lighter material, and by the spring of 1963, things were beginning to happen. He played an extended engagement at the Bitter End, where Woody Allen had just appeared. He recorded a live album. After being turned down six times by "The Tonight Show," he did an angry audition for guest host Allan Sherman and landed a booking. Then he got on "Jack Paar." Sheldon Leonard saw him and started asking questions.

Leonard wasn't intimidated by the race issue. In the early years of "The Danny Thomas Show" he'd used blacklisted writers, submitting false names to the network and failing to discuss it with Abe Lastfogel, on the theory that what Lastfogel didn't know wouldn't hurt him. No one noticed, but the show did draw nasty letters whenever Thomas put his arms around Amanda Randolph, who played his Negro maid. And Cosby wasn't anybody's maid: With Robert Culp as an intelligence agent masquerading as a tennis pro, Cosby would play his trainer and partner, a Rhodes scholar who speaks seven languages. The two characters would live together, date together, even use the same toilet. Race would be incidental, just as it was in Cosby's comedy routines. They were going to present him as if the color of his skin didn't matter.

Which was fine, except that this was broadcasting and color did matter. ABC never had found a sponsor for "Three's Company," its 1953 sitcom with Sammy Davis, Jr. NBC had given Nat "King" Cole a half-hour variety show in 1957, then dropped it after six months because most of the network's affiliates rejected it. If the same stations refused to carry "I Spy," it would go belly up as well.

Leonard and his packaging agent, Norman Brokaw, went to Grant Tinker, NBC's West Coast programming veep. Meanwhile, the personal appearance department put Cosby on the road—the Shoreham Hotel in Washington, the Diplomat in Miami Beach, the hungry i in San Francisco, Harrah's in Lake Tahoe. By the time Tinker made up his mind, the Morris office would have turned Cosby into a star.

ABE LASTFOGEL THOUGHT *ROUSTABOUT* MIGHT BE ELVIS'S STRONGEST picture yet. The script was terrific—about a nightclub singer who crashes his motorbike and ends up doing odd jobs at a fleabag carnival, where he falls for the foreman's daughter. The guy's a drifter, out for himself, and he hates the carny life. He takes off after a fight with the foreman, but when he discovers the outfit is about to go bust, he comes back as an entertainer and saves the day. To Lastfogel, this property had everything the teenagers could want—fights, bikes, black leather jackets, a girl. If it weren't for the musical numbers, it could have been a James Dean picture.

Lastfogel wasn't alone. Paul Nathan, the Paramount exec in charge of the production, saw it as something in the Tennessee Williams mold, like MGM's *Sweet Bird of Youth*, which starred Paul Newman as a Hollywood drifter who shacks up with a movie queen twice his age. Compared to this, of course, the Charlie Rogers character in *Roustabout* was a boy scout. But Richard Thorpe, who'd directed Elvis's most satisfying

film, the tough-minded black-and-white B-picture *Jailhouse Rock*, wasn't
so sure. Sleazeball carnivals might be what Lastfogel and the colonel
remembered from their youth, but they weren't exactly what was happening with the younger set these days. Did people really think this had
commercial appeal?

Hal Wallis, *Roustabout*'s producer, wasn't worried about his script. He
was worried about Elvis. By the beginning of 1964, Wallis had made six
Presley pictures, from *Loving You* in 1957 to last year's *Fun in Acapulco*,
and he'd watched in dismay as Colonel Parker used the outside-picture
clause in Presley's contract to milk his property for easy cash. The 1956
contract the Morris office had negotiated between Wallis and the
colonel allowed Elvis to appear in two outside pictures per year in addition to the one he was obligated to do for Wallis at Paramount. Wallis
used Presley in formula musicals that had more in common with the
Martin and Lewis comedies he'd produced in the fifties than with the
Humphrey Bogart classics he'd made during the war. But he saw them
as art compared to some of the outside pictures Presley had been doing.

The year before, MGM had come out with *It Happened at the World's
Fair*, with Elvis in Seattle as a bush pilot playing daddy to a winsome
Chinese orphan girl. Over the summer, they'd done another travel-
ogue—*Viva Las Vegas* with Ann-Margret, directed by the once-great
George Sidney, the man behind *Anchors Aweigh* and *Show Boat*. Then,
in October, Elvis had made a quickie with Sam Katzman, a master of
the low-budget exploitation pic. Katzman had directed *Rock Around the
Clock* with Bill Haley and *Twist Around the Clock* with Chubby
Checker, along with such gems as *Calypso Heat Wave* and *Earth vs. the
Flying Saucers*. After selling MGM on the idea that they could make
money on similar projects, he'd taken seventeen days to shoot *Kissin'
Cousins*, with Elvis in dual roles as a young air force lieutenant and a
Tennessee hillbilly who turns out to be his cousin. The results were
worse than predictable.

Neither *Viva Las Vegas* nor *Kissin' Cousins* had been released yet, but
Wallis had gotten a print of *Viva Las Vegas* and screened it at his home,
and he wasn't happy with what he saw. The picture was bad enough, but
Elvis was worse. He looked fat and jowly, and his hair was inky black
and piled on top of his head like a wig. In *Roustabout*, he'd be playing a
rough customer. He needed to be lean and rugged-looking, as he had
been in *G.I. Blues*, the picture Wallis had made with him after he got
out of the army. If he looked soft, it would be a disaster.

But the problem went beyond Elvis's weight and his pompadour. It went beyond even the quality of the outside films, which except for *Kissin' Cousins* were no worse than what he was doing for Wallis. The problem was that none of them—not Wallis, not Parker, not Lastfogel—had much idea what the younger generation was thinking. All they knew was that Elvis's popularity seemed to be on the wane. He hadn't had a number-one single since "Good Luck Charm" in April 1962, and that was nearly two years ago. The films weren't doing so well either. Wallis got the numbers on his last four pictures from Paramount's home office in New York, and after deducting distribution costs, prints and advertising, and gross profit participation (2.5 percent for Wallis, 7.5 percent for Presley), the studio's net profits showed a distinct curve: $832,000 for*G.I. Blues*, $1,015,000 for *Blue Hawaii*, $30,000 for *Girls! Girls! Girls!*, and a $350,000 loss for *Fun in Acapulco*. "These figures tell quite a story," the executive who sent them concluded.

Yes, but what did it mean? The colonel had always figured that the rock 'n' roll sound Elvis rode to stardom in 1956 was a fad that would have to be followed by other fads if the boy was to stay on top. He'd given the matter considerable reflection, and over the years he'd come up with all kinds of suggestions that he thoughtfully passed along to Wallis and Lastfogel. They'd had him singing Dixieland in Wallis's 1958 picture *King Creole*, and by the end of the year, Colonel Parker was pestering them to do a Hawaiian story, on the grounds that Hawaiian-type music seemed to be getting popular all over. The draft intervened, but Wallis liked the idea, and after Elvis got out of the army he made *Blue Hawaii*, which turned out to be Elvis's highest-grossing picture to date. On Wallis's most recent venture, *Fun in Acapulco*, Elvis had taken up a Latin beat. The fans may not have liked it, but the Lastfogels sure did: When the colonel and his wife, Marie, took them to a screening on the Paramount lot, Frances got so excited about the new single "Bossa Nova Baby" that she was all but dancing in the aisles.

Yet by 1964 there were signs that rock 'n' roll might actually be more than a fad, that it might signal big changes in the music business. The New York office of the Morris Agency had already hired a pair of agents from General Artists Corporation—successor to the old Rockwell-O'Keefe Agency, the band-booking firm Abe Lastfogel had considered buying in 1938—to sign rock 'n' roll acts. The new arrivals were a woman in her late twenties named Rosalind Ross and an even younger agent named Jerry Brandt, who'd been fired from the Morris mail room a couple of years before for delivering an envelope two hours late. The envelope, which he'd contemplated idly while smoking a joint in Central Park, turned out to contain the renewal contract for a network series; an entire roomful of executives had been waiting for its arrival. Brandt had ended up in the band department at GAC, where Roz Ross encouraged him to sign rockers like Danny and the Juniors, the New York doo-wop group, and book them in clubs he found by scanning out-of-town papers for ads that promised "Rock 'n' Roll Tonite."

GAC handled a lot of singers, from pop stalwarts like Tony Bennett and Connie Francis to teen idols on the order of Paul Anka, Frankie Avalon, and Fabian. But the head of its band department thought rock 'n' roll was a fad and nickel-and-dime bookings like Brandt's were a waste of time. On the other hand, Roz Ross was being courted by Howard Hausman of the Morris office. Hausman was Nat Lefkowitz's number-two man in New York, and he seemed to think that rock 'n' roll was going to be around for a while and that Morris should be making money off it. So in 1962, Ross had moved to 1740 Broadway and taken Brandt with her.

Roz Ross could see what was coming. In early 1963, when the Beatles released "Please Please Me" and British youth exploded into mass hysteria, she knew the Morris Agency had to sign them—mortgage the farm, do whatever you had to do, but sign them. Howard Hausman was enthusiastic, but other Morris agents thought even less of rock 'n' roll than their counterparts at GAC. Ross couldn't even muster enough enthusiasm to make it worthwhile flying to London to talk to them. She and Brandt had better luck with performers the agency already had— the Smothers Brothers, for instance, and Sam Cooke, who had a string of top-forty hits dating back to 1960 but wasn't getting many bookings because nobody at the agency knew what to do with him. They also brought some clients from GAC, including Dick Clark, the clean-cut young Philadelphia impresario whose "American Bandstand" gave the teen sound its television showcase.

Ross hadn't been at the Morris office long when she talked Clark into hitting the road with a "Cavalcade of Stars"—a dozen or more performers, none of whom qualified as headliners until you put them all together. Nobody was in the business of promoting rock 'n' roll shows, so she and Brandt called the only people they could think of who knew how to stage events at arenas—wrestling promoters. Meanwhile, the Beatles were becoming huge, just as she'd known they would. In February 1964, with Elvis about to report to Paramount for *Roustabout* and "I Want to Hold Your Hand" knocking Bobby Vinton off the *Billboard* number-one spot, the Beatles arrived at Kennedy International for their first visit to the States and the country succumbed to Beatlemania. "Multiply Elvis Presley by four, subtract six years from his age, add British accents and a sharp sense of humor," instructed the *New York Times*. "The answer: It's the Beatles (Yeah, Yeah, Yeah)."

Out on the coast, Wallis and Lastfogel and the colonel were preoccupied with plans for the shoot. All fall, Wallis had tried to get Parker to be their liaison to the carny world, but the colonel, who'd already cadged a suite of offices from Paramount and a full-time assistant from the Morris Agency—a junior agent who showed up for work each morning at the Paramount lot—held out for a deal. Finally, at the beginning of January, they'd made an arrangement—$27,500 for publicity and exploitation to Parker's All-Star Shows and a bonus of $22,500 to Elvis, in addition to Elvis's $150,000 salary and $50,000 in expense money. Now the colonel was coming through with some shtick to flavor up the atmosphere. Entrance to the midway is being watered down by a midget; next to him a man sells plastic boots for a dollar. Sign says "All the lemonade you can drink for ten cents"; pull back to show a barrel with a hose running water into it and a couple of lemons floating on top. Kid complains when he bites into a candied apple and gets a worm; Elvis says, "No charge for the meat, son. Move on!"

Meanwhile, Wallis and Paramount were casting the picture. Aside from Elvis, the main characters were Joe Lean, the foreman of the fleabag carnival Elvis falls in with; Cathy Lean, the foreman's daughter; and Maude Manulere, the carnival's owner, a hard-bitten dame who's shacking up with Joe. The Morris office was pushing hard to have Milton Berle play Joe—money was no problem, they said, plus Berle would happily go on television for free to plug the film. But the director, a "Dick Van Dyke Show" veteran named John Rich, detested Berle and refused to use him. So after considering Lee Marvin, Karl Malden, and Walter Matthau, they settled on brawny Leif Erickson for a mere $14,000. For Cathy, the love interest, they rejected Ann-Margret, Elvis's costar in *Viva Las Vegas*, in favor of Joan Freeman, who was practically unknown but a lot cheaper.

Wallis was operating on a tight budget—$1.5 million—but to play Maude, the carnival owner, he wanted someone with stature. Paramount was eager to land Mae West, the studio's great sex goddess of the

Depression, in retirement now but still represented by the Morris Agency. Paul Nathan, the studio exec, went to visit her at the Rossmore Avenue apartment where she'd lived since the thirties. At seventy-two, she was as slinky and seductive as ever, with the looks of a forty-year-old. She invited Nathan into her bedroom and got him to tell her the story. But when she found out he wanted her to play a woman who was losing a circus and had a drunk for a lover, she quickly lost interest. "She is alert, sharp, eager to do a picture," Nathan reported to Wallis. "But definitely not this one. She would probably like to play it if Elvis played a small part *opposite her.*"

There were other possibilities: Bette Davis, pulling in $100,000 a picture after landing her tenth Oscar nomination as a deranged Hollywood has-been in *Whatever Happened to Baby Jane?* Barbara Stanwyck, a Norman Brokaw client whose asking price was $50,000, though she hadn't had a hit film in years and her TV anthology series had been canceled after one season. Angela Lansbury, but she was going into Arthur Laurents's new play. Janet Leigh was offered the role and passed. In mid-February, a month before their start date, they made a deal with the Morris office for Stanwyck for $10,000 and costar billing beneath the title.

Elvis was thrilled to be working with Miss Stanwyck. He was less thrilled with the script. It was like all the rest of them, a shallow excuse to plant him in front of some scenery. But at least Hal Wallis was a producer he could respect, not a quick-shot artist like Sam Katzman. Elvis no longer had any illusions about Hollywood. It had all happened so quickly for him, from unknown to national sensation in less than a year, and then there was the army and his mama dying, and now he was locked into a treadmill, three pictures a year and three soundtracks to go with them. It wasn't what he'd wanted, but it was what he had to do. So he did it.

The glamour days were over for all of them. Wallis, Lastfogel, the colonel—they were all fighting a losing battle. Show business as they knew it was dying, and Elvis, who'd helped kill it, was trapped in the carcass. They could take it back to its carny roots in *Roustabout*, but all they'd get for their trouble were weird articles in the press about Elvis starring in Colonel Parker's life story. No one remembered that this was how it had all started, before television, before nightclubs, before Hollywood, before radio, before vaudeville—the dime museum where B. F. Keith exhibited Little Alice, "the smallest baby ever born live"; the Bowery freak shows where young Will Morris was suckered into the show world by the likes of the Skeleton Dude and Jo-Jo the Dog-Faced Boy.

No one saw that a freak show was what the star system had created. Elvis Presley, Kim Novak, Rita Hayworth—what were any of them but a high-priced collection of caged attractions, no privacy, no life, wheeled out before screaming fans for brief moments of adulation, subsisting in between on press clippings and fear? All anyone knew was that Elvis kept knocking out these Hollywood musicals, three a year, one after another, like an assembly line, and this one was about some sort of carnival.

A QUARTER-CENTURY EARLIER, IT HAD BEEN FRANCES ARMS ON THE BILL AT the Steel Pier in Atlantic City, a small but very brassy blonde belting out Yiddish-dialect numbers and sizzlers like "Let Them Ramble, Let Them Roam." Now it was June 1964, and a junior Morris agent named Wally Amos found himself on the same Steel Pier with Dick Clark's Cavalcade of Stars, shepherding a trio of twenty-year-old black girls who wore spaghetti-string dresses and silver lamé shoes and called themselves the Supremes. They had a new single out on the Motown label, an up-tempo ballad called "Where Did Our Love Go?" But they'd had other singles before and it was hot and they were tired and they were getting depressed. "We ain't never gonna get ourselves a hit record," they moaned.

The only reason the Supremes were even on the Dick Clark Cavalcade of Stars was that Amos had phoned Esther Edwards, whose brother Berry Gordy had started Motown, to book Brenda Holloway, who had an enormous hit with "Every Little Bit Hurts," and Edwards had twisted his arm. She was always telling him about these three girls who were going to be big stars, but until they had a hit, there wasn't much he could do. This time, though, she'd sent him a test pressing of their next single. He and Dick Clark had decided to offer $600 a week, which the girls would have to split three ways. They accepted. Then "Where Did Our Love Go?" was released. Two months later, in mid-August, it knocked Dean Martin off the top of the charts.

Wally Amos was the Morris Agency's liaison to Motown, the Detroit R&B label that had been racking up an incredible string of hits lately. Amos was also Morris's first Negro agent. The Morris office had handled colored acts for decades, from Eubie Blake to Sammy Davis, Jr., but this was different. Amos had been hired as a New York mail room trainee in 1961, even though he'd dropped out of high school and the agency now accepted only college graduates. Civil rights groups were putting pressure on show-business concerns to hire Negroes, and Amos came with excellent recommendations from secretarial school and from Saks Fifth Avenue, where he'd managed the supply department. Howard Hausman assured Amos he'd have every opportunity for advancement, and when he got out of the mail room, he was given a position as Hausman's secretary. Hausman became his mentor, took him to plays and concerts, invited him into his home to meet his wife, Marie, and the children. Then he offered Amos a position in the music department.

The music department was Roz Ross's bailiwick, distinct from both the nightclub department, which booked hotels and nightspots in Vegas and Miami and around the country, and the concert department, which booked acts like Eartha Kitt and the José Greco Dance Company and Hal Holbrook and Maurice Chevalier. The music department handled rock 'n' roll. Amos hated rock 'n' roll, but there weren't any openings in the television or motion picture departments, and Hausman said he should see this as a chance to make better money and establish himself. So he became Jerry Brandt's secretary.

In August 1964, with the Supremes at the top of the pops and Dick Clark's Cavalcade of Stars still touring the country, Roz Ross left the Morris office to run Dick Clark Enterprises, and Brandt took over the department. Wally Amos got back to New York that fall and came up with a find of his own—two kids from Queens who played folk music and went by the unlikely moniker of Simon and Garfunkel.

Paul Simon and Art Garfunkel—Garfunkel was the tall one with the kinky hair—had grown up in Kew Gardens, a comfortable neighborhood of tree-shaded streets and neat little row houses in Queens. In 1957, when they were sixteen and billed themselves as Tom and Jerry, they'd had a hit single called "Hey, Schoolgirl" that took them as far as Dick Clark's "American Bandstand." Then they'd finished high school, gone to college, and fallen out of touch. Paul had originally picked up the guitar because he admired Elvis, but by the time he ran into Artie again, they'd both developed an interest in the folk sound. They started performing together, first at frat parties and then at Gerde's Folk City, the Village folk club where Bob Dylan had been discovered. There they met Tom Wilson, Dylan's record producer, who talked Columbia into letting them make an album.

Wilson, who was a Negro, had become friends with Wally Amos, and he invited Amos to come by the recording studio one day. As soon as he heard them, Amos knew he had to sign them. Their music was breathtaking—an acoustic guitar that was fragile and spare, wreathed with delicate, floating harmonies. There was something pure about these two, something honest and direct and pristine. Their act, if you could call it that, was devoid of all the tired old show-business clichés that afflicted singers of their parents' generation—Frank Sinatra, Judy Garland, Dean Martin, the lot of them. It was a starkly simple presentation that spoke directly to the human condition as experienced by middle-class college students in this age of civil rights and Vietnam and continuing economic prosperity.

Of course, you could take this honesty bit too far. When Amos announced at a department meeting that he wanted to sign them, he was greeted with snickers and guffaws. A voice of disbelief sounded from the back of the room. *"Simon and Garfunkel?* Sounds like a couple of Jewish tailors from Brooklyn."

To his friends and neighbors, Bill Morris, Jr., seemed something of an eccentric. He and Red had left New York years before—left New York and show business and politics and anything resembling a public life. They lived in a beach house in Malibu, and when they got restless they went on trips, like a 1964 tour of Japan organized by the Los Angeles County Museum of Art. Morris was sixty-six now, a stoop-shouldered, kindly-looking man with a crinkly smile and a Vandyke beard and a gray fringe around his bald pate. Ambling past the surf in an old pair of chinos and a battered jersey, he could have passed for Maynard G. Krebs's beachcomber uncle on "Dobie Gillis."

Cushioned by wealth and position, Morris had survived the McCarthy years with good grace and rare style. A bigger difficulty for him had been the Twentieth Party Congress. He'd been shocked by the revelations in Moscow, when Nikita Khrushchev—once Stalin's associate, now the party's first secretary—made his seven-hour speech accusing the late dictator of unspeakable crimes. But in the end, he had to accept it. The great Soviet experiment—the system that had seemed the hope of mankind during the Depression, that he'd sacrificed the presidency of his father's agency to defend—had been as murderous as its enemies had claimed. The loss of faith was wrenching.

In 1959, at the age of eighty-six, Mother Morris had died at Camp Intermission. After her funeral, at the Little Church Around the Corner in Manhattan, and her burial at Rabbi Wise's Free Synagogue in Westchester County, Bill and Red had gone up to Camp Intermission to live with his widowed sister Ruth and her adopted son. But life in the Adirondacks didn't suit them either—the brutal winters, the isolation, the close quarters with so little diversion—so in the fall of 1961, they'd sold the place to New York State for a summer youth camp. Ruth Morris moved to a smaller house in Saranac Lake, and Bill and Red moved to Malibu, where they could pop in on the agency now and then to see how Abe was doing.

They bought a modest house in a spectacular location, a contemporary glass-and-wood structure riding on pilings above a narrow strip of sand between the ocean and the Pacific Coast Highway. It had an open floor plan, with plate-glass window-walls looking out across a wooden deck to the Pacific, which was so close that the house shook with the surf. On one side, a similar house stood a couple of feet away; on the other, a public beach gave them a sweeping view down the coast to Santa Monica and beyond. The place was minimally furnished, with bare walls and a spare, functional look. They called it Solstice because it was at the foot of Solstice Canyon, whose chapparal-covered slopes were dotted with caves from which the Chumash Indians had once observed the sun.

Bill and Red were watching television one evening when something came on about Selma. Sunday, March 7, 1965: At a civil rights demonstration in Selma, Alabama, hundreds of Negro marchers had been attacked on a concrete viaduct by state troopers and a county sheriff's posse. They'd set out for the state capitol in Montgomery to petition Governor George Wallace for basic rights—the right to register to vote, the right not to be shot by the police. Instead they were clubbed to the ground, hit with tear gas, bullwhipped by horsemen as they fell back screaming and moaning to the church they'd set out from. All on network news.

Selma was part of a campaign by the Reverend Martin Luther King, Jr., to focus national attention on the situation in Alabama, where fewer than 20 percent of the Negro population was registered to vote. King had been preaching at his church in Atlanta that day; when he got word of the bloodshed, he summoned pastors from around the country and announced an even bigger march for Tuesday, two days away. Demonstrations were breaking out in cities coast-to-coast. Bill and Red were watching the TV news when he turned to her and said, "Let's go." They threw some clothes into a bag and headed for the airport. Within hours, they were on a plane.

That Tuesday, they were among the fifteen hundred people—clergymen, civil rights leaders, students, nuns, rabbis, ordinary citizens—who set out for Montgomery. A federal judge had issued an injunction against the march, and a cordon of state troopers was waiting for them just past the viaduct. "This march will not continue," their commander intoned, echoing the command of two days before. King and his aides knelt on the ground and prayed. Then they stood up, turned around, and led the marchers back to town. A Unitarian minister from Boston was beaten to death that night when he and some friends took a wrong turn after dinner and encountered some white punks with baseball bats.

Within days, President Johnson addressed Congress and the nation on television to call for passage of his voting rights bill. Back in Malibu, Bill Morris penned an appeal to run in the "Letters" column in *Variety*:

My wife and I flew to Alabama to walk in that memorable Selma march and we believe that never again will there be official mass brutality due to the awakening that those marchers brought about.

A clarion call for a march 10 times greater in number will be made shortly. We urge with all the sincerity at our command that each and every member of the profession do his utmost to walk in that march. . . .

Start chartering planes now. Hey, Rube.

"Hey, Rube": That was a call you didn't hear much in the civil rights movement. Or in show business either, come to think of it. Ah, yes, the cry of distress among circus folk. Those buttons he'd had printed up after Pearl Harbor. It had been a while, hadn't it? Not quite twenty-five years.

DAVID GEFFEN WAS A KID IN A HURRY. TWENTY-TWO AND FRESH OUT OF THE mail room, he'd landed himself a plum job with Ben Griefer, the television agent Bill Morris, Jr., had hired in 1950 to run "Texaco Star Theater." In the years since, Griefer had handled most of the big variety programs to come out of the New York office, from "Your Show of Shows" to "Sing Along with Mitch," hosted by Columbia recording chief Mitch Miller. He'd also represented the agency's top television comedy writers—Goodman Ace, Abe Burrows, Neil Simon. Griefer was a decent soul, honest and soft-spoken and as straightforward as an agent could be. Working with him put Geffen squarely in the middle of television.

Like so many of the guys at Morris—Nat Lefkowitz, Sammy Weisbord, Phil Weltman—Geffen had grown up working-class and Jewish in Brooklyn. His mother, Batya, ran a ladies foundation-garments shop in Borough Park. "Chic Corsets by Geffen," the sign read. They lived in an apartment building two blocks away—David, his older brother, his mother, and his father, an habitually unemployed patternmaker. In high school David had wanted to become a dentist, but after graduating he answered an ad and got a drive-away car to Los Angeles, where his brother was studying law at UCLA. Beverly Hills was a revelation to him—the luxury, the money, the sheer fabulousness of it all. He spent a semester at the University of Texas and then enrolled at Brooklyn College, but studies were never his strong suit. Morris would be his ticket out.

It had taken some finagling to get there. Before going to William Morris, Geffen had applied for a job at Ashley-Steiner Famous Artists, headed by Lefkowitz's nephew, whose background was even humbler than Geffen's. He'd filled out the application accurately, only to be told that they didn't hire anyone who wasn't a college graduate. So when he went to William Morris, he put down that he had a degree from UCLA. He was savvy enough to know the agency would check with the registrar, so when a letter from UCLA came into the mail room, he steamed open the envelope, put in a new letter attesting to his status as a graduate, resealed the envelope, and sent it on.

At first glance, Geffen seemed like any other newcomer—nice Jewish boy from Brooklyn or the Bronx, socially awkward but eager to get ahead. On vacation he went to Los Angeles and hung out at the Beverly Hills office. He hit it off particularly well with Phil Weltman's secretary, Barry Diller, who was only recently out of the mail room himself. What was different about him—what separated him from Nat Lefkowitz and Sammy Weisbord and Phil Weltman and all the other Brooklyn boys who'd come to the Morris office—was that he couldn't see himself staying there forever. To him, the William Morris mail room was the Harvard School of Show Business. Better, even—no grades, no exams, small stipend, great placement opportunities.

When he got out of the mail room and went to work for Griefer and his assistant, a junior agent named Scott Shukat, Geffen became aware that his new boss kept lists of all the other agencies' television clients. As production supervisor for Morris's variety packages, Griefer routinely bought talent from competing agencies, so he and Shukat frequently asked for client lists so they'd know who was available. This enabled them to build a large file of client lists—useful information indeed. One day, the file disappeared. When Shukat asked where it was, Geffen hesitated, then confessed. The lists seemed so valuable, he admitted, that he'd taken them to Mr. Lefkowitz.

Geffen didn't realize that Lefkowitz already had the lists: Every six months or so, Lefkowitz would mumble that they ought to raid the competition, and Griefer would hand him the latest updates. All the same, Lefkowitz was impressed. It wasn't every kid out of the mail room who displayed that kind of initiative.

Ben Griefer was not impressed. As far as he was concerned, the kid had stolen from his office, and he wanted him out on the street. No, Nat said, it was a boyish mistake; let's give him another job. So Geffen found himself promoted to junior agent under Lou Weiss, a television agent who covered NBC.

Lou Weiss was a big man who smoked big cigars and wore expensive suits and happened to be George Burns's nephew. He'd started out as George Wood's secretary, then worked in the nightclub department before transferring to television. At forty-seven, he'd been with the agency for twenty-nine years. He was one of a trio of agents who covered the networks for Wally Jordan, the head of television. Weiss and Geffen got along well, possibly because it was clear that Lefkowitz had taken an avuncular interest in the newcomer. Even so, Geffen was frustrated. Everyone of any stature was twice his age. None of them paid him any notice.

It was around this time that Geffen started hanging out with Jerry Brandt in the music department. Brandt was tall and slick and a born pitchman. He was responsible for an entirely new area of business that most people in the agency knew nothing about, except that it brought in wads of cash. Junior agents watching him operate came away with their jaws hanging open, the same way Brandt himself had once been awestruck by George Wood. He was a Brooklyn kid like Geffen, but he didn't live like Geffen. He wore $200 mohair suits and Ebel gold watches. He took a limousine everywhere he went. He ate dinner with

Mr. Lastfogel at Hillcrest on his trips to the Coast. So why was he making eye-popping deals while Geffen was still trying to get Norman Jewison to return his phone calls?

Brandt fixed Geffen with a look of utter disdain. "*Schmuck!*" he cried. "You think these guys are going to listen to you? They don't care what you've got to say. They're older than you are! Deal with people your own age. Go into the music business. Nobody knows what you're doing, and nobody knows how to do it."

The way Jerry Brandt saw it, Allen Klein owed him one. Klein was a fleshy young accountant who'd demonstrated a flair for ferreting out discrepancies in record company royalty statements. He'd turned up $100,000 in back royalties and unpaid performance fees for Bobby Vinton, and he'd had similar results with Steve Lawrence, Eydie Gorme, and Bobby Darin. He was also good at winning new record contracts on better-than-average terms. In 1964 he'd approached Sam Cooke and won him an unheard-of $1 million advance from RCA. He'd also taken Cooke from the Morris Agency to GAC, which had just won the competition to book the Beatles' first major U.S. tour that August. Then, in December, the whole deal was iced when Cooke, naked except for shoes and sport jacket, was shot dead by the manager of a seedy motel on South Figueroa Street in Los Angeles.

But in the summer of 1965, Klein delivered. He'd gone to London, which was quivering with energy after a long postwar decay. Mary Quant, David Bailey, Joe Orton, Vidal Sassoon—East End gutter scum fused with the privileged issue of St. John's Wood in an explosion that bedazzled the world, with the rock 'n' roll bands at the center of it all. Klein had been rebuffed by Brian Epstein, the Beatles' manager, but he'd picked up the Dave Clark Five, Herman's Hermits, and the Animals, three groups at the core of the British Invasion. In August 1965 he approached the Rolling Stones—a squat, sinister-looking man with greased-down hair and a double chin courting swinging London's most dangerous band. "Do you want to be a millionaire?" he asked Andrew Loog Oldham, the Stones' manager from their days as an unknown pub band in the outer borough of Richmond. "Do the Stones want to be famous?"

The answer was yes and yes. Decca Records had just released "Satisfaction," which had become the Stones' first number-one U.S. hit—

American R&B, cranked through the British caste system and jolted to maximum volume. Fast and dangerous. Yes and yes. Why should they struggle while John Lennon drove a new Rolls-Royce? Offering his services on a trial basis, Klein walked into a meeting and demanded to speak personally with Sir Edward Lewis, Decca's distinguished chairman. When the meeting was over, Sir Edward had agreed to pay $1.25 million for the privilege of keeping the Stones. Before returning to New York, Klein called Jerry Brandt and offered to let Morris handle the Stones' bookings. Brandt flew to London to meet them. But he couldn't say yes without selling Nat Lefkowitz on the idea. His task was complicated by the fact that Klein did not wish to pay the standard 10 percent.

Brandt met with Lefkowitz and Lee Stevens, the starchy young deputy who'd handled the Scopitone deal. He made his pitch as Lefkowitz studied a photograph of the group—five loutish-looking fellows with shaggy hair and unfortunate complexions. "We don't represent people like that," Stevens announced firmly.

Brandt ignored him. "Mr. Lefkowitz . . . "

"Jerry," Lefkowitz said softly, "how much can you get for a night?"

"Twenty-five thousand dollars." For anyone except the Beatles, it was a preposterous figure.

Lefkowitz looked at Brandt, looked at the photo, looked at Brandt. The sanctity of the 10 percent commission was written in stone. On the other hand, 7 percent of a $25,000 advance against 60 percent of the gross in arenas and stadiums in city after city after city for ten weeks straight was . . . a lot of money. "Okay," he said at last.

That was the thing about rock 'n' roll in 1965: The business was so new that you just made it up as you went along. Wrestling promoters? Twenty-five thousand dollars? Sure, why not? Except that Allen Klein took it to mean "The Ed Sullivan Show" as well. Sullivan had ended up paying $50,000 for three Elvis appearances in the wake of Elvis's 1956 "Steve Allen Show" performance, but the Beatles had only gotten $10,000 for their three appearances in 1964. Sullivan squawked so loudly at the Stones' demand that Lefkowitz called Brandt in to complain that he was destroying the show. "It's not me, Mr. Lefkowitz," Brandt explained innocently. "It's what the act wants. I have nothing to do with it. I'm just repeating everybody else's words." Sullivan paid.

Things didn't work out as well with Simon and Garfunkel. Their album went nowhere, so Garfunkel returned to Columbia and Simon took off for London, where sensitive American folk singers were not yet a dime a dozen. Then a track called "Sounds of Silence" started getting heavy airplay in Boston, and in June 1965, while he was in the studio with Dylan recording his *Highway 61 Revisited* album, Tom Wilson got Dylan's backup group to overdub an electric guitar and rhythm tracks onto Simon and Garfunkel's fragile guitar work and tender, earnest vocals. The new, folk-rock version was released as a single in September; by December it was a number-one hit. Simon, who found out about it when he picked up a copy of *Billboard*, was soon back in New York recording a second album with his old partner. With a hit record, the Morris Agency was finally able to get them some bookings—but after they found themselves on a catch-all bill with Chuck Berry, Lou Christie, the Yardbirds, the Four Seasons, and Mitch Ryder and the Detroit Wheels, their new manager took them elsewhere.

Even so, it was a banner year for the music department. It wasn't just the Stones; the Morris Agency was also booking three of the hottest groups to come out of Southern California. The Beach Boys, back on the charts for the third straight year with "Help Me, Rhonda" and "California Girls." Chad and Jeremy, suntanned English transplants, riding the folk-rock wave the Byrds had started with their electrified version of Dylan's "Mr. Tambourine Man." Sonny and Cher, folk-rock's Romeo and Juliet, two groovy rebels who defied convention with their long hair and bell-bottomed trousers. Older agents started looking at Brandt in a whole new way: Some of his acts were pulling in more money in a night than theirs were making in a week.

And yet, he remained mindful of his elders. He was having dinner at Hillcrest one night with Mr. Lastfogel and Colonel Parker when he asked the colonel how he'd made it so big. Parker smiled expansively. "Jerry," he said, "you give me all the popcorn at all the movie theaters across the U.S.A. and you can shove Elvis up your ass. Merchandising! That's the secret."

IN SEPTEMBER 1965, AS BRANDT WAS BOOKING THE STONES TOUR TO START at the end of October, the West Coast television department was nervously anticipating the premiere of two high-stakes series. "I Spy" was making its debut on Wednesday night at ten, against Danny Kaye's variety show and Aaron Spelling's "Amos Burke—Secret Agent," a hastily revamped version of "Burke's Law," a Morris Agency package from Four

Star. At nine-thirty Friday, CBS was set to unveil another new Morris package, "The Smothers Brothers Show," opposite the phenomenally successful prime-time serial "Peyton Place" and a new comedy based on the Jack Lemmon movie "Mr. Roberts."

It had taken Sheldon Leonard two years to get "I Spy" on the air. In the fall of 1964, a year after Leonard saw Cosby on "Jack Paar," Grant Tinker and his bosses at NBC had finally given their okay to put him in the show. The question was how many affiliates—particularly in the South—would carry it. Given "The Nat 'King' Cole Show" fiasco eight years earlier, a lot of people were predicting it would fall on its face.

Cosby was frank about why he wanted it to succeed. "Money is of the utmost importance to me," he told *TV Guide*. "If this series goes five years, I will be only 33 and rich. Then I can stop and do something I'd enjoy more. I want to be a schoolteacher. That would be a real challenge." He also mentioned a desire to do a family-style sitcom on the order of "The Dick Van Dyke Show." Meanwhile, the press kept a running tally. By the Friday before the premiere, 180 stations had agreed to carry the series, including the stations in Montgomery, Alabama, and Jackson, Mississippi. The only ones to opt out were in Birmingham, Alabama; Daytona Beach, Florida; Savannah, Georgia; and Albany, Georgia.

While Sheldon Leonard was putting together "I Spy" for T&L, Aaron Spelling had been assembling the Smothers Brothers show for Four Star. Spelling had gotten his start when Stan Kamen landed him a job writing for "Dick Powell's Zane Grey Theater" and other Four Star shows back in the fifties. Later, after Kamen suggested he go into production, he produced "The Dick Powell Show," a Four Star anthology series that Powell hosted until his death in 1963. Spelling's first hit series was "Burke's Law," a "Dick Powell" spinoff starring Gene Barry as Amos Burke, a millionaire L.A. detective chief who lives in a sumptuous mansion and rides around town in a chauffeur-driven Rolls-Royce. After the Morris office got the Smothers Brothers a guest-star appearance on that program, Four Star came to them with an idea for their own sitcom. Spelling produced the pilot, and CBS bought the show.

Jug-eared and faintly geeky in their narrow ties and three-button sport jackets and shiny black shoes, Tom and Dick Smothers looked more like engineering students than network sitcom material. But now, after years as guests on other people's variety shows, they had their shot. The idea was for Dick, the straight man, to play a bachelor media executive who's constantly being tripped up by his brother Tom, a shipwreck victim who's returned to earth as a bumbling angel. A little far-fetched, perhaps, but hardly by comparison with "My Favorite Martian," a top-rated Morris package on CBS about a Los Angeles newspaper reporter who passes off a Martian as his uncle. And the brothers themselves actually liked the premise. It was everything else about the show they couldn't stand—starting with the first script, which they rejected as gimmicky and full of old jokes.

The problem was their producer, a veteran gagman who'd had his heyday writing material for Milton Berle and Jackie Gleason. If the Smothers thought it was funny, he didn't get it; if he thought it was funny, they detested it. They weren't sure what they wanted, but they knew this wasn't it. This was—this was the TV establishment, shoving lame jokes and laugh tracks down their throats.

They'd managed to get five episodes in the can when Tom McDermott called them into his office at the Four Star headquarters on the old Republic lot in Studio City, just over the hills from Hollywood. McDermott had been head of television at Benton & Bowles before joining Four Star in 1959 and taking over as president after Dick Powell's death. He was used to giving orders. If they couldn't cooperate, he told the brothers, maybe they should call it quits. "Fine," they said, rising in unison. They were halfway out the door before McDermott got them back.

Now they had a new producer—Fred de Cordova, the man behind "The George Burns and Gracie Allen Show" and "The Jack Benny Program," among others. Hollywood was predicting disaster all the same. Some thirty-five million people tuned in for the debut, enough to make it the top-rated premiere of the season, but what they saw was contrived and silly—"strictly for seven-year-olds," reported *Variety*. The following week, ratings tumbled dramatically. Score one for the TV establishment.

"I Spy" didn't get dramatic numbers at first, but its audience kept building. People seemed ready to watch a smart, hip black man play an action hero, particularly when he didn't make a big deal about it. "People can see I'm a Negro," Cosby told reporters. "We don't need to say anything else." Culp was even blunter. "We're two guys who don't know the difference between a colored and a white man. That's doing more than a hundred marches. We're showing what it could be like if there had been no hate."

SOPHIE TUCKER: NOW *THAT* WAS SHOWMANSHIP. FOR SIXTY YEARS, "THE Last of the Red-Hot Mamas" had wowed 'em wherever she appeared—in swank cafés and touring road shows, in Broadway productions and Vegas show rooms, on the silver screen and in the blue light of television. At eighty-two, she was the grande dame of the show world, capable of garbing her rotund form in orchids and beads and feathers and furs and a full-length sequined gown and belting out a song like "I'm the 3-D Mamma with the Big Wide Screen" with an assurance no one else could muster. Her Park Avenue apartment was crammed with plaques and scrolls from every charity, civic, and theatrical organization in the country. She was the agency's senior client, having signed with Will Morris himself in 1910, and one of Abe Lastfogel's oldest friends. She was playing the Latin Quarter with George Jessel and bandleader Ted Lewis when her doctor advised her to cancel. It was October 1965.

Diagnosis was cancer, lung and stomach. From her Mount Sinai hospital room, she reluctantly informed Lastfogel that her January bookings would have to be set back. In December, she told him he'd better set back those February and March dates as well. Lastfogel was so distraught, he flew to New York to be with her. The cobalt treatments were no good. At the beginning of February, her brother phoned Lastfogel in Beverly Hills to tell him he'd better come back. She died within days.

Lastfogel took charge of the funeral arrangements. It was Soph's final turn, and he wanted it to be memorable. Services were set for Riverside Chapel, the red-brick funeral home around the corner from the Ansonia Hotel, where she'd been maid of honor at his wedding nearly forty years before. The crowd was SRO and into the streets. Three thousand people stood behind police barricades while another thousand crowded inside. Softly, through the hush, the organ played "The Last of the Red-Hot Mamas." Jessel gave the eulogy, as he had for so many others. "Busboys to nitery bosses, tipsters to tycoons, stagehands to theater owners—all join today in brushing a tear," he said. "In that Great Marquee up there, Soph's name is a most shining adornment."

It wasn't just Soph they were mourning, it was the generation passing before their eyes. The Great Marquee up there could almost offer a solid bill of headliners now, just with names Will Morris had brought along. There was Jolson, of course, and Fanny Brice and Eddie Cantor, who'd gone two years before, after a decade of invalidism. Joe E. Lewis wasn't dead yet, but he'd pickled himself, his liver mostly gone, diabetes and an ulcer in its place. And Georgie Wood was there to book them.

The niteries of their era were languishing too, victims of Vegas—how could a New York supper club compete for talent with a casino show room?—and television and rock 'n' roll. El Morocco, whose zebra-striped walls had once been decorated by Howard Hughes and Tallulah Bankhead and the Duke of Windsor and Henry Ford, was never the same after it moved in 1961. The Stork Club had closed in October. The Latin Quarter, the big, brassy tourist joint that had been drawing crowds at Forty-eighth and Broadway since 1942, was fading fast.

Café society was as dead as the rhumba, replaced by an international jet set that made its transatlantic hops in hours, not days, and liked its nightspots loud and frenetic. The new places didn't even have entertainers, they just spun records at ear-shattering volume: Arthur, the discothèque that the former Mrs. Richard Burton had opened where El Morocco used to be, full of exotically slender girls in plastic dresses and op-art miniskirts, kids who'd popped in from London or Paris or Harvard or wherever, celebrities like Rudolph Nureyev, Andy Warhol, Jacqueline Kennedy, Truman Capote, Sophia Loren. . . . Le Club, which drew Gianni Agnelli and Noël Coward and Rex Harrison and the Duke of Bedford. Ondine, where Andy hung out with Ingrid Superstar and International Velvet and Edie Sedgwick, of the Boston Sedgwicks, who liked to plant herself on the tabletops and dance.

It was different in Hollywood. The pop scene was about youth, and who in Hollywood knew from youth? The studios looked like geriatric wards. Jack Warner, the sole remaining Warner brother, was seventy-four. Adolph Zukor, the chairman of Paramount, was ninety-three. Darryl Zanuck, a youngster at sixty-four, was back in the saddle at Fox. People were saying the agents had the power now, but at William Morris—the biggest and most established—Lastfogel was sixty-eight, and most of his top men were not a lot younger. The agency that was young and talked-about was Creative Management Associates, headed by forty-two-year-old Freddie Fields.

Fields operated the way the old-style Hollywood moguls might if they still had any juices. Lean and debonair, married to the actress Polly Bergen, he drove a white Bentley that came equipped with a telephone. He'd started out with a small-time agent named Abner Greshler, representing Jerry Lewis when he teamed up with Dean Martin at Skinny D'Amato's 500 Club in Atlantic City. In 1949, when Martin and Lewis were one of the hottest acts in show business, Fields had taken them to MCA and become a top television agent under Sonny Werblin. After handling such hits as "The Phil Silvers Show," "The Jackie Gleason Show," and "The George Burns and Gracie Allen Show," he left in 1960 to start a management firm. Two years later, when Justice forced MCA out of the agency business, he converted his company to a talent agency.

Fields and his partner, David Begelman, named their firm so it would have the same initials as MCA, and the influence of Jules Stein could certainly be detected in the way they did business. "Leopold and Loeb," Judy Garland called them, after the Nietzschean society lads who'd snuffed a less worthy boy in the twenties in the case that inspired the Hitchcock movie *Rope*. They started off with Fields's management clients from MCA—Garland (who'd left Lastfogel after triumphal performances at the London Palladium and the Palace in New York), Henry Fonda, Paul Newman, Phil Silvers, Joanne Woodward, and of course, Polly Bergen. Then came Kirk Douglas, Peter Sellers, and Barbra Streisand. But CMA was never intended to become as big as MCA had been: It wasn't volume Fields was after, it was stars. The rule of thumb in the agency business was that 10 percent of the clients brought in 90 percent of the commissions, and that's what he wanted—10 percent off the top of the top 10 percent. It was a brisk new attitude, and not without its admirers. "There are too many old fat cats in the agency business," an anonymous producer told Peter Bart of the *New York Times*. "Freddie and his boys are young and hungry."

BILL PALEY HAD A PROBLEM. THE CBS CHAIRMAN HAD RECENTLY WRESTED programming away from network president James Aubrey, an Ivy League wonder boy who'd taken the low road to success with hit shows like "The Beverly Hillbillies" and "The Munsters" before being canned for arrogance and insubordination. But not even Aubrey had been able to do anything about Sunday nights. For five years, NBC had owned the 9:00 P.M. time slot with "Bonanza," the color Western about big Ben Cartwright and his boys on the Ponderosa Ranch. CBS had tried everything, from "The Judy Garland Show," which went through four producers in seven months, to "Perry Mason," which bit the dust after nine years on television. Now it was December 1966, and Paley had just decided to pull the plug on "The Garry Moore Show." He called in his programming vice president, Mike Dann, and told him to have a replacement ready for January.

With twelve years at NBC and six at CBS, Dann was one of the most experienced programming execs in television. But when he left Paley's sumptuously appointed office atop Black Rock, the network's sleek new tower on Sixth Avenue, he was devoid of ideas. All he knew was that they'd have to have a variety show, since it would take four to six months to get an hour-long drama on the air and even longer to develop a pair of sitcoms. He picked up the phone and dialed the Morris office.

He got Lou Weiss and Sol Leon, the agent who covered CBS. Weiss had a thought. "Mike," he said, "I think I can get you the Smothers Brothers." That was how it always started with the Morris people: I think I can get you so-and-so. Dann didn't know much about the Smothers Brothers—they were kind of like the Kingston Trio, right? Their sitcom had slunk off the air after a single season, but Weiss assured him they were versatile performers who could carry a variety format. What he really wanted to know was, could it be ready in January?

He went to Paley with the idea. "They're nothing," Paley said dismissively, but Dann made a pitch: They sing, they dance, they'll have a lot of guest stars—it would be like "Ed Sullivan." Paley said okay. They probably wouldn't be on long anyway.

Elliot Wax, the Morris agent in charge of West Coast variety television, was supervising a Danny Thomas special in Japan when Lastfogel phoned him with the news. He flew into New York, and over the next couple of weeks, he and Sol Leon negotiated a contract with Bob Daly in CBS legal affairs—a full twenty-six-week commitment at $121,000 per show. Trouble followed almost immediately. Tommy Smothers wanted to book rock groups—Simon and Garfunkel, Buffalo Springfield, the Electric Prunes. Mike Dann, armed with years of experience, told him original music was dangerous on television; mass audiences prefer something they've heard before. Neither Dann nor anyone else at CBS suspected how quickly the Smothers Brothers would render such notions obsolete.

From vaude to vaudeo, variety theater had always depended on mass audiences responding to a broad spectrum of entertainment—novelty acts, song and dance, snippets of serious drama. But now the audience was splitting along generational lines. Kids who grooved on Sonny and Cher or Simon and Garfunkel had no use for Frank Sinatra and Sammy Davis, Jr. And in the uproar over their failed sitcom, the Smothers Brothers had become the standard-bearers of antiestablishment television.

"The Smothers Brothers Comedy Hour" made its debut on February 5, 1967. In its first month on the air, the new show knocked "Bonanza" from first place in the Nielsens to fifteenth—its lowest rating in years. But the Smothers Brothers weren't stealing its audience. "Bonanza" was a family program that appealed primarily to older, rural viewers. The Smothers Brothers drew large numbers of urban young people who normally didn't watch television. Dann had inadvertently created an entirely new audience of formerly disenfranchised viewers. Suddenly he was being hailed as the genius of counterprogramming.

Unfortunately, the youthful irreverence that made the Smothers Brothers a hit with fans also made them contentious as stars. They'd gotten artistic control, but the show still had to abide by the network's standards and practices—its censorship provisions. The first bout came over a skit in which guest star Barbara Eden played a sex education teacher and Tommy played her pupil; the network cut the words "sex" and "sex education." In April, the Smothers Brothers upped the ante with a skit for Tommy and guest star Elaine May about censorship itself. This time the entire sketch was cut: bad taste. From the Morris Agency's point of view, all this was no worse than Milton Berle's run-ins with Myron Kirk of the Kudner Agency over guests the *Red Channels* crowd might consider pink. But things had changed since Berle's day. When the Smothers Brothers ran into trouble, they didn't yell at their agents; they went to the press. On the Sunday the censorship bit was supposed to have aired, the network found it printed in the *New York Times* instead.

To CBS, "The Smother's Brothers Comedy Hour" was becoming a major headache. It was one thing to give Bob Dylan or Simon and Garfunkel an antiwar soapbox on the CBS record label, something else to carry an antiestablishment message on national television. As the Smothers Brothers' humor grew more and more barbed, they began to challenge the fundamental image the networks were in business to project—the idea of the world as the average American believed it to be. They also became socially embarrassing. Lady Bird Johnson, the president's wife, owned a CBS affiliate in Texas, and Frank Stanton, Paley's second-in-command, had been friends with LBJ since Johnson was in Congress and Truman was in the White House. The Smothers Brothers weren't the only offenders—the White House, and sometimes the president himself, frequently phoned Walter Cronkite to complain about "The CBS Evening News." But it was the Smothers Brothers Frank

Stanton had to watch with the Johnsons on his Sunday evening visits to the White House, while his friend the president went apoplectic beside him. Mike Dann always heard about it in the morning.

All spring, Elliot Wax of the West Coast office made the rounds at the networks with a thick loose-leaf notebook crammed with concepts from a new client named George Schlatter. Earlier, when he was handled by GAC, Schlatter had produced specials for a number of Morris clients—Dinah Shore, Meredith Willson, Danny Thomas. Wax had just signed him to the Morris office, and he was eager to get him a series. At the moment he was producing a special for Wayne Newton, the chubby singer from Vegas who'd come to the Morris office three years earlier when his agent moved over from GAC. But with "The Smothers Brothers Comedy Hour" gaining momentum, NBC seemed interested in an idea Schlatter had for a fast-paced comedy-variety hour called "Straighten Up and Turn Left." Wax left a copy of the presentation for the brass to peruse.

This one was sort of an updated, televised version of *Hellzapoppin'*, the Broadway revue that had so scandalized the critics three decades before. Like *Hellzapoppin'*, it would rely on blackouts, slapstick, and other timeworn devices, but it would put them in a format that seemed totally contemporary. To host it, he wanted Dan Rowan and Dick Martin, nightclub comedians who'd been a hit on NBC the year before hosting "The Dean Martin Summer Show." After the usual negotiations, the network agreed to buy it as a special to air in September, with the possibility of a series commitment if audiences responded. While they were getting it ready, one of the writers came up with a catchier title: "Rowan and Martin's Laugh-In."

"WHAT KIND OF SHITHOLE IS THIS?" FRANCES LASTFOGEL WAS BRISTLING with consternation. It was her first visit to the new offices in New York, on the top four floors of a glass-and-steel tower that had just been thrown up at 1350 Avenue of the Americas, as Sixth was now called. With ABC at Fifty-fourth Street, CBS at Fifty-third Street, and NBC in Rockefeller Center at Fiftieth, this stretch of Sixth was coming to be known as Television Row. It was lined with brittle modern boxes, but

1350 was maybe the worst, a cheaply built slab with plasterboard walls and oppressively low ceilings. The offices themselves were narrow and cramped and meanly furnished, as Mrs. Lastfogel discovered when she found one of her boys stuck at a desk with his back to the window. "This is the office they gave me, Mrs. Lastfogel," he explained apologetically.

She peered inside suspiciously, a five-foot volcano with preternaturally blond hair and a mouth ready to explode. "It's that big, tall schmuck who did this, isn't it?"

That would be Lee Stevens, the aggressive six-footer Nat Lefkowitz had brought along. Stevens was Lefkowitz's hatchet man. You could tell he was going places, and not just because he sat on the thirty-third floor with Lefkowitz and all the top television agents. He'd been known as Leo Silverman as an accounting major at New York University, but the name was already gone when he joined the Morris office in 1953. After a stint in the mail room, he'd landed on Lefkowitz's desk, where he worked hard and patterned himself after the great man. Lefkowitz was so impressed, he sent him to study law at NYU night school. Since then Stevens had made a point of learning every aspect of the business, from booking nightclubs to structuring a film deal. He represented key clients, including Barbara Walters, the NBC "Today" reporter whose father, Lou Walters, had long run the Latin Quarter. And he was no slouch at working a room.

Another thing about Stevens: He wasn't the kind to leave. Few had, except Ted Ashley. For decades, the Morris Agency had been a place where, if you made it out of the training program, you advanced in good time from junior agent to senior agent to retirement. Salaries were low—$15,000 to $20,000 for junior agents—yet nobody complained. Until now.

The generation gap that made the Smothers Brothers such a problem for CBS had hit the Morris office too. Sometimes it was just a little thing, like Nat Kalcheim saying, *Forty dollars for lunch? In our day we ate at the cafeteria!* Other times it was bigger, like the feeling among junior agents that they were being cheated—that salary and bonus together didn't add up to a reasonable percentage of the commissions they were bringing in. But ultimately it came down to a different kind of arithmetic. As the agency expanded, it needed more and more junior agents to scout for talent and service its clients. Sooner or later, most of those agents discovered there was no place for them to climb to. They could make deals, they could sign clients, but they weren't going to the top because there were too many of them, and the top was already full.

One of the first to go was Jerry Brandt, who'd bailed out of the music department at the beginning of 1967, shortly after his year-end bonus session with Lefkowitz and his deputies, Lee Stevens and Howard Hausman. After standing in line outside a conference room, he was ushered in and told his bonus for 1966 would be $6,000. "Mr. Lefkowitz," he said, "I think you made a mistake." Brandt thought he should get $25,000. "But it's already in the books!" Lefkowitz protested. So Jewish, Brandt thought as he looked at the ledger before them. "It's in pencil," he pointed out. "You can erase it." They settled on $14,000. Then he left and used the money to open a discothèque in the Dom, a Polish dance hall on the Lower East Side that he redid as the Electric Circus, a hippie joint with a light show and a health-food bar and a meditation room carpeted in Astroturf.

After Brandt left, Wally Amos was told that the music department wasn't ready to accept a black person as its boss. Also, that neither the motion picture business nor the television business was ready to accept a black talent agent. Deciding it was time to expand his horizons, he left to manage Hugh Masekela, the South African trumpet player he'd signed.

Then, out on the coast, Joe Wizan announced he was quitting. Wizan had joined the Beverly Hills mail room in 1958 and moved steadily upward—a stint as Phil Weltman's secretary, then a job in the television department booking clients onto shows at Revue. Barry Diller had been helping him, until Diller quit in frustration because Sam Weisbord wouldn't let him hire a secretary, even though they were swamped with work and Revue was the department's biggest account. Wizan stayed on, working with talented young television directors—John Boorman, William Friedkin, Sydney Pollack, Mark Rydell—and breaking them into feature films. But in the summer of 1967, as Israel was taking on Egyptian President Abdel Nasser in the Six-Day War, he quit to join Alan Ladd, Jr., as Hollywood rep for a group of London-based agencies. Weisbord was outraged. "You are worse than Nasser!" he thundered. Wizan laughed.

Then David Geffen left, shortly after signing Laura Nyro, a raven-haired singer-songwriter with a brassy voice and a reckless intensity that was so awesome it was scary. He'd heard a tape of her performance at Monterey Pop, the festival of "music, love and flowers" that for three days in June transformed the Monterey County fairgrounds into instant hippie paradise. The crowd, which had come to see the Who and Jimi

Hendrix and Simon and Garfunkel, booed Nyro off stage. Geffen figured anyone who could make that big an impression had to have something going for her. He took her to Clive Davis, president of Columbia Records, and talked him into a deal.

At that point, Geffen got an offer to join Ashley Famous (as it was known now), which Ted Ashley had recently sold to Kinney National Service, Manny Kimmel's onetime parking-lot chain, now a rapidly expanding conglomerate headed by an ex-funeral director named Steve Ross. Four years earlier, Geffen had been turned away at the door because he didn't have a college degree; now he was being offered $1,000 a week—more than twice what he was getting at Morris—and the title of vice president. He went to see Lefkowitz, who told him the Morris Agency couldn't match that kind of money but said he'd understand if Geffen couldn't turn it down. He didn't even complain when Geffen took Laura Nyro.

ABE LASTFOGEL, OLD FAT CAT THAT HE WAS, LIKED TO TALK DEALS WHILE lying on a float in the pool behind the Beverly Wilshire Hotel. He could relax, stretch out, paddle around a little. The sun was warm, the water was cool, and the muffled thwacks from the tennis court were oddly soothing. If anybody needed him, the agency was half a block away.

Abe and Frances had lived upstairs for more than thirty years now, in the same one-bedroom suite, rear corner, eighth floor. When the smog cleared, they could see above the treetops to downtown Los Angeles, nine miles away. The suite had gotten tatty, since the Lastfogels never bothered to redecorate, but it always had fresh flowers, and they had the best deal in the hotel.

Though it lacked the seclusion of the Beverly Hills Hotel, which was set amid sweeping lawns and towering palms on a majestic stretch of Sunset Boulevard, the Beverly Wilshire had plenty of cachet. The Lastfogels didn't bother with the celebrity guests—Prince Rainier and Princess Grace of Monaco, King Olaf of Norway, Emperor Hirohito of Japan. They didn't have much to do with Barbara Hutton, the Woolworth heiress, who lived in a grand suite down the hall when she wasn't in her palace in Tunisia. But they entertained lavishly at La Bella Fontana, the haute-cuisine establishment downstairs, with its leather banquettes and velvet walls and tinkling fountain. At night, they hung out in the lobby with folks like Milton Berle and Sammy Davis, Jr. And they saw a lot of Warren Beatty, who lived in the little penthouse where Elvis had once rehearsed.

Warren Beatty was a client with a problem. Tall and boyish-looking, with smoldering, blue-green eyes, he'd signed with the Morris Agency after the MCA bust-up. But by 1967 he'd been touted as Hollywood's next great film star for so long that people were beginning to yawn. He was a movie star who'd never had a hit movie, a freak of nature whose celebrity status showed just how disjointed Hollywood had become. His most compelling performances had been offscreen, in a series of much-publicized romances: Joan Collins, the London-born nymphet Fox was trying to pass off as the next Elizabeth Taylor; Natalie Wood, whose marriage to Robert Wagner broke up as a result; Leslie Caron, who left her husband after meeting him at a party given by her agent, Freddie Fields; Julie Christie, who left the man she was living with on his account.

Two years before, Beatty had finally encountered a property that engaged his passion the way women did. François Truffaut had told him about this script he'd gotten from two *Esquire* writers, David Newman and Robert Benton, about a couple of Depression-era bank robbers named Clyde Barrow and Bonnie Parker. Bonnie and Clyde hardly ranked next to John Dillinger, the man J. Edgar Hoover dubbed public enemy number one; they were just a couple of East Texas imitators who robbed banks and shot people and got themselves ambushed by a trigger-happy squadron of Texas Rangers and local deputies for their trouble. Yet they'd already inspired two other pictures, Fritz Lang's *You Only Live Once* and a B-picture called *The Bonnie Parker Story*. Benton and Newman had a New Wave version in mind—a Truffaut picture, as they imagined Truffaut would make it.

The French New Wave had been using Hollywood movies the way the British Invasion was using American R&B—as a springboard into something new and exciting. The Stones and the Beatles took their inspiration from Sam Cooke and Elvis Presley; Truffaut and his pal Jean-Luc Godard took theirs from the gangster B's of the thirties and forties. Inspired by Truffaut's penchant for swerving abruptly from comedy to melodrama and back again, Benton and Newman had written a bungled-getaway scene in which Keystone Kops slapstick suddenly gives way to a bullet in the face—the couple's first kill. They'd created a ménage à trois involving Bonnie and Clyde and their sidekick, C. W. Moss, recalling the triangle in *Jules and Jim*. Truffaut was intrigued enough to meet them and offer a few suggestions, but he was already busy in England, making *Fahrenheit 451* with Julie Christie. Then he had lunch with Leslie Caron and Warren Beatty, the Hollywood Romeo who was looking for a vehicle.

In January 1966, Beatty had optioned the script for $75,000, and he and Lastfogel had started making the rounds. Their prospects weren't good. Beatty hadn't made a movie anyone had taken seriously in four years, and here he was peddling a quirky little art film at a time when studio execs, inspired by Fox's success with *The Sound of Music*, were gambling big even as the studios themselves were headed for the auction block. Paramount had already sold off its early films, its television stations, and its Times Square headquarters and was about to sell itself to Gulf + Western Industries, a conglomerate that had grown out of a Michigan auto-parts company. Jack Warner had sold much of the Warner Bros. library to a Toronto-based licensing firm called Associated Artists and was negotiating to sell his stake in the company to an Associated Artists spinoff known as Seven Arts Productions. But when UA and Columbia turned them down, Beatty and Lastfogel went to Warner.

Warner's assistants thought the script was terrific, but Warner himself wasn't so enthusiastic. He had trouble taking Beatty seriously—a star for six years, no hit movies, and now he wants to produce? He loathed the idea of independent producers anyway, committed only to their own pictures, unbeholden to any studio. The idea of an *actor* as independent producer was utterly beyond him. As for the project, it read like a B-picture—and not one he wanted to make. Warner Bros. wouldn't have dames shooting guns. Was Beatty nuts?

One thing about Beatty, though: He could turn on the charm. He and Lastfogel drove out to Burbank, where they were waved through the studio gates and ushered into Warner's office, which looked out at a lofty water tower emblazoned with the Warner Bros. logo, emblem of the domain he'd ruled since 1928. Beatty pleaded, argued, cajoled. He got down on his knees and begged. He refused to leave until Warner offered him a deal. Finally, exasperated, Warner agreed to stake him to $2 million, which made the budget so tight that Beatty would have to throw in some of his own money. In return, the Morris office negotiated a contract that gave him roughly 30 percent of the profits, the percentage escalating on a sliding scale pegged to the gross—$20 million, $25 million, $35 million . . . To the studio lawyers, it was all funny money: They never dreamed it would hit such numbers.

Back in the Beverly Wilshire penthouse, Beatty and Lastfogel held story conferences and casting meetings. Leslie Caron was dumped straightaway—not right for the part, Beatty decided. Natalie Wood? Possibly, except that would mean being with Beatty in Texas for two months without her psychiatrist—not a good idea. Tuesday Weld? Pregnant. Shirley MacLaine? Impulsively, he rang her up from the hotel coffee shop—but she was his sister, for Christ's sake. And what about a director? Benton and Newman suggested Truffaut or Godard, but Beatty wanted someone to bring an American feel to a script with a very European edge. So they urged him to get Arthur Penn, a veteran of television and Broadway who was handled by the Morris office in New York. Penn and Beatty had teamed together earlier on *Mickey One*, an artful flop that left Beatty with an appreciation of his style. Beatty announced he was going to lock himself in a room with Penn and not let him out until he said yes.

Beatty found his Bonnie—Faye Dunaway, a twenty-six-year-old army brat who'd worked off-Broadway with Elia Kazan—at the last moment, and for the next two months he staged shootouts around the sleepy burgs of Ponder and Pilot Point. He and Warner couldn't agree about anything—the script, the casting, the sound, the music, even the need for location shooting in Texas. Beatty wanted period authenticity; he wasn't about to shoot this picture on the back lot, with phony sets and rear-projection car chases. Warner was leery, especially after Beatty refused to send dailies. When the production ran over schedule, he ordered them back to Burbank for the last two weeks of shooting. By the time he saw a rough cut, he was ready to supervise the final edit himself. He relented, but when the final cut was delivered, he emerged from the screening room with a conspicuous yawn and remarked that it was the longest two hours and ten minutes he'd spent in his life.

All spring Lastfogel worked Warner over on Beatty's behalf. Beatty was a mere kid, but Warner and Lastfogel went back forty years, past the blacklist and the USO tours and the studio wars of the thirties, all the way back to the birth of talkies. And they had common interests beyond showbiz. In June, on the day the Middle East suddenly exploded into war, Lastfogel and Warner and Lew Wasserman called an emergency meeting of the town's power brokers at the Beverly Wilshire. They came up with a plan: Warner would invite Hollywood's leading actors and directors and producers to a meeting at his estate to discuss the plight of Israel. A couple of days later, with everyone assembled in his private screening room, the doors closed and Warner rose to lecture them about their need to support the tiny nation. As Lastfogel sat beside him with a set of ledgers, Warner pointed to one person after another and asked how much. Fifteen thousand? "That's not enough," he'd say after a whispered consultation with Lastfogel, "I paid you $200,000 last year!"

To anyone accustomed to Hollywood convention, Beatty's film was almost an insult. Bad enough that it cast the ringleaders as dashing young lovers; even worse that it treated them so playfully, jokes and innuendo and violence all jumbled together. Clyde can't get it up when Bonnie wants to roll in the hay, but he's happy to let her fondle his gun. The two seem more interested in reading their press clippings than planning their next bank job. Clyde puffs a big cigar. Guns go off. Folks die.

Lastfogel and Stan Kamen had finally gotten Warner to enter the picture in the Montreal International Festival, a prestigious venue that would make the critics take notice. Even so, the release was set for August 13, weeks before the big fall pictures came out, in two theaters in New York City—two and only two. Beatty was livid. And with Warner turning the studio over to Seven Arts in July, Lastfogel's leverage was expiring.

Any hope the studio might have had that *Bonnie and Clyde* would slip out unnoticed died after Montreal, when Bosley Crowther attacked it in the *New York Times*. "A cheap piece of baldfaced slapstick comedy," he pronounced it, quivering with outrage at the spectacle of two murderous wrongos on a madcap shooting spree. *Newsweek* dismissed it as "a squalid shoot-'em for the moron trade"; *Time* called it "a strange and purposeless mix of fact and claptrap." But strange things were happening at the box office. After grossing $59,000 its first week, the film pulled in $70,000 the week after. And in the *New Yorker*, Penelope Gilliatt saw an entirely different picture from Crowther. "*Bonnie and Clyde* could look like a celebration of gangster glamour only to a man with a head full of wood shavings," she wrote. This picture wasn't about sex and violence, though Beatty had fun with both; it was about fame and death.

Beatty's Bonnie and Clyde aren't in love with death, exactly, but they're sure turned on by it, because they know the equation: fame plus death equals immortality. So they steal cars and drive fast while the law circles closer and closer, and near the end, Bonnie writes a poem about them and sends it to the newspaper. "It's death for Bonnie and Clyde," she intones at poem's end, as they lie in a peaceful meadow reading the paper. "You made me somebody they're going to remember," Clyde responds, so aroused that he successfully manages the love act at last. But the real climax comes a few minutes later, in the infamous slow-mo death scene, when the woods spurt gunfire and the two lovers writhe in ecstasy as bright red bulletholes blossom across their bodies. This wasn't about the Depression anymore, this was about Vietnam and the sixties and being a star. It was about James Dean with his neck snapped, Brian Jones of the Rolling Stones lying motionless at the bottom of his pool. No wonder college kids were lining up to see it.

Seven weeks into its release, after opening in major cities coast-to-coast, *Bonnie and Clyde* was the third-biggest draw in the country. Pauline Kael weighed in with a nine-thousand-word essay in *The New Yorker* that greeted it as a landmark. In December, it made the cover of *Time*. Suddenly it was being treated not as a bungled B but as art, like Andy Warhol's soup cans and Roy Lichtenstein's comic strips. But the dawning realization among tastemakers that *Bonnie and Clyde* was a pop masterpiece carried little weight at Warner Bros.–Seven Arts. Beatty had been doing everything imaginable to promote it—tracking the box-office returns, slipping into theaters to study the audience response, going into projection booths to complain if the sound wasn't right. Now he started pushing for a rerelease. He was told it was impossible. So he went back to the Beverly Wilshire and found Abe Lastfogel paddling in the pool.

As Hollywood's senior agent, Lastfogel enjoyed enormous prestige. He could walk into a room and all conversation would cease. He wasn't omnipotent: So far he'd been unable to make anything happen for Wayne Newton, even though the Morris office had thrown everything they had into the effort—shot a television pilot that hadn't sold, gotten Cubby Broccoli to produce a picture called *Eighty Steps to Jonah* that went nowhere. And yet, for an old fat cat, Lastfogel did have a finger in 1967's most happening pictures. Anne Bancroft was the seductive older woman in *The Graduate*, the box-office hit of the year. Tracy and Hepburn were back in *Guess Who's Coming to Dinner*, trying to confront their daughter's decision to marry a Negro. Norman Jewison came out with *In the Heat of the Night*, about a redneck sheriff and a Negro detective thrown together on a murder case. Clint Eastwood, fed up with television and despairing of getting movie work in Hollywood, had been sent to the agency's Rome office, which got him $15,000 to do a low-budget Western for Sergio Leone; now *A Fistful of Dollars* was out in the States and Eastwood was a cult star, the icy, nihilistic antihero of a new genre people were calling the spaghetti Western. But what Beatty wanted was unheard-of. Studios weren't prepared to admit they'd mis-gauged a picture's appeal. If it didn't find an audience, too bad. They had release schedules to contend with, product in the pipeline, market-ing budgets already drawn up. By January 1968, *Bonnie and Clyde* had played out its first-run dates and was showing in the nabes. Beatty threatened to sue. No deal.

Then the Oscar nominations were announced. *Bonnie and Clyde* was named in nine categories, including best picture, best direction, best original screenplay, best actress, and best actor. Finally, a new deal was struck. Beatty was forced to give back part of his percentage to cover the costs of the rerelease. But when the picture went back into first-run houses, it drew audiences five to eight times as big as it had before, not just in major cities but across the country. It wasn't just a movie, it was a phenomenon. Coeds took up the Bonnie Parker look. The two Depres-sion-era desperadoes were reborn as sixties folk heroes, counterculture rebels gunning for thrills on the far side of the law. And as for Warren Beatty—well, all Lastfogel had to do now was name his price.

"ROWAN AND MARTIN'S LAUGH-IN" MADE ITS SERIES DEBUT ON JANUARY 22. Its Monday night time slot put it up against two of the most popular shows on television—the last half of "Gunsmoke," a twelve-year-old Western that was enjoying a phenomenal comeback, followed by "The Lucy Show." Yet by Tuesday morning "Laugh-In" was the talk of the country. Here was a show unlike anything ever broadcast—wild, fre-netic, suggestive, and outrageous, an unbelievably fast-paced grab bag of pithy one-liners, ludicrous sight gags, bizarre non sequiturs, and satirical shtick. It was today. It was now. It was a TV happening.

Over the next few weeks, "Laugh-In" popularized a dozen new catch-phrases and characters. The German soldier who peered out from behind a potted palm and muttered, "Verrry interesting!" The little old lady who whacked the dirty old man on the park bench with her umbrella. "Sock it to me," followed by a bucket of water or a trap-door exit. "You bet your sweet bippy," an all-purpose rejoinder. "Beautiful downtown Burbank," home of the new NBC Studios. The Flying Fickle Finger of Fate Award. Goldie Hawn, the giggling blonde who always flubbed her lines. Rowan and Martin themselves, two suave and tuxe-doed guys who greeted the chaos around them with insouciant aplomb.

Eight weeks after its premiere, "Laugh-In" was the number-one show in America. George Schlatter had reinvented vaudeo. He'd taken all the old tricks from vaudeville and burlesque—slapstick, innuendo, black-outs, song and dance—and strung them together rapid-fire, *bam-bam-bam,* in a staccato presentation that was perfect for 1968. Television audiences were ricocheting wildly from Tet offensive to Anacin com-mercial to assassination to race riot to "Gomer Pyle." Now they had a hip and zany comedy show with the same electronic pacing. It struck them as freewheeling, almost psychedelic.

Actually, it was just the opposite. Unlike the classic Morris Agency programs from television's early years—"Texaco Star Theater" or "Your Show of Shows" or "The Colgate Comedy Hour"—"Laugh-In" was care-fully scripted and spliced together with split-second timing. Nothing happened by accident. There was no studio audience because there was no show as such, just disconnected snippets of entertainment. To get an audience response, Schlatter declared an open house and let spectators come and go as they liked. The writers toiled away in a motel in nearby Toluca Lake, where they cranked out material to be aired weeks later after being reworked to suit some guest star who needed a sketch. Only in the editing room could Schlatter create the kaleidoscopic barrage that "Laugh-In" delivered. Antic spontaneity was achieved through careful control.

The only thing freewheeling about "Laugh-In" was its bawdiness. Even more than "The Smothers Brothers," "Laugh-In" was naughty. "My fiancée just found out she's been taking aspirins instead of the pill," a regular quipped one night. "She doesn't have a headache, but I do." The off-color humor was so pervasive that even innocent bits of shtick— "Look *that* up in your Funk & Wagnalls"—provoked mass titillation. For Schlatter, it was all a cat-and-mouse game with the censors: The point was to see what he could get away with.

The show's zippy pacing and with-it graphics and liberated humor were so startlingly new for television that its audience tended not to notice how safe it was politically. Instead of taking a stand as the Smothers Brothers did, Rowan and Martin poked fun at everyone, right, left, and center. The idea was to keep it balanced. Schlatter was a liberal

Democrat; Paul Keyes, the head writer, was an unofficial member of Richard Nixon's presidential campaign staff. It was Keyes who got John Wayne, star of the soon-to-be-released gung-ho action pic *The Green Berets*, to tape a brief walk-on before the first program aired—a coup that eventually enabled them to land everyone from Jack Lemmon to Gore Vidal to Billy Graham to Dick Gregory, all at scale. For the September 16 show, Keyes got Nixon himself, popping out of a little door on the show's infamous "joke wall" with the words, "Sock it to *me?*" Hubert Humphrey, Nixon's Democratic opponent, was invited to appear as well. His advisers told him not to.

For the Smothers Brothers, it was more than a game. After a long summer in which history had gone horribly awry—Robert Kennedy shot dead in the Ambassador Hotel while celebrating his California primary win; Soviet tanks on the prowl in Prague after Czechoslovakia's brief go with freedom; tear gas on the floor of the Democratic National Convention as the police ran riot against demonstrators in the streets of Chicago—Tommy Smothers returned to the air more determined than ever.

He had the ratings to back him up. "The Smothers Brothers Comedy Hour" had ended the 1967–1968 season in the Nielsen top twenty, just two-tenths of a point behind "The Lawrence Welk Show." "War is not healthy for children and other living things," read the poster in his harborside apartment in Marina del Rey, the vast new yacht basin–singles complex on the Westside of Los Angeles. The network had censored that message from his Mother's Day show the previous spring. Now, haggard from stress, fingernails chewed to the nub, ulcer worse than ever, he sallied forth to do battle again. Harry Belafonte was invited onto the show. For seven and a half minutes he sang "Lord, Lord, Don't Stop the Carnival" while film clips of the August free-for-all in Chicago ran in the background. But when the program aired on Sunday night, that segment had been cut.

Then Tom Dawson, the network's new president, invited Tom Smothers to meet with him in his office at CBS Television City, the company's sprawling West Coast headquarters on Beverly Boulevard. Smothers, who worked out of Danny Thomas's old quarters in the penthouse, came downstairs with a peace offering—a plate of homemade brownies. Responding to this unaccustomed touch of homeyness, Dawson took the fatherly approach. He wanted to talk to them as if they were his own sons. He wanted to explain how it wasn't in their best interest to attack the network that put them on the air, to alienate the affiliates, to inspire hate mail and crank calls and presidential vituperation. Tom listened with the hangdog air of a miscreant child. Finally he stood up, fixed Dawson with his startlingly mismatched eyes—one green, one blue—and declared, "I will never forget this meeting and what you said." Then he went upstairs and let loose.

Dawson was soon gone, replaced by Robert Wood, former head of the CBS station in Los Angeles. Wood was not a fan, and with Nixon in the White House and the country more polarized than ever, he viewed the show as a major trouble spot. It was a triumph in the ratings and a favorite with the critics—a much-talked-about, award-winning program. But affiliates hated it, particularly in the South. Some said it gave aid and comfort to the enemy. Some even argued that its political slant could endanger their FCC franchise. The CBS legal department was eyeing it carefully, waiting for a slipup. Because it was such a hit, Mike Dann was anxious to keep it on the air. So was Stan Kamen, the show's chief contact at the Morris Agency. Bill Paley maintained an Olympian silence.

Tommy Smothers didn't care about network politics. All he knew was that CBS—Mike Dann, Robert Wood, Bill Paley, Richard Nixon, the establishment—was trying to censor them. He wasn't going to let them get away with it. Like any other citizen waging a righteous fight, he sought allies in Washington. He met with Massachusetts Senator Ted Kennedy and Alan Cranston of California. He met with Nicholas Johnson, the dissenter on the FCC, and fellow commissioner Kenneth Cox.

That winter, while CBS and William Morris were in renewal talks, Frank Stanton worked out a compromise that would give the affiliates some control. Even though the program had a live format, it had always been taped a few days ahead and screened by the network for content. Under the new agreement, the network would prescreen it for the affiliates as well. Tommy seemed not to care, and the Morris Agency was eager for anything that would keep it on the air. So in March 1969, a renewal agreement was reached.

Later that month, the Smothers Brothers taped a show with Joan Baez in which she dedicated a song to her husband, David Harris, who was about to go to jail for resisting the draft. When the censors cut her explanation of why he was being imprisoned, Tommy saw red. The next week's show featured guest star Dan Rowan, cohost of "Laugh-In," presenting a Flying Fickle Finger of Fate Award to Senator John Pastore of Rhode Island, who was trying to establish a review board to screen television programs for sex and violence. The tape of the show was late getting to New York.

It didn't arrive on Wednesday. It didn't arrive on Thursday. Mike Dann called Perry Lafferty, his deputy on the coast; neither of them could reach Tommy. They finally found him in San Francisco, looking for a studio where they could shoot the next season's show away from the watchful eye of CBS. He assured them he'd sent the tape. They told him they didn't have it.

At midday Friday, Robert Wood held a meeting at his office in Black Rock. He asked Dann if they'd gotten the tape. He already knew the answer.

"We've got 'em!" cried John Apple, head of legal.

Wood turned to Dann. "Cancel them," he said coldly.

THAT WAS THE SPRING THAT ABE LASTFOGEL STOPPED COMING INTO THE office. He stopped going to Hillcrest too, and he and Frances stopped going out every night for dinner. For weeks he was confined to bed in his hotel suite, and no one outside the handful of men at the top knew why. Anyone who asked was told he had a back problem. When he eventually reappeared, his back seemed fine, but his demeanor had changed—nothing dramatic, just a slight slurring in his speech, a tendency to get sentimental. He didn't have the energy he'd had before, and when he spoke to people, he tended to look past them. Finally, an agent in the television department went to Phil Weltman and asked him to level with him. Then he went to Morris Stoller, the accountant who ran the Beverly Hills office. Stoller admitted what some in the agency were beginning to suspect: Mr. Lastfogel had suffered a stroke.

Stoller and Weisbord and Lefkowitz had already decided on a course of action. This wasn't something they wanted out in the trades. Everything had to be kept hush-hush. But at the appropriate moment, an announcement would be made: Lastfogel was retiring, and Nat Lefkowitz would be succeeding him as president of the agency—the fourth president in its seventy-one-year history. Lastfogel had been spending most of his time handling clients anyway; Weisbord and Stoller and Lefkowitz had been running the agency between them for years. So the transition would be smooth. Nothing would change. Everything was going to remain the same.

PART 2

BETRAYAL

1969-1992

Where the money is, there will the jackals gather, and where the jackals gather something usually dies.

—RAYMOND CHANDLER,
"TEN PER CENT OF YOUR LIFE"

10

DAMON AND PYTHIAS

Los Angeles/Le Mans/New York, 1969-1974

THE FIRM NAT LEFKOWITZ TOOK OVER IN JUNE 1969 WAS FAR MORE impressive than the one he'd joined forty-two years before. Its annual revenues, swollen by two decades of television packages, were estimated to be in the $12 million range. It had 550 employees, many of them with titles like "executive vice president" that had never been conferred before. It had expanded beyond New York, Chicago, and Beverly Hills to London, Paris, Munich, Rome, and Madrid. And for the first time in its seventy-one-year history, it was headed by a lawyer-accountant rather than a working agent.

This made sense. Showbiz was going corporate fast. The Hollywood moguls were gone, replaced either by cold-blooded corporate raiders or by flotillas of number-crunching MBAs who answered to go-go conglomerates with interests in a dozen or more different industries. Gulf + Western was running Paramount. Transamerica, the San Francisco–based insurance and financial services company, had taken over United Artists. Kinney National Services, having expanded to embrace funeral homes, comic books, merchandising, magazine distribution, and the Ashley Famous Agency, was about to buy up Warner Bros.–Seven Arts. Kirk Kerkorian, an unschooled Armenian-American from the San Joaquin

Valley who'd made a fortune flying gamblers to Vegas, was planning a run on the most glamorous property of all, Metro-Goldwyn-Mayer, now staggering under an $85 million debt load and in danger of defaulting on its loans.

As in Hollywood, so in Vegas. With Robert Kennedy's Justice Department applying the heat, the town's gambling interests had taken cover under the umbrella of corporate respectability held out by Howard Hughes. The richest man in America, flush with cash from his $546 million sale of Trans-World Airlines, Hughes had been spirited off his private train and into the Desert Inn in November 1966. He'd been there ever since, immobilized by fear of germs, unseen by anyone except his Mormon nurses, while his chief deputy, a former FBI agent named Robert Maheu, worked with Johnny Roselli, the syndicate's man in Hollywood, to take over the Desert Inn and then the Sands and the Frontier as well. In the show rooms, Howard Hughes jokes suddenly replaced mob jokes. "You're wondering why I don't have a drink in my hand?" Frank Sinatra quipped onstage at the Sands one evening in 1967. "Howard Hughes bought it." When Hughes subsequently cut off his credit, Sinatra took a chair to casino manager Carl Cohen in the Garden Room and got a punch in the face that claimed two front teeth and sent him sprawling.

Sinatra wasn't the only one with a beef. With Hughes's crew-cut minions in place, the garish hospitality long favored by the boys gave way to a bean-counter mentality geared more toward mass than class. The age of the carpet joint, of tuxedo-clad high rollers and dames in cashmeres and furs, was over. And no one, not even Howard Hughes, did more to open Vegas to the average Joe than the new owner of the Flamingo, Kirk Kerkorian, who in the summer of 1969, shortly before announcing his bid for MGM, opened the super-colossal, thirty-story, fifteen-hundred-room International next to the town's new convention center, where pizza-product vendors and the like gathered to tout their wares.

Talent agencies were going corporate as well. In 1968, Freddie Fields had merged GAC into his Creative Management Associates to spawn an agency with annual revenues of $11 million. The new CMA was a publicly traded corporation, its shares available on the American Stock Exchange. And just before Kinney National Services purchased Warner Bros. and gave it to Ted Ashley to run, it sold his Ashley Famous Agency to Marvin Josephson Associates, a miniconglomerate that also included a TV production firm and a concert-booking bureau. Josephson, with revenues almost as large as CMA's, was about to go public as well.

The Morris office was keeping up with the times. The new headquarters on Television Row had a crisp, corporate air. Nat Lefkowitz and Morris Stoller—two-thirds of the troika running the firm—were accountants, and Sammy Weisbord, who'd soon be taking over the entire television operation with the retirement of Wally Jordan in New York, was less a functioning agent than an executive whose job was to coordinate the activities of dozens of men. Nat Kalcheim had just retired, Wally Jordan was set to go, and Harry Kalcheim was scheduled to leave in 1971—which meant that the three agents who'd dominated the New York office since the forties would soon be gone.

But compared to the studio conglomerates and its agency competitors, the Morris office still felt like a candy store in Brooklyn, a mom-and-pop operation with cousins pitching in to help and employees and clients alike made to feel like part of some enormous extended family. And that was because of the Lastfogels. When Freddie Fields and Marvin Josephson were taking their agencies public, cashing in on their holdings, Lastfogel had given his away. For years, he'd owned more than 80 percent of the agency through a Delaware corporation known as Willmor International, which had been set up in 1958, after the buyout of the Morris family left him sole owner of the agency's voting stock. But before he retired, he'd given up all future earnings on his stock and put them back into the company, which transformed its 1,000 shares of nonvoting class-B stock into 500,000, gave them full voting privileges, and made them available to its top employees.

William Morris was still no route to riches. To attain real wealth, you had to get out—like David Geffen, or Ted Ashley. Geffen had quit agenting to become Laura Nyro's manager, and when he set up a publishing company for Nyro's songs, he'd assigned 50 percent—the standard publisher's cut—to himself. Now he'd just sold the company to CBS for $4.5 million in stock. Ashley had done even better, selling his agency to Kinney National for $12.75 million, of which he got 60 percent. But there was a reward for those who stayed on despite the stingy pay and the limited opportunities for advancement and the lure of fast money on the outside. The reward was comfort and security—the security of the Morris family. At Morris, you knew you belonged. The agency functioned as mom and dad, paying a salary that was more like an allowance, lending you money when you needed it, doling out a Christmas bonus at the end of every year. Even with Abe in retirement, Frances still went from office to office, remembering birthdays, keeping in touch. You didn't want to go cuckoo like George Gruskin, but otherwise you knew you had a home.

The conglomeratization of show business coincided with the worst recession to hit the motion picture industry since the arrival of television twenty years before. Hollywood had been booming for years, riding a double-track gravy train—blockbuster hits at the box office, followed by lucrative rentals to the networks. If a picture didn't make it in the theaters, the studios could always recoup on television. Production had shot up. The price of talent headed skyward. Then, toward the end of 1969, the train stopped dead. Low-budget, made-for-television movies were replacing theatrical releases on prime-time schedules. Ratings took a nosedive. The networks slashed their bids and grew far more selective. The studios—particularly UA, MGM, and Fox—faced staggering losses, forcing cutbacks that affected everyone in town. Suddenly, the talent agencies were in the damage control business.

The worst was at MGM. Kirk Kerkorian completed his $100 million takeover in September and turned the studio over to James Aubrey, the "smiling cobra" Bill Paley had dismissed from CBS four years before. Aubrey arrived at Culver City to discover, among other things, that the studio was locked into pay-or-play commitments—payment guaranteed, whether the picture was made or not—on three big-budget epics. Two of them were Morris deals—*Ryan's Daughter*, which David Lean was directing in Ireland, and *Man's Fate*, a Carlo Ponti film that Fred Zinnemann had in preproduction in London, with David Niven in the lead.

David Lean had directed *Dr. Zhivago*, MGM's biggest money-maker since *Gone With the Wind*; Fred Zinnemann had not. In November, two days before principal photography was set to begin on *Man's Fate*, MGM's legal-affairs chief in New York phoned Ponti's attorney in London to inform him that the picture was being canceled. Phil Kellogg—who represented Ponti's wife, Sophia Loren, in addition to Zinnemann and Niven—met with MGM's attorneys in Los Angeles and flew to London to confer with his client. Then an MGM attorney informed Zinnemann that the studio would not be reimbursing him for the $3.5 million he'd already laid out for preproduction expenses and blithely suggested he file for bankruptcy. Instead, Zinnemann filed suit and, with the Morris office defraying his legal expenses, issued a bitter public denunciation of MGM's business methods. Jim Aubrey was so incensed that when he flew to Dublin to persuade David Lean to trim his budget, he refused to have Kellogg, who happened to be in town, join them for dinner.

The turmoil in Hollywood cut into the agency's revenues at a bad time. Under Nat Lefkowitz's direction, Morris had just bought several buildings adjacent to its West Coast headquarters in Beverly Hills—the building next to it on El Camino, the building directly behind it on the corner of South Rodeo Drive and Charleville Boulevard, and another building halfway up Rodeo toward Wilshire. Now economies had to be found. Nat Lefkowitz began to summon senior agents to his office.

One of them was Bernie Seligman, a twenty-four-year veteran whose clients over the years had included Anne Bancroft, Edward G. Robinson, director-choreographer Herbert Ross, composer Jule Styne, Abe Burrows, and playwright Meredith Willson. John Murray Anderson, the flamboyant Broadway showman, used to call Seligman "Hope," short for Great White Hope of the Morris Agency. But Seligman had also alienated important buyers with his negotiating stance, which was quiet and subdued but absolutely implacable. The way he saw it, he wasn't going to play the customer's game. The way Lefkowitz saw it, he was expendable.

Seligman walked into Lefkowitz's office to find the agency's new president at his desk, with Howard Hausman on one side and Lee Stevens on the other. There was some talk about the fabric of the company. Seligman said he considered himself the mortar between the bricks. Stevens made a crack about his politics not being very good. Then Lefkowitz dropped the bomb: He was being terminated.

Seligman was numb when he retreated from the office. It was a shattering blow, less like being fired than like being expelled from the fold. And the worst thing was, it had so rarely happened before.

STEVE MCQUEEN IN A RACE CAR, WITH JOHN STURGES DIRECTING: To Stan Kamen, to nearly everyone in Hollywood, *Le Mans* looked like a can't-miss proposition. With Kamen's guidance and the help of his wife, Neile, McQueen had become an enormous star. He'd teamed up with Natalie Wood in *Love with the Proper Stranger*, played a Depression-era cardsharp in Norman Jewison's *The Cincinnati Kid*, landed an Oscar nomination for *The Sand Pebbles*, even managed to impersonate a suave, white-collar crook in Jewison's *The Thomas Crown Affair*. *Bullitt*, in which he starred as a San Francisco cop who plays by his own rules, had been one of top-grossing films of 1968. The chase scene alone kept people coming back to the theater in stupefaction and awe: eleven minutes of screeching tires, grinding gears, and wailing police sirens as cars go airborne on the streets of San Francisco at a hundred miles an hour. Reunite him with Sturges, the director behind *The Magnificent Seven* and *The Great Escape*, give him creative control, and you had the makings of a box-office bonanza.

Not that it wasn't troublesome to start a $7.5 million production with no script, no storyline, and no agreement on whether they even needed a storyline—maybe they could just rely on the inherent drama of racing itself? But *Bullitt* hadn't had much of a script either until McQueen got to San Francisco, and even now its storyline was a mess. With that roller-coaster car chase and Steve's baby blues it hardly mattered, any more than it mattered that McQueen had soared dramatically over budget in his first picture as producer, or that Warner Bros.–Seven Arts, with which he had a six-picture deal, had dumped him in the middle of production. *Bullitt* was a box-office smash, so McQueen could do no wrong.

In a series of meetings in Burbank, Kamen had negotiated the separation between Warner and Solar Productions, the production company he'd originally helped McQueen set up as a tax shelter. He started shopping for a new deal immediately, while *Bullitt* was still in production. He landed them at Cinema Center Films, the instant studio CBS had just set up on the old Republic lot in Studio City, which Four Star had vacated when it left the production business for distribution. The Morris office already had William Friedkin directing Cinema Center's production of *The Boys in the Band*, the Broadway play about life in the homosexual underworld. McQueen's first picture under the Cinema Center deal was *The Reivers*, a gentle literary film directed by another Morris client, Mark Rydell. The Cinema Center execs were a lot more excited about *Le Mans*.

McQueen had wanted to make a racing picture for more than a decade, ever since he'd first taken up the sport and begun to envision himself a movie star. Sturges had come to him early on with an auto racing property he was developing at Warner Bros. called *Day of the Champion*. They'd scouted locations and interviewed racing pros, but in 1965, when McQueen was in Taiwan on location for *The Sand Pebbles* for Fox, he'd learned that John Frankenheimer was going ahead with plans to direct a rival racing picture at MGM—*Grand Prix*, with James Garner in the lead. Sturges and McQueen were two weeks away from their start date when production delays on *The Sand Pebbles* forced Jack Warner to shut down *Day of the Champion* rather than come out second. All these years since, the idea had burned in the back of McQueen's mind. And then, when Kamen moved Solar to Cinema Center, it appeared on the development slate.

McQueen was a budding tycoon now, one of a handful of Hollywood stars with his own full-fledged production company—not to mention the sister enterprise he had going in a garage a couple of miles away in Van Nuys. Solar Plastics and Engineering designed and built cutting-edge parts for racing vehicles—shatterproof plastic gas tanks, lightweight contoured plastic seats, breakthrough products that added strength and subtracted weight. The name Solar came from his first movie-star home, a Japanese-style house on Solar Drive in Nichols Canyon, a rustic enclave in the Hollywood Hills. They'd barely settled in when he and Neile and the kids moved into the truly grand establishment where they lived now, an eighteen-room stone mansion behind massive oak gates high above Mandeville Canyon, with Los Angeles spread out before them and the blue waters of the Pacific in the not-too-far distance. They called it the Castle.

Along with the pricey real estate and the business ventures, McQueen had acquired a real star complex. The constant, nagging demands he'd made on earlier shoots had mushroomed into gigantic demands whose satisfaction gave him proof of his celebrity. For *The Sand Pebbles*, it was the private gym he'd had shipped over to Taiwan. For *Bullitt*, it was the pool table he'd had installed in the San Francisco apartment he'd rented for the shoot—a twelfth-floor apartment with modest elevators, which meant they had to erect a crane and swing the pool table in through a plate-glass window that was broken out for the occasion.

Then there were the drugs. McQueen was ready to try anything new—marijuana, LSD, peyote in the desert with his auto-racing friends. Jay Sebring, the chi-chi Hollywood hairstylist who'd popularized the blow-dry look for men, had introduced him to coke after doing his hair on the 1963 shoot of *Love with the Proper Stranger*. Sebring was tough and scrappy, an ex–street punk like McQueen who'd become a star himself, with a clientele that included Peter Fonda, Peter Lawford, Paul

Newman, and Frank Sinatra. McQueen had sent all his friends to him, Kamen included, and he and Kamen and McQueen had become good buddies. Sebring and his girlfriend at the time—a shy, unassuming Morris Agency starlet named Sharon Tate—had even gone to Hawaii with Steve and Neile and Steve's friend Elmer Valentine, who ran the Whisky a Go-Go on the Strip.

By the end of the decade, McQueen was high on pot more or less continuously and snorting every day. He was also banging every chick who came his way. He'd been discreet about it before, but wasn't this the sixties? The little chickies were just his way of staying young, like the bell-bottomed jeans and the love beads and the hippie mustache he was growing. He rented Vincent Price's beach house in Malibu and carried on a torrid affair with a *Playboy* playmate. He showed up with Lauren Hutton at movie-star hangouts like the Polo Lounge and the Bistro, the see-and-be-seen bar on Cañon Drive whose backers included Tony Curtis, Jack Lemmon, Dean Martin, Frank Sinatra, and Jack Warner. He was furious when the story turned up in the gossip columns.

Neile was mortified. She'd been willing to overlook his earlier transgressions, especially since he'd made it clear that she was the one he cared about. One of the tradeoffs for her lost movie career was the pleasure of being in the tight little world of Hollywood wives who planned benefits for SHARE, the charity of choice in Beverly Hills. SHARE, which had been founded by Mrs. Dean Martin, Mrs. Sammy Cahn, and Mrs. Gene Nelson to raise money for retarded and abused children, stood for Share Happily Reap Endlessly, but Steve's blatant philandering made mock of this simple notion. She knew what was driving him—the knowledge that he was pushing forty, the groovy lifestyle of the Woodstock generation, the infantile need to have it all, and above all the phone call, that anonymous phone call he'd gotten in January 1968, when a male voice told him a book was coming out naming every homosexual in the public eye. "I thought you'd like to know that your name is on the list," the voice said, *click.* Yes, she knew what was behind it. But that didn't make it any easier to take.

McQueen was a desperately needy man, always had been. Only now he was a desperately needy man with a major coke habit and a face that made women melt. He was the same as he'd always been, a little boy who craved boundaries even as he railed against them. But he saw himself as a suave and sophisticated grown-up, an international playboy like the banker he'd played in *The Thomas Crown Affair.* He knew everything—wine, women, cars. He knew people were out to fuck him, too. Everyone wanted a piece of him, everyone was out to get him. Driving home with Neile after an evening out, he'd look in the rearview mirror and decide a car was tailing them. How much of this was drug-induced paranoia and how much was rooted in reality was hard to say—especially after August 1969.

Saturday, August 9, was the day the cleaning lady discovered the bodies at the house on Cielo Drive. Sharon Tate had rented it with her new husband, Roman Polanski—a big, comfy, isolated place on a steep road near the top of Benedict Canyon. Sharon was staying there with two friends, San Francisco coffee heiress Abigail Folger and an émigré Polish playboy named Voytek Frykowski, while Polanski finished a picture in London. Sebring had dropped by the night before after dinner at El Coyote, the Mex joint on Beverly Boulevard. McQueen had planned to join them, but he picked up a chick instead.

The news hit the radio before noon. A few hours later it was splashed across the afternoon papers. McQueen raced to the phone and ordered Sebring's house cleaned up so the cops wouldn't find the drugs. On Sunday night a second slay scene was discovered—a middle-aged super-market magnate and his wife in a mansion on Waverly Drive, miles away in East Hollywood. Seven butchered in one weekend: Gun sales went through the roof, guard dogs were sold out solid. Sinatra went into hiding, the papers reported. Tony Bennett abandoned his bungalow at the Beverly Hills Hotel for an inside room. Jerry Lewis installed an alarm system with closed-circuit cameras. McQueen bought a P.38 automatic. The only one who kept her cool was Sue Mengers, Freddie Fields's hot young agent at CMA. "Don't worry, honey," she told Barbra Streisand. "Stars aren't being murdered, only featured players."

Eventually the panic subsided, though it was unnerving to learn fourteen months later, when a messianic hippie drifter named Charles Manson and several confederates were on trial for the murders, that Manson and his followers had indeed drawn up a list of stars to be slaughtered—Frank Sinatra, Tom Jones, Liz Taylor, Richard Burton, Steve McQueen. . . . But by that time, McQueen had other things to worry about. Early in 1970, Solar became the first movie-star production company to go public, in a deal that yielded nearly $1.5 million for McQueen himself. Kamen was focused on *McCabe and Mrs. Miller* that spring—he'd been looking for a project Warren Beatty could do with Julie Christie, and when a fledgling producer suggested getting Robert Altman to direct them in a

Western about a little guy versus a big mining company, he phoned Beatty in London, got him to fly to New York to see *M*A*S*H* (which Altman had directed), had him in L.A. to meet Altman the next day, and wrapped the whole thing up in a week. Meanwhile, McQueen was pushing ahead with *Le Mans*. He broke his foot in a motorcycle race in Lake Elsinore, a resort town sixty miles southeast of Los Angeles, but he went through with the punishing twelve-hour endurance race at Sebring anyway and came in second to Mario Andretti. In June, his foot barely mended but his spirits still soaring, he left for France with Kamen and Sturges to make his big statement, the definitive racing film, the picture of his life.

Le Mans was the most exciting road race in the world—a test of endurance for man and machine, twenty-four hours across the French countryside at speeds well above two hundred miles per hour, with hundreds of thousands of people looking on and everything streaking past in a blur. The shoot looked to be just as dicey. For six months, while they argued about whether they needed a storyline and tried to cobble together a script, McQueen and company would be roaring down the road in flimsy fiberglass shells with finicky engines and tanks full of gasoline. A patch of oil, a rain slick from a summer storm, and any one of them could spin out of control and go up in a sheet of flame.

They'd been there only a couple of days when Kamen went to look after the first accident victims—a girl Steve had picked up, a member of the crew, and Steve's assistant, a kid named Mario Iscovich. It happened the night before the race, on a rain-drenched country road. Steve was driving them into town from his rented château when he lost it on a curve and sailed into a tree. He and the girl flew over the windshield; the two guys were in back with broken bones. Steve was in the race the next day, but Kamen was on hand when Iscovich came to. He got him out of the hospital, treated him to a steak and fries and a glass of wine, talked to him about life, made him feel like a person. Steve turned up the next day, worried that the kid might sue.

Neile arrived not long after with their two children, three schnauzers, and the cat. The fourteenth-century château where they were staying was too picturesque by half—surrounded by vineyards and beset by bats. The day after she got there, Steve announced he'd be spending some time with his groupies. Neile freaked. That night, he plied her with coke and got her to admit that she'd had an affair too—with a

European actor who'd recently won an Oscar. Moments later, face twitching, he had the P.38 to her head, demanding the guy's name. That started a new pattern. Night after night, he'd interrogate her, demanding to know why, waving the gun around, slapping her face, it was all her fault, fucking bitch. She felt guilty enough to take it.

Meanwhile, the production was burning money at $100,000 a week, after an initial investment of $1 million in race cars alone. By the beginning of July, Sturges had thousands of feet of film in the can but no dialogue and no script. Finally, Robert Relyea, McQueen's executive producer, hurled an ashtray against his office wall in frustration and announced that the picture was out of control. Cinema Center's production chief, who happened to be in the room, slipped out and made a phone call to Los Angeles. The top brass at Cinema Center boarded the next plane for Paris.

McQueen met them at the local airstrip and insisted on driving Gordon Stuhlberg, Cinema Center's president, back to Solar Village, the Quonset-hut camp where the production was headquartered. Stuhlberg wasn't used to that kind of driving; he emerged white as a sheet and incoherent with fear. The next day, McQueen's contingent arrived— Stan Kamen, his legal affairs chief Roger Davis, plus the Morris Agency's head of business affairs and McQueen's personal attorney. Kamen's job, as he saw it, was to tell Steve what he thought, and when the two sides gathered at the Château Lornay, they both had the same message: The game was over. Stuhlberg and his aides had thought about finding a new star, but their only real options were to finish the film with McQueen or shut it down and take a writeoff. The only way to finish was to set new ground rules. Steve would have to give up his points and his $750,000 salary; his executive producers would have to do likewise. They were shutting down for two weeks. In the meantime, Sturges and McQueen would have to come up with a workable script and be ready to start shooting.

Agreed.

McQueen seemed strangely buoyant when they finally reached an understanding. Yes, he'd lost creative control, he'd lost any hope of profits, but he'd averted a total shutdown. He uncorked a bottle of champagne and offered a toast to the people who'd saved his film. As for the script, he and Neile were going to Morocco on vacation, guests of the Princess Lalla Nehza. He'd shoot whatever they came up with when he got back.

Everyone left—Gordon Stuhlberg, Stan Kamen, Roger Davis, the execs, the flunkies, Steve and Neile. A few days later, Sturges had second thoughts: Did he really want to come up with a script while Steve was gone? He stuck his head into Robert Relyea's office. "I'm going home," he said. Relyea thought he meant to his hotel. He meant to Los Angeles.

Before they got to Morocco, Steve had already decided to fire Stan. The two of them had risen together, Steve becoming a movie star as Stan became a motion-picture agent. But Kamen was too goddamn nice, Steve realized now. The Morris crew was working for CBS, not for him. He needed a barracuda—someone like Freddie Fields. Someone who wasn't afraid to play dirty.

Fields and his wife, Polly Bergen, moved in the same social circles as the McQueens: Polly was active in SHARE, and she and Freddie gave marvelous parties at their big house on Roxbury Drive in Beverly Hills. CMA was fresh and young and in tune with the times. But Neile insisted that Steve at least break the news himself. When they got back from Morocco, Steve found out that Robert Relyea had decided to leave the Morris Agency, too, because Steve was so angry at him for throwing the ashtray and bringing the Cinema Center people on top of their heads. He asked for a copy of the wire Relyea had sent and announced he was going to send the same one. But the cable he actually sent was much more to the point:

> DEAR STAN,
> YOU'RE FIRED. LETTER FOLLOWS.
> STEVE

NORMAN BROKAW WAS EXPERIENCING HIS MOMENT. IT WAS SEPTEMBER 1972, and Brokaw had landed a client whose presence on the agency roster was both innovative and true to tradition: Mark Spitz, hero of the Munich Olympics, the swimmer from Indiana U. who'd come home with an unprecedented seven gold medals. Innovative, because Spitz and his lawyer had their eye not on an acting career but on commercial endorsements—not something Morris usually brokered. Yet true to tradition, because the Morris office did have a long and glorious history of agenting aquabelles and aquabeaus, from Annette Kellerman to Gertrude Ederle to Johnny Weissmuller, the Olympic champion MGM had turned into Tarzan. Working with Danny Thomas and Sheldon Leonard, Brokaw had picked up some of the biggest stars in television, from Andy Griffith to Bill Cosby. He'd also picked up some young leading ladies—Kim Novak, Natalie Wood—and older ones like Loretta Young and Barbara Stanwyck. During the sixties, he and Sammy Weisbord had handled many of the agency's most popular television packages, from "I Spy" to "The Mod Squad," the with-it cop show that Aaron Spelling was producing in partnership with Danny Thomas. When Weisbord was named head of television worldwide after Wally Jordan's retirement, Brokaw took over the West Coast department. Now he was moving beyond television and movie actors to public figures like Mark Spitz.

Brokaw was the perfect agent for a naïf like Spitz—straight-talking and even-tempered, a man who could look you in the eye. He had the handshake of one who paid his bills on time and was proud of his health-insurance plan. While other agents flew to Munich to court Spitz, he'd gone to the boy's parents, who were impressed enough to invite him to their home the day after their son returned. He got there to find letters overflowing the mailbox, the phone ringing off the hook, offers pouring in. Instead of trying to cash in on every offer, he recommended a conservative approach—one endorsement for every gold medal. And he had a wholesome product for Spitz to start off with: milk. It was appropriate to the "dignity" theme Spitz wanted. No Tarzan act for him, yodeling in the jungle.

Two days after Spitz signed his agency papers, the California Milk Advisory Board had him before the camera for one of its "Every Body Needs Milk" commercials. After that came the interviews. Spitz was a hot ticket, the number-one American hero at an Olympics marred by the slaughter of eleven Israeli athletes. But when reporters got him in a room and started asking him questions, they discovered he was what you'd expect of a milk lover—awkward, wooden, even a little vapid-looking. Certainly not glib, barely even warm-bodied. The wholesomeness stuck, but the dignity flew out the window.

By December, when he held a press brunch at the Beverly Hills Hotel to announce the latest endorsement deal Brokaw had worked out for him, Spitz had become something of a joke. In eleven weeks he'd come out in favor of milk and Schick electric razors; now he'd be speaking for a line of low-cost, prefab pools as well. "We're proud that Mark Spitz is joining us as spokesman for Spartan," declared the beaming chairman of Spartan Pools as the reporters and photographers eyed the brunch spread impatiently. "His outstanding record of success and personal magnetism, coupled with Spartan's record of product quality, should prove a dynamic combination in achieving our goal of making the swimming pool an essential part of the happy, healthy home."

As Brokaw looked on from the sidelines, Spitz took the podium to make a brief and only semi-incoherent statement. "I feel that with my close connection with being a swimmer and being in pools—and I've probably seen a lot of bottoms of pools more than anybody, going up and down and up and down—I felt that if I had to do something or build a pool, how would I do it? Well, a lot of people never even get that idea because they can't afford a pool. And I think that with Spartan, they enable the average person to be able purchase a pool as if they were just buying another car. I think that makes it awful nice. It brings the family together, and I'm all for that. And I'm really happy to be associated with Spartan Pools."

The first questioner wanted to know the terms of his contract—information Spitz wasn't prepared to divulge. The second questioner dispensed with the pretense and cut straight to the insults. "In recent days you've endorsed a wide variety of products," he said. "In fact, the only thing you haven't come out in favor of lately is hemorrhoids. Don't you think that if you continue endorsing products at will, you'll impair your credibility?"

That was the signal for the mob to pile on.

"What do you think of the treatment you've been getting in the media lately?"

"The treatment?" Spitz appeared nonplussed.

"Do you plan to continue endorsing products as part of your future career?"

"Is there any truth that there's a feud between you and Johnny Weissmuller?"

"Is there any truth that you're being groomed to replace Flipper when he ultimately retires?"

Finally, from far back in the room, an earnest young man with a pronounced German accent spoke up. "Do you feel comfortable and at ease in the world you are moving in now?" he wanted to know. "It has only been a very short time—how do you feel in this world that must be quite strange to you?"

All eyes turned to the champion. "I'm comfortable," he squeaked. Then he gave a nervous laugh and moved on.

THE BUSINESS WAS CHANGING, AND NOT FOR THE BETTER. MORE AND more, inside the agency and out, the name of the game was money. This was largely due to the influence of Freddie Fields and his Creative Management Associates. Headquartered in a chunky new office tower on the stretch of Beverly Boulevard where the West Hollywood decorator district folds into Beverly Hills, CMA was clearly the agency of the moment. Fields cut an aggressively casual figure—white Gucci loafers, black safari suit, shirt unbuttoned to the navel, gold chains draped across his chest. Holding court behind a six-foot-long marble table in a vast office done in tan marble and brown crushed velvet, with Oriental carpets on the floor and exotic plants creeping toward the ceiling, he looked like Mr. Hollywood himself.

Despite the rich television packaging fees his boys were pulling in, Abe Lastfogel had always presented himself as fundamentally interested in talent. At MCA, Jules Stein, Lew Wasserman, and their men had always gone after power more than money. But Freddie Fields and his partner David Begelman were clearly in pursuit of the maximum dollar. It was understood at the Morris office, for instance, that if a performer didn't have the potential of generating at least $100,000 a year in commissions, CMA wasn't interested.

CMA was a wildly competitive wolfpack whose members weren't afraid to feed on one another. CMA agents had to watch their backs at staff meetings, because if their fellow agents found out about a picture in development, they'd try to gouge the other person's client out of the deal and claw their own client in. Nobody pulled that kind of thing at the Morris Agency. At Morris, a different scam had evolved: senior agents inserting themselves into deals so the bonus money could be diverted their way. Scott Shukat had done record deals with Don McLean and Sly and the Family Stone and comedian David Frye, but after he signed David Cassidy to the agency as a solo performer, Sammy Weisbord phoned him from the coast and said he'd take care of this now. Shukat protested, in writing. Word got back to him to stop with the fuss; he'd be taken care of at the end of the year. But when bonus time came, he wasn't taken care of—so he went to Lefkowitz and asked where his money was. Lefkowitz was so honest that he paid for his own stamps, but this was Weisbord's affair. Shukat's name wasn't on the papers, Lefkowitz pointed out, and none of the money had been split to New York. These are very greedy people, Shukat said to himself as he quit.

The success of the CMA concept—a boutique agency for stars—led the Morris office to reevaluate its own relationship with its clients. The motto that had sustained the agency in Will Morris's day—"No act too big . . . no act too small"—now seemed hopelessly old-fashioned. Was it reasonable to expect the agency to devote more attention to a client than it could ever hope to recoup in commissions? Was it doing the client any favor to encourage him to hang on when his prospects were slim? That was the way it was put to the agents. So the firm began an accounting study, analyzing its clients' income to determine what it was putting in and what it was getting out.

By 1973, with the help of an IBM System/3 computer, the accounting department was running computerized projections of clients' earnings in an attempt to gauge their potential. If a performer who'd been with the office for years wasn't judged likely to bring in some minimal sum in commissions—at least $7,500 a year, say—his agent was told it might be appropriate to suggest to the guy that he go to another agency. From an accounting point of view, this made perfect sense. Not only was it pointless to throw away resources on a sure loser, it was going to give the agency a bad name when the client got disgruntled. It wasn't as if clients, from hotshot Steve McQueen to the most broken-down has-been, remained loyal to their agents. No, there was only one thing this new policy failed to take into account, and that was the nature of the business they were in—unpredictable, illogical, totally mercurial. It was as if they'd forgotten the second half of that old slogan from Will Morris's time: "Our small act of today is our big act of tomorrow."

This was hardly the kind of thing anyone with an accounting degree—like Nat Lefkowitz, or Lee Stevens, or Morris Stoller in the Beverly Hills office—could be expected to have a feel for. Especially once they realized how incredibly useful these new projections could be, not just as a basis for weeding out unproductive clients but for deciding which clients should get a push and which should not. Because it made sense, after all, to work harder for the clients who were likely to make it than for those who didn't. Of course, this meant that the projections they were making would become entirely self-fulfilling. But it was all on computer, and how could the computer be wrong?

Yet agents tended to bristle at the idea of being told who to push and who not to. For Marty Litke, who'd helped sign Bill Cosby and gotten him that first, crucial booking on "The Jack Paar Program," the last straw came at a meeting when they were discussing *The Last of the Red-Hot Lovers*, a Neil Simon comedy that was going into production at Paramount. Litke represented Anne Meara, a young comedienne who had an act with her husband, Jerry Stiller, and she'd asked to be considered for a role in the picture. But when Litke mentioned this at the meeting, he was told they couldn't put Meara up for the job because they were pushing another young comedienne, Renée Taylor, who'd costarred with her husband, Joseph Bologna, in *Lovers and Other Strangers*. What's that got to do with it? Litke countered. They could talk about more than one person for a movie role. That's when he learned the computer readout on Renée Taylor showed she was going to make a lot more money than Anne Meara was.

There was only one thing to do, and Litke did it. Slowly, deliberately, he stood up, left the meeting, walked down the hall to Nat Lefkowitz's office, and resigned.

MORRIS STOLLER WAS AN ODD ONE. FOR THE PAST QUARTER-CENTURY, he'd been administrative head of the West Coast office, functioning as Nat Lefkowitz's viceroy in Beverly Hills. The two had met at Brooklyn College in 1937, when Stoller—like Lefkowitz a CPA—had turned up in Lefkowitz's evening classes at law school. Lefkowitz asked him to join the Morris office as his assistant at $80 a week; Stoller accepted. A decade later, Lefkowitz sent him out to the coast to supervise the burgeoning operations there. Slightly built, thin, and stoop-shouldered, Weisbord bludgeoned his employees; Stoller was a scholarly, almost rabbinical presence. He was more than just a numbers man; he was liable to respond to complaints from clients and their managers with a philosophical discourse about, say, the Hittites and the Canaanites. A manager would go into his office quivering with outrage about some commission he shouldn't have to pay and come out a half-hour later with the vague understanding that the Hittites had moved into the mountains, and that was why he owed this commission. As accountants went, Stoller was pretty sharp.

Certainly he knew how to make with the psychology. He was soft-spoken and artfully manipulative, a good foil for Weisbord and his bombast. Weisbord bludgeoned his employees; Stoller encouraged them and got much better results. He was equally savvy in his business dealings. In collaboration with Nat Lefkowitz and his brother Julius, the agency's outside accountant, he'd been responsible for the Beverly Hills real-estate investments—the property on either side of El Camino that the Arms Building Corporation had purchased in the fifties, plus the adjacent parcels on El Camino and South Rodeo that the agency itself had picked up in 1969. In early 1973, he saw another opportunity: sports.

Professional athletics looked like a growth industry. The advent of cable television and pay-per-view was pumping cash into the business. Few ballplayers had agents, but they were beginning to realize that they might be worth more to the club owners than the $30,000 or so that most of them were getting. And despite the bum rap Mark Spitz was getting for his multiple product endorsements, there was a growing sense that pro sports figures could make a bundle hawking aftershave and soft drinks and the like. Stoller surveyed the landscape and decided that sports personalities would soon be as big as motion picture stars.

In years past, any such step would have been made by Abe Lastfogel in consultation with his kitchen cabinet in New York—Nat Lefkowitz, George Wood, and Nat Kalcheim, the head of the personal appearance department. But Wood was dead, Kalcheim had retired, and Lastfogel was no longer in the loop. He still came in every day, still sat in his first-floor office overlooking the corner of El Camino and Charleville Boulevard, with Sammy Weisbord on one side and Norman Brokaw on the other and Morris Stoller across the hall. He even looked the same, a beaming, white-haired cherub with twinkling blue eyes and his trademark bow tie. But he was no longer the razor-sharp seller he'd once been. He was forgetful. His mind drifted in and out. He spent most of his day reading books, or watching movies in the conference room upstairs. Nobody wanted to burden him with the problems of the agency. So when Stoller started thinking about representing athletes, he and Weisbord and Lefkowitz made the decision to go ahead on their own.

Stoller walked into Phil Weltman's office one day and casually remarked that they were going to open a sports department. Weltman

couldn't believe what he was hearing. A sports department? Who made
that decision? When Stoller told him, Weltman blew up. "Morris," he
said, "I'm sure there's nobody in the building that knows less about
sports than you three."

"You don't approve?"

"Don't approve?" Weltman fixed him with a withering stare. "I think
it's the most embarrassing thing you could do to this agency." It wasn't
as if you could just hang out a shingle and go into the sports business—
you had to have a scouting setup and go to college ball games and
romance the families, all of which the Morris Agency was no more
equipped to do than the man in the moon. Weltman was beside himself.
"How could you be so fucking stupid," he demanded, "as to get into this
situation without bringing it out in a meeting?"

But the only meeting Stoller needed was the one he'd already had,
with Weisbord and Lefkowitz. He made the announcement at the beginning of July: a new venture called WMA Sports, to be headed by an ex-
MCA man named Berle Adams. "Morris Agency's Sports Plunge," cried
the front-page headline in *Daily Variety*. WMA Sports would be active in
merchandising, commercial endorsements, television, motion pictures,
the works, all of it geared to the idea of sports-as-showbiz. Its headquarters would be not at the Morris Building on El Camino but in Century
City, the futuristic office complex that had gone up on the old Twentieth
Century–Fox backlot, just beyond Beverly Hills. Adams would report
directly to Stoller and Weisbord, bypassing the agency red tape.

Berle Adams had gotten his start in the music business, having
founded Mercury Records in Chicago in the forties before moving to
California for his health and going to work for MCA. He'd spent
twenty years at MCA, first as a television packaging agent (he'd bro-
kered the deal that put the fledgling American Football League on
ABC in 1960), then as executive vice president in charge of the operating divisions. But in 1969, with the company deeply in debt and the
Justice Department threatening its planned merger with Westinghouse
Electric on antitrust grounds, he'd gone in with Jules Stein and Taft
Schreiber on a scheme to unseat Lew Wasserman, who was under fire
for poor box-office results and suffering from a heart ailment besides.
At the last moment, Stein had second thoughts, and Wasserman
emerged from the board meeting that was to have been his undoing
with a new long-term contract instead. Adams departed not long afterward. In the two years since, he'd become cofounder and chairman of

Sports Cable, which held pay-television rights to the L.A. Lakers and the L.A. Kings, and he'd gone on the board of Jack Kent Cooke's Teleprompter Corporation, the giant cable systems operator. He knew his way around the sports world, and he knew the television business as well.

Just about the only people Adams didn't know were players. He wasn't at his new job long before he discovered he didn't much care for the breed. In television and motion pictures, he'd dealt with stars who were steeped in the ways of Hollywood. Now he was dealing with college kids, first-run draft picks who were used to lavish recruitment rituals. These boys just weren't reasonable. They wanted tax-free income. They wanted to be movie stars. They wanted flashy new cars and the world on a stick. Adams found it difficult to communicate. He wasn't a hero-worshipper. He was a fifty-six-year-old corporate executive who was used to a certain amount of deference himself. He didn't want to hang out in locker rooms. He didn't want to travel. He didn't mind going to New York now and then, but jumping on a plane to Cincinnati to woo Pete Rose, the National League's Most Valuable Player for 1973? After all the years he'd spent on the road for MCA, that just didn't fit into his way of life anymore.

Even so, Adams was able to cut some deals. For Secretariat, the three-year-old racehorse who'd just won the Kentucky Derby, the Preakness Stakes, and the Belmont Stakes—making him the first Triple Crown winner in twenty-five years—he made merchandising agreements that flooded the market with mugs and blankets and photos. He hired John Mackey, former tight end for the Baltimore Colts and founding president of the Professional Football Players League, who signed four of the year's top collegiate draft picks to the agency—Waymond Bryant of the Chicago Bears, David Jaynes of the Kansas City Chiefs, Ed "Too Tall" Jones of the Dallas Cowboys, and Henry Lawrence of the Oakland Raiders. Adams himself signed Hank Aaron, star outfielder for the Atlanta Braves, who'd started with the Indianapolis Clowns in the old Negro leagues and ended the 1973 season poised to break Babe Ruth's record of 714 home runs. When the vice president of Magnavox offered $25,000 for the record-shattering ball, Adams parlayed the bid into a $1 million endorsement deal for Aaron and threw in the ball and bat for free.

Adams might have scored more successes if he'd scrambled harder and had more rapport with the players, or if he'd been able to get the Morris Agency to throw in legal and accounting services for the 10 percent commission they insisted on charging. Lawyers were beginning to make deals for pro athletes for only 5 percent, but when Adams went to Julius Lefkowitz with the idea of offering a package of services, he was told the Lefkowitz accounting firm didn't need any more business. Meanwhile, the whole idea of sports-as-showbiz was turning into a joke. "I wouldn't be surprised if we saw *The Hank Aaron Show* before long," a rival agent told *TV Guide*. "He'll be up there singing a duet with Secretariat."

In the spring of 1974, with Hank Aaron about to hit his record-breaking home run and baseball fans showering him with hate mail because he was black, Berle Adams was working on his most ambitious deal yet. He'd signed Jimmy Connors, the young tennis star who was having a much-publicized romance with Chris Evert, and now he was trying to sell them as the king and queen of tennis. He was in the middle of talks with Pepsi when a much better offer came in—not for Connors and Evert, but for Adams himself. Berry Gordy, the chairman of Motown, wanted him to be his chief operating officer, running the company while Gordy supervised the production of Diana Ross's second movie, *Mahogany*.

A lot had happened in the ten years since Diana Ross and the Supremes had bemoaned their fate to Wally Amos on the Steel Pier in Atlantic City. After thirteen number-one hits in five years, Ross had left the group to pursue a film career at $1 million a year. Berry Gordy had left the Motor City behind for a heavily guarded Bel Air estate graced with a private menagerie that included wild peacocks and a doe named Diana. Ross's agents at the Morris office had been pushing her to do a remake of *Born Yesterday*, but neither Gordy nor his star thought much of the idea of casting her as a black dumb blonde. They'd fallen for the idea of her playing a fashion designer in love with a black politician, yet desperate to escape the poverty and deprivation of her past. As far as Berle Adams was concerned, WMA Sports was a money-losing proposition with little prospect of a quick turnaround. So in March 1974, eight months after his arrival, the trades reported that Adams would head Motown and that WMA Sports would be folded into the agency.

PHIL WELTMAN HAD NOT ENDEARED HIMSELF TO THE LEFKOWITZ REGIME. He was a maverick, Sammy Weisbord said. Take his response to the news that Sid Sheinberg, the thirty-eight-year-old executive vice president in charge of Universal Television, was being made president of MCA. In June 1973, as Morris Stoller was setting up WMA Sports, MCA had announced that Lew Wasserman was succeeding the seventy-seven-year-old Jules Stein as chairman and that Sheinberg would take over as president. Weltman was sitting in the Beverly Hills office with Weisbord, Stoller, and Lefkowitz when he remarked that the Morris Agency ought to be thinking about getting some young people into the picture too.

What did he mean by that?

He meant they ought to pick a young guy and work with him—polish him up, make him important in the industry, groom him for the top job. Then he made a crack about how they shouldn't be running the Morris office like the Mormon church, whose ninety-six-year-old president had just died and been succeeded by a ninety-five-year-old.

Lefkowitz looked as if someone had thrust a dagger in his heart. He was sixty-eight, eight years older than Wasserman. And unlike Wasserman, he'd waited forty-six years to become president—forty-six patient, self-abnegating years of cleverly structured deals and mumbled directives at meetings and awkward silences at parties, while Lastfogel flitted back and forth between New York and the coast, playing the starmaker to Hollywood and Broadway and Madison Avenue. Finally, Lefkowitz had gotten his reward, and he didn't want to see it cut short. And what about Sammy Weisbord, who was nearly sixty-two and had sat at Lastfogel's feet from the age of nineteen?

Lefkowitz and Weisbord knew they'd have to let go eventually. But Lefkowitz had his own protégés—like Lee Stevens, the one he'd sent to law school and trained in every detail of the business. Stevens was solid, dependable, a great executive. Weltman didn't want him. He thought William Morris should be headed by an agent, not an administrator.

Then there was the incident over the New York Times article. The Times reporter had hung around for days, and when his article ran, in December 1973, it was headlined "William Morris Agency Marks 75 Years of 10%." Weltman had urged the reporter to spend some time with his young fellows before going back to New York, but the reporter hadn't gotten around to it. Instead he mentioned Sophie Tucker and E. F. Albee and Fanny Brice, along with more contemporary personalities such as Clint Eastwood and Sonny and Cher. He also noted the recent defection of several promising young agents and quoted Freddie Fields as saying, "I hope I have their energy when I'm their age."

Shortly afterward, Weltman had lunch at Hillcrest with Lastfogel, Weisbord, Morris Stoller, and Norman Brokaw. That was Lastfogel's daily lunch group—Sammy and Norm, and often Stoller as well. They were telling the Boss what they thought about the article—how wonderful it was, how it captured the essence of the company, etc., etc. Lastfogel sat with a big smile on his face as they all *schmikled* up to him. Weltman spoke last, and he dropped a bombshell. He didn't like the story one damn bit. It was a beautiful obituary for the Morris office. People would read it and know nothing about the agency today, or about the young fellows coming up.

The problem with Weltman's young fellows was that they were too much like Weltman. Mike Ovitz, for instance—a gap-toothed twenty-six-year-old who'd grown up in a tract house in the San Fernando Valley and now packaged game shows for daytime TV. Ovitz had wanted to be a doctor at first, but he'd worked part-time at Universal while taking his pre-med courses at UCLA, and in 1969, shortly after graduating, he'd gotten into the William Morris trainee program. As a junior agent, he'd worked for Howard West, who handled Motown for television and put together packages for the networks. Then he'd quit to go to law school—unlike Stevens and Lefkowitz, both of whom had gotten their law degrees at night. When he finished law school, he wanted to come back to the agency. West and Weltman talked Morris Stoller into hiring him back, but Weisbord wasn't happy about it. At a meeting a couple of weeks later, he turned to Weltman and asked what was going on: "This place isn't a revolving door," he snapped. "People can't come and go as they please."

Ovitz wasn't the only one loyal to Weltman. There was Rowland Perkins, thirty-nine, a packaging agent who'd gotten into the mail room through his friend's aunt, who was Loretta Young. There was Bill Haber, a thirty-year-old packaging agent who'd been Sy Marsh's secretary until Marsh left to partner with Sammy Davis, Jr. There was Ron Meyer, a twenty-eight-year-old ex-marine from West L.A. who'd succeeded Haber as cohead of the television talent department, which booked guest stars on series at $1,500 to $2,500 a pop. Weltman had hired him away from Paul Kohner, an old-line agent on Sunset who'd handled John Huston and Ingmar Bergman for years. As a high school dropout, he'd never have qualified for Morris's training program, but Weltman had decided to take a flier on him. Now he was almost like a son.

Within the department, Weltman was as loved as Weisbord was despised. They made a peculiar pair, the drill sergeant and the martinet. Weisbord gave tremendously stirring speeches, the kind that black-and-white movie generals delivered before sending their extras into battle, all about girding their loins and going forth to attack the enemy. Weltman was the tough guy, the grizzled taskmaster they could always count on to tend their wounds, to nurse them through thick and thin. As far as clients and deals and commissions were concerned, his productive years were probably over. But to his department—the most lucrative branch of the agency—he was the glue that held them together.

The question most of them had was, what did Phil see in Sammy Weisbord? What made them so close that people compared them to Damon and Pythias, the ancient Greeks whose bond was so true they took each other's place as hostage to the tyrant of Syracuse? With Sammy and Mr. Lastfogel, it was obvious—Sammy was the picture of devotion, the son he never had. Lastfogel was blind to his faults. Weltman wasn't blind, yet he was bound to Weisbord in some inexorable way, as a brother would be. Fate conquers judgment. Family leaves no room for choice.

But did Weisbord still feel bound to Weltman? It was hard to say. Something had shifted that night Phil told Sammy he was getting married, something deeper than two buddies making room for a wife. Maybe it wasn't Mrs. Lastfogel Sammy thought he should ask for permission, maybe it was Sammy himself. No one really knew. But twice in the past few months, Mrs. Lastfogel had stepped into Weltman's office and said, "You think he's a friend of yours?" As he sat looking at her, she smiled sadly and shook her head.

MORRIS STOLLER HAD ALWAYS BEEN CONCERNED ABOUT WASTE. HE WAS AN accountant. He'd come of age during the Depression. He worried about pencils and paper clips. When Milt Ebbins, Peter Lawford's manager, pointed out that they were losing thousands of dollars on secretaries phoning their relatives back East, he forgot about the pencils and paper clips and issued telephone logs to keep track of long-distance calls. By the spring of 1974, he had a real mess to clean up: WMA Sports.

In eight months, the division had lost hundreds of thousands of dollars, maybe as much as a quarter-million. It was embarrassing, not just to the agency, but to Stoller personally. What was he to do? Hours of discussion ensued. Finally he asked Weltman if he would take over. "Morris," Weltman replied, "there's nothing to take over." They had no scouts, no infrastructure, nothing but John Mackey and a few contracts. It was latrine duty, no question. Weltman wasn't going to get involved. But he was Stoller's friend, so he did agree to let them use his name in the press release.

The trades put a positive spin on the story. Describing WMA Sports as "a semidetached R&D unit to test the waters," *Daily Variety* reported that the Morris office "has now embarked full steam into the sports environment." But the industry knew better. The agency knew better. Weltman and Weisbord and Lefkowitz knew. Stoller himself knew. The Morris Agency had taken a sports plunge, all right, and it had gotten soaked in the process.

Stoller never showed strain under pressure. He thrived on the stuff, ate it for breakfast. But that spring, he began to crack. Milt Ebbins noticed the change when Weisbord ushered him into Stoller's office to discuss a commission. Ebbins was handling Vic Damone, who was working the Rainbow Room as a career move, even though with his backup combo and commission and other expenses it was costing him money. So Ebbins went to see Sam Weisbord, gave him the breakdown, and asked if the agency could waive its commission. Weisbord suggested they go across the hall to see Stoller.

Stoller was in a conference when they walked in, but Weisbord asked if he could listen to Ebbins. "*Now,* Sam?" It would only take a minute, Weisbord said, and laid out the situation himself. "*Over my dead body!*" Stoller cried. "I'll throw him out of the office! He's going to pay a commission like everybody else!"

Ebbins was white-faced. Weisbord hustled him back into his office and shut the door. "Morris is going through something," he explained.

One morning not long afterward, Stoller was asleep at his house in Holmby Hills when his wife tried to wake him up. She shook him, called out: no response. Frantic, she dialed 911. An ambulance was dispatched to take him to the hospital, where he was quickly revived. He was back at home a few days later, but he was in no shape to come to the office. He started seeing a psychiatrist daily. Everything was kept very quiet.

*   *   *

In the fall of 1974, with Morris Stoller out of commission, Nat Lefkowitz and Sam Weisbord began planning a reorganization of the television department. After several years as head of television world-wide, Weisbord wanted to expand his portfolio to include all agency activities. Norman Brokaw, who'd succeeded Weisbord as head of the West Coast television office, would likewise be moving into all areas. The post of worldwide television chief would go to Lou Weiss, who'd been cohead of the New York department since Wally Jordan's retire-ment. The question was, who would take over West Coast television?

Phil Weltman's candidate was Rowland Perkins. He'd been groom-ing Perkins for the job, and most people on El Camino assumed Perkins would get it. Despite his casual manner, Perkins was a power-house, and he was popular in the department besides—a nice guy, someone they could work with. In the past couple of years, he'd put together a trio of packaging agents who covered the three networks on the coast. Just as Lou Weiss, Sol Leon, and a third agent named Larry Auerbach had worked with the networks' top brass in New York, Perkins and his crew had become the liaison for the networks' West Coast programming executives. Perkins covered CBS; Bill Haber, another of Weltman's boys, handled NBC; and Mike Rosenfeld, who'd been foundering as a motion picture agent until Perkins brought him over to television, took care of ABC. But New York was where the networks were headquartered, and Perkins and Haber and Rosenfeld had often found themselves second-guessed by the New York office.

Now the business was changing. Production was already centered on the coast, and more and more programming decisions were being made there as well. Costs were so high that ad agencies were buying sixty-sec-ond spots instead of entire shows, so there was little need to work with Madison Avenue. Producers were developing network series on their own rather than pay packaging fees: After his success with "The Mod Squad," Aaron Spelling had left the agency in 1972 and gone into part-nership with former ABC programming chief Leonard Goldberg, and neither Norman Lear, creator of the hugely popular "All in the Family," nor MTM Enterprises, producer of "The Mary Tyler Moore Show," saw any more need for agency representation than Spelling and Goldberg did. Morris's packaging revenues were down from $7.2 million in the late sixties to $3 million in the current 1974–1975 season, and many of the shows it did have had been sold on the coast. The New York office had less and less to do. Rowland Perkins and his group looked more and more like a bunch of young turks who needed reining in. So Lefkowitz had picked someone else for the West Coast television job: Larry Auerbach, from New York.

Auerbach was a lifer. Like Lou Weiss and Lefkowitz's protégé Lee Stevens, he was part of the thirty-third-floor group, the inner circle that sat around Lefkowitz on the top floor of the New York headquarters. He'd started in the mail room at fifteen and risen to become the main contact for ABC during the fifties and sixties. He was eager to come out to the coast. Instead they'd made him head of the New York motion picture department, but the appointment wasn't going over well with the other agents there. To Weltman he was a nebbish, a guy without fight or bite.

Weltman was irate, and Perkins and the others were no happier. It was like being told their dad was going to come watch over them. Late that fall, Sammy Weisbord chaired a special meeting of the department to discuss the changes. One by one, the guys spoke their piece, offering their reasons why Perkins should get the job. Weisbord listened, then announced that the decision had already been made. Fait accompli. Thank you very much.

There was one other matter to be settled. A bit of unfinished business Lefkowitz was eager to get off his plate. In early December, back from a trip to New York to discuss the changes, Weisbord showed up at Weltman's door, just down the hall from Lastfogel's corner office. It was mid-afternoon, about three o'clock. "How'd it go?" Weltman said, standing up to grab Weisbord's hand. Weisbord blurted out the news: "You were put in the computer," he said, "and found wanting."

11

WELTMAN'S REVENGE

Los Angeles/New York, 1974-1976

AT FIRST, WELTMAN DIDN'T KNOW WHAT SAMMY WAS TALKING ABOUT. *PUT in the computer and found wanting?* What kind of thing was that to say? As the realization that he was being fired slowly flooded his brain, he went into a kind of shock. Finally, he managed to say the only thing that came to mind: "What do you think *I* would have done if the situation had been reversed?" Weisbord gave him a long, hard look and walked out.

Weltman sat alone at his desk, numb with despair. After thirty-five years, his best friend had just told him he was worthless. His best friend, for whom he'd practically have been ready to lay down his life. He felt betrayed. He felt degraded. He felt like a charity case. He couldn't believe it was happening.

His office was quiet that afternoon, very quiet. Morris Stoller was still out, recovering. Stan Kamen stopped by for a long chat. No one else.

Weltman called his boys down, one or two at a time. When he told Mike Ovitz and Ron Meyer, they made a confession: They'd been thinking of going into business for themselves. They'd been planning it for months, but they hadn't been able to tell him. This made it easy.

Every afternoon about five, Frances Arms marched down the street from the Beverly Wilshire to pick up her Abe for dinner. This afternoon, when she got to his big corner office and found out about Phil, she became hysterical. Frances didn't share Abe's affection for Sammy—if anything, she seemed jealous—but Phil was her boy. Sammy hadn't told her what Lefkowitz was planning, probably hadn't dared to. Now Lastfogel had to ask Weltman to come talk to her. If he couldn't calm her down, Lastfogel said, he was going to have to call the doctor.

Weltman idolized Mrs. Lastfogel. To him, she had a heart as big as the world. If Sammy had been like a brother to him, Frances was like a mother. He found her sobbing and shaking in a chair. For forty minutes he held her in his arms and tried to comfort her. Then, when the shaking stopped, he stood up quietly and left.

The official, in-house explanation for Weltman's dismissal was advancing years: A mandatory age-sixty-five retirement policy had been instituted, though obviously it didn't apply to Lefkowitz. But the story of Sammy's treachery got around quickly. Only Rowland Perkins didn't hear it; he was in Europe on vacation. When he came back, his secretary told him he had a lunch meeting with Weltman at the Brown Derby. "I wanted you to hear this first from me," Weltman said when they sat down.

Perkins was stunned. *Put in the computer and found wanting?* That was because most of the deals that came Weltman's way he handed off to younger guys. And for Weisbord to have done it? Weltman was desolate, destroyed. "I feel like I've lied to you all these years," he said. "This is no family."

A few days later, the boys in the television department gave him a farewell dinner at a restaurant on LaBrea. Seventeen of them—from Mike Ovitz and Ron Meyer to Howard West and George Shapiro, who'd left the year before to open a management office down the street—pooled their money to pay for a plaque:

TO PHIL WELTMAN

With gratitude and appreciation from his team

DECEMBER 6, 1974

Ovitz and Meyer weren't the only ones who were thinking about leaving. With Weltman gone and Larry Auerbach coming in to run the department, there was little to hold any of them there. For months, Rowland Perkins, Bill Haber, and Mike Rosenfeld had talked about starting their own agency. As the holidays approached, they learned that Ovitz and Meyer had the same idea.

When Howard West and George Shapiro left the agency, Ovitz had taken over West's job, packaging daytime TV shows and handling the Motown account. Now he and Meyer went to West for advice. Should they join forces with the other three or go it alone? The only client they had with any name value was Sally Struthers, who played Carroll O'Connor's daughter in "All in the Family," the CBS sitcom that was number one in the Nielsens now for the fourth straight season. West advised them to go with Perkins and his group. Five people forming an agency would have a broad base of clients and expertise, he told them. They'd get much more than five times as much business.

Later that month, the two groups got together for the first time at Perkins's house in Bel Air. The chemistry was immediate. The timing seemed right. There were three big agencies in town—William Morris, CMA, and Ted Ashley's old firm, now known as the International Famous Agency. There were a lot of smaller agencies, but none that were bringing any new energy to the business. They saw an opening and decided to go for it.

Perkins's group had invited a sixth agent—one of Ron Meyer's best friends—to join them. He wasn't at the meeting, but a few nights later he said yes over the phone. The next morning, he called back and said no.

They set a date a couple of months away to make their move. That would give them until March—time to get organized, secure a line of credit, find office space, make a graceful exit. Then they'd tell Weisbord, and because spring was television season, they'd offer to stay until the network schedules were set.

They couldn't tell anybody yet, because they didn't want word to leak out. But they did go to Wells Fargo to ask about securing a line of credit. And they started waking up in the middle of the night. That's when it hit them: Their lives were about to change forever. They'd be working seven days a week, no pay, no guarantees. They were married men. They had responsibilities. Perkins, Rosenfeld, and Haber had kids, and Meyer was about to get married. But it was too late for any of them to pull out now.

*   *   *

Tuesday, January 7. Mike Rosenfeld got an early morning phone call from a New York entertainment lawyer who'd been told about their plans. Message was brief and to the point: They know you're leaving.

Mike Ovitz was off on a skiing trip. Ron Meyer was lying in bed in his little apartment a block down Charleville from the Morris office, immobilized by the flu. Over lunch, Rosenfeld told Perkins not to be surprised if he got a call from Weisbord. When they got back to the office, Perkins had a message: See Weisbord at once.

Weisbord had always been volatile. A couple of years earlier, he'd nearly punched out Milt Ebbins in the parking lot when Ebbins had the temerity to suggest that the Morris office wasn't God. This time he was near apoplexy. But he kept it under control. He walked Perkins over on Charleville, up and down the side streets, Camden, Bedford, Rexford, past the little stucco apartment houses full of dotty pensioners and washed-up PR men and aspiring actors, French provincial and Spanish colonial and would-be Norman, and the little stucco houses with their palm trees and rose gardens out front, up and down, over and across, burning shoe leather. Finally he said, very casually, "Morris Stoller told me he understands that five of you are leaving the company."

Perkins stopped. "Well, Sam," he said, "this is something we were going to come in and talk to you about tomorrow." Not true, and Sammy knew it.

Sammy drew himself up and stood nose-to-nose with Perkins—or nose-to-chin, since Perkins was several inches taller. "Now, Perkins," he cried, waving his finger in front of Perkins's face, "this is treason!" Ten minutes of rage, vitriol, and disbelief ensued—why, if he'd only stopped and thought, a person of Perkins's character . . . Finally Perkins yelled, "Stop it!" If that's really what Weisbord thought, he was a jerk for letting it go so long.

They walked back in silence.

Rosenfeld and Bill Haber were called in later that afternoon. Ron Meyer got a phone call at home, but he was too sick to speak. No one could reach Ovitz. Rosenfeld lived nearby, so he went to Ovitz's house and left a note on his door: You're no longer working at William Morris. Call me.

On Friday afternoon, after talks with agency attorney Roger Davis and Walt Zifkin, Morris Stoller's administrative lieutenant, the five defectors found themselves on the street—no desks, no telephones, no office. But

Davis and Zifkin did let them buy the cars the agency had provided them, and when Rosenfeld asked David Wolper, the longtime Morris client who produced the hit sitcom "Chico and the Man," if they could use his offices until they found permanent quarters, the agency didn't stand in their way. Even Weisbord managed to curb his temper when the story broke. "These are all good men," he told *Variety*. "We have no animus."

Weisbord could afford to look generous, since the renegades were going into business without any clients. Several clients did follow them over the next few weeks, but their commissions stayed at Morris until their agency papers ran out. Even so, the new partners secured a $100,000 line of credit from Security Pacific Bank, and on January 22, they announced their name—Creative Artists Agency. They figured that's what they were, an agency that handled creative artists. They found a modest spread in the Hong Kong Bank Building a few blocks away on Wilshire, and for $200, Milt Ebbins sold them some used office furniture he had in storage. They bought a conference table from a discount store in the Valley and brought card tables and folding chairs from home. They hired a secretary, but they couldn't afford a receptionist, so their wives came in to cover the front desk. They were scared.

Back at the Morris office, the mood was bleak. People were already aware of a vacuum where Morris Stoller had been. They'd seen Weltman chopped off at the knees, and with him Joe Schoenfeld, cohead of the motion picture department, who was let go at the same time. Now an enormous chunk had been ripped out of the television operation. But to the men who ran the agency it seemed like no big deal: Mike Rosenfeld they didn't care about, Ronnie Meyer they'd been ready to let go until Weltman intervened, Mike Ovitz they disliked despite his incontestable flair for agenting. . . . The only one they were actually sorry to lose was the new agency's president, Rowland Perkins, who was also the one who brought in the most income. These guys weren't *executives*, Lefkowitz announced dismissively. They were just shoe-leather agents.

Then Lefkowitz made his next move.

Morris Stoller had been out of the office for months. He might or might not be coming back. Lefkowitz had discovered him at Brooklyn College night school thirty-eight years before, had brought him into the agency, had made him his protégé and taught him the business and sent him out to the coast to run the office there. His brother and Stoller's brother were partners in the agency's accounting firm, which had moved out to Beverly Hills as well. But Lefkowitz wasn't the sentimental type. Stoller would have to go.

This time, Sammy Weisbord spilled to the Boss.

Abe Lastfogel hadn't seen fit to intervene when Weltman was fired. Lastfogel didn't intervene in much of anything anymore. He came to the office wearing his bow tie and he smiled his dazzling smile and he let his boy Sammy run the show. Phil Weltman was a maverick, just like Sammy said. Maybe even disloyal, the way Lefkowitz seemed to think. But Morris Stoller was different. Morris Stoller had had as much to do with building the company as Lefkowitz had, maybe more. Let him go, now that he was sick? Not as long as I'm here, Lastfogel declared.

The top guys in both offices were quietly lining up, taking the count, one side or the other. Nat Stoller and Julius Lefkowitz were at each others' throats. But there were only four men on the board—Lastfogel, Lefkowitz, Weisbord, and Stoller. Lefkowitz was in New York. Lastfogel and Weisbord and Stoller were in Beverly Hills. When Lastfogel and Weisbord stood up against him, Lefkowitz found himself alone.

The whole thing was kept very quiet, even quieter than the move against Bill Morris, Jr. Months later, in August 1975, Weisbord did confirm reports that he'd soon be taking over as president while Lefkowitz moved upstairs to some as-yet undefined position. By that time, Stoller had recovered and returned to the office, somewhat horrified by all that had happened in his absence. If he'd been well, he told friends, the defections would never have taken place. He wouldn't have chewed out the five guys and branded them traitors. He'd have gone to Rowland Perkins and made him an offer he couldn't refuse—an offer so rich that even if Perkins had wanted to turn it down, his wife wouldn't have let him.

Stoller also sought out Phil Weltman. He wanted to tell Weltman that if he hadn't been ill, he'd never have let him be fired. It had been nearly twenty-eight years since he and Sammy met Weltman at Union Station and ushered him to his new home at the Chateau Marmont—twenty-eight years of working together day-by-day, building the Beverly Hills office from a fragile postwar outpost to the powerhouse it was today. Stoller tried to speak, but words failed him and tears began to form in his eyes.

THE BIG NEWS IN THE AGENCY BUSINESS AS 1975 BEGAN WASN'T THE impending transition at William Morris or the puzzling defection of five television agents to form yet another diddly-squat office on Wilshire Boulevard. The big news was the December 30 buyout of Freddie Fields's Creative Management Associates by Marvin Josephson and his International Famous Agency.

By this time, Fields had established himself as the most powerful motion-picture agent in the Hollywood. In addition to Newman and Redford and McQueen, he and his people represented nearly every top star in the business—James Caan, Dustin Hoffman, Ali MacGraw, Al Pacino, Barbra Streisand. He'd negotiated development deals for directors that gave him, Freddie Fields, an agent, automatic authority to green-light a picture if any one of five actors said yes to a script—five actors, each of whom he handled, with the exception of Clint Eastwood. When Fox and Warner Bros. were developing competing pictures about an out-of-control fire in a giant office tower, he'd gotten them to merge their productions, then cast it from his own client list: Newman, McQueen, Faye Dunaway, Fred Astaire, Richard Chamberlain. *The Towering Inferno* was a blockbuster hit that Christmas of 1974—Hollywood's top-grossing disaster movie, at a time when disaster movies ruled the box office. And Josephson's International Famous Agency, successor to the old Ashley Famous, was almost as high-profile in television as CMA was in pictures.

Merger talks had been rumored for more than a year, but Fields had flatly denied that anything was in the offing. Then Fields's partner, David Begelman, was hired away to run Columbia Pictures, which was flirting with bankruptcy after dropping a cool $50 million in 1973. Another partner, Richard Shepherd, went to Warner Bros. to become a production executive. Suddenly, Fields was left to deal with everything. McQueen would phone and Fields would have to drive out beyond Malibu to Trancas, where McQueen was living with Ali MacGraw, star of *Love Story* and ex-wife of Paramount's boy-wonder production chief, Robert Evans. He'd sit around watching McQueen polish motorbikes all day, and when he finally made it back to the office there'd be a pile of angry messages from Paul Newman, who'd been trying to reach him since mid-morning. And if it wasn't the clients, it was the agents—Stevie Phillips calling from New York, where she handled Liza Minnelli and Robert Redford, complaining because Sue

Mengers in the West Coast office was getting something she wasn't. Or vice versa. Or both.

The deal was sweet. Marvin Josephson Associates, IFA's parent company, agreed to pay $6.10 a share for CMA—a hefty premium over its current price of $3.25. That gave Fields $900,000 for his 15 percent stake. Josephson agreed to pay another $900,000 for Fields's house in Beverly Hills, which it would then rent back to him for just $1,250 a month. It would also pay him $675,000 in salary over the next thirty-three months and give him an option to buy seventy-five thousand shares of Josephson stock at $1 a share.

The merger went through on January 1, creating a firm with 125 agents to Morris's 139 and revenues that would equal if not exceed the $20 million or so Morris was now said to be drawing in commissions each year. For the first time since MCA was forced out in 1962, the Morris office would face competition from another agency behemoth with muscle in every area of the business—and that behemoth would have Freddie Fields at its helm.

Except that Fields, like Lew Wasserman before him, wasn't content with being an agent. Sellers had more power than ever, but the prestige, the excitement, and the status were still reserved for buyers. So was the big dough. The money Fields was collecting from the CMA sale was chump change compared to the millions his client Irwin Allen would be raking in as producer of *The Towering Inferno*, which Fields had put together. Fields's contract with the new agency, which they'd decided to call International Creative Management, ran for almost three years, but it had two renewal options—escape hatches that would give him a chance to bail out if he got the right offer. The first option came up in September.

In June, after months of speculation, Fields confirmed reports that he'd reached an agreement with Barry Diller—Phil Weltman's former secretary, recently ensconced as chairman of Paramount—to set up a production company that would make six pictures a year for the next five years. A couple of weeks later, Guy McElwaine, who'd been head of CMA's motion picture division, took over as production chief at Warner Bros. Mike Medavoy, head of IFA's motion picture department, had already left to become production chief at United Artists. Which left the spotlight on the one figure at ICM who'd been getting more and more attention anyway: Sue Mengers.

Five-foot-two, blond, and zaftig, swaddled in caftans and shielded by enormous tinted eyeglasses, Sue Mengers was an agent with star power—not just her clients', but her own. *Time, New York, Women's Wear Daily, Ms.,* "60 Minutes"—she was getting so much attention, she made Freddie Fields look self-effacing. Stephen Sondheim and Tony Perkins used her as the model for the agent character in *The Last of Sheila,* their cinematic roman à clef about six Hollywood types trapped on a yacht on the Riviera with a sadistic producer. Joyce Haber, the Hedda Hopper replacement at the *Los Angeles Times,* dubbed her "superagent." Producers compared her to a Sherman tank. She was brash and ballsy and utterly relentless. But the key was that face-against-the-glass quality, those years she'd spent on the outside looking in.

Having escaped the Holocaust as an infant, she'd grown up in Utica, New York, until her father committed suicide; then her mother moved them to the Bronx and worked as a bookkeeper to support them. Sue started out a receptionist at MCA, then worked as a secretary at the Broadway booking agency of Baum & Newborn and later at the Morris office, where she stayed late every night and eyed the men with big expense accounts and resolved to have one herself someday. A former coworker ended her Tillie the Toiler phase, as she called it, when he took her into partnership as an agent in 1963. She got Gore Vidal to introduce her to Paul Newman and Joanne Woodward over dinner at Sardi's, and before long she was telling them about these wonderful plays they ought to be doing. That got David Begelman's attention, and in 1965 he offered her a job in the New York office of CMA. From there it was a short hop to Hollywood.

Mengers was funny and outrageous and incredibly aggressive, and she cut a broad swath through the picture community. Driving down Sunset one day, she spied Burt Lancaster in the next lane, pulled up beside him, rolled down her window, and yelled out, "Oh, Mr. Lancaster, who represents you?" "IFA," he called back. "Not for long!" she cried. She walked up to Ryan O'Neal at a party and said, "When are you going to get rid of your dumb asshole of an agent?" Lancaster resisted her charms, but O'Neal succumbed—as did Richard Benjamin, Paula Prentiss, and Tony Perkins. Freddie was impressed.

When she wasn't signing clients, Mengers was doing deals. She made her reputation with *What's Up, Doc?,* the 1972 Peter Bogdanovich picture with Barbra Streisand and Ryan O'Neal. She'd signed O'Neal four months before the release of *Love Story,* the 1970 weeper he'd agreed to do for a mere $22,500. She'd signed Bogdanovich just before Columbia released his breakthrough feature, *The Last Picture Show*. She was chummy with Streisand, who was still being handled by Begelman and Fields. So she put them together—got O'Neal $300,000 for the male lead, talked Streisand into reading for Bogdanovich. The movie turned out second-rate, but it was the deal that mattered, because it showed Hollywood that Mengers could assemble a package as deftly as her boss.

Other deals followed: Bogdanovich's next picture, *Paper Moon*, which she put together at Paramount even though Ryan O'Neal and Robert Evans had stopped speaking to each other. *Chinatown*, Evans's first picture as an independent producer, which she got for Faye Dunaway after Jane Fonda turned him down. But it was the dinner parties that took her beyond the realm of ordinary Hollywood flesh-peddler chutzpah and made her truly, truly fabulous. She cast them as if they were film packages—a couple of major stars, a director or two, an A-list producer, a top studio exec, maybe a smidgen of visiting royalty. They might complain about the food—"camel shit," groused Paramount president Frank Yablans—but they loved the company. Julie Christie met Princess Margaret at the old place in Beverly Hills, the little view house up above Pickfair. Now Sue and her Parisian screenwriter husband, Jean-Claude Tramont, were living in Zsa Zsa Gabor's place high up on Bel Air Road—a real movie-star house, all French and châteauy, with five bathrooms and marble floors and the whole city laid out below. La Mengers had arrived.

In November 1974, shortly before the IFA-CMA merger went through, amid press reports that she might assume Evans's job at Paramount or take a similar position under Begelman at Columbia, Mengers negotiated herself a package worth some $200,000 a year in stock options, expense account, and salary. Eight months later, she made a deal with the new agency, ICM, that gave her a $50,000 raise. Marvin Josephson, her new boss, didn't believe in lavish spending, but here he had little choice. With Begelman, Fields, Guy McElwaine, and Mike Medavoy all gone, Mengers now handled most of ICM's stars and many of its top directors: Streisand, O'Neal, Bogdanovich, Candice Bergen, Cher, Faye Dunaway, Bob Fosse, Gene Hackman, Sidney Lumet, Ali MacGraw, Arthur Penn, Herb Ross, Cybill Shepherd, Tuesday Weld. . . . Names that added up to a good $1.5 million a year in commissions. And she'd just been offered an extremely lucrative deal to defect to William Morris, where she'd have worked side-by-side with its newly named motion picture chief, Stan Kamen.

Stan Kamen and Sue Mengers: It was hard in that summer of 1975 to imagine two agents who resembled each other less. Kamen was a study in gray, zipped up and buttoned down. Mengers was a primary color, flamboyant and outrageous. He was the Morris office personified—conservative, old-school, operating in the shadows. She was the New Hollywood—exotic and vulgar, flourishing in the too-hot sunlight like some outlandish tropical flower. There were other agents who handled stars, among them Leonard Hirshan of the Morris office, who had Clint Eastwood and Jack Lemmon and Walter Matthau. But only Kamen played in the same league with Mengers.

A few years earlier, Stan Kamen had been nothing more than a television agent on the rise. He'd had one client who'd popped—Steve McQueen—and he hadn't been able to keep him. That hurt. But he'd held on to Jon Voight at the height of Voight's stardom, through *Midnight Cowboy* and an Oscar nomination and *Deliverance*, despite Freddie Fields's increasingly frenzied attempts to lure him to CMA. He had Goldie Hawn, the "Laugh-In" star, who'd won an Oscar playing opposite Matthau in *Cactus Flower* and starred in *There's a Girl in My Soup* and *The Sugarland Express*, by a new director named Steven Spielberg. He'd taken over Warren Beatty after Lastfogel retired and put him in *McCabe and Mrs. Miller*, and although Beatty had turned down the leads in *The Way We Were*, *The Sting*, *The Great Gatsby*, *Last Tango in Paris*, and several other major projects, Kamen had gotten him to star in Alan Pakula's *The Parallax View*.

Then, in February 1975, with Freddie Fields running the newly merged ICM, Morris Stoller had announced that Kamen would be taking over as head of the motion picture department. With Joe Schoenfeld out and his cohead, Phil Kellogg, nearing retirement age as well, a shake-up was in the offing, but Kamen hadn't gotten the job without a fight. Stoller had planned to give it to Robert Shapiro, a onetime Weltman protégé who'd been brought back to Beverly Hills after six years running the London office and handling such stars as Richard Harris, Peter Sellers, Omar Sharif, and Peter Ustinov. When Kamen found out, he told Stoller that he and Lenny Hirshan would walk if Shapiro were put in charge. Then he went to Hirshan and told him what he'd done.

Now he was heir to Johnny Hyde and Bert Allenberg—a powerful position, and a good time to be assuming it. The studios were buying again, the disaster of the early seventies forgotten after the jackpot success of *The Godfather*, Paramount's big-budget gamble of 1972, which pulled in so much dough that Gulf + Western rethought its decision to sell off the studio's venerable lot in Hollywood. The fact that Kamen and Mengers were such opposites worked to his advantage, because now there were only two major agencies left—ICM and William Morris. Stars who'd left Freddie Fields's office to go with International Famous weren't going to leave ICM for some little agent with only a couple of big-name clients. Being a star meant having a star agent, and right now there were only two flavors in town—exploding passionfruit crush and premium vanilla.

Mengers could have the headlines and the interviews and the gossip column mentions. Kamen wanted none of it. He followed Abe Lastfogel's old credo—stay in the background, let the client draw the spotlight. If Beatty was around and a photographer showed up, Kamen would drift imperceptibly away. So while Mengers collected more ink than some of the people she represented, Kamen remained in the shadows, unnoticed by the press, known only to the buyers.

Out of the office, he lived almost reclusively. He kept mum about his personal life. Every evening he made the long drive out to Malibu. He'd bought some land in the early sixties, two-and-a-half acres in Point Dume, ten miles beyond the Colony. People thought he was crazy, but to him it was paradise—a secluded hideaway on a narrow country lane, at the edge of a cliff overlooking the nude beach at Pirate's Cove, with Santa Catalina Island offshore and the Los Angeles beach towns curving off to the left. He'd planted jade trees at the edge of the lawn and installed a hot tub by the cliff, and at the end of a long drive he'd built a sprawling, one-story house that was now half-hidden by cascades of red bougainvillea. Inside it was dark and cozy, a luxurious cave with terracotta floors and brick walls and beamed ceilings and beige shag carpeting. Outside, in the enclosed courtyard with its swimming pool and its statue of a nude youth greeting the sun, bronze penis outlined against the sky, it was private and secret and sybaritic.

Despite the contrast between them, Kamen and Mengers were good friends. He thought she was a hoot. She thought he was adorable. They'd competed for years, but it was a kissy-kissy rivalry. They'd have dinner every few months, not to commiserate (that was a service they reserved for their clients) but to enjoy each other's company. When the merger happened and she didn't get that production job, he'd started courting her the way he might court one of her clients. And she was tempted—she loved the idea of working with him. But in the end it was just a lateral move, going from one big agency to another. When Josephson made it profitable to stay, she turned Kamen down.

Kamen wasn't a chaser like Mengers, but he was a signer. There aren't many signers in the business; most agents just make deals. But Kamen, like Lastfogel and Harry Kalcheim before him, could see talent where others didn't. He also had a magnetic ability to draw stars to his side. It had to do with his charm—his warmth, his sense of humor, his way of telling a good story. He didn't call a prospective client every day, asking them this, telling them about that. He was more subtle, insinuating. His Virginia schooling had taken the edge off the New York aggression that was so common in Hollywood, layered it with a patina of Southern charm. He was gentle, yet tough. Quiet, yet effective. He inspired confidence—and what is agenting but a confidence game?

There was the day Al Pacino called. Pacino was enormous—star of *The Godfather* and *Serpico* and *Dog Day Afternoon*, which was already becoming one of the top-grossing films of 1975. He'd dropped Freddie Fields and put his career in the hands of Marty Bregman, his manager-producer. Then he and Bregman had a falling out. So he called the Morris Agency in New York, told them he was Al Pacino, and asked to be put through to the top man. The switchboard operator thought he was a crank and cut him off. He called back and got her to connect him with Nat Lefkowitz's office. Lefkowitz was out, but his secretary took the message. When Lefkowitz got back, he phoned Kamen on the coast and told him to get to New York immediately. Kamen flew in the next day, met with Pacino, and signed him on the spot.

That summer he also signed Sylvester Stallone, a struggling actor who'd written a script about a would-be boxing champ and sold it to Irwin Winkler, who'd graduated from the Morris mail room and into production, and his partner, Robert Chartoff, on condition that he star in the picture himself. *Rocky* had been shot in twenty-eight days for less than $1 million, but it had a fairy-tale quality that was pure Hollywood. Kamen was good friends with Stallone's manager and with Mike Medavoy at UA, both of whom were convinced they had box-office gold. When they screened the picture for him in July, four months before its release, he responded instantly. "Saw the picture last week and it is terrific," he wrote in a memo to Lefkowitz and his top aides, Howard Hausman and Lee Stevens. ". . . it's a sleeper and he's going to be a huge star. I am commencing negotiation for him to write, star and produce his next film for Chartoff-Winkler-UA."

Other clients were harder to land. Kamen was trying to seduce Robert Redford, but so far, no dice. He was friendly with Sydney Pollack, the director who'd worked with Redford in *Jeremiah Johnson*, *The Way We Were*, and *Three Days of the Condor*, but Pollack remained loyal to ICM. And there was a limit to what Kamen would do to get a client. He honored the Morris tradition of refusing to raid smaller agencies—a tradition that had sometimes been honored mainly in the breach, as Phil Gersh discovered with David Niven. Kamen would go after an ICM client who seemed vulnerable, but if the client called him, he thought it only sporting to let the other agent know. He figured there was business enough for everybody.

That gentlemanly quality was a big part of his appeal. So was his vulnerability, in an odd way. Much of Kamen's charisma involved strength—his detachment, his reserve, his quiet self-confidence. Yet what really hooked them was his human side, the feelings he hid just beneath the surface. The experience with Steve McQueen had left him with a tough shell. "They all fuck you," he warned his nephew, who'd joined the training program in New York. "You've got to get used to it." But he couldn't help letting people know there was a person inside, not just a booker. They sensed it was more than just business to him.

Mengers shared his cynicism and took it further. She knew you could work your ass off for your clients and it wouldn't mean shit. When they're hot they want to think they did it on their own, not because their agent promised his firstborn to the director just to get them a meeting. And when they're cold they need to think it's the agent's fault, not because nobody wants them anymore. If you took it seriously, you'd be setting yourself up for a fall. "Honey," she'd tell her colleagues, "remember one thing—they'll always leave you. When you're friends, you'll get an extra month.

"So don't let 'em into your heart," she'd go on. "You may have a great time with them, they may invite you over for dinner, and they *do* love you, because you're smart and you're funny. But guess what? You can't open up to them. Sure, you can call 'em at 3:00 A.M. and they'll come over. And if you say, 'I can't stand my job and I'm so upset and frustrated I can't get out of bed in the morning,' they'll feel for you. Then they'll go home.

They'll go to bed, and then they'll wake up. And when they wake up they'll say, 'This person is responsible for my *career!*' So—don't ever forget."

But every rule has its exceptions. For Mengers, the exception was Streisand. They had such history together—the years of friendship before Sue took over from Freddie Fields, all the deals she'd done since, most recently the deal for Barbra and her hairdresser-boyfriend Jon Peters to produce their remake of *A Star Is Born*, a deal that was going to earn Streisand at least $10 million. Why, Barbra had even been matron of honor at Sue's wedding. "I know they'll all leave me," she'd sigh, "except Barbra."

LOU WEISS WAS A NATURAL AS WORLDWIDE HEAD OF TELEVISION. HE knew everybody—network chairmen, news and entertainment presidents, programming vice presidents, first-name basis. He was playing tennis one Saturday morning with ABC Television president Frederick J. Pierce—Fred—when he casually mentioned a client: Barbara Walters. It was March 1976. The weather was unseasonably warm for New York. They were on the court behind Weiss's baronial-looking mansion in Scarsdale, not far from Pierce's own house. Barbara Walters had spent twelve years as an interviewer and screen personality for NBC's "Today," the last two years as cohost. Now Weiss was suggesting that she might be amenable to a move—under the right conditions, of course, and for an appropriate sum of money.

Walters had come to the Morris Agency in the mid-sixties, shortly after being promoted from writer to on-camera reporter, because her husband, a Philadelphia summer-stock producer, was a friend of Lee Stevens. She was the "Today" girl then, the perky, effervescent counterpart to genial Hugh Downs on America's morning wake-up show. Later, with the help of a top PR firm, she'd become one of the best-known personalities in broadcasting, shedding the bubbly "Today" girl image for a new identity as a woman reporter—one of the first. She was an aggressive interviewer, eager verging on shrill. But no one could call her a ratings hog: "Today" had dropped over the past year, and a recent NBC documentary she'd narrated, "Children of Divorce," came in dead last for the week.

Lou Weiss didn't let this bother him as he made his nonchalant come-on to Fred Pierce. He knew ABC was interested in her because

Jack Hausman, an ABC board member and a good friend of ABC chairman Leonard Goldenson, had brought it up with her more than once. Hausman and Goldenson each had a child with cerebral palsy; the two men and their wives had put on benefits together since the forties and helped set up a national cerebral palsy organization. Walters had gotten to know them because her retarded sister had gone to a cerebral palsy training center on Long Island. But she hadn't been interested in ABC before because Hausman was thinking of her for its morning show, "Good Morning, America." After getting up at 4:00 A.M. five days a week for more than a decade, Walters was ready for a change.

Fred Pierce wanted to know what sort of job Barbara would be interested in. And for what kind of money.

Maybe she could coanchor the evening news, Weiss suggested. And do some prime-time specials. For, say, a million a year. Your serve.

It was no secret that ABC wanted a boost for its news department. After being locked into third place for most of its history, the network had made tremendous progress in the eighteen months since Pierce had taken over as president. It had started picking up viewers with its innovative sports coverage—the Olympics, "Monday Night Football," "Wide World of Sports," which covered everything from Formula One racing to U.S.–Soviet track meets. In June 1975, Pierce had made Fred Silverman, the CBS programming whiz, president of ABC Entertainment. Six months later, Silverman's mid-season shuffle took ABC to number one in the prime-time ratings war. Now it was only news that kept ABC behind.

"The ABC Evening News" was barely in the running with the CBS news program, anchored by Walter Cronkite, and the NBC news with John Chancellor. In the past three years its numbers had slipped alarmingly, from a respectable 22 percent of the audience to as little as 10 percent. Besides low morale, the news operation was hamstrung by limited resources and a meager budget. They could beef it up, open more bureaus, go for credibility. But a marketing study showed that audiences already considered the three newsgathering organizations to be about equal in ability. What viewers noticed was the anchorman's appeal and the popularity of the local newscasts that served as lead-ins. Harry Reasoner, ABC's white-haired anchor, was affable and droll, but he didn't convey urgency.

ABC News president Bill Sheehan had been thinking for some time about pairing Reasoner with a woman. When Pierce came in on Monday and asked what he thought about Barbara Walters, Sheehan got excited right away. This would be a shot in the arm, just what they'd all been looking for. As for the million-dollar price, he could split it with the entertainment division, which would pick up the tab for the specials she'd do.

The deal would also be a shot in the arm for William Morris, whose television business, already in decline when its West Coast packaging agents defected to form CAA, was now crippled by a bitter feud with producers over packaging fees. The Writers Guild of America West— its negotiating committee led by a former Morris client named Danny Arnold, cocreator of the hit sitcom "Barney Miller"—had refused nearly a year ago to renew its agreement okaying the practice and was locked in a court battle with the Morris office as a result. Morris, which depended on packaging for about 35 percent of its income, had been unable to sign any new writers since. If a settlement wasn't reached by December, when its last remaining writers' agreements were due to expire, it would essentially be out of the packaging business.

From the agency's point of view, $1 million a year for Barbara Walters—at a time when Walter Cronkite, John Chancellor, and Harry Reasoner each made around $400,000—made sense for reasons other than the commission. As Lee Stevens put it, why should a reporter get less for carrying a television show than a comedian does? It wasn't as if news execs got paid less than entertainment execs. And if it paid off in the Nielsens, $1 million was small potatoes to ABC. A one-point gain would mean an additional 710,000 homes, or 1.2 million people, which would allow the network to charge at least $1 million more for air time. A single point and she'd pay for herself, with dollars to spare. And that didn't even count the publicity value of snaring a million-dollar talent.

A round of meetings ensued. Walters and Lou Weiss met in a hotel suite with Fred Pierce and ABC president Elton Rule while Leonard Goldenson sat in a room down the hall, waiting for their report. Walters met at her West Fifty-seventh Street apartment with Harry Reasoner, who was less than thrilled at the prospect of sharing his post with anyone, let alone someone who'd reportedly just been offered $1 million to pose nude for *Hustler* magazine. Walters had second thoughts. She met with Reasoner and Lee Stevens and Fred Pierce and news president Bill Sheehan. Bill Sheehan met with his vice presidents and asked what they thought. They thought Sheehan and his bosses were determined to hire her despite her lack of a news background, so it didn't matter what they thought. No one had told them about the money.

On April 21, not quite seven weeks after Lou Weiss's tennis match with Fred Pierce, the *New York Times* reported that ABC had offered Walters a five-year contract at $1 million per to coanchor the evening news, and that NBC had offered to match the money, though not to put her in an anchor slot. She accepted ABC's bid the next day; an NBC spokesman told the *Times* that his network had withdrawn its offer at the last moment, not just because of the price tag but because of the "circus atmosphere" of the negotiations. "There were things that one would associate with a movie queen, not a journalist," the spokesman declared, "and we had second thoughts"—things like a hairdresser, a press agent, a limousine at her disposal. Walters said it was all absurd: NBC had been giving her these things for years. But the damage was done.

Suddenly, Barbara Walters was no longer America's first woman news anchor, no longer even the highest-paid journalist in history. She was the painted harlot of showbiz, tramping across the hallowed ground of Edward R. Murrow and Walter Cronkite and, yes, Harry Reasoner. NBC's "Saturday Night Live" aired a skit with Gilda Radner as "Baba Wawa," a million-dollar anchorwoman whose only apparent qualification was her speech impediment. "This isn't journalism—this is a minstrel show," the president of CBS News told *Newsweek*. "Is Barbara a journalist, or is she Cher?"

Five months later, Walters made her debut on "The ABC Evening News" with an exclusive satellite interview with President Anwar Sadat of Egypt. This was the coup ABC had been looking for: Pay the lady a million bucks, and world leaders would return her phone calls. As they were signing off, Harry Reasoner noted that he'd been clocking her. "You owe me four minutes," he said. Viewers thought he was kidding.

It had been a while now since Frances Arms had shown up at the office to pick up her Abe for dinner. Her health had been failing for years. First her vision started to go. Then she went into a general decline. She was nearly blind by the summer of 1976, and she died that September in their homey little suite in the Beverly Wilshire, where the furniture hadn't been changed since they'd moved in forty years before.

They'd grown old together, Abe and Frances and the agency, Abe and Frances and showbiz. Now he was alone. Bereft and alone. He couldn't even try to hide it.

The funeral was held two days later at Hillside Memorial Park in Culver City, out by the San Diego Freeway amid the West L.A. sprawl. Al Jolson was buried at Hillside, beneath a black marble sarcophagus surrounded by a columned marble temple above a waterfall that cascaded down the hill. Frances Arms's final resting place was considerably less grandiose—a travertine crypt tucked away in a simple, open-air courtyard called the Alcove of Love. George Jessel delivered the eulogy. Rabbi Magnin officiated. Then they slid her body into the wall and walked mournfully away.

Abe folded into himself after that, stopped playing the ebullient host, lost the sparkle in his eyes, abandoned himself to his grief. He still talked to her sometimes. Late at night, when it got cold and lonely in their suite and he had the night manager come up for the umpteenth time to check the heat, he'd walk into the other room and ask her if it felt warm enough. Then he'd come back in his shabby blue cardigan, the one he'd been wearing for years, and the night manager would summon an engineer and they'd go through the motions of turning up the heat, and eventually he'd put himself to bed.

Frances's death hit the whole agency hard, in ways they scarcely knew. It was she who'd kept the family feeling alive long after it had died elsewhere—who'd remembered their birthdays and asked after their wives and children and worked herself into a rage over some receptionist or secretary who was getting a bum deal. Now there was no one to do those things—only her Abe and his Sammy, the miniature Patton with the burnt-sugar tan. The doors to the first-floor offices, which had always stayed open so Lastfogel could flit in and out at will, began to shut. The hallways became a no-man's-land. The warmth was gone, just as it was gone from the suite in the Beverly Wilshire. But Mr. Lastfogel still came in every day, because the agency was all he had.

THAT SEPTEMBER WAS THE MONTH THE CREATIVE ARTISTS AGENCY LEFT the Hong Kong Bank Building on Wilshire Boulevard for the modernistic landscape of Century City. Their new offices were on the fourteenth floor of the Tiger International Building, headquarters of Flying Tiger Airlines—a professional-looking suite (no card tables) with a spacious sitting area by the elevator and a conference room beyond. To the right was Mike Ovitz's office, stark and Japanese-looking, with striking Oriental vases on lacquered tables; to the left was everyone else.

Each of the five partners had developed his own area of expertise. For Mike Rosenfeld, the packager, it was hiring—knowing who'd be good in a role. For Ron Meyer—the charmer of the bunch, a suave and athletic-looking figure who wore fashionably wide ties and aviator glasses and a blow-dry mane like Warren Beatty's in *Shampoo*—it was PR. Mike Ovitz, the youngest of the five, took care of the financial end. Ovitz had recently taken over as president from Rowland Perkins, in line with their plan to rotate the top job among themselves every two years. But though they'd started as equal partners, Ovitz was quickly emerging as the leader.

He was the most driven—dynamic and inspirational, with a hard, steely resolve and a focus on some larger prize. There was a price to success that he and his wife, Judy, seemed willing to pay. Acquaintances would see her in a restaurant at dinnertime, sitting at a table alone; two hours later, she'd still be there, waiting patiently. They still lived in the Valley, in a white-frame ranch house in Sherman Oaks, a pleasant enough community on the wrong side of the hills; but that was hardly the extent of Ovitz's ambition. Like Ted Ashley and David Geffen, he showed a Gatsby-esque desire to reinvent himself. If he saw an employee reading *Film Comment* or *Harper's* or *Art in America*, he'd ask about it. What was this magazine? Should they be subscribing to it? Would it tell him about art? Because someday, when they could afford it, he'd want real art on the walls.

The agency functioned much like the Morris office, thanks to the lessons the five partners had learned from Phil Weltman. They'd duplicated the phone sheet system, logging the day's calls and making sure nobody went home until each one had been returned. They'd embraced the dress code—suit and tie for all occasions, no open-collar shirts and neckchains à la Freddie Fields. Eventually, they'd adopt the same apprenticeship program, moving trainees from mail room to secretary to junior agent. They'd even borrowed the William Morris temperament— buttoned up, lawyerly in approach, the quintessence of professionalism. They weren't concerned with looking trendy or relaxed. They were there to get the job done.

About the only thing they hadn't taken from Morris was clients. Their biggest stars were Sally Struthers and Rob Reiner, the young couple in "All in the Family," and Talia Shire, Francis Ford Coppola's younger sister, who played Sylvester Stallone's girlfriend in *Rocky* and Al Pacino's sister in *The Godfather, Part II.* They had Bill Carrothers, producer of "The Odd Couple" on ABC, and quiz show producer Jack Barry, known to millions as the host of "Tic-Tac Dough" and "Concentration" and "Twenty-one," the program that had started the quiz show scandal back in 1958. They had some second-string television actors, like Barbara Feldon (Agent 99 on the defunct spy spoof "Get Smart") and Chad Everett (Dr. Joe Gannon on the CBS series "Medical Center"), and recently they'd picked up Ernest Borgnine, Burgess Meredith, Debbie Reynolds, and the Jackson Five. It was a grab-bag list, hardly anything to build a package around. But the worst of it was that most of them were already signed to other agencies, so until their agency papers ran out, CAA got to make their deals but not to collect their commissions.

Maybe that's why the five of them seemed to have such a siege mentality, as if it was them against the world. That was where you felt the difference between them ·and the Morris office—hunger. At Morris, they'd been kept on a short leash; now they were free to go after anyone. It didn't hurt that buyers were eager to break the two big agencies' lock on stars by throwing projects their way. As vice president of comedy development at ABC, Michael Eisner had worked closely with Mike Rosenfeld at Morris; after CAA was formed, Eisner put his programming execs in a room with Rosenfeld and his partners and refused to let them leave until each one had come up with a project the new agency could handle.

In October, Ovitz announced a new partner: Martin Baum. Marty Baum was a white-haired veteran, an old-time Broadway mugg gone Hollywood—hardly the biggest name in the picture business, but a name. He'd been a partner in Baum & Newborn, the Broadway agency where Sue Mengers worked in her Tillie the Toiler phase. Then he'd gone to Hollywood to head the West Coast office of GAC, and when ABC decided in 1968 to make feature films, he'd been put in charge. He okayed Bob Fosse's *Cabaret* and two Sam Peckinpah pictures, *Straw Dogs* and *Junior Bonner.* When ABC pulled the plug three years later, he landed a production deal at UA and made the most gruesome Western of Peckinpah's long and gruesome career, the much-reviled *Bring Me the*

Head of Alfredo Garcia. Then he left production to hang out his agency shingle again.

The stars he'd once handled were faded now—Julie Andrews, the saccharine-voiced songstress of *The Sound of Music*; Sidney Poitier, the trailblazing Negro of *Lilies of the Field* and *In the Heat of the Night.* Sue Mengers was not impressed; Stan Kamen wasn't worried. But Baum did bring CAA some real film stars—not just Poitier, but Dyan Cannon and Stockard Channing and Richard Harris and Joanne Woodward. He also brought Blake Edwards, Peter Sellers's writer-producer-director on *The Pink Panther* series, and Carroll O'Connor, who'd played character parts in the movies before becoming Archie Bunker in "All in the Family." That fall, a skywriting plane appeared over Malibu:

THANK YOU MARTIN BAUM FOR JOINING US—CAA

Ovitz wanted Baum to do what it took to get signings. Did he need to fly to the south of France to woo Peter Sellers? Absolutely, go. He soon landed Sellers and Rod Steiger, and he took Ovitz by the hand and introduced him to the film crowd. He gave them credibility. If a client had left one of the giant agencies and was dissatisfied with the other, the new office in Century City began to look like a possibility. He helped them strategize too. After a screening of *New York, New York*, the new Martin Scorsese film with Liza Minnelli and Robert De Niro, Baum suggested they sign Diahnne Abbott, the black character actress who sang "Honeysuckle Rose" in the picture. Why her? Because she happened to be De Niro's wife, Baum explained, and anything that would get them closer to De Niro, they should do.

This was a strategy the other partners picked up quickly. Before long, Ron Meyer was lending his services to people who had no intention of becoming clients or agents at CAA—to mid-level studio execs looking to move up into a new job, to freelance casting directors looking for a deal at a studio. He was just doing them a favor, no commission involved, glad to help. He knew that later, when he came back with a client or a package or a deal, the favor would be returned.

But the real secret of CAA was Weltman's final lesson: teamwork. He'd taught them to work together, trading information, leveraging off each other, putting multiple agents on every client. That was the way Abe Lastfogel had worked in the forties and fifties, passing star clients to junior agents with the understanding that the door to his office would always be open. Lastfogel's philosophy was, when you signed with the Morris office, you were represented by the entire agency. Things had changed with Lastfogel out of the action. The top agents now had their own boutiques. Junior agents were lucky to be able to hold on to the clients they brought in. But in CAA's fourteenth-floor conference room in the Tiger International Building, a portrait of a stern and balding man hung above a plaque that read:

TO PHIL WELTMAN,

Who taught us the meaning of integrity and self-respect,

WE DEDICATE THIS AGENCY.

12

THE NEW

HOLLYWOOD

Los Angeles/Memphis/New York, 1977-1984

AT THE MORRIS OFFICE, THEY STILL THOUGHT IN TERMS OF GENERATIONS. The first generation—Will Morris himself—was a portrait on the wall. The second generation—the generation that built the company, the generation of Abe Lastfogel and Nat Lefkowitz and Bill Morris, Jr.—was fading from the scene. The drama of the third generation—of Sammy and Phil, Damon and Pythias, Cain and Abel—had finally played itself out. The fourth generation was now at center stage. And the heirs apparent were Stan Kamen and Norman Brokaw.

Brokaw, now forty-nine, was making a name for himself as a fame broker, helping public figures put their celebrity on a paying basis. Mark Spitz was just the start of it. Now he had Senator Sam Ervin, the Southern-fried Constitutionalist who'd saved the republic with his handling of the Watergate hearings. He had General Alexander Haig, White House aide during the Watergate crisis. He was working on Menachem Begin, the new prime minister of Israel. But his latest coup, and by far his most spectacular, was the multimedia deal he'd just engineered for the family of outgoing President Gerald Ford.

Brokaw had met Ford in the White House two months before the election, introduced by Don Penny, an ex-client turned presidential joke writer. Letters and phone calls and more meetings followed, and in December, he won the president as a client. In March 1977, barely six weeks after Ford left office, Brokaw announced a string of media deals not just for the ex-president but for his wife and three children as well.

The cornerstone was a double book deal—a $1 million advance for separate memoirs by Gerald and Betty Ford, to be published jointly by Harper & Row and Reader's Digest. Then there was the double television deal—nearly $1 million from NBC for Jerry Ford's participation in a news special and an option on his memoirs, plus another $500,000 or so for a pair of specials from Betty Ford on a subject of her choosing, from dance to cancer. For the Fords' son Jack, there was a job at Rolling Stone as assistant to the publisher. For their son Steve, a starring role in a made-for-television rodeo movie. For their daughter Susan, a scrapbook of her photographs in Good Housekeeping.

"This is precedent-setting," Brokaw told the New York Times. "L.B.J. wrote a book and Mrs. Johnson wrote a book, but what else did they do? Eisenhower didn't have a television deal."

Then there was Bill Cosby, whom Brokaw had handled since "I Spy." On the face of it, Cosby no longer had much of a career. "I Spy" had gone off the air nine years ago, and though Cosby had tried three other series since, none of them clicked. In 1969 he'd come out with "The Bill Cosby Show," an NBC sitcom about a high school phys-ed teacher in inner-city Los Angeles. That was good for two seasons. In 1972, as variety television was finally nearing extinction, he hosted a CBS comedy-variety hour called "The New Bill Cosby Show." It was off after one season. In 1976 he turned up on ABC in "Cos," a Sunday evening variety show for kids aged two to twelve. That lasted eight weeks. He'd done films as well—costarred with Sidney Poitier and Harry Belafonte in Uptown Saturday Night, reprised that act in Let's Do It Again, starred in Mother, Jugs and Speed—but he was in no danger of becoming a movie star.

Two things kept him current: kids and commercials. "Cos" flopped, but the cartoon show he created, "Fat Albert and the Cosby Kids," was a hit on Saturday mornings. He did guest spots on other kids' shows— "Sesame Street," "The Electric Company." In 1974 he signed a lucrative contract with Jell-O to appear in television commercials pushing pudding products to tykes. That led to other gigs, hawking Kodak and Coca-Cola. Advertisers were hot for celebrities, and Cosby was Madison Avenue's dream—the universal pitchman, a black father figure who transcended the color barrier. Not that he didn't take his new role seriously—he'd gotten his bachelor's from Temple on the basis of life experience, and he was working on a doctorate in education from the University of Massachusetts, which gave him course credit for his public television appearances and let him write a dissertation on his own cartoon show. But now it was paying off. According to the head of the West Coast commercial department, between a quarter and a third of his annual income was coming from endorsements.

Stan Kamen, now fifty, stuck to movie deals, but he too was operating in a new environment. Warren Beatty, for instance—after *Bonnie and Clyde* and the McGovern campaign for president, no longer an actor but a filmmaker who doubled as a political strategist. Beatty had started negotiating his own contracts with *Shampoo*, the 1975 hit in which he sent up his own image as a great lover and the whole personal-services-to-the-stars ethos of Hollywood. He avoided paying a commission by making his own deals, but he was happy to let Kamen call him a client in exchange for friendship and advice. And in the meantime Kamen had hooked up with Jane Fonda, whom he'd landed as a client after Mike Medavoy, her agent at IFA, went to United Artists, and Paula Weinstein, her new agent, joined William Morris and left it in quick succession.

Following her Oscar-winning performance in *Klute*, Fonda had abandoned her career to campaign against the Vietnam War. Now she wanted money to fund the political ambitions of her husband, Tom Hayden, who'd just made an unsuccessful run in the 1976 senate primary. Kamen put her together with director Fred Zinnemann and sold them to Fox to make *Julia*, based on Lillian Hellman's memoir *Pentimento*. *Julia*'s success made Hanoi Jane a movie star again and gave a boost to her efforts to make *Coming Home*, a Vietnam story developed by IPC Films, which she'd set up to make politically meaningful pictures. With *Coming Home* now in postproduction at UA, Fonda too had joined the ranks of the filmmaker-stars.

In their different ways, both Kamen and Brokaw were working the New Hollywood, a kaleidoscope of celebrity in which success in one area could be parlayed into fame and fortune in all media. Despite the carping of nay-sayers—like Cleveland Amory, distinguished critic for the *Los Angeles Times*, who speculated that Menachem Begin would soon be doing ads for Hertz Rent-a-Car—it was clear that the gray-suited middlemen of the Morris Agency were inventing the future. Before long, all business would be show business.

Inevitably, there were setbacks. At the beginning of August, ABC confirmed that Barbara Walters would no longer be coanchoring the evening news with Harry Reasoner: Roone Arledge, the new president of ABC News, had decided to pull the plug. Because her contract gave her veto power over any new coanchor, Arledge decided to eliminate the anchor slot and have correspondents report directly to the viewers, with Walters in New York as a special correspondent in New York. As for Reasoner, he was rumored to be on the way out.

Losing the anchor slot was a blow, but Walters rebounded. What saved her was the success of her "Barbara Walters Specials," which ABC had sold at tremendous profit to General Electric even before she joined the network. Her very first "Special," which drew record ratings, had started off with a segment on Barbra Streisand and Jon Peters (heavily edited according to Streisand's instructions to avoid embarrassment) and concluded with a visit to Plains, Georgia, where she asked Jimmy and Rosalynn Carter, "Do you sleep in a double bed or twin beds?" In between, she took the audience on a tour of her own luxuriously outfitted apartment. The sheer pizzazz of her million-dollar deal had made her as much a celebrity as Streisand or the Carters. It was all interchangeable—the star as celebrity, the president as personality, the journalist as star, each one neatly packaged and electronically consumable.

Then, less than two weeks after Walters lost her job as coanchor, word came from Memphis: Elvis Presley had just fallen off the toilet, dead.

WHEN GINGER ALDEN, ELVIS'S TWENTY-YEAR-OLD GIRLFRIEND, AWOKE IN Graceland on the afternoon of August 16, she wasn't surprised to discover that Elvis was not in bed beside her. He'd taken a lot of downers that morning—his usual bedtime dose of Quaaludes, Seconal, Tuinal, Amytal, Valium, and Demerol, and apparently some Valmid and Placidyl as well, plus maybe some Dilaudid and Empirin with codeine, since he'd just been to the dentist—but he'd still had trouble getting to sleep. Alden remembered waking up and hearing him say he was going to the bathroom to read. That was around 8:00 A.M., six hours earlier.

Elvis wasn't looking too good by the summer of 1977. Years of good eats—cheeseburgers and French fries, fried peanut butter and banana sandwiches, ice cream by the bucket—had caused his body, once so tantalizing and erotic, to balloon to a grotesque 250 pounds. The rolls of fat around his belly testified to a yawning emptiness inside. His vanity had failed him, and one way or another, so had everything else—his dead mother, Gladys; his ex-wife, Priscilla; his manager; his guys; his stardom. Especially his stardom.

The disillusionment and self-doubt that led him to abandon his movie career in the late sixties had only intensified with his departure from Hollywood. The triumph of his comeback—his 1968 "Singer Presents Elvis" spectacular on NBC, his return to live performing at Kirk Kerkorian's International in Vegas in 1969, his 1973 "Aloha from Hawaii" special, which drew an astonishing 1.5 billion viewers worldwide—was now a memory. His career had dissipated into an endless series of one-nighters in small and medium-sized cities across America, punctuated by the occasional return to Vegas. And just a couple of weeks ago three former bodyguards had published a tell-all biography called *Elvis—What Happened?*, detailing his rampant drug addiction and even throwing in his half-baked scheme to have Priscilla's boyfriend killed.

Two years earlier he'd had one last shot at redemption, when Barbra Streisand and Jon Peters showed up backstage in Vegas, met with him in a walk-in closet in his dressing room, and talked with him about playing the lead in their remake of *A Star Is Born*. It was the perfect role for him—a defeated rock idol, victim of the machinery—but most important, it was a real role, with a real costar in a real movie, not just an excuse to sing lame songs while some floozy jiggled her assets. Elvis was so excited, he accepted on the spot. For a short while it all came back to him, the freshness and the enthusiasm, almost like he was a kid and starting over. But Streisand went away shocked by his appearance, and Colonel Parker wasn't happy at the idea of anyone approaching his boy directly. When he demanded $1 million—Elvis's customary fee—and Elvis's name alone above the title, the project went away.

Once again, the machinery got in the way. Even so, Elvis remained a star of unfathomable proportions. The tours, though increasingly dreary and listless, invariably sold out, at an average gross of $130,000 a night. Record sales had topped the 400-million mark in 1976, making him the biggest-selling singer in history. Yet somehow he managed to be broke most of the time.

This was partly the result of the contract he'd signed with Colonel Parker in January 1967, upping Colonel's take of most of his income from 25 percent—customarily the upper limit of a manager's slice—to

50 percent. Partly it was due to the highly peculiar contracts Colonel negotiated with RCA Records in 1973, signing away all rights to Elvis's existing catalogue of more than seven hundred hit songs for a flat $5.4 million, and selling all future recordings for the next seven years for an annual advance of $500,000 against royalties of fifty cents per unit—about half the royalty rate paid to other major performers, with no provision for an audit and no allowance for inflation. Partly it was due to the sweetheart arrangements Colonel made with the International (subsequently the Las Vegas Hilton), which paid Elvis a mere $100,000 to $130,000 a week while giving Parker—who was losing a million a year in the casino—a lavish suite of rooms, food and drink for his home in Palm Springs, free transportation to and from Vegas any time he wanted it, and $50,000 a year in consulting fees.

Then there was Colonel's failure to provide financial advice that would have yielded tax shelters, pension plans, any way of minimizing Elvis's income tax. And Colonel's refusal to tour Elvis abroad, despite offers of as much as $1 million for a single night's work (which only made sense if you knew that Parker was actually a Dutch citizen whose status in the United States was questionable at best). And Colonel's inexplicable failure to register Elvis's songs with either BMI or ASCAP, which would entitle Elvis to performance royalties. But none of these things was apparent. What everyone could see was Elvis throwing money around—buying ten Mercedes sedans to give away as Christmas presents, flying himself and his entourage to Denver in his JetStar for those room-service peanut butter and jelly sandwiches they remembered so fondly.

So the King kept working. To get himself psyched for his performances, to quell his chronic insomnia afterward, and to numb himself from the pain and humiliation of losing his lovely wife Priscilla to an impecunious karate champion, he'd turned increasingly to pills. In the early sixties, he was popping Demerol, Placidyl, Percodan, and Valium to go to sleep and Dexamil to wake up. By the early seventies, he was taking Dilaudid, a synthetic painkiller more potent than heroin, for the morphine kick. Among other things, the pills left him horribly constipated, his intestines virtually paralyzed, his colon distended with something that resembled chalk. When he disappeared into the bathroom that morning, Elvis hadn't had a good crap in some time.

It was Tuesday afternoon when Ginger Alden woke up, a real dog day—ninety-four degrees, the air listless and oppressive. But inside the second-floor master suite at Graceland, with the windows sealed shut and the temperature artificially low, the weather was as irrelevant as the time of day. Alden called a friend and chatted about the tour they were scheduled to begin that night, twelve days of puddle-jumping from Maine back to Memphis. She phoned her mother. Then it occurred to her to look in the bathroom.

She found him sprawled facedown across the red shag carpeting, pajama bottoms pushed down around his calves, knees bent almost into a fetal position. He felt cold to the touch. She turned his head. His face was bluish-purple, his tongue hanging out between clenched teeth. She grabbed a phone and called for help.

Graceland was in chaos by the time the fire department ambulance sped through the gates and up the winding drive. Seven or eight people were crowded into the bathroom, hovering over the body, trying to give him mouth-to-mouth, wailing, "Don't die!" Vernon Presley, Elvis's ailing father, saw the body on the floor and clutched his chest. Lisa Marie, Elvis's nine-year-old daughter, tried to run in but was pulled away. Two paramedics elbowed their way through. Clapping a life-support mask over his face, they heaved him onto a stretcher and wheeled it down to the ambulance, then raced for Baptist Memorial with four of his guys and Dr. George Nichopolous—his physician for the past ten years—in back. At the hospital, he was rushed into a trauma room and turned over to the Harvey team, the emergency crew kept on standby to resuscitate the dying. He was already well past that stage—the lips blue, the body stiff and cold—but the team worked frantically for thirty minutes or more. No response, nada, nothing. They were trying to revive a corpse.

Joe Esposito, Elvis's road manager, was waiting in an emergency room. When Dr. Nick gave him the news, Esposito commandeered an office and got on the phone. He called Colonel Parker at his hotel suite in Portland, Maine. He called Tom Huelett of Concerts West, which handled Elvis's personal appearances. Dr. Nick headed back to Graceland to break the news to Vernon—in the ambulance, just in case.

Whatever you say about Colonel Parker, he had not been greedy. By his own reckoning, Elvis owed him at present some $1.69 million— money he'd never collected, despite the pressure of his own staggering gambling losses in Vegas. The chances of his getting paid now were slim. On the other hand, the news from Memphis was sure to generate demand. Already a thousand people had gathered outside the Music

Gate on Elvis Presley Boulevard—Highway 51 South, once the main road to New Orleans, now a four-lane conduit through subdivisions and strip malls. In another hour it would be three thousand—a once-in-a-lifetime opportunity. Colonel wasted no time.

He phoned Vernon at Graceland and explained how important it was that they act quickly to protect their own interests—especially those of Vernon's granddaughter, little Lisa Marie. Vernon told him to carry on as before. Then Colonel phoned Harry Geissler, a merchandising man who operated out of the roadside hamlet of Bear, Delaware, in the shadow of the Delaware Memorial Bridge. He was ready to cut a deal.

Harry Geissler was Colonel's kind of boy—a true carny, a savvy trafficker in the flotsam of fame. He'd quit school at sixteen and started hustling straightaway, selling Christmas trees, selling supplies to the carnivals, fudge in a steel mill, food to the motel guests by the bridge, bowling shirts with names his wife stitched on. The bowling shirts led to T-shirts, a hot item for travelers on their way to the beach. Snoopy T-shirts, Muppets T-shirts, "Starsky and Hutch" T-shirts. Like many vendors, he hadn't always worried about trademarks and other technicalities. But in 1976 he'd had to shell out $100,000 in fines, and now he was more careful. He was forty-three years old, and his company, Factors, Etc., was a multimillion-dollar enterprise that owned rights to *Rocky*, *Star Wars*, and the forthcoming Warner Bros. production of *Superman*, among other things. He didn't much care for Elvis's music, but he was a big fan of Colonel Parker—the king of promoters, in his book, just as he himself was the king of merchandisers.

Geissler prided himself on his instincts. Hadn't he steered clear of Mark Spitz? Earlier that year he'd paid $300,000 for T-shirt rights to Farrah Fawcett-Majors, a Morris client who'd hit big as a private eye in "Charlie's Angels," Aaron Spelling's new tits-and-ass cop show on ABC. "Charlie's Angels" was "Burke's Law" updated for the seventies: Millionaire businessman hires three crime-busting babes who'd been languishing in desk jobs and sets them loose in exotic locales where their bods will show to maximum advantage. Farrah Fawcett was working for $5,000 a week, half what chief Angel Kate Jackson was getting. Then a company in Ohio approached her manager, Jay Bernstein, about doing a poster, and Bernstein got back to them with a one-word concept: nipples. Factors put the poster image on a T-shirt, and now, eleven months after the show's premiere, Geissler had sold so many T-shirts he'd had to pay the Morris Agency $400,000 in royalties on top of the advance.

With Abe Lastfogel in retirement, Roger Davis was handling Colonel Parker's affairs at the Morris office. A natty dresser, tall and distinguished-looking in the white-shoe manner, Davis had joined the agency in 1961 after ten years with the prominent entertainment law firm of Loeb & Loeb. He was the attorney who'd always sat in the room taking notes when Lastfogel and the Colonel talked business, and after Lastfogel retired, he was the one the Colonel turned to to get things done. Now, with William Morris as middleman, Colonel Parker flew to New York to strike a deal with Harry Geissler.

By Wednesday morning, mourners were lined up on Elvis Presley Boulevard for miles in both directions—bikers, businessmen, housewives, teenagers, reporters. As delivery vans streamed through the gate bearing elaborate floral arrangements that filled the mansion and overflowed onto the grounds, the body was laid out in the parlor beneath a crystal chandelier. That afternoon, with seventy-five thousand people massed outside in the suffocating heat, Vernon gave the word: Let the gate swing open. Let the fans pay their tribute. For three and a half hours they filed up the hill, into the mansion, past the open casket, anxious, sobbing, in thrall. Peddlers worked the highway outside, hawking T-shirts and postcards, ice cream and soda pop.

By Thursday, two days after Elvis's death, an agreement had been reached—a twelve-page contract between Factors and Boxcar Enterprises, the company Parker had created three years earlier to handle his Elvis merchandising efforts. Boxcar—the logo featured a pair of dice showing sixes—was set up to yield maximum returns to the Colonel: He owned 56 percent, with 22 percent each for Elvis and Tom Diskin, a longtime Parker associate. After expenses, which included salaries for the Colonel and several cronies, the company took half the proceeds and divided the remainder three ways—20 percent to Elvis, 20 percent to Parker, and 10 percent to Diskin. Parker ended up reaping nearly half the rewards, while Elvis saw less than a third. The new, postmortem agreement, signed by Tom Diskin for Boxcar and Harry Geissler for Factors, gave Factors exclusive rights to market the name and likeness of Elvis Presley for the next eighteen months. In return, Factors agreed to pay a $150,000 advance against royalties—$100,000 on signing, with another $50,000 to come.

Parker arrived in Memphis that morning looking incongruously jaunty in Hawaiian shirt and yachting cap. "Nothing has changed. This won't change anything," he was heard to say. "Believe me, the show is going to go on." Graceland was mournful and frenetic, overrun with relatives and reporters and celebrities and hangers-on. Ann-Margret had come with her husband, Roger Smith. Caroline Kennedy was on hand for *Rolling Stone*. Priscilla had flown in from Los Angeles with her parents and was now playing the gracious hostess. Vernon, inconsolable in his grief, was holed up in a back bedroom, watching the coverage on TV with his fiancée, his brother Vester, his sisters Delta Mae and Nash, and his eighty-five-year-old mother, Minnie Mae.

With Elvis gone, Vernon would be beset by temptation from all sides; there was no telling what he might agree to. So while Elvis's guys were busy with last-minute funeral preparations, Colonel Parker sat down with the old man and pulled out the Factors agreement. Some of the guys shook their heads at his timing, but no one said anything. Colonel was a genius at this sort of thing; if he said it was time to cut a deal, he must be right. Vernon gave his approval, putting his signature right above Colonel Parker's and Roger Davis's. Suddenly, Factors was in the Elvis business.

Soon there would be Elvis wristwatches, Elvis bubble gum, Elvis Christmas tree ornaments, Elvis dollar bills, gold-plated Elvis belt buckles, a solid gold Elvis medallion, maybe even Elvis aftershave and Elvis perfume. But with Elvis himself no longer among the living, Colonel's authority to act in his behalf might be called into question. So on August 23, one week after Elvis's death, Vernon put down in writing the sanction he'd given over the phone seven days before. "I am deeply grateful that you have offered to carry on in the same old way," he wrote, adding that as executor of Elvis's estate, "I hereby would appreciate if you will carry on according to the same terms and conditions as stated in the contractual agreement you had with Elvis dated January 22, 1976"—an agreement that gave Parker the right to sign Elvis's name to merchandising contracts, personal appearance contracts, motion picture contracts, and anything else involving him. The following day Tom Diskin wrote Vernon a letter cutting himself out of the royalty split: Boxcar would still keep half, but the other half would be evenly divided between Parker and the estate. The day after that Factors paid Boxcar the remaining $50,000 of the advance.

Bubble gum and belt buckles were but the half of it. The demand for Elvis's records was so great that for weeks, RCA had its pressing plants working around the clock. By selling off Elvis's catalogue in 1973, Parker had cut himself off from that particular gravy train. But in

September he got $1.1 million from CBS and $1.2 million from NBC for tapes of the King in performance and made a deal with RCA for a new, two-record "Elvis in Concert" album—$450,000 to be split fifty-fifty between himself and the estate, with another $50,000 to be paid directly to his alter ego, All-Star Shows. And only the week before RCA had agreed to throw him a bone—$675,000 for his "services" in packaging, promoting, and merchandising its Elvis product.

As before, the Morris office took no commission on the record money. But years of loyal service would not go unrewarded. For its role in the Factors deal, Morris would get 10 percent off the top. And in November, when Vernon wrote Roger Davis authorizing the agency as well to carry on "as in the past," Morris was assured of its cut of any movie and television deals as well.

And more deals there would be. "Elvis didn't die. The body did," Colonel told Elvis's friends and associates. "We're keeping Elvis alive. I talked to him this morning and he told me to carry on." Twenty-three years earlier, when Hank Williams kicked off, his manager—the crony who tipped Parker about this Presley kid—fell on hard times. That wasn't going to happen to Tom Parker. He knew what he had. All these years and finally he had the client he was born to promote. It was almost like handling the Skeleton Dude—only this wasn't some scrawny guy working an 1880s Bowery arcade in a skeleton suit, it was the real thing, the ultimate freak-show attraction. Colonel Parker actually had a body moldering away in a crypt, a dead body that could sell records and T-shirts and belt buckles and God knew what-all. He was the king of promoters, all right, and now he was going to show his stuff. He was going to give Elvis the gift of eternal life, with the Morris office to broker the deal.

AUGUST 1978, AND STAN KAMEN WAS FLUSH WITH SUCCESS. GOLDIE Hawn and Chevy Chase had one of the summer's top hits in the Hitchcock spoof *Foul Play*. Jane Fonda and Jon Voight had recast the debate about Vietnam with *Coming Home*, even if they hadn't drawn swarms of moviegoers. Now Kamen was ready to shop another package: *The Johnson County War*, an epic saga of the range wars between cattle barons and homesteaders in the old West, with Michael Cimino as writer-director and Kris Kristofferson in the lead. Kamen wanted a pay-or-play commitment, the principals to collect their fees ($500,000 for Cimino to direct and another $250,000 for his script, $850,000 for Kristofferson) whether the picture was made or not. The property had already been shopped around town without success, but that was before Cimino's new picture, *The Deer Hunter*, as yet unreleased but already the subject of significant buzz. This time, Cimino was hot.

It was the age of the auteur. The self-promotional efforts of the sixties New Wave had blossomed into a full-fledged theory—the director as auteur, creator, genius. With the collapse of the studio system and the emergence of directors with a distinct personal vision—Martin Scorsese, Francis Ford Coppola—it was easy to believe that in the New Hollywood, the director was king. Especially if you were a director, which Michael Cimino was.

A pudgy thirty-nine-year-old with dark, hooded eyes and an air of intense self-involvement, Cimino had started off directing television commercials in New York. In 1971 he'd moved to Los Angeles and teamed with John Milius to write *Magnum Force*, which became the second in Clint Eastwood's series about Harry Callahan, the renegade San Francisco cop. After the success of *Magnum Force*, which was violent enough to draw action fans but complex enough to make critics start taking Eastwood seriously, Eastwood bought Cimino's script for a Western called *Thunderbolt and Lightfoot*, with the proviso that Cimino would get to direct. He turned down subsequent directing offers to pursue his own vision, but nothing worked until late 1976, when he pitched EMI on an idea about the Vietnam War and its effect on three young steelworkers in the Midwest. Cimino himself was a Yale lad, product of a privileged upbringing in Manhattan and Long Island, but he had a rich kid's fascination with the gritty existence of the average Joe, and the picture he had in mind was a paean to working-class patriotism, layered with literary allusion and heavy on the portent. EMI said yes.

The Deer Hunter careened dangerously over budget, thanks to Cimino's lavish attention to detail and his determination to spend what it took. Did he need to convey the squalid delights of wartime Saigon? Then there was nothing to do but fly cast and crew to Bangkok and rent Patpong Road, the Street of a Thousand Pleasures, in order to have the perfect setting for the games of Russian roulette that would serve as his metaphor for the extremity of war, in which life could be snatched away in a second. Never mind that veterans and war correspondents could cite no instances of Russian roulette in Vietnam, either as a Viet Cong torture device or as a sicko nightclub act on the back streets of Saigon. And never mind that EMI, aghast at the rising bill, wanted to fire him and seize control. He fought them off, and the result, at $15 million and three hours plus, was impressive. More than impressive; it seemed to betoken a huge and important career.

The Deer Hunter could hardly have been more different from Kamen's other Vietnam picture, *Coming Home*, which UA had released in February. *Coming Home* was a homefront movie about suffering, loss, and the triumph of the victim—a paraplegic veteran at a VA hospital who has an affair with the wife of a gung-ho marine officer while the officer is off in Vietnam. *The Deer Hunter* dealt with loss in a way that was self-consciously heroic: It was a mytho-poetic male-bonding picture about three young men who make their passage through the death zone and back again, some whole, some not.

UA had its own mytho-poetic Vietnam epic in the works: Coppola's *Apocalypse Now*, which seemed so out of control that the press was calling it "Apocalypse Never." But the studio had worse problems. In January, a month before they were to release *Coming Home*, UA's entire senior management team had walked out in a dispute with Transamerica, the parent conglomerate in San Francisco, and launched a new company, Orion Pictures. The new president of United Artists, Andreas Albeck, was a colorless functionary with few Hollywood connections. But he did have a $100-million checkbook, and he needed to buy talent fast if he wanted to counter the rumors that Transamerica was getting UA ready for the auction block. So he'd quickly okayed a two-picture deal with Cimino, who subsequently announced that he wanted to do a remake of *The Fountainhead*, the Ayn Rand novel about the genius architect who'd rather blow up one of his own creations than compromise its integrity. Then Kamen slipped them Cimino's script for *The Johnson County War*.

Kamen's submission was both unofficial and outside the scope of the two-picture deal he'd made a few months before—unofficial, because propriety demanded he show it first to Universal, EMI's partner on *The Deer Hunter;* outside the multipicture deal, because that didn't involve much money and this was a big-budget package. In motion pictures, unlike television, a package was essentially a negotiating ploy—a felicitous combination of writer-director-story-star that the buyer would find impossible to resist, even if the price was too high. Strong studios tried to put together their own productions. Weak studios—and United Artists after the Orion defections was one of the weakest in town—were liable to grasp at anything.

There were times when a package was not a package. In March 1977, Lenny Hirshan had negotiated a deal at Columbia for *The China Syndrome*, about a near-disaster at a nuclear power plant, with Jack Lemmon playing the engineer who blows the whistle on the cover-up, Richard Dreyfuss as a documentary filmmaker who witnesses it, and Michael Douglas producing. When Dreyfuss pulled out in a money dispute, Douglas passed a copy of the script to Jane Fonda. Fonda already had a deal at Columbia for a picture on Karen Silkwood, the martyred whistle-blower at an Oklahoma nuclear plant, but she'd gotten tangled up in litigation over story rights. When she read Douglas's screenplay, she flipped. So Kamen brought her in on *The China Syndrome* and reworked the deal, with the filmmaker character turned into a bimbo television reporter who realizes the engineer is right, an experienced director brought in to justify Fonda's salary, and Columbia cosigning a note rather than providing actual financing. Kamen could claim it as a package, but Columbia president Dan Melnick, who'd gotten the submission from Michael Douglas and suggested Fonda for the Dreyfuss role, saw it as a picture with stars who happened to be represented by the Morris office.

The Johnson County War was a bona fide package, although at $7.5 million, its budget was if anything unrealistically low. Still, for a revisionist Western in which everyone gets massacred in the end, it would be good to keep expenses down. Fox passed; Warner Bros. and Universal were nibbling. In late September, a month after he'd given them the script, Kamen got a call from David Field and Steven Bach, UA's new coheads of production. He was on another line, but he got back to them a moment later.

UA was willing to accept Kamen's terms, including Christopher Walken as Kristofferson's costar. (The female lead was still uncast, though both Jane Fonda and Diane Keaton—another client, and last year's Oscar winner for *Annie Hall*—had been mentioned as possibilities.) They did insist on upping the budget to $7.8 million—still low, but at least they had their eye on the figures. Kamen said yes, and the deal was done. Not until three months later, after Cimino had gone to Montana to scout locations and returned the proud owner of a 156-acre ranch, did the project get its final title: *Heaven's Gate*.

*　　　*　　　*

By spring 1979, Stan Kamen was arguably the number-one agent in Hollywood. He'd picked up his old friend Herb Ross, one of the town's favorite directors (*The Sunshine Boys, The Goodbye Girl, The Turning Point*), who'd defected from la Mengers some months before. After years of wooing, he'd landed Robert Redford—after casting Fonda opposite him in *The Electric Horseman* when Diane Keaton didn't work out, after recommending his client Donald Sutherland to star in *Ordinary People* (Redford's first picture as director), after convincing him that he couldn't just rely on a lawyer to do his deals, that he needed an agent to keep scripts coming in and keep his name in the marketplace. Which Kamen was uniquely equipped to do, since there was hardly a power broker he wasn't chummy with or a major development project he didn't have a hand in.

He was good friends with Ray Stark, the producer who controlled Columbia and much else in Hollywood—so it was no surprise that *California Suite*, the Neil Simon picture Stark had just made at Columbia with Herb Ross directing, was studded with Morris clients: Alan Alda, Jill Clayburgh, Bill Cosby, Jane Fonda, Walter Matthau. He was good friends with Paramount's Barry Diller, which helped explain why his client Alan Pakula was producing and directing *Starting Over* at Paramount with Jill Clayburgh and Burt Reynolds, the beefcake superstar he was trying to woo away from Mengers. He was good friends with Fox president Alan Ladd, Jr., the town's favorite suit, which had something to do with the $3 million his new client Robert Redford was getting to star in *Brubaker*, a prison script that had been lying around for nine years until Kamen took it to Redford and director Bob Rafelson.

The Deer Hunter had opened in December at its full three-hour-plus length—thanks to Allan Carr, the flamboyant producer of *Grease*, who liked it so much he'd convinced Universal to scrap its fall release plans and open in New York and Los Angeles (reserved seating, limited engagement, one week only), followed by a general release in February. It was a risky scheme, a play to the cognoscenti; if the critics panned it, it would be dead before the public got a chance to see it. But the critics did like it—most of them, anyway. "An epic," cried David Denby in *New York* magazine. Others were less flattering. Pauline Kael said it had "no more moral intelligence than the Eastwood action pictures." And in *Harper's*, Tom Buckley excoriated it as the work of a charlatan, a flim-flam man who combined ignorance with megalomania. Bald-faced lie, or work of genius? Either way, it was impossible to ignore.

Another firestorm erupted when *The China Syndrome* came out in March. The Edison Electric Institute, a power industry trade group, attacked the very idea that a catastrophic nuclear accident could happen. GE withdrew its sponsorship of a "Barbara Walters Special" because Fonda was set to appear on it. Columnist George Will claimed she had "invented nuclear fantasies in the interests of satisfying her own greed." But on March 28, twelve days after the premiere, a near-meltdown occurred at the Three Mile Island nuclear plant outside Harrisburg, Pennsylvania. As TV news reports showed farms and villages being evacuated, the box office for *The China Syndrome* took off, from $4.8 million the weekend before to $5.2 million the weekend after. Even Columbia's stock got a boost.

William Morris, UA, and Cimino's lawyers were still closing the deal on *Heaven's Gate* when Three Mile Island blew. Cimino's attorneys had triggered a crisis the week before by making an extraordinary series of demands—$2,000 a week for personal expenses above his $500,000 salary, name above the title, a final cut no shorter than two and a half hours, full approval of advertising, and so forth. But the real kicker was a proviso that, since UA wanted the film for a Christmas 1979 release, any money spent to deliver it on time would not be considered over budget—even if it eventually turned out that Cimino couldn't finish on time anyway. In six months of preproduction, Cimino had racked up $2 million in expenses. The budget had already ballooned to $11.6 million. Now he wanted a blank check.

Several points remained unresolved on the evening of April 9, when the 1978 Academy Awards were presented at the Dorothy Chandler Pavilion downtown. For Cimino, it promised to be a fateful evening; for Kamen, who stood to win no matter who won, it was proof of his ascendance. *The Deer Hunter* was up for nine awards, including three for Cimino himself—best picture, best director, and best original screenplay. *Coming Home* and *Heaven Can Wait*—the latest production by Kamen's star non-client, Warren Beatty—had eight nominations each, including best picture. Jon Voight and Warren Beatty were competing for best actor; Jane Fonda and Jill Clayburgh (in *An Unmarried Woman*) were up for best actress. Beatty, the columnists pointed out, was the first person to be nominated for best actor, best director, best screenplay, and best picture (in his role as producer) since Orson Welles for *Citizen Kane* in 1941.

Outside the hall, anti-Cimino demonstrators were waving signs that read "No Oscars for Racism." The papers quoted Fonda as saying she hoped *The Deer Hunter* wouldn't win while admitting that she herself hadn't seen it. Inside, it was a Vietnam sweep: five Oscars for *The Deer Hunter*, including best picture and best director. Three for *Coming Home*, including best actor and best actress. After the ceremony, when Fonda found herself in a backstage press room where Cimino was trying to defend his Russian roulette scenes, she denounced him for his "racist, Pentagon version of the war." Cimino looked momentarily stunned. Flashbulbs popped. Fonda made her exit.

Yet it was Cimino's moment. The multiple Oscar wins made him the most celebrated filmmaker in town. The UA execs found him impossible to resist. They'd already shelled out $2 million, and if they backed out now, they'd have nothing to show for it but a gaping hole in their release schedule. So they signed the blank check. Principal photography was due to begin in a week. Once that happened, with the cameras rolling and film in the can, it would be all but impossible to pull out.

Kamen danced nimbly around the malice between Cimino and Fonda. Neither of them was easy to get close to—Cimino was arrogant and demanding, Fonda saw everything through an ideological lens. It wasn't his job to take sides between clients anyway. His job was to make the sale, to provide career counsel, to make each client feel like the only person in the world who truly mattered. That was the problem with being the top agent in town—it put you in the middle of a lot of people who were competing with each other. Usually it was career competition rather than an ideological square-off, but either way it amounted to the same thing: Hollywood was a community of people who frequently wanted to claw one another's eyes out.

Kamen handled talent with the same clear focus Abe Lastfogel once had—their desires, their needs. He also had the same lack of interest in administration. That's what Roger Davis, the in-house attorney, was for—to serve as Stan's right hand, sweating the details on motion picture contracts and handling the dirty work, like firings and bonus sessions. Stan hired 'em, Roger fired 'em—that was the joke in the department. The difference between Lastfogel and Kamen was that Lastfogel knew how to delegate. Lastfogel had no problem handing off a top client to a younger agent while watching from a distance, always attentive, always available when needed. That was how Kamen had picked up many of his clients—Fred Zinnemann, Warren Beatty. But Kamen was too much the perfectionist to operate that way. He needed to be sure everything was done right.

Not that his department was a one-man show. The motion picture agents at William Morris were a varied and eccentric lot, with a power-house talent roster and—despite a couple of intense rivalries—enormous camaraderie. There was fifty-one-year-old Lenny Hirshan, an agent of the old school whose involvement with Clint Eastwood, Jack Lemmon, and Walter Matthau gave him considerable clout. There was Ed Bondy, forty-seven, a flamboyant homosexual who'd come out from the New York office four years earlier; among his clients were Ann-Margret, Michael Douglas, Diane Keaton, Henry Winkler, and John Travolta. There was Ed Limato, a New York agent Kamen had recently lured away from ICM—along with his most promising client, Richard Gere, who'd just been hired to replace Travolta in *American Gigolo*, a Freddie Fields production at Paramount. There was Rick Nicita, a young agent who represented Sissy Spacek, Christopher Walken, and Eric Roberts. There was a trio of junior agents—Steve Reuther, Dennis Brody, Gary Lucchesi—who'd earned golden-boy status by apprenticing as Kamen's assistants.

Kamen wasn't threatened by younger agents the way some people at Morris were. He nurtured them, encouraged them, wanted them to succeed. But he was the engine that powered the department. Stars wanted to be handled by a star agent, that was the dynamic of the business—and he was the star agent. Not just anybody could meet their needs. They wanted him—that's why they were there. And he was as reclusive in business as he was in his personal life. No one else in the department knew what he was doing—who he was going to sign, what deals he was making, what he thought about any of it. They heard about it after it was done.

Unauthorized contact with Kamen's clients was a sure way to get fired. There was the overeager junior agent who saw Sally Field walking past his table at a luncheon—Sally Field, still trying to live down her television work in "Gidget" and "The Flying Nun," even though she was now Burt Reynolds's girlfriend and highly acclaimed as the star of the just-released *Norma Rae*, a picture Reynolds had talked her into doing after Jane Fonda and Jill Clayburgh turned it down. The kid stood up and introduced himself as one of her agents—an act Miss Field found highly embarrassing. He quickly became one of her ex-agents.

A junior agent in the television department was approached by Dick Berg, a Morris client who wanted Jon Voight to star in a TV miniseries he was producing called *The Martian Chronicles*, based on the Ray Bradbury novel. The agent sent Kamen a memo and followed up with a phone call: no response. He dodged Berg's calls for a week, until he realized that a couple of blocks from his house, Voight was on location for *The Champ*, a remake of the 1931 Wallace Beery film with Franco Zeffirelli directing. So he knocked on the door of Voight's trailer, introduced himself, had a nice chat during which Voight told him what he thought of television, handed Voight the script anyway, and asked Voight to please have Stan get back to him. Stan did get back to him, the next day: Voight was passing. A couple of days after that, the agent was called downstairs to see Jerry Katzman, the newly appointed West Coast head of television, and Walt Zifkin, an attorney who served as Morris Stoller's deputy. They told him he was fired.

Kamen had to be protective. Talent was volatile—actors, directors, even writers. But whatever happened, triumph or disaster, he never looked back. How could he? The action was too intense. There was always some other client who needed him, some other fire to put out, the daily blizzard of phone calls to return. Just outside his office, in the hushed confines of the first-floor hallway, Pacino or Voight or Chevy would be pacing up and down, waiting to see him. So he kept moving, plowing ahead, plowing it under, burying his feelings, on to the next crisis, feeling only the buzz.

THURSDAY EVENING, FEBRUARY 21, 1980. A SECOND-FLOOR BALLROOM IN the Beverly Wilshire Hotel. The annual meeting of the William Morris Agency, expanded to include many new stockholders. A yearly ritual, dinner and speeches. Further indoctrination into the way we do things here at the Morris office.

Around the mail room, it was said that, sooner or later, every trainee would be ushered down to the basement and shown a collection of suits. In reality, there were all sorts of odds and ends in the basement of El Camino: ancient, dusty scripts; dog-eared production notes; reel upon reel of film, including a long-forgotten screen test Frances Arms had done in the thirties; possibly the last extant model of George Wood's ill-fated Scopitone, which had proved more popular with investigators from the Securities and Exchange Commission and the U.S. Attorney's Office in New York than with bar patrons; a mounted map of the United States with colored dots across California and Texas and the Midwest to show the holdings of Willmor Properties and its sister company Morwill Properties, twin real-estate arms of the agency's parent company, Willmor International. But according to this story, there was nothing but suits, row upon row in every imaginable color and style but only one size: 36 short. The trainee would be told to look them over and pick the one he liked best. Chances were his arms and legs would stick out by three or four inches, but if he looked in the mirror and said, "Boy, this fits *great*," he was one of them.

That was the difference between the potential lifers and everybody else—whether you were *one of them*. Anyone who wasn't deemed one of them would eventually be ushered into a room and told that he looked as if he'd be happier somewhere else, that he didn't seem to be, well, one of them. But each of the forty-odd individuals who'd gathered in the Beverly Wilshire that evening was one of them. That's why they'd been given stock, to make them initiates in the family. David Geffen, returning to the business after four years on the sidelines, had discovered as much when he asked Abe Lastfogel how he'd managed to command the loyalty of those around him for so many years. It provoked one of those moments of extreme lucidity Lastfogel sometimes had, when the scales slipped away and he offered a nugget of utter truth: "Loyalty," he said, "is something you pay for."

Sammy Weisbord was running this meeting, and he believed in getting to the point. "Nineteen-seventy-nine," he declared, "was the greatest year in our entire history.

"We recorded the highest gross business and net profit we had ever attained."

The first aspect of the business he turned to was real estate. Except for sixteen acres in the Central Valley town of Lodi, now slated for development as a Kmart shopping center, all the agency's properties outside Beverly Hills had been transferred to Willmor, which was owned by Lastfogel and other senior executives. The Beverly Hills holdings had been consolidated after Frances Lastfogel's death, when the old Arms Building Corporation was dissolved and its properties on El Camino bought by the agency. Now there were big plans in the offing.

Two months ago, in December 1979, a subsidiary called William Morris Plaza had taken possession of the Arms Building Corporation property—the headquarters site and the parking lot across the street—and the adjacent parcels the agency owned on El Camino and South Rodeo Drive. The parking lot would soon sprout a new office building, three stories of black mirrored glass, with an open plaza in front and a cleft on one side leading to an underground garage. Workmen would begin transforming the dowdy old headquarters building into a black-mirrored glass rectangle, as sleek as Sammy Weisbord in his sunglasses and equally opaque. The two structures would contain 120,000 square feet of office space, with much of the new one to be leased to outside tenants. And as soon as they could buy the building behind them where Romanoff's had been, the building that stood between their other properties on South Rodeo . . .

"Nineteen-seventy-nine and into 1980, we have the highest advance bookings in our entire history," Weisbord continued. "Our business is strong, pulsating with rich, robust life and the momentum sweeps along in a surging flow."

That was the thing about Sammy. He didn't just trot out a few platitudes. He marshalled them as if for parade, puffed up their chests, marched them out before the cheering throng.

"In 1979, we made and implemented plans for a financial reorganization that will benefit every single stockholder." That was the meat of it: the new stock plan. A decade earlier, Abe Lastfogel had turned all future earnings back to the company. A thousand shares of class-B stock had been transformed into 500,000, and the third and fourth generations had become very, very comfortable. Now it was time for them to cash out their holdings and cut the younger employees in on the pie.

The reorganization plan called for the agency to retire its old stock, all of which was owned by Willmor, and create four new classes of stock, the bulk of which—400,000 shares—would be sold directly to employees. After a two-year transition period, this class-C stock would receive 100 percent of the agency's earnings. Willmor's holdings in the agency would be converted to a fixed-value preferred stock, and Willmor's owners, having profited handsomely from years of growth and investments, would cease to participate in the agency's earnings. But there was a catch. As individuals, the Willmor stockholders were eligible to buy the new class-C stock in proportion to their current holdings—as many as 23,000 shares each. New stockholders were being given options on much smaller blocks, generally 250 to 1,000 shares. The only sacrifice would come from Weisbord, Stoller, and Lefkowitz, who, following Abe Lastfogel's example, had announced their intention to buy about half the new stock they were entitled to so that more could be made available to the employees.

Weisbord was already on to his next topic—the clients and agents who had failed them. "It is a futility to decry and bemoan the frailty of human nature, the lapses of judgment, the violation of ethical codes," he lamented. "They exist and are a fact of life. But there is a victory that arises from the depths and ashes of these occasional defections and depredations, and that is the increased binding together of all of us into a tighter, more cohesive unit. What we have is rendered more precious, and anyone not appreciating our way of life, our heritage, and our support system for each other is better lost now than later."

Tighten the bond. Cut out the disloyal. Business as war.

"True also are the postures taken for the maintenance of our commission positions. Our deliberate decision to accept the loss of a Jackson Browne is amply repaid by the knowledge of the industry, as well as by our own loyal clients, that we are prepared to sacrifice easy, sure incomes if need be, to preserve and keep vital our principles."

To Weisbord, principles and commissions were synonymous. Jackson Browne and his manager had asked them to compromise those principles. The agency's position with music clients was to take 10 percent off the top, leaving them to pay their road expenses out of what was left. Jackson Browne had argued that they should take 10 percent of the net, not the gross. Jackson Browne was no longer a client.

Cut out the disloyal. Tighten the bond.

"So, too, is the refusal to reduce our package commission as some of our competitors are doing. We may lose some clients, but it is unwise in the time of our greatest financial strength, security, power, and acceptance, to 'break' and start a downward domino action that would have possible reverberations not only in TV but in other aspects of our business. . . ."

Sooner or later, it all came down to packaging. Stan Kamen could make all the high-powered film deals he wanted, but the real money was in television packages, and Morris's West Coast television operation had been a shambles ever since the CAA defections and the Writers Guild feud five years earlier. Lou Weiss still reigned as worldwide head of television in New York, but except for news and soaps, the business had

Abe Lastfogel, the world's fastest golfer, plays a round with Frank Sinatra at the new Desert Inn in Las Vegas, 1952. The agency's connections with the mob bosses who controlled the casinos made it Nevada's leading supplier of the talent during the fifties. (*UPI/Bettmann Archive*)

Rivaling the casinos for excitement were the atomic bomb tests in the desert, sixty-five miles away. Here, a Copa girl at the Sands receives a mushroom-cloud tiara from six admiring servicemen. (*University of Nevada–Las Vegas Library/Sands Collection*)

In 1953, the Morris Agency created a number of new series for ABC. The pilot that clicked was "Make Room for Daddy," starring Abe Lastfogel's favorite comedian, Danny Thomas. Here, producer Sheldon Leonard runs into trouble directing a Maxwell House commercial at the Sands in Las Vegas. (*University of Nevada–Las Vegas Library/Sands Collection*)

Pistol-packin' Mama: Sophie Tucker was a regular at the Round-Up Room in El Rancho Vegas. After the show, she'd peddle her autobiography in the lobby. *(Maurice Seymour)*

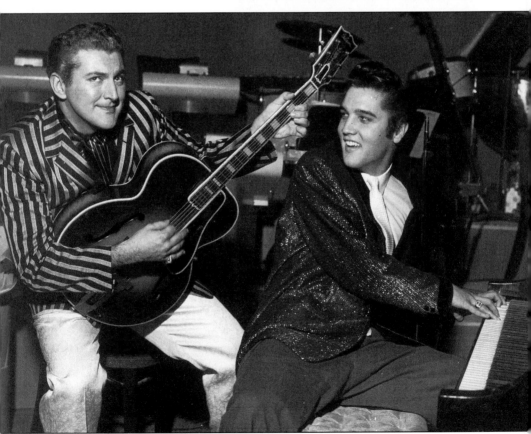

Though he was billed as "the Atomic Powered Singer," Elvis Presley's 1956 engagement at the New Frontier was a dud. Liberace *(left)* was more in the Vegas style. *(Las Vegas News Bureau)*

Steve McQueen got his start as a bounty hunter in Four Star Television's "Wanted: Dead or Alive," a Morris Agency package. McQueen (shown here with guest star Virginia Gregg) got to wear the gun, but Sammy Davis, Jr., was a better shot. (*Photofest*)

Nightclub comic Joe E. Lewis and singer Harry Belafonte (*left*) help Sammy Davis, Jr., celebrate his marriage to Vegas showgirl Loray White, hastily conducted after Davis was advised that matrimony would be good for his health. With them is Davis's little sister, Suzette Gina. (*UPI/Bettmann Archive*)

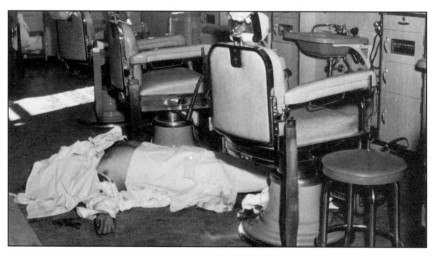

The barbershop assassination of Murder, Inc., boss Albert Anastasia was bad news for George Wood's pal Frank Costello, the mob ruler who controlled the Copacabana in New York and the Sands in Vegas. (*AP/Wide World Photos*)

Mob connection: George Wood of the Morris Agency with his bride at Idlewild, preparing to board a TWA Jetstream to Los Angeles. Jimmy Blue-Eyes Alo, close associate of Meyer Lansky, was best man. (*AP/Wide World Photos*)

Lew Wasserman led MCA into television production, making it simultaneously the largest seller of talent and the largest buyer. In 1962, Attorney General Robert Kennedy would force it out of the agency business in an antitrust suit that threw clients and agents alike onto the street. (*UPI/Bettmann Archive*)

Nat Lefkowitz was the lawyer-accountant who headed Morris's New York office. Among his protégés was David Geffen, who left for the rival Ashley Famous Agency, a progenitor of ICM. (*Matt Sultan/Television*)

Peter Lawford entertained his brother-in-law, presidential hopeful John
F. Kennedy, at the Sands during the filming of the Rat Pack movie
Ocean's Eleven. (University of Nevada–Las Vegas Library/Sands Collection)

Behind the photograph of Kim Novak sits Norman Brokaw, the first trainee in the West Coast mail room. *(Gene Daniels/Television)*

Phil Weltman headed the West Coast training operation during the sixties. Among his boys were Barry Diller and Michael Ovitz. *(Gene Daniels/Television)*

Barbara Stanwyck, another Brokaw client, was teamed with Elvis Presley in Hal Wallis's 1964 film *Roustabout*, which took showbiz back to its carny roots. *(Photofest)*

Thanks to his slavish devotion to Mr. Lastfogel, Sam Weisbord became West Coast head of television in the early sixties. His readiness to sacrifice his best friend, Phil Weltman, would help spur the formation of CAA in 1975. (*Gene Daniels/Television*)

ICM "superagent" Sue Mengers, a former secretary at William Morris, became the most glamorous seller in Hollywood in the seventies. (*UPI/Bettmann Archive*)

Michael Ovitz (*seated, center*) left Morris with four partners to form Creative Artists Agency, but it was Martin Baum (*standing, left*) who put them in the film business. Flanking Ovitz are (*from left*) his original partners, Bill Haber, Ron Meyer, Mike Rosenfeld, and Rowland Perkins, and a new recruit, Steve Roth. (*Los Angeles Times*)

Norman Brokaw cemented his reputation as a fame broker with a series of book, magazine, and television deals for former President Gerald Ford (*right*) and his family. (*Peter C. Borsari*)

NBC chairman Grant Tinker and producer Sherry Lansing salute Stan Kamen (*center*) at a $1,000-a-plate dinner in his honor at the Beverly Hilton, October 1984. With a client list that included Warren Beatty, Barbra Streisand, Jane Fonda, Goldie Hawn, and Chevy Chase, Kamen had succeeded Sue Mengers as the leading agent in Hollywood. A year and a half later, he would be dead. (*Alan Berliner/Berliner Studio*)

Toni Howard was one of several women Kamen brought into Morris's motion picture operation. (*Scott C. Schulman*)

When Sue Mengers failed to resuscitate the motion picture department after Kamen's death, Mike Simpson *(left)* and John Burnham took over. *(David Strick/Onyx)*

John Ptak *(center)* got the financing that enabled Australian director Peter Weir *(right)* to make *Green Card* with Gerard Depardieu. Then he left, along with Toni Howard and four other top agents. *(Courtesy Walt Disney Productions)*

The Godfather: When Michael Ovitz steamrolled the Morris office to become the top agent in Hollywood, Phil Weltman cheered him on. (*Scott Robinson*)

The survivors: Norman Brokaw (*left*) and Jerry Katzman were left to repair Morris's shattered image after losing most of its motion picture agents, along with such stars as Kevin Costner, Julia Roberts, Tim Robbins, and Tom Hanks. (*Peter C. Borsari*)

moved to the coast. After years of struggling, Larry Auerbach had finally turned over the West Coast department to his friend Jerry Katzman, a lawyer who'd been in business affairs until Morris Stoller sent him in to pick up the pieces. But so far, Katzman hadn't gotten a lot of results.

It wasn't just lack of manpower; the nature of the business had changed. The guild's attempt to eliminate packaging fees had finally fizzled before the Morris Agency's legal onslaught, but the golden age of packaging was clearly over. In the early seventies, with production costs rising and tobacco advertising suddenly banned, the networks had resorted to deficit financing—licensing agreements that paid less than the cost of production. Producers were now sure to lose money unless their show ran long enough to go into syndication. Agencies had no choice but to defer half their packaging fee until the show went into the black. CAA and most of the others cut their fee to 6 percent—3 percent of the licensing fee up front, 3 percent deferred. Morris held the line at 5 and 5, but its stubbornness was costing it clients.

So cut them out! Bind tighter together! "If we will but adhere to our time-honored fundamentals, even though we dress them in modern garb, we will enjoy the fruits of the second 82 years," Weisbord cried. He was unstoppable now, a force of nature, General Patton addressing the Third Army on the eve of D-Day. "And we will stand off any competition, any spurious philosophy, that may have a momentary glitter. We shall not only endure—we shall prevail!"

Most of the packaging agents in Weisbord's audience that evening would have opted for a little expediency if anyone had asked. It wasn't easy explaining to producers why they should pay 5 percent up front when other agencies were charging 3. But Weisbord was adamant: Guarantee me you can bring in twice the business, he said to agents who complained, and we'll talk about cutting the commission.

It was Jerry Katzman's job to make things work. Katzman was the son of B-picture producer Sam Katzman, the man responsible for the two worst pictures of Elvis Presley's career—*Kissin' Cousins* and the 1965 follow-up *Harum Scarum*, a humiliating exercise that Elvis had gone into thinking he could be Rudolph Valentino in *The Sheik*. Young Jerry had studied at Berkeley and gotten his law degree at UCLA, then worked as a producer himself before joining the Morris Agency in 1972. He was forty-three years old, a tough leader who was determined to get people to work together. But producers had been leaving the agency for years: David Wolper, who'd had hits with "Chico and the Man" and "Welcome Back, Kotter"—Morris packages built around standup comics the agency had brought to him. Aaron Spelling, whose new sex and fantasy lineup on ABC included four of the most popular shows on television—"The Love Boat," "Fantasy Island," "Charlie's Angels," and "Hart to Hart." Morris's prime-time lineup was down to an hour and a half each week—"Barney Miller," now in its sixth season on ABC, and George Schlatter's "Real People," a surprise success that blended audience participation with filmed reports on human oddities like the world's fastest painter: The Skeleton Dude lived.

The only bright spot on network television was in daytime, and that was due to Agnes Nixon, the soap opera producer Lou Weiss handled in New York. Once a screenwriter for drama anthologies like "Hallmark Hall of Fame" and "Philco Television Playhouse," Nixon in the late sixties had created two of ABC's most popular soaps, "One Life to Live" and "All My Children." In the process, she'd broken the taboos of daytime as effectively as "Laugh-In" had expanded the boundaries on prime time. Soap opera characters had been uniformly white and middle-class. She'd brought in blacks and Jews and pushed them all into something resembling the real world, where they had to deal with abortion and child abuse and the war in Vietnam. She also made a lot of money, both for herself and for the Morris office.

There were also new opportunities elsewhere, in made-for-TV movies and the syndication market. Nat Lefkowitz had always made a point of retaining syndication rights for the agency's clients, even in the fifties and sixties, when syndication was not a lucrative business—when reruns sold for a pittance and first-run syndication was the bargain basement of broadcasting. Syndication was so low-rent that in 1964, when Westing-house Broadcasting approached Merv Griffin about doing a syndicated version of the daytime talk show that NBC had canceled the year before, Abe Lastfogel told him it could end his career. But Griffin prospered regardless, and then, in the seventies, a series of government-imposed limitations on network programming opened up the syndication market. Now, stations were paying real money for cheaply produced first-run programs—game shows, talk shows, what-have-you—and old episodes of popular series. So a couple of young agents had started putting together shows for syndication. Nobody else in the agency paid much attention to them, but that was the way they liked it.

Larry Auerbach had assigned another young television agent, Arthur Axelman, to get them into TV movies, which Barry Diller had popularized when he launched ABC's "Movie of the Week" in 1969. Since then, TV movies had evolved from ninety-minute chase sequences shot for $350,000 to something much bigger—not art, exactly, but a reasonable form of commerce. The Morris office had a number of productions on next year's schedule, from *The Trial of Jean Harris*, a courtroom quickie with Ellen Burstyn as the prim and proper murderer of the Scarsdale diet doc, to *Kent State*, a three-hour miniseries that carefully re-created the 1970 antiwar confrontation.

What you made of all this depended on your point of view. As Morris Stoller saw it, the problem wasn't how to generate more television packages—it was how to create a situation where the company wasn't dependent on its salesmen. With Nat Lefkowitz isolated in New York and elevated to the meaningless position of cochairman, Stoller had taken complete control of the agency's financial affairs. It was his job to assure financial stability. And as far as he could tell, agents were a source of instability.

Stan Kamen, for instance. The Morris motion picture department had a hand in three of the top-grossing films of 1980—*9 to 5*, which Kamen had assembled with Jane Fonda and Lily Tomlin; *Any Which Way You Can*, the latest Clint Eastwood hit; and *Airplane!*, a loony satire that a young agent named John Ptak had put together for a pair of writer-producer clients, David and Jerry Zucker. But that fall, Michael Cimino's *Heaven's Gate* opened in Manhattan to spectacularly negative reviews. At $35 million it was not only one of the most expensive pictures ever made, it was one of the most phenomenal flops, its premiere so disastrous that Cimino and UA decided to pull it back and recut it. It was too late. Within days, *Heaven's Gate* would be shorthand for all the wretched excesses of movieland.

Real estate, on the other hand, was a good business to be in. The agency was already making new investments, bottom-fishing in the Sunbelt—a troubled office building in Austin, Texas; a distressed apartment complex in North Dallas. But no one could claim they'd forgotten their roots: The name of their investment vehicle was Radio & Television Enterprises, Inc.

EXCEPT FOR THE SUDDEN DEATH OF BERT ALLENBERG AND THE SLOW isolation of Nat Lefkowitz, the power structure of the Morris office had changed little since the retirement of Bill Morris, Jr., nearly thirty years before. No new members had been named to the board since Stoller and Weisbord went on in 1953. Bill Morris had remained a director for another ten years, but after that the company had been governed by Lastfogel and the handful of men who'd earned his approval—Sammy Weisbord, Morris Stoller, and (until his fatal move against Stoller) Nat Lefkowitz. The phone had largely ceased to ring in Lefkowitz's office now, and when he came to Los Angeles he had to hire his own car. Those who wanted power were still competing for Lastfogel's approval, usually over lunch at Hillcrest. In answer to Fanny Brice's question of thirty-five years before: Yes, they were always going to be his little boys.

But Lastfogel was eighty-two now, and he had other priorities. He still went in to the office every day, but mostly to watch old movies. He wanted to catch up on all those World War II–era pictures he'd missed while he was running Camp Shows for the USO. Every morning, dispatch would send some mail room boy out to the studios to pick up a new print and return the print from the day before. After lunch at Hillcrest, he'd go to the second-floor conference room and wait for the feature to start. If there was a meeting in progress, he'd help himself to some of the food on the table and wait for everyone to clear out. Around six o'clock, he'd show up in Sammy Weisbord's office, two doors down the hall from his own, and disappear into Sammy's private bathroom to tidy up for dinner.

Sammy might be in the middle of a meeting, but that didn't bother Mr. Lastfogel. Weisbord was holding a conference on the deal for "You Bet Your Life," the Groucho Marx quiz show that the agency was reviving for the syndie market with Buddy Hackett as host, when Mr. Lastfogel wandered in, performed his ablutions, and seated himself at Sammy's right hand. The negotiations went on around him, a tangle of issues involving a three-way partnership. Suddenly, he leaned forward as if to speak. Everyone looked at him expectantly. Sammy said, "Yes, Mr. Lastfogel?" Finally, he made his pronouncement. "You know, Sam, tonight at Hillcrest—I'm going to have the whitefish."

Aside from dinner and the movies, Lastfogel's main interest appeared to be his new woman friend, an exotic-looking young miss who wore flashy clothes and was said to be of Middle Eastern descent. Émile Chelette, his Creole chauffeur, had introduced them after picking her up by the pool at the Spa Hotel in Palm Springs. Some people thought she looked like a Vegas showgirl; he said she reminded him of Frances. Weisbord had been thrilled at first—why, having a gal might rejuvenate the old man. He was less thrilled when Mr. Lastfogel announced he was going to buy her a condo in Palm Springs. By this time, Weisbord and other people had decided she was taking him to the cleaners. But there wasn't much they could do about it, especially since he'd already given the bulk of his wealth to them.

With so many other things on Lastfogel's mind, the fourth and fifth generations had little choice but to try to please his surrogates, Weisbord and Stoller. Stoller had never been part of Hollywood, and Weisbord had cut himself off from it in his single-minded devotion to the Boss. Anyone who wanted to get in with them had to take his eyes off the business and start working the first-floor hallway. It was a situation that rewarded backstabbing rather than performance. And the bitter 1975 showdown in which Lefkowitz was shunted aside had turned the New York headquarters into an appendage of El Camino. The agency had split along two distinct lines—between agents and administrators, and between New York and the coast. The only way around it was to appoint enough people to the board to give every faction a voice.

The board expansion was the second phase of the reorganization that had begun with the new financial plan. First Mr. Lastfogel's successors had made arrangements for an orderly transfer of wealth; now they were preparing to cede power. The announcement was made in December 1980. Morris Stoller was named chairman. Sammy Weisbord would continue as president, and Abe Lastfogel and Nat Lefkowitz would be elevated to cochairmen emeriti. But the real news was the appointment of seven new board members, the first additions in twenty-seven years—three West Coast agents, Norman Brokaw, Tony Fantozzi, and Stan Kamen; two West Coast administrators, Roger Davis and Walt Zifkin; one New York agent, Lou Weiss; and one New York agent-administrator, Lee Stevens. Lenny Hirshan did not make the list—according to office scuttlebutt, because Stan Kamen blackballed him. Lee Stevens did, despite having started out as Lefkowitz's protégé. Walt Zifkin did, because he was Stoller's protégé. Tony Fantozzi did, because he handled George Schlatter, the only major prime-time television producer they had left. Norman Brokaw and Stan Kamen did, because they were Norm and Stan.

WHAT WAS HAPPENING WITH SUE? THAT WAS THE BIG QUESTION NOW. IN March 1981, at the New York premiere of *All Night Long*, the forty-four-year-old superagent was barely speaking to her star client, Barbra Streisand. Make that ex–star client, for after taking the female lead in this misguided Franco-American farce—the first Hollywood picture directed by Mengers's husband, Jean-Claude Tramont—La Streisand had left her longtime agent and friend and was now being handled by Stan Kamen and the Morris office.

Mengers had already lost Burt Reynolds, Diana Ross, and Ali Mac-Graw. *People* speculated that maybe she'd let them go because she was planning to join her ex-boss David Begelman, now head of production at MGM. Or maybe she was going to take over Columbia, the studio Begelman had run before resigning in disgrace in his embezzlement scandal. She had in fact been considered for the Columbia job when Begelman stepped down three years earlier, along with David Geffen, Freddie Fields, and Stan Kamen. But she wasn't freeing her clients now, she was losing them. And to lose Barbra, who was not only her biggest star but a veritable sister . . .

All Night Long had not been one of Streisand's favorite experiences, or anyone else's. It was a troubled production from the start—not a disaster like *Heaven's Gate*, just a great deal of *tsuris* that added up to very little onscreen. Tramont had started shooting with Lisa Eichhorn, an aspiring star who was getting $250,000 for in what was essentially a supporting role, portraying a San Fernando Valley housewife who falls for a drugstore operator played by Gene Hackman, a Mengers client and the real star of the film. But five weeks into the shoot, in what *Variety* described as "a more than surprising casting change," it was announced that Eichhorn was being replaced by Streisand. The move was surprising on several counts—Streisand replacing another actress, Streisand in a picture she hadn't developed, Streisand in a subordinate role. Mengers did get Streisand $4 million plus 15 percent of the gross for twenty-seven days' work. But Tramont wanted her to do things she found unsettling, like slide down a fire pole (she was terrified of heights) and run out into the rain (she had a cold). Finally, she had to ask herself: Was it worth it?

Far worse than the picture, however, was the bad blood between Mengers and Jon Peters, the Hollywood hairdresser who'd so brashly insinuated himself into Streisand's life. Before, people who wanted

Streisand had to go to Mengers; now they had to go to Peters as well. As far as Mengers was concerned, Peters was using Streisand to establish himself as a producer. But not everyone was eager to be involved with him—especially after they saw how he'd taken *A Star Is Born* away from its original producer, John Foreman—and Mengers felt he was keeping projects away from her client. *All Night Long* announced to the industry that Streisand was perfectly capable of doing a picture in which Peters had no involvement. At that point, the sniping between Peters and Mengers erupted into an open feud.

There was only one thing Mengers and Peters agreed on: They both disliked *Yentl*, the project Streisand had been nurturing for more than a decade. *Yentl* was based on "Yentl, the Yeshivah Boy," an Isaac Bashevis Singer short story about a rabbi's daughter who's so eager to learn the Talmud that she tries to pass as a boy so she can attend yeshivah. Streisand not only wanted to play the girl, she wanted to direct and produce and write the script. Mengers and Peters were both mollified somewhat when Streisand decided to do it as a musical—although it wasn't exactly a musical, it was a film with music, because "musical" seemed somehow inappropriate—and in 1979, they'd gotten a deal to make it at Orion, with Peters coproducing. Then, in the fall of 1980, with *All Night Long* in postproduction, everything had fallen apart. Orion put *Yentl* in turnaround—movies-peak for no go—when Streisand came in with a budget in the $17 million range. Peters, who wasn't exactly thrilled with Streisand's Jewish spiritual kick, wanted her to do a concert tour instead. Mengers couldn't imagine how she was going to produce and direct a musical that wasn't really a musical while playing a teenage girl playing a teenage boy. And she told her so.

The whole thing was a nightmare, a horror. At least Streisand hadn't left Mengers for another agent—she'd left for an attorney. But the attorney had taken her to Stan Kamen, and now, as *All Night Long* was opening to negative reviews in New York, Stan Kamen was shopping *Yentl* to the studios. It wasn't the most opportune moment to be pushing an expensive project by a fastidious megastar with zero directing experience, but Kamen appeared unfazed, even as the rejections piled up. He even sent a script to UA, which had just lost Woody Allen to Orion and was hungry for someone of Streisand's caliber—but not hungry enough, after *Heaven's Gate*, for this. UA had been tracking the project, and some people there thought they could shoot the phone book if Streisand was singing it. But one Cimino was enough, thank you. Kamen understood. UA was too unstable to be his first choice anyway.

By the end of March, however, Kamen was ready to close the deal at UA. Streisand herself had made the sale, after managing a meeting with the company's new chief (Andy Albeck had resigned in the wake of the *Heaven's Gate* fiasco) and charming him into submission. She'd invited him up to her Manhattan apartment, played him a tape of the music, even offered him the part of her father. At least, he thought she'd offered him the part; later, she denied any remembrance of it. Anyway, the deal was done. Peters was out. Shooting would start in September in Czechoslovakia. By which time, as it turned out, Transamerica would have sold the company to Kirk Kerkorian, who wanted to merge it with MGM for its distribution setup—MGM's own distribution arm having been sold off earlier in an ill-advised fit of corporate housecleaning.

So that was the outcome of *Heaven's Gate*: The studio's top execs out on the street, the studio itself dumped to the highest bidder, the director unemployed and unemployable, while the agent who'd packaged it was on to another deal, slicing cleanly through the waters in search of the next buyer. That was the way it was with agents. They didn't necessarily mean to be sharklike; it's just that they had to keep moving. Their power rode not on success or failure at the box office but on the aggregate clout of their clients—the perceived aggregate clout. With enough stars on their roster, they seemed omnipotent. Take the stars away, and who'd return their phone calls?

Streisand's shift altered the balance in Hollywood, confirmed Kamen's position as the top agent in town, gave Mengers the image of a powerhouse in decline. It was a devastating blow, not just to her career but to her self-image. Sure, she still had Ryan O'Neal and Gene Hackman and Michael Caine, and she'd picked up Farrah Fawcett-Majors from the Morris office after Farrah pulled out of "Charlie's Angels" to become a movie star. But Barbra was her magic amulet. If they wanted Barbra, they had to kiss her ass. Without Barbra, she was just exposing herself.

Mengers hadn't endeared herself to people during her years at the top. She'd been arrogant. She'd made merciless jokes. Things other people thought, she actually said. And why not? She had the stars. Those names on the phone sheet, suits waiting for their calls to be returned—let them call again. She knew what they wanted. If their number-one choice wasn't available they'd have to call back for their number-two choice, or their number-three choice. Until now. Now she didn't have so many stars. And the junior studio types she'd treated so dismissively, the readers and whatnot—some of them were important buyers now. And they remembered.

There was another thing—all those dinner parties. The whole routine was getting a bit tired. The business was changing, and even though Mengers was one of the reasons, she wasn't changing with it. Ten years before, it had been about glamour and talent and having fun with it all. You could spend the afternoon schmoozing around the pool, talking creatively about the role. Now it was about money. The $4 million Streisand pulled in for *All Night Long*? That was $3.5 million more than Mengers had gotten Faye Dunaway for *Network* five years before. So the pressure was on—on the buyers, on the sellers, on the clients. No time for poolside chitchat. Now it was conference calls with the client and his business manager and his attorney, and what they all wanted to know was, When does his gross participation kick in?

This made it easy to understand the appeal of Stan Kamen and the Morris office. What had looked stuffy and old-fashioned a few years before looked reassuringly businesslike today. Morris was where the interoffice memo pads said "Put It in Writing." It was known for meticulous deal making—for experience in contracts, attention to detail, the depth of its legal staff. That was the legacy of Nat Lefkowitz and Morris Stoller, a legacy that could be traced back to Abe Lastfogel's decision fifty years before to send Lefkowitz to law school.

Despite his studied informality—carefully pressed jeans, coffee-colored Jaguar instead of the regulation black Cadillac—Kamen was a Morris man at heart. He'd spent his life there, and he believed in the place as much as any of them, even after what had been done to Weltman. He might giggle when Norman Brokaw tried to impress the junior agents, telling them about driving Linda Darnell around to the studios—*Linda Darnell?* you could see them thinking. *Who the fuck was Linda Darnell?* But he was fond of them, even of Norman. They were family. And he subscribed to their credo, which valued loyalty above all else.

Loyalty was the bottom line. It was a good character trait, and a rare one—in clients above all. Goldie had it. Chevy had it. A handful of others. They had to realize that not every picture was going to be a hit, that you could put the best actors together with the best directors and it wouldn't always work, that the agent wasn't necessarily to blame. The more successful he became, the more critical the loyalty factor.

If he needed a reminder, he got one later that spring, when *The Pope of Greenwich Village* deal fell apart. This was a package he'd put together nearly two years before at UA—Al Pacino and James Caan in an urban crime caper about a small-time hood who gets in trouble with the mob. The script was wonderful, the casting perfect—Pacino and Caan, so riveting as the Corleone brothers in *The Godfather*, together again. It was a go picture. Then Jimmy Caan, who was getting $250,000 less than Pacino, decided he wanted the same money. Caan was a big draw—Oscar nominee as Sonny Corleone, Streisand's costar in her Fanny Brice sequel, *Funny Lady*. But Pacino was hotter, and after the *Heaven's Gate* fiasco, UA was not inclined to be indulgent— not even with Streisand, whose deal on *Yentl* specified that after $13 million, she'd be dipping into her own purse. In May, rather than meet Caan's new salary demand on *The Pope of Greenwich Village*, UA put the project in turnaround. So Caan walked—from the picture, from the agency.

That was the problem with being the top agent in town. All the stars want you to handle them because it's so reassuring to be with the number-one agent. But the reason you're the number-one agent is because you handle all the other stars—the ones they're competing with for jobs. Fear sends them into your arms, and fear drives them away. As long as you remain the star agent, they'll stay in your orbit. But at a certain point, especially with a lone-wolf agent like Kamen or Mengers, it becomes safe to leave. Someone really big defects, and that gives the others permission to think about their own nagging doubts. It had happened to Mengers, and sooner or later it would happen to Kamen, when the next star agent began to materialize.

Maybe it was happening already. He'd lost Burt Reynolds after only a couple of months—just long enough to cinch Reynolds's $5 million deal for *The Cannonball Run*, the comedy extravaganza with Farrah Fawcett, before Reynolds left in a dispute over the commission, which he didn't think he should have to pay because the producers had come to him with the project. And in the past year or two, Michael Ovitz had made some disturbing inroads into the William Morris client list. Always it was the same pitch: You're not getting the proper attention. You're not getting the right scripts. We can make things happen for your career. CAA was still a distant third behind Morris and ICM. But Ovitz had put John Travolta, whom Mengers had been trying desperately to snatch away, into *Urban Cowboy*, a hit for Paramount last year. Ovitz was working on Robert Redford. And now he and Ron Meyer were in Hawaii with Sylvester Stallone, who'd gone on vacation to lick his wounds after *Nighthawks* and *Victory*, a pair of back-to-back duds.

It wasn't just clients, either. CAA had also picked off some promising junior agents. Rick Nicita had left the year before, and taken Sissy Spacek with him. Then Jack Rapke, a young agent in the motion picture literary department, and Ray Kurtzman, who worked in business affairs under Roger Davis. Sam Weisbord got so mad when he heard about Kurtzman that he chased him screaming down the first-floor hallway. Kurtzman made it to his office, slammed the door shut, locked it, and roared, "You're outta your fuckin' mind, Weisbord!"

At the Morris office it was said that Ovitz and his partners were terrible people who'd betrayed the firm that nurtured them. CAA was the family secret, the bad seed, prodigal sons who'd brought shame upon the house. The name could be uttered only in a hush. The younger agents knew nothing about Phil Weltman, or Damon and Pythias. But they did know that CAA was starting to win Kamen's stars, and winning them, it was said, through devious means—by cutting commissions. When Redford went over, people muttered in staff meetings that he was paying only 5 percent. It went without saying that the Morris office never cut commissions—though there were rumors about that too.

Kamen himself didn't give much thought to CAA. Yes, the Redford signing put CAA on the map. But Kamen was still on top, and he wasn't one to shrink from competition. He admired Ovitz. He liked the way Ovitz handled himself. There was business enough for both of them. And after losing Steve McQueen the way he had, what could anyone do to hurt him?

There was a moment, though, that gave them all pause. It came in 1982, when Dustin Hoffman appeared in *Tootsie*—Dustin Hoffman, who'd once been handled by Howard Hausman in New York, in a movie produced and directed by Kamen's friend Sydney Pollack, the one artist in Hollywood he'd always wanted to sign and hadn't. Hoffman played a down-and-out actor who tries to pass himself off as a woman to land a part, and Pollack did a turn as his high-powered agent. There was significant buzz about the picture before it opened, and the turnout for the industry screening in New York was impressive. It was your typical show-biz crowd, jaded, self-obsessed, go-ahead-and-make-me-laugh. But an audible murmur swept through the audience when the camera panned Pollack's office, because there on the wall was something everybody was getting used to seeing: the CAA logo.

THE DEATH OF NAT LEFKOWITZ IN SEPTEMBER 1983, COMING AS IT DID just three months after the gala black-tie dinner at Hillcrest marking the Morris Agency's eighty-fifth year, was something of an anticlimax. As far as the agency was concerned, Lefkowitz might as well have been dead for the past eight years. Publicly they honored him with the title cochairman emeritus, but inside the agency he'd been a nonperson ever since his abortive move against Morris Stoller. When he expired at seventy-eight at New York University Medical Center following heart surgery, the press reports noted his many contributions to the theatrical scene—treasurer and president and cochairman of the Morris Agency, chairman of the Jewish Theatrical Guild, board member of the National Conference of Christians and Jews and of the Will Rogers Hospital in Saranac Lake, etc., etc. There was no hint of the bitterness between his family and the firm they'd built up from its vaudeville years.

But the bitterness was there. Julius Lefkowitz, Nat's brother, the outside accountant who'd been in partnership with Stoller's brother, told the Beverly Hills crowd he'd kick their ass if they showed up in Gotham for the funeral—wait outside the funeral parlor and throw them out onto the street. Sammy Weisbord was going to go anyway, but at the last minute a couple of fellow board members pulled him into a room and told him he couldn't. Services were held uneventfully at Riverside Chapel on Amsterdam Avenue, where Sophie Tucker had gotten her sendoff nearly twenty years before. Bill Morris, Jr., now eighty-four and no stranger to exile himself, flew in from Malibu to deliver the eulogy. He extolled Lefkowitz as a man who stayed always in the background.

Meanwhile, some careful maneuvering was being done along the first-floor corridors of El Camino. Sammy Weisbord was at last ready to step down as president, and someone from the fourth generation would be picked to take his place. There were really only three possibilities.

Stan Kamen was without question the most powerful agent in Hollywood in the fall of 1983. Despite the inroads of CAA, he and a handful of other agents in his department represented most of the top talent in town. Barbra Streisand was triumphant with *Yentl*, which opened in November to glowing reviews. Richard Gere was the number-one sex symbol in America on the strength of *An Officer and a Gentleman*, the 1982 box-office smash. But Kamen didn't want to be president—he was an agent, not an administrator. He didn't want Norman Brokaw to be president either. You couldn't not like Norman—he was such a wide-eyed innocent, the oldest living fan in Hollywood—but he could be embarrassing in a meeting. Every time he started to speak, it was like a trap door opened up and you were back in the forties. That left Lee Stevens, the one Lefkowitz had brought along in New York. The compromise candidate. A neutral force, acceptable to all parties.

Months later, in February 1984, after everything had been decided, the board met to elect the new leader. The vote was unanimous. Stevens would take over June 1, the sixth president in the agency's history. Weisbord would join Stoller as cochairman. The Morris office "shifts top exex with the frequency of Halley's Comet," *Variety* observed—but Halley's Comet must be coming around more and more often these days, because Stevens was the third president in fifteen years. Maybe this accounted for the strained tone of Weisbord's remarks. "We do not annul our predecessors nor do we begrudge our successors," he declared. "With tears and affection, we pass on the reins. This was done to fulfill our destiny."

Then again, that was Sammy.

NORMAN BROKAW TOOK THE CALL. IT WAS HIS OLD FRIEND BILL Cosby, phoning from New York. He was ready to try another television show.

By the spring of 1984, Cosby had become the most successful of Brokaw's celebrity clients—bigger than Al Haig, bigger than Menachem Begin, bigger even than Gerald and Betty Ford. He seemed to be everywhere—on television spots, in the record stores, doing standup in Vegas, guesting on "The Tonight Show," hosting his own specials. Abe Lastfogel had always maintained that certain entertainers—Danny Thomas being the prime example—could achieve longevity by working in every area of the business rather than focusing on pictures or television or nightclubs. Brokaw, working the fame game, had taken that idea a step further, and with Bill Cosby, he'd shown just how far you could go with it.

Cosby hadn't just stayed in the public eye, he'd grown, and he'd done it without a hit movie or television series. In the meantime, he and his wife, Camille, had had five children—but what with all the pressures and opportunities of celebrity, the man who'd made kids his career wasn't spending much time with his own. It was a little like Danny Thomas, three decades earlier. He was never home. He never saw his family. He needed a TV show to put his life in order. So he phoned his agent in Beverly Hills.

"Make Room for Daddy": This was where Norman Brokaw had come in.

Morris's television department seemed to be on the rebound. It had gone into the 1983–1984 season with five prime-time packages. George Schlatter's "Real People" was in its fifth season and sinking fast, and "Oh Madeline," a sitcom starring Madeline Kahn, was headed for cancellation after one season. But the other three looked like hits: "The Scarecrow and Mrs. King," an espionage spoof with Kate Jackson as the suburban divorcée who finds herself battling Soviet spies. "Silver Spoons," a promising sitcom with Ricky Schroeder as a precocious twelve-year-old who lives with his ultrawealthy dad. "Webster," built around twelve-year-old Emmanuel Lewis, an adorable black kid whom Lou Erlich, the current president of ABC Entertainment, had discovered in a Burger King commercial. Susan Clark and her husband, Alex Karras, the football star turned sportscaster, were Morris clients with a deal at ABC, so little Lewis found himself in their sitcom home.

Cosby was thinking of something a tad less cute. He had in mind an hour-long show about a wealthy New York private eye who rode in a chauffeured limousine and ate at "21"—"I Spy" crossed with "Burke's Law." Then Carsey-Werner called, wondering if Cosby would ever do another series.

Marcy Carsey and Tom Werner were former ABC programming execs who'd left the network to produce. During the seventies they'd worked under ABC Entertainment president Fred Silverman, who took the network to number one in prime time. Carsey, given Michael Eisner's old job as head of prime-time comedy, bought "Soap," a soap opera spoof that offended everyone from the Southern Baptist Convention to the National Gay Task Force, and "Taxi," a sitcom about a bunch of guys in a garage. Then, with two unlikely hits to her credit, she made her exit with a series commitment from ABC. Werner joined her a few months later. Their first series was "Oh Madeline," the Madeline Kahn sitcom that bombed. They were eager to try something else.

Carsey-Werner Productions wasn't a client of the Morris office, but Marcy Carsey and Tom Werner were both close to Larry Auerbach, the agency's top-level contact with ABC. They were also big fans of Bill Cosby's comedy albums, which often included takeoffs on family life. That gave them the idea of doing a family-oriented sitcom.

It wasn't exactly a commercial formula: By 1984, the sitcom seemed headed the way of vaudeo. The Nielsens were dominated by action-adventure series and prime-time soaps—"Dallas," "Dynasty," "The A-Team." "Webster" and "Silver Spoons" were bucking the trend. But Carsey and Werner wanted a family sitcom, and after he met with them, Cosby got enthusiastic too. They could do something warm and exemplary, more subtle than the usual blowhard husband–ditzy wife routines. Something positive, something that would take on the demons Cosby saw in prime-time programming—too much jiggle, not enough family. But what kind of family should he have? Cosby wanted to go blue-collar, playing a chauffeur married to a plumber, maybe in Atlanta. Three generations in the same house. Solid, wholesome, uplifting.

Then Jerry Katzman got a call from Brandon Tartikoff, a former ABC exec who now headed prime-time programming at NBC. Katzman and Tartikoff had known each other for the past eight years, ever since Tartikoff, newly arrived at ABC from Chicago, got a call from the Morris office about lunch with their top agents. Twenty minutes into the meal everyone realized a dreadful mistake had occurred: The Morris crew was expecting not Brandon Tartikoff but Brandon Stoddard, ABC's head of made-for-TV movies and miniseries. But they called a huddle at another table and decided to go on with Tartikoff. Now he was in charge of programming at NBC, though he had little to show for it but bombs. Tartikoff's baby daughter had woken up crying the night before, so he'd switched on "The Tonight Show" and caught Cosby doing his monologue about family life. That had given him an idea. "Hey, Jerry," he said when Katzman got on the line. "Has anybody thought of doing a show with Bill Cosby?"

"Funny you should ask," Katzman replied. Carsey and Werner were in Tahoe with Cosby right now, trying to develop a concept. Tartikoff had worked with them both at ABC. What did he think?

"I'd love to work with them again," he said.

A meeting was set up at ABC, which got first shot because of its relationship with Carsey-Werner. Larry Auerbach and Alan Berger, the thirty-three-year-old golden boy of the television department, made the short drive to the network's Century City offices. They met with Carsey, Werner, and Lou Erlich, the head of ABC Entertainment. But ABC already had a number of series commitments with Aaron Spelling, and a recent Cosby special on the network hadn't done well. Erlich was interested in Cosby, but he couldn't see committing to a series. Tartikoff had already agreed to Katzman's ante—a commitment for six episodes.

A few days later, Carsey, Werner, and the Morris agents went to Burbank to make their formal pitch to Tartikoff. He liked the general idea—a family show based on real life, children and parents together, humor in the situation rather than in setups and punch lines. But he had a problem with the specifics. Why Atlanta? Why not New York, where Cosby lived? And would anybody buy Cosby as a chauffeur? They should make him middle-class and successful—more believable. And they should get rid of the grandparents—too gimmicky. He wanted it to be as universal as possible, and that meant a nuclear family. They went into negotiations the next day.

But by Friday, the deal was bogged down in business affairs. Three parties wanted a piece of the program—the production company, Carsey-Werner; Bill Cosby himself; and another Morris client, Viacom International, the television distributor that syndicated such shows as "I Love Lucy" and "All in the Family." Viacom was providing Carsey-Werner with deficit financing and office space in Westwood. In return, it wanted back-end distribution rights and part-ownership of Carsey-Werner's shows. Cosby wanted creative control. And since the whole point was to be with his family, he wanted to shoot it in New York, three thousand miles from every other sitcom on television. It was late in the year to be developing a show for next season; they didn't have much time. So the Morris office set up a meeting for Tuesday morning with Tartikoff's counterpart at CBS.

Alan Berger was in his apartment on Charleville—Ron Meyer's old place, just down the street from the Morris office—that weekend when the phone rang. It was Tom Werner. He was very nervous about this, he told Berger. They really wanted to do the show at NBC. He wanted Berger to call Tartikoff and tell him what was going on.

Berger was lean and aggressive, from the ad agency side of the business—a former account exec at Leo Burnett in Chicago and Young & Rubicam in Los Angeles. Before joining the Morris Agency, he'd placed millions of dollars in spot buys in media across the country. He was used to making quick decisions. He phoned Larry Auerbach at his mansion in the hills north of Sunset. After a brief consultation, he dialed Tartikoff at his home in Coldwater Canyon. Carsey and Werner were concerned that the negotiations weren't going well, he said. They'd scheduled a meeting at CBS for Tuesday. If they didn't close the deal with NBC on Monday, they were taking that meeting.

The deal closed on Monday.

It was nice to have Cosby back on the air after all this time, but no one was expecting a hit. Still, Carsey-Werner assembled some of the best talent in television for their new star, veterans from "The Mary Tyler Moore Show" and "Taxi." By early May, they had a fifteen-minute presentation tape—there wasn't time to do a full pilot—that was laugh-out-loud funny. Alan Berger saw it for the first time in the second-floor conference room at the Morris office. When it was over, he announced that it was great, except the laugh track was too loud. That got him a funny look: There wasn't any laugh track. That was the studio audience he'd heard.

It was beginning to feel good to be a William Morris television agent again.

13

HILLSIDE

Los Angeles, 1984-1986

THE MORRIS OFFICE LOOKED RICHER AND MORE POWERFUL THAN EVER when Lee Stevens assumed the presidency that June. Its motion picture department still dominated Hollywood, despite recent inroads by CAA. Its television department, after years in the wilderness, was clearly on the rise. Its annual revenues were estimated by *Variety* to be in the $30 million range—a 150 percent increase in the fifteen years since Abe Lastfogel's retirement. It was the world's largest talent agency, with 550 agents representing an estimated two thousand clients. In fact, the complete client list—a highly confidential document—ran to fifty-seven computer printout pages and contained well over three thousand names, from Edward Albee and Kareem Abdul-Jabbar to Franco Zeffirelli and rock singer Warren Zevon. Anyone who might question the effectiveness of Lastfogel's successors had only to eye the results.

The fifty-three-year-old Stevens cut an imposing figure as president. He was a tough-talking New Yorker, uncharacteristically tall to be heading a firm whose leaders from Lastfogel on had all seemed like munchkins. He'd also gotten a new nose a few years back, a cute little button job that would have fit nicely on Grace Kelly's face but looked strangely lost on his own oversized mug. "Dress British—think Yiddish" was the watchword, and maybe he'd gotten carried away.

He had a commanding presence all the same—quiet but implacable, combative, assured that his will would prevail. He could be witty on occasion, but his reserve made him tough to read. Some saw him as warm and supportive; to others he was mean-spirited and vindictive. Either way, he was the first president to keep contemporary since Last-fogel in his prime. He read the best-sellers, knew the chart-topping records, saw all the hit plays and movies. He took his post with the easy confidence of one to the manor born. It had been years since he'd answered to the name of Silverman.

The agency had managed to weather the embarrassment of the Elvis Presley probate fight, which started when the Presley estate—controlled since Vernon's death in 1979 by Elvis's former wife, Priscilla, a Norman Brokaw client—was ordered by a Memphis probate judge to sue the agency's old buddy, Colonel Parker. Judge Joseph Evans, curious about Parker's 50 percent management fee, had appointed a Memphis lawyer named Blanchard Tual to look into Parker's dealings. Tual found that Priscilla, whom Brokaw had just put in as cohost of ABC's "Those Amazing Animals," was unaware of many of the agreements involving the Colonel, the Morris Agency, Boxcar Enterprises, and RCA. When Tual delivered a fifty-two-page report assailing the fees Parker had collected and the recording and merchandising deals he'd made, and followed up with a forty-eight-page supplement charging Parker and RCA with "collusion, conspiracy, fraud, misrepresentation, bad faith and overreaching," the ensuing barrage of lawsuits briefly threatened to expose Elvis's business affairs to full public view. But in June 1983 a settlement was reached in which Parker agreed, among other things, to remove himself from Elvis's affairs and sell his interest in Boxcar to the estate. Now Priscilla was launched as a regular on "Dallas" and presided over a reconstituted Elvis Presley Enterprises, which ran Graceland as a tourist attraction and was struggling to regain merchandising rights after a U.S. Appeals Court ruled they were in the public domain.

There were disturbing portents in Morris's motion picture operation, however. Gary Lucchesi, the department's twenty-eight-year-old golden boy, the one young agent the company administrators saw as a leader, had left the year before to take a job at Tri-Star Pictures, the joint venture recently formed by Columbia, CBS, and Time, Inc.'s Home Box Office. That December, fifty-one-year-old Ed Bondy—whose client Lou

Gossett, Jr., had won an Oscar eight months earlier for his performance as Richard Gere's drill sergeant in *An Officer and a Gentleman*—had dropped dead of a heart attack while standing at his kitchen sink. And in April, Marty Bauer, who'd recently moved to the coast after six years heading the New York motion picture department, had left to open his own agency.

Bondy's departure was involuntary; the other two had reasons. For Lucchesi, it was a chance to move to a more creative side of the business, to get into the nitty-gritty of moviemaking. For Bauer, who struck many of his coworkers as brash and egocentric, it seemed to have more to do with the realization that he was not being groomed to become Stan Kamen's replacement. Then there was the matter of a $2.50 videotape rental—an expense account item the higher-ups disallowed. A major flap ensued. Bauer left. With him went Alan Alda, directors Brian De Palma and John Avildsen, and Marty Bregman, Pacino's longtime producer, who'd rejoined his old partner at the Morris office.

Gary Lucchesi hadn't taken any clients, but losing him was almost worse. Tall and handsome and clean-cut, like all of Kamen's assistants, Lucchesi was a UCLA grad from San Francisco who'd gone into the William Morris training program after he heard David Geffen recommend it in a course he was auditing. He'd been plucked from the mail room to work on Stan Kamen's desk, then quickly promoted to agent. He was a charmer, savvy and deft, smooth but never slick. He knew how to handle Kamen—how to make him comfortable, how to save all the unpleasant phone calls to be returned until the end of the day, how to sugarcoat the bad news so it went down easy. Kamen liked him so much he'd actually started letting him share some of his clients—and not just new talents like Susan Sarandon, who'd starred in *The Rocky Horror Picture Show*, and director Roger Spottiswoode, but even Warren Beatty, whom Kamen spoke with every day.

Lucchesi had also started building his own stable of clients, which at this point showed more promise than heat. He'd signed Michelle Pfeiffer, a knockout blonde from Orange County who'd landed the female lead in *Scarface*, Al Pacino's new gangster film, which Bregman had produced and De Palma directed. Ed Limato, Richard Gere's agent, had recommended her for the role, so Limato took her over when Lucchesi left. John Malkovich, an off-Broadway actor who was making his film debut with Sally Field in *Places in the Heart*, landed with Clint Eastwood's agent, Lenny Hirshan. Sam Shepard, a client Kamen shared with him, went to Lucchesi's assistant, a young woman named J. J. Harris who'd just been promoted to agent. Then there was Kevin Costner, whose most significant role to date—as the corpse in the opening credits of *The Big Chill*—had been lost on the cutting room floor. Costner, who spent a lot of time in the lobby baby-sitting his infant daughter with Émile Chelette, Abe Lastfogel's chauffeur, was caught in a tug-of-war between J. J. Harris and Ed Limato.

That December they'd come close to losing Ed Limato too. With Limato, the problem was money. Limato was an agent in the Stan Kamen mold—quiet, persuasive, dedicated to his clients to the exclusion of all else. Tall and saturnine, with thick black hair and deep-set eyes and a brooding air, he seemed a throwback to the Hollywood of Johnny Hyde's day, when the stars dined at Romanoff's and Los Angeles was shadowy and noir. After bumming around Europe during the sixties (including a stint as Franco Zeffirelli's driver in Rome on the shoot of *The Taming of the Shrew*), he'd started in the New York mail room at International Famous, then stayed on as an agent after the merger that created ICM. In 1978, seven months after his arrival at ICM's West Coast office, Stan Kamen lured him to William Morris.

Like Kamen, like all successful agents, Limato was an action junkie. He thrived on the adrenaline rush of phone calls and crises and deals, and in the past two years he'd established himself as one of the firm's top motion picture agents. He'd persuaded Richard Gere to take the lead in *An Officer and a Gentleman*, which John Travolta had rejected as too slight—and Gere, too, until Limato talked him into meeting the producer. In the meantime, Limato had signed Mel Gibson, a blue-eyed Australian who'd starred in a postapocalyptic B called *Mad Max*, and put him in *The Year of Living Dangerously*, whose success suggested that he could be the town's next superstud. Then Limato saw the end-of-the-year bonus they were offering him.

He was so angry, he stayed home for a week. He met with Jeff Berg, who'd succeeded Marvin Josephson as president of ICM three years before, and agreed to go back to his old agency. Kamen went ballistic when he found out. With Lucchesi gone, Limato was the only one who could take over in Kamen's absence. Kamen marched down the hall to Morris Stoller's office, slammed the door, and announced that if they didn't get Limato back, he was quitting too.

Then Ed Bondy died—just like that, no warning whatever. Kamen was devastated, along with everyone else in the department. Bondy was their comic relief—funny, outrageous, wildly out of the closet. Limato felt terrible. Kamen had nurtured him, taken pride in his success. Limato felt so guilty, he called Berg and told him he had to go back to the Morris office. But he didn't go back empty-handed: Stoller and his attorney worked out a contract locking in his salary and bonus for the next three years—$250,000 for 1984, $300,000 for 1985, $350,000 for 1986. He also got a sporty Jaguar like Kamen's instead of the dowdy black Cadillac most of the top Morris men drove.

The Morris office had always disdained employment contracts—they were a family, weren't they? But at least they'd been able to hold Limato, and with him Richard Gere and Mel Gibson and Michelle Pfeiffer. Now Kamen himself was under attack. The predator was CAA—"Ca-Ca," they called it inside the department. Ca-Ca seemed to be on some kind of feeding frenzy. Ca-Ca was targeting their stars.

Nine years after leaving William Morris, Michael Ovitz had mastered the art of being in second position. He was often on the set of one picture or another to look after his clients, and it was only natural that he'd end up having dinner with some of Kamen's clients as well. He couldn't help but be charming. Kamen's stars couldn't help but admire his skill. The stars still loved Kamen, of course. Had no intention of leaving him. But now they started to develop a comfort level with Ovitz as well. That's what being in second position meant—not that you intended to displace the other agent, just that you were there in case the other agent should retire, or encourage his client in some disastrous career move, or stumble, God forbid, and fall off a cliff and die.

Ovitz was always respectful. Still, this didn't feel like the old days, when Stan and Sue made sport out of courting each other's clients. If Stan got a call from one of Sue's clients, he'd take the meeting—but only after phoning Sue and giving her a week to straighten things out. With Kamen, agenting was like fencing—ritualized combat governed by a gentlemanly code of conduct. With Ovitz, it was a hunger. Once he'd made contact, Ovitz seemed to call every day: Have you seen this script? Why haven't they told you about this property? Relentless, insinuating, planting the seed. The easy marks went first, like Farrah Fawcett, who'd returned to the Morris office after Mengers failed to make her a movie star. Others—Jane Fonda, Barbra Streisand—would take time.

Kamen's apparent weakness—the vulnerability he tried so hard to hide—was actually a strong point. It bound people to him, made them want to protect him the way he protected them. What made him look strong was in fact his Achilles heel. His perfectionism had him tightly wound, especially about his clients. His stature depended on them—not just his stature in the industry, but his influence on the first floor, which was tenuous enough already. It was taking him months to hire someone to replace Ed Bondy, even though he'd found the perfect candidate— Toni Howard, a casting director who was great with talent and plugged in at the highest levels. Toni's sister Wendy was the quintessential Hollywood hostess, active in SHARE and other socially prominent Westside charities and married to producer Leonard Goldberg, the ex–programming chief at ABC who'd hired Barry Diller away from the Morris office and then become Aaron Spelling's partner. Toni Howard was perfect, but getting her past Morris Stoller was a challenge. Without his stars, Kamen would carry no weight at all. They were his meal ticket and his life. No one else could be trusted to take care of them.

At fifty-eight, Kamen held as much power as any studio chief in Hollywood. It was right there in his office, corner of Charleville and the alley. But he couldn't spread it out, and it was so hard to hold it in. All those stars, him and him alone—the pressure was turning him into a screamer. When there was a crisis, when everyone around him was hysterical, he was a calming influence. But in ordinary circumstances, with the calls pouring in, hundreds of them every day, and just him and his assistant to handle them—inevitably the assistant would screw up and suddenly Kamen would blow, shrieking, screaming, hurling the phone. Then it would pass, and they'd go on to the next call.

It didn't help that he was starting to have these annoying little physical problems. About a year ago, he'd stepped on a rusty nail on the beach, and the wound in his foot wouldn't heal. He'd gotten a tetanus shot, seen the doctor, kept his foot soaking in a bucket for hours. Nothing seemed to help. It was driving him crazy. He kept getting shingles, too—little blisters across his back that wouldn't go away. And to have Ovitz breathing down his neck as well—but that was okay. Ovitz was a winner, and Kamen admired winners. Kamen was a winner too. Winners could take care of themselves.

ABE LASTFOGEL WAS SITTING IN HIS OFFICE, FEET DANGLING ABOVE THE floor, sporting his perennial bow tie, when the cramping hit. Abdominal pains, sharp enough to make him wince and cry out. Émile Chelette helped him out the back entrance to the alley, where a handful of top execs parked their cars. Within minutes he was at Cedars-Sinai Medical Center, the massive hospital complex in West Hollywood.

It was nothing to be alarmed about, the doctors said—a little gall bladder trouble. The operation was routine, but then complications set in—not unusual for an eighty-six-year-old. Danny Thomas got in to see him in intensive care and kissed him on the forehead. "You're the kid from the 5100 Club," Lastfogel said when he opened his eyes. Several days later, on the evening of Saturday, August 25, he was dead of a heart attack.

The funeral was held at noon Tuesday at Hillside Memorial Park, the Culver City mausoleum where Frances had been buried eight years before. Hillside was a strange oasis in the West L.A. sprawl, a patch of green beside the San Diego Freeway, with condos and shopping centers across the street and jetliners streaming into LAX not two miles away— not so much a garden of heavenly rest as a jumping-off spot into the void. Leaders of the industry gathered in the futuristic chapel to bid him goodbye—Warren Beatty, Barry Diller, Lew Wasserman of MCA. Danny Thomas delivered the eulogy. It had been more than forty years now since Abe Lastfogel had plucked him out of obscurity and made him a star—forty years during which he'd become rich and successful beyond hope or imagining. Now he was burying the man. This was like burying his father. He thought he'd buried his father already.

The old guard at the office was equally in shock—Sammy Weisbord and Morris Stoller and the generation behind them, Lee Stevens and Norman Brokaw and Stan Kamen. Despite the evidence, each one of them managed to see himself in Lastfogel's image. "I am a true clone of Abe Lastfogel," Stoller declared in his remarks.

To many of the younger agents at Morris, Mr. Lastfogel was little more than a sweet old man who puttered about the office and watched old movies every afternoon. But the sharper ones realized that even in his dotage, he was the conscience of the firm. It'll be interesting to see what happens now, more than one of them thought as they filed out of the chapel.

After the service, they trooped outside to the Alcove of Love, where, amid the dull and constant roar of the freeway, the little square man was laid to rest in the crypt beside Frances's. "Loving Husband," read the plaque on the travertine. "Loving Wife," read the plaque beside it. When it had all been done, the mourners drove back to Beverly Hills and gathered at Danny and Rosie Thomas's house to tell stories about him. Only then, as they sat beneath the murals of the Cedars of Lebanon in the living room and reminisced, did it sink in how much they'd miss him. He'd been their link to the beginnings of showbiz. He'd been their moral touchstone. He'd been their father. Now they were on their own.

The first challenge the leaders of the agency faced, now that they were on their own, was Mr. Lastfogel's will. For a man who'd owned more than 80 percent of the world's largest talent agency before he retired, it was a surprisingly modest estate: less than $2 million, before taxes. But that didn't mean it could be settled without rancor.

It seemed pretty clear-cut. Lastfogel had given away most of his fortune some sixteen years before, when he distributed his interest in the agency to a handful of his boys—the men who now controlled the company. His will was quite specific about the rest. Sam Weisbord, who, though color-blind, had amassed a sizable art collection in his penthouse in the Sierra Tower, was to receive two paintings—an André Derain still-life valued at $11,000 and an autumn landscape by "François"—and a gold Cartier wristwatch, the one Will Morris had given young Lastfogel so many years before. The rest of his personal effects were to go to Morris Stoller. Émile Chelette would receive $100,000. Modest sums were set aside for others who'd served him over the years—his masseuse, his barber, his secretary. Various charities were to get $45,000. Frances's sister-in-law, Toddy Armhaus, was to be the beneficiary of a $350,000 trust fund. All his brothers and sisters had died; none of his nieces and nephews were provided for. Everything else was to go to the Abe and Frances Lastfogel Foundation, controlled by Morris Stoller.

In the last few years of his life, however, Lastfogel had become increasingly attached to his woman friend, much to the chagrin of the men who sat on the board. Fourteen months before he died, he'd amended his will to provide her with a $350,000 trust fund. The codicil was duly witnessed by Roger Davis and Walt Zifkin, neither of whom had much choice in the matter. But Weisbord and Stoller, the executors of his estate, were as horrified by this act of profligacy as Davis and Zifkin, and they did have a choice. Mr. Lastfogel could waste his money on this gold-digging broad if he wanted to, but they didn't have to abet him. They wouldn't have anything to do with it. The Bank of America was named trustee for her account.

THURSDAY, OCTOBER 25—STAN KAMEN DAY, BY PROCLAMATION OF THE mayor of Los Angeles. It had come out of his involvement with the United Jewish Fund, which started when he met with the Israeli ambassador at the Beverly Hilton in 1973. For eight years now, he'd chaired the UJF's entertainment division, twisting arms for a good cause. For the past two years, he and Sherry Lansing—former president of Fox, now an independent producer—had led the UJF's Mission to Israel. The mission brought Hollywood heavyweights—Walter Matthau, Jack Lemmon, director Mark Rydell—to Israel for tours of army bases and meetings with political leaders. Lansing had been trying to get Kamen to accept some sort of honor for years. He always shied away from awards—the glare of the spotlight—and he'd only agreed to this one because it was a chance to raise money for something he believed in. But it made him anxious all the same.

Kamen was jumpy all day. He'd just gotten a new assistant, a twenty-seven-year-old University of Southern California law grad named Cary Woods, and that morning, Woods sent Kamen's car back to Malibu with his tuxedo in the backseat. Kamen went berserk when he found out. What was he going to wear? He threw the phones around and ran screaming into the hall. Woods ran after him, begging him not to worry—there was still plenty of time to get the tuxedo back. They both knew it wasn't the tuxedo he was worried about.

But at $1,000 a plate, the turnout that evening at the Beverly Hilton was as impressive as Kamen's client list. Edie Wasserman, the doyenne of Hollywood society, was there with her husband, Lew. The very social Wendy Goldberg was there with her husband, Leonard. Veronique and Gregory Peck showed up. Neile McQueen brought her new husband, Al Toffel. Frank and Barbara Sinatra came up from Rancho Mirage. Brandon Tartikoff came. His boss, NBC chairman Grant Tinker, was an honorary chairman of the event, along with Jack Lemmon and Barry Diller, who'd just left Paramount to become chairman of Fox. Warner Bros. chairman Robert Daly was there. Sue Mengers came with her husband, Jean-Claude Tramont. Jerry Weintraub, the flashy promoter who'd coproduced Tramont's *All Night Long* with Leonard Goldberg, came and left, apparently in a snit over his table. Robert Wagner caused a stir when he showed up arm-in-arm with Stefanie Powers, who'd just finished a five-year stint as his crime-busting costar on "Hart to Hart." Robert Evans was there, sweating the imminent release of *The Cotton Club*, the $47-million picture he'd risked everything to produce. James Caan showed up, as did Michael Cimino. And Cher, and Herb Ross, and Alan Ladd, Jr. All the top brass at William Morris turned out—Sam Weisbord, Morris Stoller, Lee Stevens, Norman Brokaw. Warren Beatty was master of ceremonies. Ted Kennedy, in town to campaign for Walter Mondale, was there to give the keynote address. Linda Gray, wife of the evil J. R. Ewing on "Dallas," was the senator's real-life dinner companion.

"We're all here out of respect," MGM/UA boss Frank Yablans told the society scribe for the *Herald-Examiner*. "And fear." For most people, it was more like respect and affection. Kamen was the most self-effacing person in town—maybe the *only* self-effacing person in town, aside from Alan Ladd, Jr.—and he looked pleasantly stunned to have all the flashbulbs snapping at him for a change. Michael Ovitz wasn't there, but he'd bought a table, which explained why his name was in the program. And he'd sent Kamen a warm personal note, which prompted Kamen to call him. Kamen had said it before: There was enough business in this town for all of them.

After dinner, and a couple of jokes from Warren Beatty, Sherry Lansing took the podium. Slim and exuberant in a white fringed gown, she told the crowd how, ten years earlier, when she was starting out as a lowly story editor at MGM, no one in town would return her phone calls—except Stan. Leslie Uggams delivered a medley of songs, and then Ted Kennedy stood up to speak. Kennedy and Kamen had been friends since the fifties, when Kamen—who'd handled Peter Lawford's short-lived sitcom, "Dear Phoebe," for the Morris office—got himself invited to a big party at Lawford's Santa Monica beach house. When Kennedy extolled him as "someone who has always asked himself what he can do for others," Kamen seemed almost to glow.

Finally, Gregory Peck introduced Shlomo Lahat, the mayor of Tel Aviv, who was on hand to present Kamen with an award from the prime minister of Israel. Kamen beamed as he accepted it. This was his peak moment, he knew it. "I will continue my efforts," he declared, "as long as God gives me the strength and ability to do so."

*   *   *

A couple of months later, Kamen received a letter from Jane Fonda. Letters were ominous: They contained things that couldn't be said over the phone. "Dear Stan," this one began.

The gist of it was that Fonda felt she was competing for roles. She loved him, he was the greatest guy in the world, but she wasn't getting the material she needed. She was going to Creative Artists.

He was looking at the downhill slide.

Kamen had already lost three of his biggest male stars—Robert Redford, Burt Reynolds, Sylvester Stallone. He still had Al Pacino and Chevy Chase, but his real strength now was in women—Jane Fonda, Barbra Streisand, Goldie Hawn, Jill Clayburgh, Diane Keaton. Too many women, all after the same jobs. If one of them was out of work for a couple of months, she might easily wonder how he could be paying enough attention to her. It wasn't as if Hollywood pictures were full of great roles for women.

Fonda wasn't the only one with a complaint. Kamen didn't seem to have the energy he'd once had. Defending himself against Ovitz left him so tired. He was too busy to throw the star-studded Saturday-afternoon parties that had once been such fun. By the time the weekend came, he was wiped.

It wasn't just Kamen who was under attack, either. His nephew, a young Morris agent named Ed Mitchell, was in a meeting with Peter Bart, the production chief at MGM/UA, when Gregory Hines came up. Mitchell had represented Hines for years—helped get him his first film role, replacing Richard Pryor in Mel Brooks's *History of the World, Part I* after Pryor torched himself; landed him the meeting with Robert Evans that got him cast opposite Richard Gere in *The Cotton Club*. Hines and Mitchell lived a few blocks apart in the funky beachside quarter of Marina del Rey, and they'd gotten to be good friends. But *The Cotton Club* had just opened to disappointing reviews, and the three-year production ordeal, in which Evans had ricocheted wildly from one investor to another in a desperate search for funds, had taken its toll on everyone.

"You don't represent Hines anymore," Bart announced as Mitchell sat in his office.

"What do you mean?" Mitchell asked blankly.

Bart pulled out a letter that had just been delivered to him. CAA stationery. Effective immediately, Gregory Hines was represented by . . .

Mitchell dug his fingers into his thighs and tried to look nonchalant.

Flo Allen, another motion picture agent, was sitting in her office on the second floor of El Camino when Rock Hudson phoned. Allen was the onetime Hollywood tennis pro who'd long accompanied Kamen to industry affairs; she'd gone into agenting in the early sixties, and in 1976 he'd brought her over to William Morris. She'd brought Hudson with her. They'd worked together for twenty years.

"I have to go," he said.

"Where are you going?" she asked, thinking he meant maybe New York.

"To CAA." *Click.*

In strategic terms, losing Rock Hudson or Gregory Hines or Farrah Fawcett was not a major blow to the Morris office. Losing Jane Fonda was. Losing Fonda, on top of Rock and Hines and Farrah, after Burt and Redford and Stallone and Caan—that created a perception problem. In a business where perception was everything, Stan Kamen was beginning to be perceived as . . . slipping. Still a power, but not necessarily *the* power. In Hollywood, or on El Camino.

It was no accident that most of these people were leaving for Michael Ovitz. Just as the arrival of big-money deals a few years earlier had motivated a lot of stars to stop schmoozing with Sue Mengers and sign with the Morris office, the emergence now of even bigger deals—bigger, more complicated deals—was encouraging them to leave Kamen for CAA. Despite his subdued demeanor and smooth professionalism, Kamen still functioned primarily as friend and confidant—a nonexotic version of Mengers. He conveyed caring, concern, personal attention. Ovitz dispensed with all that. That's what shrinks were for. Ovitz was a businessman. He came in with a plan—how to leverage, how to maximize, point-point-point. And he had an army of lieutenants to do the follow-up.

In the spring of 1985, Kamen left on a business trip to Europe. He came back a month later with a blizzard of deals—firm pay-or-play commitments for a half-dozen major clients. He also had circles under his eyes and a bad cough. He seemed to have some sort of flu he couldn't shake. He started spending more and more time with doctors, less and less with clients. By summer, status was no longer Kamen's main concern.

That August, at a regular Wednesday morning department meeting in the second-floor conference room, with Roger Davis seated at his right hand and Lenny Hirshan at his left, Kamen made an announcement. He was going to be taking it easier for the next few months. He was

going to come in less often, start doing more work from his house. Mike
Simpson, a junior agent who'd worked as his assistant four years earlier,
would be taking over as his associate.

At thirty-four, Mike Simpson was the new golden boy of the motion picture department, the one they'd developed after Gary Lucchesi went off
to Tri-Star. Like more than one of Kamen's ex-assistants, he was a lean
and handsome Texan—an air force brat who'd come to Hollywood out
of the University of Texas film school with the idea of becoming a director. He'd applied for a mail room position at William Morris to learn the
business, and after a stint on Kamen's desk, he'd been promoted to
agent. His biggest client was Kevin Reynolds, a young director who'd
put Kevin Costner in his first picture, *Fandango*; for the past couple of
years, the three of them had flown down to a friend's ranch in Texas on
Labor Day weekend to shoot skeet.

   In anointing Simpson, Kamen passed over two other agents with far
more experience. Lenny Hirshan was Kamen's contemporary. He was
always striving, always out to prove himself, always seeking the others'
approval. Though not a signer like Kamen, he was a skilled agent whose
long association with Clint Eastwood, Jack Lemmon, and Walter
Matthau gave him a high profile in the business. But like Norman
Brokaw, he had a wooden manner that made people think of him as old-
fashioned, not quite with-it, less than a power player despite his blue-
chip clients.

   Ed Limato was definitely a power player, thanks to Mel Gibson and
Richard Gere. He was also a legendary host, in the tradition of such old-
line Hollywood agents as Bert Allenberg and Charlie Feldman. He lived
in a sprawling Spanish colonial mansion in the Hollywood Hills—the
house Bela Lugosi once lived in, a movie-star hacienda built into a hillside near the top of Outpost Drive—and gave glamorously cozy parties,
redolent with stars and yet oh-so-casual, which he was famous for presiding over barefoot. But Limato was a little too charismatic for the
board's taste, a little too independent, a little too much like Kamen.
There were advantages to bringing up someone younger, less experienced, more malleable.

   Mike Simpson was soft-spoken and thoughtful, with a businesslike,
let's-get-the-job-done attitude. But he wasn't the type who was likely to
devote his life to his clients. He was married. He and his wife didn't

even live on the Westside of Los Angeles, the Hollywood-to-Malibu swath that, along with the southern flank of the San Fernando Valley just above it, defined the territorial limits of the entertainment industry. They lived forty-five minutes south of Beverly Hills, below Culver City, across the Baldwin Hills, beyond the airport, past El Segundo, in the little South Bay enclave of Manhattan Beach, a town better known to surfers and aerospace engineers than to anyone in the business.

The idea was for Kamen and Roger Davis and Lee Stevens, who'd spent only a few weeks on the coast since taking over as president the year before, to peel off Kamen's clients one by one and bond them to Simpson. No one else was to have contact unless authorized. Stevens and his wife Liz had just settled into their new apartment in New York—a splendidly decorated condo on the twenty-fifth floor of Museum Tower, the new Cesar Pelli building next to the Museum of Modern Art, down the street from Black Rock and around the corner from the agency's New York office—but it was clear he was going to have to spend more and more time on the coast. Winning the trust of Kamen's clients was a slow process, and Kamen was far sicker than he was ready to admit.

In August, he was coming in four days a week; by September, it dropped to two or three. In addition to the fatigue and the shingles and the flulike symptoms, he had a sore on his neck that wouldn't heal. And he was beginning to lose weight. In November, he didn't come in at all. Goldie came to see him at home. So did Barbra. He didn't want to see anyone else except family.

Privately, people in the department were told he had lymphoma. It was never acknowledged that he had AIDS, although Ed Limato and a handful of others had already figured it out. Kamen himself told no one—not even his nephew Ed Mitchell, or his friend Flo Allen. He'd never even told them he was gay, though of course they all knew it. He was such a private person, and it wasn't the kind of thing you'd mention.

Kamen wasn't the only one who was sick. Morris Stoller and Sam Weisbord, seventy-four-year-old cochairmen of the agency, icons of the third generation, were both suffering from cancer. Stoller had stomach cancer. Sam Weisbord—the health and fitness faddist, a man who'd never touched a cigarette in his life—was fighting lung cancer. Stoller hadn't been in the office since the end of the summer, and while Weisbord was still coming in, he seemed to be getting weaker every day. His tan was intact, but his voice was beginning to rattle in his chest, and his frame, never robust, now looked sickly and frail. Only his sex obsession was on the increase. Sometimes he'd walk out into the hallway and announce to whomever happened to be passing by that he'd just had a wonderful weekend—fucked these two girls! As for his secretaries—well, the turnover seemed faster than ever now.

Kamen's younger sister had moved out to Los Angeles a year or so before with her husband, a fraternity brother of Stan's who'd recently retired. That November they had a private Thanksgiving dinner at his cliffside estate in Malibu, just Stan and Flo Allen and his sister and her husband and their two sons, Ed and Barry Mitchell. The view was too big to look at that day, but inside it felt dark and quiet and safe. Stan had pneumonia, but he stayed up for a couple of hours. The houseboy fixed them all dinner, and Stan came out of his room long enough to eat it with them. Then he led his two nephews back to his room and gave them each a watch, one engraved from James Caan, the other a Rolex that David Niven had given him. That's when he told them he wasn't going to live much longer.

Things happened quickly after that. Word was out that Kamen was ill, but no one knew how seriously or with what. Within the department, only Ed Mitchell and Cary Woods, Kamen's assistant, were privy to the truth, and neither could betray Kamen's trust. Roger Davis even announced in a department meeting that he'd be coming back soon. They were putting a happy face on this? Mitchell shook his head in disbelief.

Davis and Mike Simpson were trying to salvage Kamen's clients, but it was a painstaking process, and they were in a race against time. Kamen couldn't let his clients go, and he couldn't hold on to them either. And no one could let on about what they were trying to do, because neither Kamen nor the agency wanted the truth to get out. All they could do was match Kamen's clients with available agents and hope they clicked. But a few years before it had taken them months just to get Raquel Welch to accept Flo Allen as her agent. And when Lenny Hirshan and John Ptak went to visit Chevy Chase on the set of *Three Amigos*—because Hirshan knew Chase and his manager, and Ptak, who represented *The National Lampoon*, had gotten Chase involved in *National Lampoon's Vacation* and *Fletch*—there wasn't much they could say beyond hoping that Stan would be all right.

So they were paralyzed. Michael Ovitz announced that, as a gesture of respect, he would sign no more of Kamen's clients as long as Kamen was sick. But that didn't prevent him from talking with them, commiserating, offering suggestions for their future. Kamen spent the holidays at home, so weak and emaciated he could barely get out of bed. He didn't want anybody to see him. Near the end of 1985, as he lay gaunt and helpless in his room, he phoned the CAA offices in Century City and got Ovitz on the line. This was no longer a sporting matter; this was the end game. "What's the matter, Mike?" he cried into the receiver. "Isn't there enough business for everybody?" Shortly afterward, he checked into UCLA Memorial Hospital under an assumed name.

As rumors about Kamen's condition swirled through the industry, the Morris office maintained an adamant silence. The black mirrored façade on El Camino, designed to look with-it and sleek, now appeared merely impenetrable, the esoteric artifact of some secret cabal. The only official announcement to come out was made at the end of January, when word was issued that Mike Simpson was being made head of a new "motion picture packaging department," effective immediately. While continuing to represent his own clients, the announcement noted, he would coordinate the efforts of talent and literary agents and work closely with Stan Kamen.

Kamen made a few more phone calls. In February he phoned Sue Mengers at her house in Bel Air. It was about nine in the evening, and Mengers was having dinner with Ryan O'Neal, whose star had faded considerably in the decade since *Barry Lyndon*. O'Neal was an unhappy client, and he and Mengers were going at it when the phone rang. "Can I call you back?" she asked Stan. "No, no," he said, "I just wanted to see how you were." They chatted for a moment, and Stan promised to call her later. It was the last she'd ever hear from him.

Aside from Flo Allen and his family, Kamen allowed only two people to visit him at the hospital. One was his friend Sherry Lansing. The other was Sam Weisbord. Kamen and Weisbord had never been chummy before, but now, after thirty-two years together, they finally felt close. Dying gave them something in common. They sat in his room and cried together, holding hands.

Ed Mitchell was just waking up at his beachside apartment on Outrigger Street when he got the call from his parents. It was seven in the morning, Thursday, February 20. Stan had just died. Mitchell threw on his clothes and dashed out the door. If he didn't get to the office soon, things would disappear—Kamen's Rolodex, for instance. He headed for

Venice Boulevard—six lanes, straight shot—and raced into town in ten minutes flat. Cary Woods and Roger Davis arrived minutes later, and the three of them worked their way frantically down Stan's client list, trying to call all the stars they could before word got out. Barbra . . . Goldie . . . Warren . . . Chevy . . . Al . . . By the time they got to Kirk Douglas, the switchboard was lighting up like a Christmas tree. Rona Barrett had gone on the air with the news.

A memo was circulated within the agency. Statements were issued. Lee Solters, of the show-business PR firm of Solters & Roskin, announced the official cause of death as lymphoma. Barbra Streisand hailed Kamen as "a sweet and gentle man." "He was reliable," Gregory Peck told Army Archerd for his *Daily Variety* column. "He never made a deal for the sake of making a deal—for any amount of money."

Kamen had made it clear he wanted no funeral or memorial service of any kind. But at noontime, after a frenzied, desperate morning, the staff gathered in the second-floor conference room for a fifteen-minute tribute. Roger Davis made the official announcement. Then Weisbord stood up to speak. He looked nearly dead himself, ashen beneath his preternatural tan, his voice a wheeze broken by a racking cough. He gave a talk that was brief but heartfelt—not his usual Patton speech but something personal, how brilliant Stan had been, how they'd all recognized it the moment he'd come out from New York so many years before. As he spoke, few could avoid looking at Ed Lebowitz, the department's forty-nine-year-old business affairs chief, once hearty, now pale and wraithlike and hobbling on a cane. He too was suffering from AIDS. Would he be the next to go? Or would it be Weisbord? Or Morris Stoller, who hadn't been seen in months? Then the gathering was over, and they all went back to work, almost as if nothing had happened. Except it had.

First Lefkowitz, then Lastfogel, now Kamen—there was death in the air, and yet the television department was on a roll. The incredible success of "The Cosby Show" was revitalizing William Morris, NBC, and situation comedies all at once. As Dr. Cliff Huxtable, Bill Cosby was the everydad of the Reagan era—stern yet gentle, old-fashioned yet undeniably contemporary, jocular yet ever so instructive as he addressed a nation that had somehow lost its way.

Now in its second season, the show had been number one in the Nielsens for more than a year and had just won an Emmy for Marcy Carsey and Tom Werner. As the lead-in for a blockbuster Thursday night lineup that included "Family Ties," "Cheers," "Night Court," and "Hill Street Blues," it had taken NBC from last place in prime time to first. Doubleday was coming out with a Cosby book, a slim volume of humor and advice called *Fatherhood*, which was shaping up as the runaway bestseller of the spring. Bill Cosby was golden, and Brandon Tartikoff looked absolutely clairvoyant. As for Lou Erlich, his opposite number at ABC, the story was that when a bum accosted him with a sob story on the street, he turned to the man and cried, "You think *you've* got problems? I'm the guy who turned down 'Cosby'!"

"Cosby" was as important to Jerry Katzman and Larry Auerbach of the Morris office as it was to Tartikoff. When Tartikoff publicly credited the Morris Agency with changing his life, Morris's television operation became hotter than hot. It didn't hurt that "Murder, She Wrote," the detective series that had debuted on CBS that same September and now stood at number three, starred Katzman's client Angela Lansbury, though it wasn't a Morris package. Suddenly, agents were making network sales over the phone. Producers were so eager to sign on with a winner that the 5-and-5 packaging fee no longer looked so bad. Better to pay 5 percent and make it on the air, they figured, than to pay nothing and never get out of development.

Capitalizing on his relationship with Viacom, Katzman had recently engineered a deal to set up a subsidiary, Viacom Productions, to deliver prime-time series and made-for-TV movies to the networks, with Morris collecting a packaging fee. On December 1, NBC had aired *Perry Mason Returns*, a successful TV movie from Viacom and Fred Silverman, who'd gotten the rights to the series from the estate of its creator, Erle Stanley Gardner. This spring, they were doing a pilot for NBC for a new Andy Griffith series, a legal drama called "Matlock," starring the onetime sheriff of Mayberry as an aw-shucks defense whiz whose clients turn out as innocent as Perry Mason's. And after seven years of trying, Morris's TV movie operation had put together *Return to Mayberry*, a $3.4 million reunion special on NBC with Griffith as Sheriff Taylor, Don Knotts as his sidekick Barney Fife, and Ron Howard—now the highly successful director of *Splash* and *Cocoon*—as his grown-up son Opie. Viacom was producing on a $2.6 million network licensing fee, meaning that while Viacom stood to lose $800,000 if it flopped, Morris's 5 percent up front guaranteed it $130,000. If the show succeeded, Morris would get double that, plus 10 percent of any syndication sales. Air date was set for April 13.

Upstairs in the motion picture department, everyone was back at work, numb but functioning. They'd all worked more or less independently under Kamen anyway, so they tried to carry on as before. Lee Stevens sought to fill the vacuum, with Roger Davis's help. It was obvious Stevens was going to have to spend most of his time on the coast, so he and his wife bought a condo in the secluded residential enclave of Century Woods, a five-minute drive from El Camino. Stevens had worse things to worry about than the motion picture department.

Within days of Kamen's death, Sammy Weisbord had been hit with a sexual harassment suit. One of those secretaries he'd made a play for— the born-again Christian who used to come in wearing those tight miniskirts, until the day she ran screaming out into the hall and woke up the entire first floor. They'd barely had time to digest that news when, on March 24, the morning before Oscar night, Morris Stoller died at Cedars-Sinai. Another funeral at Hillside, another trek to the bleak beyond in Culver City, another reminder of the void Abe and Frances had left. Phil Weltman came, and after the service, when he saw Norman Brokaw on the hillside above the chapel, he beckoned for Brokaw to come down. Weisbord walked down the hill with him and tried to shake hands, but Weltman ignored him. It was the last time they'd meet.

Stoller's death left Weisbord sole chairman of the agency. But Weisbord was slipping fast, and he was the target of a highly embarrassing lawsuit. Rather than wait out the inevitable, the six remaining board members resolved to award the chairman's slot to one of their own. It was complicated, of course. There were many candidates, many considerations, many maneuverings. But at the beginning of April, a week after Stoller's death, a solution was reached. The board agreed to elevate Weisbord to chairman emeritus and name not one but two new chairmen—in Beverly Hills, Norman Brokaw; in New York, Lou Weiss, the worldwide head of television. Lee Stevens made the announcement, which noted pointedly that the promotions had the support of the other three board members. Unanimity reigned.

Weisbord died at Cedars-Sinai a month later. By this time the deaths felt like depth charges, *kaboom-kaboom-kaboom*, rolling the place with a slow, sickening heave. Funeral was May 9 at Temple Beth-El, the

modest synagogue below the Sunset Strip where Weisbord had wor-
shipped for years—first with Phil Weltman, then without him. Danny
Thomas had been asked to deliver the eulogy, but he refused: It felt
like they were burying too many Morris people now, felt like some sort
of jinx. Tony Orlando, whom Weisbord had signed years earlier and
packaged in the "Tony Orlando and Dawn" show, a last-gasp variety
series on CBS, was pressed into service instead. But where were the
stars? Where were the industry execs? Why did the town that had lion-
ized Abe Lastfogel seem so indifferent to his successor? As they gathered in the half-empty synagogue just down the hill from the Chateau
Marmont, the men and women of the Morris office were hard-put not
to wonder if Danny Thomas wasn't right. Had some sort of curse been
laid upon them all?

Stan Kamen's funeral had been a private affair, a quiet family service at
a Jewish cemetery in New York. Despite his wish not to be publicly
eulogized, however, Barbra Streisand had gone ahead with an invitation-
only memorial at her house in Holmby Hills. Guests arrived in
limousines. Stars and producers made grand entrances. Much was said
about what a true gentleman Stan had been. Meanwhile, Lee Stevens
was holed up at this office in Beverly Hills, phoning Michael Ovitz at
CAA, Jeff Berg and Sam Cohn at ICM, begging them to give him some
time. Six months he asked for. Six months to solidify the relationship
with Stan's clients. Then they could move in.

Lee Stevens and Roger Davis were smart guys. They knew their business. But Davis's business wasn't agenting, and Stevens's business
wasn't Hollywood. Davis was a lawyer, an administrator, the nuts-and-
bolts guy who handled complicated contracts and did Kamen's dirty
work. He didn't read scripts, cast pictures, sign clients. He didn't have a
lot of relationships. He didn't exist on the Westside social circuit. And
Stevens was a New Yorker. He didn't know the movie business—didn't
know the players, didn't know the lingo, didn't know the pictures in production, didn't know the properties in development. The star he kept
mentioning in meetings was Barbara Walters.

Word spread. Within weeks, the image of power and professionalism
that Kamen had cultivated over the years began to erode. Studio execs
wondered out loud what was happening. Clients began to freak. Their
loyalty was to Kamen, not to some board. With Kamen gone, their tie

was cut. The stability that made Morris so attractive ten years before, when ICM was cobbled together and all its key agents left except Mengers, had given way to infighting among a group of apparent nonentities. Lee Stevens, Roger Davis, Walt Zifkin—who could keep them all straight, let alone be bothered to care what they did in their black box behind the Beverly Wilshire? No, it was time to go.

But not to ICM. In April, after twenty years as an agent, Sue Mengers announced that she was quitting the business. Her contract was up, her client list had largely evaporated, and agenting had stopped being fun. And while ICM was dominated by two other powerhouse agents—Jeff Berg, who'd recently been named chairman, and Sam Cohn in New York—neither of them provided a suitable alternative to Kamen. Berg, thirty-nine, was a highbrow with an aggressive streak, so cool and remote he was known as "the Iceberg." A Berkeley grad with a degree in English lit, he'd gotten his start reading scripts for the Ashley Famous Agency, then worked for a time as Freddie Fields's assistant. He got on well with directors—James L. Brooks, Bernardo Bertolucci, Roman Polanski—but he lacked the free-floating empathy it took to nurture a stable of stars. Sam Cohn was the last of the seventies superagents, a peer of Mengers and Kamen who operated as they had, up close and personal. He kept a classy list—Meryl Streep, Mike Nichols, Woody Allen—but he was famous for not returning phone calls, and he was firmly ensconced in New York.

The first to leave was Mark Rydell, Kamen's longtime friend, the director he'd put together with Steve McQueen for *The Reivers* seventeen years before. Rydell signed with ICM. But unhappy stars had only one place to go: CAA. Within weeks, the exodus was on: Streisand . . . Goldie . . . Chevy. By summer, virtually all of Kamen's remaining stars were gone. Morris's motion picture agents were in a state of panic.

It wasn't just Kamen's stars; their clients were being raided too. Like Tom Hanks, the young comic they'd signed when he was doing television and turned into a movie star with the 1984 hit *Splash*. Hanks was ready to walk when he heard one of his agents was using his name to get better tables in restaurants. They pulled that one out when Hanks's manager, who figured he'd be out of the picture if Hanks went to CAA, decided to place him with Mike Simpson. But clearly, they couldn't go on this way. Ca-Ca was all over them. They needed a leader—someone to turn to for advice, someone with the clout to make clients feel secure, someone who could ring up a studio chief at home on Sunday afternoon when a problem came up.

As it happened, Roger Davis had already been scouting candidates.

The picture business was as it always had been—a small circle of players who knew one another well and switched hats willy-nilly. Davis was talking with former competitors, for the most part, people who'd started as agents and moved on during the agency diaspora of the mid-seventies. Mike Medavoy, who'd left ICM after the 1975 merger and was now production chief at Orion. Guy McElwaine, an ICM veteran who'd just stepped down as chairman of Columbia. Even Freddie Fields, the agency's would-be nemesis in the sixties, now back to independent production after a woeful stint as president of the MGM side of Kirk Kerkorian's MGM/UA Entertainment Company. Plus Bernie Brillstein, who'd started in the Morris mail room in 1955 and was now a manager-producer with a string of television and motion picture hits, from "Hee-Haw" to "The Muppet Show" to *Ghostbusters*.

Davis was dangling a hefty piece of bait—$1 million a year, plus stock. But it was as tough to recruit a major executive as it was to sign a top star. He and Lee Stevens had had a nice meeting with Mike Medavoy, who was very polite but apparently uninterested in returning to the agency business. Guy McElwaine, on the other hand, he thought he had. As a studio exec, McElwaine could claim credit for a number of Columbia hits—*The Big Chill*, the phenomenally successful *Ghostbusters*, a sleeper called *The Karate Kid* that ended up grossing $91 million. But the place was owned by the Coca-Cola Company now, which meant long trips to company headquarters in Atlanta every couple of months, less time working with the talent. And Columbia's slate for 1985—the year McElwaine was promoted from president to chairman—had included some embarrassing failures, from a disastrous remake of *The Bride of Frankenstein* to a Neil Simon flop called *The Slugger's Wife*. In April, after months of speculation, McElwaine had resigned.

Davis and McElwaine had been good friends for years; they spent Christmas together with their families in Hawaii. When Davis asked McElwaine over to his house to talk about running the motion picture department, McElwaine was intrigued. He asked for a meeting with the rest of the board. He met them all—Walt Zifkin, who administered the television department just as Davis administered the motion picture operation; Lee Stevens; Lou Weiss, still a powerhouse in television, though he was becoming isolated in New York; Tony Fantozzi, the tough-talking ex-Chicagoan who handled George Schlatter; Norman Brokaw, who proudly displayed photographs of himself standing next to Jerry Ford. He was almost ready to say yes. But if he were to take this job, he wanted to do what it took to put Morris back in the game—court stars, wine and dine, fly wherever, hire new people, spend money. And he sensed some unease there—not that anything was said, exactly. What they actually disagreed about was whether he would go on the board.

Putting a new man on their board—that was a big step. They were willing to take it, they said, but they wanted to wait a year. In the meantime, they proposed that McElwaine head an executive committee that would report to the board and run the agency—subject, of course, to board approval. To McElwaine, this made no sense. Why wait a year? They were trying to make a statement; that's why they wanted to hire him. They were going outside the family, bringing in a division head who wasn't even Jewish. If you're going to make a statement, you put the guy on the board right away. You don't wait a year.

That's when he learned that the board had a requirement: unanimity. Davis and Zifkin seemed ready to do almost anything in their power to lure him to the company, and most of the others seemed willing to go along. But Tony Fantozzi was not. Why should they spend a lot of money to stay in the motion picture business? They were rich already. What if it didn't work?

Roger Davis was reporting to the department on the negotiations with various prospects when he mentioned McElwaine. One agent said she'd heard he'd just landed a lavish production deal at United Artists—which, as it happened, was now run by Jerry Weintraub, who'd produced *The Karate Kid* at Columbia. Bullshit, Davis exploded—he's signing with us. The next day, the McElwaine/UA deal was all over the trades.

Bernie Brillstein was a candidate for McElwaine's position at Columbia. But when they contacted him about the Morris job, he was as intrigued as McElwaine had been, maybe more so. Who wouldn't want to come home a king? Then he mentioned the word "autonomy," and after that, he never heard back.

Davis and Stevens were continuing to meet with studio execs, feeling their way into the business, learning as they went. One afternoon,

Lenny Hirshan got a call from Warner Bros. president Terry Semel; John Ptak got a call from Mark Canton, Warner's production chief. The two Warner Bros. execs had just had lunch with Lee and Roger, who'd asked what they should do with the motion picture department. Hirshan and Ptak were horrified. Sellers didn't ask buyers what to do. If this got out on the street, they'd all look like idiots. Something had to be done.

To Ptak, there was only one solution: Put Hirshan in charge. Ptak was one of the more influential agents in the department, a quiet but force-ful deal maker who, besides putting together such pictures as *Airplane!* and *Fletch*, had helped Bruce Beresford and Peter Weir make the leap from directing in Australia to directing in Hollywood. He and Hirshan had worked for years in adjacent offices at the back of the first floor. He thought Hirshan's constant striving made him a good agent, and several of the others thought he had a point. They knew that Hirshan wasn't a galvanizing figure—that he came off as wooden and robotic, that he could be domineering at times. But he was a senior agent who was plugged into the upper levels of the industry. The only such person they had left.

A few days later, the motion picture department asked the board of directors to come upstairs for a meeting. With most of the department gathered in the second-floor conference room, Ptak and several other agents told Lee Stevens and Roger Davis and Walt Zifkin that their activities in the field were disruptive to the department. The only solu-tion, they felt, was to put Lenny Hirshan in charge. The directors were not happy about being challenged in a public forum, but shortly after-ward, they reached a decision. At the end of June, four months after Kamen's death, Lenny Hirshan was named West Coast head of the motion picture department. Boaty Boatwright, a former MGM/UA pro-duction exec whom Kamen had hired two years earlier, was named to head the New York motion picture office. The post of worldwide motion picture chief—Kamen's position—was left unfilled.

Hirshan was thrilled all the same. He'd spent his entire career in Kamen's shadow, toiling away unnoticed while Kamen got the glory. Even Clint Eastwood was someone else's to claim—Norman Brokaw had signed him, and Brokaw never let him forget it. But if other people overlooked Hirshan's contributions, Hirshan himself had kept careful track. Natalie Wood's profit participation in *West Side Story*, for instance—that had been his idea. Now he'd have a chance to prove himself.

Hirshan wanted to jump-start the place. He wanted to reinvigorate the department, give it new direction. He scheduled meetings to improve the lines of communication, to find out how they could work together, to get information flowing once again. On weekends, he even invited people to gather at his house, a sprawling fifties ranch high above Beverly Hills in Benedict Canyon.

Roger Davis was stressing the communication theme, too—how they were all going to share, how it wasn't going to be the way it had been under Stan. But they had an uphill fight. In September, when the department's business affairs chief died of AIDS and the papers ran front-page headlines about a nurse being accused of murder for allegedly phoning in a change of medication that sent him into a coma, it seemed to sum up the mordant and chaotic state of affairs that prevailed at the Morris office. The place was a sick joke. A CAA trainee couldn't even ask a Morris trainee, "How ya doing?" without a snicker.

There was another problem that few people knew about. The clue was the baseball cap Lee Stevens had taken to wearing around the office when he was there at all—an incongruous touch for a man who invariably wore expensive, well-tailored suits. Stevens had been diagnosed with lymphoma. He was being treated, and the prognosis looked hopeful. But he didn't have the luxury of a lengthy convalescence. Though he was thin and pale, he forced himself to come in. He had to lead the agency through its crisis. He had to fight for his authority on the board.

They hung on to a few of Kamen's clients. Alan Pakula went with Boaty Boatwright in New York. Norman Jewison, whom Kamen had shared with Larry Auerbach, stayed with Auerbach and Boatwright. Diane Keaton's manager put her together with John Burnham, a well-connected young agent who'd come from ICM three years before. But Keaton had stopped getting offers, and she was ready to go with Sam Cohn at ICM when Burnham asked her to give him a month. She was up for the lead in *Baby Boom*, a comedy in development at UA, but UA seemed ready to put the property in turnaround. Burnham called his friend Ned Tanen, the president of Paramount, and asked for a favor: Call UA and tell them you want to pick up *Baby Boom* and put Diane Keaton in the lead. The next day, Burnham got a call from UA: *Baby Boom* was a go picture, and they wanted Keaton to star.

By the end of the year, most of the rest of Kamen's clients had signed with CAA. And that's when the media discovered Michael Ovitz. It started in December, a week after Ovitz's fortieth birthday, when the *Wall Street Journal* ran a page-one profile of the new agency kingpin. Ovitz, "all but unknown outside of Hollywood's clannish creative community," was said to be power-hungry and publicity-shy. In classic *Journal* style, a multideck headline told the story:

Hollywood Star

An Agent Dominates
Film and TV Studios
With Package Deals

—

Michael Ovitz Puts Together
Clients of Creative Artists
In Single High-Fee Unit

—

Muffled Voices of Protest

Stan Kamen was already history, locked in the vault with Abe Lastfogel, Johnny Hyde, and Will Morris himself. Now, more than three-quarters of a century after Will Morris assembled a touring company around Harry Lauder and took them to Teddy Roosevelt's White House, Michael Ovitz was about to become synonymous with the package deal. Before long, people would even start to think he'd invented it.

14

RAPE AND PILLAGE

Los Angeles, 1987-1992

It was in the regular Wednesday morning department meetings that Lenny Hirshan's weaknesses as a department head first showed up. The meetings had always been a little chaotic—thirty agents crammed into the second-floor conference room, fifteen or sixteen of them sitting around a large, doughnut-shaped table, the rest shoe-horned in against the wall, everyone furiously calculating the need to share some juicy tidbit of information versus the advantageousness of holding it back. But at least when Stan Kamen was in charge, the meetings were brief and to the point. Kamen himself never said much. He announced deals after they happened. He spoke last. He led by example.

Now, with Lenny Hirshan running the show—at the end of Roger Davis's leash, or so it seemed—the meetings were a disaster. Hirshan spoke first, though he often had to struggle to make himself heard above the other agents, who whispered and giggled like schoolchildren. He'd go on for half an hour, then look bored and distracted while the others made their reports. Occasionally he'd cut someone off mid-sentence, while Davis shot him a look. Finally a group of agents went to him and asked him to speak last.

But that was only a stopgap. By the first of the year, several of the top agents in the department—Ed Limato chief among them—were raising red flags, lobbying the board members to bring in someone with real clout, someone they and their clients could feel confidence in. Guy McElwaine and Bernie Brillstein were out of the running. So Limato was pushing another candidate: Sue Mengers.

Mengers claimed she wasn't interested—but what if they could talk her into it? The idea had a lot of support in the department. Mike Simpson was for it. So was Cary Woods, Kamen's ex-assistant, who'd been promoted to agent after Kamen's death. And John Burnham, who'd salvaged Diane Keaton. And Toni Howard, and Toni's friend Boaty Boatwright, the New York motion picture chief. Even John Ptak, Lenny Hirshan's main champion, was in favor of the idea. As for Hirshan, he was getting sick of the job. He wasn't an administrator. He didn't need to baby-sit thirty obnoxious agents. He was fed up.

But the six men on the board weren't eager to put a woman in the job—that had been Stan Kamen's thing, filling the place up with broads. Many of the board members had a hard time thinking of women as agents, period. Nor were they in any rush. Why should they be? The Morris office was in no danger of foundering; far from it. Despite all the grumbling in the motion picture department, the agency was performing tremendously.

First, of course, there was the real estate—not a bad business to be in in southern California in the 1980s. At the end of 1986, the agency's William Morris Plaza subsidiary had finally closed on the mid-block building behind the headquarters on El Camino—the one that housed the moribund Chinese restaurant Liu's and, before that, the legendary Romanoff's. Since the agency had bought the buildings on either side of it in 1969, this gave them title to the half-block stretch of South Rodeo Drive between the Beverly Wilshire Hotel and Charleville Boulevard. In the three decades since Morris had started buying property there, downtown Beverly Hills had gone from a sleepy little hometown for movie stars to a high-gloss jumble of designer boutiques and prestige office towers, a commercial vortex so hot it was known in real-estate circles as the Golden Triangle. And the agency had a prime development site on the Triangle's southern edge, a few steps from the Beverly Wilshire and across the street from the offices of Drexel Burnham Lambert, where Michael Milken conducted the junk-bond deals that were reshaping corporate America.

Meanwhile, the television side was thriving. "Matlock" was a solid hit. "The Cosby Show" was the kind of jackpot you only get to dream about in Vegas. The "Cosby" syndication rights were being sold that spring, and the bids were coming in higher than anyone had expected. WOR in New York was paying $250,000 an episode, three times what it had ever paid before for a sitcom. Stations were ready to pay whatever it took, even if it meant losing money on the deal, to grab a winner for their schedules. When all the syndie sales were added together, the agency stood to make upward of $50 million. Not counting the commissions from Cosby's *Fatherhood*, by far the bestselling hardcover book of 1986.

Now they had a "Cosby Show" spinoff in the works—"A Different World," starring Lisa Bonet as Denise Huxtable, out of Brooklyn and off on her own at the black college where her father and grandfather had gone to school. They had Diane English, a promising writer-producer who was constantly being pushed in department meetings by Lou Weiss's son Steve, in her second season with a popular sitcom called "My Sister Sam." Plus pilot commitments for any number of potential new series, including "Jake and the Fatman," a "Matlock" spinoff from Viacom, and "Frank's Place," an offbeat sitcom created by Hugh Wilson, who several years earlier—before coming to Morris with John Burnham, unfortunately—had come up with the hit sitcom "WKRP in Cincinnati."

As part of his reward for the turnaround, Jerry Katzman had just been awarded Lou Weiss's position as worldwide head of television. But from the board's perspective, finding someone to engineer a similar revival in the motion picture department hardly seemed the most pressing priority. None of the board members was in the film business. None of them seemed to realize what the motion picture department really contributed—not the money television brought in, but glamour, prestige, the stature that lures clients who do television while waiting to break into pictures. Besides, it wasn't their fault, what was happening. It was Stan Kamen's, for not bringing in his associates to help with his star clients. So things were allowed to slide.

That spring, as every spring, twenty actors and five directors were competing for Oscars. Nine were represented by CAA. ICM had six. A new agency, Triad Artists, had three. Not one was a Morris client.

AN ASSISTANT LOOKED OUT MIKE SIMPSON'S SECOND-FLOOR WINDOW ONE day at the end of July and saw a plainclothes security detail that looked sufficient to guard a president. They were clustered on the other side of El Camino, wearing earphones and talking into their hands outside the garage entrance to the black-mirrored William Morris Plaza Building, the one they called "Danny's building," because the packaging fees from Danny Thomas's television shows had paid for it. Must be somebody really important here, the assistant thought.

But there were no important visitors that day. The guards worked for Gavin de Becker, a Hollywood security consultant who'd been on retainer for the Morris Agency for years. They were out to bust Bobby Harris, the superintendent of the agency's underground parking garage. Harris was a middle-aged black man, friendly and soft-spoken, who'd worked there for twenty-seven years, first on the asphalt lot and then in the building that went up on the site. Besides getting visitors in and out, he took care of the agency's fleet of cars—washed them, polished them, gassed them up. His wife was a receptionist in the main building across the street. After having him under surveillance for months, de Becker's men had observed him dealing cocaine.

Drugs were no stranger to the Morris office, any more than they were to any other place in the business. Agents used drugs. Clients used drugs. Producers and studio executives and shopaholic Hollywood wives used drugs. Trainees in dispatch assumed that any package they were given that was particularly well-sealed probably contained drugs. The third floor, where the music department was located, was known as a drug haven. In 1982, a twenty-nine-year-old music agent had drowned when he fell facedown in his bathroom sink while getting ready for work one morning. Nothing had changed.

Bobby Harris was a connection. Had been for years, by his own account, for agents and clients alike. Did it as a favor, not to get rich. Drug dealers did it to get rich. He wasn't a drug dealer. You didn't see drug dealers washing cars ten hours a day.

A phalanx of security guards escorted Harris from the garage to the main building, then down the first-floor corridor to an empty office. Walt Zifkin was waiting for him. Zifkin was their new éminence grise, fifty-one years old with steel-gray hair, hard eyes, and a USC law degree. He'd joined the agency's administrative team in 1963, after two years in the legal department at CBS Television City. He sat on the boards of Cedars-Sinai and the Beverly Hills Chamber of Commerce, but otherwise he was little known outside El Camino. If, as the joke went, the office was divided into talent agents, packaging agents, and real-estate agents, he'd be the chief real-estate agent. Certainly he'd done okay in real estate himself, having scored a lovely pink Spanish number on Bedford Drive, in the flats just below Sunset. But essentially he was the hatchet man.

Bobby Harris was escorted inside. Zifkin pushed a button on his desk and the door to his office swung shut via remote control. Zifkin was blunt and to the point. They were going to ask him to resign, he told Harris. If he didn't, they'd fire him. In the meantime, he might as well tell them what he knew.

A short time later, Harris's wife was called in and offered $5,000 in severance if she chose to resign. She told him she had no reason to resign. She had nothing to be embarrassed about. If they weren't embarrassed, why should she be? They were the ones using the drugs.

Zifkin looked shocked.

Still, it was a surgical operation. Very neat, very clean, very private. Three agents, sent out for rehab. One parking lot attendant, cut loose. No police, no clients, no publicity. Until Monday—and even then, the *Daily Variety* headline put the right spin on the story:

WM Agency Moves Quickly
To Stamp Out Drug Problem

It wasn't until two months later that things threatened to get out of hand. Bobby Harris, angry at taking the fall for a bunch of well-paid white guys he'd been doing a favor for, went to Gloria Allred, the attorney who'd represented the born-again Christian who sued Sam Weisbord the year before. On September 10, Allred wrote a blistering letter to Norman Brokaw that was somehow leaked to a number of publications, including *Daily Variety* and the *L.A. Weekly*. The letter charged widespread drug abuse within the Morris office and noted that "the agents involved were not terminated from their positions." The only difference, Allred concluded, was that the agents were white and her clients were black.

Morris attorneys replied angrily to the charge: "He was found selling for profit. [The agents] were purchasing for their own use. Society makes a difference between the two." As for the Beverly Hills cops, they were left out in the cold. A couple of detectives came by to question

Harris, only to have him blast them for not questioning the three agents instead. And furthermore, Harris went on, your chief told William Morris I would not be prosecuted.

The two gumshoes looked at each other. "We've been had," one said, and they got up to leave.

FOR THE MOTION PICTURE AGENTS, IT WAS LIKE BEING BURIED AT THE bottom of a mudslide, after starting at the top. But toward the end of 1987, after tumbling helplessly for a year and a half, they began to think they might be able to claw their way out. Good things were happening to them, or at least to a few of their clients. Steve Guttenberg, a lower-echelon actor who'd gotten a big break when he landed a lead role in Hugh Wilson's *Police Academy* series, was one of the leads in Disney's *Three Men and a Baby*, which turned out to be the runaway hit of the year. Mel Gibson and Danny Glover starred in *Lethal Weapon*, a take-no-prisoners action picture from Joel Silver, successful producer of maximum-body-count thrillers. Kevin Costner got the industry's nod for stardom for his portrayal of crime-buster Eliot Ness in Brian De Palma's *The Untouchables*.

Costner was one of those actors who'd seemed fated for stardom from the start. He had an aura of destiny about him, self-confidence buoyed by sense of purpose, not to mention charisma. Mike Medavoy at Orion had seen it the year before when he gave Costner his first starring role in *No Way Out*, based on the 1947 thriller *The Big Clock*. But he hadn't been Paramount's first choice to play Eliot Ness, the Chicago G-man whose pursuit of Al Capone had already yielded a hit series for ABC. The producer, Art Linson, wanted Mel Gibson for the part. Then J. J. Harris, who was still fighting Ed Limato to represent Costner, got a look at the script. Forget Gibson, she said, the guy you want is Kevin Costner. Gibson was Limato's client, of course, but J. J. and Ed were so competitive that this little breach of etiquette hardly seemed worth noticing. Costner soon had second thoughts—his character seemed such a goody-two-shoes, next to Sean Connery, who was playing an experienced older cop, and Robert De Niro, who was playing Capone. But Harris talked Costner into it as well, and later, when the picture was finished and Paramount's test marketing showed it had huge appeal, she urged Orion to hold back its release of *No Way Out* so they could capitalize on the push he'd be getting from Paramount. It was good advice.

Now Costner was trying to decide between *Bull Durham*, a baseball picture that Orion had in development, and *Everybody's All-American*, a football melodrama in the works at Warner Bros. Baseball pictures were notorious underperformers at the box office, and Ron Shelton, the screenwriter who was set to direct *Bull Durham*, had never directed before and had shopped his script to every studio in town before Orion said yes. But Harris thought it was a good part—a sinewy baseball player meets a smart, seductive fan as he's approaching obsolescence on a North Carolina farm team—and the script was wonderful, with finely etched characters, crisp dialogue, and wry, distilled humor. Costner said yes.

Harris had a good friend in the department named Elaine Goldsmith, a forthright young woman with an outsized personality. The two of them made a sort of wacky duet—they'd both started out as secretaries before being admitted to the training program in the early eighties, and Harris's bubbly good humor made a nice foil for Goldsmith's more acerbic disposition. Goldsmith had recently signed Tim Robbins, a twenty-nine-year-old actor she'd lured away from a little agency on the Strip after meeting him on the set of *Howard the Duck*. Robbins was gangly and offbeat, a kid who'd grown up in the Greenwich Village folk scene and studied theater at UCLA and founded a repertory group called the Actors' Gang. Goldsmith was eager to show him what she could do, so the day after Costner agreed to do *Bull Durham*, she sent him the script.

Robbins had been offered a part in another baseball film at Orion, *Eight Men Out*, about the legendary 1919 Chicago Black Sox. But he loved the *Bull Durham* script as much as J. J. and Elaine did, and after meeting with Costner and Ron Shelton, he passed on *Eight Men Out* because Goldsmith said they wanted him for *Bull Durham*. He was ecstatic, at first. Then weeks slipped by, and the offer didn't come in. Goldsmith found out that Orion was considering Anthony Michael Hall, the blond teenager from *Sixteen Candles* and *The Breakfast Club*, for the *Bull Durham* role. When she went to the board to get someone to intercede, she was told to concentrate on bigger fish. Then Susan Sarandon—formerly with the Morris office, now with ICM—won the female lead. She met with Robbins and liked him so much that she and Costner persuaded Orion to give him the job. Goldsmith kept her client; Robbins got the part; and, as it turned out, Sarandon found her mate.

*   *   *

One flight down, in the stillness of the first floor, the wheels of decision were slowly grinding. Stan Kamen had been dead nearly two years when Roger Davis finally placed the phone call to Sue Mengers. Mengers had been getting calls from the Morris office for months—from Ed Limato, whom she knew from his days at ICM. From Toni Howard, whom she adored, whom she'd known from the day she arrived in California because Toni had been Freddie Fields's secretary at CMA. From Boaty Boatwright, whom she knew from even further back, because Boaty had been a casting director for Universal when Sue was first made an agent in 1963 in New York. But those were her friends, begging her to come. They didn't have the authority. Roger Davis did. And from her point of view, his timing was excellent.

By the start of 1988, Mengers was beginning to get a little antsy in her retirement. For a while it had been a whirl—staying with Gore Vidal at his villa in Ravello, lounging on a yacht on the French Riviera with Wendy and Leonard Goldberg and their good friends the Poitiers, flying off to Israel, celebrating Jerry Weintraub's fiftieth at that party he gave at Blue Heaven, his eight-acre estate in Malibu. She and Jean-Claude had taken advantage of the real-estate boom to sell their fabulous Bel Air mansion—the Zsa Zsa house—and buy apartments in New York and L.A. They'd thought about making New York their home, but now they'd decided to stay in L.A. after all, and they'd just seen a house they liked in Beverly Hills, a darling little ochre number nestled among the estates north of Sunset. Now she wondered—had she made a mistake, leaving the business the way she had? Coming in to rebuild the department, acting as a mentor to the younger agents—maybe it would be nice for a couple of years. And there was that $1 million salary . . .

Mengers wasn't stupid. She could see that the six men who sat on the board didn't really want her—that the idea of a woman running the department made them squirm, that after Kamen, they didn't want anyone strong in the job. What she didn't realize, being an outsider, was how much power they wielded. They seemed like nice old men who'd leave her alone. So she didn't insist on a seat on the board. She did insist on Kamen's title—head of the motion picture department worldwide. Lenny Hirshan wasn't happy about it, but he got used to the idea.

All this happened slowly, very slowly, a period of months. Every issue on the table had to be discussed among six board members on two coasts. Meanwhile, half-emboldened, half-desperate, the motion picture agents upstairs had decided to take the initiative. With Kevin Costner and Mel Gibson, they had two among the handful of leading men whose name on the marquee was enough to open a picture. Now they drew up a hit list—a list of dream clients. Clients they wanted for their own. Three pages, single-spaced, with one to three agents assigned to each name. If this was the way the game was played now, this was the way they'd play it. No more marquess of Queensbury. No more waiting until they'd heard some star was dissatisfied. If they weren't dissatisfied already, make 'em that way.

Lenny Hirshan met with Francis Ford Coppola in San Francisco in February. He had a good breakfast meeting with Albert Finney. He had lunch with Arthur Hiller, the *Love Story* director, who seemed to be on the brink. He was meeting next with Kathleen Turner. John Burnham met with Madonna at the beginning of February. A few weeks later, he had lunch with Martin Short. He and Toni Howard were set to have lunch with Ted Danson. Cary Woods was talking to Emilio Estevez. No progress at all, unfortunately, on Kevin Bacon, Kim Basinger, Tom Berenger, Billy Crystal, Robert De Niro, Goldie Hawn, Tim Hutton, Michael Keaton, Oliver Stone, or John Travolta.

Right—so who were they kidding? They needed a leader, a heavy hitter, somebody the town could respect. Somebody who could go straight to the head of Orion and get Tim Robbins that offer. As far as Ed Limato could tell, the board was never going to act. And Limato was no longer in a position to wait. Richard Gere, who was virtually his oldest client, was unhappy at the Morris office. And why not? *The Cotton Club* had bombed, and so had every picture he'd done since—*King David*, Bruce Beresford's ill-advised sword-and-sandals pic; *Power*, Sidney Lumet's star-studded essay on corruption; *No Mercy*, a substandard thriller that left audiences cold. His next release was *Miles from Home*, a road movie that was clearly beyond redemption. Gere hadn't scored a hit since *An Officer and a Gentleman*, six years ago. And in the meantime, Mel Gibson, Limato's other leading man, had zoomed right past him—hailed by *People* as "the sexiest man alive," propelled into the $4 million salary range by the box office on *Lethal Weapon*.

A waning star made a vulnerable client. Studio execs might not be interested in Richard Gere any longer, but to competing agents he was prime meat. Mike Ovitz was making a play for him. Sam Cohn of ICM was putting him together with a director he represented who was making a killer-on-the-loose picture called *Far from Home*. Limato wasn't in their league, and he had no one at the Morris office to turn to. Lenny Hirshan? Norman Brokaw? Not unless he wanted the Linda Darnell stories again. Limato might be retro, a self-conscious throwback to the old Hollywood, but the guys he was working for were relics. And in the difference, he smelled disaster.

Then he got a call from Jeff Berg, the chairman of ICM. Sam Cohn wanted to fly out to meet with him.

Berg had been calling Limato at regular intervals for some time. But for Sam Cohn, who seldom ventured closer to Hollywood than the Russian Tea Room on West Fifty-seventh Street, a flight out to the coast was a rare event. He had a good reason for doing it this time. ICM needed stars, but it also needed star agents, and Cohn and Berg both realized that it made no sense to steal Gere from Ed Limato when they might be able to get Gere and Limato both, and probably the rest of Limato's clients as well. Berg wanted Limato to meet them at a bungalow on the sprawling, palm-studded grounds of the Beverly Hills Hotel—a secluded hideaway in one of the industry's leading fishbowls. Limato told him he was staying at William Morris. But he agreed to take the meeting.

When he got to the bungalow, he found that Berg and Cohn had brought along ICM's forty-one-year-old president, Jim Wiatt. A product of Beverly Hills High and USC, Wiatt had joined the agency after a stint as an aide to California Senator John Tunney. He was the warm and congenial one, the foil to Berg and Cohn, the New York eccentric who was legendary for his ratty sweaters and his odd paper-chewing habit. The three of them struck Limato as not just intelligent but enthusiastic. They were on the way up, not down. They were exactly what he needed—a group of top-level agents he could go to in a crisis. He walked out convinced.

There was one complication, however. Limato was still under contract to William Morris—or was he? The three-year contract they'd negotiated at the end of 1983 had expired more than a year ago. A new three-year contract had been negotiated but never signed, although Morris was adhering to its terms—a new Jaguar and a salary and bonus package of $550,000 a year, more than anybody in the department was making except Hirshan. While ICM's lawyers looked into the situation, Limato broached the subject to his clients—to Gere, to Mel Gibson, to Michelle Pfeiffer, to Matthew Modine and Nicolas Cage. All of them were prepared to go over with him.

Meanwhile, Sue Mengers was hammering out her agreement with the board of directors, unaware that Morris's leading motion picture agent was planning his exit. Months went by. He didn't tell her. He felt guilty about it, but he couldn't.

APRIL 6, 1988, STARTED AS A NORMAL ENOUGH MORNING ON EL Camino—agents pulling into the underground garage across the street, filing past the squat cylindrical columns by the front door, disappearing into the elevators on their way upstairs. It was Wednesday, the day of the motion picture department's regular weekly meeting, and by ten o'clock, the conference room was full. Lenny Hirshan started the meeting, though neither Ed Limato nor Roger Davis had come in. They were used to seeing Limato drag himself in late, hair askew, face a mask of stubble, slurping black coffee to bring himself around. And Davis was a board member; he had other things to do.

In fact, Davis had been trying to get Limato on the phone. He'd come in that morning with a tremendous surprise to announce: Sue Mengers and the board had finally come to terms, and Sue was arriving that afternoon to assume command of the department. Then he realized Limato was missing. No one had seen him in nearly a week. J. J. Harris had told Davis she'd heard Limato was going to ICM. And there was no answer at his house.

They were ten minutes into the meeting when Davis walked in, white-faced. He had one question: Had anyone seen Limato?

No.

Then they had a problem.

What?

They had reason to believe he'd left for ICM.

A pall fell across the room. Disbelief. Then, uproar. Panic. Limato was their last real claim to credibility. What were they going to do without him?

But don't worry, Davis continued, moving on to the good news. Sue Mengers was coming in as head of the department.

Davis left. The meeting fell apart. People retreated to their offices, angry, excited, hysterical, depressed. Some were in tears. Some walked by Limato's empty office and peered inside, as if by staring at his telephone they could conjure him up.

Before noontime, a messenger arrived with a letter from Limato:

Dear Roger:

After much consideration, and in light of the continuing at-will status
of my employment with William Morris Agency, I have decided to ter-
minate my . . .

By the time Mengers arrived that afternoon, everybody in Hollywood
had heard about Limato. Mengers was horrified. It wasn't bad enough
that the only high-profile agent they had left was taking off with three of
the agency's biggest stars. No, he had to do it the day she walked in, so
the whole town would think it was because of her. And he'd told her
working at Morris would be fun.

Anyway, there was nothing to do but go through with it. She was a
trouper, a survivor, a fucking legend, for Christ's sake, and she was back
in the game, even if she was holding only a pair of deuces. So she spent
the afternoon in Stan Kamen's old office—Lenny Hirshan's office
now—holding court with the *alter kockers* on the first floor while the
remaining motion picture agents were brought down and introduced,
one by one. Hirshan was there, of course, and Roger Davis, and Walt
Zifkin, and Norman Brokaw, and Jerry Katzman from the television
department. She cut an ebullient figure, brash, sarcastic, irrepressible,
bumming cigarettes, blowing smoke about the difference she was going
to make. And if her agents squinted really hard when they walked into
the room, it was just possible for them to believe that this wasn't going
to be a disaster.

The problem with stepping into Stan Kamen's shoes was that they were
no longer there. It had been two years since Kamen died, two years
since Mengers quit ICM. The era of Stan and Sue was over, finis, rele-
gated to the memory bin along with bell-bottomed jeans, mood rings,
and Ma Maison, the perpetual French garden party on Melrose where
tout Hollywood used to frolic. The business had undergone a sea change
since then. It was Mike Ovitz's game now—cool, calculated, ruthless.
Armani suits in Century City. Big shoulders, swagger and attitude.
Power lunch.

Mengers set up shop in Ed Limato's office, the second-floor corner
suite directly above the executive conference room that had been built

where Abe Lastfogel's office used to be, at the corner of El Camino and Charleville. By rights, she should have been on the first floor, next to Lee Stevens and Norman Brokaw and Roger Davis and Walt Zifkin and the top packaging agents in the television department. But Lenny Hirshan had taken over Kamen's office, and besides, it made more sense for Mengers to be accessible to her troops. It was kind of nice up there, spacious, tree-shaded, a little removed from the traffic on the street. On her coffee table sat a large bowl of lemons.

The way she figured it, the Morris office had nowhere to go but up. The place had been flattened. Kurt Russell had stuck with them after Kamen died, even after Goldie Hawn, the mother of his child, went to CAA. On the day Limato left, Russell announced he'd be joining her there. That left them with maybe two dozen movie stars on the client list: Lauren Bacall, Anne Bancroft, Katharine Hepburn, Sophia Loren, Joanne Woodward, and Loretta Young. Gary Busey, Kevin Costner, Matt Dillon, Danny Glover, Steve Guttenberg, Tom Hanks, Ralph Macchio, John Malkovich, and Eric Roberts. Candice Bergen, Carrie Fisher, Anjelica Huston, Diane Keaton, and Andie MacDowell. Clint Eastwood, Jack Lemmon, Walter Matthau, Peter O'Toole, and Omar Sharif. Two dozen out of three thousand, and most of them either well past their prime or yet to hit it.

There were things you could do with such a list, but not much that involved motion pictures. Take Candice Bergen. Age: forty-two. Daughter of famed ventriloquist Edgar Bergen, "sister" of Charlie McCarthy, Bergen's wooden-headed sidekick. Wife of classy French director Louis Malle. Actress who'd landed an Oscar nomination nine years ago for her work with Burt Reynolds and Jill Clayburgh in Alan Pakula's *Starting Over*. Nice job in *Gandhi* (1982), reteamed with Burt in the Elmore Leonard crime drama *Stick* (1985). Nothing since. Cold, cold, cold.

But that winter, Diane English, the writer-producer whom Steve Weiss in the television department had been pushing for years, had gotten a pilot commitment from CBS for a sitcom called "Murphy Brown"—a TV newsroom series built around a tough woman reporter fresh out of the Betty Ford Clinic, "Mary Tyler Moore" updated for the eighties. English had developed the show with JoBeth Williams in mind, but when Williams decided to pass, the television department started looking for someone else to fill the role. Candice Bergen's agent got her a script. Bergen was skeptical, but when she read it—on a plane to New

York—she got so excited, she phoned the Morris office in mid-flight and asked what she had to do to get the part.

A meeting was arranged. English decided she was perfect. But CBS entertainment president Kim LeMasters had his doubts. Could she really do comedy? Would she be able to stand the pace—week after week, knock it out, bam-bam-bam? He even had her come over to his office at CBS Television City and read for him—a demand she found vaguely insulting. Yet that February, despite her pique, she'd signed up for the job—her first television series. In March she'd filmed the pilot, with Jerry Katzman and Larry Auerbach and half a dozen other William Morris television agents on hand to tell the CBS brass what a hit they had. Now she was in New York, dazzling the ad agency types who'd come to view the pilots and decide what to buy.

All of which was very nice for Candice Bergen and Diane English and Jerry Katzman and the television department. But in terms of contemporary box office, Mengers was left with maybe a half-dozen viable names on the client list. Tom Hanks was about to come out in *Big*, playing a thirteen-year-old trapped in a grown-up's body. Sixteen-year-old Ralph Macchio had hit pay dirt as the wimp hero of *The Karate Kid*. Danny Glover was using *Lethal Weapon* to move from character actor to leading man. *Three Men and a Baby* made Steve Guttenberg look like the luckiest white man on earth—sweet guy, little talent. Clint Eastwood was three hundred miles up the California coast, having gotten himself elected mayor of the picture-postcard village of Carmel; what time he had left was spent indulging his desire to become a filmmaker with uncommercial projects like *Bird*, his Charlie Parker biopic. Which meant that the biggest working star the Morris office could claim was Kevin Costner.

At this point in his career, Kevin Costner was a very busy man. Orion had scheduled a summer release for *Bull Durham*. Now he was working on yet another baseball picture, a quirky, sentimental yarn called *Field of Dreams*, about an Iowa farmer who plows up his cornfield after voices tell him the ghosts of Shoeless Joe Jackson and the 1919 Chicago Black Sox are waiting to play ball. He was about to start shooting a thriller for Columbia called *Revenge*. And he'd fallen in love with *Dances with Wolves*, a novel a friend was writing about a nineteenth-century cavalry officer who goes native in the Old West. He liked the era, liked the character, liked the thundering herd of buffalo, liked the revisionist approach to Western history. He liked it so much that he'd gotten Nelson Entertainment—one of the small, independent studios that had sprung up in Hollywood in the past few years—to option the screen rights so he could star in it and direct it himself.

If the Morris office had few other stars of Costner's rank, it had no shortage of wannabes. The client list was so large and cumbersome, so cluttered with music and television acts hoping to make it in pictures, that it was hard for anyone to break out of the crowd. The department was divided up into covering agents and responsible agents—agents who covered a particular studio, and agents who were responsible for a particular client. The agent who covered Warner Bros. would meet with the casting director on a picture there and run down the list of ingénues who might be right for a part: Valerie Bertinelli, Ann Marie Bobby, Lisa Bonet, Belinda Carlisle, Sheena Easton, Jamie Gertz, Robin Givens, Valeria Golina, Isabelle Huppert . . . The casting director would respond as if to a word association test: no, no, like, no, no, no, like, like, no . . . Then they'd start in on the younger leading men and the character actors and the ethnic males and so forth until they'd gone through a couple of hundred names, 70 percent of whom no casting director would ever be interested in—actors and actresses whose autographed glossies served largely to adorn the interiors of L.A. car washes and dry-cleaning establishments. Celebrities no one had heard of.

So Mengers set out to sign real celebrities. Not that she'd come in to be a signer—she thought of herself as a builder, a teacher, someone who could reorganize things and get them back on their feet. But the board expected her to sign stars, and the industry too. If that's the way it was, that's the way she'd play it. She had the contacts. She knew the stars—the older ones, anyway. If only she hadn't told them how much she hated the business when she left ICM . . .

As a signer, Mengers imagined herself in a role not unlike Michael Ovitz's—someone who reels in the stars and passes them on to other agents who handle them day-to-day. But the domineering attitude that had worked so well for her in the seventies—"Your career sucks! Get smart. Get out of there. They aren't doing dick for you!"—didn't cut it anymore. The Ovitz approach was smooth, professional, salesmanship cut with a hint of servility—"What's happening in your life? What would you like to have happen? Here's what I can do for you. . . ." Mengers seemed loud and bullish and dated by comparison. Not that she didn't have supporters: "William Morris must be spinning in his grave from happiness," Ray Stark told the *Wall Street Journal* when asked about her appointment. But to others, her arrival merely confirmed the impression that the Morris office was out of the loop. It didn't help that she'd made enemies over the years, or that many of her contacts were of the mogul-emeritus variety, or that many of the assistants and story editors she'd dismissed so rudely when she was on top were senior studio executives now, calling the shots. She was still a big name; she got her phone calls returned. But the reaction was wait-and-see.

It was a short wait. Within weeks, the Wednesday morning meetings devolved into a somber ritual. "Let me tell you who turned me down *this* week," Mengers would say tartly, and then she'd rattle off a couple of more names. Goldie Hawn. Sidney Lumet. Sylvester Stallone—the Victor Mature of the nineties. Her former clients had other agents now, and they weren't eager to come to the Morris office in any case. Michael Caine and Jonathan Demme had already left ICM for Morris and gone back. Barbra Streisand had fled to CAA after Kamen's death. No one who wasn't in trouble was signing with the Morris office. It was a place you left, not a place you went to. It had an aura.

When things failed to click, Mengers's profile in the industry underwent a polar reversal. Overnight, tentative attraction turned into magnetic repulsion. At the same time, she realized she couldn't reform the department the way she'd planned to because the board had all the power. She lacked the authority to hire and fire. She couldn't even set salaries and bonuses. Changes she wanted to make, like putting key agents under contract, were simply ignored. Around Memorial Day, her attitude suddenly shifted. Maybe she couldn't build Morris back into a powerhouse, but she could certainly make trouble.

What was Morris's strong point? It was their writers—never the glamour set in Hollywood, but where would the business be without them? They were the jewel of the agency, the people who generated the ideas that turned unknowns into stars and kept stars from fading back into unknowns. The list included bestselling authors with screenplays to their credit—people like Susan Isaacs, whose *Compromising Positions* had starred Susan Sarandon three years earlier, and Dominick Dunne, whose novel *The Two Mrs. Grenvilles* had yielded a miniseries for ABC. It included playwrights on the order of Martin Sherman, whose Holocaust drama *Bent* had once lured Richard Gere to Broadway, and Harvey Fierstein, now costarring with Anne Bancroft in the screen version of his *Torch Song Trilogy*. It included such well-known Hollywood figures as Buck Henry, who'd made his name collaborating on *The Gradu-*

ate, and Carrie Fisher, now writing a screenplay for MGM based on her novel *Postcards from the Edge*. And it included newcomers like James Orr and Jim Cruickshank, the writing team Disney Studios chief Jeffrey Katzenberg had brought in to rescue *Three Men and a Baby* after the writer-director of the French film it was based on decamped for Paris five weeks before the start of production.

With gold like that in their vaults, it made sense to be careful whom they shared it with. If some producer was going to let CAA negotiate a studio deal for him, let CAA come up with material. So they divided the town into three camps.

The first camp consisted of clients who were looking for projects—Clint Eastwood, Tom Hanks, Diane Keaton, directors Bruce Beresford and Costa-Gavras and Alan Pakula and Franco Zeffirelli, among others—and independent producers who were considered friendly to the Morris office. Bernie Brillstein. Norman Lear. Ray Stark. Freddie Fields, Mengers's old boss. Joel Silver, who was always on the prowl for projects. Mel Brooks, whom Mengers always referred to as "the funniest man in America." Guber-Peters-Barris Entertainment, headed by ex–Columbia exec Peter Guber and ex–Streisand boyfriend Jon Peters, who'd produced Costa-Gavras's *Missing*. Simpson-Bruckheimer Productions, headed by Don Simpson and Jerry Bruckheimer, the guys who gave *Beverly Hills Cop* and *Top Gun* to Paramount. Steven Spielberg's Amblin Entertainment, probably the biggest production outfit in town. Weintraub Entertainment, the company Jerry Weintraub formed after Kirk Kerkorian fired him from UA. Frank Yablans, effectively ousted as head of MGM/UA three years earlier and grateful for any material he could get. They were to get first crack.

Then there were the neutral independents—producers who did business with everyone. Irwin Allen. Allan Carr. Marty Bregman, Al Pacino's producer. James L. Brooks, creator of "The Mary Tyler Moore Show" and "Taxi," Oscar-winning writer-director of *Terms of Endearment*. Larry Gordon, ex-president of Fox, now producer of action pictures on the order of *Predator* and *Die Hard*. Imagine Films, Ron Howard's highly successful outfit at Universal. Interscope Communications, the independent production company that kept feeding hits to Disney, *Three Men and a Baby* among them. Irwin Winkler, coproducer of the *Rocky* series. The Zucker brothers, whose latest picture, *The Naked Gun*, starred Priscilla Presley in her first film role. They weren't to get first crack, but there was no reason to keep material away from them.

Finally there were the "nonclients"—most of them clients of CAA or closely allied with it. Many were ex-clients of Stan or Sue or both—Chevy Chase, Cher, Sally Field, Jane Fonda, Goldie Hawn, Herb Ross, Sylvester Stallone. Others were producers who'd moved into the CAA orbit: Keith Barish, Stan Kamen's ex-friend, who'd allied himself with CAA after Kamen helped launch him as a producer with *Sophie's Choice*. Carolco Pictures, the indie responsible for Stallone's *Rambo* series. Castle Rock Entertainment, headed by Carl Reiner's son Rob, one of CAA's earliest clients. Half-assed stars like Michael Douglas who'd send some bimbo out to take a meeting so she could go back and dump on them. They should get nothing—no meetings, no screenplays, nothing. Let 'em wonder what they were missing.

Once again the agency business was in flux. In February, as Mengers was negotiating her contract with the William Morris board, two young agents had left Creative Artists to join Bill Block, a hyperaggressive thirty-four-year-old from ICM, in a new firm called InterTalent. New agencies formed and dissolved all the time, but not out of CAA. When Laura Dern, Kyle MacLachlan, and Kiefer Sutherland left too, Ovitz was reported to be "on the warpath." A lot of good it did him: InterTalent quickly joined Triad Artists and Marty Bauer's Bauer-Benedek Agency to form a trio of small, high-profile firms that promised the kind of personal attention it could be hard to get at the big three agencies.

Then, in July, Marvin Josephson finally succeeded in taking ICM private. After years as a patchwork assemblage of semi-independent boutiques within a miniconglomerate that included a brokerage firm, an office supply company, and several other outfits (some of which the agency's profits were supporting), ICM was suddenly independent and employee-owned. The deal left it with $62 million in bank debt, but it also left it free from the interference of outside stockholders, free to lure star agents with the same astronomical salaries CAA was paying, free to match Ovitz at his own game. Snaring Ed Limato from the Morris office, it appeared, was just the beginning.

In the void left by Limato and his stars, a handful of younger clients were beginning to emerge at the Morris office. With *Predator* and *Die Hard*, John McTiernan had moved out of television commercials to become one of Hollywood's top action directors. Tim Burton, the quirksome young director of *Pee-Wee's Big Adventure*, scored the surprise hit of the year in *Beetlejuice*, a wacky look at the afterlife. In October, he was due to fly to London to start *Batman*, a Warner Bros. project that had been through ten scripts and almost as many directors before he took it on. *Bull Durham* came out in June and sent Tim Robbins to the top of the list of the town's interesting new faces. Eric Roberts bolted, his career in free-fall after starring roles a few years before in *Star 80* and *The Pope of Greenwich Village*. But his kid sister Julia had just given a winning performance in *Mystic Pizza*, a low-budget ensemble picture due to be released in October, and she had a pair of agents, one on each coast, doing everything they could think of to make things happen. Maybe they couldn't sign stars, but there was no reason they couldn't create one.

Julia Roberts had come to the Morris Agency in 1985, when her manager set up a lunch with Risa Shapiro, a junior agent in the New York office who was already beginning to show a keen eye for talent. Roberts was seventeen years old and totally green—a fresh-faced Georgia teenager, frail and doe-eyed and innocent, smile so bright she could light up a room. Shapiro was rather doe-eyed herself—thin and fragile-looking, an ex-model with flaming red hair that cascaded across her shoulders. Armed with a master's in educational psychology, she'd planned to work with disturbed children; when that didn't pan out, she switched to actors. She looked at Julia Roberts and was mesmerized.

Risa Shapiro and Elaine Goldsmith were good friends, and together, they'd set out to find the right parts for their new client. After a lot of legwork, Shapiro got her in with a casting director who was looking for a New England pizza shop waitress for *Mystic Pizza*, a female coming-of-age picture in development at the Samuel Goldwyn Company, the independent outfit headed by Sam Goldwyn, Jr. Her first screen test wasn't too good, but she came back for another and won over the director, if not Goldwyn himself. The film turned out to be charming and engaging, and Roberts was so special in it that Goldwyn had to kick himself for not getting an option on her. But in the meantime, she'd landed a role as Sally Field's diabetic daughter in *Steel Magnolias*, Ray Stark's big-budget adaptation of an off-Broadway play about a small-town beauty parlor in the South, with Herb Ross directing a star-studded cast. The next step was to get her a starring role.

The question that kept them all spooked was, How long could they hold on to their clients once they built them up? Not just Julia Roberts, but Kevin Costner and Tim Burton and Tom Hanks and the lot of them.

With the Writers Guild locked in an angry strike that had kept film and television production shut down since March, agents had little to do except raid one another's lists. The Morris office had already lost Steve Guttenberg to Creative Artists and Danny Glover to Triad. John Burnham scored Roseanne Barr from Triad because her manager, who also handled Diane Keaton, was impressed with his performance on *Baby Boom*. But it was too late to get the package commission on her new sitcom, a not-exactly-uplifting slice of family life from Carsey-Werner that premiered in October and quickly started crowding "Cosby" for the number-one Nielsen slot. As for Mengers, the biggest signings she could claim were Christopher Walken, who'd left Morris to be with her when she was at ICM, and Treat Williams, an ICM client whose career had peaked ten years earlier with the screen version of the sixties rock musical *Hair*.

But Mengers wasn't ready to admit defeat yet. This was business. This was war. This called for someone like John Burnham, who screamed and threw phones around but managed to get the job done. Besides Diane Keaton, Burnham handled Carrie Fisher, rock singer Belinda Carlisle, performance artist Sandra Bernhard, and producer Hugh Wilson. He showed his flair for the new order in November, in the memo he sent to announce that a heart attack had just claimed one of his more distinguished screenwriter clients:

To: All Agents East/West

Re: Lukas Heller

I regret to inform you that Lukas Heller passed away yesterday. That's the bad news. The good news is that shortly before his peaceful passing he defeated a fellow writer in tennis and was putting the finishing touches on his screenplay for RALPH MACCHIO.

WHEN THE NUMBERS WERE TALLIED, 1988 TURNED OUT TO BE THE BIGGEST year the Morris Agency had ever had: $60 million in revenues, much of it attributable to "The Cosby Show" bonanza. They had five and a half hours on prime time this season, including "Matlock," "The Cosby Show," "A Different World," and "Murphy Brown." "Frank's Place" had gotten the ax from CBS, but Hugh Wilson was hanging around the mail room to soak up color for a new sitcom he was developing, a spoof of the agency business called "The Famous Teddy Z." It was a risky project—the networks were notoriously resistant to shows about show business—but an appealing one, an inside look at a Beverly Hills talent agency that looked a lot like William Morris.

Teddy Z himself, a Greek-American mail room temp who's sent to pick up a temperamental movie star at the airport and comes back as his agent, was based on the real-life experience of Jay Kantor, who was working in the MCA mail room in 1947 when he was dispatched to meet Marlon Brando. But the rest of the show was unmistakably William Morris, from fast-talking, ultraslick agent Al Floss (a play on Hal Ross, the packaging agent who covered CBS), to company chairman Abe Werkfinder, a doddering old soul whose fatherly presence is all that keeps the firm's hyperaggressive employees from clawing each other's eyes out.

The Morris office could afford to laugh at itself. It was doing so well that its class-C stock, distributed among seventy-seven officers and employees, had risen 14 percent in value, to more than $20 million. Television packaging provided much of the cash, but it wasn't carrying them single-handedly. The news division in New York represented a lucrative stable of clients, including Barbara Walters, ABC News anchorman Peter Jennings, NBC weatherman Willard Scott, and tabloid news personality Geraldo Rivera, who'd recently augmented his syndicated show with a two-hour prime-time special on devil worship for NBC. The New York literary department had just gotten Tom Clancy a $4 million advance for *Clear and Present Danger*, his fifth novel, and had auctioned U.S. and foreign rights to an as-yet unwritten sequel to *Gone with the Wind* for more than $10 million. The William Morris Plaza Building in Beverly Hills generated more than $2 million a year in rental income. The lecture department booked everyone from world heavyweight champion Mike Tyson to professional fitness maven Richard Simmons to "Lifestyles of the Rich and Famous" host Robin Leach to New York Mets star Darryl Strawberry, who was available to speak out against drug abuse. Only the motion picture department continued to languish.

But there was another problem that didn't show up on the balance sheet. Lee Stevens hadn't been to the office in months. He'd been diagnosed with cancer once before, and he thought he'd beaten it. He hadn't. In February 1989, at the age of fifty-eight, he died at Cedars-Sinai. Funeral was at Hillside.

Like Norman Brokaw and Stan Kamen, Larry Auerbach and Lenny Hirshan, Stevens had been a lifer—thirty-six years with the Morris office. They'd grown up together, the fourth generation of Morris men, and now they were dying together. It seemed all but incomprehensible—two of them struck down by fatal illness before they were sixty. But their shock was mitigated by the vacuum he left behind.

For weeks, as Stevens fought for his life, the five remaining board members had been meeting in the first-floor conference room where Abe Lastfogel's office had once been, struggling to choose his successor. There wasn't one of them who didn't secretly covet the job. Lou Weiss, the television powerhouse in New York. Roger Davis, the attorney who'd tried to run the motion picture department. Walt Zifkin, the attorney who administered the television department and managed their real-estate investments. Tony Fantozzi, though his star had faded as George Schlatter fell from the ranks of major television producers. Norman Brokaw—most of all, Norman Brokaw. Of the three golden boys of the fourth generation, only Brokaw was left alive. Which meant there was no one to stand in his way—except Jerry Katzman.

Katzman was a newcomer. He'd joined the agency in 1972, after spending the first seven years of his career as a producer at MGM. But as head of television worldwide, the man who'd breathed new life into their cash cow, he was in a strong position. He'd been close to Lee Stevens. He was everything Brokaw was not—dynamic, connected, a leader. He'd watched in frustration as the board allowed the agency to drift. Now was his chance to make a play.

Katzman had support within the agency, especially in the television department. But how did you lobby a board whose members all wanted the job for themselves? At least Brokaw had a legitimate claim. He was their link to the past, to the days of Mr. and Mrs. Lastfogel. He was their link to Bill Cosby. Through Priscilla Presley, under whose leadership the Presley estate was now grossing some $15 million a year, he was their link to Elvis. He'd just lost the race to sign Ronald Reagan to Morton Janklow, the New York literary agent with close ties to CAA. But to deny him the presidency now, five years after Stevens had snatched it away, would be tantamount to public humiliation.

On February 6, four days after Lee Stevens's death, the board's decision was announced. Brokaw would become president and chief executive officer. Lou Weiss would stay on as chairman. Walt Zifkin was named chief operating officer. As usual, the vote was unanimous.

Brokaw was ebullient. A couple of nights later, he was on the phone with Bill Cosby at his house in the Trousdale Estates section of Beverly Hills when someone broke in on the line to sing him congratulations—Jesse Jackson, Cosby's friend and Brokaw's client, just back from a trip to Moscow to negotiate the release of four Soviet Jews. Brokaw was right in his element, playing the fame game with the nation's big men of affairs—only now, he was president of the William Morris Agency!

For Katzman, who at fifty-one was ten years younger than Brokaw, the course of action was obvious. Wait. Watch. Bide your time. Before any significant changes could be made, the board would have to be adjusted. A change was overdue in any case. It had been nine years since the board had first been expanded, and in the interim, more than half its members had died: first Nat Lefkowitz, then Abe Lastfogel, then Stan Kamen and Morris Stoller and Sam Weisbord, and now Lee Stevens. Of the five remaining board members, only Lou Weiss was based in New York, and only Norman Brokaw had any relationship with the Hollywood entertainment community. It was time for a realignment.

A week after Brokaw was made president, it was announced that four new members had been elected to the board of directors. Jerry Katzman, of course. His friend Larry Auerbach, also from the television department. Lenny Hirshan from the motion picture department. And fifty-year-old Owen Laster, the youngest of the bunch, a twenty-seven-year agency veteran who headed the literary department in New York and handled such best-selling authors as Robin Cook, Dominick Dunne, Susan Isaacs, James Michener, and Gore Vidal. Sue Mengers was conspicuously absent. Once again, the vote was unanimous.

Another change drew far less notice. On February 13, the same day the election of the new board members was made public, a four-page document was faxed to the New York County Clerk's Office on Foley Square. It was an amendment to the agency's incorporation papers, and its purpose was to set up an executive committee to manage the agency's affairs. This committee would consist of two to seven people elected by the holders of class-A stock, which was much more tightly held than the class-C stock that was routinely made available to employees. The committee was empowered to hire and fire everyone in the corporation (including directors), to set compensation, to manage the day-to-day affairs of the corporation, and to instruct the board to "take any and all actions" it deemed appropriate. So Katzman and the others got on the board but the board itself became nothing but a front.

IT WAS FUNNY. MORE AND MORE, ALMOST AGAINST HER WILL, ELAINE Goldsmith found herself in Sue Mengers's office with Julia Roberts, arguing ferociously while Roberts sat there with her mouth open. Mengers had always hoped to be a mentor to the younger agents, particularly the women, and that's what was happening now. Goldsmith had started as a secretary, just as Mengers had. Then she'd gone to work for Ed Limato, who'd signed Nicolas Cage on her recommendation and encouraged her to help with some of his younger clients. She'd always known she'd make a great agent, because to turn nos into yesses you need to believe in what you're selling, and she did—she believed in herself. But she had to admit, she always came away from these shouting matches with Mengers having learned something.

For months now, Goldsmith had been preoccupied with a property called *3000*. It had started when a producer sent her the script for a low-budget picture he planned to do at Vestron, a marginal video distributor that had gone into the independent film production business and scored a hit with *Dirty Dancing*. The script was dark and bleak, a morality tale about a drug-addicted Hollywood prostitute who's hired for a week of luxury and then thrown back on the streets—and yet, reading it, Goldsmith realized that this was Julia Roberts. They'd been waiting for the right story, and this was it. She was so excited, she got in her car and drove it straight to Roberts's house.

Then Vestron chief Steve Reuther—the same Steve Reuther who'd once been Stan Kamen's assistant at the Morris office—left to become a producer at Touchstone Pictures, the Disney subsidiary that had been set up to produce grown-up fare. He took *3000* with him. Goldsmith began a full-court press, pestering Touchstone president David Hoberman to give Roberts the part, pestering Ed Limato and Sam Cohn to look at the script for Richard Gere, who'd already passed on it once. Finally, to shut Goldsmith up, Hoberman agreed to see *Mystic Pizza*. He was impressed enough to give Roberts a screen test, and then to give her the part. Gere still wasn't interested, but Hoberman and his boss, Jeffrey Katzenberg, were having the script rewritten, lightened up, given a romantic twist. Katzenberg called Sam Cohn at ICM's New York office and urged him to get Gere to reconsider. Cohn called Limato. Limato called Gere. At this point in his career, Gere didn't have many choices. He met with the director—Garry Marshall, who'd started out years before writing comedy material for Danny Thomas and Joey Bishop— and liked him enough to say yes.

Julia Roberts had completed *Steel Magnolias*, which Herb Ross was readying for a Christmas 1989 release. *Mystic Pizza* had turned into the sleeper hit of 1988. The buzz on Roberts was good, very good. Suddenly, the girl these two agents from the Morris office had been hawking was hot. Which was why Goldsmith picked up her phone one day not long after Norman Brokaw was named president and found Bill Block on the other end.

It had been a year since Block left ICM to start InterTalent. At ICM, he'd been part of a small clique of agents who called themselves the wolverines, after the weasellike carnivores with the flesh-ripping teeth. Their motto was "Kill, maim, and package." David Hoberman had been one of them until Disney's Jeffrey Katzenberg hired him away to help run Touchstone. Then Block went in with two partners from CAA to form InterTalent, which was going to be the CAA of the nineties. Now he wanted to meet Julia Roberts's agent.

Goldsmith panicked. Like other junior agents in the motion picture department, she'd fantasized for years about going off on her own, being part of a hip, creative office instead of the dinosaur outfit she was in. Actually doing it, however, was something else. She ran down the second-floor hallway and burst in on her friend J. J. Harris, who handled Kevin Costner. "What do I do?" she cried. Harris, being the practical sort, suggested she have dinner with him.

J. J. Harris was a tall, slender woman, loose-limbed and deceptively scattered in appearance, with curly blond hair that fell in soft curls around her face. As usual, she was preoccupied with Costner. She'd enlisted John Ptak to put the financing together for *Dances with Wolves*, which Nelson Entertainment had dropped after running into financial difficulties. What *Yentl* had been to Streisand, *Dances with Wolves* was to Costner—a project from the heart, and Harris was going to do everything she could to help him make it.

The problem was that he wanted control. He didn't want to argue with studio execs about whether it should run for three hours, or if it should have Sioux dialogue with English subtitles, or what title to give it. That was the fight he was having now with Universal over *Field of Dreams*, which he wanted to call *Shoeless Joe*, after the novel it was based on. Universal had tested that title and found zero interest. Harris was arguing feverishly for *Shoeless Joe*, but she was getting nowhere. And Ptak was having only marginally better luck making a deal for *Dances with Wolves*.

Ptak had always been interested in where the business was going, and right now it seemed to be going international. With the arrival of multiplex theaters and cable and satellite television, Europe was experiencing a demand for entertainment that local producers couldn't hope to satisfy. So instead of selling packages to the major studios, or going to an independent like Nelson or Vestron or Goldwyn, a handful of Hollywood agents—Jeff Berg of ICM chief among them—were beginning to make international cofinancing deals for their clients' pictures, selling off distribution rights one territory at a time and using the money to bankroll production. The focus at William Morris was on bookings—you never leave where you start, as the saying went, and the Morris office was still a vaudeville-booking agency at heart. All the same, Ptak had been building relationships in Europe and Japan, which made him one of the few agents in Hollywood with overseas financial connections on his Rolodex.

Several months earlier, when Nelson Entertainment dropped out, he'd told Costner they should forget the Hollywood studios, which weren't going to give him free rein to direct his first picture, and trade on his box-office appeal overseas. They could cut a deal with a foreign sales agent who could sell the picture territory by territory, then come back and make a studio deal for domestic distribution. Costner agreed. So Ptak had gotten in touch with Guy East, the head of a London-based film sales company called Majestic Films. East had gone to various European distributors and come up with nearly $9 million—almost three-quarters of the projected cost of the film. Costner himself had convinced Chris Blackwell, the rock entrepreneur behind Island Records, to serve as executive producer and help finance the picture. But at the end of January, with shooting only two months away and $250,000 needed to tie down the locations, Blackwell backed out. So

Ptak phoned London again, this time to speak to a man named Jack Eberts.

Eberts was an experienced international producer, the man behind such films as *Chariots of Fire* and *Gandhi*. Ptak was already talking with him and Guy East on another project, the film adaptation of a Pulitzer Prize–winning off-Broadway play called *Driving Miss Daisy*, which Bruce Beresford had been set to direct until MGM put it in turnaround. At $12.5 million, it was a chancy project, a talk-heavy period piece about an elderly Jewish lady and her black chauffeur in the South, and one studio after another turned it down. Finally, Warner Bros. agreed to pick it up, but not at $12.5 million or even the revised budget of $7.5 million; Warners would put up no more than $5 million, for domestic rights only. Eberts took the script on a cross-country skiing trip in the Canadian Rockies and phoned from his helicopter to say he'd buy the rest of the world and make up the difference.

Driving Miss Daisy was a big gamble overseas. *Dances with Wolves* was not. Eberts knew that *No Way Out* and *Bull Durham* had been big hits in Japan, so big that Costner had just done a beer commercial there. But he was still worried about the budget, and about Costner's directing ability. As for Ptak, he was spending most of his time looking over his shoulder. Michael Ovitz had been courting Costner for nearly a year, visiting him in Cuernavaca on location for *Revenge*, maneuvering into second position. Ptak was taking Costner to Lakers games in his spare time; so was Ovitz. Ptak and Ovitz both had floor seats—folding chairs on the edge of the court, a couple of feet from the action. The picture had been in limbo for four weeks when, on the last Sunday in February, Ptak and J. J. Harris and Costner's attorney went to Eberts's room at the Beverly Hills Hotel and made their pitch. Eberts was leaving town that night. The next day, he phoned from London to tell them he was in.

Then Elaine Goldsmith, J. J. Harris's friend, got her phone call from InterTalent. Harris had been a schoolteacher in her former life, before she joined the Morris office as a secretary in accounting. She was a cheerleader type, perky and boisterous and irrepressibly enthusiastic, and aside from Kevin Costner, her chief enthusiasm was William Morris. She wasn't pleased when Elaine drove over to her house one evening to say she'd taken the meeting with Bill Block at InterTalent and told him she and her friend J. J. Harris wanted to talk with him together. As far as Harris was concerned, she was staying with Morris. These people had given her every opportunity. On the other hand, Elaine was her pal, and J. J. owed it to her to take the meeting. So they drove up to Block's house, in the hills above Hollywood on Mulholland Drive, and listened as he and his partners made their spiel.

When they came back to earth, Goldsmith concluded that the risks of joining a fledgling agency were too great. Harris, on the other hand, was excited and ready to go. They'd have to take a pay cut, they'd be vulnerable to CAA and ICM, but here was a once-in-a-lifetime opportunity. She cut herself a deal. As with all deals, word leaked out.

She was in Goldsmith's office when Mengers walked in. "Are you two broads leaving?" Sue barked. "I am," Harris said. "She's not." Elaine started sobbing. Sue looked at J. J. and chewed her out. She was making a huge mistake. She was going to lose Costner and Inter-Talent was going to dump her. Mike Simpson and John Burnham came to her office a little later to talk her into staying—they'd be taking over the department soon, they informed her, and they'd make sure she got anything she wanted. But when she went downstairs to see Roger Davis, he said that if she'd made up her mind to leave, she should leave.

By then it was lunchtime. As she was getting ready to go, J. J. stopped by Elaine's office, where Elaine and Julia Roberts were eating lunch. Toni Howard heard the three of them inside and started banging on the door. The head of accounting came up and escorted her to the street. She got a cab to the InterTalent offices on Sunset.

A week later, Costner announced his decision. He loved J. J., she'd been great for him. Ptak had done a great job of setting his picture up. But now he needed somebody with real clout. He was going with Creative Artists.

In April 1989, a month after Costner's defection, the Morris office celebrated its ninetieth birthday with the usual black-tie dinner at Hillcrest. This time, the ranks were sadly thinned. Norman Brokaw presided, the leading survivor of the fourth generation. No one from the old guard was left at all, except for one frail old man being pushed around in a wheelchair by an attractive young nurse: Bill Morris, Jr., eighty-nine years old, a widower now but still living in his Malibu beach house by the pounding surf. "He's probably the only one here who'll get laid tonight," Mengers quipped.

They were celebrating a year late this time, and yet within a month it came to seem as if they'd celebrated prematurely. On May 15, the *Los Angeles Times* ran an article headlined "William Morris: Is the Movie Luster Slowly Fading?" which noted the loss of Kevin Costner, among others, and focused on Mengers's apparent inability to turn the motion picture operation around. In June, *Forbes* came out with a more extensive piece called "Living Off the Past." Unlike the *Times*, *Forbes* had gotten full cooperation—interviews from top to bottom, permission to sit in on meetings, the run of the place. Mengers had tried to warn the board—did they really think the Morris Agency had anything good to say?—but she was ignored. After all, Caspar Weinberger, the former defense secretary who'd just become *Forbes*'s publisher, was a client. Cap Weinberger wouldn't attack his own agency, would he?

The *Forbes* article began with a joke: "How do you commit the perfect murder? Kill your wife and go to work for the Morris Agency. They'll never find you." It went downhill from there, but the zinger came on the final page: "Cut through the details of Morris' decline and what do you find? A vacuum at the top. . . . William Morris has never found an adequate replacement for Abe Lastfogel."

IT WAS ONE OF THOSE INTERCHANGEABLE INDUSTRY SEMINARS AT WHICH A half-dozen agents, or studio execs, or producers, pontificate sagely before a roomful of people who are desperate to break into the business, who care less about the knowledge these wise ones have to impart than about cornering one or two of them when the session breaks up and maybe walking away with a business card. A name! A phone number! A contact! This particular seminar was organized by an outfit called the Independent Feature Project for an audience of would-be filmmakers, few of whom could boast of agency representation. The topic was, "What Does an Agent Really Do?" The question for most of those present was, How do I get one?

But, okay, what does an agent really do? "In many ways, agenting is all about hype," offered a young agent from Triad, one of the boutiques that had taken its place behind Creative Artists, ICM, and William Morris. There was much discussion of packaging. One panelist said the term was too loaded; he preferred something like "accumulation of elements." But Jeremy Zimmer was for calling a package a package. Zimmer was from ICM, the last remaining wolverine. "There is no such thing as bad packaging," he maintained. "Bad packaging is packaging that doesn't get you financing."

But what does an agent *really* do? Zimmer had an answer for that too. "The big agencies are all like animals, raping and pillaging one another day in and day out," he declared, wallowing in his wolverineness. "We're all out there doing business. It's very competitive. And at the end of the day the question is always who's doing what to whom, how much are they doing it for, and when are they going to do it to me."

Jaws dropped. Eyes widened. People took notes.

Rape and pillage: It was as succinct a summation of the agency situation as anyone had come up with. Maybe too succinct. After Zimmer's comments were reported in *Daily Variety*, his boss, Jeff Berg, issued a formal repudiation. Not long afterward, Zimmer departed ICM to "pursue other career opportunities"—possibly because of Berg's embarrassment over the rape-and-pillage remarks, or maybe because Zimmer had reportedly gotten himself in hot water with Jeffrey Katzenberg for selling Paramount a script by a screenwriter who was under contract to Disney. In any case, Zimmer turned up shortly afterward as a partner at the Bauer-Benedek Agency, possibly the hottest of the new boutiques. There he'd be working with Marty Bauer, the former Morris agent who'd left with Brian De Palma and Alan Alda five years earlier—a man who'd been known to pull a fake shark snout out of his briefcase and say, "I put this on when I'm making deals."

Not that anyone seriously disputed Zimmer's assessment. For weeks, Hollywood had been transfixed by the spectacle of Joe Eszterhas, the highest-paid screenwriter in town, taking on Mike Ovitz over his decision to leave CAA for ICM. Jeff Berg had set the play in motion that August when he wooed Guy McElwaine—the onetime Columbia chief William Morris had tried to land but couldn't—back to the agency business. McElwaine was a good friend of Eszterhas, who was pulling in $1.25 million a script on the strength of the disco musical *Flashdance* and the 1985 thriller *Jagged Edge* (which Columbia had made during McElwaine's tenure there). Naturally, Eszterhas wanted to join his buddy at ICM. But when he went to CAA's new headquarters in Beverly Hills to tell Ovitz—according to his subsequent account, set down in a four-page letter that caused fax machines to overheat on both coasts—

Ovitz went ballistic. "My foot soldiers who go up and down Wilshire Boulevard each day will blow your brains out," the letter quoted Ovitz as saying. "If somebody came into the building and took my Lichtenstein off the wall, I'd go after them. I'm going after you the same way. You're one of the agency's biggest assets."

The Eszterhas move, the McElwaine snare, the leveraged buyout, Ed Limato and all his stars—ICM had pulled off a stunning series of coups. In a year and a half, Jeff Berg had transformed it into a serious competitor to Creative Artists. A parallel transformation seemed to be taking place within Berg himself. Berg had long been considered intellectual (never a plus in Hollywood) and abrasive, but now his profile in the industry was shifting from smart and forbidding to smart and aggressive. Over at the Morris office, Elaine Goldsmith was beginning to think he was the most persistent person she'd ever encountered. She kept getting these calls from him, one a month.

In November 1989, two weeks after the rape-and-pillage speech, John Burnham and Mike Simpson were officially named coheads of Morris's West Coast motion picture office. In theory, they would report to Mengers. In fact, they would supersede her. Mengers, who still had seventeen months to go on her three-year contract, stormed into Roger Davis's office and informed him that she did not approve. Davis, elegant and unflappable in his impeccably tailored suit, told her he hoped that she'd change her mind and that they could continue to work together. She spat out the words: *"No chance."*

The accent was on youth. "We're the oldest agency in the business," Mike Simpson proclaimed, "and we're the youngest." It was March 1990, and Simpson and Burnham were leading the department on its first-ever corporate retreat—a weekend therapy session at which they could debate their goals, their problems, and their strengths. Corporate retreats were not the Morris style, but CAA's retreats were the talk of the industry, and CAA set the benchmark in everything now. So here they were, gathered not around the doughnut-shaped table in the second-floor conference room, scene of one disaster after another, but in the serenity of the Ojai Valley Inn and Country Club, looking out across a secluded mountain vale carpeted with pin oaks and orange groves and sheltered by a wall of rugged peaks. Fifty miles northwest of Beverly Hills, they'd found Shangri-la.

They needed it. Morale had hit a new low. Sue Mengers had made it clear she wouldn't be staying once her contract ran out. Their big attempt to rebuild Stan Kamen's stable of stars had fizzled. They were experiencing wild mood swings, from feelings of impotence and depression to hope fantasies that veered toward grandiosity and omnipotence. The only measure of success they had left was money—big expense accounts, first-class air travel, hefty year-end bonuses—and they weren't getting it. They were angry at management, Davis and Zifkin in particular. Their facilitator noted an unwillingness to admit personal responsibility for the department's failures. Mostly, they just wanted to feel valued, and they expected Simpson and Burnham to do something about it.

Simpson and Burnham might have youth on their side, but they were definitely the odd couple—Burnham the society dude, graduate of Bev Hills High, good buddy of Morgan Mason, the indie film producer who was James Mason's son and Belinda Carlisle's husband; Simpson the homebody, driving back to Manhattan Beach every night. Of the two, Simpson was considered the more accomplished agent. He'd hung on to Tom Hanks when Hanks was on the verge of leaving for CAA four years before. He'd salvaged their once-iffy relationship with Tim Burton and gotten him launched on *Beetlejuice*. But neither Simpson nor Burnham was in the same league with Ovitz or Berg. And the agency's reputation was so bad that clients who went into meetings with producers and studio execs often ended up having to explain why they were still there.

Agenting was a game of confidence, and there seemed to be no one left in Hollywood who still had confidence in William Morris. Yet they'd managed to lure Jeffrey Katzenberg up to Ojai to give the keynote speech, if only because it was in Katzenberg's interest as a buyer to encourage competition. He expanded on Simpson's youth theme, comparing the Morris Agency's youth focus with the approach he'd taken when he took over Disney's moribund film division in 1984. Since then, Disney had spewed out hit after hit—*Down and Out in Beverly Hills*, *Ruthless People*; *Three Men and a Baby*; *Good Morning, Vietnam*. With *Who Framed Roger Rabbit?* and *The Little Mermaid*, it was even reestablishing its tarnished reputation in animation. Tactfully, he failed to mention that all this had been accomplished only after a companywide housecleaning that swept away Disney's sclerotic leadership and left him and Michael Eisner in control.

Yet the youth theme made sense for Morris too, if only because most of their established stars had fled. Tim Burton was in Florida directing *Edward Scissorhands* after the spectacular success of *Batman*, a $50 million production that had grossed five times that amount in the United States alone. Roseanne Barr was doing a voiceover in *Look Who's Talking Too*, the sequel to the baby-talking novelty flick that had been one of 1989's other giant hits. Andie MacDowell had costarred with James Spader in *sex, lies, and videotape*, the sleeper of 1989; now she was set to star in *Green Card*, Peter Weir's upcoming comedy for Touchstone, which owed its existence to John Ptak's ability to assemble financing from French and Australian banks. Tom Hanks, whose multipicture deal at Touchstone had so far yielded only the unfunny hit *Turner & Hooch*, was set to star in *The Bonfire of the Vanities*, Brian De Palma's big-budget adaptation of the Tom Wolfe bestseller—as close to a sure thing as you could get in Hollywood. Julia Roberts was up for an Academy Award for her performance in *Steel Magnolias*, the only member of its star-studded cast to be nominated. And *Pretty Woman*—the 3000 project, which Katzenberg had had rewritten as a deliciously improbable Cinderella story, with Roberts playing the hooker who's swept away by her beneficent Prince Charming—was scheduled to be released in a week.

Oscar night came and went. Julia Roberts didn't win, but by April, it was clear that *Pretty Woman* would be a runaway hit. Suddenly, Julia Roberts was a sensation—the strongest female box-office attraction the business had seen since Barbra Streisand appeared in *A Star Is Born* in 1976. With Mengers disengaging from the agency's remaining stars, John Burnham was chosen to step in, and the success of *Pretty Woman* made Roberts a number-one priority. The board did not want a repeat of the Stan Kamen situation, when a single agent was the agency's sole contact for most of the top stars. So Elaine Goldsmith was informed that she and Risa Shapiro, who'd moved to the West Coast office the previous June, would have to share Roberts with Burnham or with a member of the board.

Goldsmith wanted to know why.

Because the board decided it.

But the client doesn't want it, Goldsmith protested. What she meant was, the client doesn't want those Linda Darnell stories. Doesn't need them. Won't profit from them. It wasn't as if the board had Mike Ovitz or Jeff Berg to give her career advice.

We'll educate her, she was told. We'll do it slowly. But this is what the board has decided. When you work here, you work for the board.

It was a flat-footed move, almost calculated to arouse resentment. But to Goldsmith and her friends in the department, that was true of most of the things the board did. As agents, they were charged with keeping million-dollar clients happy, but if they asked for a better car for themselves, they'd be told, If we do it for you, we'll have to do it for everybody. If a client turned down a lucrative booking, the agent was liable to get in trouble. But what really galled them about the board was the way it passed judgment on them. Its sessions were secret, but its members made it clear what their deliberations concerned: every one of them. Their performance. Their attitude. Their contribution. Not that the board members were close enough to the film business to have much insight into what the agents actually did. Attempts to sign people, to bring some coordination to the department, carried less weight than how much money you brought in.

Goldsmith ignored the board's instructions. Jeff Berg continued to call. Ed Limato was phoning Goldsmith and Toni Howard. Limato was the reason Toni had joined the Morris office. Elaine was practically his protégé. She and Toni were good friends with each other.

The summer wasn't all bad. Renny Harlin, an impoverished young Finnish director who was being handled by a junior agent named David Goldstein, scored a major box-office hit with the hyperviolent action picture *Die Hard 2. Pretty Woman* pulled in nearly $160 million in its first four months and was poised to become the top-grossing film of the year. But with Michael Ovitz advising Japan's giant Matsushita Electrical Industrial Company in its $7.5 billion bid to acquire MCA—after picking up a multimillion-dollar fee the year before for brokering the sale of Columbia to Sony—the Julia Roberts phenomenon seemed tame. Morris had been turning ingénues into screen stars for decades, but selling film studios to Japanese industrial corporations—Ovitz was reinventing their business.

Fall was worse. There was the indignity of seeing Kevin Costner, the actor they'd picked up off the cutting-room floor, score a surprise hit with *Dances with Wolves*, the picture Ptak had arranged the financing for. Anjelica Huston was turning heads with her portrayal of a small-time confidence woman in *The Grifters*, a well-received picture whose talented young director, Stephen Frears, was handled by the agency as well. But *The Grifters* was a low-budget film, its success a succès d'estime; the big money was riding on *The Bonfire of the Vanities*, a $50 million production from Warner Bros. that seemed likely to make or break Tom Hanks's career.

Hanks had starred in three bombs after the 1988 hit *Big*—*Punchline*, a painfully honest look at the life of a standup comedian; *The 'burbs*, a comedy from Imagine that never caught on; and *Joe Versus the Volcano*, a failure so dismal it was all but released in a coffin. His only hit in two years was *Turner & Hooch*, and it was so stupid it embarrassed him. He and Simpson both were counting on *The Bonfire of the Vanities* to revive his career—especially Simpson, since Michael Ovitz was courting both Hanks and his manager with increasing urgency. But the buzz wasn't good. What Hanks had seen as a challenge—the chance to play a Wall Street WASP—now looked like miscasting. Columnist Liz Smith and the *Los Angeles Times* both reported that the test-screening results were dicey, and as the December 21 release date neared, *Bonfire*'s swollen budget and poor word-of-mouth made it an irresistible target for pundits on the prowl for waste in movieland. The advance reviews were devastating. "A strained social farce," opined the *Daily Variety* critic. "Will be quickly extinguished at the box office," predicted the *Hollywood Reporter*.

December was always stressful at the Morris office. It was when bonuses were awarded to those who measured up to expectations, when those who didn't were fired. One by one, like miscreant children, the agents would be called down to the first floor and ushered into an office and presented with a computer printout that summed up their clients' earnings and their own involvement in every deal, based on a tally of the booking slips the agents had filled out during the year. Every phone call was accounted for. Agents who shared a client were assigned a percentage of that client's business. It was axiomatic that you'd get less than you had a right to expect. A couple of agents had managed to negotiate their bonus upward, but most were still debating how to react. Should you look at your check and make a face? Return to your desk and write a memo? Or did it make any difference what you did, since the main purpose of the exercise appeared to be to foil your negotiating skills and lower your expectations?

December 1990 was the worst yet. There was a Christmas party on December 13 to hail the agency's latest real-estate venture—the completion of the new office building on South Rodeo, a three-story, $22 million structure built of rose-colored brick. It was a dubious celebration, since the Beverly Hills office market had cratered nine months earlier with the collapse of Drexel Burnham Lambert, which put Michael Milken out of business and emptied 250,000 square feet of office space across the street just as four other buildings were being completed a few blocks down Wilshire Boulevard. The market had been weakening even before the Drexel Burnham collapse: There were vacancies in the William Morris Plaza Building, despite the presence of such high-profile tenants as Burt Sugarman, the film producer turned corporate raider whose holdings included a Porsche, a Ferrari, a cement company, and 44 percent of a chain of hamburger stands. Now Morris had to compete with see-through office buildings up and down Wilshire. As for the rest of the agency's fabled real-estate holdings, they consisted of a 12 percent interest in an apartment complex in suburban West Covina and a concrete warehouse in a Phoenix industrial park that had gone vacant for months.

So far, it had been possible to ignore the bad press they'd been getting and focus on the good news—their resurgence in television, the "Cosby Show" windfall, the flashy new real-estate development. Now even the real estate had egg on its face, and the continuing debacle in the motion picture department was threatening to undermine the entire agency. It had been less than two years since Norman Brokaw had beaten out Jerry Katzman for the presidency of the firm. But Brokaw's claim to leadership seemed less compelling now than the turnaround Katzman had engineered in television. Though still a newcomer by Morris standards, Katzman did have proven administrative capabilities. He also had a power base. He hit all the buttons, checked all the boxes. Even so, they weren't entirely ready to hand him the keys. The board agreed to make him president, but Brokaw managed to hang on as CEO. The announcement would be made . . . sometime. When they were ready.

On December 17, the Monday before the *Bonfire* premiere, the board finally confirmed what most people in Hollywood had known for months: Sue Mengers was leaving. Her contract, which was due to expire in April, was being bought out. She would not be returning in the new year. The department would continue to be led by Simpson and Burnham, who'd been heading the West Coast office for thirteen months now. In his announcement, Roger Davis spoke of the agency's "respect and appreciation for all that Sue has accomplished." Unidentified sources in the trades cited its disappointment at her inability to sign new clients.

Coincidentally with Mengers's departure, Davis announced that three agents were being canned. One of them—a junior agent who'd just lost Richard Grieco, a costar of the Fox cop show "21 Jump Street" and of its short-lived spinoff, "Booker," to CAA—was so popular that Toni Howard, Elaine Goldsmith, Risa Shapiro, and four others trooped down to the first floor to speak up for her. To no avail. So they knew their opinions didn't count; now they got to open their bonus checks.

"The gross is up," Roger Davis liked to say when they looked at the check and saw how small it was, "but the net's down." This time, the net was apparently under water. Boaty Boatwright looked at her bonus check and resigned on the spot. Toni Howard and John Ptak had to lobby her for a week before she changed her mind. Sue Mengers went to Davis and Walt Zifkin and said, "Do you really want her to leave? Because she'll take people you don't think will go. She'll rip the core right out of this agency. You'd better watch it."

Nearly all of them—Howard and Ptak included—had a contingency plan. An option they were keeping open; someone to call if the situation got desperate. Ptak had been talking with ICM and CAA for nearly a year. Ed Limato had been wooing Toni Howard and Elaine Goldsmith for longer than that, urging them to join him at ICM. They wanted to think of themselves as loyal—loyal to the agency, loyal to Mengers. But Mengers was gone now, and the agency was nickel-and-diming them while the men who ran it tried to horn in on their clients. They were reaching a point where it wasn't loyalty that kept them there, it was fear of leaving.

Toni Howard was doing a slower burn than Boaty, but if anything, she was even angrier. Three months after starting at the Morris office, she'd flown to New York and signed Joanne Woodward. Her thanks was a note from a board member that said congratulations, and we're deducting $40 from your expense account because we don't take limos at Morris. She'd be happy now with an extra $15,000—a lousy $15,000 that they weren't prepared to part with. It was true that none of her clients was bankable, but she knew how to handle talent, and she had a social spin that gave her cachet. And she was responsible for a lot of actors who were much in demand. If she went, the covering agents— the grunts of the department—would see half their livelihood walk out the door.

Shortly after Christmas, when it became apparent that no more money would be forthcoming, she decided to take Limato up on his offer. It must have been a wonderful time when Abe Lastfogel was here, she reflected as she sat in her condo above Wilshire Boulevard, in the high-rise strip overlooking the rolling greens of the Los Angeles Country Club and the movie-star mansions of Holmby Hills. But it just wasn't about that anymore.

IT DIDN'T SOUND LIKE BIG NEWS AT FIRST—JUST A TERSE ANNOUNCEMENT in the January 23 *Daily Variety* that senior William Morris agent Toni Howard had ankled her post for ICM, taking with her such clients as Anjelica Huston, James Spader, Anne Bancroft, and Jason Robards. A week later, when Elaine Goldsmith and Risa Shapiro joined her, and with them Julia Roberts, Tim Robbins, Andie MacDowell, and Ralph Macchio, it began to look more ominous. The next day, when Boaty Boatwright announced she was leaving for ICM's New York office, the men who headed the Morris office were reported to be "shocked and angered by the defections."

For Hollywood, it was almost beyond belief. Three years after winning Ed Limato, ICM had come back for his friends, a tight little circle of agents who happened to represent most of the stars Morris still had. Suddenly, William Morris was all but out of the picture business. Jokes about the Morris office ("Why did it take the American forces in Panama so long to find Noriega? Because he was represented by William Morris") gave way to a morbid fascination. It was like an auto accident, everyone rubbernecking and hoping for the worst. Yet El Camino remained as opaque as ever. Privately, some of the top men expressed bitterness toward the defectors—nobody liked them anyway, they were disloyal and incompetent and about to be fired—but most maintained the same this-too-shall-pass attitude they'd displayed for years. There was little else they could do, since they'd refused to let Mengers offer contracts.

The feeding frenzy continued. Seven months earlier, Jeff Berg had approached David Goldman, who handled Billy Idol and Gus Van Sant in addition to Renny Harlin; now Berg was back on the phone, repeating his offer. John Ptak, their financing whiz, was talking with ICM and with CAA, which had much more need for his contacts. The big question was what Mike Simpson would do. With Tom Hanks and Tim Burton on his client list, Simpson would be worth big money to another agency. Simpson had already met with Michael Ovitz at Hanks's manager's suggestion, but Ovitz had reported afterward that Simpson wasn't his kind of agent. Simpson had also talked with ICM. But he believed in loyalty, not just to the Morris office but to the memory of Stan Kamen. He would not be quick to jump.

Two weeks after Toni Howard's exit, John Ptak became the fifth to leave—not for ICM but for Creative Artists. "I didn't leave the William Morris motion picture department," he reportedly quipped on the way out the door. "The William Morris motion picture department left me." The following day, hoping to diminish the impact, the agency announced its new executive lineup. Rather than spotlight the fact that Jerry Katzman would be taking over as president, however, the announcement emphasized Norman Brokaw's ascension to the chairmanship and Lou Weiss's move from chairman to chairman emeritus. The agency insisted that the changes had been in the works for months. Press reports treated this with disbelief and noted that they were overshadowed by Ptak's departure. No one mentioned unanimity.

The following week, David Goldman joined the others at ICM. Mike Simpson was still rumored to be leaving, this time to CAA. That was something Jerry Katzman could not afford to let happen. Within the week, Katzman nailed down Simpson and Burnham with lucrative three-year contracts. He started meeting with studio executives to convince them that Morris was still in the film business. He gave an interview to the *Los Angeles Times* in which he mentioned the possibility of buying a smaller firm—a step the Morris office had taken in Nashville a year earlier, when it made itself the world's largest country music agency by absorbing the Jim Halsey Company, whose roster included such stars as Waylon Jennings, Tammy Wynette, and the Oak Ridge Boys. He even suggested that something might be done about the board. What made him so self-confident? "Basically, I'm a winner," he declared, "and because I'm a winner, people will believe in me."

Tom Hanks was not convinced. Having let his manager serve as a go-between for years, Hanks dismissed him politely and announced he wanted to see his agents. He wanted material. He already had a second project in development at Touchstone, a picture about alcoholism and codependency called *Significant Other,* which he'd loved when it came in and which had then been rewritten for Michelle Pfeiffer and rewritten again for Debra Winger. Now he wanted something funny, but with weight—*Big,* not *The 'burbs.* Those left in the department worked frantically to come up with projects they could pitch him, but they already knew what the outcome would be.

In April, after an Oscar ceremony in which former client Kevin Costner swept the field with the movie that former agent John Ptak had gotten made, a second wave of defections began—only this time, it wasn't just agents heading for the exits, it was Morris's remaining clients. Alan Pakula and Joanne Woodward had already followed Boaty Boatwright to ICM; now Norman Jewison did the same. Tom Hanks left for CAA shortly after Debra Winger pulled out of *Significant Other*. Hugh Wilson, the man behind the *Police Academy* pictures and "The Famous Teddy Z," went to CAA as well. Steven Starr, the agent in charge of the New York motion picture office, simply left. When an ex-Morris agent saw a former coworker on the street and asked what they were doing, he grinned helplessly and said, "Just trying to keep the doors shut."

Losing Tom Hanks was the worst thing that could happen to them. The board members were devastated by the blow and furious at Mike Simpson for letting it happen. Now they had exactly one bankable star left—Clint Eastwood, who'd been there so long he was part of the family. The question they kept asking was why. Why is this happening to us? It was a matter of loyalty and betrayal, the twin forces that had governed the Morris office from the beginning. But to answer the question, you first had to decide who were the true heirs of Will Morris and Abe Lastfogel, the real custodians of the William Morris tradition. Was it the lawyers and accountants Lastfogel has chosen to succeed him, or was it the renegades they'd expelled from the fold so many years before? And that was the question no one on the first floor could afford to ask.

THE RUMORS STARTED ALMOST IMMEDIATELY: MORRIS WAS TALKING WITH Triad (Bruce Willis, William Hurt, Patrick Swayze, Whitney Houston). Morris was talking with InterTalent (Charlie Sheen, Andrew Dice Clay). Morris was talking with United Talent Agency, which had just been formed in a merger involving Marty Bauer's Bauer-Benedek Agency and had set up shop in Drexel Burnham Lambert's old quarters on Wilshire Boulevard. Morris was trying to buy its way back into the picture business.

In other areas, the Morris office was as strong as ever: "Murphy Brown," "The Cosby Show," and "Matlock" were still high in the

Nielsens, and the music, country music, and New York literary departments all boasted mega-selling clients. But the collapse of the motion picture department was crippling. To begin a turnaround, Jerry Katzman had had to abandon the pretense that they were still a family and implement the reforms Sue Mengers had tried to put in place and failed—agent contracts, scheduled annual raises, automatic bonuses. Shortly after Mike Simpson and John Burnham were put under contract in February, they themselves had been put in charge of offering similar deals to others in the department. But it wasn't an offer so much as a demand: Simpson and Burnham would walk into an agent's office, close the door, and start talking terms, good cop-bad cop, no time for a lawyer. The terms were generous—50 percent raises or more, with two thirds of the money coming as salary and one third as a locked-in, year-end bonus. But the pressure was on. Fail to sign, and your loyalty was suspect.

The Triad talks fizzled almost as soon as they began, and the negotiations with InterTalent never went beyond a couple of conversations with Bill Block. In July, Morris managed to generate some positive ink by hiring Burnham's friend Morgan Mason, who'd coproduced *sex, lies, and videotape* and was currently working with Diane Keaton on two other film projects. But the agency's most visible motion picture effort was its tangled legal battle with Paramount over the Eddie Murphy picture *Coming to America*, which a Los Angeles Superior Court judge had ruled was based on a screen treatment that Art Buchwald had sold to producer Alain Bernheim—a Morris client—eight years before. In July, with the judge preparing to set damages and Morris's West Coast business affairs chief set to testify on Buchwald's behalf, Paramount subpoenaed every William Morris motion picture contract and deal memo involving writers or producers from 1975 to 1987. The subpoena was duly quashed, but the bare-knuckles demand—from a studio that would get to examine deals its competitors had made for a dozen years—gave Morris a bad case of jitters.

Talks with Marty Bauer's United Talent Agency heated up in October but quickly cooled off. Once again, the issue was autonomy: Bauer was being offered a seat on the board, but he'd still have to report to the executive committee. Two months later, in an effort to streamline its image, Morris announced a revamping of its much-vaunted board of directors. Roger Davis, Tony Fantozzi, and Lou Weiss were stepping down, and four "young whippersnappers," as Davis called them, would take their place. The new inductees were thirty-seven-year-old Bob Crestani, the onetime head of syndication and pay television, who'd succeeded Jerry Katzman as West Coast head of television after big wins with "Geraldo" and "It's Garry Shandling's Show"; Jim Griffin, Crestani's forty-two-year-old counterpart in New York; Alan Kannof, forty, the administrative head of the New York office; and Robert Gottlieb, thirty-eight, a New York literary agent whose latest coup was a $12-million-plus deal for Tom Clancy's new novel. But there was still no fresh blood for the motion picture department, and the board remained largely a ceremonial body in any case.

Not everyone accepted the board restructuring quietly. In April 1992, after forty-seven years with the agency, Larry Auerbach abruptly resigned. Merger talks continued sporadically throughout the spring; so did client defections. Mike Simpson lost his sole remaining high-profile client when Tim Burton—awed by Michael Ovitz's stunning contemporary art collection and seduced by talk of interactive video technologies, art exhibitions, maybe even his own theme park—left for CAA. Then, at the end of May, John McTiernan, whom Morris had put in as director of Clancy's *The Hunt for Red October* two years before, went to CAA as well. "Their goal is to put us out of business," a Morris executive told the *Los Angeles Times*. Morgan Mason had just signed Elizabeth Taylor, but that was cold comfort: Legends are not commissionable.

That spring and summer were among the bleakest in recent memory for Hollywood. Buyers were disappearing—Orion in bankruptcy, Carolco losing millions after a string of big-budget flops, MGM a black hole. Those that remained were skittish. Sony was turning off the money spigot at Columbia. Disney, never a fountain of bucks, had tightened the screws after Jeffrey Katzenberg issued a much-publicized memo on costs the year before. Agents were finding themselves with more clients than they had jobs to fill. Writers and directors were cutting their prices. Rival agents were playing the wooing game: We can get you work, we can get you better deals, we have more clout. A Santa Monica psychotherapist put together an entertainment-industry-career support group. The whole town was running scared.

Morris just had an image problem; other agencies were facing bigger difficulties. InterTalent was split by internal dissension and spilling money from an ill-advised expansion into the music business. Triad, formed eight years earlier in the merger of three smaller agencies, boasted a number of hot music acts in addition to its roster of movie stars—Ray Charles, Nirvana, Pearl Jam, the Red Hot Chili Peppers. But the agency was poorly managed and radically overstaffed, with some 250 employees servicing a client list a fraction of the size of William Morris's. Arnold Rifkin, the forty-six-year-old partner who ran the motion picture division, was a go-for-broke deal maker whose taste for scented candles and New Age music masked an alter ego as a screamer. Rifkin's phenomenal negotiating skills—five years earlier he'd gotten Bruce Willis, costar of ABC's hit show "Moonlighting," an unprecedented $5 million to star in *Die Hard*—seemed likely to guarantee him the loyalty of his biggest client. But Melanie Griffith had recently left Nicole David, the agent who'd nurtured her career from the beginning, for ICM. William Hurt had just left as well. People were stopping Triad agents on the street to say they'd heard the company was going out of business. Something had to give.

Talks between Triad and William Morris had resumed informally in February, when Rifkin and Mike Simpson met for a drink. Secrecy was essential, so discussions were resumed in an out-of-the-way hotel whose aura Rifkin found highly dubious. The pace picked up over the summer, when Jerry Katzman, Norman Brokaw, Walt Zifkin, and other Morris execs started meeting under assumed names with their Triad counterparts at the more agreeable J. W. Marriott Hotel, not far from Triad's Century City headquarters. With Zifkin and Triad president Richard Rosenberg as chief architects, a plan began to take shape. Rosenberg would go on the William Morris board. Arnold Rifkin would come in as worldwide head of the motion picture department, superseding Simpson and Burnham. The music operation was almost a deal breaker—John Marx, head of the Morris's successful contemporary music department, had defected from Triad several years before and brought clients and other agents with him—but a compromise was reached, egos were soothed, and on Friday, October 16, the purchase of Triad Artists was finally agreed to. The price was stiff—in the $25 million range, considerably more than the $15,000 that would have kept Toni Howard from starting the run that had finally finished them off in the film business—but everyone professed happiness.

That night the calls went out—calls from board members and department heads to the rank and file, telling them about the deal, telling them to show up for the big meeting the next day. Or telling them not to: Morris stood to lose sixteen to twenty agents, including several who'd been there for a decade or more. One agent in the personal appearance department was covering a client's act at the Greek Theater in Griffith Park when he got a tap on the shoulder: Jerry Katzman on the phone, waiting to tell about the great move they were making but how, unfortunately, they'd have to make some changes. . . . A New York agent with forty-three years under his belt returned from a Bill Cosby show in Atlantic City to find a message to phone Lou Weiss at home: They'd just closed a deal with Triad, and it hurt Lou to report that his job had just gone south. A West Coast television agent who flew back from New York that night was awakened by a 6:30 A.M. call from Jerry Katzman: They'd be having meetings all weekend to discuss manpower, and there was a possibility . . .

At Triad, where dozens of agents and hundreds of support personnel learned they were being dismissed, it was far worse. Partners got death threats in the middle of the night, bombs might go off, police and security guards had to be summoned. But for the lucky ones at both agencies, Saturday was a day of new beginnings. There was understandable elation as they gathered in Morris's black glass citadel on El Camino to celebrate this union, this shotgun marriage of Hillcrest Country Club and the Tribeca Grill, the chic Beverly Hills eatery that was headquarters for Hollywood's junior players. They'd pulled it off! They'd done something right! But what they were really toasting was the end of the William Morris family, the death of all pretense. No longer could anyone profess the importance of loyalty and devotion. From now on they'd be sharks in a shark's world—a point that Arnold Rifkin, their new Armani-clad zen master, understood perfectly as he touched his fingertips together, adjusted his aura to suit the demands of this very special moment, and stepped forward to take command of the department that Johnny Hyde and Bert Allenberg and Stan Kamen had once made great.

PHIL WELTMAN WAS IN HIS OFFICE AROUND THE CORNER, A PAIR OF rooms at the back of a small, red-brick office building on South Beverly Drive, just below Charleville. It was snug and warm, an old-fashioned place on the first-floor rear, lined with paneling and mementoes of a life in the talent trade—signed photos, the director's chair from his boys at CAA that identified him as "The Godfather." Hanging on the wall across the room was the most cherished item of all, the plaque the fellows in the television department had given him at his farewell luncheon.

He only had one client these days—Tim Conway, the comedian he'd put in "McHale's Navy" back in 1962. But he still came in every day, and he was as hard and crusty as ever, an old bulldog who wouldn't let go. Nearly twenty years had passed since the day Sammy Weisbord showed up at his office door, and the bitter taste had never left. *Put in the computer and found wanting?* As if he were worthless, no good, a fucking charity case? And look what had happened to them since.

Weisbord, Lefkowitz, Lastfogel—it was funny how he'd outlived them all. He wished to hell it hadn't happened that way. He wished they were still around to see what his young fellows were doing—like Barry Diller, for example, and Mike Ovitz and Ronnie Meyer and all the boys at CAA. Particularly the fellows at CAA. They treated him right—had him sit in on meetings, asked his advice, called him all the time. Weltman was probably the only person in America who could talk to Mike Ovitz as if he were a small boy. Right now, he was concerned about the lad's health. Ovitz was working too hard. If he wasn't careful, he'd end up keeling over like Johnny Hyde and Will Morris himself. Heart attacks, that's what this business was about—heart attacks and nose jobs. "You should stop and smell the roses," Weltman snapped.

"Why should I?" Ovitz barked back. "You never did!"

NOTES AND SOURCES

It is now ninety-nine years since William Morris first went into show business. Over the ensuing decades, the agency he founded and the clients it represented have been involved in every aspect of entertainment—vaudeville, radio, movies, theater, music, television, books, sports. The client list is so enormous, the range of activities so vast, that to cover everything in a single volume would be impossible. Instead, I decided to focus on the key individuals at the agency—the people who made it what it has become—and a small coterie of core clients. This has meant concentrating on certain fields—vaudeville at first, then broadcasting and motion pictures, and nightclubs until they were overtaken by rock 'n' roll—while relegating such enterprises as book publishing and Broadway theater to the sidelines.

Not coincidentally, the areas that drew the most attention at the Morris office over the years were the ones that brought in the most money; from a business point of view, literary and legit functioned mainly as feeders for more profitable enterprises. The exception is nightclubs, a natural outgrowth of vaudeville that not only fed radio and television but yielded big money in Las Vegas before being supplanted by rock. I chose to follow Morris's nightclub business because it was key to the firm's identity; by the same token, after its formative years I disregarded rock, an antishowbiz form of show business that remained an alien presence within the Morris office even as it generated enormous profits.

Even within the areas I elected to focus on, enormously difficult choices had to be made. Of the many hundreds of screen stars Morris has represented over the years, only a handful could be treated in much detail. I decided to fix on those whose careers were central to the story of the agency itself, to the exclusion of others who may have been with the agency for years but contributed little to its development beyond their commissions. Tracy and Hepburn, for example, despite their close ties to Abe Lastfogel, had less impact than Marilyn Monroe did. Clint Eastwood's years of loyalty to Lenny Hirshan yield less insight into the agent-client relationship than the tandem rise of Steve McQueen and Stan Kamen and McQueen's final, stark betrayal.

This book is based on information from a wide range of sources, including author interviews with agents, managers, clients, attorneys, network and studio executives, law enforcement officials, and friends and family members; archival material in research libraries in New York, Boston, Washington, Memphis, Las Vegas, Los Angeles, and elsewhere; files obtained under the Freedom of Information Act from the Federal Bureau of Investigation, the Securities and Exchange Commission, and the antitrust and criminal divisions of the Justice Department; federal and county court records in New York, Memphis, and Los Angeles; corporate filings in New York, Delaware, and California; memoranda, client lists, and other documents made available by former Morris Agency employees; and newspapers, magazines, and books from the turn of the century to the present. In addition, my account of the life of William Morris relies heavily on an unpublished biography by his children, William Morris, Jr., and Ruth Morris White, which was made available to me through the generosity of Morris, Jr.'s stepson, Albert Ruben.

My work began in February 1991 with an assignment from *Premiere* to report on the sudden defection the month before of six agents from the Morris motion picture department, together with such star clients as Julia Roberts, Tim Robbins, Anjelica Huston, James Spader, Andie MacDowell, and Joanne Woodward. When I discovered that the agenting business had never been the subject of a major book and only rarely of a magazine article, I began to think the William Morris story deserved much fuller treatment than I could give it in a single magazine piece. In August 1991, as the *Premiere* article hit the stands, I went back to Los Angeles to reinterview many of those I'd spoken to before and to start tracking down individuals and documents that could show me how the Morris Agency, and show business itself, had evolved over the past century. Many of those I interviewed were extremely generous with their time, agreeing to repeated questioning and sharing records they'd kept to help me pin down elusive data. While every effort was made to encourage them to go on the record, the tangled web of relationships in the entertainment business made it necessary for some to request anonymity.

Because the William Morris Agency itself refused to cooperate, despite repeated entreaties, no current officer or employee was available to speak. With minor exceptions, every other living person mentioned in this book was interviewed or asked for an interview and given an opportunity to comment. Morris's chief competitors, CAA and ICM, took no corporate position on the book, but many individuals at both firms were quite helpful, as were a large number of former Morris agents at other agencies, in the motion picture studios, in independent production, and in retirement. Anecdotes and characterizations in the book represent a composite of the recollections of as many sources as possible. Where sources failed to agree, I have either noted the conflict or chosen the version which seemed most probable, given the sources involved and my own assessment of the situation.

Full publishing information for books cited in these notes can be found in the bibliography.

PROLOGUE

Descriptions of the William Morris mail room and of the anniversary celebration come from author interviews with a number of former Morris agents. Other sources include:

1   Groucho Marx at Hillcrest: Gabler, *An Empire of Their Own*, 275.
1   Ben Siegel at Hillcrest: Friedrich, *City of Nets*, 258.
1   Jews only: Birmingham, *The Rest of Us*, 254.
3   WMA's 85th anniversary: *Daily Variety*, June 3, 1983; *Los Angeles Times*, June 4, 1983.
6   Misty Mountain: Guy Trebay, "Stein's Way," *Vanity Fair*, July 1991.

1: THE SHOWMAN

The primary source for this chapter is the unpublished biography of William Morris by William Morris, Jr., and Ruth Morris White. Many details about the early years of Abe Lastfogel and William Morris, Jr., come from author interviews with Lastfogel's niece, Henrietta Lastfogel Prince, and with Albert Ruben and Laddie Marshak Delaplane. Other sources, many of them located in the William Morris Collection at the Billy Rose Theatre Collection of the New York Public Library for the Performing Arts at Lincoln Center (hereinafter cited as Morris Collection/NYPL), include:

14   "Give him room when he falls": *Variety*, March 13, 1912.
14   Albee dropped dead: Ibid., March 19, 1930.
15   "NO ACT TOO BIG": Ibid., January 5, 1932.
15   "When I go": "Put Their Names in Lights," *Fortune*, September 1938.
17   Morris's death: *New York Times*, November 2, 1932; *Variety*, November 8, 1932.
18   Morris's early life: Robert Grau, "A Napoleon of the Vaudeville World," *Theatre*, October 1910.
20   Morris and Liman: *Variety*, December 12, 1908.
20   Morris opens his own office: *Theatre*, October 1910.
22   Independent agents v. the Combine: *Variety*, December 12, 1908.
22   The white death: Taylor, *Saranac*, 43–44.

23 As welcome as Jews: Kaiser, *Great Camps of the Adirondacks*, 135.

24 Will Rogers: Contracts, 6/14/05, 7/1/05, 7/21/05, Will Rogers Memorial.

25 Keith wasn't slow: *Variety*, June 2, 1937, January 4, 1939.

27 Defection of the Morris managers: *Variety*, December 12, 1908, October 27, 1926.

27 Morris and Erlanger: *Theatre*, October 1910.

29 Morris Amusement Company: *New York Telegraph*, June 29, 1907.

29 American Music Hall: Ibid., June 12, 1908.

29 Morris and Lauder: Ibid.

30 Morris at the White Rats meeting: *Variety*, January 23, 1909.

30 Morris laid the cornerstone: *San Francisco Post*, January 12, 1910.

32 Morris in retirement: *New York Telegraph*, December 30, 1911.

35 Wonderland: Program, 2/24/13, Morris Collection/NYPL.

36 Chaplin and Sennett: Chaplin, *My Autobiography*, 129–38.

36 Morris and Selig: *Moving Picture World*, April 11, 1914.

38 Joint venture with Casey: *New York Telegraph*, February 2, 1917.

38 The Morris Agency: Though it traces its roots to William Morris's first agency venture in 1898, the current William Morris Agency, Inc., dates from this period. The agency was officially incorporated on January 31, 1918, with $5,000 in capitalization and William Morris, William Morris, Jr., and Abe Lastfogel as its directors. New York County Clerk, certificate of incorporation of WMA, Inc., 12/20/17; amendment, 2/21/18.

38 Letter from Morris to Selig: Selig Collection, Margaret Herrick Library, Academy of Motion Picture Arts and Sciences (hereinafter cited as AMPAS).

38 Morris attractions: *Variety*, October 27, 1926.

42 "WILLIAM MORRIS CALL BOARD": Ibid., August 22, 1928.

42 Vitaphone: Geduld, *The Birth of the Talkies*, 168–73.

43 Jolson and Jessel: Ibid.; H. Goldman, *Jolson*, 145–49.

45 Zeppo and Zukor: Rosenberg and Silverstein, *The Real Tinsel*, 96.

47 Stock swap with Paramount: *Variety*, September 4, 1929; New York County Clerk, amendments to the incorporation papers of WMA, Inc., 8/14/29. The amendments expanded the number of directors from three to six and created two classes of stock, each of which was entitled to elect half the directors.

49 "Didn't you know, Ed?": Stein, *American Vaudeville as Seen by Its Contemporaries*, 336.

50 Letter from Selig to Morris: Selig Collection/AMPAS.

2: THE PRINCE AND THE PAUPER

Characterizations of key figures in this chapter are largely derived from author interviews with Jane Harvey, Sam Jaffe, Nat Perrin, Henrietta Lastfogel Prince, Albert Ruben, and Bernie Seligman. Many of the newspaper accounts cited are from the Billy Rose Theatre Collection, NYPL, and from the Hearst Collection in the Department of Special Collections at the University of Southern California (USC) Library.

53 "Fadeout for Agents": *Variety*, January 15, 1932.

53 Suit against a screenwriter: Ibid., January 29, 1932.

53 Cagney had been discovered: Cagney, *Cagney by Cagney*, 37–39.

54 Studios piled with debt: Balio, *The American Film Industry*, 255–56.

54 Paramount stock swap reversed: *Variety*, February 2, 1932.

55 "Actors are like children": Frances Marion, *Off with Their Heads* (New York: Macmillan, 1972), cited in Stine, *Stars and Star Handlers*, 110.

55 The star system: Balio, *American Film Industry*, 353–55.

55 Starstruck hopefuls: *Variety*, May 9, 1933; Ross, *Stars and Strikes*, 65.

56 A rootless boomtown: McWilliams, *Southern California Country*, 334.

57 Set him off at the Ambassador: *Los Angeles Examiner*, March 1, 1928.

57 New Year's Eve 1931: Ibid., January 10, 1931.

58 Agents were despised: Alva Johnston, "Hollywood's Ten Percenters" (Part 1), *Saturday Evening Post*, August 8, 1942.

58 Warner Bros. movies: Schatz, *The Genius of the System*, 136–40.

59 Warners retaliated: *Los Angeles Examiner*, April 30, 1932; *Variety*, April 29, May 10, 1932.

59 Selznick and Joyce tried: *Variety*, June 10, June 24, 1932.

60 Face-off resolved: *Los Angeles Examiner*, September 22, October 1, 1932.

60 Faced a lot of situations: *Fortune*, September 1938.

60 Harry Lauder limped: *Variety*, January 24, 1933.

60 Trouble in radio: Ibid., February 7, 1933.

61 "Sprinkled with stardust": E. J. Kahn, Jr., "The Quiet Guy in Lindy's" (Part 2), *The New Yorker*, April 27, 1946.

62 Bill Morris had come to her: West, *Goodness Had Nothing to Do with It*, 146.

63 The academy set up committees: *Variety*, January 31, 1933.

63 Box-office receipts: Ibid., March 7, March 14, 1933.

63 Academy losing credibility: Ibid., March 28, 1933.

64 New York industry bosses: Ibid., April 18, April 25, 1933.

64 The code proposed: Ibid., August 29, 1933.

64 If the studios couldn't: Wills, *Reagan's America*, 218.

65 Agents circulated petitions: Ibid., September 12, 1933.

65 The new Screen Actors Guild: Ibid., October 10, October 17, 1933.

66 Press luncheon at Sardi's: Ibid., November 14, 1933.

66 Roosevelt invited Cantor: Ibid., November 21, 1933.

67 Dispute with Joan Blondell: *Los Angeles Examiner*, November 10, 1933, June 19, 1934.

67 Lastfogel's usual method: *The New Yorker*, April 27, 1946.

68 *The Big Broadcast of 1936*: *New York Times*, April 27, 1935.

68 Al Jolson's 1932 debut: H. Goldman, *Jolson*, 206–7.

69 By the 1937–1938 season: *Fortune*, September 1938.

69 An estimated 3.2 million sets: Ely, *The Adventures of Amos 'n' Andy*, 196.

70 Agency headquarters in the RKO Building: *Variety*, June 22, 1936.

71 Lastfogel and Hyde functioned as nursemaid: *Fortune*, September 1938.

72 Frances Arms on tour: *Variety*, August 17, August 31, 1938, September 13, 1939.

72 Morris's town house: "Blond Wood," *House & Garden*, July 1938.

72 Signed Aldous Huxley: Dunaway, *Huxley in Hollywood*, 56–57.

73 Bootlegger named Tony Cornero: Fox, *Blood and Power*, 36–37.

73 One of the leading agencies: *Fortune*, September 1938.

73 Olsen and Johnson's *Hellzapoppin'*: *Variety*, September 28, 1938.

74 Lastfogel to head negotiating committee: Ibid., November 2, 1938.

74 A reassuring presence: *The New Yorker*, April 27, 1946.

75 Metro's most valuable star: *Variety*, January 4, 1939.

75 Lastfogel offered to represent her: Frank, *Judy*, 107–8.

75 That wasn't going to happen: Rooney, *Life Is Too Short*, 148–50.

3: BROADWAY BOOGIE-WOOGIE

Characterizations come primarily from author interviews with Vincent "Jimmy Blue-Eyes" Alo, Irving Brecher, Harold Cohen, Milt Ebbins, Robert Elswit, Rose Marie Guy, Dorris Halsey, Jane Harvey, Sam Jaffe, Lloyd Kolmer, Erle Krasna, Henrietta Lastfogel Prince, Sam Sacks, Lee Salomon, Bernie Seligman, Phil Weltman, and Charles Wick. Many of the newspaper accounts cited are from the Hearst Collection, USC, and the James R. Dickinson Library of the University of Nevada, Las Vegas.

77 Stein's early life: Moldea, *Dark Victory*, 14–18; Pye, *Moguls*, 19–22.

78 Guy Lombardo: David G. Wittels, "Star-Spangled Octopus" (Part 2), *Saturday Evening Post*, August 17, 1946.

78 Talks with Rockwell-O'Keefe: *Variety*, April 27, May 4, 1938.

79 Productions for trade shows: Ibid., September 21, September 28, 1938.

79 Alexander joins WMA: Ibid., April 12, 1939.

80 Rockefellers were taking in $7 million: Ibid., January 4, 1939.

80 This was just slumming: Selznick, *A Private View*, 228.

80 Stein and Bette Davis: David G. Wittels, "Star-Spangled Octopus" (Part 4), *Saturday Evening Post*, August 31, 1946.

81 Wasserman's first million-dollar deal: Ronald Reagan with Richard Hubler, *Where's the Rest of Me? The Ronald Reagan Story* (New York: Duell, Sloan and Pearce, 1965), 123, cited in Wills, 262.

81 USO–Camp Shows: Coffey, *Always Home*, 25–26.

82 "Hey Rube!": *Billboard*, December 27, 1941; *Radio Daily*, December 24, 1941.

83 Benefit for Russian War Relief: *New York Times*, October 10, 1941.

83 Helped found the National Council of American-Soviet Friendship: Notice, 3/6/43, and minutes, 3/7/43, National Council of American-Soviet Friendship Collection, Tamiment Institute Library, New York University (hereinafter cited as NCASF Collection/NYU).

83 Fund-raising drive: Minutes, 6/9/43, 8/11/43, NCASF Collection/NYU.

83 Russian War Relief pageant: Program, 6/22/44, Southern California Library for Social Studies and Research.

83 Lastfogel shuttled: E. J. Kahn, Jr., "The Quiet Guy in Lindy's" (Part 1), *The New Yorker*, April 20, 1946.

84 Six-week tour of Britain: *New York Times*, December 17, 1942; *Variety*, December 23, 1942.

84 Camp Show performers: Coffey, 26–27.

84 "Abe dear": Camp Shows, Inc. *Reports of Activities, 1941–1953*, Vol. 4, 11.

84 Some people were offended: *The New Yorker*, April 20, 1946.

85 Entertaining the wounded: Coffey, 27–28.

86 Hollywood Canteen: *Saturday Evening Post,* August 31, 1946.

86 Larry Finley's troubles: Moldea, *Dark Victory*, 41–42; Pye, 29–32.

87 Hayward-Deverich Agency: "The Octopus," *Time*, April 23, 1945.

88 Selznick's divorce: *Los Angeles Examiner*, October 21, 1939; *Los Angeles Times*, February 8, 1940.

88 Selznick's death: *Los Angeles Examiner*, March 22, 25, 1944.

88 Finley decision: *Saturday Evening Post*, August 31, 1946.

89 Louella Parsons reported: *Los Angeles Examiner*, August 12, 1946.

89 Luncheon at the Waldorf: *New York Times*, December 12, 1945.

89 Keynote address: Camp Shows, *Reports*, Vol. 5, 9–31.

90 The agency's band effort: *Variety*, June 26, 1944, February 27, 1946.

90 Management took orders from Costello: Lacey, *Little Man*, 87.

90 Nightspots run by the Mob: Fox, *Blood and Power*, 78–80.

91 Hoover and Billingsley: Gentry, *J. Edgar Hoover*, 216.

92 Costello's early life: "'I Never Sold Any Bibles,'" *Time*, November 28, 1949.

92 The Piping Rock: *New York Times*, September 13, 1944; undated report, New York County District Attorney's files, Box 410, New York City Municipal Archives.

92 The Colonial Inn: Lacey, 87.

92 The Beverly Club: "'I Never Sold Any Bibles.'"

93 Tight not only with Costello: Kelley, *His Way*, 208.

93 Having dinner with Joe Adonis: Conrad, *Dear Muffo*, 3–5.

96 Ashley's early life: Karl Fleming, "Who Is Ted Ashley? Just the King of Hollywood, Baby," *New York*, June 24, 1974.

99 "Goldwyn is ripe": Berg, *Goldwyn*, 381–83.

99 Sensational charges: *Los Angeles Herald-Express*, July 24, 1941.

99 Hyde won his divorce: *Anne Hyde v. John Hyde et al.*, Los Angeles County Superior Court, testimony of Frederick Charles Moore.

99 $24,000 trust fund: *Los Angeles Herald-Express*, July 29, 1941.

99 Wed his secretary: Ibid., September 11, 1943.

100 Trouble again: Ibid., April 13, 1946.

100 Hyde attacked her: *Mozelle Hyde v. John Hyde et al.*, Los Angeles County Superior Court, wife's questionnaire.

100 The dick was as tiny: Kazan, *A Life*, 405. The starlet in question was Marilyn Monroe.

101 Hyde bought out her contract: *New York Telegraph*, June 26, 1941.

101 Lana Turner's abortion: Morella and Epstein, *Lana*, 37–41; Turner, *Lana*, 62–66.

102 Hayworth and Eddie Judson: Leaming, *If This Was Happiness*, 36–41, 64–66.

104 Hayworth would receive 25 percent: Ibid., 127–28. Hyde's coup was overshadowed a few years later by Lew Wasserman's deal for James Stew-

art to star in Universal's 1950 Western, *Winchester 73*. Universal, which had no stars at all on its talent roster, agreed to pay Stewart 50 percent of the profits. The terms were unprecedented, but *Winchester 73* was not, as is sometimes reported, the first back-end deal.

106 First big-time performer Las Vegas had ever seen: Knepp, *Las Vegas*, 43.

106 Offshore gambling ships: Fox, *Blood and Power*, 154–58.

107 Ben Siegel and Billy Wilkerson: Lacey, 151–53.

107 Opening of the Flamingo: *Las Vegas Review-Journal*, December 26, 27, 30, 1946.

4: Vaudeo

This chapter is largely based on author interviews with Helen Gurley Brown, Harold Cohen, Michael Dann, Milt Ebbins, Buddy Hackett, Dorris Halsey, Jane Harvey, Dorothy Healey, Eleanor Hittelman, Leo Jaffe, Garson Kanin, Corliss Lamont, Ring Lardner, Jr., Sam Sacks, Bernie Seligman, Elliot Wax, Phil Weltman, Charles Wick, and Tiba Willner. Additional sources include:

109 Bill Morris, Jr., named: U.S. House of Representatives, Committee on Un-American Activities, *Testimony of Walter S. Steele Regarding Communist Activity in the United States*, Eightieth Congress, July 21, 1947, 1–5.

110 Hollywood had been softened up: Friedrich, *City of Nets*, 167–68.

111 He identified Morris: HUAC, *Testimony of Walter S. Steele*, 65–66, 146–47.

111 Cited its chairman: Notes, 4/13/46, NCASF Collection/NYU.

112 Banquet at the Waldorf: Program, 2/21/46, NCASF Collection/NYU.

112 Morris vice chairman: Minutes, 6/12/46, NCASF Collection/NYU.

112 Cover story: "Enemy Within the Gates," *Newsweek*, June 2, 1947.

113 "The Baby Snooks Show": H. Goldman, *Fanny Brice*, 283.

115 The subpoenas: Friedrich, 306–7.

116 Walter Winchell broadcast: Press release, 10/17/47, NCASF Collection/NYU.

117 The show began: Goodman, *The Committee*, 207.

117 The first day's witnesses: *New York Times*, October 21, 1947.

117 John Charles Moffitt: U.S. Congress, House Committee on Un-American Activities, *Hearings Regarding the Communist Infiltration of the Motion-Picture Industry*, 80th Congress, October 21, 1947.

119 Weber's secretary: The little mouseburger grew up to become Helen Gurley Brown, author of *Sex and the Single Girl* and editor of *Cosmopolitan*.

119 Indefinite adjournment: *New York Times*, October 31, 1947.

119 Sworn statements: HUAC, *Motion-Picture Hearings*, exhibits 30–32.

120 "Now's the Time": *Advertising Age*, May 3, 1948.

120 "Vaude-Tele Mated": *Variety*, May 19, 1948.

121 Athlete's foot: Fox, *The Mirror-Makers*, 98.

121 Stellar Radio Enterprises: New York County Clerk, certificate of incorporation, 2/1/40.

121 Palace would shut its doors: *Variety*, May 26, 1948.

121 Foote, Cone & Belding survey: Ibid.

124 Morris Agency shows on DuMont: *Advertising Age*, May 3, 1948.

125 A frenzied comic: "The Child Wonder," *Time*, May 16, 1949.

126 Kalcheim had his hands full: *Variety*, February 2, February 9, 1949.
127 Socialist Party resort: LoMonaco, *Every Week, a Broadway Revue*, 2–7, 37–38.
127 Admiral Broadway Revue": *Variety*, January 12, 1949.
128 *Herald-Tribune* review: Sennett, *Your Show of Shows*, 18.
129 CBS raids: *Variety*, January 5, January 26, 1949.
130 Sarnoff couldn't believe: Bilby, *The General*, 249–51.
130 Murray's death and funeral: *Variety*, March 16, 1949.
131 Suit against Gosden and Correll: *New York Times*, May 12, 1949.
131 Burns and Allen: Letter to MCA, 5/9/49, George Burns and Gracie Allen Collection, Cinema-Television Library, USC.

5: PYGMALION

Personal recollections from this period are from author interviews with Morey Amsterdam, Irving Brecher, Milt Ebbins, Sam Goldwyn, Jr., Ben Griefer, Dorris Halsey, Jane Harvey, Garson Kanin, Erle Krasna, Albert Ruben, Sam Sacks, Elliot Wax, Phil Weltman, and Charles Wick. Other sources include:

132 Ann Miller nose job: *New York Telegraph*, June 26, 1941.
132 They just laughed at him: Kanin, *Hollywood*, 273–74.
133 In way over her head: Spoto, *Marilyn Monroe*, 147.
133 A bad scene ensued: *Mozelle Hyde v. John Hyde et al.*, wife's questionnaire.
133 Divorce terms: *Los Angeles Examiner*, April 31, 1947. The widely reported story that Hyde left his wife for Marilyn is not true: By the time he met Marilyn, he'd been married and divorced three times.
134 She'd met Joe Schenck: Pepitone and Stadiem, *Marilyn Monroe Confidential*, 96–98.
134 Not the way he treated her: Kazan, *A Life*, 406.
135 He bought out her contract: Spoto, *Marilyn*, 146–48.
136 Rita Hayworth in *Born Yesterday*?: *New York Times*, June 12, 1949.
140 Paramount followed suit: Ibid., February 26, 1949.
140 Sam Goldwyn argued: Goldwyn, "Hollywood in the Television Age," *The New York Times Magazine*, February 13, 1949.
140 Variety show with Ed Wynn: *Variety*, April 27, 1949.
141 Merger with Berg-Allenberg: *Hollywood Reporter*, December 16, 1949.
141 Developments like Phonevision: Zenith's Phonevision was one of several pay-per-view systems whose introduction was delayed for more than a decade by the Federal Communications Commission, thanks to the appeals of broadcasters and theater owners.
142 Variety Club dinner: Program, 10/27/49, Morris Collection/NYPL.
142 Vishinsky dinner: Guest list and press release, 11/10/49, NCASF Collection/NYU.
142 Tenney committee report: California Senate, *Fourth Report of the Joint Fact-Finding Committee on Un-American Activities in California, 1948: Communist Front Organizations*, 200–1, 262–63, 322, 357–58.
142 Vishinsky speech: Press release, 11/10/49, NCASF Collection/NYU.

143 Activities on the agenda: Press release, 11/8/49, leaflet and program notes, 12/20/49, NCASF Collection/NYU.

144 "Your Show of Shows" reviews: Sennett, 18.

145 The "atomic" sales force: *Variety*, April 27, 1949.

146 A growth industry: Barnouw, *Tube of Plenty*, 109–10, 127–29.

149 Hyde's death: *Los Angeles Examiner, Los Angeles Times*, December 19, 1950.

150 Hyde's funeral: *Hollywood Reporter, Los Angeles Examiner*, December 20, 1950.

6: COMMUNISTS AND MOBSTERS

Recollections in this chapter are from author interviews with Vincent Alo, Morey Amsterdam, Betty Garrett, Harold Cohen, Richard Collins, Michael Dann, Harvey Diederich, Milt Ebbins, Robert Elswit, Dorris Halsey, Jane Harvey, Stan Irwin, Leo Jaffe, Paul Jarrico, Garson Kanin, Lloyd Kolmer, Henrietta Lastfogel Prince, Albert Ruben, Sam Sacks, Elliot Wax, Tiba Willner, and anonymous sources. Information on the day-to-day activities of the West Coast literary department comes from the Reece Halsey Collection at the American Heritage Center of the University of Wyoming. Other sources include:

152 Robinson's agency representation: Contracts, 10/9/34, 4/15/37, 3/15/43, Edward G. Robinson Collection, Cinema-Television Library, USC.

152 "Film Stars Listed": *Los Angeles Times*, June 9, 1949.

153 Garland at the Palladium: Shipman, *Judy Garland*, 269–70.

154 Monroe and Kazan: Kazan, *A Life*, 402–4.

155 Sat in the Morris office for three weeks: Spoto, *Marilyn*, 181–2. The contract was for forty weeks a year at $500 the first year, $750 the second, $1,250 the third, $1,500 the fourth, $2,000 the fifth, $2,500 the sixth, and $3,500 the seventh. Morris split her commissions with Famous Artists.

155 Nothing definite against him: Robinson with Spigelgass, *All My Yesterdays*, 242–43.

156 Announced he'd been cleared: Gansberg, *Little Caesar*, 144–46.

157 Accused of being a rabbit: Holtzman, *Judy Holliday*, 142.

157 A bumpy ride: Ibid., 144–45.

157 The model was Harry Cohn: B. Thomas, *King Cohn*, 285.

157 Holliday's contract with Columbia: Holtzman, 150.

158 Whittaker Chambers: Halberstam, *The Fifties*, 11–12.

158 Nevada Proving Ground: Titus, *Bombs in the Backyard*, 55–59.

158 People were excited: Ibid., 93–94.

159 April 1950: Rappleye and Becker, *All American Mafioso*, 137–38.

159 "A senator from Nevada": A. J. Liebling, "Our Footloose Correspondent: Action in the Desert," *The New Yorker*, May 13, 1950.

160 The best part: E. Wilson, *The Show Business Nobody Knows*, 2–5.

162 Fred and Midge Elswit: *Variety*, March 7, 1951.

163 The Kefauver revelations: Lacey, *Little Man*, 200–1.

164 Regarded by millions: *Time*, November 28, 1949.

164 Wood had been trying: Strauss, *A Talent for Luck*, 85.

165 Parks admitted: Navasky, *Naming Names*, vii–ix. Parks, who'd been with the Morris office only a couple of years, did not receive any guidance from the agency on his testimony. Shortly after his appearance before the committee, however, he and his wife, Betty Garrett—the M-G-M contract player who'd costarred with Frank Sinatra, Gene Kelly, and Ann Miller in *On the Town*—were quietly and without explanation dropped as clients. They were likewise dropped by their respective studios, Columbia and M-G-M.

165 When they asked him about Edward G. Robinson: Gansberg, 147–48.

165 The 1950 Academy awards: Carey, *Judy Holliday*, 117–19; Holtzman, 146–49.

167 Courtesy of Dmytryk: "'Operation Hollywood,'" *Time*, May 7, 1951.

168 Negotiations with NBC: Berle, *An Autobiography*, 294–95.

169 Columbia's story editor: U.S. Congress, House Committee on Un-American Activities, *Hearings Regarding the Communist Infiltration of the Hollywood Motion-Picture Industry*, 82nd Congress, September 10, 1951.

169 Heard from Leo Townsend: HUAC, *Motion-Picture Hearings*, September 18, 1951.

170 Appointed the detention board: *New York Times*, September 19, 1951.

170 Martin Berkeley: HUAC, *Motion-Picture Hearings*, September 19, 1951.

171 Interest in Robinson: Correspondence, 2/18/52, 2/26/52, Jack Warner Collection, Cinema-Television Library, USC.

171 "Please, Eddie": Gansberg, 153–54.

172 The questions were sharp: U.S. Senate, Subcommittee to Investigate the Administration of the Internal Security Act, *Subversive Infiltration of Radio, Television, and the Entertainment Industry*, 82nd Congress, March 26, 1952.

173 A charge Lamont contended: *Daily Compass*, September 27, 1951.

174 Kazan summoned before HUAC: Kazan, 445–47, 453–55.

176 Handled the story deftly: *New York Post, Variety*, April 30, 1952. It remains unclear why Morris, Jr., resigned at precisely this time. Was he being targeted? The HUAC papers are sealed, and a search of Pat McCarran's papers at the National Archives in Washington, at the Nevada Historical Society in Reno, and at the Department of Special Collections in the University of Nevada, Reno Library gave no such indication. Morris's FBI file might yield the answer; however, although I requested it under the Freedom of Information Act in May 1992, at the time this book went to press, nearly three years later, the file still had not been released.

176 Fête at the Waldorf: Program, 5/3/52, Morris Collection/NYPL.

176 2:00 P.M. board meeting: New York County Clerk, amendment to the incorporation papers of WMA, Inc., 5/8/52.

176 Robinson was shattered: Gansberg, 155–59; Robinson with Spigelgass, 263–64.

177 Robinson was a tough sell: Gansberg, 163–64.

178   Pleaded for the role: Kelley, *His Way*, 187–89.
179   Cohn was furious: Ibid., 192–95.
180   Eclipsed by the Sands: *Las Vegas Review-Journal*, September 11, 1952.
180   Nevada Tax Commission: Best and Hillyer, *Las Vegas*, 80–82.
181   Shareholders at the Sands: *Las Vegas Review-Journal*, September 5, September 11, October 30, 1952.
182   Opening night: Ibid., December 15, 1952.

7: PACKAGE DEAL

This chapter is largely based on author interviews with Berle Adams, Flo Allen, Vincent Alo, Ed Becker, John Bonomi, Irving Brecher, Bernie Brillstein, Harold Cohen, Milt Ebbins, James Farrar, Leonard Goldenson, Ben Griefer, Leo Jaffe, George Klein, Lloyd Kolmer, Don Kopaloff, Richard Linke, Sy Marsh, Ed Mitchell, Joe Nellis, Robert Nicholson, Rowland Perkins, Sam Sacks, Lee Salomon, Jerry Schilling, Murray Schwartz, Bernie Seligman, George Shapiro, Elliot Wax, Phil Weltman, Bill Willard, Bill Wright, Jerry Zeitman, and anonymous sources. Additional information was provided by an unpublished 1989 interview with Danny Thomas that was made available by a confidential source. Details of George Wood's mob connections were buttressed by his FBI file, which was obtained under the Freedom of Information Act, and by records in the New York City Municipal Archives.

183   Danny Thomas was back: Thomas with Davidson, *Make Room for Danny*, 185–86. Goldenson disputes the assertion, which Thomas makes both in his book and in the 1989 interview, that to get Bolger ABC had to take Thomas.
185   Cantor and the Will Mastin Trio: S. Davis, *Yes I Can*, 148–53.
185   "Three's Company" pilot: "Can Sammy Davis, Jr. Crash Network TV?", *Ebony*, October 1954.
185   Edelman came over: Thomas with Davidson, 186–88.
187   Van Heusen had arrived: Kelley, *His Way*, 207–8.
187   Frank was having dame trouble: Ibid., 202–6.
188   Lawford at M-G-M: Spada, *Peter Lawford*, 145–47.
189   Allowed to buy into the Sands: *Las Vegas Review-Journal*, March 23, 1953.
189   The idea came from Doc Stacher: Kelley, 219–20.
190   Sinatra's kind of guy: Ibid., 208. "George was supposed to keep Frank from slashing his wrists again," Abe Lastfogel told Kelley in June 1983. "He was perfect for Frank because he knew all the gangsters—Meyer Lansky, Vincent 'Jimmy Blue-Eyes' Alo, Frank Costello—all of them!"
191   He and Sinatra went everywhere together: Ibid.
194   Revue Productions: Edward T. Thompson, "There's No Show Business Like MCA's Business," *Fortune*, July 1960.
197   A tiny portion of the old Rancho: Los Angeles County Tax Assessor.
197   New West Coast headquarters: *Variety*, May 11, 1955.
197   Arms Building Corporation: California Secretary of State, articles of incorporation, 9/21/53.

199 He met David Susskind: Robert Fure, "The Wizards of Oz" (Part 3), *W&L*, May 1983.

200 A baby-faced greaser: Marsh, *Elvis*, 62–63.

201 The Royal American Shows: A. Goldman, *Elvis*, 133–36.

204 No agency papers: Shelby County Probate Court, Estate of Elvis Presley, Report of the Guardian Ad Litem, 15 (hereinafter referred to as the Tual Report; the subsequent Amended Report of the Guardian Ad Litem will be cited as the Amended Tual Report).

205 Seven-year deal: Contract, 4/2/56, Elvis Presley-General file, Hal Wallis Collection, Margaret Herrick Library, AMPAS.

205 The pay was modest: Memo, 4/2/56, Elvis Presley-General file, Wallis Collection/AMPAS.

206 Call from Leonard Hirshan: Memo, 4/5/56, Elvis Presley-Col. Parker Correspondence file, Wallis Collection/AMPAS.

206 Due at the Morris office: Letter, 4/6/56, Presley-Parker Correspondence file, Wallis Collection/AMPAS.

206 Maybe *The Rat Race*: Memo, 4/10/56, Presley-Parker Correspondence file, Wallis Collection/AMPAS. The picture was eventually produced by William Perlberg, the former Morris agent, with Tony Curtis and Debbie Reynolds in the starring roles.

206 How to sweeten: Letters, 4/10/56, 4/27/56, Presley-Parker Correspondence file, Wallis Collection/AMPAS.

206 Prestige engagements: Memo, 3/6/56, Presley-Parker Correspondence file, Wallis Collection/AMPAS.

207 Opened at the New Frontier: *Las Vegas Review-Journal*, April 19, April 20, 1956.

208 Merchandising deal: Tual Report, 4, exhibit 4. A. Goldman declares (*Elvis*, 235) that in six months, Saperstein reported gross sales of $26 million.

209 So Davis walked into: Davis, Boyar, and Boyar, *Why Me?*, 77–78.

211 Harry Cohn's replacement: B. Thomas, *King Cohn*, 225–30. The Hitchcock film Novak was to make with Jimmy Stewart was eventually released as *Vertigo*.

211 Brokaw had grown up: WMA bio.

212 Novak called a truce: *New York Post*, September 11, 1957.

212 Within days: Davis, Boyar, and Boyar, 81–86.

212 When Harry Cohn found out: B. Thomas, *King Cohn*, 353–55.

213 Davis was in trouble: Davis, Boyar, and Boyar, 87.

214 "Nigger weasel": Giancana, *Double Cross*, 195.

214 A well-connected friend: Davis, Boyar, and Boyar, 93–97. Some of Wood's associates say it was Wood himself who broke the news to Davis, but their accounts do not entirely agree. Burt Boyar, who with his wife Jane was Davis's coauthor, says that Davis never revealed the identity of the man who came to his dressing room. As for the hit itself, it's obvious the threat was more important than the follow-through, since it would be unfortunate (though not unprecedented) to have one of the mob's top nightclub performers incapacitated. Neither Novak's agent nor Davis's would have

been aware of Wood's activities, as this was not the type of thing that would be brought up in a meeting.

215 It was Neile Adams: Spiegel, *McQueen*, 94–98; Toffel, *My Husband, My Friend*, 72–75.

216 Four Star Productions: Lloyd Shearer, "Three 'Hams' Bring Home the Bacon," *Weekend*, April 12, 1959.

216 Things weren't going as smoothly: Davis, Boyar, and Boyar, 89–91.

218 Power play on *The Young Lions*: Bill Davidson, "MCA: The Octopus Devours the World," *Show*, February 1962.

219 "The Frank Sinatra Show": Goldenson, *Beating the Odds*, 144–45.

220 Eager to meet Sinatra: Spada, 203–4.

221 "What difference does it make?": Kobal, *People Will Talk*, 144.

221 Lawford ended up: Spada, 214.

221 Allenberg had a visitor: Niven, *Bring on the Empty Horses*, 366–70.

222 Allenberg's death: *Los Angeles Examiner, Los Angeles Times*, November 28, November 29, 1958.

8: JUSTICE

Much of this chapter is based on author interviews with Vincent Alo, Peter Andreotti, Irving Brecher, Harold Cohen, Michael Dann, Harvey Diederich, Milt Ebbins, Roy Gerber, Lloyd Kolmer, Nat Laurendi, Lee Loevinger, Jeremiah McKenna, Sy Marsh, Daniel Melnick, Ernest Mittler, Robert Nicholson, Robert Relyea, Joe Sanpietro, Edgar Scherick, Elliot Wax, Ed Wright, and Jerry Zeitman. Details of the antitrust investigations of William Morris and MCA are primarily from the files of the Justice Department's Antitrust Division, which were obtained under the Freedom of Information Act. Details of the New York County District Attorney's Office investigation of Scopitone were augmented by papers from the files of Robert Nicholson, who as of this writing was chief investigator for the New York State Task Force on Organized Crime.

223 Record-breaking season: *Variety*, October 7, 1959.

225 "The $64,000 Question": Barnouw, *Tube of Plenty*, 184–86.

226 "Dan," he asked: Halberstam, *The Fifties*, 660.

227 "Sonny, look at the schedule": *Fortune*, July 1960.

227 Abe Lastfogel and Wally Jordan: Memo, 11/3/60, MCA file, Antitrust Division, U.S. Department of Justice (DOJ).

227 Problems of Hugh O'Brian: Burt Boyar, "The Marshal Meets His Match," *TV Guide*, undated clipping, DOJ.

228 MCA was already the biggest: Moldea, *Dark Victory*, 127.

228 Justice was investigating: *New York Herald-Tribune, New York Times*, February 26, 1958.

228 Not that MCA showed: Moldea, *Dark Victory*, 131–33.

229 Frankie Carbo: Fox, *Blood and Power*, 355–57.

230 Criticizing Sinatra: Kelley, *His Way*, 255–56.

231 For nearly a month: Press release, Box 25, Sands Collection, James R. Dickinson Library, University of Nevada-Las Vegas.

231 A party every night: Spada, *Peter Lawford*, 215–16.

232 Sinatra introduced his new friend: Tosches, *Dino*, 325.

232 Booze and broads: Kelley, 268–69.

232 "How's your bird?": Ibid., 255.

232 Sinatra would be leaving: *Variety*, March 30, 1960.

233 Nearly a year had passed: Barnouw, 247.

233 Weisbord testimony: Memo, "A Digest of FCC Hearings on Programming (LA)," 2/13/61, MCA file, DOJ. Other witnesses included Loretta Young, Ozzie Nelson, Desi Arnaz, and Dick Powell, who testified that Four Star went from zero shows on the air to twelve after signing with William Morris in 1956.

235 Exposé of MCA: *Fortune*, July 1960.

235 Taft Schreiber: Memo, 2/13/61, DOJ.

235 Black Tuesday: Barnouw, 299–300.

236 Brennan note: Letter, 10/27/61, Attorney General Files, General Correspondence, John F. Kennedy (JFK) Presidential Library.

237 Civil or criminal indictments: Memo, 3/21/61, DOJ.

237 Posner wanted a grand jury: Moldea, *Dark Victory*, 155–57.

237 The perfect gift: *Los Angeles Examiner*, June 28, 1961.

237 Grand jury investigation: Memo, 10/5/61, Attorney General Files/JFK.

237 The only solution: Memos, 9/15/61, 9/18/61, DOJ.

238 Memo to Bobby Kennedy: Undated memo, Attorney General Files/JFK.

239 A Who's Who of shady characters: Memo, 9/14/66, New York County District Attorney's Office, prepared by Robert Nicholson for his commanding officer in light of the then-current investigations into Scopitone by the Securities and Exchange Commission and the U.S. Attorney's Office in New York.

244 Wood was making progress: Ibid.

245 The Morris Agency was as bad: Memos, 7/7, 7/11, 7/12/61, DOJ.

245 "Decides what you see": *Show*, February 1962.

245 "Vampirous attacks": "Period of Adjustment," *Time*, undated clipping, DOJ.

245 Bob Hope quipped: Bill Davidson, "MCA, Part 2: A Case Study in Power," *Show*, March 1962.

245 On Friday, July 13: Moldea, *Dark Victory*, 207–8.

246 MCA immediately filed suit: *Daily Variety*, July 20, 1962.

246 The firm was out of business: *Wall Street Journal*, July 20, 1962.

246 Hollywood was in chaos: *Daily Variety*, July 23, July 24, 1962.

246 Other agencies were competing: *New York Times*, August 6, 1962; *Variety*, August 8, 1962.

9: MAD, MAD, MAD, MAD WORLD

This chapter is based largely on author interviews with Flo Allen, Al Alweil, Wally Amos, Morey Amsterdam, Rosalind Ross Bell, Robert Benton, Jerry Brandt, Bernie Brillstein, Burton Cohen, Michael Dann, Laddie Marshak Delaplane, Milt Ebbins, Robert Elswit, Joe Esposito, David Foster, David Geffen, Ben Griefer, Leo Jaffe, George Klein, Don Kopaloff, Alan Ladd, Jr., Sheldon

Leonard, Marty Litke, Sy Marsh, Fred Moch, Rowland Perkins, Robert Relyea, Mike Rosenfeld, Albert Ruben, Lee Salomon, Edgar Scherick, Murray Schwartz, Bernie Seligman, George Shapiro, Scott Shukat, Roy Silver, Peter Stamelman, Harry Ufland, David Warden, Elliot Wax, Mimi Weber, Phil Weltman, and Joe Wizan. Many details of the Morris Agency's involvement with Scopitone are from documents obtained under the Freedom of Information Act from the SEC and from the Justice Department's Criminal Division.

250   The FCC was backing the networks: *Variety*, August 22, 1962.

255   Represented his balls: Toffel, *My Husband, My Friend*, 90.

255   His way of keeping score: Spiegel, *McQueen*, 183–87.

256   A system for dealing with scripts: Toffel, 118–19.

256   On location in Bavaria: Spiegel, 129–34; Toffel, 114–16.

258   The Morris Agency's playwrights and directors: *Variety*, December 25, 1963.

259   Abe Burrows's twenty-fifth anniversary: Ibid., October 4, 1963.

261   Working the Scopitone deal: Option agreement and confirmation memo, 5/29/63, Scopitone Files, U.S. Securities and Exchange Commission.

261   The investor group: *Wall Street Journal*, April 26, 1966.

261   The deal was worth: License agreements, 10/25/63, 11/6/63, and memo, 12/3/63, Scopitone Files/SEC. Eight months later, in July 1964, 80 percent of the stock of Scopitone was acquired by a Chicago company known as Tel-A-Sign, Inc., which until then had been essentially controlled by an investor group headed by Roy Cohn and including Floyd Patterson, the former heavyweight champ. The deal was rich: According to the *Wall Street Journal* article of April 26, 1966, ten Scopitone stockholders, among them Aaron Weisberg of the Sands and Abe Green of the Runyon Sales Company, traded an $8,000 investment for Tel-A-Sign stock worth $3.3 million. By the time of the article, both the SEC and a federal grand jury were looking into Scopitone. Nat Lefkowitz, contacted by the *Journal*, declined to comment on the investigation or on the Morris Agency's involvement in Scopitone. However, documents received under the Freedom of Information Act show that on September 22, 1965, Gerry Catena of the Genovese family was questioned by the SEC about his involvement in the Scopitone deal. Among other things, Catena was asked if he'd been introduced to Scopitone by George Wood, and if he had any stock interest in the William Morris Agency. He took the fifth on these as on all other questions, even as to his home phone number. Roy Cohn and the current management of Tel-A-Sign vehemently protested any suggestion that they were connected with undesirable elements, and both the April 26 story and a subsequent *Wall Street Journal* article stressed that the honesty and integrity of Tel-A-Sign's current management was not in question. No one was convicted as a result of these investigations. Tel-A-Sign experienced financial difficulties after its California distributor was unable to pay for machines that had been delivered, and in August 1967 the company went into chapter 11 bankruptcy.

262   Wood's death: *New York Times*, November 11, 1963; *Variety*, November 13, 1963.

262 Wood's funeral: Report, 11/12/63, Central Investigation Bureau, New York Police Department. The CIB regularly covered mob-related funerals.

263 The hottest producer in television: Deborah Haber, "The Men from Morris: All the Talent Isn't on Stage," *Television*, September 1964.

263 Ashley had some popular shows: Richard K. Doan, "Ted Ashley: The Biggest Little Packager in TV," *New York*, January 5, 1964.

265 Cosby's act: "Riiight," *Newsweek*, June 16, 1963.

266 Lastfogel thought *Roustabout*: Memo, 2/24/64, Roustabout file, Wallis Collection/AMPAS.

266 Lastfogel wasn't alone: Undated memo, Wallis Collection/AMPAS.

266 Thorpe wasn't so sure: Memo, 1/14/63, Wallis Collection/AMPAS.

267 Worried about Elvis: Letter, 9/10/58, Wallis to Parker, Elvis Presley file, Wallis Collection/AMPAS.

268 Wallis got the numbers: Letter, 3/3/64, Wallis Collection/AMPAS.

268 Rock 'n' roll was a fad: Letters, 12/13/58, 12/18/58, 12/26/58, Presley-Parker Correspondence file, Wallis Collection/AMPAS.

268 The Lastfogels sure did: Letter, 9/27/63, Parker file, Wallis Collection/AMPAS.

270 The Beatles arrived: *New York Times*, February 8, 1964.

270 Liaison to the carny world: Memo, 8/19/63, *Roustabout* file, Wallis Collection/AMPAS.

270 Made an arrangement: Memo, 3/12/64, Presley file, Wallis Collection/AMPAS.

270 Colonel was coming through: Letter, 2/17/64, notes, 2/18/64, *Roustabout* file, Wallis Collection/AMPAS.

270 Casting the picture: Memos, 1/16/64, 3/11/64, Wallis Collection/AMPAS.

270 Eager to land Mae West: Letter, 9/6/63, Wallis Collection/AMPAS.

271 Other possibilities: Memos, 10/2/63, 1/4/64, 1/16/64, Wallis Collection/AMPAS.

271 Deal for Stanwyck: Contract, 2/14/64, memo, 3/11/64, Wallis Collection/AMPAS.

273 Ross left the Morris office: *Variety*, August 5, 1964.

275 Mother Morris's death: *Adirondack Enterprise*, March 7, 1959.

275 Sale of Camp Intermission: Ibid., October 26, 1961.

276 Morris penned an appeal: *Variety*, March 17, 1965.

279 "Want to be a millionaire?": Dalton, *The Rolling Stones*, 55.

280 The sanctity of the 10 percent commission: Written in stone, yes, but not in indelible ink. According to his widow, Al Jolson paid only 5 percent in the forties; but when Dustin Hoffman offered to come back to Morris in the early eighties if he could pay 5 percent, he was turned away. The sanctity of the 10 percent figure depends on any number of factors, chief among them the hunger of the agent.

282 "Money is of the utmost": Robert de Roos, "The Spy Who Came in for the Gold," *TV Guide*, October 23, 1965.

282 The press kept a running tally: *New York Times*, September 10, 1965.

282 Smothers Brothers show for Four Star: Leslie Raddatz, "They're Tilted," *TV Guide*, February 5, 1966.

283 "People can see I'm a Negro": R. Smith, *Cosby*, 65.

284 Sophie Tucker's death: *Variety*, February 16, 1966.

285 Freddie Fields: *New York Times*, May 15, 1966.

286   Paley had wrested programming: S. B. Smith, *In All His Glory*, 429–33.

288   Challenge the fundamental image: Barnouw, 403–4.

289   The new offices in New York: *Hollywood Reporter*, June 26, 1966.

293   Beatty had finally encountered a property: "The Shock of Freedom in Films," *Time*, December 8, 1967.

294   Morris office negotiated a contract: *New York Post*, May 31, 1968.

295   He and Warner couldn't agree: Parker, *Warren Beatty*, 131–34; Thomson, *Warren Beatty and Desert Eyes*, 222–23.

296   *Bonnie and Clyde* reviews: Thomson, 243–45.

300   For the Smothers Brothers: Metz, *Reflections in a Bloodshot Eye*, 299–303.

PART II: BETRAYAL

303   "Where the money is": Chandler, "Ten Per Cent of Your Life," *The Atlantic*, February 1952.

10: DAMON AND PYTHIAS

This chapter is primarily based on author interviews with Berle Adams, Milt Ebbins, David Foster, Mario Iscovich, Leo Jaffe, Don Kopaloff, Marty Litke, Sy Marsh, Ben Melniker, Rowland Perkins, Robert Relyea, Mike Rosenfeld, Bernie Seligman, George Shapiro, Scott Shukat, Alan Somers, Lee Steiner, Harry Ufland, Elliot Wax, Phil Weltman, and anonymous sources.

305   Lefkowitz took over: *Daily Variety*, *Hollywood Reporter*, June 11, 1969.

305   Going corporate fast: Balio, *American Film Industry*, 439, 576–77.

305   Kirk Kerkorian: Bart, *Fade Out*, 29–30.

306   Hughes in Las Vegas: Moldea, *The Hoffa Wars*, 128–29; Rappleye and Becker, *All American Mafioso*, 278–84.

306   Howard Hughes jokes: Graham, *Vegas*, 48.

306   Sinatra took a chair: "Render Unto Caesars," *Time*, September 25, 1967.

306   Kinney National Services: *Box Office*, August 11, 1969.

307   Retirements: *Variety*, November 4, 1970.

307   Lastfogel had given his away: Delaware Secretary of State, certificate of incorporation of Willmor, Inc., 10/9/58; New York County Clerk, amendments to the incorporation papers of WMA, Inc., 10/8/58, 1/31/68, 11/26/69. Within a month of its incorporation, the name of the Delaware company was changed from Willmor, Inc., to Willmor Enterprises, Inc., to Willmor International Corp. The 1968 New York amendment transformed WMA's 980 issued shares of Class B (nonvoting) stock into 157,500 and its 20 unissued shares of Class B stock into 342,500, presumably to be made available to employees. The 1969 amendment transformed the 500,000 shares of Class B into voting stock. The story of how Lastfogel gave his wealth back to the company is a staple of agency lore.

308   Aubrey arrived at Culver City: Bart, 32–36.

308   An MGM attorney informed Zinnemann: Ibid., 36–38. Zinnemann's lawsuit was eventually settled.

309   Bought buildings in Beverly Hills: Los Angeles County Tax Assessor.

311 Sebring introduced him to coke: Toffel, *My Husband, My Friend*, 109–10.

312 His way of staying young: Ibid., 177–79.

312 Anonymous phone call: Ibid., 165.

313 McQueen had planned to join them: Ibid., 198–99.

313 The news hit the radio: Bugliosi with Gentry, *Helter Skelter*, 20–21, 41–44. There was a fifth victim at the Tate house, first unidentified—an acquaintance of the nineteen-year-old caretaker.

313 "Don't worry, honey": Rosenfield, *The Club Rules*, 127–28.

313 Solar went public: Spiegel, *McQueen*, 249–50; Toffel, 188.

316 Kamen was too goddamn nice: Toffel, 238–40.

316 Brokaw had landed a client: *Variety*, September 27, 1972.

317 "Every Body Needs Milk": *New York Times*, September 20, 1972.

317 Press brunch for Spartan Pools: Tape recording provided by a confidential source.

319 Description of Freddie Fields: *New York Times*, December 3, 1973.

323 Announcement of WMA Sports: *Daily Variety*, July 9, 1973.

323 Scheme to unseat Lew Wasserman: Moldea, *Dark Victory*, 253–55.

325 "I wouldn't be surprised": Peter Greenberg, "Good Things Come in Big Packages," *TV Guide*, July 27, 1974.

326 MCA had announced: *New York Times*, June 6, 1973.

326 "75 Years of 10%": *New York Times*, December 3, 1973.

329 Positive spin on the story: *Daily Variety*, March 25, 1974.

330 Reorganization of the television department: Ibid., December 18, 1974.

330 Morris's packaging revenues: U.S. District Court, Central District of California, *Adams, Ray, Rosenberg* v. *William Morris Agency, Inc.*, affidavit of Roger Davis, 12/10/75.

11: Weltman's Revenge

This chapter is largely based on author interviews with Danny Arnold, Robert Elswit, Leonard Goldenson, Ed Limato, Guy McElwaine, Mike Medavoy, Ed Mitchell, Rowland Perkins, John Ptak, Mike Rosenfeld, Edgar Scherick, George Shapiro, Robert Shapiro, Alan Somers, Peter Stamelman, Harry Ufland, Elliot Wax, Mimi Weber, Phil Weltman, and anonymous sources.

336 When the story broke: *Variety*, January 15, 1975.

336 Announced their name: *Hollywood Reporter*, January 23, 1975.

338 Begelman hired away: McClintick, *Indecent Exposure*, 29–30.

339 The deal was sweet: *Daily Variety*, December 11, 1974.

339 Fields confirmed reports: *Hollywood Reporter*, June 10, June 17, 1975.

339 Attention on Sue Mengers: Marie Brenner, "Is Sue Mengers Too Pushy for Hollywood," *New York*, March 17, 1975; Louise Farr, "And Now from Hollywood: The Sweetening of Sue Mengers," *Ms.*, June 1975.

340 Early life of Mengers: Rosenfield, *The Club Rules*, 131–34.

340 Mengers's career: *New York*, March 17, 1975; Rosenfield, 135–40.

341 Deal with ICM: "Intelligencer," *New York*, August 4, 1975.

342 Stoller had announced that Kamen: *Daily Variety, Hollywood Reporter,* February 26, 1975.

344 "Saw the picture last week": WMA memo, 7/28/76.

346 Deal for *A Star Is Born:* "The Sherpas of the Subclause," *Time,* June 13, 1977.

346 He was playing tennis: Oppenheimer, *Barbara Walters,* 247–48.

347 A child with cerebral palsy: Goldenson, *Beating the Odds,* 80–83.

347 Her retarded sister: Ibid., 393.

347 "The ABC Evening News": *New York Times,* April 23, April 24, 1976.

348 Bitter feud with producers: *Adams, Ray, Rosenberg v. William Morris Agency, Inc.,* defendant's response, 8/17/76, and affadavit of Roger Davis, 6/17/76. The case was settled in December 1976.

348 As Lee Stevens put it: *New York Times,* May 2, 1976.

349 "Circus atmosphere": Ibid., April 23, 1976.

349 "This isn't journalism": "The $5 Million Woman," *Newsweek,* May 3, 1976.

349 Made her debut: Oppenheimer, 265–67.

349 Frances Lastfogel's death: *Variety,* September 8, 1976.

350 Frances Lastfogel's funeral: *Hollywood Reporter,* September 3, 1976.

352 Eisner put his programming execs: *Wall Street Journal,* Dec. 9, 1986.

352 CAA's new partner: *Daily Variety, Hollywood Reporter,* October 5, 1976.

12: The New Hollywood

Most of the information in this chapter is from author interviews with Flo Allen, Arthur Axelman, Alan Berger, Jay Bernstein, Marty Caan, Émile Chelette, Richard Clayton, Joe Esposito, David Geffen, Jeff Griswold, J. J. Harris, George Klein, Ed Limato, Gary Lucchesi, Daniel Melnick, Deborah Miller, Ed Mitchell, Rowland Perkins, Henrietta Lastfogel Prince, John Ptak, Jerry Schilling, Alan Somers, Peter Stamelman, Arnold Stieffel, Anthea Sylbert, Tom Tannenbaum, Brandon Tartikoff, Sam Thompson, David Warden, Mimi Weber, and anonymous sources.

356 Brokaw deal for Ford family: *New York Times,* March 23, 1977.

357 Speculated that Menachem Begin: *Los Angeles Times,* January 8, 1978.

358 Walters no longer a coanchor: *New York Post,* August 4, 1977.

358 Her very first "Special": Oppenheimer, *Barbara Walters,* 278–82.

358 Ginger Alden awakes: A. Goldman, *Elvis,* 562–64.

358 Elvis Presley's diet: Thompson and Cole, *The Death of Elvis,* 53.

359 His vanity had failed him: Greenwood and Tracy, *The Boy Who Would Be King,* 298.

359 Tour grosses and record sales: Hopkins, *Elvis: The Final Years,* 224–25, 228–29.

359 Colonel Parker's 50 percent commission: Tual Report, 7.

360 RCA contracts: Ibid., 16–18; Amended Tual Report, 15–18.

360 Deal with the International: Amended Tual Report, 25, 37–38.

360 Failure to provide financial advice: Tual Report, 10.

360 Refusal to tour abroad: Amended Tual Report, 38–39.

360 Failure to register Elvis's songs: Tual Report, 41.

360 Presley's drug intake: A. Goldman, 346–47, 501–4.

360 His colon distended: Thompson and Cole, 52–53.

361 Presley death scene: A. Goldman, 564–69; Thompson and Cole, 2–3, 16–17.

361 Presley owed Parker $1.69 million: Tual Report, 6.

361 Parker's gambling losses: Amended Tual Report, 38. In the early 1970s, the general manager of the International estimated these at $1 million per year.

362 Colonel wasted no time: A. Goldman, 571.

362 Geissler paid $100,000 in fines: Amended Tual Report, 9.

362 A big fan of Colonel Parker: Tony Schwartz, "The Spoils of Elvis," *Newsweek*, January 30, 1978.

362 $400,000 in royalties: Hopkins, 299.

363 Davis was handling Colonel's affairs: Tual Report, 15.

363 Parker flew to New York: A. Goldman, 577.

363 Agreement reached with Factors: Tual Report, 27. The Amended Tual Report, p. 7, notes that Parker maintained that the agreement, while dated 8/18/77, was actually entered into several weeks after Presley's death. This contradicts both Goldman's account and the impressions of several of Presley's closest associates. The term of the agreement was for eighteen months commencing 8/18/77. Tual was finally unable to determine the date the agreement was actually executed.

363 Ownership of Boxcar: Tual Report, 12–14.

363 Royalty split for merchandising: Ibid., exhibit 17.

363 Agreement between Boxcar and Factors: Ibid., exhibit 13.

363 "Nothing has changed": Stanley, *Elvis, My Brother*, 261.

364 Colonel sits down with Vernon: A. Goldman, 577; Stanley, 261.

364 Vernon's letter to Parker: Tual Report, exhibit 14.

364 Diskin's letter to Vernon: Ibid., 7, exhibit 15.

364 The remaining $50,000: Ibid., 27.

365 Parker's deals with CBS and NBC: Ibid., 38.

365 New agreements with RCA: Amended Tual Report, 21–23.

365 Morris commission on Factors: Ibid., 8.

365 Vernon's letter to Davis: Tual Report, exhibit 19.

365 "Elvis didn't die": Hopkins, 301.

365 Kamen wanted a pay-or-play commitment: Bach, *Final Cut*, 121.

367 $100-million checkbook: Ibid., 66.

367 Cimino wanted to do *The Fountainhead*: Ibid., 91–92.

368 Kamen got a call from Field and Bach: Ibid., 135–37.

370 Power industry attacks on *The China Syndrome*: *New York Times*, March 11, 1979; *Variety*, March 21, 1979.

370 Box office response to Three Mile Island: *Variety*, April 4, 1979.

370 Cimino's demands: Bach, 205–9.

370 The 1978 Academy Awards: Wiley and Bona, *Inside Oscar*, 560–63, 566–67.

374 Weisbord speech: Text made available by former WMA agent.

374 Real estate transferred to Willmor: Report of Julius Lefkowitz & Co., January 1980, made available by former WMA agent.

375 William Morris Plaza transactions: Los Angeles County Tax Assessor.

375 Building plans: *Daily Variety*, October 17, 1980.

375 Stock reorganization plan: Lefkowitz Report, January 1980; New York County Clerk, amendments to incorporation papers of WMA Inc., 5/30/80, 3/6/81.

377 Presley in *Harum Scarum*: Presley, *Elvis and Me*, 211–12.

379 Bottom-fishing in the Sunbelt: Report of Wallin, Simon, Black, & Co., February 1981, made available by a former WMA agent.

381 Board of directors expanded: *Variety*, December 10, 1980.

382 *All Night Long* premiere: "What Agent Can Lose Barbra and Burt and Stay on Top? Only a Girl Named Sue (Mengers)," *People*, March 23, 1981.

382 Considered for Columbia job: McClintick, *Indecent Exposure*, 390.

384 Streisand herself had made the sale: Bach, 393–94.

388 Lefkowitz's death: *Variety*, September 7, 1983.

389 Stevens elected president: Ibid., February 29, 1984.

13: HILLSIDE

Most of this chapter depends on author interviews (for this book and/or the *Premiere* article) with Flo Allen, Arthur Axelman, Alan Berger, Bernie Brillstein, Marty Caan, Émile Chelette, Joseph Evans, J. J. Harris, Ed Limato, Gary Lucchesi, Guy McElwaine, Mike Medavoy, Daniel Melnick, Fred Milstein, Ed Mitchell, John Ptak, Anthea Sylbert, Tom Tannenbaum, Brian Taylor, David Warden, Phil Weltman, Cary Woods, and anonymous sources. Additional details were provided by the 1989 Danny Thomas interview.

395 Priscilla Presley unaware: Amended Tual Report, 7

395 Tual's conclusions: Tual Report, 46–49; Amended Tual Report, 46.

395 A settlement was reached: *Variety*, June 29, 1983.

396 Ed Bondy's death: Ibid., December 21, 1983.

396 Marty Bauer leaves Morris: *Daily Variety*, April 2, 1984.

398 Limato's contract: Los Angeles County Superior Court, *William Morris Agency, Inc. v. Edward F. Limato et al.*, letter, 12/28/83.

400 Lastfogel's death: *Daily Variety, Los Angeles Herald-Examiner, Los Angeles Times, New York Times*, August 27, 1984.

400 Lastfogel's funeral: *Daily Variety*, August 31, 1984.

401 Lastfogel's will: Los Angeles County Superior Court, Estate of Abe Lastfogel.

402 Stan Kamen Day: *Daily Variety, Hollywood Reporter, Los Angeles Times*, October 29, 1984; *Los Angeles Herald-Examiner*, October 30, 1984.

409 Simpson working with Kamen: *Daily Variety, Hollywood Reporter*, January 30, 1986.

410 Postmortem comments on Kamen: *Daily Variety, Los Angeles Herald-Examiner*, February 21, 1986.

412 Sexual harassment suit: *Hollywood Reporter*, February 28, 1986.

412 Stoller's death: *Variety*, March 26, 1986.

412 Brokaw and Weiss named cochairmen: *Daily Variety*, April 2, 1986.

412 Weisbord's death: *Daily Variety, Los Angeles Times*, May 8, 1986.

415 Guy McElwaine's resignation: *Los Angeles Times*, April 10, 1986.

417 Hirshan named motion picture chief: *Variety*, July 2, 1986.
418 Business affairs chief's death: Ibid., October 1, 1986.
419 Michael Ovitz profile: *Wall Street Journal*, December 19, 1986.

14: RAPE AND PILLAGE

This chapter is primarily based on author interviews (for this book and/or the *Premiere* article) with Arthur Axelman, Michael Chapman, Sam Goldwyn, Jr., Bobby and Anthea Harris, J. J. Harris, Bruce Kaufman, Ed Limato, Gregg Mayday, Fred Milstein, Ed Mitchell, John Ptak, Lee Salomon, Beth Swofford, Tom Tannenbaum, Brian Taylor, David Warden, Phil Weltman, and anonymous sources.

421 Morris Agency real estate: Los Angeles County Tax Assessor; *Los Angeles Business Journal*, March 19, 1990.
422 "Cosby" syndication rights: Randall Lane, "Bill Cosby, Capitalist," *Forbes*, September 28, 1992; *Wall Street Journal*, June 20, 1988.
422 Representation of Oscar nominees: *Los Angeles Times*, March 31, 1987.
423 Music agent drowned: *Variety*, May 12, 1982.
424 Bobby Harris asked to resign: *Daily Variety*, August 3, 1987.
424 Threatened to get out of hand: *Daily Variety*, October 12, 1987; *L.A. Weekly*, November 6, 1987.
424 Gloria Allred letter: Ibid.
424 Beverly Hills cops: *Daily Variety*, October 13, 1987.
427 Mengers in retirement: Rosenfield, *The Club Rules*, 130.
428 List of dream clients: WMA memo, 3/21/88.
429 Limato's contract: *William Morris Agency, Inc. v. Edward F. Limato et al.*, letter, 1/5/87.
430 Limato's departure: *Hollywood Reporter*, April 7, 1988, April 11, 1988.
431 Limato's resignation letter: *WMA v. Limato*, letter, 4/6/88.
431 Mengers joins Morris: *Daily Variety, Hollywood Reporter*, April 7, 1988.
434 "Morris must be spinning": *Wall Street Journal*, June 20, 1988.
435 Morris Agency writers: WMA client list, December 1, 1988, made available by a former WMA agent.
436 Divided the town into three camps: WMA memo, 5/20/88, made available by a former WMA agent.
437 Ovitz "on the warpath": "Intelligencer," *New York*, May 16, 1988.
437 ICM is taken private: *Daily Variety, Hollywood Reporter*, July 22, 1988.
439 Lukas Heller memo: WMA memo, 11/3/88, made available by a former WMA agent.
439 1988 Morris's biggest year ever: Lisa Gubernick, "Living Off the Past," *Forbes*, June 12, 1989.
440 Class-C stock rose in value: *Los Angeles Times*, May 15, 1989.
440 William Morris Plaza Building income: Wallin, Simon Report, March 1990, made available by a former WMA agent.
440 Lecture clients: WMA brochure, January 1989, Morris Collection/NYPL.
441 Stevens's death: *Los Angeles Times, New York Times*, February 4, 1989.

441   Income of Presley estate: Robert Hilburn, "Eternal Revenue," *Los Angeles Times Magazine*, June 11, 1989.

441   Race to sign Ronald Reagan: *Los Angeles Times*, January 26, 1989

441   Brokaw named president: *Daily Variety*, February 7, 1989.

442   On the phone with Bill Cosby: *Los Angeles Herald-Examiner*, February 10, 1989.

442   Four new board members: *Daily Variety*, *Hollywood Reporter*, February 13, 1989.

442   Executive committee formed: New York County Clerk, amendment to incorporation papers of WMA, Inc., 2/9/89.

446   *Driving Miss Daisy* deal: *Daily Variety*, June 27, 1990; *New York Times*, March 6, 1990.

446   *Dances with Wolves* deal: *Daily Variety*, June 27, 1990; *Los Angeles Times*, April 11, 1991.

447   J. J. Harris goes to InterTalent: *Daily Variety*, March 13, 1989.

447   Celebrated its ninetieth birthday: Ibid., April 21, 1989.

448   Industry seminar on agenting: *Daily Variety*, November 16, 1989.

449   Zimmer reportedly in hot water: *Hollywood Reporter*, November 21, 1989.

449   Hollywood had been transfixed: *Los Angeles Times,* October 19, 1989.

450   Burnham and Simpson named coheads: *Variety*, November 29, 1989.

450   Corporate retreat in Ojai: Report of Ian Russ, Ph.D., made available by a former WMA agent.

451   The youth theme made sense: *Daily Variety*, March 14, 1990.

454   *Bonfire of the Vanities* word-of-mouth: Salamon, *The Devil's Candy*, 375–76.

454   *Bonfire of the Vanities* reviews: Ibid., 403–5.

454   Beverly Hills office market had cratered: *Los Angeles Business Journal*, March 19, 1990.

455   Vacancies in the William Morris Plaza Building: Wallin, Simon Report, March 1990.

455   Mengers leaves Morris: *Daily Variety*, December 18, 1990.

457   Howard leaves Morris: Ibid., January 23, 1991.

457   Goldsmith and Shapiro leave Morris: Ibid., January 29, 1991.

457   Boatwright leaves Morris: Ibid., January 30, 1991.

458   Ptak leaves Morris: Ibid., February 6, 1991.

458   Katzman named president: Ibid., February 11, 1991.

458   Simpson and Burnham sign contracts: Ibid., February 13, 1991.

458   "Basically, I'm a winner": *Los Angeles Times*, February 15, 1991.

459   Merger rumors: *Daily Variety*, October 24, 1991; *Los Angeles Times*, April 12, April 19, 1991.

460   Morgan Mason hired: *Hollywood Reporter*, July 17, 1991.

460   Legal battle with Paramount: *Daily Variety*, August 7, August 23, 1991; *Los Angeles Times*, August 7, August 23, 1991.

460   Morris Agency board revamped: *Daily Variety*, December 6, 1991.

461   Auerbach leaves Morris: Ibid., April 16, 1992.

461 That spring and summer: *Los Angeles Times,* February 2, 1992.

461 InterTalent difficulties: Lynn Hirschberg, "The Players," *Vanity Fair,* January 1993.

462 Talks between Triad and Morris: *Variety,* October 26, 1992; *Vanity Fair,* January 1993.

463 Death threats at Triad: *Variety,* October 26, 1992.

463 Gathering at William Morris: *New York Times,* October 19, 1992.

BIBLIOGRAPHY

Adams, Joey. *Here's to the Friars: The Heart of Show Business*. New York: Crown, 1976.

Adamson, Joe. *Groucho, Harpo, Chico, and Sometimes Zeppo: A Celebration of the Marx Brothers and a Satire on the Rest of the World*. New York: Simon & Schuster, 1973.

Allen, Steve. *Hi-Ho, Steverino! My Adventures in the Wonderful Wacky World of TV*. Fort Lee, N.J.: Barricade, 1992.

———. *More Funny People*. New York: Stein & Day, 1982.

———. *Ripoff: The Corruption That Plagues America*. Secaucus, N.J.: Lyle Stuart, 1979.

Alley, Robert S., and Irby B. Brown. *Murphy Brown: Anatomy of a Sitcom*. New York: Delta, 1990.

American Business Consultants. *Red Channels: The Report of Communist Influence in Radio and Television*. New York: Counterattack, 1950.

Anderson, Christopher. *Hollywood TV: The Studio System in the Fifties*. Austin: University of Texas Press, 1994.

Anger, Kenneth. *Hollywood Babylon*. New York: Dell, 1975.

Atkinson, Brooks. *Broadway*. Rev. ed. New York: Macmillan, 1974.

Auletta, Ken. *Three Blind Mice: How the TV Networks Lost Their Way*. New York: Random House, 1991.

Bach, Steven. *Final Cut: Dreams and Disaster in the Making of Heaven's Gate*. New York: Morrow, 1985.

Balaban, Carrie. *Continuous Performance: The Story of A. J. Balaban*. New York: Putnam's, 1942.

Balio, Tino, ed. *The American Film Industry*. Madison, Wis.: University of Wisconsin Press, 1985.

———. *Hollywood in the Age of Television*. Boston: Unwin Hyman, 1990.

Balsamo, William, and George Carpozi, Jr. *Under the Clock: The Inside Story of the Mafia's First 100 Years*. Far Hills, N.J.: New Horizon, 1988.

Banham, Reyner. *Los Angeles: The Architecture of Four Ecologies*. London: Penguin, 1971.

Bankhead, Tallulah. *Tallulah: My Autobiography*. New York: Harper & Brothers, 1952.

Barnouw, Erik. *Tube of Plenty: The Evolution of American Television*. 2nd rev. ed. New York: Oxford University Press, 1990.

Bart, Peter. *Fade Out: The Calamitous Final Days of MGM*. New York: Morrow, 1990.

Basten, Fred E. *Beverly Hills: Portrait of a Fabled City*. Los Angeles: Douglas-West, 1975.

Bedell, Sally. *Up the Tube: Prime-Time TV in the Silverman Years*. New York: Viking, 1981.

Behlmer, Rudy, ed. *Inside Warner Bros. (1935–1951)*. New York: Viking, 1985.

———. *Memo from David O. Selznick*. New York: Viking, 1972.

Berg, A. Scott. *Goldwyn: A Biography*. New York: Knopf, 1989.

Bergen, Candice. *Knock Wood*. New York: Linden Press/Simon & Schuster, 1994.

Berle, Milton, with Haskel Frankel. *An Autobiography*. New York: Delacorte, 1974.

Bessie, Alvah. *Inquisition in Eden*. New York: Macmillan, 1965.

Best, Katharine, and Katharine Hillyer. *Las Vegas: Playtown U.S.A.* New York: McKay, 1955.

Bilby, Kenneth. *The General: David Sarnoff and the Rise of the Communications Industry*. New York: Harper & Row, 1986.

Birmingham, Stephen. *Our Crowd: The Great Jewish Families of New York*. New York: Harper & Row, 1967.

———. *The Rest of Us: The Rise of America's Eastern European Jews*. Boston: Little, Brown, 1984.

Booth, Stanley. *Dance with the Devil: The Rolling Stones and Their Times*. New York: Random House, 1984.

Boyer, Peter J. *Who Killed CBS? The Undoing of America's Number One News Network*. New York: Random House, 1988.

Braudy, Leo. *The Frenzy of Renown: Fame and Its History*. New York: Oxford University Press, 1986.

Britt, Albert. *Turn of the Century*. Barre, Mass.: Barre, 1966.

Brown, Les. *Televi$ion: The Business Behind the Box*. New York: Harcourt Brace Jovanovich, 1971.

Brown, Peter Harry. *Kim Novak: Reluctant Goddess*. New York: St. Martin's, 1986.

Brownstein, Ronald. *The Power and the Glitter: The Hollywood-Washington Connection*. New York: Pantheon, 1990.

Bruck, Connie. *Master of the Game: Steve Ross and the Creation of Time Warner*. New York: Simon & Schuster, 1994.

———. *The Predators' Ball: The Junk-Bond Raiders and the Man Who Staked Them*. New York: American Lawyer/Simon & Schuster, 1988.

Buckley, William F., Jr., ed. *The Committee and Its Critics: A Calm Review of the House Committee on Un-American Activities*. Chicago: Regnery, 1963.

Bugliosi, Vincent, with Curt Gentry. *Helter Skelter: The True Story of the Manson Murders*. New York: Norton, 1974.

Burk, Bill E. *Elvis: A 30-Year Chronicle*. Tempe, Ariz.: Osborne, 1985.

Burns, George, with David Fisher. *All My Best Friends*. New York: Putnam's, 1989.

Burrows, Abe. *Honest, Abe: Is There Really No Business Like Show Business?* Boston: Atlantic Monthly Press, 1980.

Caesar, Sid, with Bill Davidson. *Where Have I Been? An Autobiography.* New York: Crown, 1982.

Cagney, James. *Cagney by Cagney.* Garden City, N.Y.: Doubleday, 1976.

Cantor, Eddie, with Jane Kesner Ardmore. *Take My Life.* Garden City, N.Y.: Doubleday, 1957.

Capra, Frank. *The Name Above the Title: An Autobiography.* New York: Macmillan, 1971.

Carey, Gary. *Judy Holliday: An Intimate Life Story.* New York: Seaview, 1982.

Carter, Randolph. *Ziegfeld: The Time of His Life.* London: Bernard, 1988.

Caute, David. *The Great Fear: The Anti-Communist Purge Under Truman and Eisenhower.* New York: Simon & Schuster, 1978.

Ceplair, Larry, and Stephen Englund. *The Inquisition in Hollywood: Politics in the Film Community, 1930–1960.* Garden City, N.Y.: Anchor/Doubleday, 1980.

Chaplin, Charles. *My Autobiography.* New York: Simon & Schuster, 1964.

Chase, Francis, Jr. *Sound and Fury: An Informal History of Broadcasting.* New York: Harper & Brothers, 1942.

Chernow, Ron. *The House of Morgan: An American Banking Dynasty and the Rise of Modern Finance.* New York: Atlantic Monthly Press, 1990.

Coffey, Frank. *Always Home: 50 Years of the USO.* Washington, D.C.: Brassey's, 1991.

Cohen, Sarah Blacher, ed. *From Hester Street to Hollywood: The Jewish-American Stage and Screen.* Bloomington, Ind.: Indiana University Press, 1983.

Cohn, Art. *The Joker Is Wild: The Story of Joe E. Lewis.* New York: Random House, 1955.

Cole, Lester. *Hollywood Red: The Autobiography of Lester Cole.* Palo Alto, Calif.: Ramparts, 1981.

Collier, Peter. *The Fondas: An American Dynasty.* New York: Putnam's, 1991.

———, and David Horowitz. *The Rockefellers: An American Dynasty.* New York: Holt, Rinehart & Winston, 1976.

Connor, Jim. *Ann Miller: Tops in Taps.* New York: Watts, 1981.

Conrad, Harold. *Dear Muffo: 35 Years in the Fast Lane.* New York: Stein & Day, 1982.

Cressey, Donald R. *Theft of the Nation: The Structure and Operations of Organized Crime in America.* New York: Harper & Row, 1969.

Csida, Joseph, and Jane Bundy Csida. *American Entertainment: A Unique History of Popular Show Business.* New York: Billboard, 1978.

Dalton, David. *James Dean: The Mutant King.* San Francisco: Straight Arrow, 1974.

———, ed. *The Rolling Stones: The First Twenty Years.* New York: Knopf, 1981.

Dannen, Fredric. *Hit Men: Power Brokers and Fast Money Inside the Music Business.* New York: Vintage, 1991.

Davidson, Bill. *Jane Fonda: An Intimate Biography.* New York: Dutton, 1990.

————. *The Real and the Unreal*. New York: Harper & Brothers, 1961.

Davis, Genevieve. *Beverly Hills: An Illustrated History*. Northridge, Calif.: Windsor, 1988.

Davis, Sammy, Jr. *Hollywood in a Suitcase*. New York: Morrow, 1980.

————. *Yes I Can: The Story of Sammy Davis, Jr.* New York: Farrar, Straus & Giroux, 1965.

————, and Jane and Burt Boyar. *Why Me? The Sammy Davis, Jr. Story*. New York: Farrar, Straus & Giroux, 1989.

Dunaway, David King. *Huxley in Hollywood*. New York: Harper & Row, 1989.

Edwards, Anne. *A Remarkable Woman: A Biography of Katharine Hepburn*. New York: Morrow, 1985.

Eels, George, and Stanley Musgrove. *Mae West: A Biography*. New York: Morrow, 1982.

Einstein, Charles, ed. *The Fireside Book of Baseball*. 4th ed. New York: Fireside/Simon & Schuster, 1987.

Ely, Melvin Patrick. *The Adventures of Amos 'n' Andy: A Social History of an American Phenomenon*. New York: Free Press, 1991.

Evans, Robert. *The Kid Stays in the Picture*. New York: Hyperion, 1994.

Fadiman, William. *Hollywood Now*. London: Thames & Hudson, 1973.

Federal Writers' Project. *The WPA Guide to California*. New York: Pantheon, 1984.

————. *The WPA Guide to New York City*. New York: Pantheon, 1982.

Fein, Irving. *Jack Benny: An Intimate Biography*. New York: Putnam's, 1976.

Fell, John L. *A History of Films*. New York: Holt, Rinehart & Winston, 1979.

Fox, Stephen. *Blood and Power: Organized Crime in Twentieth-Century America*. New York: Morrow, 1989.

————. *The Mirror Makers: A History of American Advertising and Its Creators*. New York: Morrow, 1984.

Frank, Gerold. *Judy*. New York: Harper & Row, 1975.

Freedland, Michael. *Jack Lemmon*. New York: St. Martin's, 1985.

————. *Jolson*. New York: Stein & Day, 1972.

Friedrich, Otto. *City of Nets: A Portrait of Hollywood in the 1940s*. New York: Harper & Row, 1986.

Gabler, Neal. *An Empire of Their Own: How the Jews Invented Hollywood*. New York: Crown, 1988.

Galbraith, John Kenneth. *The Great Crash: 1929*. Boston: Houghton Mifflin, 1988.

Gansberg, Alan L. *Little Caesar: A Biography of Edward G. Robinson*. London: New English Library, 1983.

Gardner, Ava. *Ava: My Story*. New York: Bantam, 1990.

Gavin, James. *Intimate Nights: The Golden Age of New York Cabaret*. New York: Grove Weidenfeld, 1991.

Geduld, Harry M. *The Birth of the Talkies: From Edison to Jolson*. Bloomington, Ind.: Indiana University Press, 1975.

Geist, Kenneth L. *Pictures Will Talk: The Life and Times of Joseph L. Mankiewicz*. New York: Scribner's, 1978.

Gentry, Curt. *J. Edgar Hoover: The Man and the Secrets*. New York: Norton, 1991.

Giancana, Sam, and Chuck Giancana. *Double Cross: The Explosive, Inside Story of the Mobster Who Controlled America*. New York: Warner, 1992.

Goldenson, Leonard H., with Marvin J. Wolf. *Beating the Odds*. New York: Scribner's, 1991.

Goldman, Albert. *Elvis*. New York: McGraw-Hill, 1981.

Goldman, Herbert G. *Fanny Brice: The Original Funny Girl*. New York: Oxford University Press, 1992.

———. *Jolson: The Legend Comes to Life*. New York: Oxford University Press, 1988.

Goldman, William. *Adventures in the Screen Trade: A Personal View of Hollywood and Screenwriting*. New York: Warner, 1983.

Goodman, Walter. *The Committee*. New York: Farrar, Straus & Giroux, 1968.

Graham, Jefferson. *Vegas: Live and in Person*. New York: Abbeville, 1989.

Green, Abel, and Joe Laurie, Jr. *Show Biz: From Vaude to Video*. New York: Holt, 1951.

Greenwood, Earl, and Kathleen Tracy. *The Boy Who Would Be King*. New York: Dutton, 1990.

Griffin, Merv, with Peter Barsocchini. *Merv: An Autobiography*. New York: Simon & Schuster, 1980.

Guiles, Fred Lawrence. *Legend: The Life and Death of Marilyn Monroe*. New York: Stein & Day, 1984.

Guralnick, Peter. *Last Train to Memphis: The Rise of Elvis Presley*. Boston: Little, Brown, 1994.

———. *Lost Highway: Journeys & Arrivals of American Musicians*. Boston: Godine, 1979.

Halberstam, David. *The Fifties*. New York: Villard, 1993.

———. *The Powers That Be*. New York: Knopf, 1979.

Hamilton, Ian. *Writers in Hollywood, 1915–1951*. New York: Harper & Row, 1990.

Hart, Harold H. *Hart's Guide to New York City*. New York: Hart, 1964.

Hayward, Brooke. *Haywire*. New York: Knopf, 1987.

Hepburn, Katharine. *Me: Stories of My Life*. New York: Knopf, 1992.

Higham, Charles. *Hollywood at Sunset*. New York: Saturday Review Press, 1972.

———. *Kate: The Life of Katharine Hepburn*. New York: Norton, 1975.

———. *Merchant of Dreams: Louis B. Mayer and the Secret Hollywood*. New York: Donald I. Fine, 1993.

———. *Warner Brothers*. New York: Scribner's, 1975.

Hine, Thomas. *Populuxe*. New York: Knopf, 1986.

Hirschhorn, Clive. *The Columbia Story*. New York: Crown, 1990.

Holtzman, Will. *Judy Holliday*. New York: Putnam's, 1982.

Hopkins, Jerry. *Elvis: The Final Years*. New York: Berkley, 1983.

Hotchner, A. E. *Blown Away: The Rolling Stones and the Death of the Sixties*. New York: Simon & Schuster, 1990.

Houseman, John. *Entertainers and the Entertained: Essays on Theater, Film, and Television*. New York: Simon & Schuster, 1986.

Howe, Irving. *World of Our Fathers*. New York: Simon & Schuster, 1976.

Humphries, Patrick. *Paul Simon: Still Crazy After All These Years*. New York: Doubleday, 1988.

Jessel, George. *This Way, Miss*. New York: Holt, 1955.

———, with John Austin. *The World I Lived In*. Chicago: Regnery, 1975.

Jones, Landon Y. *Great Expectations: America and the Baby Boom Generation*. New York: Ballantine, 1981.

Kahn, E. J., Jr. *Jock: The Life and Times of John Hay Whitney*. Garden City, N.Y.: Doubleday, 1981.

Kaiser, Harvey H. *Great Camps of the Adirondacks*. Boston: Godine, 1982.

Kanin, Garson. *Hollywood: Stars and Starlets, Tycoons and Flesh-Peddlers, Moviemakers and Moneymakers, Frauds and Geniuses, Hopefuls and Has-Beens, Great Lovers and Sex Symbols*. New York: Viking, 1967.

Katz, Ephraim. *The Film Encyclopedia*. 2nd ed. New York: HarperCollins, 1994.

Katz, Leonard. *Uncle Frank: The Biography of Frank Costello*. New York: Drake, 1973.

Kazan, Elia. *A Life*. New York: Knopf, 1988.

Kelley, Kitty. *His Way: The Unauthorized Biography of Frank Sinatra*. New York: Bantam, 1986.

Kent, Nicholas. *Naked Hollywood: Money and Power in the Movies Today*. New York: St. Martin's, 1991.

Kidd, Charles. *Debrett Goes to Hollywood*. London: Weidenfeld & Nicholson, 1986.

King, Moses, ed. *King's Handbook of New York City*. 2nd ed. Boston: King, 1893.

Kleinfelder, Rita Lang. *When We Were Young: A Baby-Boomer Yearbook*. New York: Prentice-Hall, 1993.

Klurfeld, Herman. *Winchell: His Life and Times*. New York: Praeger, 1976.

Knepp, Donn. *Las Vegas: The Entertainment Capital*. Menlo Park, Calif.: Lane, 1987.

Kobal, John. *People Will Talk*. London: Aurum, 1986.

———. *Rita Hayworth: The Time, the Place, and the Woman*. London: W. H. Allen, 1977.

Koskoff, David E. *Joseph P. Kennedy: A Life and Times*. Englewood Cliffs, N.J.: Prentice-Hall, 1974.

Kouwenhoven, John A. *The Columbia Historical Portrait of New York: An Essay in Graphic History*. New York: Icon, 1972.

Lacey, Robert. *Little Man: Meyer Lansky and the Gangster Life*. Boston: Little, Brown, 1991.

Lasky, Jesse L., with Don Weldon. *I Blow My Own Horn*. Garden City, N.Y.: Doubleday, 1957.

Leaming, Barbara. *If This Was Happiness: A Biography of Rita Hayworth*. New York: Viking, 1989.

Leonard, John. *A Really Big Show: A Visual History of the Ed Sullivan Show*. New York: Sarah Lazin, 1992.

Leonard, Maurice. *Mae West: Empress of Sex*. London: HarperCollins, 1991.

Levi, Vicki Gold, and Lee Eisenberg. *Atlantic City: 125 Years of Ocean Madness*. New York: Potter, 1979.

Levy, Emmanuel, *And the Winner Is: The History and Politics of the Oscar Awards*. New York: Ungar, 1987.

Litwak, Mark, *Reel Power: The Struggle for Influence and Success in the New Hollywood*. New York: Morrow, 1986.

LoMonaco, Martha Schmoyer. *Every Week, A Broadway Revue: The Tamiment Playhouse, 1921–1960*. New York: Greenwood, 1992.

MacGraw, Ali. *Moving Pictures: An Autobiography*. New York: Bantam, 1991.

Madsen, Axel. *The New Hollywood: American Movies in the '70s*. New York: Crowell, 1975.

Mankiewicz, Joseph L. *More About "All About Eve."* New York: Random House, 1972.

Manso, Peter. *Brando: The Biography*. New York: Hyperion, 1994.

Marc, David, and Robert J. Thompson. *Prime Time, Prime Movers*. Boston: Little, Brown, 1992.

Marcus, Eric. *Making History: The Struggle for Gay and Lesbian Equal Rights, 1945–1990*. New York: HarperCollins, 1992.

Marcus, Greil. *Dead Elvis: A Chronicle of a Cultural Obsession*. New York: Doubleday, 1991.

———. *Mystery Train: Images of America in Rock 'n' Roll Music*. New York: Dutton, 1976.

Marsh, David. *Elvis*. New York: Rolling Stone Press/Times Books, 1982.

Martin, Ralph G. *A Hero for Our Time: An Intimate Story of the Kennedy Years*. New York: Macmillan, 1983.

Marx, Groucho. *Groucho and Me*. New York: B. Geis Associates, 1959.

McBride, Joseph. *Frank Capra: The Catastrophe of Success*. New York: Simon & Schuster, 1992.

McClintick, David. *Indecent Exposure: A True Story of Hollywood and Wall Street*. New York: Morrow, 1982.

McCrohan, Donna. *Prime Time, Our Time: America's Life and Times Through the Prism of Television*. Rocklin, Calif.: Prima, 1990.

McCullough, David. *Truman*. New York: Simon & Schuster, 1992.

McGilligan, Patrick. *George Cukor: A Double Life*. New York: St. Martin's, 1991.

McWilliams, Carey. *Southern California Country: An Island on the Land*. New York: Duell, Sloan & Pearce, 1946.

Messick, Hank. *The Beauties and the Beasts: The Mob in Show Business*. New York: McKay, 1973.

———, and Burt Goldblatt. *The Mobs and the Mafia: The Illustrated History of Organized Crime*. New York: Galahad, 1972.

Metz, Robert. *CBS: Reflections in a Bloodshot Eye*. New York: Signet/New American Library, 1976.

Michaels, Leonard, David Reid, and Raquel Scherr, eds. *West of the West: Imagining California*. San Francisco: North Point, 1989.

Miller, Jim, ed. *The Rolling Stone Illustrated History of Rock & Roll* (rev. ed.) New York: Random House/Rolling Stone Press, 1980.

Millichap, Joseph R. *Lewis Milestone*. Boston: Twayne, 1981.

Mitgang, Herbert. *Dangerous Dossiers: Exposing the Secret War Against America's Greatest Authors*. New York: Donald I. Fine, 1988.

Moldea, Dan E. *Dark Victory: Ronald Reagan, MCA, and the Mob*. New York: Viking, 1986.

———. *The Hoffa Wars: Teamsters, Rebels, Politicians, and the Mob*. New York: Paddington, 1978.

Morella, Joe, and Patricia Barey. *Simon and Garfunkel: Old Friends*. New York: Birch Lane, 1991.

Morella, Joe, and Edward Z. Epstein. *Lana: The Public and Private Lives of Miss Turner*. New York: Citadel, 1971.

Morris, Jan. *Manhattan '45*. New York: Oxford University Press, 1987.

Murray, Albert. *Good Morning Blues: The Autobiography of Count Basie*. New York: Random House, 1985.

Navasky, Victor S. *Naming Names*. New York: Viking, 1980.

Niven, David. *Bring on the Empty Horses*. New York: Putnam's, 1975.

Norman, Philip. *Symphony for the Devil: The Rolling Stones Story*. New York: Linden/Simon & Schuster, 1984.

Oates, Stephen B. *Let the Trumpet Sound: The Life of Martin Luther King, Jr.* New York: Plume/New American Library, 1983.

O'Donnell, Pierce, and Dennis McDougal. *Fatal Subtraction: How Hollywood Really Does Business*. New York: Doubleday, 1992.

Oppenheimer, Jerry. *Barbara Walters: An Unauthorized Biography*. New York: St. Martin's, 1990.

Osborne, Robert. *Fifty Golden Years of Oscar: The Official History of the Academy of Motion Picture Arts & Sciences*. La Habra, Calif.: ESE California, 1979.

Paley, William S. *As It Happened: A Memoir*. Garden City, N. Y.: Doubleday, 1979.

Parker, John. *Warren Beatty: The Last Great Lover in Hollywood*. London: Headline, 1993.

Partridge, Marianne, ed. *Rolling Stone Visits Saturday Night Live*. New York: Rolling Stone Press/Dolphin/Doubleday, 1979.

Pearl, Ralph. *Las Vegas Is My Beat*. Secaucus, N.J.: Lyle Stuart, 1973.

Pepitone, Lena, and William Stadiem. *Marilyn Monroe Confidential: An Intimate Personal Account*. New York: Simon & Schuster, 1979.

Phillips, Julia. *You'll Never Eat Lunch in This Town Again*. New York: Random House, 1991.

Polanski, Roman. *Roman by Polanski*. New York: Morrow, 1984.

Powdermaker, Hortense. *Hollywood, the Dream Factory: An Anthropologist Looks at the Movie-Makers*. Boston: Little, Brown, 1950.

Presley, Priscilla Beaulieu, with Sandra Harmon. *Elvis and Me*. New York: Berkley, 1986.

Pye, Michael. *Moguls: Inside the Business of Show Business*. New York: Holt, Rinehart & Winston, 1980.

Rappleye, Charles, and Ed Becker, *All American Mafioso: The Johnny Roselli Story*. New York: Doubleday, 1991.

Riese, Randall. *Her Name Is Barbra: An Intimate Portrait of the Real Barbra Streisand*. New York: Birch Lane, 1993.

Robinson, David. *Chaplin: His Life and Art*. New York: McGraw-Hill, 1985.

Robinson, Edward G., with Leonard Spigelgass. *All My Yesterdays: An Autobiography*. New York: Hawthorn, 1973.

Rooney, Mickey. *Life Is Too Short*. New York: Villard, 1991.

Rosenberg, Bernard, and Harry Silverstein. *The Real Tinsel*. New York: Macmillan, 1970.

Rosenfield, Paul. *The Club Rules: Power, Money, Sex, and Fear—How It Works in Hollywood*. New York: Warner Books, 1992.

Ross, Murray. *Stars and Strikes: The Unionization of Hollywood*. New York: Oxford University Press, 1941.

Roxon, Lillian. *Lillian Roxon's Rock Encyclopedia*. New York: Grosset & Dunlap/Universal Library, 1971.

Sackett, Susan. *The Hollywood Reporter Book of Box Office Hits*. New York: Billboard, 1990.

Salamon, Julie. *The Devil's Candy: The Bonfire of the Vanities Goes to Hollywood*. Boston: Houghton Mifflin, 1991.

Salwen, Peter. *Upper West Side Story: A History and Guide*. New York: Abbeville, 1989.

Sarlot, Raymond, and Fred E. Basten. *Life at the Marmont*. Santa Monica, Calif.: Roundtable, 1987.

Scaduto, Anthony. *Bob Dylan: An Intimate Biography*. New York: Grosset & Dunlap, 1971.

Schatz, Thomas. *The Genius of the System: Hollywood Filmmaking in the Studio Era*. New York: Pantheon, 1988.

Schlesinger, Arthur M. *Robert Kennedy and His Times*. Boston: Houghton Mifflin, 1978.

Schulberg, Budd. *Moving Pictures: Memories of a Hollywood Prince*. Briarcliff Manor, N.Y.: Stein & Day, 1981.

Schwartz, Nancy Lynn. *The Hollywood Writers' Wars*. New York: Knopf, 1982.

Selznick, Irene Mayer. *A Private View*. New York: Knopf, 1983.

Sennett, Ted. *Your Show of Shows*. New York: Collier, 1977.

Server, Lee. *Screenwriter: Words Become Pictures*. Pittstown, N.J.: Main Street, 1987.

Simon, George T. *The Big Bands*. New York: Macmillan, 1967.

Shaw, Arnold. *Honkers and Shouters: The Golden Years of Rhythm & Blues*. New York: Macmillan, 1978.

Shaw, Artie. *The Trouble with Cinderella (An Outline of Identity)*. New York: Farrar, Straus and Young, 1952.

Shevey, Sandra. *The Marilyn Scandal: Her True Life Revealed by Those Who Knew Her*. New York: Morrow, 1987.

Shipman, David. *Judy Garland: The Secret Life of an American Legend*. New York: Hyperion, 1993.

Skolsky, Sidney. *Don't Get Me Wrong—I Love Hollywood*. New York: Putnam's, 1975.

Slide, Anthony. *The American Film Industry: A Historical Dictionary*. Westport, Conn.: Greenwood, 1986.

————. *The Vaudevillians: A Dictionary of Vaudeville Performers*. Westport, Conn.: Arlington House, 1981.

Sloane, Arthur A. *Hoffa*. Cambridge, Mass.: MIT Press, 1991.

Smith, Bill. *The Vaudevillians*. New York: Macmillan, 1976.

Smith, Ronald. *Cosby*. New York: St. Martin's, 1986.

Smith, Sally Bedell, *In All His Glory: The Life of William S. Paley*. New York: Simon & Schuster, 1990.

Sobel, Robert. *Panic on Wall Street*. Rev. ed. New York: Talley/Dutton, 1988.

Spada, James. *Peter Lawford: The Man Who Kept the Secrets*. New York: Bantam, 1991.

Spiegel, Penina. *McQueen: The Untold Story of a Bad Boy in Hollywood*. Garden City, N.Y.: Doubleday, 1986.

Spitzer, Marian. *The Palace*. New York: Atheneum, 1969.

Spoto, Donald. *Laurence Olivier: A Biography*. New York: HarperCollins, 1992.

————. *Marilyn Monroe: The Biography*. New York: HarperCollins, 1993.

————. *Stanley Kramer: Film Maker*. New York: Putnam's, 1978.

Stagg, Jerry. *The Brothers Shubert*. New York: Random House, 1968.

Stallings, Penny. *Forbidden Channels: The Truth They Hide from TV Guide*. New York: Harper Perennial, 1991.

————. *Rock 'n' Roll Confidential*. Boston: Little, Brown, 1984.

————, with Howard Mandelbaum, *Flesh & Fantasy*. New York: St. Martin's, 1978.

Stanley, Billy, with George Erikson. *Elvis, My Brother*. New York: St. Martin's, 1989.

Starr, Kevin. *Material Dreams: Southern California Through the 1920s*. New York: Oxford University Press, 1990.

Stein, Charles W., ed. *American Vaudeville as Seen by Its Contemporaries*. New York: Knopf, 1984.

Steinem, Gloria. *Marilyn*. New York: Holt, 1986.

Stern, Jane, and Michael Stern. *Jane & Michael Stern's Encyclopedia of Pop Culture*. New York: Harper Perennial, 1992.

Stern, Robert A. M., Gregory Gilmartin, and John Massengale. *New York 1900: Metropolitan Architecture and Urbanism 1890–1915*. New York: Rizzoli, 1983.

Stine, Whitney. *Stars and Star Handlers*. Santa Monica, Calif., Roundtable, 1985.

Stoddart, Dayton. *Lord Broadway: Variety's Sime*. New York: Wilfred Funk, 1941.

Stokes, Geoffrey. *The Beatles*. New York: Rolling Stone Press/Times Books, 1980.

Strauss, Helen. *A Talent for Luck: An Autobiography*. New York: Random House, 1979.

Strauss, William, and Neil Howe. *Generations: The History of America's Future, 1584 to 2069*. New York: Morrow, 1991.

Summers, Anthony. *Goddess: The Secret Lives of Marilyn Monroe*. New York: Macmillan, 1985.

Taraborrelli, J. Randy. *Call Her Miss Ross: The Unauthorized Biography of Diana Ross*. New York: Birch Lane, 1989.

Taylor, Robert. *Saranac: America's Magic Mountain*. Boston: Houghton Mifflin, 1986.

Thomas, Bob. *Clown Prince of Hollywood: The Antic Life and Times of Jack L. Warner*. New York: McGraw-Hill, 1990.

———. *King Cohn: The Life and Times of Harry Cohn*. New York: Putnam's, 1967.

———. *Selznick*. Garden City, N.Y.: Doubleday, 1970.

Thomas, Danny, with Bill Davidson. *Make Room for Danny*. New York: Putnam, 1991.

Thompson, Charles C., II, and James P. Cole. *The Death of Elvis: What Really Happened*. New York: Delacorte, 1991.

Thompson, Douglas. *Clint Eastwood: Riding High*. Chicago: Contemporary, 1992.

Thomson, David. *Warren Beatty and Desert Eyes: A Life and a Story*. Garden City, N. Y.: Doubleday, 1987.

Titus, A. Constandina. *Bombs in the Backyard: Atomic Testing and American Politics*. Reno and Las Vegas: University of Nevada Press, 1986.

Toffel, Neile McQueen. *My Husband, My Friend*. New York: Atheneum, 1986.

Torrence, Bruce T. *Hollywood: The First Hundred Years*. New York: New York Zoetrope, 1982.

Tosches, Nick. *Dino: Living High in the Dirty Business of Dreams*. New York: Doubleday, 1992.

Tucker, Sophie. *Some of These Days: The Autobiography of Sophie Tucker*. Garden City, N. Y.: Doubleday, Doran & Co., 1945.

Turner, Lana. *Lana: The Lady, the Legend, the Truth*. New York: Dutton, 1982.

Valentino, Lou. *The Films of Lana Turner*. Secaucus, N.J.: Citadel, 1976.

Vellenga, Dirk, with Mick Farren. *Elvis and the Colonel*. New York: Delacorte, 1988.

Von Hoffman, Nicholas. *Citizen Cohn: The Life and Times of Roy Cohn*. New York: Doubleday, 1988.

Wagner, Walter. *Beverly Hills: Inside the Golden Ghetto*. New York: Grosset & Dunlap, 1976.

———. *You Must Remember This*. New York: Putnam's, 1975.

Wallock, Leonard, ed. *New York: Culture Capital of the World, 1940–1965*. New York: Rizzoli, 1988.

Walton, Richard J. *Henry Wallace, Harry Truman, and the Cold War*. New York: Viking, 1976.

Warhol, Andy, and Pat Hackett. *POPism: The Warhol '60s*. New York: Harcourt Brace Jovanovich, 1980.

Warren, Doug, with James Cagney. *Cagney: The Authorized Biography*. New York: St. Martin's, 1983.

Watson, Mary Ann. *The Expanding Vision: American Television in the Kennedy Years*. New York: Oxford University Press, 1990.

Weaver, Pat, with Thomas M. Coffey. *The Best Seat in the House: The Golden Years of Radio and Television*. New York: Knopf, 1994.

West, Mae. *Goodness Had Nothing to Do with It: The Autobiography of Mae West*. Englewood Cliffs, N. J.: Prentice-Hall, 1959.

Whitcomb, Ian. *After the Ball: Pop Music from Rag to Rock*. New York: Simon & Schuster, 1972.

White, William Chapman. *Adirondack Country*. New York: Duell, Sloan & Pearce, 1954.

Widener, Don. *Lemmon: A Biography*. New York: Macmillan, 1975.

Wiley, Mason, and Damien Bona. *Inside Oscar: The Unofficial History of the Academy Awards*. 4th ed. New York: Ballantine, 1993.

Wilkerson, Tichi, and Marcia Borie. *The Hollywood Reporter: The Golden Years*. New York: Coward-McCann, 1984.

Williams, Huntington. *Beyond Control: ABC and the Fate of the Networks*. New York: Atheneum, 1989.

Wills, Garry. *Reagan's America: Innocents at Home*. Garden City, N.Y.: Doubleday, 1987.

Wilson, Brian, with Todd Gold. *Wouldn't It Be Nice: My Own Story*. New York: HarperCollins, 1991.

Wilson, Earl. *The Show Business Nobody Knows*. Chicago: Cowles, 1971.

———. *Sinatra: An Unauthorized Biography*. New York: Macmillan, 1976.

Wolf, George with Joseph DiMona. *Frank Costello: Prime Minister of the Underworld*. New York: Morrow, 1974.

Wolfe, Tom. *The Right Stuff*. New York: Farrar, Straus & Giroux, 1979.

Wynn, Ned. *We Will Always Live in Beverly Hills: Growing Up Crazy in Hollywood*. New York: Morrow, 1990.

Yagoda, Ben. *Will Rogers: A Biography*. New York: Knopf, 1993.

ACKNOWLEDGMENTS

This book could not have been written without the assistance of a great many people—good friends, professional colleagues, total strangers. I owe a particular debt to Peter Biskind, my editor at *Premiere*, who had the foresight to have me look into the situation at William Morris while waiting for a celebrity interview to come through. I'm still waiting for that interview—perhaps in the intervening four years I somehow slipped to the bottom of his publicist's phone sheet?—but thanks to Peter I've kept busy nonetheless. I'm also indebted to senior editor Howard Karren, to Nancy Griffin in the West Coast office, and especially to Susan Lyne, *Premiere*'s editor, who had enough faith to send me out to cover the picture business in the first place, when I barely knew turnaround from a tent pole.

A number of people have taken it upon themselves to help educate me since, but none so purposefully as my good friend Peter Graves. I'm also indebted to Richard Rouilard for further tutoring in the ways of Hollywood. And I'm particularly grateful to Ariel Swartley, whose love of Los Angeles inspired me to see beyond freeways and minimalls to the oasis Carey McWilliams once described as "an island on the land."

A number of other writers and journalists have assisted me at key junctures. Victor Navasky helped me find my way through the thickets of the Red Scare. Robert Lacey supplied the leads that enabled me to crack the George Wood story. Lisa Gubernick of *Forbes* opened the door to areas that would otherwise have been closed to me. Patrick Goldstein, Paul Rosenfield, and Dan Moldea all made helpful recommendations. Stephen West gave me access to *Daily Variety*'s archives. Mike Russell was equally generous at the *Adirondack Daily Enterprise* in Saranac Lake, New York. Kit Rachlis of the *Los Angeles Times Magazine* was there at every juncture with a suggestion, an idea, a contact.

My understanding of the first William Morris would have been immeasurably poorer without the generosity of his stepgrandson, Albert

Ruben, who granted me access to the unpublished biography written by William Morris, Jr., and his sister, Ruth Morris White. Henrietta Lastfogel Prince and Mark Lastfogel, among others in the Lastfogel family, were kind enough to share their family memories with me. Judge Joseph Stone served as my guide to the New York law enforcement community: Of those he sent me to, I'm particularly obligated to John Bonomi, Nat Laurendi, and of course Robert Nicholson, all of whom went to great effort to see that I got the story straight. I also interviewed more than two hundred people in the entertainment industry in New York and Los Angeles, many of whom spent long hours giving me insight into the workings of the Morris office and the business in general. It would be impossible to cite them all here, especially as several of those who were most helpful have requested anonymity. Suffice it to say that without the help of seven or eight people—they know who they are—I would never have gotten started. Thank you.

A project like this requires a great deal of archival work, which I could hardly have undertaken without expert help. At the Billy Rose Theatre Collection at the New York Public Library for the Performing Arts, where the William Morris Collection serves as the centerpiece of a vast series of collections that shed light on the evolution of the agency and its clients, I received particularly valuable help from curator Robert Taylor as well as from Kevin Winkler, Brian O'Connell, and Richard Buck. I got courteous guidance from the staffs of the Local History Division and the Economic and Public Affairs Division of the New York Public Library on Fifth Avenue. Marty Jacobs of the Theatre Collection of the Museum of the City of New York was extremely helpful, as were Terry Geesken of the Film Stills Archive at the Museum of Modern Art and Eleanor Mish at the American Museum of the Moving Image. The staff at the Museum of Television and Radio guided me through hundreds of hours of vintage programming. Peter Filardo of the Tamiment Institute Library at New York University helped me sort through its unparalleled collection of socialist and Communist materials, while Kenneth Cobb of New York City Municipal Archives was my guide to the files of the New York County District Attorney's Office.

Beyond New York City, a number of other libraries were equally helpful in my research. For my view of the Morris family's life in the Adirondacks I'm indebted to the volunteers at the Adirondack Research Center in the William Chapman White Room (named after William Morris's son-in-law) at the Saranac Lake Free Library in Saranac Lake. The staff of the John F. Kennedy Presidential Library in Boston made it possible for me to gain otherwise inaccessible insights into the workings of Robert Kennedy's Justice Department. At the National Archives in Washington, D.C., Rod Ross of the Center for Legislative Archives helped me comb the records of the Congressional investigations of the fifties. The staff of the Library of Congress gave me access to the William Morris Collection there. The staff at the Memphis Room of the Memphis/Shelby County Public Library helped me with details of local history and Presleyana. Patricia Lowe of the Will Rogers Memorial in Claremont, Oklahoma, tracked down rare documentation of William Morris's dealings with the Cowboy Philosopher. Rick Ewig of the American Heritage Center at the University of Wyoming was particularly helpful in leading me through its holdings. At the James R. Dickinson Library of the University of Nevada-Las Vegas, Susan Jarvis of the Department of Special Collections guided me through voluminous archives, while the staff of the Nevada State Museum in Las Vegas enabled me to get a much fuller picture of that city's development than I would otherwise have had. At the University of Southern California, Steve Hanson and Ned Comstock of the Cinema-Television Library were especially helpful, while Dacy Taube of the Department of Special Collections gave me a view of early Los Angeles it would otherwise have been impossible to achieve. And I am particularly indebted to Sam Gill and the staff of the Margaret Herrick Library of the Academy of Motion Picture Arts and Sciences in Beverly Hills; their patient guidance was essential to my understanding of Hollywood in general and the agency business in particular.

For all their help, this book might not have been published at all without the support of Craig Nelson, my initial editor at Harper, and the enthusiasm of Susan Moldow and Bill Shinker. It certainly would not have been published as well without the efforts of my current editor, Cynthia Barrett, and the people she works with—the publisher of HarperCollins, Jack McKeown; the publishing director of HarperBusiness, Adrian Zackheim; and Genie Gavenchak, Lisa Berkowitz, Linda Dingler, Suzanne Noli, Pam LaBarbiera, Lorie Young, and Elissa Altman, all of whom have worked extremely hard on my behalf. Minda Novek and Nicolai Ouroussoff provided excellent research assistance at critical junctures in my work. And I'm particularly indebted to my agent, Kris Dahl of ICM, and to Dorothea Herrey and Gordon Kato, whose faith in me has been heartening at all times.

A great many friends worked overtime to help me as well, but none more than George Bennett and Georges Piette. Special thanks are due to Tom Cherones and Joyce Keener, whose generosity not only introduced me to the joys of canyon living but made it possible for me to complete this project. I would also like to thank Penny Stallings, Joan Peters, Bill Stern, Peter Stamelman, Howard Mandelbaum, Ron Mandelbaum, Steve Mizel, Joy Steinberg, Ellen Rashbaum, and John Wallace, all of whom made major contributions at different stages in the game. As she has so many times before, Beth Rashbaum gave me the faith and support I needed to see a long project through to the end. And I owe a special debt to the mysterious blonde, who gave me this idea in the first place.

INDEX